1/09

2

MW01199307

Constituting EMPIRE

STUDIES IN LEGAL HISTORY

Published by the

University of North Carolina Press

in association with the

American Society for Legal History

Thomas A. Green, Hendrik Hartog,
and Daniel Ernst, *editors*

DANIEL J. HULSEBOSCH

Constituting EMPIRE

New York and the

Transformation of

Constitutionalism in

the Atlantic World,

1664–1830

THE UNIVERSITY OF NORTH CAROLINA PRESS
CHAPEL HILL

© 2005
The University of
North Carolina Press
All rights reserved

Designed by Eric M. Brooks
Set in Janson and Trajan
by Keystone Typesetting, Inc.
Manufactured in the
United States of America

Portions of this work have appeared
previously, in somewhat different form,
in "The Ancient Constitution and the
Expanding Empire: Sir Edward Coke's
British Jurisprudence," *Law and History
Review* 21 (2003): 439–82; "The
Constitution in the Glass and the
Constitution in Action," *Law and History
Review* 16 (1998): 397–401; and "*Imperia
in Imperio*: The Multiple Constitutions
of Empire in New York, 1750–1777,"
Law and History Review 16 (1998): 319–79,
and are reproduced here with permission.

Library of Congress
Cataloging-in-Publication Data
Hulsebosch, Daniel J.
Constituting empire : New York and the
transformation of constitutionalism in the
Atlantic world, 1664–1830.
p. cm. — (Studies in legal history)
Includes bibliographical references
and index.
ISBN 0-8078-2955-2 (cloth: alk. paper)
1. Constitutional history — New York
(State) 2. New York (State) — Politics and
government — To 1775. 3. New York
(State) — Politics and government —
1775–1865. 4. Great Britain — Colonies —
Administration — History. 5. Political
culture — New York (State) — History.
6. Constitutional history — United States.
I. Title. II. Series.
KFN5681.H85   2005
342.74702′9 — dc22   2004029987

09 08 07 06 05   5 4 3 2 1

In memory of my mother

CONTENTS

Constituting EMPIRE

Introduction

Constitutions and Empire

THIS BOOK EXPLORES the formation of the United States' distinctive constitutional culture in early New York, from the British takeover of the province to its emergence as the Empire State in the early nineteenth century. During that time, New York was transformed from a modest Dutch trading outpost on the edge of the Atlantic world into a bustling entrepôt and exporter of goods, people, and culture. Its most important cultural export may well have been its constitutional culture. Decades of political and legal turmoil generated a new understanding of constitutionalism that New Yorkers published in books that circulated across the new United States and beyond. The institutional matrix for this creativity was empire, and the catalyst was an intraimperial struggle that culminated in a civil war known as the American Revolution. Afterward, New Yorkers played leading roles in reconfiguring Anglo-American constitutional resources into a new genre of law, constitutional law, as the province moved from the periphery of Britain's Atlantic empire to the center of a new continental one.

New York was a geographic, military, and commercial linchpin of the British Empire, the center of loyalism during the Revolution, and a fount of legal ideas in the early Republic. A seventeenth-century royal governor reported home that "this Province by its scituation (being much in the center of the other Colonies) . . . ought to be looked upon as the capital Province or the Cittadel to all the others; for secure this, and you secure all the English Colonies."[1] Its port lay where the Hudson River fed into the harbor and where the Atlantic pushed into the river, an estuary that the Mahican Indians called Mahicannittuck, or "great waters constantly in motion." European explorers referred to it as the "great River of the Mountains" because it cut through the Appalachians about 150 miles north of the harbor. The Dutch called it the North River, and the British renamed it "Hudson's" for the Englishman who explored the river under Dutch contract.[2] Whatever its name, all viewed it as "the Center and Key of the Continent."[3] "Every Thing conspires to make *New-York* the best Mart on the Continent," exclaimed a New York lawyer in 1753, better than Boston or Philadelphia. No other province had "a River so far navigable into the Country as ours; whence the Indian Trade from those vast Territories on the North, determines its Course to *Albany*, and thence down the *Hudson's* River to *New-York*, as naturally as a Stream gliding in its proper Channel."[4] Built by wind and water, then improved with landfill and wharves, New York seemed perfectly fitted for trade — nature's port.

By the middle of the eighteenth century, New Yorkers operated on the edge of a vast ocean marketplace, and their province helped connect the British Isles and the West Indies. Commerce linked the colonies and British port cities, and most New Yorkers had no reason to imagine a world without those ties. From this perspective, New York was much like Bristol, its trading partner on the west coast of England: both measured their distance from London by sailing time; only the unit of measurement, weeks versus days, differed. But diversity and specialization engendered conflict among the provinces, such as between the continental colonies and the West Indies. And New York was itself regionally diverse: the port city and its hinterland; the Hudson Valley, with its large manors and commercial farming; Albany, a hub for Indian trade; eastern Long Island, a place of farms and fishing villages close in space and identity to New England; scattered western settlements; and forts and trading posts even farther west in land still governed, to all intents and purposes, by the Iroquois. Although they were not royal subjects and had no formal representation in the province, the Iroquois made New York different from other crown dominions. On the other hand, New York shared with its neighbors a reliance on slave labor. There was a large slave population in New York City — 20 percent of its population in 1740 — and a significant number of slaves throughout the countryside.[5] Slaves, like Native Americans, were not members of New York's political culture, but they too affected its constitution before and after independence. This regional and demographic diversity produced rivalries as well as connections, a sense that New York was a separate jurisdiction, and reminders that it was enmeshed in a larger empire. The Native Americans had long observed that the province's main river flowed up through the mountains and down to the sea. New Yorkers' perspective shifted likewise, north and south, east and west, into the continent and across the Atlantic. This oscillation between the local and the cosmopolitan defined what it meant to be provincial and generated conflicting constitutional visions among colonial New Yorkers.

New York was, therefore, both representative and unusual. Colonists elsewhere in British North America were at least as protective of their local liberties as the provincial elite in New York. Those in Massachusetts, for example, were unrivaled when articulating their colony's charter-based autonomy and their claim to English liberties, and they strove relentlessly to minimize the power of their royal governor. Likewise, there were competent imperial officeholders in several of the other colonies. Georgia, in particular, had a strong group of military and civilian officials in the mid-eighteenth century.[6] Yet no other colony had as coherent a group of imperial agents as that based in New York after 1750. More important, in no other colony were the provincial elite and the imperial agents so well balanced during the last quarter century of imperial rule. That tension between a corps of officials trying to reform imperial administration and a provincial elite jealous of its local power, in a marchland colony full of opportunities and threats, made New York's path to revolution indirect and not inevitable.

After the Revolution, New York remained a strategic port and became a headquarters for continental expansion. It was then that people began calling it the Empire State. That nickname probably derives from George Washington's reference to New York City as "the seat of the empire" in 1785 when he received the golden key to the city, then the Confederation's capital.[7] A seat of empire was geographically central, commercially vibrant, and internationally formidable. Rome was the classical model, London its contemporary successor. Washington invoked the prospect of an American empire to urge the city's residents to resist localism, which he thought threatened "to sap the Constitution of these States" and "destroy our national character."[8] In 1785 it was unclear whether New York was truly the seat of an empire, for it was too early to tell whether the Confederation would succeed as one. This was the issue — "the fate of an empire, in many respects, the most interesting in the world" — that Alexander Hamilton framed for New York voters two years later in *Federalist* 1.[9] New York's unusually rich debate over the federal Constitution reflected its geopolitical importance and tradition of articulate political opposition. In turn, New York's ratification literature helped translate the tropes of imperial and provincial power into American constitutionalism.

The recovery of the imperial origins of American constitutionalism is not only a matter of historical interest. Although legal scholars often declare that

American constitutions are living documents that adapt to changing times, even those who eschew reliance on the framers' original intent try to identify historically legitimate restrictions on constitutional meaning.[10] Some fundamental meanings were encoded long ago, and each generation must work within or against them. The first American constitutions, state and federal, were drafted after two centuries of colonization in which English legal culture structured relationships between province and metropolis, among the provinces, and within each province. Consequently, the constitutional ideas and practices of the first British Empire still influence American constitutionalism today.

Most Americans, however, equate the founding with the writing of the federal Constitution and view that event as an exceptional break with the past. They accept the framers' claim to have established *Novus Ordo Seclorum* at face value rather than ask why the framers wished to distance themselves from some, but not all, legacies of the British Empire — why they wished to see themselves as *founders*.[11] Returning the Constitution to the context of imperial resistance, rebellion, and state constitution making reminds us that the founders looked backward as well as forward.[12] In both directions they saw empire. Although crown officials and parliamentary legislation were gone, the legacies of British rule — its legal institutions, practices, and languages — remained as the raw material for the American constitutions.

Now "empire" has negative connotations. Modern empires are seen as expansive and exploitive. According to the conventional historiography, the United States has, except for an aberrant moment in the late nineteenth century, been free of imperial ambition.[13] Since the Second World War, historians have shifted focus away from even the incontestably imperial aspects of its history. A century ago, historians examined "the colonial period of American history," the "colonial background of the American Revolution," and the structure of the British Empire in the Atlantic world.[14] The imperial school fell out of favor in part because its practitioners had successfully outlined colonial institutions. Others examined how those institutions — colonies, administrations, courts, interest groups — functioned and recovered their social histories.[15] In addition, much scholarly energy in the midtwentieth century was spent trying to understand, criticize, and explain the meaning of American civilization to its citizens and a world caught in the Cold War.[16] Though some warned against returning to a complacent Whig history that celebrated freedom, the United States' imperial legacy was deemphasized.[17] Constitutional history in particular became a story of the growth of American liberty.[18]

New interpretive models within the academy and skepticism about nationalism outside it allow us to return to the eighteenth century and recover the imperial strand of American constitutional history. The renaissance of Atlantic history and imperial studies remind us that the American colonies were much like the other British provinces across the ocean: each was protective of its autonomy while participating fully in Atlantic trade and culture.[19] Historians have begun to recover the political, social, and economic connections that integrated the Atlantic and the individual empires within it.[20] Constitutional culture was a crucial means of integration. From its beginning, the British Empire could not have expanded so successfully without the integrating symbols of English constitutional liberty, and constitutionalism would not be so strong a force in the modern United States without that imperial legacy. But the empire was also marked by legal pluralism and polyvalent authority. Relationships that today appear vertical were then horizontal, as the empire was a collection of competing power centers rather than a pyramid of sovereignty. Who governed what? The answer turned on who asked whom, when, and why. The empire's legal architecture was baroque but unfinished: ornate in some areas, rude in others. Most Britons adhered to no single theory of the empire or its constitution; legal integration remained a controversial goal, not a reality.[21] As the empire spread, the resources of English constitutionalism became more malleable. What had served integration soon disguised diversity behind familiar terms. The failure to create a unifying constitution — a legal environment that could account for and contain disputes within the empire — contributed to its disintegration.

Some officials in eighteenth-century New York recognized that a special category of imperial law was necessary to bind the empire. In a legal world with no imperial or British law superior to the local law of its parts, these officials tried to manufacture one, carving out a space either within the common-law tradition or separate from it in which to administer imperial policy. The common law had served this purpose in medieval England, as royal judges centralized justice in toward the crown and away from local customary courts. But although England had become Great Britain, and Great Britain the British Empire, the dominant constitutional resources within those extended territories remained English, particularly the common law. This was now a hybrid resource of institutions and rhetorical strategies plastic enough to bolster central control or defend local autonomy, especially when the common law became closely identified with the "liberties of Englishmen" in the seventeenth century. Overseas, provincial New Yorkers successfully used those components of common-law constitutionalism upholding local autonomy, which forced the imperial agents to search for a separate imperial law. But the agents' attempts to create it helped precipitate rebellion, and today they are forgotten. A generation later, American lawyers created constitutional law to bind the states together. In so doing, they succeeded where the British imperial agents had failed and figure prominently among those whom Americans call "founding fathers." Other jurists built on this foundation of federal constitutional law to revise state common law and make it more integrative too. When the founders created a new republic, they did so in dialogue with their own colonial past, forging tighter bonds than the old imperial administrators had ever imagined: "a more perfect Union."

Recovering the nexus between empires and constitutions should also help revitalize British-American constitutional history. "Constitutional history is certainly not dead," historian Stanley N. Katz remarked twenty years ago, "but it is not flourishing and its significance for colonial history is not altogether obvious."[22] Not long before, there had been much excitement in the field, centering around the work of Bernard Bailyn and Gordon S. Wood. "The word 'constitution' and the concept behind it," Bailyn observed, "was of central importance to the colonists' political thought; their entire understanding of the crisis in Anglo-American relations rested upon it." He and Wood argued that the concept "was forced apart, along the seam of a basic ambiguity, to form the two contrasting types of constitutionalism that have remained characteristic of England and America ever since."[23] In England, they argued, "constitution" signified only the extant arrangement of government, a framework of power that Parliament could change as it pleased. The English constitution had no fundamentality about it. The American innovation was to fix constraints on government. The colonists invoked anachronistic fundamental-law arguments to protest the new imperial regulations of the 1760s, and, Bailyn concluded, "[o]nce its utility was perceived and demonstrated, this process of disengaging principles from institutions and from the positive actions of government and then of conceiving them as fixed sets of rules and boundaries, went on swiftly." Writtenness, the extralegislative convention, and the doctrine of popular sovereignty all play important roles in this story that culminates in the federal Constitution of 1787 becoming fundamental law.[24] The descriptive and positivist English constitution, the argument concludes, became the prescriptive, restrictive, and aspirational American constitution.

This version of the American constitutional transformation has become the conventional wisdom. Some legal historians have amended it. John Phillip Reid, Barbara A. Black, and Jack P. Greene argue that there were two versions of the British constitution: London's interpretation, in which Parliament was omnipotent; and the colonial interpretation, premised on the belief that there were limits to Parliament's authority to legislate for the colonies.[25] These historians accept the Atlantic constitutional divide charted by Bailyn and Wood but argue that the American Whigs drew on a competing, live tradition within English constitutionalism. Indeed, the innovation, gradually developing in Britain, was that Parliament as a legislature reigned supreme above other sources of constitutional authority *at home*, and perhaps overseas too. In short, the equation of a constitution with fundamental law that restrained government, helped define a people, and, when violated, provided a set of remedies was not an American invention. The English remedy was the right of resistance, with its graduated steps of petition, riot, rebellion, and finally revolution. Postrevolutionary Americans did change constitutional meanings and remedies, but they did not move the constitution to the center of cultural identity. It was already there.[26]

The evolving definition of "constitution" is analyzed throughout this book. For now, it is helpful to think of constitutions not as documents but rather as relationships among jurisdictions and people mediated through highly charged legal terms. Before and after the Revolution, a constitution was a way of thinking about, and practices for carrying out, the project of government that never depended on a single institution of enforcement.[27] Instruments and rules were not enough. Well-understood practices, resting on a shared commitment to the society that a constitution serves, are needed to make constitutions work. The premise of Anglo-American constitutionalism has always been that constitutions are largely self-enforcing through a mixture of popular acceptance and deft administration. However, constitutional ideas and practices resting on this premise of convention varied across space at any given moment and changed over time in the eighteenth century. Britons in New York before the Revolution, and Americans after, struggled to define constitutions to accommodate and shape British legal culture as it traveled with colonists abroad. The focus here is on the way people experienced constitutions rather than on constitutional theory. It is futile to classify Anglo-American constitutionalism as, for example, either republican or liberal. Most people believed that a constitution should protect both the public interest *and* individual liberties.[28] Similarly, early modern constitutions were not simply descriptive blueprints for government or lists of prescriptive ideals. A constitution could be either or both, depending on who invoked it and for what purpose. Too much has also been made of the distinction between unwritten and written constitutions.[29] Much of the English constitution *was* written. Although no single document captured all English constitutionalism, there was an evolving canon of great documents. Magna Carta (1215), the Petition of Right (1628), and the Bill of Rights (1689), for example, were on everyone's list, while the Levellers' Agreement of the People (1648) was on few. These documents were not exhaustive. Commentary in treatises, essays, and judicial reports fleshed out their significance, as did oral tradition. Beyond the documents and the commentary were the institutions that interpreted and applied them, the practical conventions that gave constitutions life.[30] Collectively, these documents, ideas, and practices formed the empire's constitutional culture.

This culture was not sealed off from the rest of Anglo-American culture. Control over it was decentralized; no one held a monopoly on constitutional meaning. There were no constitutional law casebooks or professors of constitutional law; indeed, there was no genre of constitutional law. Early modern English-speakers also conveyed more than strictly legal meanings when they employed constitutional scripts. Modern Americans sometimes do the same, slipping political visions into well-crafted legal interpretations. Early moderns did so explicitly because the legal had not been divorced from the political. Constitutional discourse was a legalist idiom that highlighted arguments not just about courts, legislatures, and executives but also the fate of political society. Consequently, constitutional culture provided a primary language for constructing the British Empire, revolting against it, and writing the new American constitutions.[31]

Conventional wisdom tells us that the American revolutionaries rejected the principle of legislative supremacy along with parliamentary regulation and carefully distributed authority between the states and federal government in an arrangement called federalism.[32] However, if we change the prerevolutionary image of the British Empire, the new Union looks different too. Instead of dual, limited governments emerging from an omnipotent sovereign, provincial Britons moved from a fluid constitutional environment to a much more structured and constraining one. If "federal" means diffuse authority, government became *less* federal after the Revolution because there were fewer legitimating ideas and institutions for Americans to draw on than for Britons a generation earlier. Indeed, the American constitutional doctrine of federalism entailed just this concentration of power. Centripetal, not centrifugal, forces characterized the constitutional settlement that followed the American Revolution. Soon legitimate constitutional authority operated at only two levels: the federal government and the states, with local authority subsumed beneath the latter.

The shift from common-law constitutionalism to American constitutional law also tended to submerge the political dimension of constitutions as the realm of politics became more clearly separated from law. In the first two generations of the Republic, state legislatures enjoyed something very close to supremacy. With the crown gone and executive governance suspect, state legislatures inherited the lion's share of legitimate authority after the Revolution. No longer were there horizontal competitors, reaching in like the crown or the British Parliament. The vertical alternatives — the federal and local governments — were not serious competitors. The party system, which flourished in early nineteenth-century New York, raised the state government's political power to its high water mark. But partisan politics, and the large internal improvement projects that party-led states undertook, led to a backlash as state voters demanded new constitutions to rein in state government. Those nineteenth-century state constitutions clarified the line between ordinary politics and constitutional law, but they also demonstrated that constitution making remained a form of politics too.[33] In short, state legislative power did not exhaust the people's constitutional power. The backlash also allowed Federalist jurists, who for three decades had been working to draw legal boundaries around legislative power, to enjoy newfound influence as commentators and treatise writers — greater influence, perhaps, than they had in the Federalist heyday of the 1790s.

So there was a transformation in constitutionalism in the early United States, but it was not a shift from descriptive to prescriptive constitutions. Instead, Americanization involved the reorganization of the sources of a constitution, new institutions of enforcement, and a new conception of law as a hierarchy of substantive genres rather than, as in England, a collection of courts and procedures for resolving disputes, each jostling with the others for preeminence. This new conception of law did not develop directly out of English legal ideas and was not invented by the American founders in the 1780s but rather passed first through a stage that might be called Britonization or imperialization in which colonial subjects and administrators adapted British legal sources for their purposes. Where in England law was defined in terms of jurisdiction — who had the power to determine right and wrong and what were the boundaries of that power? — abroad it was increasingly conceived as jurisprudence, a rational system of rules that bound governments and private parties. The jurisdictional lines that defined the ancient constitution were difficult to police overseas. In contrast, short, powerful statements of fundamental law traveled well across space.[34] For the colonists to claim English liberties, they had to conceive of them as an abstract jurisprudence operative in all the crown's dominions, not as a system of licenses to sue in territorially bounded courts. Substantive notions of liberty, like negotiable instruments, became transatlantic currency that could be traded anywhere English was spoken. This jurisprudence of liberty could be used many ways. It could be imperial and integrative here, provincial and disintegrative there; liberating in one place and enslaving in another — or even liberating and enslaving in some places at the same time.[35] To understand the legal culture of the British Empire and the early United States, we must understand the intellectual transformation in the idea of law on which colonial resistance was premised: the shift from jurisdiction to jurisprudence, the rules in a legal system to the rule of law, English liberties to American liberty. The fundamental legal tension of empire was between the rule of law and the expansion of rule, a striving toward universals of government and rights on the one hand and toward increasing territorial jurisdiction on the other. The American founders' resolution was to attempt to control a space by law that could not possibly be controlled by men.

The expansive space could not be controlled by traditional means because the people moving across it would not submit to such control. This relentless mobility was the paramount expression of popular sovereignty in America, and it expressed more than traditional "customs in common."[36] Popular constitutionalism, which was performed in petitions, protests, parades, and mobbing, persisted after the Revolution and connected white Americans to their British past.[37] But overland emigration, which only with nationalist hindsight can be called internal migration, had always distinguished North American constitutional culture. That movement, which expressed radical notions of liberty and property, infuriated the British imperial agents while also making some of them rich from land speculation. Frustration fell away after the Revolution, and mobility became the country's most important capital investment; without it, the Union's greatest resource — land — remained worthless. And without ties of cultural identity, foremost among which was constitutional identity, much of that land might not have become part of the United States. People moved west, acting out what they believed were their liberties; their governors called them American; lawmakers incorporated them into the Union; because that incorporation offered the settlers the prospect of equal citizenship, they accepted it.[38] In retrospect it is manifest destiny. At the time it was a speculative project, a kind of political speculation.

The hard fact of mobility — of popular disregard for jurisdiction in the traditional sense of legal boundaries of both liberty and power — was a fundamental fact of early American constitutionalism. It contributed to the Revolution, and it shaped all the American constitutions. The colonies and states that succeeded them existed in a market for people that turned on legal incentives called rights and liberties, and the imperial, then federal, government struggled to maintain the perception, true in most places at most times but fictional in all once in a while, that it exercised control over all whom one government called "subjects" and its successor called "the people." Here was the radical potential of "we the people." The relentless mobility of the people proved as momentous as their increasing participation in the electorate and their occasional performances of their power in parades and mobs. Men, women, often children, sometimes slaves, pushed where they were told not to go and encountered Native Americans unschooled in the legitimating language of Anglo-American liberty. They conquered the continent less with violence than with the confidence with which they carried forward their notions of constitutional liberty, notions forged in the matrix of empire.[39] That too is what was meant by a government of law rather than of men.

A word about sources. One cannot trace *the* constitutional experience of even a single province. The focus here is on the people who debated, enforced, and lived within constitutions while following their serendipitous ways of thinking and practices. New York was a large, diverse, and complicated place even three centuries ago; much of its constitutional history is left uncovered. On the other hand, much important to its constitutional history occurred outside its borders, so the study travels beyond the stipulated boundaries of time and space. In a world in which law was first and foremost procedural, legal culture was keyed to law-making and law-enforcing institutions; those are the backbone of its history. Courts and legislatures were the most important but not the only institutions that mattered. Also relevant were the many smaller regulatory bodies within the province, as well as the literature though which early modern Britons and Americans expressed old and new senses of legality. Although these institutions generated precedent and learned traditions, the historical focus should remain on the people who built and used those institutions. This book, therefore, concentrates on competing and successive groups of legal administrators and consumers and thus relies on prosopography.

Part I of this book lays out the imperial context of New York's founding. The seventeenth century was an age of territorial expansion and political innovation, and in the English world the polestars were the empire and constitution, which are explored in chapter 1. Empire and constitutional liberties were related and reinforcing, yet there was little consensus about the meaning of these key terms in the early modern British Atlantic world and even less about whether the liberties of Englishmen traveled overseas to other crown territories. Chapter 2 reconstructs the institutional framework of colonial New York and how its settlers gradually demanded, and got, many of those liberties.

Despite these institutional changes, New York's constitution remained contested. Part II explores the multiple interpretations of the constitution and the mid-eighteenth-century project of legal reform. Chapter 3 examines the three different versions of the constitution that crystallized in the middle of the eighteenth century: one held by the imperial agents who served the British Empire on the ground; another by the provincial elite jealous of maintaining their local control; and a third, less articulate version expressed in the cities and the marchland by socially marginal colonists who were suspicious of all but the most local forms of authority. Chapter 4 describes the reforms that the imperial agents proposed to control provincial law, politics, and settlement. These reforms failed and contributed to the Revolution.

Part III relates New York's constitutional history during the Revolution. When colonial government dissolved, the British military imposed an extreme version of legal centralization: martial law. As chapter 5 explains, the British government debated continuously whether to restore civil government but never did, much to the disillusionment of loyalist New Yorkers. In contrast, the revolutionary provincial government wrote a new constitution that preserved what many colonists believed were the liberties that they had long enjoyed—or should have enjoyed. The state's new constitution is detailed in chapter 6. This constitution rested explicitly on the authority of the people, and most New Yorkers probably believed that legislation was the paramount expression of the people's will. But when state legislation conflicted with Confederation treaties and the law of nations, some New Yorkers sought ways to curtail that legislation. As the case of *Rutgers v. Waddington* reveals, one new and controversial way was through strong judicial interpretation of the state constitution.

Part IV sketches New York's constitutional significance in the new Union. No other state had as articulate a debate on the ratification of the federal Constitution as New York. Chapter 7 analyzes the main themes of that debate. *The Federalist Papers* were written in New York for New York voters and inspired some of the most powerful Antifederalist essays too. The literature that New York's Federalists and Antifederalists left behind had little effect on ratification but did influence the way the new document was interpreted. Together they created the new genre of constitutional law to bind the states. In the early nineteenth century, New York, like most states, rewrote its own constitution and made its political culture more democratic and less centralized. Suffrage barriers fell for white men, and more offices became elective rather than appointive. In short, as chapter 8 concludes, the state government's power was curbed. At the same time, chapter 9 argues, the state's unusually sophisticated legal culture produced works that influenced law throughout the United States. Paramount among these was James Kent's *Commentaries on American Law* (1826–30), a Federalist-inspired primer for students and practitioners. Works like *The Federalist Papers*, Kent's *Commentaries*, and other legal treatises were shipped west on the Erie Canal and helped forge a national legal culture.

The Imperial Origins of New York

> *Nothing in law springs entirely from a sense*
> *of convenience. There are always certain ideas*
> *existing antecedently on which the sense of*
> *convenience works, and of which it can do no*
> *more than form some new combination; and*
> *to find these ideas in the present case is exactly*
> *the problem.*
>
> Henry Maine, *Ancient Law* (1861)

THE ENGLISH BEGAN VENTURING across the Atlantic at the same time that they were consolidating their national identity around the English language, Protestant religion, commercial expansion, and a legal order soon known as the ancient constitution.[1] Overseas expansion and the English constitution developed simultaneously and reciprocally, each structuring the other. The English compared their legal order not only with that of other kingdoms in continental Europe but also with that of other dominions in their empire, and national borders served to insulate the realm from both. To the modern eye, it almost appears as though England had shed its prenational characteristics and passed them on to the colonies: as in the medieval realm, the empire's government was primarily royal, its borders were fluid, and it was legally and culturally pluralist. These characteristics set the colonies apart from the English nation, which was increasingly perceived as a well-defined jurisdiction under a constitutional monarchy.

The English believed they were perfecting liberty at home, in part through colonization abroad, and although they always intended to keep those colonies within the pale of civilization, at first no one thought that the overseas dominions enjoyed the full range of English liberties. Those were, literally, the birthright of *Englishmen*. The legal culture of the colonies received little attention at home, and the design of governmental institutions abroad was haphazard.[2] Stronger executive government distinguished most colonies from England, as did tighter restraints on trade and migration. These restrictions were necessary to prevent settlers from trading directly with, and encroaching on the lands of, other European empires and the Native American tribes. The executive was especially strong in New York. Compared with neighboring colonies, by the middle of the eighteenth century it had a cohesive group of imperial agents, and frequent imperial wars made the British military a regular presence in its harbor and on its marchland.

Even though all the empire's subjects were aware of its jurisdictional diversity, most also believed that they differed from people outside it, and part of what those subjects shared was access to England's constitutional culture. Over the course of the seventeenth and eighteenth centuries, settlers abroad appropriated metropolitan law and constitutionalism to hold the crown administration to standards then being set in England, and they invented some new standards too. In this respect, New York was typical. New Yorkers shared institutions and ideologies with England but reconfigured them to serve local needs. The crown and its imperial agents believed that they could control the colony through their commissions and instructions, but settlers demanded a representative assembly and many "liberties of Englishmen" associated with the common law. Officially, legal authority descended from the crown. In practice, it was layered with ambiguity, compromise, and an assortment of local institutions derived from all over the British Atlantic world. Helping to hold it together was a common devotion to English legal ways.

Empire and Liberty

Our constitution is a prescriptive constitution; it is a constitution whose sole authority is that it has existed time out of mind. . . . [I]t is a constitution made by what is ten thousand times better than choice, it is made by the peculiar circumstances, occasions, tempers, dispositions, and moral, civil and social habitudes of people, which disclose themselves only in a long space of time.

Edmund Burke, "Speech on the Representation of the Commons in Parliament" (1782)

T HE HISTORY OF LAW IS LIKE the archaeology of an ancient yet living city. Structures and artifacts of the past endure, but their historical meanings are disguised by the twin illusions of continuity and obviousness. The words "empire," "constitution," and "liberty," for example, seem to mean now what they will forever, the same as they did in the beginning.

But there was a beginning. Each of these keywords owed its origin to many causes. Still, it is striking that just as Anglophone people began expanding beyond the bounds of medieval England, creating an entity they called an empire, they came to believe that they enjoyed a constitution, a term used both to describe government and to prescribe how it should function to safeguard the liberties of Englishmen.[1] These dual quests for nationhood and empire reinforced each other. As the English created a national identity and built an empire, they also reconfigured parts of their common law and political tradition in new terms of a constitution of liberty. In a transatlantic circle of meaning, the nation gave life to the empire, the empire preserved liberty,

liberty helped define the English nation, and the English constitution was the repository of liberty. This link between the British Empire and the English constitution had dramatic consequences across the globe, especially in British North America, and its legacy persists, as the expansion of rule and the rule of law remain central to modern history.[2]

The Origins of Empire

The early modern English lived in a dynamic place. They were on the one hand schismatic, breaking after a millennium from the Roman Church, and on the other expansive, taking to the seas in search of markets, land, and glory. The term "empire" captured both internal consolidation and external expansion; it was a claim of immunity from foreign power, and it described an authority that held together fragmented territories under one king.[3] The word derived from the Latin *imperium*, which meant simply authority without any territorial connotation, but also served as a shorthand for expansive kingdoms such as the Holy Roman Empire. The term had positive and negative connotations. To some, empire involved the conquest of enemies, but to others it was a divine instrument for spreading Christian civilization. The term also conveyed a claim of independence. The word became prominent in Henrician England, where it signified the realm's autonomy from Rome.[4] After the union of England and Scotland in 1603, the accent on its meaning shifted from the autonomous kingdom to the whole collection of crown territories. The idea of a British Empire preceded this union and derived from the myth of an ancient, united Isle of Britain under Brutus. The union of crowns, many thought, reunited what for too long had been divided.[5] This broader conception of empire also included Ireland, which some viewed as a coordinate realm in a system of multiple kingdoms and others as a colony of a united Britain.[6] Either way, by the eighteenth century the core of the British Empire was Great Britain, and the dominant partner there was England. From Great Britain it spread outward to the West Indies, North America, India, and beyond.

Most colonies began as private commercial ventures that received the crown's blessing to establish dominion abroad in return for the promise that the venturers would possess the land within some time period and, if not, the grant would revert to the crown. The colonizers got dominion, a property interest, from the crown; in return they extended the crown's sovereign jurisdiction, its *imperium*, abroad. They could not settle land without the royal grant, and the crown had little land to grant until they settled it. This was the elemental pattern of empire: crown power and the liberty of the subject were mutually dependent, and the public mixed imperceptibly with the private.[7]

Yet the whole was greater than the sum of its parts. Lawyer and crown officer Francis Bacon, in a Machiavellian essay entitled "Of Empire" that was part of the early seventeenth-century campaign for political union with Scotland, equated the term with kingdoms that were expansive and "aim at greatness," a category that implicitly included England.[8] According to Machiavelli, whose republican theory was at the core of early modern English political philosophy, expansion was the only way to achieve greatness because territorial gain brought trade, strength, and opportunity. But expansion also led to standing armies, corrupt rule, and the decline of liberty. In 1656, James Harrington reminded his republican readers that "Empire is of two kinds, domestic and national, or foreign and provincial." Every nation was a "domestic or national" empire, and its political system could be a monarchy, mixed monarchy, or republican commonwealth. "Foreign and provincial" empire, in contrast, referred to overseas plantations. In Harrington's utopia, which he imagined amid the disappointments of Cromwell's republic, these "foreign" provinces were safety valves for ambitious citizens who sought more wealth than permitted at home under the agrarian law's limitation on property holding. Because of these disparities in wealth in the provinces, ordinary subjects there would enjoy fewer liberties, while great landholders might seek independence from the republic. Accordingly, Harrington warned that provincial interests should not be permitted to wield "the balance of dominion in the province, because that would bring the government from provincial and dependent to national and independent," and, in an increasingly frequent analogy, he reminded his readers that distant and unmanageable provinces contributed to Rome's decline.[9]

Rewriting these tragic scripts of republicanism in progressive terms was a challenge facing imperial thinkers for the next two centuries.[10] One strategy was to strengthen imperial government abroad. Strong administration would yield the benefits of colonization while preventing fragmentation. A different approach was to inoculate the dominions with liberty. If settlers enjoyed the full panoply of English liberties, corruption would never take root in the colonies and thus would not spread back home.[11] The English pursued both strategies in North America.

Ideologically, the empire was more than a series of business ventures. Indeed, the ideology of empire was quite similar to English national ideology. "Protestantism, oceanic commerce and mastery of the seas provided bastions to protect the freedoms of the British Empire," observes David Armitage, and "[t]hat freedom found its institutional expression in Parliament, the law, property and rights, all of which were exported throughout the British Atlantic world."[12] Although some elements of this ideology were contested, most agreed that the empire would help preserve English liberties, and those liberties would guarantee the success of the empire.

But whose liberties did the empire serve, and what were they? Were they English liberties, for the realm of England alone? British liberties for Scotland too and perhaps parts of Ireland? Or were these liberties common to all white English-speakers in the empire? Because English culture dominated within the empire, British liberty was defined in English terms, and the degree to which this English liberty was exported to the empire's provinces was never clear. At the outset of transatlantic colonization, most believed that the overseas dominions had their own, separate legal systems. When the crown established its jurisdiction over a territory, it did not convey all of English law to that land. Royal imperium and English freedom overlapped but were not identical; most of the latter was restricted to England. But many Britons came to believe that the overseas colonists enjoyed core English liberties, especially representative government and common-law protections of property and person.

The Liberties of Englishmen beyond England: Calvin's Case

The legal definition and spatial boundaries of liberty arose immediately on the union of crowns in 1603. When Elizabeth died without a lineal heir, the crown of England descended to her cousin, King James VI of Scotland. After centuries of war and suspicion, the two kingdoms were joined at the head, though not for another hundred years did they unite politically. One king ruled two kingdoms with separate national legislatures, court systems, and churches.[13] It seemed to many that the fabled empire of Great Britain would be restored.

James established a commission to recommend reforms that would facilitate trade, and the commissioners proffered three proposals: the abrogation of "hostile lawes" in each nation targeting the other; the creation of uniform commercial law; and the treatment of natural subjects in one nation as subjects in the other, which would ensure that Scots and Englishmen could migrate into either kingdom without fear of discrimination based on nationality.[14] The Scottish Parliament accepted all the proposals, but the English Parliament balked at the third: the Commons did not want to recognize Scots as English subjects. While most agreed that people born in one kingdom before James ascended the English throne (*antenati*) could not be treated as natural subjects in the other kingdom, opinion was divided about the status of those born after union (*postnati*). James issued a royal proclamation in support of all three proposals and added that English law already authorized treating Scottish *postnati* as English subjects.

Parliamentarians supported expansion but did not want to treat inhabitants of the other dominions as equal to themselves when those other subjects came to England. They also feared setting a precedent. "This case," warned member of Parliament (MP) Sir Edwin Sandys, "might give a dangerous example for mutual naturalizing of all nations that hereafter fall into the subjection of the king, although they be very remote, in that their mutual commonalty of privileges may disorder the settled government of every of the particulars." Each constituent "nation" of the king's expanding dominions had its own "privileges" and "birthright," which had been "acquired for patrimony by their antecessors of that place."[15] While supporting expansion, parliamentarians feared that reciprocal subjectship would erase jurisdictional borders—*national* borders—within the king's composite monarchy.[16] Through force of example and immigration, something like Gresham's law would reduce legal privileges throughout the king's lands: bad constitutional currency minted abroad would drive out good at home, sending England into despotism.[17]

Two aspects of the parliamentary protest are notable. First, parliamentarians presumed that England was the center of the royal territories and, correlatively, that English law was superior to the others and *not* operative outside England. The script of ancient English liberties was drafted, or at least revised, amid uncertainty about whether the Scottish king would try to impose a new legal order on England, perhaps one based on the continental civil law. The threat was actually minimal. There was no such program, and the difference between English and continental law was exaggerated.[18] Nonetheless, the fear helped generate the political fiction of a timeless legal framework guaranteeing liberty.[19] If the English nation shaped the empire, the expansion also sharpened English subjects' perceptions of their national legal culture.

Second, exporting cherished English liberties throughout the empire was no priority. Martial law, for example, was permitted by the London-based governors of the Virginia Company at the same time that these same men, serving in Parliament, decried its use at home.[20] Liberties were national, meaning native, and once earned they became birthright property: bought with the blood of ancestors and held in trust for posterity. Nations existed along a chain of being measured in degrees of liberty; each got as much as it deserved.[21] This held true within the empire too. Parliamentarians conceived of the emerging empire in pluralist terms in which each of the king's dominions enjoyed a different quantum of liberty.

James's proclamation on mutual subjectship, and parliamentary opposition to it, reveal that legal pluralism characterized not only the emergent empire but also England itself. No institution had a monopoly on legal interpretation. The king speaking alone or through his Privy Council was one interpreter of law, the common-law judiciary was another, and Parliament, embracing the king and two Houses, still one more. The jurisdictional politics among these and other institutions to define English law reflected all the tensions of Jacobean England and contributed to the Civil War in the 1640s.[22] Early modern parliamentarians traded on the institutional pluralism within England to oppose James's program to open up the boundaries between his multiple kingdoms.

Calvin's Case, therefore, arose within an early modern borders debate in which many parliamentarians feared that the right to hold land might attract immigrants from the north and elsewhere. Unaccustomed to freedom, the newcomers might lay England's most important property — its liberty — to waste. The question was whether a Scotsman could sue in the common-law courts to vindicate title to land located in England. Everyone agreed that an alien "can have no real or personal action for or concerning land"[23] and that Scots born before the king of Scotland became the king of England were aliens. The only issue was whether Scottish *postnati* were not aliens but rather subjects of the king as an English king. The court answered affirmatively. Drawing on the political fiction of the king's two bodies, the judges held that "ligeance" bound the subject to the person of the king rather than to the king in his "politick capacity" as head of a particular kingdom.[24] This ligeance was created naturally on birth within the king's territory from parents who were under the king's obedience. A feudal logic lay behind this birthright: property was the root of sovereignty and legal authority; it provided the bond between lord and tenant, king and subject. Reciprocally, the king was bound to protect the property claims of his subjects on his land.[25]

The jurisprudential upshot of *Calvin's Case* for the empire was that the king's natural subjects in any of his territories could hold land in England and file suit in the royal courts for that English land, unless they were born before the English king obtained that territory. When in England, those subjects owed obedience to the king as an English king and were entitled to common-law rights in English courts. But the court did not hold that these subjects enjoyed English liberties in those other dominions. The king's "mandatory and remedial writs," which included all common-law writs, did not run to any land outside the realm of England.[26] These remedial writs "cannot by any means be extended into any other kingdom, country, or nation, [even] though it be under the king's actual ligeance and obedience."[27] In contrast, the English king's "mandatory and non-remedial writs," which commanded a subject to return to the realm and answer the king in person, "are not tied to any place but do follow subjection and ligeance, in what country or nation soever the subject is."[28] In other words, the king and his Privy Council had jurisdiction over those other dominions; his common-law courts did not. Coke's ancient constitution was an English constitution. While in England, the English king's other subjects deserved its liberties and privileges, such as the right to hold land there by common-law tenures. This was the holding of the case, and no more was necessary for the decision.

The decision seems limited today, amid claims of human rights and calls for universal jurisdiction. But the doctrine of ligeance was radical for its time because it encouraged mobility throughout the king's composite monarchy. Here is the *British* aspect of *Calvin's Case*: a subject born in another royal territory, like Scotland or Virginia, could immigrate to England, and if he bought or inherited land there, he could sue in the English common-law courts to vindicate his title. This was the meaning of British liberty. But *English* liberty was for England. In Coke's legal world, remedy defined right, and the common law's remedial writs ran no farther than the English border. A Scot or a Virginian could not sue in the English common-law courts for possession of land in Scotland or Virginia. For that, he had to resort to a local legal forum, with a right of appeal to the king's Privy Council. Given this jurisdictional conception of law, no one in the early seventeenth century interpreted *Calvin's Case* to mean that the common law and liberties of Englishmen were exported to the king's other dominions.

Coke also used his opinion to bolster the legal fiction for which he is most famous: the "ancient constitution."[29] When he wrote that lands inherited by descent retained their ancient laws, and so too conquered Christian land, he was pleading in the alternative to support the claim that England enjoyed an ancient legal order that originated before William I's assumption of the English throne in 1066 and endured that event, whether viewed as a conquest or an inheritance. Either argument would explain how the "ancient common laws" of the Anglo-Saxons survived 1066 and were not superseded by Norman law. Latin charters referring to fundamental institutions like the jury, sheriffs, Chancery, and escheat for treason "prove that the common Law of England had been time out of minde of man before the Conquest, and was not altered or changed by the Conqueror."[30] Similarly, jurist and parliamentarian John Selden, in his 1610 history of "our *English Brittish* Law," argued that "new acquired Empires, do run some hazard by attempting to make new Laws: and the *Norman* did warily provide against this danger, by bestowing upon the yielding conquered Nation the requital of their ancient Law."[31] Like Coke, Selden wrote of "ancient law," not an "ancient constitution." He too associated that ancient law with *English* law, a characteristic move of common lawyers as they came to grips with the rule of a Scottish king. Still, there was some truth to the myth of an ancient legal order. The Normans had taken over "a going concern," an island with many local legal systems as well as the rudiments of a centralized one.[32] These principles of legal survival might also explain why the common law extended to Coke's own day, in the face of Tudor and Stuart centralization.[33] Again, common lawyers were most concerned about England and its constitution, not the other dominions.

However, in obiter dicta elaborating the reasons for the decision, Coke sketched the outlines of a constitutional jurisprudence for the overseas territories. These dicta educated lawyers about the legal status of the colonies when they read the case in the Inns of Court or elsewhere in preparation for careers in law, enterprise, or royal administration.[34] For generations, imperial officials and colonists went to school on Coke's opinion in *Calvin's Case*.

Three aspects of Coke's dicta influenced the empire's legal culture: his reasoning style; his distinction between inherited and conquered territories; and his remarks on the legal rights of emigrant settlers. First, Coke used the same reasoning to analyze the status of non-English territories that he used to interpret English law: he championed the "artificial reason" of the legal community above the natural reason of the individual.[35] In other words, law was custom of a special sort. The law's reason differed from "the reason of the wisest man" and could be grasped only "by diligent study and long experience and observation." A close student of the laws could see that "[t]here be multitudes of examples, precedents, judgments, and resolutions in the laws of England, the true and unrestrained reason whereof doth decide this question."[36] The precedents concerned the old Norman provinces, the Channel Islands, and Ireland. Today the opinion reads like a crabbed medieval tract on the king's dominions, and even though it read the same way to a few contemporaries, it remained the most sophisticated legal interpretation of the British Empire for at least two centuries.[37] Later, in the fourth volume of his *Institutes of the Laws of England*, Coke drew a "map" of "all the high, honourable, venerable, and necessary tribunals, and courts of justice within his majesties realms and dominions." This map included about one hundred English courts and several others in Scotland and Ireland.[38] It was imperative for the lawyer to know these boundaries because "as the body of man is best ordered, when every particular member exerciseth his proper duty: so the body of the commonwealth is best governed when every severall court of justice executeth his proper jurisdiction."[39] Coke's "map" of the empire's jurisdictions was authoritative. New discoveries had to be fitted within its medieval dimensions.

Second, Coke categorized all overseas territories as inherited or conquered. This distinction derived from the classical period and was current throughout Europe.[40] In lands obtained by inheritance, like Scotland, the king "cannot change [the] laws of himself, without consent of parliament." Until then, the laws extant before the descent remained in force. A king could not revise the laws of inherited land wholesale; he had to rule with the "consent of parliament."[41]

Conquered lands were different. Coke divided conquered territories into Christian and infidel. The native laws of infidel lands were "abrogated" immediately upon conquest because they were "not only against Christianity, but against the law of God and nature." Accordingly, "until certain laws be established among them," the king could govern infidel lands by "natural equity, in such sort as Kings in ancient time did with their kingdoms, before any certain municipal laws were given."[42] In contrast, the laws of a conquered Christian people remained in force until the conqueror changed them.

This second aspect of Coke's British jurisprudence received much commentary in the eighteenth century and some from modern historians because it bears on the American revolutionaries' claim that their colonies were outside the British Parliament's jurisdiction and could be governed only by the king-in-council.[43] The controverted point is what Coke meant by the "consent of parliament." Many historians, following Robert L. Schuyler, believe that Coke was referring to the *English* Parliament. If so, Coke was silent about the form of government within overseas dominions.[44] But some, like Barbara A. Black, interpret Coke to mean that the king had to rule most of his overseas colonies with the consent of a *local* parliament rather than alone or through the English Parliament.[45] "Coke's position," Black argues, "was that of a parliament-man, not a Parliament-man."[46] If so, the revolutionaries rested on good authority.

Little can be resolved on the basis of Coke's few words on the matter. Given his jurisdictional orientation, when he stated that the king could make no new law in an inherited land except with the "consent of parliament," he could well have meant a local representative body, not the English Parliament. But Coke did not explain what he meant by "consent of parliament" or whether this was the only means of governance. His equivocation reflected the legal pluralism of early modern England. The three methods of governance — through a local parliament, through the metropolitan Parliament, and through the Privy Council — were not exclusive alternatives.[47] Although Coke quite possibly intended to say that the king could not alter the native laws of an inherited kingdom without the consent of its own local parliament (the Scottish Parliament, for example, in the inherited kingdom of Scotland) and that the same was true in conquered lands where the king introduced English law (such as Ireland), he probably envisioned areas of governance not affecting native laws in which the king could govern without local consent and with or without the metropolitan Parliament. This approximates the imperial modus vivendi that developed over the next century.[48] Coke was content to list the precedents for parliamentary jurisdiction overseas rather than justify it, guide its exercise, or treat the examples as exceptions. Whether or not the king governed those places through his prerogative institutions or through the metropolitan Parliament turned, in practice, on metropolitan and imperial politics rather than on constitutional principles located in the writings of Sir Edward Coke or elsewhere.[49]

The irony is that Coke identified precedents for English parliamentary power to legislate for overseas dominions at the same time that he and the other English judges maintained that the common-law courts' jurisdiction — the common law as it was then understood — did not extend outside the realm of England. The former was a knotty problem; the latter was not. Soon after Coke died, colonists began to argue just the reverse, that they enjoyed the common law and the liberties of Englishmen but were not subject to parliamentary legislation.[50]

At the dawn of transatlantic colonization, English jurists were less concerned with mapping the constitutional rights and duties of the center and peripheries of the emergent empire than with defining those constitutional rights and duties *within* the realm of England. In the curiously Anglocentric formulation of *Calvin's Case*, Coke's analysis of inherited and conquered Christian dominions seemed to counsel the English king to respect Scottish law and political institutions. However, it also meant that the Scottish king had to respect English legal and political institutions. While handing King James a political victory over the House of Commons, Coke told him that he had to respect English liberties.[51] He agreed with James that Scottish and English subjects should enjoy reciprocal rights, but he implied that England was preeminent on the Isle of Britain. This supremacy would prevent the constitutional regression that parliamentarians feared.

The third part of Coke's opinion that influenced imperial legal culture was his assertion that *some* of the rights of Englishmen emigrated with natural subjects who settled in newly conquered lands, especially property rights and consent. The former meant that emigrant Englishmen should be able to hold property in the same tenures available in England. Under the latter, emigrants would benefit from parliamentary government. The right to parliamentary governance was implicit in the ambiguous dicta suggesting that the king would, in kingdoms obtained through descent or Christian lands got by conquest, rule with the "consent of parliament." Again, Coke did not elaborate on this mandate's form: Did it require a representative assembly? a council of notables? Nonetheless, it does seem that he was a "parliament-man." Emigrant settlers as well as natives in those overseas territories would benefit from the right to some form of parliamentary rule, whether local or metropolitan.

The property rights strand of Coke's exportable core of English liberty was unequivocal and more important to the spread of common-law culture. The king's subjects, "as well Antenati as Postnati," Coke wrote, "are capable of lands in the kingdom or country conquered, and may maintain any real [i.e., property] action, and have the like privileges and benefits there, as they may have in England."[52] Coke did not mean that those emigrants could sue for colonial land in the *English* common-law courts, for he made clear that remedial writs from those courts did not run outside the realm of England, and these common-law property actions were remedial.[53] Nonetheless, Coke intended for the king to respect the emigrants' property rights abroad, such as the common-law rights to inherit and devise land or a widow's claim to dower. But he did not specify how emigrants would vindicate these property rights. Was the king obligated to establish colonial courts along the lines of his English common-law courts to administer common-law actions? Or could the king hear cases himself, through his governors or Privy Council? In practice, there was a mixture. Formally, the Privy Council delegated its power to hear disputes to local executive courts and reserved the power to review appeals itself.[54] In practice, lawyers and judges in those local courts gradually replicated many common-law rules and procedures.[55] The right to hold property by common-law tenure—the "marrow of English law," Coke called it, that was contained in Littleton's *Tenures* and glossed in the first volume of his *Institutes*—went abroad even though the jurisdiction of the common-law courts did not.

Here is a clue to the conceptual transformation that Coke catalyzed and that went the farthest fastest in the colonies: the shift from a predominantly jurisdictional to a substantive understanding of the common law. Coke's minimalist constitution, which envisioned parliamentary government and common-law tenures for British emigrants in the colonies, went abroad as the imperial *lex franca*. The simplicity of this exported version of English liberty was its strength. Again, Coke wrote of emigrants' ability to "maintain any real action"; he did not write of a transcendent common law. However, he linked "real actions" and "privileges and benefits" in the same sentence. Syntactically and logically, remedy still preceded right, but the remedy was being liberated from the jurisdiction of the court system in which it had been created. The unsystematic mass of common-law property writs were flowering into rules that could be understood apart from the executive directives in which they originated. Writs were becoming rights.[56]

English Common Law as Imperial Fundamental Law

The availability of many real actions to vindicate property interests may not seem momentous today. Some of those actions never went abroad.[57] Others, like the right to devise property by will, are now taken for granted. These rights are so ingrained in liberal legal culture that it may be forgotten that in the Middle Ages they were matters of the king's grace that slowly became routinized into privileges vindicable in the king's courts and then spread across oceans with the early modern empire as rights. John Baker remarks that "[l]iberty and freedom will not be found as titles in the books of common law before 1600." English lawyers spoke of plural "liberties" and "franchises" as "specific privileges or exemptions" from royal jurisdiction.[58] A franchise, wrote F. W. Maitland, was "a portion of royal power in the hands of a subject," granting him immunity from a royally-imposed burden or the power to exercise some aspect of royal power.[59] Baker concludes that the general concept of liberty—freedom writ large—"developed through the cumulative effects of decisions which were not widely known to outsiders and became unknown to posterity save through laborious research."[60] Although early modern jurists sincerely desired to increase, in Coke's memorable phrase, "the freedom and liberty of the subject,"[61] their handiwork had the more immediate effect of distancing their own courts, and the whole common-law community over which they presided, from the crown. The predominance of the common law as the *lex franca* of empire began with the triumph of common-law institutions within England.

The term "common law" originated in medieval canon law "to distinguish the general and ordinary law of the universal church both from any rules peculiar to this or that provincial church, and from those papal *privilegia* which were always giving rise to ecclesiastical litigation." Secular continental jurists then used the term *ius commune* for the law of the Holy Roman Empire as a whole, as opposed to local laws, which were known as *ius proprium*.[62] Medieval English legal thinkers borrowed the term to distinguish the general laws of the king's courts from the law of manors and other local units that continued to enjoy legal authority after the conquest. The king's own judges led this consolidation, struggling to centralize justice in toward the crown and away from local, customary municipal and feudal courts.[63] The process by which the common-law courts displaced much local justice, then trespassed into the jurisdiction of their royal competitors, was a procedural and administrative triumph rather than an intellectual one.

The substantive gloss that Coke and other common lawyers placed on the common law helped abstract the common law from its procedures. The cases he reported were subtle and slow to yield general principles because common-law writs — the formulaic letters from the crown to its legal agents demanding them to resolve certain disputes in royal courts, and from the courts to parties before and after judgment — originated ad hoc and then solidified into an unsystematic mass.[64] Substantive law developed "gradually," wrote legal historian Henry Maine, "secreted in the interstices of procedure."[65] It did so in concrete controversies. While Coke and his generation strove to present the common law as a "barrier against absolutism," they also reconceived at least part of it as a set of immutable principles from which those rules were derived.[66] In other words, the "historical turn" in common-law thought was a political strategy.[67] Among other virtues, this theory of transcendental principles helped explain how and why common-law rules changed. Legal thinkers continually discovered errors and brought those rules into closer relationship with eternal principles. Correctly considered, the common law was the perfection of reason, what Coke called "artificial reason . . . , which requires long study and experience, before that man can attain to the cognizance of it." The common law was not comprehensible with only the natural reason of those who, like the king, were untutored in law.[68]

This artificial reason was transmitted through the legal culture's educational institutions, and central to these were Coke's writings. He mined property law for analogies to express the claim that common law was fundamental law.[69] In the didactic prefaces to his *Reports*, Coke used property-law metaphors to explain why he published judicial opinions: "the ancient and excellent laws of England are the birthright, and the most ancient and best inheritance that the subjects of this realm have, for by them he enjoyeth not only his inheritance and goods in peace and quietness, but his life and his most dear country in safety."[70] To protect the subject, those laws had to be publicized and certain. Later, in the parliamentary debate over the Petition of Right, Coke invoked a series of "fundamental laws" demonstrating that the king could not take property from or imprison his subjects without due process of law, and the last was the boldest: "the common law hath so admeasured the King's prerogative, as he cannot prejudice any man in his inheritance; and the greatest inheritance a man hath is the liberty of his person, for all others are accessory to it."[71] The liberty of inheritance was vindicable in common-law courts, and on this analogy the king could not take away a person's liberty in a general sense. Once more Coke used a property maxim to express the idea of political liberty. The metaphor of liberty as property — a birthright — circulated throughout England and then beyond in Coke's writings, with unintended consequences.[72]

Excellent examples of the abstraction of common-law rules are the reports of *Darcy v. Allen* and *Bonham's Case*. In *Darcy*, King's Bench narrowly construed a royal monopoly to vindicate the right of a subject to practice his trade, which was the manufacture of playing cards. The court held simply that the monopolist had no remedy in the common-law courts; he had to go directly to the crown. But Coke's report of this case — in which he was not a judge — contained broader language that came to stand for the erroneous proposition that English law forbade monopoly.[73]

One of Coke's most famous opinions came in *Bonham's Case*. In that case his own Court of Common Pleas held that the common-law courts would not uphold the London College of Physicians' statutory monopoly over medical practice in the city of London.[74] The problem was that the college had the power to enforce its monopoly. When proceeding against competitors, it was judge and party.[75] The holding was narrow: the common-law courts had no writ to remedy the college's claim, which violated the principle that a party should not be a judge in his own cause. This became a bedrock common-law principle. But Coke added that "when an Act of Parliament is against common right and reason, or repugnant, or impossible to be performed, the common law will controul it, and adjudge such Act to be void," a sentence that provided grist for those who wished to restrict legislative authority in the future.[76]

These cases were, in an informal way, constitutional cases. Although *Bonham's Case* was not an early instance of what Americans now call judicial review, in his opinion Coke construed a statute so strongly, and contrary to its plain meaning, that it has understandably been interpreted as advocating something close to judicial review.[77] More important, his opinion was intended to check *royal* authority rather than legislative power in the abstract. Such cases demonstrate that early modern jurists used common-law ideas to counter the centralizing momentum of the Stuart kings. Over time the controversies that gave rise to those cases, and even their holdings, were forgotten, while their abstracted meanings gained a deceptive clarity.[78] Coke encouraged this abstraction in many of his opinions, including that in *Calvin's Case*, in which common-law liberties began to escape their jurisdictional matrix and started to become a jurisprudence of British liberty.

In addition, Coke and others elevated the common law above other sources of law within England. This ensured that the common law would trump the others as English rule spread across the Atlantic. "There be divers lawes within the realm of England," Coke wrote in his *Institutes*, and common law was only one of them, though the most important and "sometimes called *lex terrae*."[79] But Coke listed fourteen other types of law, from "*lex coronae*, the law of the crowne," the law merchant, and parliamentary statutes to equity and local customs.[80] Despite this legal pluralism, common lawyers and parliamentarians argued in the early seventeenth century that the common law was "the law of the land" in the broader sense that it embraced all others. Similarly, John Selden argued that "the Common Law . . . [is] the principal and general law," and although each other type of law, like the ecclesiastical law, admiralty law, law merchant, martial law, and the law of the state, "may justly be called *a* law of the land, yet none of them can have the pre-eminence to be stiled *the* law of the land."[81] Another common lawyer, John Davies, believed that the common law provided "the most excellent form of government" and "is so framed fitted to the nature and disposition of this people, as we may properly say that it is *connaturall* to the Nation, so as it cannot possibly be ruled by any other law."[82] The competitor Davies had in mind was continental civil law; it was foreign and ill suited to England. In contrast, the common law was no longer simply the procedures and rules prevalent in the king's central courts. It was the heritage and resource of the English people. Most important, it was controlled by the members of the common-law profession, who were increasingly separated from the crown that had established their courts. This movement tended to flatten the pluralistic legal landscape of England. The common law became more abstract and less tethered to the jurisdiction of the common-law courts; it was becoming a cultural commons accessible to all and exportable to distant lands. A mechanism for controlling jurisdiction was becoming a jurisprudence that transcended borders. The omnivorism of the common law was its strength. It adapted to changing circumstances, and it absorbed useful bodies of law from elsewhere.[83] Analytically and territorially, the common law became the law of the land.

A dozen years after *Bonham's Case*, Coke was in the Commons advocating its powers and liberties.[84] His ideas did not simply serve his new institutional interests. The statute that Coke curtailed in *Bonham's Case* merely confirmed royal letters patent to a guild; it was the monopoly patent, not the legislation, that offended him. In that case, the Houses of Parliament had functioned as a facilitative rather than a deliberative body. Later, Coke partook in the struggles that helped shift the balance of power within Parliament from king to Commons. He now viewed the Commons as a partner with the courts in the enterprise of identifying fundamental laws.[85] The legislative side of the effort culminated in the Petition of Right in 1628, which was a bill of particulars against the Stuart kings and instantly a part of the constitutional canon.[86] Once again, a gambit to restrain the crown contributed to the constitutional ideal of separated powers, and gradually these various strategies became known as the ancient constitution.

Constructing the Constitution: Royal, Whig, and Popular Constitutionalism

Legal historian John Reid quips that in the early modern period the "British Constitution was a composite of whatever views could be plausibly argued and forcibly maintained" and that its meaning was "more a matter of personal usage than of judicial certainty."[87] This goes a little far. The number of valid constitutional arguments was not infinite. Still, Reid captures the fluidity of constitutional discourse in its formative period, when it was not primarily a matter of judicial definition. The term "constitution" did not gain widespread currency until the latter half of the seventeenth century. For example, Coke did not use the term "constitution" in its modern sense. He frequently referred to "the whole frame of the ancient common laws of this realm" and "the fundamentall lawes of the realme," but not the ancient constitution.[88]

Though obscured by its later career, the first prominent uses of the term "constitution" were to protect *royal* power, not individual or parliamentary liberties.[89] Renaissance humanists used "constitution" to refer to the composition of the human body, and from this arose the political connotation of constitution: the organization and tendencies of the body politic. Although the image of the body politic was current across Europe, this use of "constitution" was an English idiom and remained unique in Europe for a century until Montesquieu, after studying English government, injected it into continental legal thought as a universal concept.[90] In *A Comparative Discourse of the Bodies Natural and Politique* (1606), justice of the peace and member of Parliament Edward Forset compared the sovereign to the heart and soul of a body and argued that political diagnoses required one to "know the constitution and complexion of the bodie politique" just as medical ones demanded knowledge of the human body. Forset, a supporter of James I, was drawing on Jean Bodin's concept of sovereignty. The "soveraigne," Forset wrote, is the soul of the body politic, and reason is "the soule of the soule," meaning that "in the State the Soveraigne is governeth by lawes."[91] The king was governed by reason, but not by any other force or institution. Here was a new way of expressing the old idea that the king was superior to all his subjects but was himself subject to fundamental law, and this was no contradiction. Bracton had articulated this idea in England in the thirteenth century, deriving it from Roman law: "*quod Rex non debet esse sub homine, sed sub Deo et lege.*"[92]

Those wishing to restrict the crown tried to make this fundamental law less abstract. In the fifteenth century, Sir John Fortescue categorized England as *dominium politicum et regale* rather than *dominium regale*: it was a political kingdom, not an absolute monarchy, because it balanced the liberties of the subject and the prerogatives of the king to prevent the tyranny of the latter.[93] The constitutional battles of the Stuart era were fought using these once compatible, now increasingly exclusive, legal ideas of royal prerogative and fundamental law.[94]

The most prominent early use of "constitution" came on the eve of the English Civil War. In 1642, the Houses of Parliament demanded a joint power to appoint the king's advisers. Demurring in *His Majesty's Answer to the XIX Propositions of . . . Parliament*, King Charles praised "that excellent Constitution of this Kingdom" and characterized it in the Polybian terms of mixed government, another humanist rediscovery. The drafters of the *Answer*, Lucius Cary, the second Viscount Falkland, and Sir John Colepepper, who was Charles's chancellor of the exchequer, were "constitutional Royalists." These men supported parliamentary power but also respected the crown and feared their more extreme colleagues.[95] They assured the Commons that the English constitution mixed the three social estates (the king, nobility, and commons) and balanced the three corresponding classical forms of government (monarchy, aristocracy, and democracy). The king controlled foreign relations, appointments, and pardons; the lords possessed judicial power; and the Commons possessed the right of taxation and power of impeachment. The gravamen of the *Answer* was that joint power of appointment violated this functional division. (In modern terms, it was a claim for executive privilege.) While the triadic estates model was ancient, the equation of the three estates with the three functional forms of government was new to English thought. Conventionally, the estates were the Lords Temporal, the Lords Spiritual, and the Commons. Now, the Lords were united, and the king became the third estate. For the first time, the king conceded that he was one of the three estates of the realm rather than separate and above them.[96] "Constitution" entered English political discourse as a term expressing a vision of politics that positioned the king in a horizontal relationship with the other governmental institutions. In short, constitutional discourse could be used against the king as well as for him.

English constitutionalism absorbed fragments of other languages besides mixed government, like fundamental law and popular consent.[97] All were available to express the idea that English society adhered to the rule of law. Today the rule of law primarily defines the boundary between the public and the private, but early modern Britons invoked it as a defense when one part of the social order overreached, vertically across social lines or horizontally across space, to trespass on the liberties of another. Maybe it was a central court extending its jurisdiction into the provinces, the Privy Council scrutinizing a borough charter, imperial officials restraining settlement on colonial frontiers, or, as in the *Answer*, the king defending his power of appointment. The crown was most often the target, and constitutionalist notions such as fundamental law and mixed government emerged as ways to restrain it. Fundamental law was defined with metaphors of foundations, contracts, pure reason, ancient law, and evolving custom.[98] There were tensions between these definitions. Ancient law and contract, for example, do not always sit well together. When English jurists used the term, they usually employed the plural: fundamental laws.[99] Because Coke and others identified the core of the common law as fundamental, soon much constitutional discourse derived from the common law.[100] Not all of the common law was part of the ancient constitution, and the constitutional canon also contained other sources. During the early modern period this canon expanded to include the

Petition of Right of 1628, the Declaration of Rights of 1689, and the Act of Settlement of 1701. These documents were unusual in their articulation of political rights and duties, and although they were often treated as restatements of existing principles, many of the rights were new. The popular conception of this constitutionalism is summed up in the title of one compilation of key documents published first in London in 1682 and reprinted in the colonies a generation later: *English Liberties, or the Free-Born Subject's Inheritance, Containing Magna Charta, The Petition of Right, the Habeas Corpus Act, and Divers Other Most Useful Statutes.*[101]

Common-law constitutionalism contributed to the English Civil War in the 1640s. Parliamentarians strove to protect legal liberties from what they saw as royal abuses such as the extension of martial law to civilians, the supplanting of local officials by lords lieutenant, and new forms of taxation.[102] A primary language of resistance was common-law constitutionalism and its celebration of freehold tenure, local institutions like the jury, and parliamentary government. In short, the substance of a royal court system's jurisprudence was marshaled against royal power. Most parliamentarians viewed the common law as a repository of liberty, but other revolutionaries disagreed. Levellers saw the common law as a tool imported from Normandy to suppress truly ancient liberties.[103] But even here, those ancient liberties were similar to Coke's, though they supposedly antedated the common law. Even though most rejected the Levellers' distinction between ancient and common-law liberties, the idea of immemorial law further separated substantive liberties from the common-law courts.

The greatest constitutional legacy of the English Civil War and the Interregnum that followed was the increased emphasis on popular consent. The language of mixed government receded, not least because the commonwealthmen executed one-third of the triad. Faith in fundamental laws remained, but commonwealthmen thought it important to put them into print. This trend toward consensual written statements of fundamentals derived in part from written manorial custumals and corporate by-laws. Probably more important was the centrality of the written word in reformed Protestant culture. In addition, some reformers also doubted the "artificial reason" of common lawyers, whom they suspected of manipulating unwritten law.[104] Although the serial Agreements of the People, Instrument of Government (1654), and Humble Petition and Advice (1657) were not termed "constitutions," the reformers' emphasis on the written word accelerated the trend of memorializing fundamental laws in print.[105] These liberties were ancient, and this ancientness was evidence of past consent, a consent that was confirmed through popular participation in the declaration of the nation's fundamental laws. Writing was supposed to confirm ancient liberties and reduce the role of "artificial reason" in their interpretation. It was not a positivist replacement of custom.

Soon after parliamentarians gained hold of English government, they asserted control over the whole empire. One example is the first Navigation Act. Beginning in December 1651, all "Goods or Commodities whatsoever, or the Growth, Production or Manufacture of Asia, Africa or America" had to be shipped on vessels belonging to "the People of this Commonwealth, or the Plantations." The act was supposed to increase the shipping and encourage the navigation of England rather than benefit the plantations.[106] Colonists who opposed this or other measures of Cromwell's administration appropriated common-law constitutionalism to protect themselves from metropolitan interference. The first to do so were crown loyalists in Barbados in 1650.[107] Overseas, common-law constitutionalism offered defense against the positive legislation of Parliament.

"Constitution" became a commonplace term in Whig political discourse between the Restoration of the Stuarts in 1660 and the Glorious Revolution of 1688/89. Champions of the House of Commons accented the consensual element in constitutionalism and deemphasized the crown as an independent estate.[108] But the Glorious Revolution, unlike the Civil War, did not threaten the monarchy as an institution. Kings were supposed to govern for the public good; if they did not, they could be ousted in revolution. The mixed estates model persisted, and other connotations of the constitution lingered and mingled. Matthew Hale, chief justice of King's Bench during the Restoration, depicted the common law as an alternative source of authority to the newly empowered Commons as well as the crown. Common lawyers like Coke had long claimed that the common law enjoyed some autonomy from the crown. Now Hale, like the colonial royalists of the previous generation, claimed that the common law provided ballast against both the royal prerogative *and* parliamentary legislation. Common law was the glue of a nation defined as having a limited central government, not just a limited monarchy. Hale, to rebut Thomas Hobbes's positivist criticism of customary law, argued that the common law rested on accumulated practice, which was more protective of liberty than the individual will of a king or the collective will of a legislature. The most legislators could hope for was that statutory law would someday accumulate the respect due custom. Hale's custom was, however, more evolutionary than Coke's. Changes to law were "partial and successive," some by legislation and some not. Nonetheless, "in the general" English law was the same as it had been six hundred years earlier, just "as the Argonauts Ship was the same when it returned home, as it was when it went out, tho' in that long Voyage it had successive Amendments, and scarce came back with any of its former Materials." Hale was sending a signal to legislators to respect common-law rights and proceed cautiously when reforming the laws.[109] He also claimed that common law controlled the king's prerogative. The law, meaning the courts of law, could offer remedies to subjects injured by the king's actions. As he put it, "the Laws also in many cases bindes ye Kinges Acts, and make them void if they are against Lawe." When operating under his prerogative, the king was outside the "coercive" power of the law, meaning beyond the remedial jurisdiction of his courts. The king nonetheless remained subject to the law's "directive" power, or some fundamental check on his decision making. This explained the maxim that the king could do no wrong. While deeds done by the king himself might be beyond legal remedy, those of his agents were not. *How* these remedies would be enforced remained uncertain. Hale maintained that crown ministers who committed wrongs were "liable to the coercion of the law to make satisfaction."[110] Alternatively, the king could dismiss those ministers. Or the people could dismiss the king, through revolution. The point is that Hale's work kept alive the tools of extraparliamentary popular constitutionalism and included the courts among them.

This gradual domestication of the crown, in the sense of reducing its independent power within the realm of England while increasing that of Parliament beyond it, accelerated after the Glorious Revolution. When the Houses of Parliament declared that James II had abdicated, and then invited William and Mary to replace him, the trend in which Parliament became the central fount of national law became a constitutional principle. The Commons in particular became a partner in imperial governance with the crown. Nation was replacing crown as the symbol of English identity.[111] With Parliament eclipsing the king-in-council, the need to insulate the English realm from the crown dominions decreased. The borders between realm and dominion became more porous, with Parliament assuming the power to rule those territories and colonists claiming the liberties of Englishmen. Thus, a new tension arose, between those ancient liberties and Parliament's legislative power at home and abroad.

The tension between legislative constitutionalism and the older sort based on Coke's identification of common and fundamental law persisted in England into the eighteenth century. In a tract criticizing Robert Walpole and his Whig ministry, the Tory Viscount Bolingbroke distinguished "the constitution" from "government." Governments came and went; some were good and some bad, depending on whether their ministers adhered to the transcendent constitution. This he defined as "that assemblage of laws, institutions and customs, derived from certain fixed principles of reason, directed to certain fixed objects of public good, that compose the general system, according to which the community hath agreed to be governed." Accordingly, a "good government" acted in "strict conformity to the principles and objects of the constitution," whereas a bad one deviated from them "either by obtaining new laws, which want this conformity, or by perverting old ones which had it." In sum, "constitution is the rule by which our princes ought to govern at all times; government is that by which they do govern at any particular time. One must remain immutable; the other may, and, as human nature is constituted, must vary." Again, the constitution was "the rule by which we are to try [government]," in the legal sense of rendering judgment on its administrators. This conception was more constraining than Coke's fundamental common law. The degree to which statutes "conform[ed]" to the constitution "prescribes the measure of our submission to them, according to the principles of the revolution."[112] Bolingbroke's constitution was a collection of fundamental rules against which the people could measure ministerial behavior to gauge whether it was corrupt. Enforcement depended primarily on popular supervision of legislators to ensure that they did not succumb to the crown's corrupting influence. "Government is the business of those, who are appointed to govern," Bolingbroke explained, "[b]ut the British constitution is the business of every Briton."[113] The people had to demand frequent elections and monitor legislative activity. As a last resort, enforcement might require revolution, something many of Bolingbroke's readers had experienced firsthand. In between electoral supervision and the right of revolution were several strategies for opposing unconstitutional government. Some modes were the privilege of the literate and propertied (voting, petitioning), while others were available to all (protest, resistance). One strategy did not preclude another.

In contrast to Bolingbroke, David Hume found that the English constitution lacked the integrity that many assumed it had. Instead of a single constitution, England had several successive constitutions. Refuting the common notion that the Stuarts introduced arbitrary governance to England, Hume—a Scot—argued that it was actually the beloved Queen Elizabeth who "was the least possessed of . . . a tender regard for the liberties and privileges of her people" and "exercised the royal authority in a manner so contrary to all the ideas which we at present entertain of a legal constitution."

The Tudors, not the Stuarts, had introduced the Star Chamber, the Court of High Commission, martial law over civilians, and monopoly charters. Hume then unpacked England's serial constitutions:

> By the ancient constitution, is here meant that which prevailed before the settlement of our present plan of liberty. There was a more ancient constitution, where, though the people had perhaps less liberty than under the Tudors, yet the king had also less authority: the power of the barons was a great check upon him, and exercised great tyranny over them. But there was still a more ancient constitution, viz., that before the signing of the charters, when neither the people nor the barons had any regular privileges; and the power of the government during the reign of an able prince was almost wholly in the king. The English constitution, like all others, has been in a state of continual fluctuation.[114]

Finding multiple constitutions, Hume implicitly rejected the idea that there was one ancient constitution. For him as for many "Court Whigs" loyal to the governing administration, the term "constitution" was descriptive, and he used it to refute critics like Bolingbroke and the eighteenth-century commonwealthmen.[115] They, in turn, would have argued that Hume was describing transitions of governments rather than changing constitutions.

But it was William Blackstone, not Bolingbroke or Hume, who penned the orthodox account of the English constitution in the mid-eighteenth century. In every society, Blackstone wrote, there must be "a supreme, irresistible, absolute, uncontrolled authority, in which the *jura summi imperii*, or the rights of sovereignty, reside." In England, this was Parliament acting in its legislative capacity. Blackstone even disowned the constitutional doctrine of popular resistance. "No human laws will suppose a case," he declared, "which at once must destroy all law." He warned that English "political or civil liberty . . . can only be lost or destroyed by the folly or demerits of its owner: the legislature." Although he harbored reservations about the wisdom of much legislation, the theory of indivisible sovereignty struck him as incontrovertible.[116]

The consequences for the common law were clear: legislation trumped the artificial reason of jurists. Blackstone did add that "no human legislature has the power to abridge or destroy [natural rights]" and that "acts of parliament that are impossible to be performed are of no validity." These restrictions echoed Coke's opinion in *Bonham's Case*. Yet they had less bite because Blackstone added: "[I]f the parliament will positively enact a thing to be done which is unreasonable, I know of no power that can control it: and the examples usually alleged in support of this sense of the rule do none of them prove, that where the main object of a statute is unreasonable the judges are at liberty to reject it; for that would set the judicial above the legislative, which would be subversive of all government."[117] Here Blackstone rejected the broad interpretation of *Bonham's Case* in favor of the narrow one: that case merely involved statutory construction, not judicial review. He encouraged judges to prevent "absurd" consequences "not foreseen by the parliament," but an unjust law must nonetheless be enforced if clearly intended because, he noted wistfully, "there is no court that has power to defeat the intent of the legislature."[118]

The legislature was becoming supreme, but what was the legislature? Analyzing the outcome of the Revolution of 1688/89, Blackstone argued that celebration of the two Houses of Parliament, to the exclusion of the king, went "too far" and risked upsetting the "equilibrium" among the three. It was not true that the Convention of 1689 had dissolved all government and returned England to "a state of nature." Instead, the convention found King James II guilty of attempting to subvert government. Even then, the crown remained a critical part of government. "It is highly necessary for preserving the ballance of the constitution," Blackstone maintained, "that the executive power should be a branch, though not the whole, of the legislature." Although each branch alone would push government in a different direction, together they forced it along "the true line of the liberty and happiness of the community." He concluded that "whatever may have become of the *nominal*, the *real* power of the crown has not been too far weakened by any transactions in the last century. The stern commands of prerogative have yielded to the milder voices of influence." Beneath constitutional discourse was the stable politics of the eighteenth-century constitution. At least at home.[119]

Although the term "constitution" developed a broad connotation that outlined political society and, for some, prescribed limits on governmental behavior, the term "constitutional law" was all but unknown in the English-speaking world before the American Revolution.[120] Yet early modern legal thinkers did believe that there were special customs, rules, and enactments that were pieces of their constitution. No single document contained the whole of the constitution; no single organ of government enjoyed the role of preeminent interpreter. The English constitution was not a thing. Rather, it was a cultural commons, a customary repository of rhetorical strategies that could be invoked to assert powers, rights, and duties, as well as simply to make sense of the political landscape. In practice, the constitution was what people in particular places and at specific times made of those traditions. So the Anglo-American constitutions would continue to be: English words generating divisible constitutional traditions, at once forged and awaiting use in concrete controversies in England, Britain, and beyond.

This is why the English constitution might seem "a composite of whatever views could be plausibly argued and forcibly maintained." Yet not all rhetorical moves were legitimate. Apart from the pliable scripts of custom, fundamentality, consent, and balance, the primary source of this constitution remained the English common law. In addition, the reasoning process used to analyze the constitution was similar to that used for more mundane legal problems. With the common law, this constitutional canon traveled throughout the empire.

Time Immemorial
The Foundations of Common-Law Culture
in an Imperial Province

> *Province* (Provincia) . . . *Amongst the*
> *Romans it was used for a country without the*
> *limits of Italy, gained to their subjection by*
> *conquest; but, in general, it is used to denote*
> *the division of a kingdom or state.*
> Anthony Stokes, *A View of the*
> *Constitution of the British Colonies* (1783)

A S PEOPLE TRAVEL ACROSS SPACE, time seems both to slow down and to accelerate. Migration has the confusing effect of congealing loose ideas into fixed concepts while simultaneously, as individuals encounter new environments, transforming everyday practices. So it was with the diffusion of law in the British Empire. Colonists carried with them or inherited familiar legal ideas, but what they made of them on the periphery often seemed foreign at home.

By the late seventeenth century, two elements stood out in the legal landscape of British America. The first was the provincial elite's devotion to English legal culture.[1] They lived in a constitutional world shaped by the English Civil War, and for the rest of the colonial period British American legal thought was suffused with seventeenth-century presuppositions about fundamental restraints on government, suspicion of the crown and, especially, its agents, and the declaratory nature of the legal process.[2] The seventeenth-century revolutions cast the common law as the primary guarantor of English liberties; this idea traveled beyond England to the rest of the British Empire, and not just among English emigrants and their offspring.

Complementing this embrace of English liberties was a devotion to local autonomy.[3] Localist claims and the centralizing demands of the common law had frequently conflicted in early modern England, but tension between them lessened after the Stuart Restoration. Many seventeenth-century mythologists of the ancient constitution had invoked common-law tropes and procedures to defend decentralized government. The common law was, many lawyers thought, a means of negotiating the relationship between the crown and locality. So too abroad. For North American colonists, the common law vindicated local authority while at the same time tethering them to Britain. Though provincial institutions were frequently compared to metropolitan complements in London, they just as often seemed in theory and functioned in practice like those in English counties and cities, which still enjoyed substantial freedom to order everyday life.

New York, like the other American colonies, did not fit English institutional models. It was part proprietary, part corporation, part county, and part replica of the whole of England. People called it a plantation, colony, and province. When it was one and not the other depended on who was arguing for what, when, and where. These were the leitmotifs of colonial development: local power and English rights, each reinforcing the other in New York, as the argument went, time out of mind.

Conquest and Charter: Creating New York

New Netherland was renamed New York in 1664, after a war between England and the United Provinces of the Netherlands fought mainly on the seas for control of the west African slave trade and hardly at all in America. The peace treaty determined the fate of trading posts from the Caribbean to the Indian Ocean; the transfer of the Dutch West India Company's North American colony was only one exchange. Most English-speakers probably agreed with John Dryden's summary: "The Dutch confess'd Heav'n present, and retir'd, / And all was Britain the wide ocean saw."[4] The alleged penitents might have demurred. New Netherland was primarily a trading post, and much of the trade violated its company charter. It was not intended to be a settler colony like its English neighbors. With the exception of Rensselaerswick, even the fabled patroonships along the Hudson River failed.[5] And two decades later, at Parliament's invitation, a Dutch prince ascended the British throne as William III.[6]

In the meantime, the Stuart king of England, Charles II, granted the proprietary colony of New York to his brother, James, Duke of York, in return for his service in the Dutch war. The grant extended beyond the uncertain boundaries of New Netherland and stretched east into Connecticut and Massachusetts, including what is today western Maine, New Hampshire, Vermont, New Jersey, part of Pennsylvania, many of the islands off the coast of New England, and a piece of Quebec. The western boundaries were particularly unclear. The duke received "the Hudsons River and all land from the west side of Conectecutte River to the East side of De La Ware Bay."[7] James originally planned to make New York City a center for the export of furs and the import of goods into the northern and middle colonies, but his own largesse and that of his brother curbed those plans. James quickly granted East and West Jersey to associates, giving them governmental authority too, although it was not clear that he had the power to do so. The Jersey ports competed well with New York, especially for illegal trade. James tried to reclaim this grant but was too late: the king had confirmed it.[8] Then Charles granted the southern Delaware Valley to William Penn, creating another rival for the fur trade.[9] Still, James possessed vast lands stretching deep into the continent, and Charles gave him a free hand to govern it. Through a charter conveyed in letters patent, his most formal instrument of delegation, the king bestowed on his brother "full and absolute power and authority to Correct punish Pardon Governe and Rule all" inhabitants of the province, including the power to grant land, collect quitrents on that land, and levy taxes. In an age of liberal grants, this was the most sweeping delegation of power to an American proprietor.[10]

There were a few restrictions. First was annual service. The patent for New York, as for other colonies, was modeled on "our Manor of East Greenwich in the County of Kent in free and common soccage," meaning that the duke owed an annual quitrent but no military service. The rent for New York was forty beaver skins. This was largely symbolic, but what it symbolized was the crown's ultimate title to the province. The duke was a great lord holding of the king; any who received land from the duke would hold of him in turn. Property still had political dimensions.[11]

More important was the repugnancy clause. The proprietor was to make laws "not contrary to but as near as conveniently may be agreeable to the Laws, Statutes & Government of this Our Realm of England." Each American colonial charter contained a similar injunction to make no law "repugnant" (as it was usually termed) to those of England, which was the basis for Privy Council review of legislation. The idea was to restrain the proprietor from creating a wholly un-English legal culture. The next clause, empowering the Privy Council to hear judicial appeals too, was more unusual: "And saving and reserving to us Our Heirs and Successors the receiving, hearing and determining of the Appeal and Appeals of all or any Person or Persons of in or belonging to the territories or Islands aforesaid in or touching any Judgment or Sentence to be there made or given." In a narrow but profound way these clauses contained the germ of colonial political development, but what exactly they meant was never clear. One thing was clear: they did not grant English law to the duke's subjects. Rather, the first clause was an indefinite limitation on James's law-making power and the next a restraint on his judicial administration, permitting litigants recourse to the Privy Council in London. Council appellate jurisdiction had been implicit and controversial in some of the earlier colonies, especially Massachusetts, so the appeals clause spelled out the review process. It soon became standard in all colonial charters.[12] As in most colonies, few litigants in New York availed themselves of Privy Council appellate review. Between 1664 and 1776, New Yorkers brought only nine appeals, suggesting that they believed they would receive a fair hearing in their own province or no more fairness in London. At the very least, the chance of reversal may not have been worth the cost.[13]

Finally, the duke and his provincial subjects had to obey all imperial trade regulations and remit "the Customs and Duties therefore due and payable according to the Laws and Customs of this Our Realm," including the Navigation Acts, which regulated colonial trade, the first of which Parliament passed in 1651.[14] Beyond this, James's power was unrestricted.

Provincial Political Institutions: Conceptualizing Local Government

On his island of autonomy within the Atlantic empire, however, the duke could not play Prospero. Quickly the proprietary colony began to function like a self-governing corporation.[15] From the beginning, there was a gap between the official constitutional theory of colonial governance—an institutional hierarchy, with power flowing from London—and the practice of substantial local autonomy. The institutional model for the province was also ambiguous. Along with the Stuarts' feudal ideal, there remained the models of British local government, such as the county and the municipal corporation, and English metropolitan government, centering on Parliament and its emboldened House of Commons. Both models, county government and Parliament, were invoked throughout the colonial period by those hoping to expand as well as those trying to restrain provincial power.[16]

Whatever the theory of government, the legal environment of New York was too complicated for the proprietor to control at will. Impediments included the conquered population: about five thousand European settlers of various ethnic and religious backgrounds.[17] The most prominent of these were Dutch. Not long after the duke received his grant, England fulfilled its treaty promise to the Netherlands to respect the property, contracts, inheritance customs, and religious liberty of the Dutch who remained, along with the Albany merchants' monopoly on the fur trade with the Iroquois, who formed another largely self-governing population in the province. These Articles of Capitulation (1664) curtailed the duke's power in exchange for the obedience of the conquered inhabitants.[18]

Ruling an overseas plantation also entailed practical limitations. One was self-imposed: James never intended to rule New York directly. He was a military officer and a potential heir to the throne. He also held proprietary interests throughout the empire. Just one of his commissions was "High Admiral of Dunkirk, Tangier, and all foreign possessions in Africa and America." From the beginning, the duke selected a deputy governor to serve as his agent within the colony and delegated much of his authority by commission.[19] His first choice, Colonel Richard Nicolls, was a royalist during the Interregnum and led the conquest of New Netherland. He was one of the Stuarts' many loyal military governors.[20]

Second, from the outset James required his governor to rule with the advice of a provincial council, a group of "the most eminent inhabitants of New Yorke, not exceeding tenn." The governor nominated and the duke appointed these men, many of whom were recent emigrants and retained commercial and political ties to England. Governing with the consent of a council was common in the colonies. The council was identified with various models: the House of Lords, the Privy Council, and corporate councils. As a result, the hybrid council served as an advisory board, a legislative body, and, sitting with the governor, the highest provincial court. Appointment, which usually lasted for life, also confirmed social status within the colony.[21]

The provincial council, James hoped, would be the only concession to local participation in government. The younger Stuarts planned to make New York the staging ground for imperial reorganization and resisted pressure for a representative assembly. "[A]n assembly," James told his governor in 1676, "would be of dangerous consequences, nothing being more known than the aptness of such bodies to assume privileges destructive to the peace of the government."[22] Governor Nicolls divided the colony into two parts. Stretching east was Long Island, which he planned to rule along the lines of the New England colonies. Pushing north and west was the Hudson Valley, containing several manors and anchored at each end by the cities of New York and Albany.

For New York City and Long Island, Governor Nicolls drew up "The Duke's Laws" after consulting with their inhabitants.[23] Arranged alphabetically, like most legal reference works at the time, the Duke's Laws did not provide for an assembly but were acceptable because they were modeled on the laws of the New England colonies and preserved a prominent role for town government.[24] Nicolls retained the power to appoint justices of the peace. At the top of the administrative pyramid sat a Court of Assizes, an annual tribunal comprising the governor, his council, and the justices of the peace. This body exercised judicial, legislative, and executive duties. In between the court's sessions, the governor and the council administered all the business of provincial government.[25]

Nicolls complemented the Duke's Laws with four manors in the Hudson Valley. The manors, which built on the Dutch West India Company's failed patroonships, were administrative units as well as land grants.[26] They replicated the proprietary government itself, a chain of personal kingdoms loyal to the crown. This subdivision of a royal grant of jurisdiction, known as subinfeudation, was forbidden under the common law within England but not outside the realm.[27] In addition to stimulating development, the colonel intended these pockets of dominion and loyalty to secure the colony's northern and western reaches, just as the marchland manors had on the Scottish and Welsh borders. The manor lords had the power to collect rent from and, to some degree, govern the people on their lands. Like medieval English manor lords, they had the power to hold courts for criminal and civil disputes, though these courts were all but moribund at home and never vital in New York. For most subject matter, the manors were included within the jurisdiction of the county courts. Still, the manors were economic, social, and political boons to their owners. They also inspired loyalty to the grantors. Governors used them to ensure the support of provincial grandees they helped create through the grants.[28]

Similar to the manors were the cities of New York and Albany. The Dutch West India Company built New Amsterdam and Fort Orange to secure the Hudson River. Later, New Amsterdam received the privileges of a Dutch municipality, and the company referred to it as a city.[29] After the conquest, the predominantly Dutch citizens of New York and Albany persuaded their new rulers to incorporate their communities as cities. The municipal corporation was a legal form common to all Europe, and it helped ease the transition from Dutch to English rule. The cities enjoyed much autonomy. Successive governors, for example, confirmed the right of the Common Council of New York City, "a body politic and corporate," to make laws and ordinances within its boundaries "not repugnant" to the law of England or of the province.[30] In the cities and manors, the genetic pattern of English governance emerged again: layered authority, one institution replicated in another. The governor's manorial delegation mirrored his commission from the duke, just as the duke possessed letters patent from the king. In turn, the tenants owed the lord rent, the lord owed the duke quitrents, and the duke remitted to his brother forty skins a year.

Despite this pyramid of authority, power did not flow smoothly. Each institution was answerable to the next, but to what degree and in what ways remained unclear, which hampered central authority while allowing local government much freedom. Within the buffer zone between this theory and the practice of administration grew competing visions of the empire. A complicated constitutional environment was, however, not the best place for ordinary administration. Revenue collection, in particular, met with stubborn resistance. Merchants in New York City resented the duke's port duties. When some of them refused to pay, the duke's customs collector, a man named William Dyer, seized their goods. The merchants, a mostly Dutch community aided by Anglophone colleagues familiar with English law, responded by forming a grand jury — the province's first — and indicted Dyer for treason in 1681. The merchants seem to have had the support of the governor, whose jurisdiction sometimes collided with the collector's. Dyer was charged with plotting "Inovacons in Government and the subversion and change of the known Ancient and Fundamentall Lawes of the Realme of England" because he used a collection procedure — seizure — that violated Magna Carta, the Petition of Right, and "other statutes." The grand jury assumed that the English constitutional canon, including parliamentary statutes, applied to New York. Already the colony's diverse population claimed the rights of Englishmen. The collector challenged the court's jurisdiction and, because of the gravity of the charge, was shipped to London for trial, where he was not prosecuted.[31]

Nonetheless, this suit, along with persistent petitions for an assembly and competition with neighboring colonies for British settlers, accomplished its goal.[32] The duke realized that another compromise with the centrifugal forces of colonization was necessary. In 1683, he instructed Governor Thomas Dongan to summon "a General Assembly of all the Freeholders, by the persons who they shall choose to represent them," to make laws that were "fitt and necessary . . . for the good weale and governement of the said Colony." The assembly was to have legislative power subject to the governor's veto and Privy Council review. The duke's instruction took a cue from the merchants' protest and paraphrased Article 39 of Magna Carta, while also echoing the king's directive that he respect English law: "I doe hereby require and command you," James instructed his governor, "that noe mans life, member, freehold, or goods, be taken away or harmed in any of the places under your government but by established and knowne laws not repugnant to, but as nigh may be agreeable to, the laws of the Kingdome of England." Finally, he authorized the governor to reorganize the judiciary.[33]

The governor ordered local sheriffs to hold elections in their judicial districts for members of the assembly. Some were direct elections; other were indirect, by local governing bodies. In the direct elections, only men holding forty-pound freeholders could vote, as in England, and they did so viva voce.[34] The assembly met in New York City in October 1683 and immediately passed "The Charter of Libertyes and priviledges granted by his Royall Highnesse to the Inhabitants of New Yorke and its dependencyes," the title of which assumed a great deal. It was a legislative substitute for a royal charter that did not exist. The drafters drew on the English constitutional canon and the charters of neighboring colonies, thus mixing corporate and English liberties, local and imperial identities.[35] The liberties and privileges the assembly presumed to have been granted included the assembly itself, triennial sessions, the privilege of determining members' qualifications, jury trials, civilian immunity from martial law, and the "due Course of Law," among other old and new rights of Englishmen. Two decades after the English takeover, the first provincial assembly invoked the rights of Englishmen as reflected in Magna Carta, or the "Great Charter of Liberties," the Petition of Right, and the charters of incorporated colonies. The assembly contained several Dutch-descended members, who had their own tradition of local control. But now this transnational European principle was funneled into English legal words and forms, which became the raw material of constitutional argument for the next century.[36]

Although the peace treaty with the Netherlands provided that the English government would respect Dutch property arrangements, non-English legal forms were marginalized, as were those people who resisted Anglicization. This resistance peaked during Leisler's Rebellion of 1689, in which German merchant Jacob Leisler, who had married a Dutch widow, rallied those displeased with the political and religious trajectory of New York—toward England, Anglicanism, and aristocracy—and who longed for either New

Netherland or a political community premised on reformed Protestantism. Even though Leisler's Rebellion led to minimal bloodshed (mostly his and his lieutenant's on the arrival of a new royal governor in 1691) and his reign lasted less than two years, the schism between a royalist, Anglicizing elite and a heterogeneous faction of reformed Protestants persisted for more than a generation. The rebellion, along with uprisings in other colonies, also sank plans for uniting the northern colonies in one large royal dominion.[37]

After writing its own charter, the assembly divided the province into counties, thereby reproducing the jurisdictional structure of England. The counties provided ballast against proprietary rule, as they did in England against royal government, and against the manors. They also formed the skeleton of a new provincial judiciary so that, according to Eben Moglen, "the essential adjudicatory business of the colony would be done in courts at or below the county level." While this system of county courts satisfied the desire for local government, the provincial Supreme Court of Judicature, which the assembly created in 1691 and which had the power to hear writs of error and receive transfers from the counties, centralized some administration. The courts were more centralized in New York than in England because the supreme court's jurisdiction was simple and broad. It had jurisdiction over cases that in England were divided among all three central common-law courts: King's Bench, Common Pleas, and Exchequer. Accordingly, there was less horizontal friction at the top of the colonial judicial system than within the realm of England: all review proceeded vertically in one direction, toward the supreme court.[38] Finally, the familiar county structure would help draw English immigrants into the province, or at least keep them from moving to its more Anglicized neighbors.[39]

As the fundamental administrative unit, the county was extremely important. In addition to county courts, there were numerous county commissions for specialized problems, each limited in jurisdiction and duration.[40] The same individuals might sit on different courts and commissions, which often convened at the same time and place. All of this fitted into the tradition of English local government. The assembly passed many statutes requiring taxes to be levied, roads to be constructed, militias to be formed, wolves to be killed, and so on, but it did not specify how each task would be accomplished. Instead, the assembly depended on the counties for implementation. It was at the county level that most of the governmental business transpired, including tax collection, church and road maintenance, care for the poor, organization of the militia, and dispute resolution. In turn, county officers often depended on town and village officers.[41]

Localities executed provincial laws, but they also initiated many of them through petitions, which were central to the assembly's business.[42] As a result, provincial government served local interests. An assemblyman was the agent of his constituents as members of a county as much as individuals. The agency model, which dated from at least the medieval period, paralleled the notion of interest representation in local government throughout the empire, but it differed from the emergent idea of virtual representation in the English Parliament.[43] Recovery of how the assembly's committees actually decided these petitions may be impossible. The regional partnerships, family alliances, and favors that went unrecorded would probably demonstrate that these petitions involved much patronage and deal making. This narrow orientation led provincial lawyer William Smith Jr. to complain that the views of most in the assembly "seldom extended farther than to the regulation of highways, the destruction of wolves, wildcats, and foxes, and the advancement of the other little interests of the particular counties, which they were chosen to represent."[44] As a result, factional fights in the assembly centered on the control of public payments to individual New Yorkers.

In addition, county offices provided opportunity for much self-government because of the English tradition of rotating local offices. Sparse population, combined with a limited supply of genuine grandees, necessitated a high level of participation in government and contributed to the felt sense of autonomy that distinguished colonial political culture from England's. Yet in some towns certain family names dominate the records throughout the colonial period, suggesting local patterns of familial domination and deference.[45]

The county was more than a model for local government within the colony. The province itself resembled a county or municipal corporation. Specific practices that developed over centuries in English counties and cities were worked into colonial government, often by way of the experience of assemblymen who had previously administered local government. For example, tax collection and reimbursements for the publicly beneficial activity of private actors absorbed most of the effort of local government. Within a generation of the assembly's existence, such activity dominated its time as well. Consequently, the assembly functioned more like a county or town government, both familiar to its members, than like the House of Commons, which most of them knew only from their agents' reports, parliamentary manuals, and newspapers.

The influence of county administration on the provincial assembly is illustrated by the local compensation of assemblymen. Each representative had to return home to petition a county or municipal board for expenses, sometimes with receipts in hand. This was how members of Parliament were compensated in England until the eighteenth century, and it resembled the way counties reimbursed citizens for other public services at the local level. Representatives in the assembly were familiar with this tradition through their own petitions and, many of them, from earlier service as county or municipal administrators. They brought this method of petition and reimbursement with them into the assembly, deriving it unselfconsciously from the practices of local government as they operated throughout the empire.[46]

Consequently, colonial legislators did not just emulate Parliament but also assumed the broad administrative powers of local institutions. The rise of the colonial assembly was premised on the seventeenth-century rise of the English county.[47] Yet to explain their legislative privileges, especially after the Glorious Revolution of 1688/89, assemblymen turned increasingly to parliamentary literature.[48] The assembly was, then, a conceptual hybrid. Squeezing the colonies into preexisting institutional categories was the English way of empire. The Charter of Libertyes—with its corporate form, localist substance, and parliamentary rhetoric—nicely memorializes the province's institutional ambiguity. Creole provincials spoke from parliamentary scripts here and administered their jurisdiction like a county there. Their articulate representatives were lawyers used to pleading in the alternative, not political philosophers elaborating a theory of sovereignty. In New York as everywhere in the early modern empire, government remained undertheorized, which allowed creative minds to draw on several legal scripts at once to pursue their political ends. For generations, elite New Yorkers would alternate between viewing themselves as members of a semiautonomous corporation within a larger empire and as leaders of their own imperium.

Back in London, the duke signed the Charter of Libertyes while still proprietor. But before transmitting approval he ascended the throne, transforming New York into a royal colony, and changed his mind. James II and his Privy Council did "not think fitt to confirm" what they called "The Charter of Incorporation of the Province of New York." They also objected to the wholesale claim to English law and believed that the list of liberties would interfere with the royal prerogative.[49] To raise taxes, the governor called another assembly in 1685, but he soon dissolved it and never called another. In 1688, the king extended the Dominion of New England to include New York and New Jersey. He had created the dominion in 1685 to centralize government in the northern colonies, and its governor ruled only with the advice of an appointed council.[50] New Englanders had lost their chartered privileges, including elected representation, and now New

Yorkers, who claimed chartered rights and liberties too, did as well. From an orthodox perspective, all this was constitutional. Power flowed from the king. The governor's authority rested on the king's commission, given to him in England and published when he arrived in his domain. Additional directions to the governor came in private instructions.[51] These instruments fell under the rubric of the royal prerogative. New York and all the plantations were in theory ruled by the king-in-council — the king *outside* Parliament, not *in* Parliament. Yet the king-in-Parliament, and Parliament without the king during the Interregnum, had also legislated for the colonies. As the prerogative's scope contracted during the tumultuous seventeenth century, Parliament became more involved with the overseas dominions. The most controversial imperial regulations, the Navigation Acts, were acts of Parliament. From the beginning of New York's history, therefore, it was unclear which metropolitan institutions were responsible for the colonies.[52]

The Revolution of 1688/89 did little to clarify the locus of authority in England. This complex event culminated in the ouster of James II. The Houses of Parliament offered the crown to his daughter Mary and her Dutch cousin and husband, the Prince of Orange.[53] Parliament's role in governing the overseas dominions remained uncertain for decades. What is clear is that the revolution ended James's reign in Britain and that simultaneous rebellions in North America brought down his Dominion of New England.[54] The new king, William III, authorized his governor in New York to call a new representative legislature. This new assembly passed a bill even more liberal than the old Charter of Libertyes and entitled "An Act Declaring What are the Rights and Privileges of Their Majestyes Subjects Inhabiting within Their Province of New York," which the governor signed in May 1691. The assembly thanked the king for "restoring to them the undoubted rights and privileges of Englishmen," meaning the assembly and local government, which had been lost under the dominion. They also asked the governor to confirm additional "rights, Priviledges, Libertyes and francheses according to the Lawes and statutes of their Majesties Realm of England." These included freeholder suffrage, common-law tenures, the jury trial, due process, freedom from martial law, freedom of conscience (excepting Catholics), and other familiar parts of the English constitutional canon. These liberties, they observed, formed the "most excellent constitution . . . much esteemed by our ancestors."[55] The governor had granted the people the right to form an assembly, but the assembly tried to define its own powers as well as other liberties and privileges. This statute was shipped back to London for review by the Board of Trade, which advised the king's Privy Council in 1697 that the act assumed "too great and unreasonable privileges" and contained "several large and doubtful expressions." The council disallowed the act. The board also attached a marked-up extract from the Virginia charter granted by Charles II for the assembly's consideration. Charles had revoked many charters, at home and abroad, and regranted stricter ones, such as the Virginia charter. The extract stressed the colonists' "immediate dependance on the Crown" and on his agent, the governor.[56] The New York redaction of real and contested common-law rights had been rejected again. Although the Stuarts were gone, imperial orthodoxy at the center remained.

As a practical matter, disallowance had little effect. The assembly continued to meet throughout the remainder of the colonial period, as the king's instructions said it should, subject to prorogation and dissolution by the governor. Similarly, a week before it declared New Yorkers' rights and privileges, the assembly created justices of the peace, county courts, and the supreme court. All these violated the governor's commission, which gave him the exclusive power to create courts. This judicial act contained a two-year sunset provision, but the assembly renewed it three times before 1698, when an anti-Leislerian assembly refused to do so. This forced the Leislerian governor, the Earl of Bellomont, to issue an ordinance recognizing the court system, which from then on rested on the governor's authority. Still, to most New Yorkers it remained the creature of the assembly.[57]

Because the principles on which the assembly and the courts rested were never articulated in an official instrument again, the constitutional basis of the legislature and the legal rights claimed by New Yorkers remained contested. Formally the king's gift, these liberties and privileges seemed always, in the minds of many New Yorkers, to rest on additional bases. At times New Yorkers proclaimed that they did indeed have a charter, their Charter of Libertyes, and that the assembly was akin to the governing council of a corporation.[58] At others they invoked the customary rights of Englishmen and viewed the assembly as a provincial version of the House of Commons. The New York assembly, like those in the other colonies, produced dozens of acts each year that, together, carved out a zone of corporate positivism within a common-law empire. Inside its borders, New Yorkers, or at least their legislative elite, thought that they could rule freely. When they did protest Parliament's legislation, they objected to the British claim to have a free hand to legislate within New York. Rarely before the 1760s did they protest the abstract principle of legislative sovereignty. Claims of legislative autonomy sat without tension next to claims of fundamental law.

Physically, the assembly was more like a county institution than the House of Commons. It had no dedicated home. Instead, it shared City Hall with the Common Council of New York City. This building had originally served the New Amsterdam council and symbolized the way authority in New York was layered across time and at every moment. By the mid-eighteenth century, the assembly had twenty-seven members. New York City sent four representatives; nine counties sent two; and the borough of West-Chester, the township of Schenectady, and each of the three manors sent one each. As in the House of Commons, there was a mix of bodies represented: a municipal corporation, an unincorporated city, counties, manors, and a borough. The enumeration of representatives reflected the principle of proportional representation, although New York City in particular was underrepresented throughout the colonial period.[59]

Legislative procedure followed parliamentary lines. The assembly initiated most bills, which then went to the council and the governor, who held an absolute and oft used veto.[60] With the governor's signature, a law was published, which meant it was read aloud "in the open street, near City Hall, his Excellency and the two Houses being present," and occasionally printed in newspapers.[61] In addition, from the early 1690s on, the assembly printed its journal, which contained a limited record of debates, vote tallies, and session laws. Compilations of revised statutes were rare. Consequently, practitioners had difficulty discovering which laws had been repealed or had expired.[62] William Livingston and William Smith Jr., who revised the assembly's statutes in 1751, found that in previous collections "several Acts have been published, which probably have been practised upon, that never were passed by the whole Legislature; and others, that have been duly *Enacted*, wholly omitted." Accordingly, the revisers published "all the publick Acts now in force," but for "those that are *Repealed*, *Expired*, *Obsolete* or *Private*, we have only given the Title," indicating which was which.[63] The last category — private acts — included most of the statutes that originated in petitions, such as those for debtor relief, reimbursements, licenses, and naturalization. The British Parliament published only public acts; indeed, publication rather than generality of effect defined an English public act.[64] But Peter Van Schaack, who revised New York's statutes in 1773, thought it was important to include the titles of private acts because many of them, such as those that naturalized immigrants and allowed them to hold land, were "the Foundation on which very considerable real Estates in the Province are held."[65] At the end of each term, usually twice a year, new laws were sent to London for review by the Board of Trade. Based on the board's report, the Privy Council approved or disallowed the statutes.[66] Most colonial laws went into effect immediately and were voidable by the Privy Council; others contained suspending clauses and were not effective until approved in London.

The governor was powerful, more so than any county official. He was the political head of the province, captain general of its militia, chancellor, and, along with his councillors, judge on its highest court. Functionally, he was an exalted lord lieutenant, magistrate, and landlord rolled into one.[67] He had the power to grant land, appoint local officials, and veto colonial legislation, a prerogative last used by the crown over an act of the Houses of Parliament in 1707. He could dissolve the provincial assembly at will, with no requirement for convening it again within a definite time period, which was guaranteed in England by the triennial and septennial acts; he also had the power to appoint and dismiss judges at will, whereas at home, after the Revolution of 1688/89, the king granted his judges good behavior tenure.[68] Formally, the crown enjoyed powers in the colonies that had not been exercised at home since the seventeenth century. In practice, however, the governor was limited by the dynamics of colonial politics and his tenuous, often mercenary relationship to the province.[69] As just one example, a governor depended on local notables to nominate the provincial officers he appointed. In the case of sheriffs and justices of the peace, he had to appoint men acceptable to the local population or else they not be able to carry out their duties.[70]

Contemporary governors were aware of this paradox of, in Bernard Bailyn's phrase, "swollen claims and shrunken powers."[71] As early as 1711, Governor Robert Hunter complained to ministers in London that the assembly was "claiming all ye priviledges of a House of Commons and stretching them even beyond what they were imagined to be." If the provincial council conspired with the assembly, together they might become "a body pollitick co-ordinate with (claiming equall powers) and consequently independant of ye Great Councill of ye realm," meaning the king's Privy Council. Recalling James Harrington's categorization of empires, he warned that New York risked moving "from Provinciall and dependant, to Nationall and independent."[72] To prevent provincial groups from wielding "the balance of power" in the colony, Hunter recommended appointing officials from outside it. He followed his own advice. Hunter brought several fellow Scots to New York and placed them in office. Though governors never abandoned the policy of co-opting provincial leaders, several patronized immigrants with few local ties.[73] Hunter's effort was only the beginning, and the problem still remained of what law those provincials enjoyed—what procedures and claims of right they could interpose between themselves and imperial officials.

Provincial Law: Sources and Myth

In theory, all law began as the duke's law, which after James's ascendancy became royal law. The colonies did not enjoy the common law because they did not fall within the jurisdiction of common-law courts. But seventeenth-century jurists like Sir Edward Coke had helped abstract the common law into a national law that safeguarded various liberties, and a minimalist version of this common-law constitutionalism went abroad: parliamentary government and common-law tenures for settlers overseas. The simplicity of this conception of English liberty gave it strength and endurance across the empire.

The emergence of the doctrine of "settlement" further contributed to the sense that the colonies enjoyed English law. Beginning at least as early as the 1640s, colonists claimed that they enjoyed the liberties of Englishmen. In the late seventeenth century, this protest gained some recognition at home. Chief Justice John Holt declared from King's Bench that English law followed Englishmen when they peopled uninhabited lands, and he thereby constructed a new category in between Coke's poles of conquered and inherited land: discovered land with settler colonies.[74]

What Holt meant by "English law" was not clear: the common law? parliamentary statutes? something else? Nonetheless, it was a theory that served two needs: it recognized that the colonies were developing political cultures, and it tethered them to England. The colonies were changing. "Settlement" was taking root in the colonies as second- and third-generation English-speakers were born there. In addition, metropolitan officials were increasingly concerned about the possibility of colonial revolt after the Restoration and sought greater control. Some colonies received new charters, as royal colonies. The crown also created the Board of Trade within the Privy Council.[75] The notion of settlement, and the recognition that colonists deserved some English liberties, helped tie the colonists to Britain. Holt's discovery-and-settlement doctrine emerged amid these developments. As applied to most of the American colonies, discovery was a fiction, for the continent was neither unclaimed nor uninhabited. Holt himself realized this several years later and held that Virginia was a conquered province.[76] Similarly, Chief Justice Lord Mansfield opined from King's Bench in 1774 that the settlement doctrine was not applicable to New York and several other American colonies because they were indisputably conquered land. As a result, "they have their whole constitution from the crown."[77] However, building on Holt's first opinion, a government attorney advised the Board of Trade in 1720 that "[l]et an Englishman go where he will, he carries as much of law and liberty with him, as the nature of things will bear," though the effect and precedential value of this statement are uncertain.[78] This was never the orthodox view, leaving aside the question of how much of that law an Englishman carried and who decided what the nature of things would bear.

Fictitious and contested as it was, the doctrine of settlement offered an escape from Coke's rigid theory of conquest. Many colonists did not need to cite the doctrine to express their belief that they enjoyed English law. William Smith Jr. approvingly quoted a Virginia lawyer who opined that "there is undoubtedly a great Difference between the People of a conquered Country, and Colonies reduced by the King's Consent by the Subjects of *England*." Coke would have agreed with the Virginian too. But he would not have agreed with what came next: the common law followed the English subjects "wherever they go."[79] The law of their land was English law, which increasingly meant the common law, as this mass of rules and procedure was recreated in New York.[80] The colonists' construction of their legal system looks in retrospect like a "selective imitation and adaptation of English law," though they did not follow a conscious program.[81] When encountering the practical problems of institution building and dispute resolution, provincial New Yorkers relied on their interpretations of imported legal materials and their sense of what it meant to live in an English legal jurisdiction. In turn, these interpretations were shaped by colonial experience. Two or three decades into the eighteenth century, most New Yorkers agreed that English law was operative in New York.

What it meant to have English law in an overseas province was a question that arose every day in litigation. But only rarely were lawyers and judges conscious that the larger issue at stake was the applicable body of legal rules within different parts of the empire.[82] In daily litigation, there was little to prevent lawyers and judges from imitating many English ways. Flashpoints of jurisdictional friction made the problem manifest. Encounters with other imperial institutions forced New Yorkers to justify the legal autonomy they experienced most of the time and claimed by right. Such conflicts were frequent enough to remind New Yorkers that they lived in a pluralistic legal environment, which royal officials viewed vertically as a hierarchy and most provincials saw horizontally as a series of separate jurisdictions spread across space. New Yorkers claimed the common law but were reluctant to recognize other well-established English courts and institutions, such as crown-controlled chancery courts and military courts. Anglicization in New York was never total.

Royal governor William Cosby's attempt to invest the provincial supreme court with equity powers without the assembly's consent, for example, stimulated a lively debate about the status of English law in New York. Today, this controversy is best known for giving rise to the trial of John Peter Zenger, whose acquittal on charges of seditious libel stands in American legal mythology as a landmark on the road to a free press.[83] A petty political dispute over patronage sparked the controversy. When Governor Cosby arrived in New York, he sought the customary moiety, or half, of the governor's salary earned by Lieutenant Governor Rip Van Dam in between Cosby's appointment and his arrival in the province. Van Dam, who as the senior member of the council served as lieutenant governor in the governor's absence, refused unless Cosby also proffered half of what he had received in England for the appointment. Cosby demurred, and the dispute went to the courts.

Cosby was loath to submit his suit against a local politician to a common-law jury. That left the governor's chancery court. Cosby never wanted to hear any cases in his capacity as chancellor because he left New York City often, going to Albany, for example, to negotiate with the Iroquois; he did not want to add to the delays that already plagued the regular business of chancery, such as enforcing quitrents. In addition, even the most mercenary governor would hesitate to judge his own cause.[84] Instead, Cosby tried to invest the supreme court, sitting as a court of exchequer, with equitable powers. He claimed that the idea of using the equity side of the supreme court to collect quitrents preceded his suit against Van Dam and that in doing so he placed the crown's interest above his own. The transfer of his own equity jurisdiction to the supreme court, he told the Board of Trade, provided "very evident proof" that he "had no arbitrary view or design," an accusation others had leveled at him.[85] Two of the three justices on the court agreed that it had an equity side to its exchequer jurisdiction. Chief Justice Lewis Morris did not. Cosby removed Morris for this challenge to his command, as well as for "other reasons arising from his partiality and neglect of duty." Under a new and loyal chief justice, James DeLancey, the supreme court soon began hearing cases without juries, and popular outrage ensued.

DeLancey was the son of a Huguenot exile who had made his way into the Albany fur-trading community. He went to England for social seasoning and on his return married the daughter of Councillor Caleb Heathcote, gaining by dower the Manor of Scarsdale and the eminence to launch a public career.

At this early stage of his public life, he was a gubernatorial loyalist.[86] It was worth inciting popular outrage to gain office. Van Dam, for example, accused Cosby of subverting New Yorkers' "rights and liberties" by taking away the jury trial, "which is the distinguishing birth right of Englishmen by Magna Charta and other laws."[87]

Still, a governor's attempt to wrest fees from a provincial stalwart, and his alteration of supreme court jurisdiction to do so, cannot explain the extent of that outrage. Behind both controversies lay the struggle by the governors and imperial agents to collect quitrents for the crown and for their own support.[88] Royal governors at least since Robert Hunter had advocated the use of jury-less equity courts to enforce quitrents, and with limited success they did establish such courts.[89] Many colonial landholders refused to pay quitrents, and the imperial agents struggled for decades to devise ways to enforce them. In England, the crown could resort to the Court of Exchequer, which had jurisdiction over all disputes concerning the royal revenue and had an equity side on which the judges sat without a jury.[90] While the provincial supreme court had all the jurisdiction available to the three central English common-law courts, this juryless dimension had not yet been explored.

New York did have a juryless chancery court. Equity jurisdiction in New York had a curious history. New Yorkers objected to the personnel in such courts — usually crown appointees rendering decisions without juries — rather than the law of equity itself.[91] Although the governors' commissions empowered them to establish a chancery court, resistance on the ground made it controversial and, when operating, inefficient. New Yorkers objected less, however, to equity courts that were created jointly with the assembly and administered by New Yorkers. An established chancery bar in England made the chancery courts something less than an arm of the crown; there was no such bar in most colonies. New Yorkers viewed assembly participation as a way to prevent the governor from using the courts arbitrarily. The assembly could refuse to consent to establish such a court, or it could pass legislation limiting its jurisdiction. In fact, after Cosby left the province, the assembly did agree to invest the supreme court with power to enforce quitrents in its capacity as a court of exchequer, and it permitted distraint of personal property to satisfy judgments, though quitrents still remained difficult to collect.[92] Although colonists had always been concerned about equity courts, such concern sparked a crisis only when Governor Cosby sought to give the supreme court, now staffed by judges loyal to him, equity jurisdiction. In other words, Cosby appropriated the well-oiled equipment of the province's leading court to decide cases without juries that concerned crown revenue, land patents, and his own salary.

The quitrent symbolized the tenurial structure of English landholding. It originated as a commutation of fealty due one's lord, a monetary or commodity payment to absolve, or make "quit," some service. Sometimes the dues were substantial. When nominal, they reminded the landholder that, no matter how free the tenure on paper or in practice, the king was his lord. Quitrents were unpopular throughout the colonies. Those who owned large, sparsely settled tracts as speculative investments could not raise the money to pay those quitrents from the land itself. Many colonists simply considered their property to be allodial. In addition, the Dutch West India Company had granted land without quitrents, and the Articles of Capitulation of 1664 guaranteed Dutch property rights as they were enjoyed before the English conquest. Consequently, land descended from Dutch holdings was free of quitrents, whereas neighboring plots derived from English patents were not.[93] Here was one more example of the limits of Anglicization. This time, imperial officials strove to assimilate colonial property law to English standards, while colonists viewed this bit of English law as oppressive, at least as applied to unproductive land.

Enforcement was weak. Sheriffs, charged with quitrent collection, were easily intimidated, and juries often refused to convict landowners of default. Although quitrents were transplanted to most North American colonies, some of the crown's remedies, such as distraint of personal property, were not developed to enforce them until the mid-eighteenth century, another example of selective Anglicization.[94] Even then, slight improvements in quitrent enforcement went hand in hand with an understanding that old, dubious patents would not be questioned.[95] Yet year after year, the imperial agents held out hope that quitrents, like an unmined lode of gold, would provide support for royal administration and free them from relying on the assembly for their salaries.[96] Early in his tenure, Governor Hunter invoked his power as chancellor to hear quitrent cases. In 1723, he appointed a new, loyal receiver general, Archibald Kennedy, who stepped up enforcement and hired Philadelphia attorney Andrew Hamilton, who later gained fame as Peter Zenger's defense attorney, to pursue chancery prosecutions.[97] Hunter's successor, Governor William Burnett, continued to exercise equity jurisdiction. The court was never popular, however, and Governor Robert Montgomerie abandoned it in 1729, despite repeated instructions from the Board of Trade to use it to collect quitrents.[98] The board then instructed Van Dam to do the same, but he dallied. When Cosby arrived, he complied. He also threatened to use the chancery court to vacate dubious land patents, several of which were held by members of the provincial elite. Finally, to increase the flow of quitrent cases *and* to create a forum in which to sue Van Dam for fees collected in his absence, Cosby asked the supreme court to hear chancery cases too.[99]

Thus it was not just Cosby's pursuit of his moeity that turned Peter Zenger's press. And although Zenger's *New York Weekly Journal* was a Morrisite instrument, Cosby's removal of Lewis Morris from the supreme court was not the only motor, either. Beyond factional politics lay quitrents and the financial independence they could give crown administration. Zenger's readers feared effective revenue collection, especially when it could be used by a governor who lacked Montgomerie's charm or Hunter's diplomatic sense.[100] Zenger printed essays and verse that lambasted Cosby for giving equitable powers to the supreme court and removing Morris for refusing to exercise them. Both the new jurisdiction and the assertion of at-will tenure, Zenger's paper claimed, violated English liberties. After elections for the New York City Common Council in which Morrisites won most of the seats, the *Weekly Journal* toasted the victors and promised revenge on supporters of the governor.

> *Exchequer courts, as void by law,*
> *great grievances we call;*
> *Though great men do assert no flaw*
> *in them; they shall fall,*
> *And be condemned by every man*
> *that's fond of liberty. . . .*
> *Though pettifogging knaves deny*
> *us rights of Englishmen;*
> *We'll make the scoundrel rascals fly,*
> *and ne'er return again.*
> *Our judges they would chop and change*
> *for those that serve their turn. . . .*
>
> *. . . . .*
>
> *While [those who] with us resolve to stand*
> *for liberty and law,*
> *We'll drink their healths with hat in hand.*[101]

For publishing these and other criticisms of Cosby, Zenger faced charges of seditious libel. Again, the underlying constitutional issue was whether the governor could create courts. Creating new courts without consent was, the

Morrisites claimed, against English law. Their premise was that English law operated in New York. Because the province was "part of the Dominions of *Great Britain,*" Lewis Morris argued, New Yorkers were "entitled to the Liberties of *English-men.*" One of those liberties was the right to participate, through the legislature, in the creation of an exchequer court. Almost all disputants agreed that English law operated in New York, but they disagreed about what English law required. Chief Justice James DeLancey argued that, according to Edward Coke, the English Court of Exchequer "did not derive its Jurisdiction in Equity from [a] Statute, but from the common Law." Therefore, because New York's constitution was "formed upon the Model and as nearly similar as Circumstances will admit, to that of *England,*" De-Lancey argued that there was no need for the provincial assembly to approve the court of exchequer. Morris maintained that the Court of Exchequer in England rested on a parliamentary statute and that, far from originating in common law, it represented a desire to bypass common-law courts. But were the statutes establishing that court in England operative overseas? "The Extent of the Laws of *England* into the Plantations has been a Question often Debated, but never satisfactorily resolv'd," Morris reported; "some thought the common Law only, some that the common and statute both, did extend." While the question was unsettled in theory, in practice lawyers and judges simply "adapt[ed] such of them as were needful to our particular Circumstances."[102] The controversy reveals the ambiguity of both the content of English law and colonial necessity.

The assembly sought two legal opinions answering the question of whether the governor could establish new courts without its consent. The opinions tracked those of the judges. William Smith Sr., father of the future historian of the province, denied the governor's right to establish a court without legislative consent. He argued that the colonists enjoyed "the same *fundamental* Rights, *Privileges,* and *Liberties*" as those in England. There, he argued, a statute established the Court of Exchequer; the same was required in New York. Attorney General Joseph Murray, on the other hand, defended the governor's prerogative to establish courts, arguing that this power too was part of the common law and "incident to [the English] constitution." But he agreed with Smith's premise. New Yorkers were "entitled to the *Liberties and Privileges of English Men,*" and they were "under the *same Constitution* and entitled to the *same Laws* as are in *England.*" These, Murray agreed, included the right to form an assembly. This right rested not on the governor's commission; it derived instead "from the *common Custom and Laws of England,* claimed as an *English-man's Birth Right,* and as having been such by *Immemorial custom in*

England."[103] Despite this disagreement about whether the governor could unilaterally establish a court, all assumed that the province had the right to an assembly, that the common law was in effect, and that these two liberties were essential to constitutional government.

In all the American colonies, slavery and common-law liberties were also seen as complementary. Imperial administrators had little power to control the colonial trade and regulation of slaves. Most times, they had no desire to do so. Although there was little slavery in Great Britain, the metropolis benefited greatly from excises and investment income from colonies based on slave labor.[104] But occasionally colonial control over slavery caused problems, such as when it imperiled relations with other European empires. On 16 August 1748, Robert Troup seized the Spanish ship *Carmen*, which was manned by forty-five dark-skinned sailors. Troup assumed that the sailors were slaves and sold them in New York's marketplace, along with the rest of his prize. Two problems distinguished this captured ship from the many hauled into New York's port during the War of Austrian Succession (known in North America as King George's War) between 1740 and 1748. First, the preliminary articles of peace, which preceded the Treaty of Aix-la-Chapelle, provided that all parties would return prize captured after 9 August 1748, a week before Troup captured the *Carmen*.[105] Second, the forty-five men sold into slavery claimed to be freemen. Troup had violated a peace treaty and the law of nations, yet no institution could punish him or force the buyers to liberate the captured men. The Spanish governor of Florida repeatedly petitioned New York's governor and New York's vice admiralty court, which had condemned the prize, to let the men go. Apparently the Spanish hired a New York lawyer to plead their case too. That was not enough. Under colonial law throughout British America, a black-skinned person was presumed a slave; the burden to prove otherwise lay on him.[106] So the buyers demanded that the captured men prove that they were free, which required them to obtain proof of freedom or free birth, attested by three notaries public, from their homes in the Spanish Caribbean. This was not a swift process, nor one that all could satisfy.[107]

The case of the *Carmen* was just one example in which provincial courts serving provincial merchants endangered imperial diplomacy. Those courts also threatened military discipline, as during the murder trial of James Parks, a gunner on the HMS *Greyhound*. On 7 June 1750, merchant William Ricketts sailed his small pleasure boat from the Battery into New York's harbor and flew a burgee flag, a pennant that naval rules prescribed should be lowered when passing a royal ship. Ricketts knew of this rule, for he had been out sailing the previous afternoon and was ordered by the commanding officer on the *Greyhound* to lower the flag or risk seizure. Ships like the *Greyhound* were in the harbor not just for defense but also to help enforce the Navigation Acts by inspecting cargo ships. It was no secret, as Cadwallader Colden observed, that "illicit trade" with other European empires "can not be so effectually prevented as by the men of War & if they cannot fire a shot at any vessel without being subject to a trial by a Jury in this Country it is not probable they will be of much use for that purpose."[108] It was not just the intrusion that merchants like Ricketts resented; it was the actual interruption of trade that produced an important stream of profit.[109]

Lieutenant John How's commanding officer, Captain Robert Roddam, was in New York City with his new wife, who was the daughter of Governor George Clinton.[110] Because of Ricketts's insubordination, How decided to inspect the sailboat. He ordered Parks to launch warning shots across Ricketts's bow as a signal to come to and await inspection. The first shot had no effect, but the second flew through Ricketts's mainsail and hit his children's nurse in the head. Ricketts turned back to shore, but soon the nurse was dead. The city's coroner concluded that she had been murdered in the waters of New York City and County.[111] He convened a coroner's inquest — a jury — to determine the cause of death and its perpetrator, and he asked Roddam to send the relevant parties ashore to tell the inquest what had happened. The captain sent Parks because he had already placed Lieutenant How under military arrest. (How was later tried, and acquitted, by the Commissioners of Admiralty in England.) Parks told the inquest that How had ordered him to shoot, which he had done. The coroner's inquest indicted Parks for manslaughter, and Chief Justice DeLancey jailed him to await trial.[112]

Roddam then petitioned both DeLancey and the governor, his father-in-law, for Parks's release. He explained to DeLancey that the governor's commission provided that all crimes committed by servicemen on crown ships be tried by military law. This was no mere technicality. The substitution of provincial for military jurisdiction, he warned, "may affect the discipline, on Board His Majesty's ships and every officer's authority."[113] Military discipline was a constant problem in the colonies. Royal troops, for example, mutinied on New York's northern frontier during war three years earlier because the DeLancey-controlled assembly refused to fund their salaries.[114]

The commission clause Roddam referred to denied provincial jurisdiction over any person "who shall be in actual Service & pay, in or on Board of any of Our ships of War or other Vessells," and gave it instead to the Commissioners of Admiralty in London. The colonial courts had jurisdiction only over "Disorders & Misdemeanors committed on shore" by members of the military.[115] On the other hand, New York City's most recent charter, granted by Governor John Montgomerie in 1730, declared that "the compass, precincts, circuit, bounds, liberties, and jurisdictions, of the [city], do reach, extend, and stretch forth ... to the low water mark on the west side of the North River." In other words, the city's, and thus the province's, jurisdiction extended across the Hudson River and the harbor to New Jersey.[116] No metropolitan jurist or imperial agent interpreted the city charter as superseding the governor's commission; military jurisdiction over soldiers on ships was an exception to the province's jurisdiction, not in conflict with it. Provincial lawyers and judges saw matters differently. They might have responded without reflection when they argued that the supreme court's jurisdiction followed New York's boundaries. Perhaps DeLancey could not imagine forgoing the common-law trial process and denying a local jury its right to render a verdict in the case of a violent offender. He never confronted the commission clause directly; nor did he cite the charter. Location determined jurisdiction. The murder had been "committed within the city and County of New York," DeLancey informed the captain, "and therefore I ... must lett him remain to be delivered by a due course of Law."[117] DeLancey used to be a close associate of all the governors, from Cosby on and including Clinton, but he had broken with Clinton and now headed a vigorous opposition. He must have known that he was tweaking Governor Clinton and increasing his own popularity.[118] But he may also have believed that the province — the abstraction of New York greater than its royal status or the names of its leading families — operated under its own rule of law, which was different from that of the royal officials, who acted on the premise of another abstraction: the crown. It was axiomatic for DeLancey that New York governed the river. Geography defined jurisdiction. The dispute was what neither would, or *could*, say it was: a conflict of laws, a clash of jurisdictional claims within the empire.

The governor complained to London that the DeLancey "faction" made political hay of the incident, especially the connection between Roddam and the governor. It was as if Parks were a proxy for Captain Roddam and Roddam in turn a proxy for Clinton. The governor ordered the attorney general to publish the jurisdictional clause from the commission in the papers "to quiet the minds of the people, who were exasperated by the clamours of the Cabal."[119] A publicity battle was all he could muster.

Attorney General Richard Bradley obeyed these orders, but the role of the colonial attorney general was ill defined, and the crosscurrents of New York politics further blurred his responsibilities and loyalties.[120] Captain Roddam asked Bradley to explain how the supreme court could have ignored the commission clause and why he had not demanded that the court turn over Parks. Bradley reported that the supreme court had followed correct common-law procedure; beyond ensuring that, there was little he could do without risking "severe censure from the Chief Justice for my impertinence and arrogance in matters of Law." DeLancey, the strong head of the province's leading faction, was the fount of provincial legal authority. Bradley, on the other hand, was old, timid, and uncertain of his own authority.[121] Because the attorney general was no help, Clinton advised Roddam to get another lawyer.[122]

The governor did use his channel of communication to the Board of Trade to complain of DeLancey's arrogance and his own inability to discipline the chief justice, at least not "without endangering the peace of the province, and of throwing all into confusion." Little could be done to reprimand DeLancey because he had received his commission with good behavior tenure. Even if he could be tried for contempt of crown authority, "it seems no way probable, that a Jury of this Country, would find him guilty, much less, as he sits himself at the head of a popular Faction."[123] Colden bluntly summarized what he saw as the constitutional ramifications of DeLancey's behavior: "This consequence to me seems to suppose that the Clause in his Majesty's commission restraining the Jurisdiction of the ordinary courts in New York is illegal & that the C[hief] J[ustice] of New York has authority to interpret the Royal Commission in such manner as to declare any part of that Commission to be illegal which he shall judge so & consequently not to be observ'd. To what length such a power claim'd in the Colonies may go your Lordships can best judge."[124] It was the legal world turned upside down, with the provincial court modifying a foundational document of imperial law. There was no other way for the governor and his council to describe the problem of competing jurisdiction — no other understanding of the empire's institutional pluralism — other than in terms of defiance and division.

A criminal defendant like James Parks was not entitled to a lawyer under the English common law. But the supreme court did allow attorneys to raise jurisdictional issues in criminal trials.[125] When the case came to trial, William Smith Sr. introduced the governor's commission and argued that the incident fell within the military's jurisdiction. Joseph Murray, a close friend of James DeLancey's, argued in favor of provincial jurisdiction. As during the Zenger controversy two decades earlier, these two lawyers squared off in defense of different interpretations of imperial law. Smith now vindicated the governor's commission, while Murray defended the right of provincial juries to pass judgment on alleged wrongdoers. This time Murray won. "Mr Smith was ready to prove his assertion by the Books," one member of the audience reported, "but it was not allowed, [DeLancey] saying he was fully persuaded that it was cognizable in Banco Regis [i.e., King's Bench] & so proceeded to Tryal."[126] The trial jury found Parks guilty.[127]

Throughout the proceeding, those who supported Clinton, or at least opposed the DeLancey faction, hoped that the chief justice had finally gone too far. James Alexander, a Morrisite who was loyal to the governor, speculated hopefully that the case "may be a finishing stroke to him."[128] Months later, a contact in London informed Colden that the crown was sending an order directing the New York Supreme Court to deliver Parks "in order for his coming home to give Evidence at Mr Howe's Tryal & we Suppose a Smart Reprimand to the magistrates for committing him in pursuance of the Civil Law."[129] This proved partly accurate. The crown demanded delivery of Parks and later found him and Lieutenant How innocent. But no official criticism of DeLancey ever arrived.[130] Indeed, a few years later, after Clinton's successor committed suicide, DeLancey became lieutenant governor and sought revenge on his provincial opponents.

Since the passage of the Charter of Libertyes, New Yorkers had claimed that some parliamentary statutes were effective in their province. None of this was new. In *Calvin's Case*, Edward Coke had provided several examples of parliamentary statutes that reached the dominions, though metropolitan officials usually understood him to mean that parliamentary statutes were effective abroad if Parliament expressed that intent, not if the settlers there claimed to enjoy their benefits. By the mid-eighteenth century, as jurists in London began to concede that the colonists enjoyed some version of English law, they transformed that interpretive presumption into a rule of law. Parliamentary statutes passed before colonization were in force in the plantations; those passed after were not, except when Parliament specifically mentioned the colonies in individual acts.[131] Again, colonial understanding and practice were less coherent. Usually colonists claimed to enjoy the rights represented in parliamentary statutes rather than the statutes *as* statutes. Even when they demanded statutory rights, such as the good behavior tenure for judges announced in the Act of Settlement (1701), they often referred to them as common-law liberties that they enjoyed on an equal basis with Englishmen.[132] Here again was the logic of custom and the persistent belief, denied by metropolitan theorists, that colonies were merely distant provinces deserving all the liberties of Englishmen.

While embracing some parliamentary statutes, New Yorkers rejected others that regulated the colonies.[133] Such statutes, colonists argued, were inconsistent with common-law principles. This approach to statutes may also have reflected the corporate tradition that had long influenced New Yorkers' felt sense of autonomy. Statutes, even parliamentary statutes, were like by-laws that applied only to a finite territory and did not cross those boundaries. New York's statutes governed New York; British statutes governed Britain. The common-law principles surrounding those British statutes were, on the other hand, transcendent. Consequently, the colonists took the common law and the best that the British statutes had to offer, but often not the statutes themselves.[134] Late in the colonial period, the assembly passed a bill recognizing a long list of British statutes passed after the conquest of New York "to prevent all Doubts and Scruples" about their effect. The purpose was to confirm the transatlantic migration of common laws, including statutes, rather than to incorporate specific legislation. The governor signed the bill, but the Privy Council disallowed it because it deprived "both the Crown and its Governor of that distinct approbation or dis-approbation that is essential to the Constitution of the province."[135] Yet this did not stop New Yorkers from claiming the rights bundled in their failed statute, just as they never relinquished their Charter of Libertyes and the principle that legislative consent was necessary to establish new courts.

Despite this colonial development, William Blackstone adhered to the tripartite scheme of imperial lands created by Coke and Holt. He told his readers in the mid-eighteenth century that the American colonies were "conquered or ceded countries." Consequently, "the common law of England, as such, has no authority there; they being no part of the mother country, but distinct (though dependent) dominions." He accounted for any resemblances by supposing that the colonists had "copied the spirit of their own law from the original." They remained "subject however to the control of parliament."[136] This was essentially the same theory of the imperial constitution that Coke had espoused a century and a half earlier, except that Blackstone said nothing about a core of imperial liberties and was more certain of Parliament's power, at home and abroad. One reason that he was less concerned about the legal culture of the dominions than Coke was that they were more Anglicized than anyone in the previous century would have imagined and there was less worry, at home, about excesses committed in the name of the prerogative. This made Coke's theory of an irreducible core of imperial liberties unnecessary.

By Blackstone's day, even imperial liberals did not subscribe to Coke's theory that the core of the ancient constitution traveled to all settlements under the English crown. Edmund Burke, for example, understood New

York's situation quite well. Burke served as the New York assembly's agent in London, and he owed his seat in the Commons, representing Bristol, to the support of the father-in-law of Henry Cruger, Bristol's other MP and a native New Yorker. He was also a native Irishman well aware of provincial suspicion of Parliament throughout the empire. While Burke referred incessantly to prescriptive government, immemorial rights were not for him. Burke cautioned, "We Englishmen stop very short of the principles upon which we support any given part of our constitution; or even the whole of it together." Instead, constitutions rested on compromise. "We balance inconveniences; we give and take," Burke told the Commons in 1775; "we remit some rights that we may enjoy others; and we choose rather to be happy citizens than subtle disputants." That was his message to both those in England, who sought to regulate the colonies at will, and his clients abroad, who claimed, among other ancient liberties, an immunity from parliamentary regulation. "Man acts from adequate motives relative to his interest," he opined, "and not on metaphysical speculations."[137] It was in everyone's interest to keep the empire working.

When Welshman Anthony Stokes traveled at midcentury to North America, where he held a variety of colonial offices including judge, he also concluded that the colonists did not deserve the common law by right, citing Blackstone. However, "the Crown has from time to time established the common law of England in all the British American Plantations, except Quebec."[138] Here was one imperial agent's way of expressing the practical operation of the common law in his courts, an explanation still based on the royal prerogative. In a more accurate, passive construction, the last prerevolutionary governor of New York observed that "[t]he Common Law is considered as the Fundamental law of the Province," though there was never any instruction supporting this proposition and many statements to the contrary.[139]

Most day-to-day governance rested on local legislation responding to conditions unknown in England. When necessary, however, colonists invoked the common law to defend their corporate privileges. That their neighbors in other colonies also claimed the common law as their own seemed logical and right. That the individual legal systems of the colonies — each envisioning itself as a zone of corporate autonomy — differed in important ways went unexamined. Opposition to external regulation was a common denominator. Finally, imperial administrators at home and in the colonies had their own ideas about the colonies' autonomy, and they too expressed them in terms of the English constitution. Who, then, had the authority to determine the province's jurisdiction? Who defined its constitution?

Imperia in Imperio:
Property and Sovereignty
in a Frontier Province

Abroad your empire shall no limits know,
But, like the sea, in boundless circles flow.
John Dryden, "Astraea Redux" (1660)

AT LEAST ONCE DURING HIS TENURE, the governor of New York received a list of questions from London. The Board of Trade, which recommended colonial policy to the king's Privy Council, sought information about the province's geography, population, trade, and legal regime. This last question often came first: "What is the constitution of the Government?" The responses, from New York's first governor in 1669 to the last before the Revolution in 1774, perfunctorily described the outline of colonial government. In 1738, for example, the lieutenant governor wrote that "[t]he constitution is such as his Majesty by his commission to his Governour directs, whereby the Governour with the Council and Assembly are empowered to pass laws not repugnant to the laws of England."[1] But sometimes the board got more. In 1749, for example, Governor George Clinton replied more insightfully, with the help of his closest adviser, Cadwallader Colden. "The constitution of this Government," Clinton reported, "is founded on His Majesty's Commission & Instructions to his Governor. But the Assembly have made such Encroachments on his Majesty's Prerogative by their having the power of the purse that they in effect assume the whole executive powers into their own hands & particularly claim the sole right of Judging of and rewarding all Services, as well by fixing Sallaries on the Officers annualy, and by rewarding particular contingent Services."[2]

Colden, a longtime imperial official who more than once drafted responses to this query, maintained that "the Government is form'd as near as may be upon the same Plan as that of our Mother Country." He praised the original and, after summarizing English history from the Norman Conquest to the Civil War, emphasized the importance in it of "a proper Ballance between the Monarchical Aristocraticall & Democratical forms of Government." He warned that whenever the balance was altered "by an overbearing power in any of these three parts . . . the Constitution it self is so far alter'd & such Alteration has been allwise accompanied with many Disturbances & often with Civil Wars & Revolutions of the State." In New York, provincial over-reaching threatened the balance. The governor was "without Force, without money (which he can only obtain of an Assembly), without Friends or any Natural Interest," leaving him vulnerable to the ambitious provincial legislature.[3] Most troubling, Colden believed, was the absence of the aristocratic element. The council, on which he served for fifty years, was too weak to help counter the popular forces associated with the assembly. He lamented the mistreatment of the councillors and other faithful crown servants, and he sought ways to insulate them from provincial harassment.

In a 1751 report, the Board of Trade drew on these local analyses to condemn the assembly for encroaching on "the Legal prerogative of the Crown" and taking over "the most essencial powers in the Governor." These included control over "the disposal of publick money, of nominating Officers and fixing their salaries, of superceding the Governor's warrant in the issuing of publick money, with the custody of Naval Stores of the Colony, the direction of the Fortifications, and the power of regulating the Militia." Here was a contemporary analysis of what historians call "the rise of the assembly" and its control over the local treasury, appointments, salaries, supplies, and defense; the board viewed it as the decline of crown authority. On the eve of another war with France, the board also feared that the assembly's failure to support Indian diplomacy would alienate the Iroquois, "always the most constant and best allies of the British Interest in America." To remedy these problems, it recommended that the Privy Council give the next governor "new . . . and still stricter Commission and Instructions," give him an independent salary, and direct him to "reunite the Assembly, and prevail upon all Men to assist in reestablishing the proper and ancient Constitution of Government."[4]

These orthodox accounts of the constitution of New York are interesting for what they reveal and what they do not. The board's question presupposed that one could analyze colonial government in terms of a constitution, like English government and its constitution at home. The relationship between the colonial constitution and the English constitution, gradually known among some as the constitution of the empire, was, however, unclear. In turn, the responses indicate the documents, discourses, and images that the agents of the British Empire associated with the word "constitution": royal commissions and instructions, local legislative power, the model of the English constitution, the baseline of English law, and the lessons of English history.

These answers offered more than a blueprint of New York's government. They also contained an interpretation of its history and suggestions for reform. Yet, because they remained the formulaic answers of appointed officials, they also failed to convey the constitution as most New Yorkers experienced it. While the imperial agents answered questions about geography and climate in detail, their analysis of the political environment lacked specificity. Asked about the colonial constitution, they replied with ambiguous phrases — "balance," three "forms of government," "the laws of England" — that had gained currency during the constitutional battles of the seventeenth century. These catchwords did not fully capture the dynamics of colonial governance in the eighteenth century. Beyond these platitudes lay disagreement about how the colonial government and the imperial system of which it was part should be described and how they should function. The imperial agents recognized that the fit between English constitutional lore and colonial experience was imperfect — hence the anguished replies to Whitehall's questionnaire. But to them the discrepancy revealed the ominous potential of colonial politics, not the limitations of the lore. They could, for example, only interpret the politicking of the provincial elites in New York, and their lobbying in London, as corruption. As much as they pushed, pulled, and pleaded, the agents remained trapped by the discourse of English constitutionalism. If provincial society did not conform to historical models, it would erupt in civil war or revolution. Only a change in emphasis was needed to transform this royalist analysis into a Whig interpretation of colonial constitutional history: the assemblies rose against an oppressive royal administration, and with their triumph came democracy and liberty.[5]

To overcome the limitations of this interpretation, some historians have argued that in the 1760s and 1770s there were two conflicting interpretations of the imperial constitution. One was the colonial interpretation, premised on the belief that there were limits to Parliament's authority to legislate for the American colonies. The other was the metropolitan interpretation, in which Parliament was omnipotent.[6] Jack P. Greene documents how authority in the British Empire "was negotiated in a perpetual tug-of-war between the center and the peripheries," and the central site of the colonists' "quest for power" was their lower legislative houses.[7] This bipolar constitutional world gave rise to a conflict between what John Reid calls "the two constitutions": imperial law at the center and Whig law in the colonies.[8] But the dispute over parliamentary sovereignty was only one, late episode in a long debate over the relevance of the English constitution to the colonies, a debate that erupted repeatedly throughout the century.[9] Most of the controversies that ignited the debate occurred between groups within the colonies. Constitutional disagreements did not, therefore, map neatly along a division marked by the Atlantic. The divisions were as much intracolonial as between the colonies and the metropolis. New York bred especially articulate and searching colloquies because its peculiar geopolitical environment made it a linchpin of Britain's Atlantic Empire. Recapturing the legal importance of New York's dynamic marchland, and of New York *as* a marchland—an imperial buffer zone of commercial, diplomatic, and military exchange—decreases the importance of metropolitan interpretations of the constitutional relationship and shifts focus to those who claimed and performed authority on the ground: the imperial agents; the creole elite that dominated the assembly, courts, and countinghouses; and the urban and frontier populations that both leading groups tried to govern. Constitutional discourse was the site where all these social groups, from the elite to the popular, interacted to assert their interests and make sense of their shared colonial world. Between the center and the unknown periphery, between Whitehall and the wilderness, lay a thriving province bounded on one side by the Atlantic, on the other by Indian and French territory, and uniting New England with the rest of the British colonies.

New York's centrality and diverse population, including its combustible mix of British imperial agents, Anglicized lawyers, aggressive settlers, and Native Americans, meant that many of the most sophisticated debates about the meaning of the English common law and the imperial constitution took place on the margins of the empire in a factious colony containing a large number of people without English blood who, according to the eighteenth century's foremost commentator on English law, did not enjoy the common law by right. Rather than a blueprint drafted by metropolitan administrators, New York's constitution emerged out of its local political environment as refracted through the legal languages that circulated through the British Atlantic world. No one could conclusively explain this dynamic relationship between English phrases and provincial practice. So the missive kept coming, decade after decade: What was the constitution of New York?

The Multiple Constitutions of Empire in New York, 1750–1777

Do not dream that your letters of office, and your instructions, and your suspending clauses are the things that hold together the great contexture of this mysterious whole. These things do not make your government. Dead instruments, passive tools as they are, it is the spirit of the English communion that gives all their life and efficacy to them. It is the spirit of the English Constitution, which, infused through the mighty mass, pervades, feeds, unites, invigorates, vivifies every part of the empire, even down to the minutest member.
Edmund Burke, "Speech on Conciliation with the Colonies" (1775)

T HE CONSTITUTION OF COLONIAL NEW YORK was a contested, shifting arrangement of political power that was expressed in the traditional terms of English constitutionalism. That fluid source was the font of constitutional debate. Yet it was often the only common element, as New Yorkers emphasized different parts of it to serve their interests and make sense of their identities within the empire. A shared political vocabulary and grammar functioned at times as an important cultural glue; at others it obscured fundamental differences in the way groups interpreted colonial experience.

By the mid-eighteenth century, three versions of the colonial constitution had emerged. Each constitutional perspective seemed to be English because each was signified by similar phrases about the liberties of Englishmen, the dominion of the crown, imperial glory, custom, balance, and other key terms of English constitutionalism. But each differed from the original, reflecting the influence of American conditions as perceived by different cultural groups, collectives defined by ethnicity, family, status, and region. Each group grasped those strands of English constitutionalism that best expressed its situation and aspirations, resulting in glosses whose metropolitan phrases disguised colonial innovation. Pieces of one looked much like parts of another. Cooperation and shifting alliances between the three groups occurred frequently and always remained possible. Yet from a distance it appears that New Yorkers used similar words to describe different worlds and that there was no single constitution but rather competing constitutions.[1]

The first constitutional perspective was that of a group of imperial agents. To them the common law — any law — was a set of procedures to integrate the British Empire. When that law failed to do so, reform was necessary. The second perspective focused on the province's internal development and was expressed by the creole provincial elite who hoped to "improve" New York — politically, economically, and culturally — while carrying forward the progress of English liberty. The third involved frontier settlers and oceangoing sailors who moved freely across the empire's borders and defied local authorities. Migration and lawless behavior in New York's marchland, especially, reflected a disregard for the formalities of legal jurisdiction that became constitutionally significant. This extralegal activity struck many as extraconstitutional, but its participants also drew on English legal traditions to defend their interests.[2]

These groups disagreed not only about the content of the constitution but also about its nature and sources. Both the provincial elite and common people conceived of New York's constitution as fluid in source and rigid in substance. They drew on a wide range of English constitutional resources but held firm to the particular liberties they claimed. The imperial agents, on the other hand, relied on fixed sources but wish to keep its substance fluid to permit administrative flexibility. In other words, the provincial versions of New York's constitution were essentially lists of political and legal liberties selected from the English tradition that defined local government and individual freedom, while that of the agents identified hierarchical procedures that would ensure that the right personnel controlled government. On the one hand were two definitions of the substantive liberties of localism; on the other was the authority of imperial personnel.

The Epistolary Constitution: A British Empire in New York

The most elaborate constitutional perspective was that of the imperial agents serving in the colony. Silently, they conflated the constitution of New York with the constitution of the British Empire. They considered New York a subsidiary unit of the empire and, when forced to put this belief into legal terms, explained that the constitution of the royal colony flowed from the crown's prerogative and was therefore subordinate to the overarching British constitution. The colonial constitution was "an Emblem, or faint Representation" of the English original, argued New York councillor Archibald Kennedy, and its sources were the commissions and instructions from London to the royal governors. He conceded, as many of his colleagues did not, that "Every Subject within the King's Dominions . . . ha[s] a Right to the common Law of *England*," but this was only a vague baseline. Beyond it, all aspects of government were derived from the prerogative. "If we abuse, or make wicked Use of his Majesty's Favours," Kennedy warned, "we are, of them, but Tenants at Will; we only hold them during Pleasure, and good Behaviour."[3] Liberties abroad were defeasible grants from the crown.

The imperial agents reached back to the arguments of royalist lawyers in the seventeenth century and invoked the royal prerogative and the ballast of aristocracy, just as such rhetoric was becoming anachronistic in England. Cadwallader Colden complained to London that the governor was financially dependent on the assembly and, therefore, relied more on provincial politicians than on imperial agents like Colden. Many of these local men were "educated in republican principles & great numbers of them (perhaps the greatest number in some of the Colonies) Foreigners who know nothing of the English constitution & can have no esteem of it." Consequently, "little more than a shadow of the royal authority remains in the Northern Colonies," and some of them were approaching "a state of anarchy." He urged London to free the governor from dependence on the assembly by granting his true supporters, the imperial agents, permanent tenure of office, independent salaries, and land. In short, he advocated the creation of an imperial aristocracy on which to rest royal power within the province. Similar was Kennedy's lament that each governor was forced to ask on appointment, "Into whose Hands shall I throw myself?" Inevitably the answer was "[i]nto whose but can best manage the Assembly."[4] In the hope of creating an administrative counterweight, Kennedy also lobbied for independent salaries that would release him and his colleagues from the grip of provincial forces.

This vision of prerogative power vested in a privileged bureaucracy, rather than the gradually developing idea of the supremacy of Parliament, was the imperial agents' mainstay throughout the colonial period.[5] The prerogative and aristocracy, like parliamentary supremacy for some others, were ways of justifying their policies but were not intrinsic to them, for their goal was to create an administrative elite in North America, not to empower the crown or Parliament. Yet colonial governance as the agents described it actually mapped well onto the contemporary English constitution, which in practice depended on informal accommodations between the crown and the Commons. Ironically, some of their recommendations belied the premise that the colony was England writ small. And gradually, they denied that analogy and tried to fit the colonies into a different conception of the imperial constitution.

The agents' theory of empire was less sharp, and more realistic, than their analysis of New York's constitution. They assumed that the colonies ought to serve the economic and political good of the home country, a loose collection of ideas now referred to as mercantilism and embodied in the Navigation Acts.[6] But the British Empire was not a coherent system. William Knox, who cut his teeth as an imperial agent in Georgia and then served as undersecretary to the Board of Trade, complained of the "total lack of plan or system" to govern the colonies.[7] Ministers at home did not theorize much about the constitution of New York or of the empire; their directives aboard packet ships sailing west tell only part of its story. In addition, focus on the governors, who served temporarily, obscures more perceptive correspondents.[8] The key figures maintaining the imperial perspective were semipermanent imperial agents such as Cadwallader Colden, William Johnson, and Archibald Kennedy. They made their lives and families in North America. For them, unlike the governors, it was "home."

Colden, who was born in Scotland during the Glorious Revolution and died in New York two months after the Declaration of Independence, embodied the long eighteenth century.[9] He trained as a physician in Edinburgh and London and then emigrated to Philadelphia in 1710. Shortly after his arrival, he impressed the Scottish governor of New York, Robert Hunter, who appointed Colden surveyor general of crown lands in New York. Colden tried to reform land distribution in the province, was well rewarded with land of his own, and soon joined the governor's council. For a half century, from Hunter's administration through the long reign of George Clinton in the 1750s and his own brief interludes as lieutenant governor, Colden remained loyal to the crown and almost always loyal to the governor. The only exception was Governor William Cosby, who alienated many New Yorkers with his condescending style in the 1730s and made Colden fear for his offices.[10] This experience taught Colden that his fortunes depended as much on the good favor of ministers in London as on New York's governors. As his then friend Lewis Morris reported to a London minister, Surveyor General Colden was "not only a check upon the people to prevent them from imposing upon the Crown but also a Check upon the Governours to prevent them from granting of Lands in other manner than the Crown intended."[11] The imperial agents strove to become an independent force in imperial politics, a check on the governor and a balance against "the people."

Away from politics, Colden's first love was science. He corresponded not only with Benjamin Franklin in Philadelphia and William Douglass in Boston but also with the Dutch botanist Gronovius and various scientists across Europe. His naturalism extended beyond horticulture. Land surveying brought him into contact with Native Americans, which made him aware of their strategic importance to the empire, and in the 1720s he began to write the first English history of the Iroquois.[12]

Within New York, Colden's preferred companions were other imperial officials, such as Archibald Kennedy (1686–1763), a fellow Scottish immigrant.[13] Kennedy was a longtime councillor, custom collector, and receiver general, posts that gained him a small fortune made larger when invested in New York City real estate.[14] The son of a justice of the peace, he arrived in New York in 1710. Hunter soon gave him a key to the city, symbolizing his access to power. Kennedy had one brother in New York, a merchant with ties to the West Indies; another was a merchant in Surinam. His son was a captain in the British navy. The Kennedys represented a common type: an energetic, far-flung Scottish family expanding with the empire.[15] Kennedy was among the first to see that the colonial assemblies were more powerful in practice than in theory and thought that the contentions between them and the governors were no more than petty disputes about "a few Pounds, when even our All is at Stake." The "all" was the prospect of becoming "Masters of this Continent."[16] The imperial imperative was never out of his mind. He led a Palatine regiment in Queen Anne's War soon after arriving in America and headed the four companies of British soldiers guarding the Canadian frontier, a post that showed him New York's strategic importance as well as the need for intercolonial cooperation.[17] He also developed an appreciation for the Indian trade and considered the Albany merchants who dominated it traitors for doing business directly with the French. Accordingly, he and others proposed that ministers in London appoint a superintendent of Indian affairs to control relations with the Iroquois.[18] The choice was Whitehall's to make, but there was only one man fit for the position: William Johnson.

Johnson (1713–74) was a brawny, gregarious Irishman who immigrated to New York in 1738 to manage the Mohawk Valley land of his uncle and patron, Sir Peter Warren. He also acquired tracts of his own.[19] Johnson soon developed a close relationship with the Iroquois and by the 1750s was the Briton they trusted most.[20] Especially after the failed Albany Congress of 1754, at which the Iroquois learned that they could not rely on provincial officials to hold back settlers, they looked to Johnson for protection.[21] Because of this trust, Whitehall made Johnson the first superintendent of Indian affairs for the northern colonies in 1755, a post that went to his son when Johnson died in 1774.[22] He also became a New York councillor, though he rarely attended meetings two hundred miles away in New York City.

If Colden was the continent's first British botanist, Johnson was among its earliest anthropologists. His home on the Mohawk River became the site of Indian conferences and cultural exchanges.[23] The Iroquois were, in addition to allies, his business partners and family. Johnson was initiated as a Mohawk brave in the 1740s, and his second wife, Molly Brant, was a Mohawk. Their son Peter captured Ethan Allen during the revolutionary attack on Montreal in 1775. Molly's half brother, Joseph Brant, fought alongside another of Johnson's sons in the Revolution, made a diplomatic trip to London, and died in Canada a United Empire Loyalist, as did Molly.[24] So far from London, Johnson's racially mixed family was among the most loyal to the crown. In official and personal correspondence, Johnson rebutted claims that Native American civilization, language, and government were primitive.[25] His relationship with the Iroquois provided a model of acculturation similar to the one used by the French and Spanish elsewhere on the continent but rarely followed by the British. Colden, with his history of the Five Nations, and Kennedy, urging closer alliance with the Native Americans, complemented his efforts.[26] The British lacked the premise of cultural exchange laid in other European empires by the Jesuits ("worthy," Johnson thought, "of our Imitation"), leaving it to the imperial agents to forge analogous links — the Jesuits of the British Empire. They similarly respected native ways but always expected conversion to fundamental principles.[27]

Other imperial agents included George Croghan, an Irish immigrant who was William Johnson's chief deputy; Andrew Elliot, a Scot who succeeded Kennedy as customs collector and held a variety of offices during the Revolution; George Clarke, a longtime councillor and secretary of the colony who emigrated from provincial England after failing as a lawyer in Dublin; Goldsborough Banyar, a deputy secretary of the colony who emigrated from pro-vincial England; Thomas Pownall, who began his long career as an imperial agent in New York as an aide to Governor Charles Hardy in the 1750s; and the Welsh cartographer Lewis Evans. Most of the family members and depu-ties of the leading agents conformed to the profile, sharing and inheriting offices as property. Related coteries were the Anglican missionaries of the Society for the Propagation of the Gospel and the military officers, such as General Thomas Gage, who arrived to fight the French.[28]

Though there were differences among the agents, political orientation, administrative routine, and recreation brought them together.[29] Each relied on patronage connections in London.[30] Yet most came from lands peripheral to the metropolis and traveled as young men to a place even more marginal. Consequently, they shared a perspective at once provincial and imperial. The farther they traveled from Whitehall and the more they settled into lives different from those of officials at home, the firmer their commitment to the reign of Britain over the colony. Their empire was not just about trade, though all participated in the mercantile economy on which New York was founded and reaped its fees.[31] It was not just about cultivation, though they were interested in peopling the province, especially their own lands.[32] Each supported the Anglican Church and missionaries, but their empire was not primarily about theology.[33] It had much to do with imperial rather than na-tional pride, a cosmopolitanism bred in the provinces that could sound for-eign in London. It was pride felt most deeply by men like Colden, Johnson, Kennedy, and others, who because of birth and residence were doubly con-cerned with their position in the empire. These provincials-turned-colonists were the ones who negotiated the meaning of British Empire in America, and the key word is *British*, not English, a distinction they helped draw. No longer just an island, Great Britain was an expansive empire, they declared, they who were supposed to make its authority real.[34]

The administrative and commercial networks of the empire rested on similar social foundations but were not identical. The mercantile "citizens of the world," whom David Hancock has chronicled, offer an illuminating com-parison. The "citizens" migrated from the margins of Great Britain to Lon-don, its geographic and social core. They helped construct the infrastructure of the empire: employment and interest group networks, trade routes, and integrating media of exchange. They too built and exploited the resources of the empire.[35] But the American agents' location on the fringe, their move-ment from one province to an even more remote outpost, and their official positions gave them a different perspective on the imperial project. They were forced to grapple with and articulate the whole enterprise as an empire, a political and legal unit, not just a series of business opportunities.[36] *This* empire was distinguishable from the Atlantic commercial network with which it partly overlapped. Trade occurred wherever merchants could profit; definition of the empire demanded self-conscious thought about the role of law in its expanding periphery. Those who administered authority overseas were compelled to put pressure on these often rudimentary legal ideas. The empire was, ironically, best served by provincials, its constitution articulated most clearly far from London.

The imperial agents acknowledged the existence of a place named New York, but for them the empire flowed west across the Atlantic and would roll naturally across the continent. The boundaries of individual colonies, on the other hand, were the accidental lines of settlement. To be sure, New York was the continental headquarters of the military as well as the northern terminus of the imperial postal service. And the Hudson River was, in Kennedy's phrase, "the Center and Key of the Continent."[37] But a key opens something of greater value.

Johnson's title exemplified this transcolonial perspective. Though based in New York, he was superintendent of Indian affairs for "the northern colonies." (His counterpart for the southern colonies was John Stuart.) Another example is Kennedy's statistical approach to the continental colonies, treating them in the aggregate as "the northern colonies," as opposed to the West Indies in the Caribbean.[38] Most illustrative is Colden's map of the marchland province appended to the second volume of his *History of the Five Indian Nations*.[39] This map represents New York as aqueous, full of rivers and lakes leading to the heart of the continent and beyond, "a Scene of inland Navigation as cannot be parallel'd in any other Part of the World."[40] The land east of these lakes, including New York, seems foreshortened: there is not much of it, and there is as much water as land on the continent. But this makes sense from Colden's perspective. He came from an island nation and crossed the Atlantic three times as a young man.[41] The British of his day were comfortable on water, which was the transportation network of their empire and easier to navigate than land, with its human and topographical barriers. On Colden's map, the Hudson and Mohawk Valley waterways offered a way to transect the mountains, a familiar element passing through an unknown environment, making New York the staging area for imperial aggrandizement.

Imperial agents such as Colden, Kennedy, and Johnson were charged with enforcing the constitution of this empire. But constitutional practice was not a purely legal affair, and none of these men was a lawyer. The imperial scheme was not defined in letters patent or statute books, though there were laws designed to shape some imperial activities. Restricted by the verbal conventions of the English constitutional canon, the colonial and imperial constitutions were rarely defined sensitively by its official representatives even when they responded to the Board of Trade's query. More precise answers would have required an assessment of the very process of inquiry because the imperial constitution was primarily a network of those loyal not just to significant ministers but ultimately to the crown: an abstract symbol of the empire. These agents of the crown were more anxious about defining its interests in America than were the mercenary governors or the Board of Trade in London.[42] By the mid-eighteenth century, the agents supplied most of London's information about the colonies, eclipsing informal interest group networks.[43] They also recommended policies and enforced those policies as best they could. As such, they were mirror images of the assembly-sponsored colonial agents who lobbied for provincial interests in London. The agents invoked the crown's prerogative as if it had independent constitutional force, yet they were the ones who, in the colonial setting, gave meaning to royal power. Closer to the experience of colonization, their pursuit of empire largely *was* the empire. Consequently, the crown's interests blended imperceptibly with their own, and some saw them as self-interested. This conflation of public and private gain, however, also meant that these agents believed that there was a transcendent imperial interest. They represented the crown along with the successive governors, serving those holding that commission but also holding their own. They developed a sharp imperial perspective working with one another on the ground. Day after day these agents grappled with the concrete problems of imperial administration and wrote about their efforts to one another and to ministers back in London. In these letters they repeated themselves, developing a stock of images and phrases that formed a discourse of report, complaint, analysis, and policy recommendation. In those letters they accumulated the administrative capital of empire.[44] As a result, a working description of the imperial constitution of New York is located in the correspondence of the imperial agents. Theirs was an epistolary constitution.

The Provincial Constitution of Improvement

Andrew Elliot, the Scot immigrant who succeeded Archibald Kennedy as customs collector, complained at midcentury that colonists did not act for "the Good of the Country," meaning North America. The idea of the public interest, which he admitted was manipulable, "must sometimes be of Service." But on the west side of the Atlantic, "theres no such word known for no Body owns this as their Country, even country borne call Britain or Holland home & it really cant well be otherwise for when people come out here its with a view to gett Money & then return but when they find thats not to be done they're obliged to Settle here where to the last they are railling at the Country & wishing to end their days at home. The Children learn the same from their parents but I make doubt but it will be quite otherwise with the next Generation & it will be good for the Country when it is so."[45] There were always mercenaries in New York. But Elliot made the mistake of equating his arrival with the province's origins and failed to see that there were already second- and third-generation New Yorkers beginning to own the province as their country.

Constitutional authority did not only flow transatlantically. Local sources of power, epitomized for the imperial agents by the assembly, hindered the enforcement of the imperial policy. But this force involved much more than "the power of the purse."[46] By the mid-eighteenth century, a provincial self-consciousness, defined in part against London but also in relation to neighboring colonies, emerged. Many began to imagine New York — long a glorified trading post — as a place with a distinct cultural identity. These cultural initiatives were premised on a felt sense of legal autonomy and helped generate an interpretation of New York's constitution expressed in the familiar terms of English constitutionalism, especially the common law. In the press, new periodicals, and assembly journals, New Yorkers were articulating a provincial constitution of improvement.

The process was creolization. "Creole" has many connotations, but here it means simply one who was born in the province and treated it as home yet still could be considered, perhaps considered himself, "not ancestrally indigenous to it."[47] Born in New York, these people were not natives in the existential sense — not, as they informed the metropolis, like the "savages." They were civilized.[48] Creole New Yorkers had a kind of dual identity. They were of European extraction, usually from some provincial part of Great Britain, and they considered this lineage an important source of political and cultural definition; they also began to look at their daily relationships with the place and people around them as primary reference points for identity. They were colonists in comparison with people in the metropolis, and they were colonizers in relation to the Native Americans. In short, elite creoles were proudly part of an empire larger than their piece of it, but they were becoming ever more proud of that piece. Empire and province, like province and city, were overlapping and interdependent, but not identical, categories. These axes of identity coexisted with only minor tension for a century.[49]

Empire, province, city: each jurisdiction fitted into the other, and each was the object of improvement. The spirit of improvement was a defining characteristic of the eighteenth century and not limited to one place within the empire or to one group in each place.[50] One of its earliest promoters in New York was Cadwallader Colden. During a respite from politics in 1728, Colden withdrew to his country estate in the Hudson Valley, studied botany, and pondered the Newtonian universe. But the drawback of retirement — a concentrated form of the drawback of being in America — was the loss of friendly communication familiar to this Edinburgh native. "I wish that a certain number of Men would enter into a Voluntary Society for the advancing of Knowledge," Colden wrote Boston physician William Douglass, "& that for this purpose such in ye Neighbouring provinces as are most likely to be willing to promote this design be invited to enter in to it."[51] Many felt similarly, but although his epistolary society was never founded, others, mostly local and specialized, were.

Voluntary associations designed to enliven colonial society flourished in the mid-eighteenth century, and New York City was in the vanguard.[52] The title of a projected issue of the *Independent Reflector*, one of the first colonial periodicals and modeled on English magazines like the *Tatler* and *Spectator*, conveyed much of the New York improvers' anxious hope: "On Our Defect of Public Spirit: Its Beneficial Influences in *Philadelphia*."[53] Though many participated in the movement, the creole elite took the lead.

This provincial improvement cannot be labeled either Anglicization or Americanization, as the participants were becoming at once more metropolitan and less a part of the British Empire as it was conceived by its agents.[54] Imperial officials did not forcibly Anglicize the American colonists. Rather, the settlers Anglicized themselves as a strategy of colonial empowerment.[55] Although most of their improvements were confined to New York City, the identity of names and its relative importance blurred, for them, the distinction between the city and the whole colony. Their seaport opened onto an ocean highway, up and down the continent and back to Britain. New Yorkers operated on the edge of a vast marketplace and helped link the British Isles to the West Indies, and most had no reason to imagine a world without those ties.[56] Oriented longitudinally along the Atlantic coast, the provincials' competitive ethos and striving for improvement could have divided the colonies, internally and intercolonially, and to some extent they did, sowing longlasting animosities. This was especially true between the mainland colonies and the Caribbean colonies, which seemed to New Yorkers to receive more favorable treatment in London.[57] However, this spirit of improvement also laid the groundwork for cooperation.[58] Trade generated rivalries as well as connections, visions of New York as part of a large empire and also as an empire itself. "Every Thing conspires to make *New-York* the best Mart on the Continent," exclaimed lawyer William Smith Jr. in 1753.[59] Provincialism always contained its opposite, and Smith's celebration of New York's geographic advantage was an argument directed to London, not a prelude to independence. Life on the empire's edge involved endless comparison with other parts of the empire and shifts in perspective to assess economic, political, and cultural opportunities.

Sponsored with a pride born of feelings of inferiority, these associations included, in addition to the assembly itself, a bar association called the Law Society, New York Society Library, New York Hospital, ethnic fraternal organizations, the chamber of commerce, the Society for the Promotion of Useful Knowledge, the Society of Dissenters, and other incorporated and quasi-corporate bodies.[60] They involved families such as the Livingstons, Smiths, Morrises, DeLanceys, and Philipses, among other Scottish, Huguenot, and Dutch descended families that had been in the province for two or more generations. These families were related by blood, marriage, education, trade, and land, creating less a caste than a skein of complementary social, commercial, and political interests.[61] The provincial families could often divide against one another, as with the famous Livingston-DeLancey feud in the late colonial period.[62] But this confirms the flexibility of their connections as well as their shared concerns. Moments of conflict did not undo underlying patterns of association.

These creole improvers built on the province's position as an entrepôt. It would still be that, but its residents would also manufacture culture for themselves and neighboring provinces. And this required substantial legal autonomy. Creole New Yorkers were bred in an environment thick with claims of autonomy in a place that was, in fact, governed largely from within. English law both helped create the perception that New Yorkers were free and provided the lexicon to express the experience of self-regulation. The provincials fastened on certain legal traditions, particularly corporate freedom and the liberties of Englishmen, which in turn fueled their perception that within New York they were free to carry on civil and social business as they pleased.[63] The issue was not legislative supremacy in the abstract. It was a question of jurisdiction: Which institution had power where? New Yorkers wanted the political, or legislative, freedom of an equal dominion and the legal liberties of an English county. These traditions were impeccably English. Yet they were used to express legal and political innovations that were not fully apparent even to the provincials and to beget numerous self-governing institutions of which the colony itself was only one. In short, they created the discrete legal space of New York and declared jurisdiction over its essential activities.

William Smith Jr.'s *History of the Province of New-York* (1757) was an expression of this provincial coming-of-age. Smith was the son of a Morrisite lawyer, and he learned his law and politics from his father. He dedicated the history to Lord Halifax, first lord of the Board of Trade, and wished to inform metropolitan English readers that "the provinces are different in their Constitutions, and with respect to government, independent of each other." On the title page, he quoted *Liberty* by James Thomson, a Scot who was the unofficial poet laureate of the empire:

> *Lo! Swarming o'er the new discover'd World,*
> *Gay Colonies extend; the calm Retreat*
> *Of undeserv'd Distress. . . .*
> *. . . Bound by Social Freedom, firm they rise;*
> *Of Britain's Empire the Support and Strength.*[64]

Across the Atlantic in the "new discover'd World," creole Britons built cultural organizations within their internally free province that would, they promised, redound to the glory of the empire.

The Incorporation of New York

The provincials' most interesting legal innovation was their use of the corporate form. The corporation originated in Roman law as a political subdivision with internal autonomy, a collective body to which the ultimate authority delegated part of its dominion. It was a labor-saving device for an overextended central authority. As such, the Norman conquerors of England used it to subdue competing sources of authority.[65] On the other hand, pockets of power, such as towns and boroughs, already existed throughout England, and a corporate charter at once recognized their relative autonomy and subjected them to the crown. Hence there was some ambiguity when the crown "granted" a charter, especially prescriptive charters, which involved the legal fiction of delegating authority to existing towns.[66] As a result, the corporation, wrote legal historians Frederick Pollock and Frederic W. Maitland, was "a very contentless idea, a blank form of legal thought," but one that everywhere "is implicated in a system of local government."[67] This ambiguity pervaded colonial corporations. Colonial trading companies emerged in the late sixteenth century as a means for merchants to gain royal approbation and for the crown, in turn, to regulate this new brand of foreign policy. Following this precedent was the corporate form of the colonies themselves, even of the proprietary, later royal, colony of New York.

Practical autonomy throughout most of the colonial period supported this premise of common-law corporateness. In practice, the colonies seemed close to realizing that "Solecism in Politicks" feared in the eighteenth-century: *imperium in imperio*, each a sovereign body within a sovereign body.[68] An ambiguous reciprocity of power pervaded the colonial arrangement and belied the theory that the crown had created it. "We are no more than a little Corporation," Archibald Kennedy argued to deflate provincial power, "in the same manner as a Mayor, Alderman, and Common-Council are impowered, by his Majesty's Letters Patent. . . . [E]very Law made, that in any Shape clashes or interferes with the Laws of *Great-Britain*, are *ipso Facto*, void."[69] The provincial improvers agreed.[70] To them, however, a charter was a license for internal autonomy. New Yorkers had no official charter, but they had the experience of corporate freedom, a kind of customary charter, which to them was just as good.[71] They also had their legislative Charter of Libertyes of 1683, a corporate platform for English rights that they cited for generations even though the crown had disallowed it. In addition, the tradition of corporate thought affected the way New Yorkers structured their improvements. The cities of New York and Albany, the college, the chamber of commerce, the hospital, the library, and some churches received corporate charters from the governor. There were many other quasi-corporate bodies with structures and by-laws approximating those of corporations.[72]

The debate over the incorporation of King's College in the 1750s illustrates the improvers' innovative use of the corporate form. "He must be a Stranger to History and the World," wrote William Smith Jr., "who has not observed, that the Prosperity, Happiness, Grandeur, and even the Strength of a People, have always been the Consequences of the Improvement and Cultivation of their Minds." Education was a means to improve the province. However, "we are not only surpassed by several of our Neighbours, who have long since erected Colleges for publick Instruction, but by all others, even in common Schools." At the least, a college deserved the assembly's immediate attention.[73] While most elite New Yorkers supported the idea of a college, they disagreed about how it should be established. Some creoles opposed a crown-chartered, Anglican college because they believed that "Societies have an indisputable Right to direct the Education of their youthful Members," an argument complementing claims for political autonomy.[74] William Livingston, a younger son of the upper manor Livingstons, proposed instead a nonsectarian Protestant school founded on a charter bestowed by the provincial assembly, called an "Act of Incorporation."[75] Like the legislative Charter of Libertyes seventy years earlier, this hybrid form defied legal orthodoxy, for it was an established common-law principle that the king's consent was necessary to create a corporation, and one corporation could not incorporate another.[76] Livingston, Smith, and John Morin Scott — the three Yale-educated lawyers known as the "New York triumvirate" that engaged in provincial boosterism for a generation — devoted several issues of their *Independent Reflector* and a series of newspaper articles entitled "The Watch-Tower" to support the provincially chartered college. They believed that this power of incorporation fell within New York's jurisdiction.[77]

The proposal was denounced by Anglican minister Samuel Seabury, whose *In Defence of the Constitution*, published under the pseudonym "John Englishman," demonstrated that the triumvirate did not have a monopoly on constitutional argument.[78] At issue was "the true meaning of the words, *English Constitution.*" Seabury viewed the nonsectarian proposal as a Presbyterian gambit. "The want of *secular power*," he claimed, "not of *religious* liberty, is what they greatly lament, and ardently wish." The bill proposing a legislatively controlled, nondenominational college was the first step toward abandoning the constitution. After that, the "transition [would] be made easy, from a state of *irreligion* and *prophanity*, into a state of the worst *superstition* and *slavery*." Though the vision of a society based on common rather than individual interests was held by both sides, the Anglicans could not separate common creed and common interest. The remedy for religious diversity was to leave education to "the true religion established."[79] Seabury, who became the first president of King's College, had a point: the push for an ecumenical Protestant college was at least as much a local political maneuver as it was an expression of religious principle. Most opponents of the triumvirate were provincials themselves, revolving around the DeLancey family rather than the Livingstons. The DeLanceys controlled the assembly at the time and were Anglican. At this moment, at least, their service to the province coincided with the crown's interest.

In the end, King's College received a charter from the governor, as agent for the crown. But provincials of all denominations attended the college and were its "governors," controlling that corporation as they did others.[80] With or without royal charters, most of these institutions were, as a practical matter, corporations within a corporation. They were part of the construction of the legal space of New York in which creole improvers assumed jurisdiction over many essential civic activities: law, commerce, police regulation, discipline of military personnel, and the disputes that were heard in England in ecclesiastical courts. They sought liberty inside the empire. They never intended for that liberty to become something more. Neither would they allow it to become anything less.

English Liberties in Creole New York

The provincial improvers never doubted their own loyalty because "the rights of Englishmen" were central to their legal thought, and only one of those was the right of internal legislation. They spoke a constitutional idiom of Britain, though a localist dialect derived from seventeenth-century England that fitted the improvement of eighteenth-century New York.[81] An anonymous writer in 1747 warned that the days when the kings "were Subject to the Rules of Law, and Reason"—when, for example, they had relied on local revenue collection—were passing.[82] About the same time, New Yorkers protested a parliamentary bill that declared that the assembly ought to obey royal instructions. "If such act Doe pas in a law," warned Henry Beekman, "[it would] strike Immediately at the Liberty of the Subject and Establish arbitrary power to all the Continent and Islands in America & Else under the King's Dominions."[83] Once again New York's Anglicization followed a peculiar path, making it less like a little England than a large self-governing, and jealous, county.

British American colonists were always reluctant to raise revenue. In the mid-eighteenth century, the target of this resistance shifted from the governor and king to the whole Parliament, which of course included the king. The demand for local autonomy remained constant. During Queen Anne's War, while pressed by metropolitan officials to provide supplies, Governor George Clinton demanded that the assembly raise adequate funds.

> Consider, Gentlemen, by what Authority you sit, and act as the General Assembly of this Province! I know of none but the Authority of the King's Commission and Instructions to me, which are alterable at his Majesty's Pleasure. You seem to place it upon the same Foundation with the House of Commons of *Great-Britain*. . . . If so, you assume a Right to be a Branch of the Legislature of the Kingdom, and deny your Dependence and Sub-

jection on the Crown and Parliament. If you have not the Rights of the House of Commons of *Great-Britain*, then the Giver of Authority by which you act, has, or can put Bounds and Limitations, upon your Rights and Privileges, and alter them at Pleasure.[84]

This had been the official version of New York's constitution from the beginning, although the crown's agents sometimes flattered the assembly to garner support for imperial projects like war against France. If New Yorkers deserved the liberties of Englishmen, they owed the duties of Englishmen too. In one attempt to raise revenue, Governor Benjamin Fletcher told the assembly that "there are none of you but [t]hat are bigg with the priviledge of Englishmen, and Magna Charta, which is your right." Liberties carried duties, which if shirked would bring metropolitan scorn. "[L]et not any opportunity be given to any person to asperse you with that new coind name of *Jacobites*," he warned, "but let us show a zeal and good affeccon for their Majesties and their government."[85] Fletcher's successor, the Earl of Bellomont, similarly spoke of the reciprocal relationship between rights and duties. Because New Yorkers were "under the best Constitution of Laws, . . . they must be obedient to English laws."[86] A generation later, in a plea for financial support, Lieutenant Governor George Clarke told the New York assembly that "Your constitution is built upon a plan nearly resembling that of England, as the nature of the thing would admit of: Why would you not then tread in the steps of a British Parliament?"[87] Provincial envy of the metropolis could work for as well as against royal officials.

The key to provincial reasoning about parliamentary regulation was not whether that body could legislate for the colonies. Clearly it could and had. Rather, provincial logic rested on the distinction between internal and external regulation, taxation and regulation, or between the part of governmental authority possessed within the province and that still held in London. The assembly conceded that "his Majesty, and the Parliament of Great Britain, have a right to regulate the trade of the colonies and to lay duties on [imported] articles that may interfere with the products or manufactures of Great Britain, or any other parts of his Majesty's dominions." But this right "exclud[ed] every taxation, internal or external, for the purpose of raising a revenue on the subjects in America, without their consent."[88] This distinction had deep roots in English history, and the crown's violation of it was one cause of the English Civil War. New Yorkers also invoked the example of Ireland. "The Fidelity and Dependance of the Kingdom of *Ireland*, and the Colonies," the assembly wrote in 1765, "have always been firmly secured, though untaxed by the Parliament of *Great-Britain*."[89] The line between regulation and taxation defined English freedom. Councillor and merchant John Watts complained to Governor Robert Monckton that if London ignored the distinction between trade regulation and taxation, "the Atlantick makes the difference between a Freeman & a Slave."[90]

William Smith Jr. was the most consistent advocate of New York's corporate autonomy. The Revenue Act of 1764 was the British Parliament's first serious attempt to raise support for imperial administration by taxing colonial trade. Although the act actually cut duties on molasses in half, it included new means of enforcement, the most controversial of which was the prosecutor's power to try cases in a new, juryless vice admiralty court.[91] Smith wrote a petition to the House of Commons on behalf of the colonial assembly. The petition was a familiar mode of resistance literature; it was one of the few formal ways that subjects could raise their concerns to the metropolitan legislature and the crown. The American colonists turned increasingly to petitions as successive ministries levied new taxes and imposed new regulations. Smith explained that local autonomy was necessary to secure all other rights "established in the first Dawn of our Constitution." If these were lost, "Liberty, Property, and all the Benefits of Life, [would] tumble into Insecurity and Ruin." In addition, the deprivation of such rights would "dispirit the People, abate their Industry, discourage Trade, introduce Discord, Poverty and Slavery; or, by depopulating the Colonies, turn a vast, fertile, prosperous Region, into a dreary Wilderness; impoverish *Great-Britain*, and shake the Power and Independency of the most opulent and flourishing empire in the World."[92]

Smith's petition was the model for similar ones by the other members of the New York triumvirate, William Livingston and John Morin Scott. "By improving a Country inhabited only by Savages," Livingston wrote in his petition to the House of Lords, New Yorkers had increased Britain's trade so that it might soon "equal the greatest Empire recorded in the Annals of Fame." Growth would continue unless "checked by a new Model of our Constitution, and an Abridgment of the essential and fundamental Rights of *Englishmen*."[93] The power of local taxation, which the Revenue Act abridged, was supported by English custom and history, survived the Norman Conquest, and was even a "natural Right of Mankind." Such a durable liberty surely extended to the British colonies.[94]

In his parallel petition to the king, Scott focused on the right to representation and to a jury trial. He also made explicit an additional basis for English liberties abroad: the successful settlement of a "wilderness." Taxation was a matter for local legislation, and the jury trial was inviolable. The former was an indisputable English right and the latter an "antient Badge of *English* Liberty." Both were guaranteed in the "Charter of Libertyes and Priviledges," in which "a political Frame was erected, in the nearest possible Resemblance to that of our Mother Country." Although the crown had rejected the charter twice, this was a legal world in which such formalities seemed not to matter; the customary principles beneath them did matter. Scott argued that there were, in addition to the charter, three other bases of New Yorkers' constitutional equality with Englishmen: the liberties earned by settlement, the structure of their government, and custom. New Yorkers had a Charter of Libertyes; their immigrant ancestors carried with them the rights of Englishmen; they replicated English government by establishing a governor, council, and assembly; and this system had persisted for nearly a century. The right of self-taxation, "whether inherent in the People, or sprung from any other Cause, has received the royal Sanction, is the Basis of our Colony State, [has] become venerable by long Usage," and was "fundamentally woven into our Constitution." The colonists had further earned these rights by long service against New France, culminating in the conquest of Canada, "the most luminous Event, that ever adorned the Page of *English* History." These were the arguments of a lawyer accustomed to pleading in the alternative. In sum, the enjoyment of the liberties of Englishmen abroad and "the Lustre of the *British* Empire" went hand in hand.[95]

Similar petitions followed the Stamp Act in 1765, the New York Restraining Act in 1767, and the Coercive Acts in 1774.[96] William Smith Jr. reflected sadly on the "new and awful Idea of the Constitution" that Great Britain expounded over these years. "You Americans are absolutely ours," Parliament seemed to say: "We may dispose of you, your Commerce, your Lands and Acquisitions as we please — You have no Rights — The Patents of our Kings to your Ancestors do not bind this Nation. The Privileges and Securities of English Men cannot be yours, unless you return to the old Realm. — Our antient Indulgences, were temporary Permissions."[97] From the east side of the Atlantic, New York's constitution was a matter of "grace" rather than "right" and could be repossessed at will. What New Yorkers wanted was to retain the local autonomy they had long experienced, "restoration" rather than revolution. They wanted the ministry to recognize their "unalienable Rights as Englishmen" such as consent to taxation, jury trials, good behavior tenure for judges, and the right to print paper currency. There were also some new grievances, called the "intolerable acts." One was the Quebec Act, which restricted the fur trade and permitted Catholicism in the French cession. Another was the statute that closed the port of Boston, punishing an entire city "without the Formality of a Trial." Again, the petitions, which proliferated in the 1760s, and resistance, which increased in the 1770s, were qualitatively distinct from rebellion, the ultimate recourse available to vindicate the English constitution. The protests, the assembly informed the House of Commons at late as 1775, were designed to make the "Union" between Britain and American colonies "permanent and solid." The way to do so was to allow the colonies "to participate of that Constitution, whose direct End and Aim is the Liberty of the Subject."[98] Provincial interests and the liberty of the colonial subject served the empire's interest.

The triumvirate wrote these memorials for the assembly, and the assembly helped organize provincial resistance to the crown and Parliament. But defense of the colonial constitution was not limited to the assembly. Many people involved were not assemblymen, and the movement included other institutions. Nor did all the provincial improvers become revolutionaries. Some remained loyal, including Smith, who spent his last years as chief justice of Quebec.[99] Smith lamented that the metropolitan government had "opened Pandora's box" with the new taxes of the 1760s and failed to see that "to tax the colonies by act of Parliament, was totally to *disanglify* them." It was part of the colonists' constitutional heritage to insist on this freedom. The settlement of North America confirmed that they deserved such English liberties. Even people unfamiliar with liberty, like "Russians and Turks," would claim this right if they had "conquer[ed] America."[100]

Smith here made the point of contention too fine. He knew that behind the issue of taxation lay the larger problem (in his words) of disanglification. The creole improvers began to see that their cultural institutions were integral not only to the functioning of their daily lives but also to their identities as Britons in New York. For generations, local associations and government, not metropolitan directives, had given form to colonial life.[101] The practical experience of self-government was at the root of their protest, and New York lawyers expressed this felt sense of freedom in the terms of the constitutionalism learned from the common-law canon. Gradually the lawyers' conception of liberty became the interpretive lens for many, though not all saw the same landscape of freedom.

The protesters never made precisely clear what they meant by "constitution." They were looking for words to express their sense that they should control their society. Constitutional arguments created a discursive site where the colonists could maintain, within and outside established political institutions, that they enjoyed some autonomy and deserved the liberties of

Englishmen. Some of those institutions were political, like the assembly in New York and the right of petition. Some were legal, like the colonial courts that New Yorkers dominated and that served their interests so effectively that they rarely sought review of their cases in the Privy Council. Other institutions were not clearly legal or political. The provincial elite, for example, resorted to printed literature and boycotts. John Reid points out that the colonists collapsed most political debates into legal terms.[102] This was true of their behavior as well as their words. There was no clear distinction between law and politics; colonists believed that policy should serve and be amenable to legal norms — to the norms of the English constitution, whose basic function was to restrain power and protect liberties. Representation and common-law procedures were the most effective means of enforcement but, again, not the only ones. This experience of local self-rule, defended with traditional English means, was their constitution.

Rather than a precise set of institutions and rights, this constitution captured claims for autonomy that involved political and cultural institutions. There was a federal quality to the provincials' thought, but they developed no theory of federalism.[103] The flexibility and eclecticism of their constitutional resources served them so well for so long that there was little incentive to define their conception of empire more precisely. Indeed, they chafed at *any* rigid conception of the imperial constitution. Despite all their pamphlets and petitions, the provincials rarely explored the relationship between the colonial constitution and the English constitution. The exceptions came in the decade before the Revolution. Some colonists sketched plans for an American parliament that would have the same jurisdiction on the west side of the Atlantic that the British Parliament had on the east. For decades there was no contradiction between provincial and imperial loyalty, and the very diffuseness of the colonists' constitution allowed them to petition for English liberties without ever asking whether such was consistent with membership in the empire. They assumed that the two constitutions were similar. To the degree they differed, the colonial constitution was somehow coordinate, not, as for the imperial agents in New York and the ministry in London, subordinate to the English constitution. This allowed many of the colonists to resist royal administration at one moment and participate in it the next. When William Livingston received a copy of Catherine Macaulay's *History of England* from the author, who praised Livingston as "one of the most distinguished Guardians of the American Liberty," he complimented her history of their shared culture and observed "that nothing will satisfy us short of a Constitution similar to that enjoyed by our fellow Subjects at home and established upon such a basis that any infringement of it by the Parliament be deemed so fundamental a violation as would absolve us from all dependence on the Mother Country."[104] English and American liberty were identical to him. While the creole elite often celebrated the empire, they increasingly reserved primary loyalty for the province. The ambiguous relationship between the two was, for them, the constitution of the empire.

Sometimes that loyalty was more narrowly circumscribed, limited to the seaport city and its immediate hinterland. Sometimes the empire, and its constitution, might exist on an altogether different plane. "Never had a nation such a prospect as Britain of erecting a vast and durable empire," William Livingston proclaimed five years after the end of the Seven Years' War. Then he shifted his focus from the Atlantic to the continent, "an inheritance from ocean to ocean" that was the "indispensable substratum of empire." There was land "amply sufficient for hundreds of millions" that could be settled "without the guilty effusion of human blood." There was, characteristically, little notice of the native population. Following this came the familiar trope of *translatio studii*, which Livingston may have derived from Bishop George Berkeley. The difference was that liberty, not learning, was the cargo of his westward moving empire. Rather than imagine independence outside the British Empire, Livingston envisioned "a *Phoenix state*" in America that might, someday, take the lead within it: "The day dawns in which the foundation of this mighty empire is to be laid, by the establishment of a *regular* American constitution. All that has been hitherto done, seems to be little beside the collection of materials, for the construction of this glorious fabrick. 'Tis time to put them together. The transfer of the European part of the great family is so swift, and our growth so vast, that, before seven years roll over our heads, the first stones must be laid." [105]

New Yorkers, drawing on the corporate tradition and the liberties of Englishmen, layered sovereign body beneath sovereign body in their effort to construct that empire, and the resulting lines of power were difficult to trace. Solecism of political theory though it was, the colony was an experiment not just of *imperium in imperio*. Its epigraph might have been *imperia in imperio*: multiple empires within the empire.

The Marchland Constitution and the "Lawless" Frontier

Such were the coordinates of the midcentury British Atlantic empire: London to New York; Canada to the West Indies. But, as William Livingston's paean revealed, there was another geographic factor at work: a continent of unknown extent. Land speculators among the provincial elite thought that the northern and western parts of the province would be the scene of the most promising improvement. Similarly, the imperial agents never fixed their eyes only on London; they also looked west. Out there was the future of the empire.

Many small farmers, traders, liberated servants, sailors, and newly arrived immigrants agreed. While not consumed by the civic consciousness of the more established provincials, they too embraced the ethos of improvement, especially involving agriculture and trade.[106] Sailors best embodied this ethos on the oceanic frontier, usually working within the discipline of their ships but occasionally running away from their captains in protest and sometimes turning the world of the sea "upside down" as pirates.[107] In the colonial backcountry there were similar negotiations between settlers and speculators, each hoping to use the other as together they evaded imperial law. Settlers and speculators carried a variant of English enclosure into the American continent. From one angle, the pattern of settlement looked like a safety valve for the effects of enclosure at home; from another, it appeared to be a transplant of that elemental English institution.[108] On the west side of the Atlantic, however, the common landholders displaced were not British, and landholding became in practice less tenurial and more allodial. No one seemed seised of the land except those who could put it to cultivated use.

The constitution of New York and the empire in the mid-eighteenth century cannot be grasped without an account of this popular energy that was channeled into migration.[109] The belief that one could move at will, leave social and political ties in one jurisdiction and resettle in another, repeatedly, was expressed in the perpetual migrations from the British Isles and northern Europe to the mainland colonies and the continuation of this movement on the American continent. This migration provides the context in which to understand the few legal expressions of its participants. Here was a roughly articulated marchland constitution, a fundamental law carried on the legs of thousands of endlessly migratory Europeans of various ethnic backgrounds. Unlike most modes of resistance, it was not choreographed by custom or the elite.[110] It was, nonetheless, a vital strand of popular constitutionalism—a kind of lived constitutionalism that reflected how thousands of colonists experienced authority and how they wished to restructure it.

There was a tradition of migration in Europe, and many of the North American settlers may have considered the transatlantic voyage simply another leg in a multigenerational journey.[111] But the dynamics of space and people, of land and labor, changed in the colonies. The persistent migration in North America toward land viewed as underpopulated has been long studied but is not fully understood. Recently, historians who observe that neither geographic determinants nor Malthusian imperatives can fully explain "the impulse to move" to and across the American continent have focused on the complex web of land speculation.[112] The search for a causal relationship between speculation and migration is circular.[113] But the supply-side argument should not be exaggerated. Although speculative interests promoted and facilitated migration, they cannot fully account for the cease-less mobility in New York or any other colony. Speculators would not have taken risks without believing that there would be enough buyers and tenants to cover their investments of time, money, and their own journeys into the unimproved landscape. Behind this mobility lay an ambivalence about authority, though not one that should be termed democratic.[114] When the settlers did express themselves, they too used the phrases of the English constitution and common law. The popular will to relocate beyond established towns and counties, disregard provincial jurisdiction, and ignore imperial law demonstrated the limits of popular respect for government. The popular use of the constitutional canon also demonstrates how malleable that canon became as the empire extended its boundaries farther west.

This mobility affected property law most immediately. Traditionally in England, property carried governmental authority.[115] In New York, the equation held, and the new patterns of land possession altered the dynamics of power. The land contained diverse groups of people subject to conflicting claims of authority. It was often unclear who owned what or who ruled where.

Marchland Development

For all the conflicts among competing land users, many contemporaries complained that there were not *enough* land users: New York's population was smaller than most of its neighbors'; there seemed to have been less movement there than elsewhere. Some historians argue that the province developed slowly because Dutch manor lords spread themselves thinly along the fertile banks of the Hudson, forcing land-poor settlers into neighboring colonies.[116] Others blame the early English governors for transforming the unsuccessful Dutch manorial strategy into a massive land giveaway. But the thrust of the argument is the same: large manors discouraged settlement by honest yeomen.[117]

Historian Sung Bok Kim's analysis of tenant leases, however, casts doubt on the thesis that the governors and elite were to blame for the slow population growth and supports William Smith Jr.'s contemporary report that tenants of the Van Rensselaer and Livingston families "have free farms at the annual rent of a tenth of the produce, which has as yet neither been exacted nor paid." The landlords had every reason to people the land; cultivation of one parcel raised the value of others near it. They often lacked the leverage to extract rents from their tenants or did not try.[118] There were egregious cases of exploitation, such as Robert Livingston's early eighteenth-century attempt to build a plantation on the backs of Palatine refugees. But many tenants stayed and prospered, making the manorial counties among the fastest growing in New York.[119]

It was not, some contemporaries thought, so much the size of the grants that accounted for New York's slow improvement as the lack of a policy to attract immigrants. Land cultivation and manufacturing suffered, the New York triumvirate complained in the *Independent Reflector*, because of "the high Price of Labour" and the poor quality of that available, which they saw as "low, profligate, drunken and faithless." Consequently, "nothing is more wanted to open a vast Fund of Riches into the Province, in this Branch of Trade, than the Importation of Foreigners."[120] In fact, New Yorkers did exert themselves at least as hard as those in other colonies to attract immigrants, and New York's population grew quickly in the late colonial period. Still, as in all the colonies, there was always more improvement needed than there were hands available, and New York's absolute population lagged behind that of most of its neighbors at a time when the census was becoming an index of improvement. Against this measure, New York fell short. Something other than the manors was at work.[121]

The map offers some clues. The Appalachian Mountains obstructed the flow of western migration and penned in early development. The Mohawk River, stretching northwest from Albany, did provide the most promising western passage through the range, but it was a slim gateway hostage to seasonal water flows. Another factor was imperial diplomacy. The colony's boundaries were never established with finality during the colonial period. The contiguity of New France in particular made for uncertainty, and New York hosted some of the most significant battles of the eighteenth century. William Smith Jr. attributed some of the undercultivation of the province to "the French and Indian iruptions, to which we have always been exposed." Before the end of the Seven Years' War, he could describe New York's northern boundary no more precisely than "the line between us and the French."[122] The peace treaty of 1763 eliminated the French threat, but it did not terminate French claims to land within New York.[123] The colony's boundaries also remained uncertain because of disputes with its neighbors about conflicting charter rights. Massachusetts's claim to land in western New York was not resolved until after the Revolution. Contested eastern boundaries had a similar stifling effect. There were sporadic border skirmishes between those holding New York titles and those claiming land under grants from New Jersey, Connecticut, Massachusetts, and New Hampshire.[124] Violence in provincial borderlands also hindered productive land use. This was one area in which provincial landowners turned willingly to imperial decision makers, who usually vindicated titles from the royal colony over those from neighboring corporate colonies.[125]

There was also Britain's promise to the Iroquois that it would protect their hunting grounds in return for military aid. The northwestern regions of New York contained relatively dense populations of Native Americans, though they were not included in the colony's census and their cultivation went unrecognized by colonial statisticians and settlers.[126] They were, however, integral to the province's economy, especially the fur trade, and to its defense against France. Native American participation in colonial society was diminishing almost everywhere in the established colonies except New York, where it remained important for Euro-Americans to seek accommodation along a "middle ground" that included the colony's western reaches and in which British, French, and native cultures interacted in peace and war.[127] To obtain a patent, every land speculator first had to extinguish Indian title. This required meeting with the Native Americans who controlled the parcel and purchasing a release. The practical fact of Indian control, and British willingness to acknowledge the fact in most colonies, existed side by side with the common-law principle that all land already belonged to the crown either by right of conquest or, in the eyes of some, settlement by his subjects. The practice and principle were reconciled not so much by a recognition of the Native Americans' preexisting property interest as by the fiction that the king had granted them the right to occupy the land. But purchase of that bare right alone did not confer title on the purchaser. After extinguishing the Native Americans' right, the claimant then obtained an official survey and petitioned the governor for a patent. Only after this long and costly process did title vest in the speculator.[128]

Amid these barriers were Sir William Johnson and his associates, who attempted to manage the settlement of the strategic Mohawk Valley.[129] Along with diplomacy, indeed part of its definition, was self-aggrandizement. When the land was divided in the late colonial period, Johnson controlled the distribution and took the best pieces.

The geopolitics of the empire, not the Dutch manorial policy or early British governors, dictated the pace of settlement. The imperial agents and provincial elites tried to manage what was left to local control, with limited success.

Common Law in a Contested Marchland

If geopolitics shaped marchland development, so too did the late colonial demographic revolution. Beginning in the 1760s, the colony's population grew rapidly, fueled by a spike in immigration after the Seven Years' War.[130] One by-product was the erosion of colonial law enforcement. Already in 1750 Archibald Kennedy observed that "where People are numerous and freed, they will push what they think is for their Interest, and all restraining Laws will be thought Oppressive; especially such Laws as according to the Conceptions we have of English Liberty they have had no hand in contriving or making."[131] This attitude hindered law enforcement. Thirty-seven percent of the criminal prosecutions in eighteenth-century New York that historian Douglas Greenberg was able to track did not reach completion, and the number jumps to 60 percent in the northern counties.[132]

One problem was that New York's criminal law institutions were inadequate. The amateur, rotating personnel were undertrained, ill equipped, and not respected. This last fact is particularly striking. The deferential political culture that historians attribute to colonial America was not strong in its marchland. Law officers, at least, received little deference. Sheriffs and constables were routinely assaulted, some murdered, while carrying out their duties. Typical was the experience of Sheriff Jacob Van Schaack of Albany County. He reported to Lieutenant Governor Colden in 1760 that an arrest was frustrated when the suspect "seized a pistol, swore he would blow my Brains out, and so kept me off from further prosecuting the arrest, uttering all the time the most violent oaths and other abusive Language against me. It is impossible for me to execute my office . . . not only my life, but my fortune also is in the utmost danger by these insults."[133] Greenberg calculates that 70 percent of the contempt-of-authority cases he compiled involved attacks on law officers. Others never came to court. Jurors, like these officers, were difficult to select, subject to intimidation, and errant.[134]

Geography and demography also hindered law enforcement. Large, sparsely settled counties facilitated evasion.[135] Contested borders were again important. Encroaching New Englanders, often with the tacit approval of the Massachusetts government, were a constant problem. In the 1750s, Robert Livingston Jr., William Livingston's older brother and third lord of Livingston Manor, implored Sheriff Abraham Yates of Albany to remove the "new England men" who trespassed and squatted on his land.[136] Livingston petitioned the governor and council for help, and they issued a bland proclamation that migrants should obey New York's property laws and not squat on other people's land. Still, Livingston could not depend on local law enforcement officials. When one vengeful tenant and his son were released from jail after charges of murder were dropped, Livingston sought Sheriff Yates's aid but got none, leaving him to mix lamentation and disgust: "Good God what an affair is this; pray how came it about that he is sett at liberty[;] be so good as to advise me, & whether I am left to defend my Self without the assistance of Government or Laws; if so, I will remove Immediately with my family, as it is impossible for me to defend my Self against a Government bent on my distruction, and seek Some place of refuge."[137] After Yates informed him that the tenant received a proclamation of freedom from the governor and council (a document not reserved for substantial landlords), a frustrated Livingston warned, "[Y]ou'll I suppose not be surprised when you hear that I have shott him, which I am determined to do the first time I see him."[138] When needed most, on one of the colony's largest manors, deference was scarce.

More violence followed in the 1760s. To protest the Stamp Act, the provincial bar refused to file stamped paper in the courts, effectively closing them during the winter of 1765–66. Rents on the Hudson Valley manors went unpaid in larger numbers than usual. The boycott on the courts ended when Parliament repealed the Stamp Act, and lease enforcement actions flooded the courts. This in turn sparked rent riots up and down the Hudson Valley.[139] Attorney General John Tabor Kempe was unsuccessful in apprehending many of the rioting tenants. When he did prosecute one ringleader, the crown granted the defendant a pardon on the royal governor's recommendation, hoping that leniency "will have a better effect in recalling these mistaken People to their Duty than the most rigorous punishment."[140] The crown's strategy upset the creole elite, much of which depended on tenanted land, but it also reflected the inability of the imperial agents to keep order. The long campaign by Colden and others against the landed elite made the imperial agents allies of a sort with the tenants.[141] Neither the elite nor the agents wanted violence, but the rent riots taught the elite lessons about its utility. They too were prepared to embrace violence if the law did not serve their ends. Hugh Wallace, a member of the council associated with the DeLancey family, complained that Colden's plan to force the sale of unsettled portions of land on which quitrents were in arrears would endanger titles across the colony's frontier. The original patents had required the grantees to settle the lands or forfeit them, so Colden was merely attempting to enforce terms of the grants. But Wallace knew that limited enforcement was part of the bargain of the rule of law in the colonies. "If Men will do all that the Law will support," he observed, then "it's well there is a Law against picking Pocketts or we should not be able to walk the Streets with a Dollar about us." Some rules were enforced regardless of formal law; others could never be enforced, again regardless of formal law. The Irish-born Wallace reminded William Johnson that "there is a Law called in our Country *Shillalagh* & If any Man was to wrest my property from me in such a Manner, I would apply that law to him."[142] The agents were on notice of the possibility of violent resistance.

If settlers did not hold a monopoly on violence, the provincial elite did not hold a monopoly on legal arguments, for the language of "lawless" New Yorkers was often similar to that of the provincial lawyers. They too conveyed their sense of right in terms of English liberties, occasionally leavened with the Old Testament righteousness of New England.[143] A good example is the way Ethan Allen and his associates defended their New Hampshire land grants west of the Connecticut River, which was part of New York under its 1664 patent. The Green Mountain Boys relied on foul language, intimidation, and violence. They threatened to skin sheriffs alive, placed a bounty on the head of Attorney General Kempe, and referred to their guns as sources of authority almost as often as they invoked the common law.[144] Still, there was more to their rebellion than land grabbing and riot. The squatters possessed title, however disputable, from New Hampshire governor Benning Wentworth, and they mimicked the procedures of New York's criminal law when, for example, they "tryed" Justice of the Peace Benjamin Hough in the place they called Bennington. They found Hough guilty of the crime of accepting his commission from New York's government, sentenced him to "two hundred stripes on his naked back," and banished him from the region on pain of five hundred more lashes. If this was "rough music" of the sort heard throughout the British Atlantic world, the tune was the common law. These procedures and punishments, though not the substantive charge, were common in colonial courts, and the New Hampshire grantees adopted them wholesale.[145] When the assembly passed a riot act calling for the arrest of Allen and others for assuming "Judicial Powers" and other offenses, the New Hampshire grantees invoked the liberties of Englishmen and protested that the legislature "had no Constitutional right or power to make such Laws and consequently they are Null and Void from the Nature and Energy of the

English Constitution."[146] They denied New York's jurisdiction, just as many in New York denied that of the crown, and they too would write a new constitution in 1777.

IT WAS THE IMPERIAL DYNAMICS of this marchland, a contested territory viewed differently by different groups of British Americans, that gave rise to multiple constitutions. The people moving across it experienced conflicting claims of authority: the crown and its agents; provincial law, itself subject to contesting groups; the Iroquois; and claims of those from other colonies and empires. These multiple sources of authority were perhaps too diffuse to constitute *imperia*; yet together they precluded the operation of *imperium*. Out there, on the edge of New York, the British Empire barely existed. Still circulating was its constitutional currency: the English common law.

The Search for Imperial Law
in the 1760s

I am realy vexed at the Behavior of the
Lawless Banditti upon the Frontiers, and
what aggravates the more, is, the Difficulty to
bring them to Punishment. . . . The Disorder
lyes in the Weakness of the Governments to
enforce obedience to the Laws, and in some,
their Provincial Factions run so high, that
every villain finds some powerfull Protector.
Commander in Chief Thomas Gage to
Sir William Johnson (1766)

T HE MULTIPLE VISIONS OF New York's constitution — that of imperial authority, provincial jurisdiction, and common-law claims in the marchland — coexisted for many years until the events of the 1760s forced their contradictions into relief. The tumultuous decade that followed the Seven Years' War compelled the imperial agents to conclude that common law, as imported into the colony, was no longer integrative. Throughout the colonial period, many had argued that the colonists did not enjoy English law and especially the common law by right, but the imperial agents in New York were the first to attempt to withdraw parts of the common law from the colony. They targeted three common-law institutions that obstructed imperial policy: property-law doctrine, the jury, and the personnel of the legal system. The imperial agents hoped to reform these institutions and establish a new administrative regime with themselves at the helm. The provincial improvers, on the other hand, strove to preserve those common-law institutions as their birthright. Without much explanation but with plenty of righteousness, so too did less coherent communities, especially on New York's frontier. At stake was the meaning of the common law. What had long helped hold the empire together now, in the eyes of the imperial agents, was pulling it apart. Their goal was to link the province more firmly to the rest of the British Empire.

The Property Law of a Marchland

As he made his way from his hilltop mansion overlooking the Mohawk River to the far side of the valley, Sir William Johnson must have thought that the year 1766 was a good one, for himself and the British Empire. He had been knighted during the Seven Years' War, and his renown was spreading throughout Great Britain and the colonies as His Majesty's superintendent for Indian affairs, the man who had helped defeat the French and then negotiated peace with the Native Americans in the western cession. Turning in his saddle, he saw everywhere land that was his; and if he did not own what he saw, he knew who did because he had been involved in the granting or because it was still possessed by the members of the Mohawk nation, which included himself. In the imperial tradition of naming what one controls—or attempting to control the landscape by naming it—he lived in Johnson Hall, in Johnstown, New York. It was the largest building west of the Hudson, and its simple elegance would have looked impressive not just in the provincial capital in New York City but also back in the British Isles, as he modeled it on the estate of his uncle and patron, Sir Peter Warren.[1] An intercultural meeting place supplanting the modest Fort Johnson, the neoclassical structure symbolized the evolution of his self-perception. Sir William had arrived.

Yet he was on the move again, constantly meeting with Native Americans, tenants, settlers, and soldiers. This day it was a white squatter on Mohawk soil who had ignored warnings to leave. He had to struggle to maintain his power, the power of the British Empire on the American continent. Accordingly, Johnson recommended various reforms to the Board of Trade in London, including the restriction of Indian trade to military posts, the establishment of a network of Indian commissaries, the prevention of fraudulent land purchases, and the clarification of boundaries between European and Indian lands.[2] Through these initiatives he hoped to control diplomacy and land disposition in the marchland. A key part of this strategy was the displacement of provincial law. He wanted to replace some common-law property rules and, more important, the decision makers who applied them.

London gave Johnson some of what he wanted. Foremost was the royal Proclamation of 1763, which he and other imperial agents helped formulate. The proclamation forbade private land purchases from the natives, required licenses and bonds of traders, and restricted settlement west of the Appalachians so "that the Indians may be convinced of our justice and determined resolution to remove all reasonable cause of discontent."[3] But the laws of motion eclipsed those of restraint. "I do assure your Lordships," Sir William wrote to the Board of Trade, "that the much greater part of my time is occupied in composing differences occasioned by the lowest of the People who either from views of Trade, Lands or some other interested motives take upon them to convene Indians then say what they please."[4] In letter after letter, he pleaded for more authority to resolve frontier disputes, complaining that he was powerless to discipline "the Frontier Inhabitants, who seem regardless of the Laws, and not only perpetrate Murders whenever opportunity offers, but think themselves at liberty to make settlements where they please."[5]

Land patents, provincial laws, and even the king's proclamation had little effect. Settlers kept saying and doing what they pleased. After returning from that squatter's cabin in 1766, for example, Johnson warned in a dispatch to the president of the Board of Trade that "the thirst after Indian lands, is become almost universal, the people who generally want them, are ignorant of, or remote from the consequences of disobliging the Indians." He concluded that the main culprits were not the "ignorant settlers." They were, rather, large speculators. These he described as

persons of consequence in the Capitals, who . . . make use of some of the lowest and most selfish of the Country Inhabitants, to seduce the Indians to their houses, where they are kept rioting in drunkenness till they have effected their bad purposes, to prevent which, the Gentlemen of the Law here say, my Commission is not sufficiently expressive, nor will any Act of an American Legislature be obtained, that affects their private interest. . . . [T]ho' Proclamations are issued, and orders sent to the several Governours, experience has shewn that both are hitherto ineffectual and will be so, whilst the Gentlemen of property and Merchants are interested in finding out evasions or points of Law against them, and whilst many of these, and the much greater part of the commonalty entertain such contracted ideas of sovereign power, & authority.[6]

Johnson reported how he had written the squatter at the Mohawks' request, showed him the proclamation personally, and referred the case to the governor and attorney general. None of this had any effect. The squatter, Johnson reported, simply "laughs at" such threats, "well knowing the party that is ready to support him, in so much, that it would only weaken the prerogative to prosecute him, as may be evinced in many similar cases."[7]

Johnson was involved in several of these cases. One concerned George Klock, who purchased part of an old, disputed Livingston family patent known by the Indian name Canajoharie and plied additional acreage loose with rum. Klock's first scheme was selling rum to the natives and stealing their clothing, which he then resold to them. Then he moved on to buying land fraudulently. An Albany jury refused to find him guilty.[8] Johnson wrote him twice to stop. Klock's answer, Johnson reported, was that "I might hang myself."[9] Partly because Klock was able to hire William Livingston as his attorney, the cases against him persisted through the Revolution.[10] Similarly, Eve Pickard, "a Mullatto Woman," obtained a deed from "three Indians dead drunk." She went unprosecuted.[11] Then Iroquois chiefs returning from North Carolina were set upon by white frontiersmen, who could not be prosecuted because "these sort of Lawless people are not easily detected, being screened by one another."[12] Incidents like these compelled Johnson to conclude that Indian affairs had to be reorganized and his own authority enlarged, at the expense of provincial jurisdiction.

Land purchases were the main problem. Settlers and speculators often bought land from the natives without first obtaining a patent from the governor as required. They also sought patents from neighboring colonies like Massachusetts and New Hampshire, which granted land on both sides of their contested borders. Settlers then claimed that possession was most of the law. Thomas Young, a doctor born in Ulster County and a companion of Ethan Allen's, defended leaseholders on contested parcels east of Albany with the "maxim in law, that the possessor's title is ever good till paramounted by a better." Possession and cultivation represented the spirit of the imperial enterprise, which Young believed overrode boundary descriptions in old patents. "The settling and improving of the wild lands of *America*," Young wrote, "has ever stood confest an object worthy of the attention of our Most Gracious Kings, as well as every subordinate lover of either king or country." These leaseholders — "We, the common people" — improved the land in the plain sense, unlike most large proprietors. Imperial administrators argued that such lands were reserved for soldiers as payment or in lieu of pensions for service in the Seven Years' War. The settlers simply responded that they, cultivators of the soil, were as useful to the empire as soldiers and that their "undoubted rights" of property deserved protection.[13] A central figure in this case was John Henry Lydius, a land speculator and longtime troublemaker for the imperial agents. But he, like the agents, thought his personal interests complemented the empire's. Indeed, he thought that challenges to his titles delayed "settlements & improvements of part of those lands, to his great loss & damage, but much more of the British interest in North America."[14] Squatters too could invoke legal maxims, the language of improvement, and the crown to defend their land.

Most troublesome for Johnson was the infamous Kayaderosseras patent. This huge tract, which stretched from Saratoga to Schenectady, had been sold in 1703 by the chiefs of two Mohawk tribes who did not represent the whole Mohawk nation; Mohawk custom required that all chiefs consent to such land sales.[15] But, with this proof of purchase, the buyers had procured a patent from an early New York governor. As a result, the claims could not be revoked without calling into question common-law land titles, the cornerstone of English society made even more important overseas, where colonists anxiously drew lines and affixed names. "Tear *Indian* Title to pieces," Thomas Young exclaimed, "and tear the country to pieces!" The patentees had paid some Native Americans for some land and then paid fees to the governor and other officials to obtain a patent. Now, complained the assembly, the Native Americans simply denied the sale. This was "very common," for they were "unlettered Barbarians, who keep no certain Memorials; have very indistinct Notions of private Property, live by Hunting; use no land Marks, nor have any Inclosures."[16] No landmarks, no records, no cultivation: all of this was contrary to the letter and spirit of the common law. Provincials often characterized the Native Americans as ignorant of English law and incapable of fair dealing. In their eyes, it was a contest between the king's loyal subjects and unlettered "savages." To them, it should have been no contest. If provincial judges and juries decided the matter, it would not be one.

Yet if provincial landholders won, Johnson's influence with the Iroquois would suffer.[17] He needed their loyalty for defense against other European empires and Indian nations, to fulfill promises made to them during the war with France, and to justify his own authority in the marchland. Colden reported to Johnson that the Kayaderosseras patent was under review in London, and although "[t]he Proceedings there from the nature of things, are slow and require patience, . . . their effects are certain and effectual, which the greatest and richest Man cannot withstand."[18] Dissatisfied, Johnson explained that the Native Americans would feel "neglected unless the means of relief are speedy, and I am not Sufficiently Acquainted with the Nature of a process on a Scire facias to know when the Affair may come to a conclusion."[19] Paeans to the rule of law did not solve diplomatic problems.

Johnson turned to Attorney General John Tabor Kempe for more advice. Kempe concluded that the grant was valid even though the patentees had not first purchased the land legitimately from the Mohawks. The Privy Council had instructed the governors that purchase from the Native Americans was required to perfect land titles. If the governor granted patents to settlers who had not purchased the land as instructed, were those patents valid? In a letter that was unusually thoughtful in its justification of provincial titles, Kempe opined that

> it is the Policy of our Constitution, that wheresoever the Kings Dominions extends he is the Fountain of all Property in Lands, and to Deny that Right, in the Crown, in any place, is in Effect denying his Right to Rule there. Hence it follows, that in a legal Consideration the King can grant Lands within his Dominions here, as well without a previous Conveyance from the Indians, as with. Nevertheless the Crown has thought fit by its Instructions to its Governors here to direct them not to Grant Lands before they were purchased from the Indians, but this is not a Restriction contained in his Commission by which he has the power to Grant, but exists in the private Instructions. And tho if a Governor should act contrary to his Instructions it would justly expose him to the Kings Displeasure, yet perhaps his Acts might be nevertheless binding, and a Grant contrary to the Instructions good, if the Governor pursued the powers in his Commission.[20]

It had been English practice since the establishment of New York, and Dutch policy before that, to require buyers to extinguish Indian claims before the governor granted a patent. Nonetheless, legally all land belonged to the king with or without prior purchase from the natives, who held no common-law interest. This part of Kempe's analysis was conventional. The gloss on the relationship between the commission and instructions was, however, new. Kempe believed that the commission investing the governor with the power to grant land trumped the instruction that required grantees to purchase the land from the natives before receiving a patent. Commissions were indeed superior to instructions. That, however, did not mean that an action authorized by the broad terms of the commission but violating an instruction was legal. A commission conferred powers on the governor. Instructions explained how he was supposed to use these powers. Accordingly, instructions supplemented a commission; they should have been reconciled with the commission rather than interpreted as conflicting and subordinate.[21] But under Kempe's interpretation, a governor could dispose of land as he pleased under his commission and the grants would be valid, notwithstanding instructions that the land be purchased first.[22] Kempe, who held questionable land titles himself, crafted a rationale for vindicating provincial titles in every case. This did not help answer the question of *which* governor's patent was valid when there was more than one, but it did eliminate the legal necessity of extinguishing aboriginal title. Under the common law, the king was the original owner of all land. Kempe's bottom line was that a governor could grant land whether or not the patentee had first purchased it from the Native Americans.

A frustrated Johnson responded by repudiating the common law. "[H]ow it would appear at Common Law does not appear to be the Question," he wrote to Kempe, "for I perceive that the Common Law is not at all calculated for enquirys between White people & Indians."[23] While dealing with another case of fraudulent purchase, Johnson concluded that "at Common law, where they stick to Letter, and Word, the Indians may Expect little redress."[24] In the colonies, "justice" toward the Native Americans was more important than preserving the integrity of the common law. Earlier he had suggested "throwing" such matters "into Chancery," which he said less out of respect for the law of equity, with which there is little reason to believe he was familiar, than in the hope of evading provincial judges and juries, for the governor was the chancellor and the chancery court operated without a jury.[25] His goal had been to displace provincial decision makers. Now he concluded simply that the Native Americans "were not known when the greatest part of our Laws were made, nor has there been since a proper provision made for them in such Cases, consequently measures must be pursued of a different Nature, at Least from the Common Law, to obtain Justice for them, for whether under it or not does not appear to me Material so Long as Justice & good policy demand our attention to their Grievances." Although the common law was "happily devised for our use," its rules were made "before the discovery of America" and in "many cases prove a bar to [the Indians] getting justice."[26] New laws were necessary. For example, he assured the Board of Trade that, contrary to provincial protests, the Iroquois did have a concept of property. Their rules of ownership were, however, different: nations, not individuals, owned land. "Each Nation is perfectly well acquainted with their exact original bounds," and each divided its land into tribal allotments. These, in turn, were subdivided "into shares to each family," which had the right to use the land. Johnson thought the system worked well. Unlike Euro-American settlers, the natives did not "ever infringe upon one another, or invade their neighbours' hunting grounds."[27] His reports countered the popular image of the land as empty and revealed the fraudulence, under the Native Americans' conception of property, of land sales by individual members of a tribe.

Johnson's argument for a special imperial law was not disinterested. His role as a cultural mediator helped him monopolize the late colonial land grant process. In return for his diplomacy, the Mohawk Indians gave him one hundred thousand acres on the Mohawk River, which the crown eventually confirmed despite its being one hundred times larger than ordinarily permitted.[28] But Johnson's concern for the orderly disposition of western land and trade cannot be reduced to his interest in gaining tracts for himself and friends, though he thought these were due after twenty years of service. Johnson feared another Indian war like that in the Ohio Valley in 1763. Those western tribes, brought into the empire with the French cession, did not accept the idea that they were subjects of the king of England. They wanted to keep their traditional trading contacts, they wanted to prevent further British settlement, and they wanted gifts in return for friendship. Johnson tried to deliver all three. He also valued his special relationship with the Iroquois.[29] His personal gain complemented the interests of both the Iroquois and the empire. English property law, as adopted in New York, did not.

As concerned as Johnson was about British-Indian relations, he too lost patience with the nations west of the Iroquois when they did not respond to his diplomacy. European settlers violated treaty lines and encroached on native lands. Nonetheless, he believed, those tribes overreacted. "The least provocation," he wrote Lord Hillsborough in London, "suffices as a pretext for acts of Violence."[30] Still, the colonists were more to blame for the violence than the Native Americans, as in the case of an alcohol-fueled dispute between a white trader and some western Indians on Lake Erie. One Captain Ramsay killed six men, a woman, and a child, scalping some of his victims, which according to Indian custom was a declaration of war. Commander in Chief Thomas Gage agreed to have Ramsay prosecuted for murder, but this would not satisfy the Native Americans, for "(as is usual on such occasions) the Interest which his creditors will make with those who are his jurors, and the prejudices of the Commonalty against Indians, will probably prove the means of his being acquitted, altho he makes use of threats that he will do much more mischief when enlarged." Johnson partook in the funerals for the victims, explained that Ramsay acted in defense, and proffered gifts in apology. But he despaired of long-term peace with the western tribes.[31] The only way to ensure peace was to separate colonial land, available for settlement, from native land, reserved for hunting.

Johnson's final treaty conference, at Fort Stanwix in 1768, was a dramatic scene. The Iroquois confederation and the British Empire, embodied in sachems and a superintendent who were all friends and family, negotiated a deal to ensure British title to the Ohio Valley while safeguarding native hunting grounds. Guy Johnson, the superintendent's nephew, drew a map that memorialized the treaty, a thick line separating native from colonial land. Eventually the line would shift. Johnson never intended for the continent to remain a hunting preserve forever — perhaps part of it for a century, he speculated, but not forever. The line was farther west than the Board of Trade had authorized, leading some in London to suspect that Johnson had grabbed land for himself and friends. They were right. Eventually the board approved the Stanwix Treaty, though it also forced Johnson to negotiate an amendment to the treaty that did not include grants from the Iroquois directly to Johnson's associates.[32] Here was another instance in which London ministers ratified, in large part, policy that originated in personal encounters between the imperial agents and the natives. Though some in London criticized Johnson, there too men anticipated a land boom, sooner or later. In just a few years, Johnson supported the establishment of a new colony in the Ohio Valley in which he was a large shareholder. He claimed that a well-planned settlement under the "judicious management" of a loyal governor and himself would "appear to the Indians as the most necessary check . . . [on] unrestrained licentious which prevailed long before the Cession, was daily gathering strength, and would have done so had no purchase ever been made in that country."[33] Self-interest was at work, but he believed that disciplined settlement within a colony that he would help govern was best for the Native Americans and the empire, as well as for himself. A man like Johnson would have prospered under most circumstances. He chose, however, to tie his fate to the empire. Soon he died, the empire was divided, and the Iroquois scattered, some fleeing to Canada while a remnant stayed to claim bits of tribal land in the new states. The parties to the Stanwix Treaty drew a line on a map, and the Privy Council ratified it, but none of them had the power alone to give it meaning. Three weeks before Johnson died, Parliament passed the Quebec Act, which transferred much of the Ohio Valley to the loyal colony of

Quebec, governed by a strong executive and no assembly.[34] All these imperial measures were mooted by the coming rebellion; none forestalled the transformation of western New York and the Ohio Valley.

Closer to that future was the provincial civil war under way in the northeast. In their 1777 constitution, Vermonters accused New York's governors, Cadwallader Colden, and provincial "land jobbers" of violating the Tenth Commandment by coveting the land of their neighbors, such as New Hampshire, which had granted the settlers "many charters of land and corporations." They also excoriated the new state of New York for continuing to demand quitrents, implicitly criticizing them as feudal. And in their bill of rights they proclaimed that "all people have a natural and inherent right to emigrate from one State to another, that will receive them; or to form a new State in vacant countries, or in such countries as they can purchase, whenever they think that thereby they can promote their own happiness," one of the earliest expressions in Britain or America of the freedom of movement.[35]

Twelve Peers in a Hybrid Province

The jury was another problem for the imperial agents. To the provincials, the jury was just as fundamental a constitutional liberty as freehold tenure. There was no greater symbol of the British constitution than the jury of one's peers, and it attained even more symbolic importance in the colonies than in England. New York lawyer William Livingston proclaimed that jury trials "are justly esteemed by all true Britons, as one of their most inestimable privileges. . . . It is undoubtedly the most impregnable fortress of our civil rights, which cannot be easily invaded without either abolishing or overawing those incorruptible judges of matters of fact. And hence, we find the common law confirmed in this excellent bulwark of our liberties by Magna Carta."[36] Livingston also argued that the jury was "used in England before the Norman invasion." That claim remains debated, but the jury had at least functioned as a check on government since not long after that time.[37] But where Livingston saw a bulwark of liberties, the imperial agents found colonial obstructionism.

Even for the provincials, or at least the creole elite, the jury had limits. When it came to crime *within* the colonies, provincial legislators were skeptical of the jury's value. Colonial legislatures granted courts summary criminal jurisdiction without juries, at least over misdemeanors.[38] What was considered sufficient for urban rowdies, frontier squatters, and slaves was not good enough for land speculators, their clients, and transatlantic merchants. Most of these summary cases are lost to history; minimal paperwork contributed to their efficiency. A rare protest against summary proceedings came from Attorney General John Tabor Kempe. Justices of the peace in Suffolk County, on Long Island, prosecuted one Wheeler for breach of the peace. Wheeler was a servant of Andrew Seaton, an acquaintance of Governor Sir Henry Moore's. The governor instructed Kempe to threaten the justices with criminal prosecution if they did not rescind their judgment. This strategy was too blunt for Kempe. Instead he questioned the validity of a conviction without a jury trial. A provincial statute did permit the justices the power to decide some criminal cases without a jury. But, according to Kempe, there were limits to the justices' personal jurisdiction. In short, some defendants deserved a jury and some did not. The statute was intended "to affect only Vagrants and other disorderly Persons not able to maintain themselves in Goal and to prevent their imprisonment from being a Charge to the County and must not be extended beyond that, as it destroys the Trial by Jury," Kempe explained to the justices, "and yet I have understood it has been too frequent a Practice to extend this Act to almost every Case whether the Offender comes within the Purview of the Act or not." The problem was not simply that the justices had tried a man with good connections or that the act was probably "void for its repugnancy to the Laws and the first Principles of the Constitution (and so no Person able to justify himself under it)." Summary procedure also denied the king's courts and lawyers, like Kempe, their usual fees and fines.[39] The justices retreated swiftly.

Seaton and men like him got what they wanted. Native Americans rarely did. New York juries did not protect tribal claims, there was no use of mixed juries (half native, half European American) in the province, and native forms of evidence carried little weight. "The Indians . . . frequently observe that our Governments are weak & impotent," Johnson informed the Earl of Dartmouth, secretary of state for the colonies, "that whatever these people do their Jurys will acquitt them, the Landed men protect them or a Rabble rescue them from the hands of Justice."[40] Jury nullification extended beyond criminal cases to civil controversies with imperial ramifications. The agents viewed the jury less as the voice of the people, community, or ancient rights than as a screen for local interests. Consequently they sought to shield Native Americans from juries and thus protect imperial policy.

Colden recommended to the Board of Trade that the natives should have "an easy method of obtaining justice in every dispute." Distant venues and complex procedures handicapped the natives, not least because of their "ambulatory Life." So did common-law restrictions on the admission of oral evidence. Colden believed that the natives were as truthful as "Christians" and deserved to be treated as "rational or human creatures." So he pleaded the "absolute necessity of allowing Indian evidence; for, where evidence is on one side of the Question, it is impossible that Justice can be done; and yet, this is the practice in the Courts of Law, I believe, all over North America."[41] Throughout the colonies, judges and juries did not have to ignore the testimony from Native Americans, for they rarely encountered it.

A related problem was the stream of settlers into the French cession. General Thomas Gage, the commander in chief of British forces in America, sought to prosecute all those accused of crimes in the cession in courts-martial. While the Proclamation of 1763 enjoined the military and the Indian service to return any fugitive found in the territory and charged with a felony to "the colony where the crime was committed of which they stand accused," it did not cover crimes committed in the territory.[42] In a draft amendment to the British Mutiny Act, Gage proposed that the military be given jurisdiction over any "Crime or Trespass committed at any of the [military] posts, not in the inhabited parts of the Country, and where Civil Judicature hath not taken place." In other words, Gage believed that the cession was outside the borders of any colony; a local court-martial should try civilian defendants rather than send them to the nearest colony. In London, Secretary of State Halifax agreed with Gage that the new territory did not fall within any of the colonies. But Secretary of War Wellbore Ellis thought that Gage was wrong. The cession did fall within the several old colonial boundaries, so that "[a]ll the posts in North America are within some civil jurisdiction." Parliament embraced Ellis's interpretation. The Mutiny Act for North America, passed in 1765, extended the logic of the proclamation and instructed the military to deliver civilian wrongdoers "to the Civil Magistrate of the next adjoining Province." Parliament was not prepared to expand the jurisdiction of military courts to cover civilian wrongdoers.[43]

Johnson's plan for resolving controversies between Native Americans and settlers in the western territory met a similar fate. When he got the chance to shape the legal system west of the Appalachians, he eliminated juries in cases involving Native Americans. The Board of Trade approved of a network of Indian commissaries beyond the proclamation line, a continental replica of the epistolary constitution in the area Johnson called "the Jurisdiction of the Marches & Frontiers . . . not comprised within any Colony." He hoped that "the Superintendant & his deputys [would] have certain powers given them as conservators of the peace throughout that district."[44] The commissaries reported directly to Johnson, could forgo common-law procedures, and had jurisdiction over all settler dealings with the natives including, according to him, "judicial authority."[45] Finally, Johnson had jurisdiction over all native-settler controversies. During their two-year tenure, however, the commissaries were often ignored and undercompensated.[46] In 1768, the Board of Trade disbanded them because of traders' complaints and the cost of their gifts to the western tribes. Regulation of Indian trade reverted to the individual colonies, though Johnson retained supervision over land disputes and Indian diplomacy.[47]

The problem for Johnson and the other agents was that colonial traders and merchants had influence in London too. These contacts persuaded Lord Shelburne, still the southern secretary, to select provincial rather than imperial control over Indian trade.[48] This option was also less expensive, as metropolitan administrations strove to shift the financial burden of empire to the colonies. In addition, the far-flung trading posts, like much of Johnson's "Marches & Frontiers," were beyond effective control.[49] Finally, Johnson never enjoyed the confidence of all the Native Americans who were collected under the rubric "Iroquois." Where he saw nations, there were in reality much looser connections of villages, and many of these still had relationships with colonial families that dated from the Dutch period. Before Johnson emerged, Indian affairs were managed by Livingstons, Schuylers, Philipses, DeLanceys, and other prominent provincials, while daily contact involved many more.[50] Thus, a case concerning one Schermerhorn, "a cunning fellow" who purchased land without Johnson's permission, may have involved something other than exploitation by "ignorant settlers." It is difficult to determine how much actual negotiation took place in these unofficial transactions. But Johnson fitted this case in with the others, reporting again that it had become "verry Customary of late for People unauthorized to assemble Indians on many Affairs contrary to his Majestys express Intensions, but it Seems the Law will not admit of a remedy for it, for in any Trial by Jury I am certain they would be acquitted."[51] To him, the Iroquois were unitary, and his relationship with them excluded competitors. In addition, his knowledge of native America was local, confined mostly to the Mohawk Valley, and his understanding of the western tribes was filtered through Iroquois informants, who had their own reasons for exaggerating their influence in the west. The Mohawks, "like true friends," confirmed their allegiance to him and therefore the king.[52] But the Mohawks were only one of the Six Nations, and the Six Nations were only one constellation of many tribal groupings. Johnson kept believing that the Iroquois had "a great influence over the rest" long after this was true.[53] He and the other imperial agents never accepted the fragmentary nature of imperial authority over both settlers and natives, even though they experienced it firsthand everyday.

At the same time in New York City, a civil battery case gave Colden the chance to propose imperial review in London of jury verdicts rendered in the provincial supreme court. The case, *Forsey v. Cunningham*, involved a bitter commercial dispute between two merchants that culminated in a waterfront sword fight. Waddell Cunningham got the better of Thomas Forsey, stabbing him in the chest. Forsey sued for assault and battery, and a jury in the New York Supreme Court awarded him damages of fifteen hundred pounds.[54] Cunningham, in London at the time of the suit, wanted to appeal the unusually large award to the governor and council, then if necessary to the Privy Council. His New York lawyers, John Morin Scott and William Smith Jr., refused to pursue the appeal to the governor and council. Much to the chagrin of his counsel, he relied on his friend George Harison, a merchant, to make the motion in the supreme court, which violated the Law Society's monopoly on supreme court litigation. The court entertained the motion only to confirm the principle that appeals of jury verdicts were impermissible. The strategy backfired. Colden, serving as lieutenant governor while Governor Robert Monckton was in London, supported the appeal, arguing that the governor and council had the power to review jury determinations. The governor and council had always had the power to review the legal judgments of the provincial courts by a writ of error. But that writ allowed the reviewing court only to examine the record for errors, not to reexamine its underlying facts. The *Forsey* controversy turned on Colden's interpretation of an amended royal instruction of 1753 that omitted "in cases of error only" after the directive that governors should "allow appeals." Colden argued that this omission broadened the scope of review to factual determinations, which would have made every provincial common-law case open to complete retrial, first in front of the governor and council, then again in the Privy Council.[55]

William Smith Jr., who was Cunningham's own lawyer, maintained that his client had no right to appeal. He protested that Colden's interpretation followed "the ministerial principle, that the King's Will is Law in the Provinces." Smith associated the appeal with the continental civil law, feared because it was not common law. "The Term appeal is borrowed from the Civilians," Smith advised Governor Monckton, "and I suppose those who introduced it intended to give it a Civil Law operation, and render the administration of Justice amongst us, controlable by the King, as that of the Praetor in the Roman Provinces by the Emperor, on the appeal to Caesar."[56]

Here was the negative image of the agents' vision of empire—centralized, arbitrary decision making—and it was one reason that they rarely drew on the civil law when reforming imperial administration. Supreme court justice Daniel Horsmanden invoked the Charter of Libertyes to complain that appeal of jury determinations was "nothing less than the entire subversion of the Constitution of the Province, so wisely plan'd & Established at the time of the Revolution in 88, to give us the full Enjoyment of the Laws of Our Mother Country; what Mr. Colden seems to aim at, is to introduce the Scotch law, Civil Law Courts, without Jurys, (a priviledge so highly valued by every Englishman)."[57] Justice Robert R. Livingston doubted whether even a clear royal instruction could authorize review of a jury verdict. The mention of appeals in the instruction did not refer to the technical civil-law procedure, he surmised, but rather only to the traditional writ of error. Even John Watts, a councillor suspicious of the provincial legal establishment, "told the old Gentleman a Jury was the Bulwark of English Freedom." Undeterred, Colden "coldly answerd & with seeming indifference 'that there were no Jurys in Scotland & he did not see but Justice was as well Administer'd as in England,'" leaving Watts to hope that the Privy Council would not "cram the old Mans Scott's unconstitutional Doctrine upon the Colony."[58] It did not.

Although Colden failed, his justification for appeals of jury determinations revealed his grasp on the problem of legal uniformity in an expanding empire. The proposal had elements of Scottish law, civil law, the royal prerogative, and common law. It could be seen as derived from any of these sources. For Colden, its virtue was instrumental. The appeal was, Colden told the New York council, a legacy of the early common law and was used "both before and after the Conquest." By contrast, the writ of error was a recent development, "not by common Law" and therefore "confined to the Courts where such usage prevails." He artfully turned the common-law notion of immemoriality on the provincials to argue that writs of error were relatively new and appeals were ancient. One precedent came from the Channel Islands, where jury verdicts could be appealed to the Privy Council: "The reason given is, *that tho those Islands are parcel of the Dominion of the Crown of England, they are not parcel of the Realm of England.*" The colonial courts, like the Channel Islands, were creatures of the royal prerogative. Procedures not used in England might be valid in the colonies without being repugnant to English law. Writs of error were strictly English, while appeals to the crown were allowed from wherever else he ruled.[59]

Even more interesting than this legal history of crown dominions was Colden's citation of Matthew Hale's *History of the Common Law of England* to argue to the Board of Trade that the crown could never have intended for colonial law *or* fact to be decided without central review because juries were subject to local influence. Colden analogized the colonial courts to medieval county courts that, as Hale recounted, were controlled by local lords. A party fearing local prejudice could remove his cause to the king's circuit courts or directly to Westminster. However, "in the Colonies neither the Crown nor the subject can have such security and relief against interested Judges and an overbearing Faction; their only security and relief is by appeal." He admitted that "the King appoints all the Officers of Government, but while they (from the Governor to the meanest Officer in the Government) depend on the Assembly for their daily bread, they must very unwillingly quarrel with such powerfull Factions." The power of appointment did not protect the crown's interests. For one thing, the assembly nominated many justices of the peace and sheriffs.[60] Another check was necessary. Provincial judges had developed transfer jurisdiction to remove cases from obstructionist county courts to their supreme court, countering some of the centrifugal pressure that juries generated within the province.[61] But Colden drew no distinction. The provincial supreme court was no more sympathetic to the crown's interests than local colonial courts or those in medieval English counties. To him, the common law was designed by the crown to subdue competing jurisdictions. Specific procedural attributes, such as the jury trial, were secondary.

The controversy surrounding a pamphlet defending Colden's stance in the *Forsey* case reveals the source of his apprehensions. The author was anonymous, but most readers assumed that Colden wrote it. The assembly sought an indictment of the author for perpetrating "a very vile, false, infamous and libellous reflection on His Majesty's Council, Assembly, Courts of Justice and the whole Body of the Law in this Province." Representative Robert R. Livingston, who was also a supreme court justice, led the cause in the assembly and then presided over the grand jury that considered the indictment. When the jurors refused to indict an anonymous defendant, Livingston told them they would not be dismissed until they did so. It was a way to try Colden indirectly, a judicial analogue to the mob's burning of his effigy during the Stamp Act riots. To Colden, it all seemed to be the work of a cabal.[62]

Archibald Kennedy in the customs house also encountered provincial obstruction. Juries routinely found local merchants not guilty of violating imperial trade laws. Everyone knew that smuggling was rampant in New York. The most prominent merchants were the greatest offenders.[63] A list of "Recognizances taken by Mr. Justice [Daniel] Horsmanden relating to illicit

Trade" with the French during the Seven Years' War reads like a who's who of New York's mercantile community. Several of them went on to found the chamber of commerce.[64] Insurance was even available in London to cover losses flowing from seizure, but the risk was so low as not to be worth a large premium.[65] And the Tea Act of 1773, which gave the East India Company control over the tea trade, led Hugh Wallace, a merchant and member of the council, to proclaim "in Favor of Smuggling & against monopolies," while merchant Philip Livingston quipped that "there was not a Man in Town that was not a Smuggler in some sense."[66]

As early as 1757 William Smith Jr. criticized the "clandestine trade" with Hamburg and the Netherlands as "impolitick and unreasonable; how much soever it may conduce to advance the interest of a few merchants, or this particular colony." Yet he did not advise increasing enforcement. That, because of its cost and the character of customs officials, was "a remedy worse than the disease." Rather, the colony should be allowed to import certain popular commodities, like tea, free of tariff. The price of these items would decline, reducing the market for contraband.[67] The advice went unheeded, though London did eventually reduce customs duties in the 1760s. But this only persuaded the colonists that they were being taxed for revenue rather than regulated.

The provincial supreme court and the vice admiralty courts had concurrent jurisdiction over violations of the Navigation Acts. But during the 1750s, provincial lawyers and judges, including the creole judges of the vice admiralty court, had decided that the New York harbor was not part of the high seas, which came under vice admiralty jurisdiction, but rather fell within the province. A notorious instance of this jurisdictional claim came in the case of the *Greyhound* in 1750. The supreme court tried and convicted a naval gunner for manslaughter, even though he committed the crime while on a royal ship and following military orders.[68] Although the facts of this case were unusual, the principle of provincial jurisdiction over the harbor had large ramifications. Consequently, most prosecutions took place in common-law courts because the owner of a ship caught with illicit goods in the harbor could seek a writ of prohibition against the vice admiralty proceedings and move them to provincial courts.[69] The agents enforcing the Navigation Acts then had to prosecute each case in front of a jury of the smuggler's peers. In practice, customs collectors never enforced the letter of those laws and permitted much illegal trade. They had to. And much smuggling went on without official knowledge, for informers were subject to violent abuse.[70] A merchant's ability to remove enforcement proceedings from the vice admiralty court did not alter this unstated policy of accommodation, but it did tip the balance even more in his favor. In response to the complaints of customs officials, the new parliamentary legislation of the 1760s gave the vice admiralty courts exclusive jurisdiction over violations. But these initiatives generated considerable provincial outrage and little revenue.[71]

The imperial agents saw juries as pawns of the provincial elite. But this image was distorted, and the conclusion that the legal community had usurped royal authority simplified a terribly complex situation. Nonetheless, conveyed in countless letters, it became the conventional wisdom in London. Edmund Burke, whom the assembly hired to represent its interests in Parliament, complained that colonial lawyers "snuff the approach of tyranny in every tainted breeze" and then perpetuated a half-truth at once disturbing and reassuring: "In no country, perhaps in the world, is the law so general a study. The profession itself is numerous and powerful; and in most provinces it takes the lead."[72] All would be well, the imperial agents persuaded themselves and London officials, if the legal profession was reformed.

Reforming the Creole Legal Establishment

In report after report, the imperial agents returned to what they thought was the root of the problem: the legal community. The lawyers dominated provincial politics, agitated against royal policies, and obstructed imperial laws. The agents wanted to displace this powerful group with a loyal corps of their own: themselves, their children, and new recruits from elsewhere in the British Empire. However, the agents never succeeded in creating the sort of institutional network and professional reproduction that New York's lawyers had in place by midcentury. Consequently, the creole legal establishment survived the threat and was left poised to assume even greater authority if the imperial agents ever departed from the province. In short, this late colonial struggle determined who would govern the province for decades and with what resources.

"Were the people freed from the dread of this Domination of the Lawyers," Lieutenant Governor Colden informed a London minister in 1765, "I flatter myself with giving general joy to the People of this Province." The bar, he thought, stirred up urban crowds during the Stamp Act controversy, who in turn destroyed his property and sense of safety.[73] William Johnson agreed, blaming the political turmoil of the 1760s on the "Independent Gentry" and "the Menaces of a few party Men."[74] He predicted no relief "whilst every Interested Individual has it in his power by Words or Actions to Counteract the proceedings of a General, a Superintendent or any other person in Office."[75] So too believed General Thomas Gage, the commander in chief of the British military in America stationed in New York City: "The Lawyers are the Source from whence the Clamors have flowed in every Province." They in alliance with the merchants "stirred" up the "inferior People" and sailors into a "Mob."[76] If the agents could subdue the provincial elite, they could also control the "inferior people." That, at least, was the view from Fort George, Johnson Hall, and the customs house.

The problem, went the venerable argument, was that the colonial governor was weak; provincial lawyers and judges streamed into the vacuum of crown authority. The remedy was for the executive — meaning the imperial agents themselves — to gain greater control over legal administration. In the backcountry, Johnson wanted the governor to appoint justices of the peace from outside the province. He opposed local judges because "there is no Justice to be expected by any Englishman in this Country, nor never will, whilst the Bench of Judges & Justices is composed entirely of Dutch, who pride themselves in the appellation, which alone, in my opinion should render them odious to everry Britton." By "Briton" Johnson meant his Irish and Scottish family, colleagues, and leaseholders, the last recruited in droves during the 1760s. By contrast, "Dutch" was a loose category that included all who obstructed imperial justice as Johnson defined it rather than those tracing their roots to the Netherlands or Germany. While Johnson was sophisticated when countering the provincial image of the Indian-as-savage, he quickly denigrated non-British white settlers who violated English legal ways, as he construed them. In 1772 he persuaded Governor William Tryon to carve a new county, named Tryon, out of the western part of Albany County to give him control over the Mohawk Valley. He had tired of negotiating with Albany and Hudson River notables over the appointment of sheriffs and justices. Now his nominees would be unopposed.[77] Only in a specially drawn county could Johnson control Mohawk Valley law and politics, and then only briefly. He died in July 1774. The rebellious Tryon County Committee of Safety, full of men with Dutch and German names, was established the next month.[78]

Colden also pleaded for heritable offices so that the agents' positions would descend to their children. He also called for the appointment of men without provincial connections to key posts on the bench and in the bar. As early as 1747 Colden sought the replacement of longtime nemesis Chief Justice James DeLancey with a lawyer from England. Provincial-born men were susceptible to local influence, and, protected by good behavior tenure, chief justices like DeLancey and Colden's erstwhile friend Lewis Morris before him became "as formidable at the head of the Laws as the Popes formerly were in the days of Ignorance at the head of Monks & friars."[79] When DeLancey died in 1760, Colden asked the Board of Trade to appoint a successor with no interests in New York and loyal to the crown's prerogatives. He got one in Benjamin Prat.

Born in Massachusetts, Prat began life as an artisan. An injury led him to Harvard College and the law, where he climbed the professional ladder by dint of wit and loyalty to imperial agents like Governor Thomas Pownall. Though an accomplished lawyer, Prat encountered obstacles everywhere in New York. "His haveing no connection in this Province is a Principal Reason with me why he should be appointed preferably to any other in this place who make pretensions to the office," Colden wrote to John Pownall, secretary of the Board of Trade. The provincials, on the other hand, wanted "a Chief Justice with whom they have strong connections, & in order to obtain their end find pretences to refuse a salary to Mr. Prat."[80] Prat complained to the Board of Trade that as long as judges depended on the assembly for salaries, their rulings would follow local interests. Consequently, provincial law would diverge from English law without judicial check because "the Colonies are vested with Legislative Powers, by which the Systems of their Laws are gradually varying from the Common Law, & so diminishing, in that Respect their connection with the Mother Country."[81] This was the frequent criticism, made in the familiarly vague way, that the common law did not function in New York as it did in England. It divided rather than integrated the empire.

Colden too realized that the appointment of a sympathetic chief justice and other officials was not enough. Behind the obstreperous judges, officers, and juries was a corrupt provincial establishment. "The distinguished families in so small a country as this," he complained in 1762, "are so united by inter-marriages and otherwise, that in few cases a cause of any consequence, especially where the King's Rights are concerned, can be brought before a Judge who is one of these families, in which he can be supposed intirely disinterested, or free from connections with those interested either in that case, or in other cases similar to it."[82] The reason for the strength of "faction" lay in the colony's social foundation: "In a young Country, like this, where few Men have any acquired learning or knowledge, where the Judges and principal Lawyers are proprietors of extravagant grants of land, or strongly connected with them in Interest, or family alliances, it is possible, that a dangerous combination may subsist between the Bench and the Bar; not only greatly injurious to private property but likewise dangerous to His Majesty's prerogative & Authority."[83] When lawyers allied with large landholders, there was no ballast against their power.

In another version of this analysis that tracked the Scottish Enlightenment idea that civilizations developed through stages, Colden divided the province into four "ranks": "Proprietors," "Gentleman of the Law," "Merchants," and "Farmers." He recognized that the "ranks" were permeable. The lawyers, for example, were often related to and served the landowners, a nexus institutionalized in New York's Law Society. The farmers were "the most usefull and the most Morall, but allwise the Dupes" of the others. The great men used newspapers to sway their inferiors. He concluded that the press was to the provincial elite what "the Pulpit was in times of Popery": the means of "deluding an ignorant mob."[84] Land, the bar, trade, and provincial print culture: here was the matrix of provincial improvement that had developed over two or three generations; the imperial agents saw it as a conspiracy. The new sociology helped them frame a powerful but simplistic picture of provincial society.

The agents did not just recommend replacing the creole elite with loyal imperial servants. They also sought financial support independent of the assembly. Colden drew up a plan in which the crown would transform the council into a permanent "senate" with each senator receiving ten thousand acres of land. This loyal branch of government would bolster the crown's interest in the province and restore balance between the three parts of the colony's constitution, for then "the Ballance between the three is kept so even that no one can be too strong & every one may be a Sufficient Check upon the others." In short, he advocated a new colonial aristocracy. He did not publicize this plan in London or the province.[85] But its elements—proprietary office holding and land grants—were constant themes in the agents' correspondence, and a similar proposal was published in a provincial newspaper in 1770 under the title "The Dougliad." The author was probably James Duane, who was at the time within Colden's ambit of influence. "The Dougliad" echoed Colden's long-standing analysis of the unbalanced colonial constitution and proposed replacing the council with a permanent upper house. In England, "[a]n August Peerage, forms a Barrier, between *the Prince* and *the People*; and preserves within due Bounds, the prerogative of the *One*, and the Privileges of the *other*."[86] In its present form, the council could not play the same role. A new upper house secure in its social and political power would restore that balance.

The twelve "Dougliad" essays were published during Alexander Mac-

Dougall's libel case. MacDougall had published a letter criticizing the assembly for financing both Colden's administration and British troops quartered in the province. The assembly, dominated after the elections of 1768 and 1769 by the DeLancey faction, had provided this support to avoid being suspended by the British Parliament. In the Restraining Act of 1767, Parliament had targeted New York because of its particularly vociferous petitions and protests against the postwar regulations. In response, the assembly provided the supplies. The legislators did not, however, view their grant as conceding Parliament's right to demand support; that, they claimed, "would have been repugnant to the Sentiments we entertained of our constitutional Rights." The justification for the compromise had been that the appropriation was like others in the past: it was "*a free Gift*; and if it should be accepted as such, the Right of Parliament would rest on their own Conception, and not on our Admission."[87] But MacDougall, called by some "the American Wilkes" and others "a beggarly Scotchman," thought that the assembly had taken "money out of our pockets without our consent." The Livingstons, now out of power, agreed. Colden was again identified as the greedy mastermind: "Mr. Colden knows, from the nature of things, that he cannot have the least prospect to be in another administration again; and therefore, that he may make hay while the sun shines, and get a full salary from the Assembly, flatters ignorant members of it, with the consideration of the success of a bill to emit a paper currency; when he, and his artful coadjutors must know, that it is only a snare to impose on the simple; for it will not obtain the royal assent."[88] London finally did allow the assembly to issue bills from a land bank, which alleviated the credit crunch.[89]

It is likely that Colden helped a temporary ally, James Duane, write the "Dougliad." The major theme of the essays was that truth should not be a defense to the seditious libel charge against MacDougall, just as it was not under English law. (Here was one of those opportunities when the imperial agents found it useful to invoke a common-law rule.) A judicial determination of truth in such cases would violate "the Spirit of our English constitution" because it required examination of the motives behind the assembly's appropriations. Judicial assessment of the truth of MacDougall's charge against the assembly would "convert the Seat of Justice, into a Cabinet of State" and "transform those venerable Sages, into a Cabal of visionary Politicians!"[90] The same charge concerning the truth defense arose in the Zenger case four decades earlier; Colden had been referring to the provincial elite as a cabal for almost as long.[91] The difference now was that provincial opposition aimed not just at a single governor but rather at the entire imperial establishment. In addition, Colden was no longer a silent partner with the governor's foes; he was their target. He and his allies further depersonalized the attacks by portraying the problem as one involving the separation of judicial and legislative powers. They sought only to criticize judicial interference with a legislative compromise designed to preserve peace within the empire, but they also raised the stakes of the constitutional controversy by focusing attention on the fundamental question of imperial constitutionalism: Who defined the law of New York? According to what sources and to what end?

More successful was Colden's opposition to good behavior tenure for judges. Chief Justice Prat's colleagues on the supreme court, Daniel Horsmanden and John Chambers, briefly refused to serve and shut down the court to protest Colden's claim that their tenure was at the king's—which meant Colden's—pleasure. The problem arose because Governor William Cosby granted James DeLancey's commission as chief justice for good behavior when he expanded the supreme court's equity jurisdiction. Legal advisers to the Privy Council criticized the departure from "usage; but as the power given by the commission is general, we apprehend the grant is good in point of law, and cannot be revoked without misbehaviour."[92] The question was whether future grants were for good behavior too, as all judgeships were in eighteenth-century England. In answering that the offices were at will, the Privy Council accepted Colden's analysis, which distinguished the colonial judiciary from that at home. In England, the crown ceded the power to dismiss judges at will after the Glorious Revolution. Permanent salaries and tenure drew qualified jurists to the bench. "The same circumstance does in no degree exist in the American Colonies," Colden argued. Because there was no support apart from assembly funding, "men of learning and ability" refused to take the position. Consequently, governors "are frequently obliged to appoint such as offer from amongst the Inhabitants however unqualified to sustain the character tho a more fit person should afterwards be found, yet if the Commission was during good behavior such unqualified Person could not be displaced."[93]

Leading lawyers admitted that there were some unqualified judges and lawyers among them. Their remedy was not, however, greater superintendence by the imperial agents. Indeed, part of the problem was that governors had too liberally granted licenses to practice law. Tighter admission standards were needed *within* the provincial legal community. New York's lawyers had for two generations worked to limit membership in the bar by imposing educational requirements monitored by the quasi-corporate Law

Society.[94] Self-regulation by the provincial elite, independent of the imperial agents and to the detriment of local interests, was their answer here as elsewhere.

British colonies did not develop a hierarchy of functions and titles like that within the common-law bar in England. But in New York, as in several other colonies, the prerequisites of general education and apprenticeship divided an elite corps of practitioners from all other advocates. By the 1750s, only members of the Law Society could practice in the supreme court, and this was similar to the restriction of practice in the Westminster courts to members of the Inns of Court.[95] The creation of the Law Society was part of the project of cultural improvement and reinforced the sense that New York was a discrete legal jurisdiction. It reflected at once Anglicization, in the development of sophisticated legal techniques similar to those used in England, as well as cultural differentiation, since it generated a power center apart from the British Empire's official representatives.[96] Bar formation was a part of the process of creolization. It contributed to the creation of a distinct provincial identity *within* the empire.

Creolization of the legal community was gradual. Key markers include the collection and revision of provincial statutes in 1752 by William Smith Jr. and William Livingston, the bar's increasing control over its own training and membership, and the formation of a viable bar association.[97] The Law Society required members to accept only clerks with at least two years of college education. The sixteen signatories agreed to ensure proper training of lawyers and "to prevent the unrestrained Admission of Clerks for the future." The clerks had to pay two hundred pounds for the privilege of their service and were bound for five years. Each attorney could have only two clerks at a time, thus limiting the number of prospective lawyers. After five years, the clerks needed a recommendation from their mentor before they could take the bar exam.[98]

Some elite New Yorkers continued to send their sons to England for college and enrollment at the Inns of Court. They also adapted to the changes within English legal education. New Yorkers knew that William Blackstone became the first Vinerian Professor of English Law at Oxford in the 1750s, and some wanted their sons to experience this mixture of legal and liberal education. In 1762, John Watts wrote a letter of introduction for Peter DeLancey (a son of his wife's brother), who was off to study at Oxford. "We have a high Character of a Professor at Oxford," Watts reported, "who they say has brought that Mysterious Business to some System, besides the System of confounding other People & picking their Pockets, which most of the Profession understand pretty well." But the economic imperative inducing most New Yorkers to rely on provincial training was evident in the same letter: "As the Youth is one of a half a Score Children, it is meant that he be educated with as much frugality as decency & Character will admit of." Finally, provincial fears of the corrupting effect of metropolitan education offered another reason to forgo English training.[99]

The Law Society, with its requirement of college education, internal regulations, and methods of instruction, offered an alternative to overseas instruction in law and the liberal arts. Prospective lawyers had long been required to receive a license from the governor after examination by the supreme court justices, but this was largely a formality. Lawyers like Smith and Livingston argued that the test must separate the good lawyer from "the Pettifogger." The problem, in their eyes, was that the governor too readily accepted the private recommendation of ignorant judges. They proposed that candidates be examined in open court. "By this Means, the Honour of the Profession would be retrieved and preserved, and the good of the Public promoted."[100]

Under the new system of licensing, prospective lawyers clerked for five years before examination. Those who passed had to sign the bar agreement and promise to submit to the society's rules. Violators, after a "full Hearing," were "treated by the Rest with Contempt and held to strict practice."[101] Education continued after bar admittance. To polish their forensic skills, some lawyers joined debating societies, like the Moot, named after a traditional exercise in the English Inns of Court.[102] By 1758, leading lawyers could claim that "the Practice of Law in this Province, is more conformable to the Course of Practice in England, than in any other of his Majesty's Colonies upon this Continent."[103]

The bar did have local critics. In 1768 an assembly campaign was organized around the slogan "no lawyer in the Assembly." But wherever constitutional disputes flourished, lawyers were involved. So it is less ironic than typical that the "no lawyer" campaign was engineered by the DeLancey family, chock full of lawyers, and that John Watts, partaking in an American tradition, reviled the bar and "the hatefull Labyrinths of the Law" while encouraging his son John Jr. to join and enter.[104] Watts knew that the bar had substantial power and influence. Its formation was part of New York's improvement. It grew in tandem with the sense that New York was a discrete legal space. New York had its own jurisdiction, a bar to police that jurisdiction, and an assembly to legislate for it.

The lawyers succeeded not only in limiting the number of lawyers collecting litigation fees. Their Law Society was more sound and self-perpetuating than the royal bureaucracy. The profession's quality was not just a matter of local concern, and more was at stake than autonomy and pride. The imperial agents' reports of a provincial cabal were having effects in Britain, if not on official policy, then on the way metropolitan merchants viewed their colonial partners. Robert R. Livingston wrote his son Robert R. Livingston Jr., a student at King's College, that "Mr. Colden by writing a vindication of himself [in the *Forsey* case] has thrown aspersions on every station of men amongst us." The immediate threat was to transatlantic trade. "[S]o much are matters misinterpreted at home against us," Livingston senior wrote in 1767, "that several principal houses have refused to send over goods, imagining that we are running headlong into a rebellion."[105] The creole elite worked their transatlantic connections to counter Colden's reports. When Prat died after one tumultuous year on the bench, the Board of Trade picked a compromise candidate to replace him: provincial councillor and puisne justice Daniel Horsmanden. Horsmanden was the longest-serving justice on the court and was enmeshed in provincial networks. Yet he was also pliable and loyal, and he usually found himself negotiating the gray zone between the resistant creole elite and the imperial agents, a space occupied by many New York colonists. Horsmanden would serve at pleasure. In practice, tenure at pleasure usually meant life tenure. Horsmanden continued as chief justice until his death in 1778 at the age of eighty-four.[106]

The imperial agents and Privy Council saw that New York's legal culture deviated from their ideal of empire. They were wrong, however, to conclude that one system would guarantee impartial justice while the other did not. The difference was between two conceptions of the empire and its constitution, not between justice and injustice. They failed to see that they were dealing not with a primitive outpost but rather with a province that conceived of itself as maturing and autonomous, in a state of improvement.[107] Self-government meant a government staffed by their own: the creole elite. The agents, on the other hand, were trying to create an administrative caste devoted to the empire's welfare and their own within it. The bureaucratic infrastructure supporting military adventure that John Brewer calls "the English/British state" did not stretch far beyond its island shores. "Sinews of power" required sense, understanding, and judgment.[108] The imperial agents believed the latter were missing from North America and tried to provide them. Their proposal had two parts: the promotion of an administrative elite, and the maintenance of records to preserve institutional wisdom.

First, they couched much of their criticism of the province and their legal reforms in terms of aristocracy. Again this was in part a social gambit. But the language of aristocracy—by which they meant a group of men loyal to something greater than their interests in the province—was one of the only ways to express the notion of conscientious administration. The ideal of disinterested civil service had not yet surfaced, not at least in the colonies; the agents may have been working toward it, though they linked their interests to the crown rather than to some disembodied public good.[109] They sought ample compensation, but that was supposed to insulate them from provincial harassment. There were several such plans. Colden drafted one that called for a provincial aristocracy. He, Johnson, and other agents acted on a similar idea when they sought guaranteed salaries, land grants, and patronage for their family, including hereditary offices. Secure in property and office, they would form a bulwark against local interests.

Complementing the idea of an administrative caste, the agents sought to maintain written records to generate precedents. One example is Colden's diligent epistolary practice. He maintained a letter book with drafts or copies of his correspondence, allowing him to refer to old advice and construct his own chronology of events. It appears that Colden was more cautious in keeping his papers than most ministers in Whitehall.[110] But he was not alone. Other imperial agents, in New York and elsewhere, called for the preservation of records, new law codes for the colonies, and handbooks of administration for imperial agents.

Beginning at midcentury, the agents proposed several plans for collecting institutional wisdom. Dr. William Douglass, Colden's friend in Boston, proposed appointing to the Board of Trade "gentlemen returned home, who have formerly been governors of colonies, judges of vice-admiralty, consuls at foreign ports of trade, commodores who have served some time in plantation-stations, surveyor-generals, and collectors of the customs in the colonies, planters, merchants, and factors who follow the plantation trade." These experienced men could survey all colonial laws, consult "eminent lawyers," and draft "a body of general laws for all the plantations (it may be called the Magna Charta of the British Colonies in America)." This code, which would be passed in Parliament and compact enough for "a one-pocket volume," would be like the Roman Pandects or the civil code of Louis XIV. Douglass was ready with a draft. It included a revision of the Navigation Acts to liberalize colonial trade and forbid intercolonial tariffs.[111]

Thomas Pownall was the kind of returning crown servant that Douglass had in mind. Pownall began his long career as an aide to Governor Danvers Osborne, assisted Governor George Clinton at the Albany Congress of 1754, and then moved on to the governorship of Massachusetts before returning to

England. A decade and a half after Douglass published his book, Pownall made similar recommendations. His premise was that *"the British Isles, with our possessions in the Atlantic and in America, are in* Fact, United into One Grand Marine Dominion: *And therefore, by policy, [should] be united into a one Imperium, in a one center, where the seat of government is."* He recommended the appointment of a special colonial secretary who would sit on the Board of Trade. The secretary should have the power to convene all the governors and survey "the *actual* state of the crown's authority." Together they would examine colonial legislation and judicial proceedings to ensure that they conformed with the colonial charters, royal commissions, and English law. They should also enforce the Navigation Acts, vacate fraudulent land grants, and implement other imperial policies. Then the secretary should draft "a general bill of rights, and an act for the establishment of government and commerce on a great plan of union" in which "the colonies will be considered as so many corporations, not without, but united to, the realm." This new arrangement might mollify disgruntled colonists and make them less inclined to unite together against the empire.[112] Pownall agreed that Parliament "must have, from the nature and essence of the constitution, has had and ever will have, a sovereign supreme Power & jurisdiction over every part of the dominions of the state, to make Laws in all cases whatsoever." But it had to exercise restraint, for "you can never govern an unwilling people: they will be able to obstruct and pervert every effort of your policy and render ineffectual every exertion of your Government."[113] Pownall was trying to theorize the practical situation of authority within the empire, to make respectable the idea that *imperia* could exist within *imperio*. "One supream comprehending community [may] govern another subordinate comprehended community by a sovereign jurisdiction which still leaves the inferior jurisdiction all and every right privilege & liberty which constitutes the free agency of a Political state."[114] The empire had done so in the past, and it could continue to do so in the future. A more solid theory and structure would help.

There was also William Knox, an imperial agent who began his career in Georgia. He returned to London and held a variety of offices in the 1760s and 1770s, including undersecretary of state.[115] Knox was shocked to discover that the secretaries of state treated their correspondence as "private property" and took official letters with them when they left office. George III stopped this practice; the crown began to retain official correspondence. John Pownall, Thomas's brother, was similarly disconcerted by the state of colonial records. While serving as an undersecretary to the Board of Trade, he sought some century-old Privy Council records and was told that he might find them in a room above the gateway to the Privy Garden. This was supposed to house the "State Paper Office" created under Queen Elizabeth. So he climbed a "rotten staircase" and found a door secured by a lock that "had not been opened for many years and to which there was no key to be found." Pownall got a locksmith to break the lock, and when the door opened, he "was covered with a cloud of dust, raised by a flock of pigeons, who had long made that room (the windows being broken) their dwelling place. When the cloud was dissipated, he removed the filth, and there found the books he was in search of, with many other ancient and public records."[116]

For crown officers serving overseas, precedents were even more difficult to locate. Welshman Anthony Stokes held judicial offices in the West Indies and the southern colonies, but when he first traveled across the Atlantic at midcentury "he in vain sought for some Book that would afford him an insight of the Constitution and Mode of Proceeding in the Colonies: he was equally unsuccessful in his search after Colony Precedents; for in all the English Law Books he met with, he does not remember to have found half a score Colony Forms." There was no such precedent book. When he returned to London during the Revolution, he penned his own handbook to guide future agents, although many of the details concerned the newly independent provinces and soon became worthless.[117]

These recommendations, intended to generate manuals for imperial administration, reveal that there were no educational institutions for imperial servants. The empire and its agents in America had nothing to match the training of the provincial legal community. The agents' complaints about the dominance of the lawyers testified to this institutional gap. Things were no better anywhere else within the empire. Oxford and Cambridge did not yet produce colonial civil servants. The Inns of Court, which John Baker calls England's "third university," did not play the role for the empire that they had for medieval and early modern England: the school and library for the king's courts, facilitating consolidation of the island and the growth of a politically self-conscious class of administrators.[118] Neither was there a literature to guide the agents nor manuals like those that justices of the peace used to administer local government. For more than two centuries after establishing the first transatlantic colony, Britons engineered few new institutions for imperial governance. When in the 1760s some in London did investigate the problem of empire, they attempted both too little and too much, all too late. And they did so primarily for domestic rather than imperial reasons.

The View from London

The multiple interpretations of English constitutionalism in New York were not simply rhetorical strategies in a political struggle for local control; they also shaped the ways in which the empire was conceived by those on its dynamic fringe. The modern distinction between law and politics would have made little sense to eighteenth-century Britons. Legal discourse shaped political expression and provided the structure for understanding and articulating the felt differences in interest developing across the empire. Contests over the relevance and content of the common law, jurisdiction, and the personnel of the legal system divided the inhabitants of New York into slowly cohering political groups: the imperial agents, the creole provincial elite, and scattered associations of settlers in the marchland province. These divisions, more than the tension between the abstractions of "London" and "the colonies," help explain the indirect path in New York that ended in rebellion.

Yet imperial policy in Parliament and Whitehall changed in the 1760s and contributed to colonial discord. It remains unclear how government ministers could have formulated such policies without predicting the resistance they met across the Atlantic. Despite various avenues of information — from the governors and imperial agents, as well as from the creoles through interest group contacts — key decision makers did not understand that there were divergent perspectives on the imperial constitution. Instead, there arose in London a remarkably simple view that the imperial constitution was whatever those controlling Parliament wanted it to be. In some ways this represented still another interpretation of the imperial constitution. Logically, this definition resolved the ambiguities of the empire. But its very logic, its compelling simplicity, revealed its adherents' distance from colonial political culture. Metropolitan officials failed to gauge the depth of the provincials' devotion to a particular conception of legality and therefore did not take the imperial agents' recommendations for reforming legal administration seriously enough. Instead, Parliament, under Lord North, enacted one blunt regulation after another.

Perhaps the most radical regulation was the Quebec Act of 1774, the brainchild of old imperial agents William Knox and John Pownall. The whole French cession, from the Stanwix line to the Mississippi, was incorporated into the royal colony of Quebec. Much of this land was within the boundaries of older colonies such as Virginia, Massachusetts, and New York, according to their charters or letters patent. In addition, Governor Guy Carleton administered Quebec without an assembly. Finally, Parliament granted the Roman Catholic inhabitants the right to maintain their churches, complete with legally enforceable tithes to support their priests, and also preserved other legacies of French rule such as seigneurial land tenures. From one angle the Quebec Act was enlightened because it respected the rights of the conquered population. The initial policy of conquest a decade earlier was to replace French law wholesale with English law, and many of the French inhabitants in the eastern provinces were deported to other English colonies. At that time, Lord Mansfield had thought it "rash and unjust" to abolish the legal system of a conquered people with one stroke of a pen. Perhaps recalling dicta in *Calvin's Case* about conquered Christian nations, Mansfield maintained that England "has always left to the conquered their own laws and usages, with a change only so far as the sovereignty was concerned." He referred explicitly to the gradual replacement of local law in Ireland and the maintenance of local laws in Berwick and Minorca. In addition, the Scot may have had the 1707 Act of Union's legal compromise in mind. The complete displacement of French law was not just cruel; it was also unwise because it stirred discontent among the conquered people. "Is it possible," Mansfield asked George Grenville, the king's first minister, that an official who did not know "a syllable of their language or laws, has been sent over with an English title of magistracy unknown to them, the powers of which office must be inexplicable, and unexecutable by their usages?" If so, the policy had to change. "For God's sake," Mansfield concluded, "learn the truth of the case, and think of a speedy remedy." The remedy came in the Quebec Act, but this attempt to learn from the empire's history did not contribute to its well-being.[119]

Yet more was at work behind the Quebec Act than fair treatment of French Catholics. The act ensured that the new territory would be under the firm control of a loyal administrator. All prior colonial claims to the western lands were denied; French property law, the thought was, would discourage western migration by British settlers.[120] The act was supposed to say to British settlers, in the words of Solicitor General Alexander Wedderburn, " 'this is the border, beyond which, for the advantage of the whole empire, you shall not extend yourselves.' " The North administration's opposition in Parliament criticized the act. "[I]t is evident that this constitution is meant to be both an instrument of tyranny to the Canadians," complained Edmund Burke, "and an example to others of what they have to expect; at some time or other it will come home to England." Burke was concerned about British settlers in Canada and elsewhere, like those in New York who paid him to represent their interests in Parliament. But the opposition's ultimate fear was one that had haunted parliamentarians since the dawn of the empire: the colonies could become a training ground for innovations in crown rule. "Despotism" abroad might return home.[121]

The threat to New Yorkers was closer and more urgent. "What can speak in plainer language, the corruption of the British Parliament," wrote a precocious King's College student, than an act that gave the king "absolute power" in a province populated by Roman Catholics? They "will be the voluntary instruments of ambition; and will be ready, at all times, to second the oppressive designs of administration against the other parts of the empire."[122] The student, Alexander Hamilton, would soon get his chance to oppose imperial administration.

How come metropolitan officials did not predict this reaction to their American polices? First, the colonists were at the edge of the empire. While imperial value did not always decline in proportion to distance from London (witness the fascination with India), often it did.[123] More important was the parochialism of parliamentary politics. Extraparliamentary public opinion was just coalescing among the "middling" and others excluded from high politics.[124] English political life was still dominated by shifting political alliances held together more by patronage than principles. Elections turned on "a number of local forces, personal rivalries, struggles for local consequence and importance." The key word is "local." London was a temporary stage. The roots of politics lay in the English provinces.[125] Members of Parliament spent much of their time at their country seats and were only in the capital for sessions in the winter. When one American colonist went to London 1771 to defend the colonies, he found the place empty. "The great ones of the Earth, being at their seats in the country or at Paris and there is the greatest inattention to the affairs of the State you possibly can conceive of. The Kingdom is like a ship laying to, in a storm. Her helm lashed and the mariners all below asleep."[126] The "great ones" had fought to protect this social world in the seventeenth century, and provincial pride inspired an "urban renaissance" outside London in the eighteenth. But it also led to the neglect of imperial administration.[127]

There were metropolitan institutions responsible for colonial affairs. But Whitehall was a gold mine of patronage. The colonial offices, especially, were not professionally managed.[128] The Board of Trade was formally responsible for the colonies. This body had its roots in Oliver Cromwell's attempt to reorganize the various British dominions during the Interregnum and was made permanent during the Restoration. The board's commission enjoined it to recommend colonial policy, especially that promoting "the

Trade of Our Kingdom of England," to the King's Privy Council.[129] It was primarily interested in commercial policy, but much of its time was spent reviewing colonial legislation and corresponding with the governors and imperial agents. This narrow focus weakened the board's policy-making influence.[130] More important, the board had no executive power; this resided in the Privy Council. What appointment power the board did have it usually let pass to the southern secretary, except when it had a strong leader.[131] Horace Walpole lamented that membership on the board degenerated "almost into a sinecure" during the long administration of the Duke of Newcastle before midcentury. "It would not be credited," Walpole lamented, "what reams of papers, representations, memorials, petitions, from that quarter of the world [i.e., the American colonies] lay mouldering and unopened."[132] Because the colonists could not help one get power in the House of Commons, leading ministers discounted colonial policy.

For about a decade at midcentury, the board was rejuvenated under Lord Halifax. In 1752 the Privy Council, at Halifax's insistence, gave the Board of Trade more influence in the appointment of imperial agents.[133] In addition, Halifax got the Privy Council to instruct the royal governors to respond directly to the Board of Trade, which gave it executive authority for the first time.[134] Halifax was soon appointed to the Privy Council, though not in his capacity as the Board of Trade's president. This meant that while he gained much personal power, the board as an institution did not.[135] In 1761 Halifax left the board to become lord lieutenant of Ireland. The man to whom William Smith Jr. had dedicated his history of New York in 1757, and whose epitaph in Westminster Abbey would read "the Father of the Colonies," had grasped the main chance, far from America, as soon as it was offered. Meanwhile, the board became again a depository of facts, figures, and sinecures.[136]

The Board of Trade turned to Parliament for legislative support after the Seven Years' War. In doing so, it conceded its weakness amid the great changes in the colonial situation now that France was expelled from Canada. Parliamentary support was contrary to the intention of the board's architects, like King William III, who had envisioned board members as the king's personal advisers. But like many curial bodies throughout English history, the board gravitated out of the king's sphere and closer to the full Parliament, of which the king was part, but only part. The parliamentary alliance was forged by a new generation of politicians and administrators who took the increasing power of the Commons for granted and were insensitive to the practical compromises of Robert Walpole and Newcastle. Suddenly the imperial constitution was equated with parliamentary authority, with the Commons dominant. "We are reduced to the alternative of adopting coercive measures, or of forever relinquishing our claim of sovereignty or dominion over the colonies," concluded Lord Mansfield, adding that either "the supremacy of the British legislature must be complete, entire, and unconditional or on the other hand, the colonies must be free and independent."[137]

Since the Revolution of 1688/89, political thinkers had expounded the position that the Houses of Parliament were sovereign.[138] During the first half of the eighteenth century, few elaborated this theory. It did not reflect the reality of parliamentary politics, in which the king remained a vital element. But a new generation, raised on the Whig slogans of the revolution, entered government around midcentury and began to perform from these revolutionary scripts. These younger men assumed that Parliament was sovereign and that within Parliament the Commons was supreme. Seventeenth-century polemics and schoolboy stories were transfigured into human form. The theory of unitary sovereignty became real through that familiar sort of revolution: a generation coming of age.[139]

The colonies were not the only parts of the British Empire threatened by the new legislation. So were George III and his court. The theory of unitary sovereignty was a political instrument across Europe. In Britain, it helped the Commons reduce the crown's ability to make law outside Parliament. The crown, along with the colonies, was the target of the Commons' ambition. In other words, the new colonial legislation of the 1760s had as much to do with metropolitan politics as with reorganizing the empire. In response, the king created a third secretary of state, for America, to coexist with the secretaries of the northern and southern departments. This new secretariat would help the king retrieve control over colonial administration and its patronage. Thus, for their own political reasons, George III and his court also took an uncompromising position toward the American colonies.[140]

This new metropolitan constitutionalism, forged through competition between the Commons and the crown, eventuated in the Declaratory Act of 1766 and then Lord North's conciliatory proposal of 1775, which passed with a large majority in the Commons. These acts would have forced the colonies to acknowledge the right of parliamentary taxation, while Parliament agreed not to exercise it as long as the colonies continued to contribute to the common defense. This was the maximum point of compromise in the capital. The belief that the colonists would accept this constitutional principle in exchange for a promise that it would not be enforced reflected metropolitan indifference toward the colonists' constitutional scruples. This indifference grew as informal contacts with the colonies declined. Colonial interest group representatives—agents for the assemblies, religious denominations, and mercantile houses—lost influence after the ascension of George III, whose ministers' clear vision of the imperial constitution left little room for unofficial input.[141] What mattered most in London was the relationship between king and Commons, not between Parliament in the abstract and the colonies.

Back in New York, the issue for the imperial agents was their own authority. A new parliamentary stamp tax on official documents followed a new sugar excise a year earlier. "Trade is the support of America," customs collector Andrew Elliot explained to his brother, who sat on the Board of Trade. "All the people of fortune are in trade more or less, their lands bring in no rent so that what ever touches the trading Interest all ways makes a noise here." New imperial taxes brought complaints "that [New Yorkers] are to pay money that does no good to the nation but only to support Court offices."[142] Robert R. Livingston wrote his father from the intercolonial Stamp Act Congress that the three key issues were "trials by juries, a right to tax ourselves, [and] the reducing of admiralty courts within their proper limits."[143] The congress opened just before the act became effective (1 November 1765) and met in New York City because of its central location. To a contact in London, Livingston explained that resistance to the Stamp Act was designed to preserve, not fracture, the empire. "We know not how matters appear to you on the other side of the Atlantic," he wrote, "but here we seem to think it clear as any proposition of Euclid, that if America submits to be taxed at the pleasure of the house of Commons the power will be too great & uncontrolable to remain long unabused, & that the abuse of it will naturally render the Colonies independent." Opposition to the tax flowed not from a "factious spirit" but rather "from a real patriotic desire of promoting the general interest of the Empire."[144]

On 31 October 1765, city merchants gathered to organize a partial boycott of British goods to protest the stamp tax. Over the next few nights, mobs roamed the city and erupted in violence here and there, some of it linked to traditional celebrations of Guy Fawkes Day. Lawyers dared not file official papers that required the new stamp, which kept the courts closed for six months. As Judge Robert Livingston reported to former governor Robert Monckton,

> Merchants have resolved to send for no more British manufactures. Shopkeepers will buy none, Gentlemen will wear none[;] our own are encouraged, all pride in Dress seems to be laid aside, and he that does not appear in a Homespun or at least a Turned Coat is looked on with an Evil Eye.

The Lawyers will not Issue a writ, Merchants will not clear out a vessel, these are all facts not in the least exaggerated and it is of Importance that they should be known. But the worst of all is this, that should the Act be enforced there is the utmost danger I speak it with the greatest concern imaginable of a Civil War.[145]

Realizing that the Stamp Act could not be enforced and bombarded by threats against him as "the Chief Murderer of [New Yorkers'] Rights & Privileges," Colden moved the stamps offshore to a naval ship under the command of Captain Archibald Kennedy Jr. Colden was yet again lieutenant governor. He decided not to enforce the Stamp Act "but leave it to Sir Harry Moore," on his way to assume the governorship, "to doe as he pleases." For this compromise — his acceptance of the principle of parliamentary taxation while refusing to collect taxes — a mob burned Colden's effigy in the streets of New York City and the crown administration condemned him in London. "Whatever the wisdom of the Ministry may suggest to be the true policy of Great Britain with respect to her Colonies," a despondent Colden wrote Lord Mansfield, "they never can think it good policy to deliver up their faithfull servants supposing they may have erred in Judgment to the violent resentment of a virulent Faction who stood in opposition to the Authority of Parliament."[146] He took it from both sides, which was nothing new.

New York soon became the target of metropolitan punishment, an example for all colonies. When in 1766 the assembly refused to provide supplies required by the Quartering Act, Parliament passed the New York Restraining Act, which directed the governor not to consent to any statute until the assembly complied with the Quartering Act. Essentially, it suspended New York's legislature. Governor Moore accepted the assembly's next appropriation as acknowledgment of the Quartering Act, which permitted both sides to act as though they had vindicated their competing principles. But the lawyers in the assembly who drafted the appropriation bill "carefully avoided to acknowledge the Authority of Parliament," reported Colden, and as a result "[a]n opinion is industriously infused into the Minds of the People, that the legislative authority of Great Britain does not extend to the Colonies, by Men who from their Profession are supposed to understand the Constitution best."[147] As late as 1767, the practice of accommodation continued even as interpretations of that practice diverged.

Merchant John Watts offered shrewd insight on the situation. Son of a Scottish immigrant, Watts inherited his father's commercial contacts and ascended to the governor's council. Throughout the period of resistance he was loyal to the empire and suspicious of provincial lawyers. But his business ties and friendships sensitized him to the provincial interpretation of the imperial constitution. "I really believe some New Constitution will be form'd in time between the Mother Country & the Colonys," he wrote friend and former governor Robert Monckton. To a London associate and in-law, he warned,

> If America is to be governd & their Lives & propertys dispos'd of by people sent out meerly because they had no Character or Credit at home or are a burthen upon some great Man. If their property is to be thrown into dependent Courts of Admiralty & their Causes to be carry'd at pleasure to an obscure Corner of his Majestys Dominions, called Hallifax, wither they cannot attend them. If Verdicts from Jurys are to be overruled by a Governor & a Council appointed at will & of course all mens Estates lay at Mercy. If internal Taxes are to be laid by fellow Subjects who know Nothing of their Circumstances & whose Interest it will be to make them beasts of burthen, & it is meer mercy if they do not [rebel].[148]

Even a loyal councillor understood provincial fear of foreign-born officers and the popular demand for juries and self-taxation. But Watts was born in New York, and he hoped that the compromises of eighteenth-century constitutional practice would continue.

Parliament's attempt to simplify the imperial constitution failed. So too provincial attempts. Few in London took seriously proposals for an American parliament equal to that in Britain. The loyalist William Smith Jr. went to the grave with faith in this solution. The problem with Smith's proposal for an American parliament was that he had reduced the whole conflict to representation. It was about more than this, as tensions among the colonies would soon reveal. Nonetheless, throughout the Revolution Smith hoped that "an American constitution" establishing a "grand Wittenagemoot," perhaps meeting annually in New York City, would bring lasting peace.[149] Few colonists embraced this idea, which would have required extensive cooperation between the colonies. Intercolonial congresses like the Albany Congress and the Stamp Act Congress, both held in New York, were not encouraging precedents. It took a war and another decade before the American provinces were ready to agree to a constitution that gave substantial authority to a "grand Wittenagemoot." London officials were not interested in such an institution either. They kept declaring their power to govern without colonial restraint.

In the end, the imperial agents were left to enforce new imperial policies amid the ambiguities and compromises that had marked imperial administration for decades. While Parliament could draft Declaratory Acts, few in New York believed what they read. The real battle was not transatlantic; it went on within the province. The failure of the imperial agents' plans for reform led them to send dire reports back to London. These in turn led to more drastic curbs on provincial autonomy: restraints on property; limitations on territorial jurisdiction; restrictions on the jury trial; and the appointment of government officials born elsewhere in the empire. The agents tried to do too much and succeeded with little, except in conveying to London officials the impression that the colony was ungovernable. When the tumult of the 1760s reappeared in the mid-1770s, more radical responses followed. Common law gave way not to a new imperial law but rather to martial law.

ON MANHATTAN AS WELL AS on the frontier, the imperial agents had struggled to reconfigure the common law for the empire's benefit. Their interpretations of ancient phrases and institutions were screened through their experiences in supporting the imperial system, a system in which they pictured themselves prominent: Johnson ruling the "Marches & Frontiers" with diplomatic skill; Colden in the city challenging provincial attempts to secure internal governance; Kennedy and Elliot regulating trade from the customs house. There were elements of truth in these self-images, sent repeatedly, with pleas for more power, to London. However, for all the agents' perceptive reports about the limits of imperial power on the margins, the conclusion that land grabbing, unpredictable juries, and weak law enforcement were the functions of a conspiratorial legal establishment obscured the powerful, anarchic energy within the province. Ironically, the clarity of their imagined empire helped ensure that it would never come to pass. The reality of colonial New York was more indistinct, blurred by the shadows of movement mentioned only indirectly and that, for all the complaints about trespassers, went largely unexamined.

Some provincials began to perceive that volatility, but they also explained it with inadequate historical analogies. Suddenly, feared some of the elite, the province abounded with "levellers." In 1774, Gouverneur Morris, scion of illustrious provincial families, King's College alumnus, and legal clerk to William Smith Jr., lamented that provincial turbulence was fast becoming a struggle over "the future forms of our government, whether it should be founded upon Aristocratic or Democratic principles." The "gentry" had initiated the resistance, but it was slipping out of their control. "The spirit of the English Constitution has yet a little influence left, and but little," Morris reported to a friend. "The mob begins to think and to reason. Poor reptiles! it is with them a vernal morning, they are struggling to cast off their winter's slough, they bask in the sunshine, and ere noon they will bite, depend on it. . . . I see, and I see it with fear and trembling, that if the disputes with Britain continue, we shall be under the worst of all possible dominions. We shall be under the domination of a riotous mob."[150]

Morris became one of New York's reluctant revolutionaries, a delegate to the 1787 Constitutional Convention, and a federal senator: his attempts to control that "mob." As the imperial agents had attempted to freeze a dynamic situation by reforming — even supplanting — the common law, their American successors would try the same with other innovative uses of English legal ideas, hoping finally to solve the persistent riddle of New York's constitution.

Before leaving the story of the prerevolutionary constitutions of New York, recall what colonial political culture was like on the ground. There in 1766, for example, was Sir William Johnson knocking on the rude door of the Mohawk Valley squatter, an invader of sorts, who, when shown the royal Proclamation of 1763, chuckled, a sneer that was not really even a challenge, as he felt secure in his appropriation of land that seemed to belong to no one in a jurisdiction that would enforce neither the king's dominion nor the Native Americans' claim. Who, then, was the squatter? It is a laugh that echoed through the hills of North America for some years, belying the severity of legal declarations, following the momentum of empire west. The unnamed squatter, the German George Klock, the irrepressible Ethan Allen, and countless others were more than the pawns of speculators. They, as much as the provincial elite's incorporated associations, entered that American vacuum of public authority that the imperial agents could not fill with their many desperate letters. The frontier settlers invoked the spirit and phrases of the common law, but the degree of their politicization is uncertain. What is clear is that they were loyal foremost to the freedom of movement, ignored jurisdictional claims, and laughed in the face of the titled, those deemed meritorious, and the letter of imperial law.

This third constitutional force was ultimately the most revolutionary. The mobility that lay beneath colonization, when coupled with common-law constitutionalism, was the primary cause of the Revolution. Common-law constitutionalism conditioned the way the colonists viewed their relationship to the empire and the American continent. In turn, they invoked that notion of legality to protect themselves from imperial reforms. Like most early modern crowds in the Atlantic world, New York's settlers adhered to customary rules, such as the maxim that possession was most of the law and that land claims should be made in common-law ways in front of a local judge and jury.[151] Unlike most crowds, this one got what it wanted. The Revolution constitutionalized provincial control, including its most local form: allodial land title. Allied sometimes with the provincials and at others with the expositors of empire, but always part and parcel of both, the settlers' mobility persisted, with migrants pursuing their own notions of improvement, never fully trusting the printed statements of popular sovereignty. As the imperialists and provincials printed ever more words, the migrations continued with the same urgency and persistence, destruction paired with improvement, that the articulate always claimed to understand and pretended to manage. Through the years that echo might still be heard, still in the hills, but not just there and ever less with one of the British accents, as people reconstituted themselves in those ancient, fertile landscapes with their contingent legal names: Johnstown, Canajoharie, Manhattan, New York.

Imperial Civil War and Reconstitution

America is at eve of a civil War.
James Duane (1774)

T HE AMERICAN REVOLUTION was first a British civil war that divided regions, institutions, families, and individual consciences. Sources of law and authority in New York, already plural, increased even more. Which ones would predominate was far from clear. State formation was not the only response to the imperial crisis. The thirteen provinces also joined together in the Continental Congress. But the states could not have viewed their limited cooperation in the congress as a prelude to the federal Constitution of 1787. Most government remained local government. Loyalist judge and historian Thomas Jones exaggerated somewhat, but only somewhat, when he wrote that after the Declaration of Independence "the courts, and justice itself ceased, all was anarchy, all was confusion. A usurped kind of Government took place, a medley of military law, convention ordinances, Congress recommendations, and committee resolutions."[1] During the war New York, like only a few other colonies, had dual governments: royal and rebel. The revolutionaries' legal manifestos — their constitutions — were written to oppose the form the empire had begun to take: imperial control over provincial legislative and judicial power, a trend that culminated in martial law in New York City during the war. Drafters of the new state constitutions sought to secure the internal, corporate autonomy of each province and the related liberties of Englishmen, pieces of the transatlantic constitutional tradition that had formed the idiom of provincial resistance. They also assumed, in the words of New York's constitution, that a "league of friendship" would exist among all the states. New Yorkers resisted the *new* manifestations of the imperial constitution, but not the English constitution or the idea of an empire as a union of provinces.[2]

The Continental Congress, representing thirteen of the mainland colonies, proclaimed that all colonists were "entitled" to the common law, at once a principled stand against British policy and an evasion of the diversity of colonial law. Everyone claimed the liberties of Englishmen and the constitution that contained them, but together the colonists had no truly common law, only many laws in common, or thirteen variations on the English common law.[3] For now, they could agree that the common law was fundamental law, that certain principles transcended the multiplicity of rules, statutes, and procedures operative in each of the states. This distillation sounded as though it fitted the English constitutional tradition — a refinement based on infinite particulars — but in practice it obscured differences between the new states, each enthusiastically embracing the freedom associated with the common law while engineering a variety of innovations.

This problem of legal federalism could wait. The relationships between the state and the Confederation and between local and state governments remained undertheorized for years. War took priority over constitution making. In addition, many New Yorkers assumed that they would enjoy all the benefits of the old empire — especially security and trade — without accounting for them in the state constitution. They were familiar with war. They were not familiar with a world without the empire. Making sense of this fast-changing constitutional order was the task of those who negotiated the relationships between the state and Confederation government, between the states, and within the state.

All three of these relationships were explored in *Rutgers v. Waddington*, a 1784 case in the Mayor's Court of New York City in which a landowner sued under the state Trespass Act to recover rent from a loyalist who had occupied her property during the war. Attorneys for both sides aired arguments about key legal relationships — between the city and province, judiciary and legislature, assembly and Continental Congress, state law and international treaty, written and unwritten law — that would be restructured over the next several years. Struggling to define the state constitution, New Yorkers contributed to the movement for a new federal union and supplied much of the vocabulary used to construct it.

Provincial Resistance and Garrison Government

> *The friendly part of America keep up their*
> *spirits . . . that the re-union of the Empire*
> *will be yet happily established.*
> Governor William Tryon (1780)

I N 1765, WILLIAM SMITH JR. warned New York's absentee governor, Robert Monckton, that "Great Britain has indeed lost the affection of all the Colonists, and I am very fearful not only of Discontent and partial Tumults amongst them, but that a general Civil War will light up and rage all along the Continent." Smith feared that tensions had reached the ultimate crisis. "I tremble at the Thought of your recurring to Force," he wrote Monckton, warning that "our People" would "resist to the last" in order to "preserve or regain our Liberty."[1] Smith did not predict independence. He meant civil war, like that in Britain a century earlier: an internal rebellion to "preserve or regain our Liberty."

Force was not used in the 1760s. But a decade later the pattern reemerged: parliamentary taxation and limitations on provincial courts, which triggered resistance. Invective returned to the presses, mobs to the streets. "I suppose we shall repeat all the Confusions of 1765 & 1766," Smith lamented. "Our Domestic Parties will probably die, & be swallowed up in the general Opposition to the Parliamentary Project of raising an Arm of Government by Revenue Laws."[2] This time Britain used force, rending Smith's world in two.

By the end of 1776, the British military had secured all of New York City, once again its continental headquarters, as well as Long Island and parts of the Hudson and Mohawk valleys. "As long as you maintained New Yorke," believed Secretary of State for the Colonies Lord George Germain, "the continent was divided."[3] But neither side "maintained New York." Who controlled what land was unclear throughout the war. Two governments claimed jurisdiction over the whole colony; each actually governed limited parts, and areas in between became true marchlands.[4]

If royal and rebel jurisdictions were never clearly divided, their respective ideas of legality were. Royal civil government collapsed in 1776, and for years imperial officials equivocated about restoring it. Residence in royal New York meant living under martial law. Meanwhile, while retreating up the Hudson, the provincial rebels composed their new state constitution. Their devotion to constitutional legality contrasted starkly with military governance in the royal sector. Each side claimed legitimacy, and neither succeeded in establishing impartial legal institutions. But never before had the competing provincial and imperial constitutions been so clear. The crown's military government kept promising to restore civil government, while the state constitution of 1777 declared that "no authority shall, on any pretense whatever, be exercised over the people or members of this state, but as shall be derived from and granted by them."[5] In the coming years, the state continually tried to make popular sovereignty a fact and not just an ideal, while the British Empire moved ever closer to executive government.

The Provincial Constitution, Improved: Committees, Congresses, and Convention, 1775–1777

The division of New York was gradual, and colonial protesters did not know where their hesitant steps would lead. After the tea boycott of 1773, the British Parliament passed the Coercive Acts and closed the port of Boston. Many of the continental colonies supported Massachusetts. In New York, the political lead was taken in New York City. With the assembly reluctant to support an intercolonial nonimportation agreement, city activists formed a local committee of correspondence, a parallel governing body that would "consult upon the present state of affairs [and] correspond with the Neighboring colonies." The original committee, the Committee of Fifty-One, recommended a colonial congress to coordinate responses to the Coercive Acts, for the "Cause concerns a whole Continent." The Continental Congress was intended to prevent radical resistance and other "mischief and disappointment." It would protest parliamentary abuses, but the colonies would agree to support its policies and engage in no more extreme resistance on their own. New Yorkers, who were enmeshed in the Atlantic economy, hoped that a complete boycott would not be the greatest common denominator.[6]

When committees from eleven other colonies agreed to establish the first Continental Congress, the New York committee nominated five representatives: John Alsop, James Duane, John Jay, Philip Livingston, and Isaac Low.[7] A group of mechanics nominated a rival slate of five, replacing Alsop and Duane with Alexander MacDougall and Leonard Lispenard, and this latter group was selected. Confirming elections were held on 28 July 1774. The Committee of Fifty-One soon recommended its replacement by an elected committee of sixty. These elections took place in November 1774. Five months later, the committee selected members of the "Provincial Convention," charged in turn with selecting delegates to the Second Continental Congress. The committee, now numbering one hundred, also moved to create a more permanent governing body. After a new round of elections, the Provincial Convention became the Provincial Congress, which governed the rebellious parts of the colony until the passage of the new state constitution in 1777.[8]

All of this was extraordinary and extralegal but not unconstitutional. The right of resistance included the right to establish extralegal assemblies for temporary governance. Cadwallader Colden reported to London that many committee members admitted that such "Assemblies of the People, without Authority of Government, are illegal . . . but they deny that they are unconstitutional when a national grievance cannot otherwise be removed."[9] Although committee government increased popular participation in politics, it was not a radical innovation. The colonial tradition of legally ambiguous, self-governing institutions reached its culmination.

Yet only with hindsight does committee government appear as a prelude to independence. That, thought one revolutionary as late as 1774, was "the most vain, empty, shallow, and ridiculous project that could possibly enter into the heart of man."[10] In the early months of resistance, New York Whigs assumed themselves to be as independent as ever — and no more. Most wanted to remain within the empire. All hoped to prevent the disintegration of civil authority. During the elections for the new Provincial Congress in April 1775, the New York City committee stated its support for "a reconciliation between Great Britain and America" to preserve "our constitution," prevent "anarchy," and protect "good order, and the safety of individual and private property."[11] But the fact remained that the governor did not summon this assembly. New Yorkers convened it themselves.

This new Provincial Congress comprised two representatives from each of the counties, three from the city of Albany, and four from New York City, an apportionment similar to that in the colonial assembly. The two manors that had enjoyed assembly representation, Van Rensselaer and Livingston, lost their seats. Much has been made of this loss in telling the story of the decline of aristocracy in New York.[12] But the Livingston family had never been a monolith. Only one part, the "upper manor," enjoyed direct representation. Several Livingstons continued to influence provincial politics after 1775, and some gained new influence beyond New York's borders, as did some Morrises, Schuylers, Van Rensselaers, and others. Provincial elites were becoming continental leaders. While they may not have had much choice in trading local for interstate leadership, they did not lament the change either.

Continental government, independence, and state constitution making were gradual developments. For a long time there were few institutional changes. The Provincial Congress looked much like the colonial assembly and sounded like it too. In the summer of 1775, the congress instructed its delegates in Philadelphia to "point out such moderate terms, as may tend to reconcile the unhappy differences which threaten the whole Empire with destruction." This letter accompanied a draft plan of accommodation that conceded Britain's right to regulate trade but demanded legislative autonomy within the colonies "in all cases of internal polity whatsoever, subject only to the negative of the Sovereign in such manner as has been heretofore accustomed."[13] Such claims continued for months. The Provincial Congress repeatedly instructed its Philadelphia delegates to seek conciliation; the New York delegates assured their home province that they were "[d]eeply sensible of the calamities of a civil war" and wanted to be "instrumental in compromising this unnatural quarrel between the two countries, on the basis of natural justice and constitutional liberty." Those in the Provincial Congress thought they still lived in a colony and sought to preserve their "ancient and established form of Government."[14]

Traditional claims of self-governance held against the Continental Congress as well. In its first session, Provincial Congress president Isaac Low introduced a resolution that his government controlled "the internal police of this Colony" and would obey only those Continental directives concerning intercolonial matters.[15] Several members deemed even this too deferential, and the final resolution promised merely to "pay the highest attention to every recommendation of the Grand Continental Congress." For its part, the Continental Congress assured the colonies that they enjoyed internal autonomy and the common law.[16] Beyond these platitudes, there was for months no discussion of the constitutional relationship between the two governments.

Relations between the province and the Continental Congress remained amicable because each was becoming more frustrated with the empire than with each other, especially after the British used force in Boston.[17] Once the military struggle began in earnest, the Continental army added yet another layer of authority within New York, and new conflicts arose. Late in the winter of 1776, for example, General Charles Lee urged the New York congress to adopt a loyalty test, warning that "the crisis will admit of no procrastination." Rather than waiting for a legislature he never fully trusted, Lee instituted a test oath himself, eliciting protest from the New York delegation in Philadelphia and a provincial resolution that "[t]here can be no liberty where the military is not subordinate to the civil power in every thing not immediately connected with their operations."[18]

Similar jockeying for authority emerged within the province. The relationship between the Provincial Congress and local units of authority, from committees to towns, was never clear. Resolution and exhortation, rather than legislation and execution, characterized wartime government at all levels. When the Provincial Congress tried to direct the war effort, it could only resolve, not command, that local governments should organize the militia, regulate trade, fix prices, contain disease, garrison troops, limit liquor distribution, and so forth.[19] Hortatory price controls followed for blankets, hats, shirts, wool, and leather. Sometimes the congress offered interest-free loans and premiums to encourage the manufacture of necessary military supplies.[20] At others it granted Commander in Chief George Washington the authority to impress carriages and boats.[21] Persuasion was occasionally backed by threats. When the committee of Richmond County (now Staten Island) refused to send delegates to the Provincial Congress in December 1775, the congress alluded to the possibility of coercion: "[R]est assured, gentlemen, that the neighbouring Colonies will not remain inactive spectators if you show a disposition to depart from the Continental Union."[22] Richmond, glad host of the British navy throughout the Revolution, took its chances.

Elections offered another opportunity for influence. When in January 1776 the Provincial Congress asked the county committees to elect men who supported the resistance, threats gave way to obsequiousness. The congress appealed to the local committees' "sense of duty," their "desire to promote the union of Colonies," and "that ardent love which you have for the liberties of America" to persuade them to nominate Whigs and then take "pains to secure their election."[23]

Careful diplomacy was also necessary when handling intercolonial disputes. As throughout the colonial period, New York asked the distant government to mediate its grievances with neighbors, such as old boundary disputes and new ones rising with the pitch of rebellion. When Ethan Allen and the Green Mountain Boys stirred up secessionist sentiment in New York's northeastern counties, the provincial government asked the Continental Congress "to interpose their authority, and recommend to the said insurgents a peaceful submission to the jurisdiction of this State."[24] When a band of men from Connecticut destroyed the printing press of a loyalist in New York City and imprisoned Anglican minister Samuel Seabury, the New York congress warned Connecticut governor Jonathan Trumbull that it would seek from the Continental Congress "such a general regulation on this subject as may well prevent such jealousies."[25]

Ignored here, called on to mediate there, the Continental Congress remained without a clear legal basis. "We are in a State of Nature," Patrick Henry opined to his colleagues in Philadelphia, but his was a minority opinion. John Jay did not think "that We came to frame an American Constitution." The mandate was instead "to correct the faults of an old one — I can't yet think that all Government is at an End."[26] Conventional wisdom in the British world held that constitution making was a legitimate enterprise, but only after some political apocalypse. In the continental colonies, most government had not ceased because most government remained local government. Town and county institutions continued to regulate everyday affairs and rallied support for resistance. Yet they were unable to collect taxes and raise troops on the scale necessary to wage what was becoming a full-fledged civil war.[27] Constitution making could not await the end of all government.

As throughout the colonial period, military problems catalyzed constitutional reform. Despite the apparent pyramid of power among governments, one level could not command another. The members of the Continental Congress assumed that they could tell the state congresses what to do, and the provincial authorities assumed in turn that they could get what they wanted from local committees. But nobody had coercive authority.

Individual compliance with the military effort was another problem. Agents of the new state government could not — or, to satisfy their constituents, would not — engage in the sort of interference into civil life that had been common in the colonial period. The Continental Congress asked its commanders to stop demanding that skippers follow European naval custom and lower their mainsails when passing the forts; the colonies had "sufficiently suffered through punctilio, and we beg you [to] desist from exacting marks of submission or respect of any kind."[28] In 1778, John Jay implored the new state assembly to establish clear rules for the impressment of military supplies. It was "the undoubted Right and unalienable Priviledge of a Freeman not to be divested, or interrupted in the innocent use, of Life Liberty or Property, but by Laws to which he has assented." It did not matter whether the breach was "by the King of Great Britain, or by an American Quarter Master"; they were "equally partaking of Injustice." The assembly followed Jay's advice. During its first session, it passed a law that directed quartermasters to apply to the local justice of the peace for a list of potential suppliers, and it required compensation for supplies taken.[29] Abuses in supply did not cease, but there was now an established process to take citizens' property for the war effort.

New forms of persuasion were needed to meet the demands of military supply. For instance, the provincial government requested use of shoreline property for a military shipyard from James Livingston, a request he had refused when made by the local commissioners. "Though neither the Continental nor Provincial Congress would choose to dispossess themselves of any man's property against his will," the New York government wrote Livingston, "yet you will readily see that your refusal to comply with the request above mentioned will render you obnoxious to all the friends of liberty. It is therefore recommended to you by this Committee to permit the ship builders to occupy the spot they have applied for, and we engage to make you a proper compensation for the same."[30] It was not clear that these governments had the authority to condemn property, but they could "recommend" a sale, and they guaranteed just compensation in the common-law tradition. When the Continental Congress urged the production of certain scarce goods that the imperial trade regulations had long forbidden, like cloth, the Provincial Congress exhorted, threatened, and appealed to the self-interest of farmers "to devote a larger part of our lands than usual to the culture of hemp and flax, and the pasturing of sheep." Suddenly the land was "ours" and subject to the moral imperative of successive "oughts." The shortage of materials "ought, from motives both of private interest and public utility, to be compensated for by the improvement of our lands, in such a way as will infallibly be attended with great profit to the land holder." Appeals to private interest were always part of the mix. The Provincial Congress assured farmers that "the advantage will be so highly improved by the enhanced prices of hemp, flax and wool, that every farmer who neglects to take uncommon pains for the increase of those necessary articles, will be most culpably inattentive to the general weal and his own private interest."[31]

Suspected loyalists encountered harsher measures. The Provincial Congress investigated rumors of loyalism and then tried and punished suspects. In short, the congress was prosecutor, judge, and jury. Shame was the penalty of choice. In April 1776, the Committee of Safety tried Peter DuBois for allegedly expressing unpatriotic thoughts about the valor of New England troops, "that they fought behind walls, and in secret places, and were afraid to show themselves openly"; that the British commander in chief, Thomas Gage, was "a gentleman and a man of honour"; that those who tarred and feathered loyalists were "a damned set of rascals"; and that "it was no sin to break [a loyalty] oath." But DuBois also claimed to be a Whig and opposed parliamentary taxation. Colonel Alexander MacDougall scolded DuBois: "[I]t is the opinion of the Committee that he has discovered a temper inimical to his country; that such conduct is inconsistent with the philosopher, the soldier or the good man." Yet the penalty was light. The committee told DuBois "to impress a more careful conduct."[32] Similarly, those accused of bearing arms against the Continental cause were usually released from jail after promising not to do so again.[33]

The Provincial Congress also acted as an appellate tribunal when it reviewed local committees' prosecutions of loyalists. It empowered the county committees and its own Committee of Safety to summon and examine witnesses and suspects, issue certificates of loyalty, grant parole, take security, and detain probable loyalists. Each committee was to keep a "just record of all proceedings" and judgments to enable review. The congress rarely reversed those judgments but did impose sanctions and occasionally granted pardons to those who promised to support the rebellion. Informed that committees in the mid–Hudson Valley were subjecting suspected loyalists to hard labor, the congress approved only detention until the accused posted security.[34] The state congress also listed as suspects those who held crown offices, did not join the rebellion, or failed to demonstrate "by their conduct a zeal for, or attachment to, the American cause" as "suspicious." Even an "equivocal neutrality" was suspicious.[35] Soon many of the people so listed were attainted, which meant that the state legislature convicted them of treason and confiscated their property.[36] Among the fifty-nine people convicted were leading imperial agents, like Colden, the Johnson family, the past and present governor, and

Attorney General John Tabor Kempe, along with dozens of leading provincials who chose to remain loyal, such as the DeLancey family.[37]

The rebel government had difficulty enforcing loyalty provisions even on Whigs. Many men sympathetic to the rebellion refused to take the Continental loyalty oath because they feared that this oath would force them into the Continental army; they preferred to fight in local militias and argued that the oath violated long-standing militia regulations, another invocation of local custom to trump new central directives. The Provincial Congress capitulated and made an exception for those who preferred to fight locally.[38]

The Continental Congress had informal ways of goading provincial citizens as well. In May 1776, General George Washington informed the Provincial Congress that he was worried about the concentration of loyalists in New York City and requested that it appoint a committee to meet with him about those "intestine enemies." This committee recommended that all those holding British military commissions and civil offices be apprehended. Another committee drew up regulations to carry out the "spirit and intention" of the resolutions.[39] Antiloyalist prosecutions at the local, state, and continental levels increased throughout the war.[40]

Although the accretion of military authority by the Continental Congress was almost inevitable, the primary means—constitution making—was not and revealed much about revolutionary ideas of legitimate government.[41] Whenever dissatisfied with governmental efficiency, members of the Continental government talked in terms of constitutions, implying that conscious reconstruction of government would streamline administration. This dissatisfaction with committee government began almost immediately; paradoxically, some of the ideals of the rebellion, like localism, were undermining it. In the spring of 1775 John Jay wrote home from Philadelphia that the colonies should "erect good and well ordered Governments . . . [to] exclude that Anarchy which already too much prevails," foreshadowing James Madison's analysis of the "vices of the political systems of the states" a decade later.[42] But it was primarily to increase military efficiency that, in May 1776, the Continental Congress advised each colony to "constitut[e] a new form of government and internal police." Because the king had breached his duty to the colonies, the Continental Congress resolved, crown authority should be "suppressed, and all the powers of government [should be] exerted under the authority of the people of the colonies."[43] Like all congressional resolutions, it was only a recommendation. It was nonetheless, as James Duane observed, "a Machine for the fabrication of Independence."[44]

Loyalty and Rebellion

Why did some New Yorkers rebel and others remain loyal? The reasons were economic, religious, ethnic, familial, and factional. The cases of the imperial agents and related coteries are simple: most never considered rebellion.[45] Division within the provincial elite was more complicated. A majority of those within the DeLancey family orbit, for example, remained loyal, while most Livingstons rebelled. In part this was because the De-Lancey faction was in power during the 1770s, which led to a rapprochement between its members and the imperial agents.[46] But there also were cultural reasons why the DeLanceys felt stronger ties to Britain. Most were Anglican, many had been educated in England, and they had tighter commercial and interest group connections with Britain.[47] Still, several people associated with the DeLanceys, such as James Duane, joined the revolution, while some in the Livingston circle — most prominently William Smith Jr. — did not. As in all civil wars, even families were divided, siblings against siblings and parents against children.[48] Rather than stark political or social divisions, there were thousands of individual decisions. Many colonists could have gone either way. Some who at first resisted later adhered to the crown. Some loyalists remained within the rebel-controlled sectors of the colony through-out the war. Others fled to Britain but returned to New York after the war, suggesting that the differences between loyalists and revolutionaries were not irreconcilable.

On the marchland, the loyalty of the Johnsons and four of the Six Nations inspired many in the region who opposed them to rebel.[49] In the Green Mountains, the New Hampshire grantees viewed the British Empire as hostile to their land claims; they had a better chance in rebellion and formed Vermont. Vermonters waffled when they realized that many New York land-owners were involved in the new Continental government, and in the middle of the war they explored a separate peace with Britain.[50] On the Hudson Valley estates, most tenants sided with their landlords except where, as on Livingston Manor, there had been recent hostilities.[51] In the city, artisans and mechanics generally supported rebellion, many because of the restrictive imperial trade laws that hurt their business.[52]

Few of these decisions were inevitable. Often they were relational: the choice could turn on the loyalty (or disloyalty) of adversaries within the province. Although the Revolution reverberated throughout the empire, the decision to participate in it was a local one. Yet because of its ultimate success, many historians view the Revolution as inevitable, and those who remained loyal are treated with contempt or nostalgia. The way those loyalists governed and were governed has been forgotten. But that government—the seven years of martial law—reveals much about the possibilities for reconstituting imperial rule in mainland North America and what that rule might have looked like.

Martial Law in Royal New York

Practically defunct since the rise of the rebellious committees, royal civil government ceased when the military took command of New York City in the latter half of 1776.[53] As always, there was little guidance from London about how to govern the colony on a daily basis. The one significant statement was the Prohibitory Act, which took effect on 1 January 1776 and forbade trade between the rebellious colonies and any other part of the empire. The King's Commissioners for Restoring Peace to the Colonies were, however, empowered to declare any colony or town "at peace" and restore trading privileges.[54] The British military entered this vacuum of government, and by the fall of 1776 much of southern New York was under martial law.

Martial law was not unusual in the eighteenth century.[55] However, by the mid-eighteenth century, the custom of protecting British civilians from martial law had migrated across the Atlantic, as the New Yorkers who drafted the Charter of Libertyes had long ago claimed.[56] Case law from across the empire held that military courts had jurisdiction only over members of the military and civilians serving it. Statutes endorsed this rule too. In the Mutiny Act for North America (1765), Parliament forbade the military from assuming criminal jurisdiction over civilians in the French cession. Nonetheless, the British routinely tried civilians during the American Revolution in military courts, and not only for military offenses. The uncertain loyalty of many civilians made military officers reluctant to leave civil authority in their hands, even in cases involving only loyalists. Consequently, the military administered criminal law and controlled civil dispute resolution.

To justify this extension of military authority, some officials claimed that the Prohibitory Act implicitly extended the jurisdiction of the military courts in the rebellious colonies. Others candidly invoked the principle of necessity.[57] In London, Judge Advocate General Charles Gould objected mildly to the trial of civilians in colonial military courts. In 1777, he wrote Commander in Chief Sir William Howe that while he understood "the necessity of executing speedy Justice," he felt compelled to "point out a material distinction . . . between Military persons, who are the proper and immediate objects of the Articles of War, and Civil persons, who are certainly not within the purview of them." But, having stated the law, Gould suggested how to avoid it: the military courts should "not . . . call attention to any of the Articles of War in the penning of their Sentence."[58] The customary interpretation of the Articles of War could be put aside. Necessity was sufficient ground for subjecting civilian loyalists in New York to military jurisdiction. This quick displacement of civil institutions revealed a fundamental difference between how creole loyalists and imperial officials viewed New York: the former saw a British province deserving English law, whereas the latter saw a hostile overseas outpost.

As soon as British forces subdued New York City and its environs, loyalists sought the restoration of imperial trading rights and civil government. To many of them, martial law was not law.[59] In October 1776, more than one thousand New Yorkers signed a petition to the Howe brothers, who were commanders of the army and navy as well as peace commissioners, asking them to restore trade and civil government in the city. The petition began as a loyalist answer to the Declaration of Independence. The merchants pledged "allegiance" to the king and conceded "the constitutional Supremacy of Great Britain, over these Colonies and other depending parts of his Majesty's dominions, as essential to the Union, Security, and Welfare, of the whole Empire." But they also requested the restoration of the city "to his Majesty's Protection and Peace." The signers were not disgruntled neutrals. They were prominent loyalists, including four members of the governor's council, supreme court justices Daniel Horsmanden and George Duncan Ludlow, Mayor Whitehead Hicks, Attorney General John Tabor Kempe, the present and future rectors of Trinity Church, a son-in-law of Governor Tryon, and hundreds of other lawyers, officeholders, and merchants. In his reply, Governor Tryon thanked them for their "attachment to the British Constitution" and promised to ask the peace commissioners to reestablish "the ancient Constitutional authority of Government."[60] The petition had no effect. At the beginning of the imperial conflict, when it remained in British eyes an insurrection, the loyalist plea found little reception.[61]

However, when France and Spain joined the rebels and the conflict became a global war, pacification of the colonies climbed the list of priorities. Officials in New York repeatedly recommended that civil government be restored, and the ministry sent back orders to do so when "convenient." But it never happened. A turning point seemed to come with the arrival of the Second Peace Commission under Lord Carlisle in 1778. After failing to negotiate a settlement with the Continental Congress, the commissioners recommended that Britain bypass that body and appeal directly to the colonists. The lure was the restoration of civil government, within the empire. The commissioners also reopened New York City and Newport to imperial trade. A chorus of pledges to restore civil government soon followed. After returning to London, two peace commissioners urged that civil government be restored "as far as practicable" to gain loyalist support. They also suggested joining several colonies "under one Government," perhaps giving them "a constitution like that of Ireland" or creating an intercolonial congress "in opposition to the usurped power." These and similar plans, however, came to naught. The situation in New York never seemed "ripe" for restoration.[62]

The model for restoration was Georgia, the centerpiece of "the southern strategy" to win loyalist support for the war. Restoration of civil government had begun in the south because there the loyalists outnumbered rebels. The trial never got far and weakened the already disastrous southern military campaign, which culminated in Lord Cornwallis's surrender in Virginia in 1781.[63] When the Georgia courts reopened, loyalists filed a civil suit against the military quartermaster for billeting troops in private homes "without the consent of a civil magistrate." To many, the prospect of civil litigation against the military was reason enough not to revive the courts elsewhere. Yet one New York loyalist believed that the challenge to the "unconstitutional act" in Georgia "was so far from operating as an objection against reviving the civil law, that it was one of the most forcible arguments that could be adduced in its favour." He maintained that restoration elsewhere would have stifled the rebellion. Instead, the British behaved in an "impolitic" way that was "repugnant to the Constitution, the spirit, the honour, and the sentiments of Englishmen."[64] Would restoration in New York have led to a different military outcome? Loyalists in and around the city might have responded as ambivalently as those in the south, but it is possible that the empire would have reaped large rewards from more favorable treatment of those taken for granted in the most secure city on the continent south of Quebec.[65] At least, vocal loyalists craved restoration, and they predicted great rewards would flow from it.

The trappings of civil government did not all vanish. There was still a crown-appointed civilian governor, William Tryon, a military man himself. But the Howe brothers asked him to keep "the executive powers of civil government dormant."[66] Two courts still operated: admiralty, which heard some of the wartime prize cases, and the governor's Prerogative Court, which issued marriage licenses and administered estates.[67] But the supreme court, chancery court, and local county courts did not meet. The bulk of civil administration was left to the commandant, a military officer appointed by the commander in chief. Ministers in London never sent instructions to discontinue the assembly, courts, or the other civil institutions. Indeed, Parliament in the Prohibitory Act assumed that civil government would continue. The act specified that only disloyal sectors should be put outside the king's peace, which meant that they could not trade with the rest of the empire. Parliament said nothing about military government.

The losers were the loyalists. For them, martial law was evidence of government gone awry and denied the colonists "the common law, the laws of the land, [and] the liberties and privileges of Englishmen."[68] Thomas Jones was representative of their plight. Jones was a lawyer, supreme court judge, historian, and scion of a prominent Long Island family. His grandfather was an Ulsterman of Welsh extraction who, though Protestant, fought for James II during the Glorious Revolution and then left for the American colonies, landing in Jamaica before moving to Rhode Island in 1692. There he married Freelove Townsend, the daughter of a Quaker merchant from Long Island. The couple settled on Long Island's north shore, where the Jones family spread roots and became prominent merchants, lawyers, and officeholders. The historian's father, David Jones, was a longtime member of the provincial assembly and a supreme court judge. In 1762 Thomas married Anne DeLancey, daughter of recently deceased Chief Justice James DeLancey, and built a large townhouse in New York City named Fort Pitt, in honor of the empire's recent success against the French. Family influence won Thomas the office of recorder of the city in 1767, which meant that he sat on the Mayor's Court. In the tradition of hereditary colonial offices, he replaced his father on the supreme court in 1773. The elder Jones built Thomas a substantial house on Oyster Bay, soon named "Tryon Hall," in gratitude to the governor. Its foundation stones were quarried in Rhode Island, its floorboards cut from southern pine, and the large elkhorns hanging in the entrance hall bagged in the Mohawk Valley, a gift from Sir William Johnson. The house symbolized the family's ascent and its dependence on the empire's fortunes. There was no reason for a young Thomas Jones to think that the trajectory would change. But the royal supreme court convened for the last time in 1776, and an ailing Jones fled to England in 1781. He died ten years later, after penning his *History of New-York during the Revolutionary War.*[69]

As a piece of exile retrospective, the *History* is reminiscent of those of Thomas Hutchinson and Peter Oliver, less satisfying in its assessment of the causes of the conflict (which Jones attributed to Presbyterianism and Yale College, his alma mater) but exceeding both in describing the war's effects. It is the record of one loyalist's gradual disenchantment with the empire while never seeing any alternative. For its acerbic sketches and endless vituperation (almost eight hundred pages when published a century later), there is nothing like it. Jones heaped invective on the "New York triumvirate" and other rebels, and his loyalty to the crown never wavered. But he was as critical of royal administration during the Revolution as any provincial pamphleteer had been before it. Jones believed that Britain never used adequate force against the rebels. Instead it abused loyal subjects. He offered the example of Oliver Cromwell, who succeeded in pacifying Ireland because he put "every soul to the sword." In contrast, the British never relied on their loyal colonists in America. Cromwell was a curious model for a crown loyalist, and most colonists had struggled to distinguish North America from Ireland. But Jones's point was that a timely counterattack in late 1776 might have saved all the colonies. It never came. The only fusillade was verbal. "The American rebellion was the first (I believe) in the universe attempted to be crushed, and reduced, by proclamations." Meanwhile, Jones estimated that sixty thousand loyal New Yorkers were denied "the liberties and privileges of Englishmen."[70]

The abridgment was particularly offensive in New York City. Its charter provided that the freemen's liberties and privileges would be guaranteed in "a *legal* court of law, before legal sworn judges" and "an honest, *legal*, jury of twelve men upon oath." But the Common Council and the Mayor's Court were disbanded, and the city's revenue was diverted toward the military governors and their favorites.[71] New York had become a "garrison town." Jones knew that there were garrisons throughout the British Empire, like Gibraltar and Portsmouth. But garrisons were usually limited to urban centers, and civilians there were not subjected to military law and "deprived of the laws of the land."[72]

The leading complaints were that the military government confiscated loyalist property without justification or compensation and that the civil courts were closed throughout the war. Jones lamented that New York's military governors established "arbitrary, illegal, despotic, and unconstitutional Courts, called 'Courts of Police,' " which were "in lieu of the Courts of common law."[73] The first of these juryless police commissions was established in New York City in May 1778. Superintendent Andrew Elliot, the longtime customs collector, now regulated an array of activities formerly handled by the Common Council and the Mayor's Court. He monitored cartmen; he licensed taverns, ferries, and pumps; he policed markets; he managed fire companies and night watchmen. He also set commodity prices and specifications in consultation with the chamber of commerce. Similarly, Elliot referred trade disputes to the chamber of commerce. If the parties did not obey the chamber's decision, which was rare, the case moved up the chain of authority to the commandant. Elliot tried not to confiscate too much rebel property because he feared upsetting arrangements with British creditors, but he rented some in lieu of taxes to provide for poor relief and other "exigencies."[74] There were repeated proclamations from military officials guaranteeing civilians that "they may obtain proper Redress" from the commandant or "the Officers commanding the nearest Post of his Majesty's Troops," but these men were often the source of civilian complaints.[75]

The appointment of James Robertson as governor in 1779 reactivated that office, and the crown instructed him to call an assembly as soon as he and his council thought fit, for it was London's intention "to allow them all the benefits of a local Legislature, & their former Constitution." In addition, Robertson was told to confiscate rebel land and give it to loyalist refugees, "those meritorious sufferers," who had lost property outside loyalist lines.[76] Upon arrival, Robertson established a council, appointed William Smith Jr. as the new chief justice, and promised to restore the full complement of courts and the assembly. He also ordered the expropriation of all rebel estates within British lines for "the use of his Majesty's loyal refugee subjects, such only *excepted* as should be wanted for his Majesty's service." Commodities needed for the war effort were to come from rebel estates first, then only if necessary from loyalists, who were supposed to receive compensation.[77]

But in the meantime, Robertson expanded the system of commission government. Under a compromise reached with Sir Henry Clinton, the governor would have the "management," subject to Clinton's "inspection," of additional commissions — one each for Staten Island and Long Island and another in the city to handle civil cases — to complement the original police commission.[78] In addition to general regulatory power, each commission had plenary jurisdiction to decide civil causes according to the principles of "equity and justice."[79] ("Equity" here had a lay connotation.) The Board of Enquiry, composed of three field officers and two magistrates of police, heard disputes between military officers and citizens. The board's decision went to the commandant, who enforced or dismissed it or sent it to a court-martial for further investigation. Civil disputes between citizens were decided by the police or through arbitration.

Though these police commissions were not courts, they functioned much like English local commissions. The new governor thought they made a difference. "[M]en who for years have had nothing they could call theirs," Governor Robertson reported to London, "find in security, and freedom [from] military misrule unspeakable blessings." The return of some civil government symbolized a future very different from the arbitrary government *outside* the loyalist sector. "The contrast between the happiness and order that has taken place within our limits," he wrote to Secretary of State for America Lord Germain, "and the anarchy tyranny and exactions exercised among the rebels, could not long escape observation." This persuaded Germain that partial restoration should "remove those unjust prejudices entertained of the vindictive disposition of Great Britain towards the revolted Provinces."[80]

Still, the commissions were creatures of the military. Thomas Jones thought that the commissioners were incompetent, corrupt, or both. Robertson was "a Jack-of-all-trades in the money-getting way" and possibly a pedophile. Elliot "had a large family, loved money, and was a Scot"; he was also "wholly unacquainted with the law." David Matthews, Elliot's assistant and mayor of the city, was "low in estimation as a lawyer, profligate, abandoned, and dissipated, indigent, extravagant, and luxurious, over head and ears in debt, with a large family as extravagant and voluptuous as himself, and no method of supplying his wants till this 'judicious' appointment." George Duncan Ludlow, the superintendent on Long Island, was a "tyrant." Admiralty judge Robert Bayard was "totally ignorant as to all matters of law." William Smith Jr. was competent but "hated Loyalists."[81]

Jealousy was at work here, for Jones received no new office. But Smith also criticized the military officers as "unfit . . . for Civil Trusts." He felt that most officials paid only lip service to the goal of restoring civil government. Andrew Elliot opposed civil government, thought Smith, because he wanted to retain the perquisites of his superintendency. Robertson claimed always to support the goal, but once he got "the Military Police under his Thumb," he too seemed "indifferent whether Civil Authority was set up."[82] The bar and most courts were gone; dispute resolution was left to military officers and their dependents. All officials answered to the commander in chief. Here was centralized administration beyond the imagination of even Cadwallader Colden.

Property rights suffered most. According to Jones, military officers expropriated loyalist property for the war effort because they had already taken rebel property for their own "ease, pleasure, diversion, and emolument." The military took all kinds of buildings: "sacred edifices, brewhouses, dwelling-houses, the college, barns, store-houses, and stables." These expropriations violated the English constitution because "by *magna charta* no man can be disseized of his freehold without a *legal* trial by his peers in a *legal* court of law." No trials were held and no compensation given.[83]

Jones recounted several cases, some of which involved his own property or that of relatives.[84] A revealing case was that of Micah Williams, "a young gentleman of fortune, character, and loyalty." Williams forbade an African American military driver to enter family property on Long Island to search for supplies. The driver reported the incident to his superior, who told the officer in charge of the foraging party. Williams was marched toward New York City for trial by a court-martial. "For what?" asked a disgusted Jones. "For kicking a negro runaway, in the very act of committing a trespass upon his uncle's property." Williams's friends interceded, and the military released him after he apologized to the officer and the driver. "Such cruelties did his majesty's loyal subjects suffer," a disgusted Jones recalled; "such insults were they obliged to bear."[85] Jones conceded the gravamen of the charge: Williams refused to allow the military to enter his family's property. But Jones assumed that a jury would have dismissed any complaint against the property holder, either on the grounds of defense against trespass or because the sole witness was black, possibly a former slave who joined the British military in return for a promise of freedom and who would have had no credibility in colonial courts.[86]

Some loyalists had greater claims to sympathy than Micah Williams. William Smith Jr. tried to prevent the expropriation of timber from the estate of loyalist Roger Morris, which his wife, Sarah Gouverneur Morris, needed to support herself while her husband was serving in the British military. When Smith told Governor Tryon that it was a crime "to destroy the property of King's friends," Tryon responded that the Morrises would be compensated. " 'Will they?' " asked Smith. " 'May be so,' says [Tryon], 'after the War is over' — with a Smile."[87] During the war military officers, including those holding civil offices like Tryon, did not fret over the daily travails of loyal civilians. Men as different as Jones and Smith agreed on two basic principles: loyalty itself, and the operation of the English constitution in even the rebellious colonies.

Martial law was an obscure strand of the English legal tradition. Jones may have learned about martial law in the other parts of the empire from Stephen P. Adye's *Treatise on the Courts-Martial*, published in New York in 1769. It was the only English treatise on martial law published in the eighteenth century and one of the very few legal treatises written and published in the colonies before the Revolution.[88] Adye claimed that, under the Articles of War, civilians on Gibraltar and elsewhere where there was "no Form of Civil Judicature" were tried in military courts for capital offenses. Actually, the Judge Advocate General's Office in London had long held that civilians on Gibraltar were *not* subject to military jurisdiction unless they were attached to the military. Adye was, however, not alone in believing that military courts could substitute for civil whenever practicable. Throughout the empire interpretations of jurisdictional provisions of the Articles of War varied.[89]

Adye's treatise offers another clue why martial law persisted so long in revolutionary New York: it followed many common-law ways, which closed some of the gap between martial and civil procedures. Adye, a second lieutenant stationed in New York after the Seven Years' War, lamented like so many imperial agents that London provided little instruction about overseas administration. He tried to fill the void for military justice.[90] It was time for a manual, and it was written where most needed: New York City, the British military headquarters in North America.

The book has two parts. The first treats martial law as a coherent body of law, examining the personal and subject matter jurisdiction of a military court and its procedures. Most British lawyers had harsh words for martial law, which they characterized as informal and capricious. Adye argued that martial law was not a renegade area of English justice but rather a cousin of the common law and shared fundamental elements with it. One example was the jury. In courts-martial, the jury comprised the defendant's peers, which in this context meant other military men, though usually superior in rank. True, a military jury required only a majority to convict, not unanimity. But Adye believed that this was an improvement because unanimous verdicts in common-law trials often resulted from judicial compulsion. Majority verdicts were purer.

Adye conceded that the Articles of War often did not specify procedures for trying violators. He proposed that where they did not, military courts should imitate the procedures of "the other established Courts of Judicature." Accordingly, he walked the reader through the elements of an English criminal trial, citing familiar common-law authors like Coke, Hale, Plowden, and Hawkins. It was a step-by-step guide to a military trial, from indictment to judgment and execution, that paralleled an English criminal trial.[91]

Whether military trials in wartime New York followed these recommendations is unclear. Since Adye was the local judge advocate general, it is reasonable to suppose that they did. The trials were not perfunctory. A record of military trials of civilians for criminal or martial offenses conducted in America during the war reveals that the vast majority (187 of 228) occurred in the southern part of New York, most of those in New York City. Just under half of the defendants were acquitted, though a few of these defendants received penalties anyway. Black defendants, for example, were deported to the West Indies, which probably meant that they were returned to slavery. Twenty-nine of the New York defendants were sentenced to death; three of those were pardoned.[92] It is, however, difficult to conclude from these numbers that civilians fared well in courts-martial, especially in light of the informal sanctions meted out by the military of the sort Thomas Jones noted in his *History*. Still, martial law was not arbitrary. These courts seem to have been just fair enough to prevent popular protest against them.

Although they were not arbitrary, even military officers conceded that courts-martial for civilians were temporary expedients. Momentum for the restoration of civilian justice gathered after Governor Robertson's arrival, but the timing never seemed right to those in charge. It was even unclear who had the authority to make that decision. Month after month, Robertson declared that restoration was an important strategy. "[A] loyal American Assembly," he wrote home in 1781, "might at this time hold to Americans a language useful to Britain." Yet he always deferred to Commander in Chief Clinton. For his part, Clinton assured William Smith Jr. that he was "as much for Civil Government as any Man and for the speedy Erection of it as soon as it consisted with the general Good." But eighteen months later he still believed there was "not Loyalty enough in the [loyalist] Lines for setting it up with Hopes of Success." Smith again argued that the suppression of civil government contributed to "the Disloyalty he apprehended to be within our Lines." What else could be expected? Smith asked Clinton "whether a County in England could be held quietly for a Month at Military Discretion." He assured the general that "Nothing would so terrify the Rebels as a Loyal Legislature — Nothing so thoroughly shift the People here as a grand Jury."[93] Representation and the common law were keys to the hearts and minds of New Yorkers. Like Smith, they believed that their colony possessed all the liberties of an English county.

Yet even Smith did not advocate a quick reestablishment of *all* civil institutions. Courts were one thing; legislatures another. There could no be no return to legislative government, he maintained in 1778, until New Yorkers again "united with Great Britain in Affection . . . and an aristocracy becomes a Part of our Establishment, to prevent the Revival of that spirit of Democracy, which [Britain] neglected till it acquired strength to shake and indanger the whole Empire."[94] For a decade, Smith had described the colonial mobs as Levellers. Like the imperial agents, he had come to believe that New York's constitution was unbalanced and that a local legislature could not be trusted. Smith, like Colden before him, recommended the establishment of a political caste instinctively loyal to the empire: "an aristocracy." In the meantime, an assembly could wait.

As defeat became clear in early 1782, Clinton relented and encouraged the immediate reestablishment of civil government "to quiet the minds of the loyalists." It was one of his last official statements before leaving America, and his reasoning was not clear. Other officials who earlier had inclined toward restoration, such as Governor Robertson, now doubted its wisdom. No one wanted responsibility for the decision. Clinton in particular, "wild and distressed" while preparing to return to London, was "wholly ingrossed by a justifying Review of his own Conduct and the Censure of others." The council too remained divided, with all but Smith agreeing "that the Present was not the proper Moment" for restoring civil courts. "What shuffling Conduct!" a frustrated Smith exclaimed.[95]

In London, the Marquis of Rockingham replaced Lord North in March 1782, and the new ministry decided to recognize the colonies' independence. Sir Guy Carleton, the new commander in chief, was instructed to prepare for evacuation. Restoration now played another role: proof to loyalists that they would not be abandoned in defeat. The catalyst was a court-martial of a loyalist accused of hanging a rebel. Carleton, on Smith's advice, thought that the defendant did not belong in a military court. Smith, Attorney General Kempe, and Chief Justice Frederick Smyth of New Jersey all recommended that Carleton erect a "Court of Errors" above "the lesser Distributions of Power" as a way to bring justice closer to "the Spirit of the Laws."[96] It might not have been coincidental that the highest court in the parallel state government of New York was named the Court of Errors, though this court was not yet functioning either.

William Smith remained the strongest advocate of restoration. He conceded that the exigencies of war might not permit the full operation of civil government; and he cautioned against restoration of the assembly if there was no "Determination" in London "to maintain this Post and the Controversy."[97] Still, Smith continued to urge restoration of the civil courts. First, as he had long argued, martial law was not "a Law, but Power exercised by Necessity for Government, Order and Discipline over the Army, and those of the opposite Army; and not upon others . . . when the King's Courts are open." A related reason was practical. Until restoration of civil government, all government officials, including himself, were operating beyond the authority of law and were therefore liable in common-law courts once they reopened, just like officials in Georgia. "[W]ho can hope for an indemnity," Smith asked, "that has proceeded against the Life of the King's Subjects, without his Authority?"[98]

Smith's criteria for legal or constitutional government (for him the two were identical) were not stringent. A quorum in the assembly would be impossible because several counties were beyond royal control. To surmount this problem, he suggested the creation of new cities and boroughs within the loyal sector to reach a quorum. He also recommended a trial period during which the army would continue to govern until the new assembly proved its ability to legislate responsibly. His models for this rump assembly were "the Convention Parliaments" of the English Civil War a century earlier, hardly the high point of representative government in English history.[99] Smith's point was that royal New York had not met even this standard. It was an extralegal regime. For years he hoped that the regime might be made legal, that the colonies could be reunited with the empire. As late as September 1782, he expressed faith that reconciliation could bring "the Common Salvation of the Empire."[100] His hope endured the peace treaty, first while he was exiled in London and then while serving as chief justice of Quebec. There in 1785, he wondered whether the American states would erupt in another "civil war," and a year after they had ratified the federal Constitution, Smith retained hope that the imperial breach could be "sewed up still, and that is no small consolation in this Region of self Deniance, Frost and Snow."[101]

Others in the British Empire looked forward rather than back. Historians are still unraveling the lessons that the British learned from the American Revolution. Most agree that administration grew stricter *outside* the British Isles, in places like India, the South Pacific, and later Africa and the Middle East. There were many strategies for avoiding another colonial revolution; building a strong administration around the executive was one of the most successful. Some of the framers of the second British Empire, like Lord Cornwallis in India, had cut their teeth in America.[102] The experience of martial law during the Revolution provided a positive and negative model for reform: positive because it permitted stronger executive government, but negative because of its effect on the morale of loyal subjects who saw themselves as Britons abroad. Government by executive commission became more common, and it was to administer its remaining colonies around the globe that nineteenth-century Britain developed its professional civil service. For decades imperial civil servants would struggle to find the right balance between firm and respectful governance and, more important, to distinguish between British settlers and indigenous peoples, between those who de-served English liberties and those who did not.

The failure to reestablish civil government in New York hampered British efforts to control New York and frustrated many loyal subjects. In practice, the revolutionaries did not always come much closer to the ideal of civil government. But they came much closer in theory. The new state constitution of 1777 was designed to accomplish what Smith wanted the British to do: reestablish the "ancient Government" of New York.

The State Constitution of 1777

We have a government, you know, to form;
and God only knows what it will resemble.
Our politicians, like some guest at a feast, are
perplexed and undetermined which dish to
prefer.
> John Jay (July 1776)

W HEN THE CONTINENTAL CONGRESS recommended in May 1776 that the rebellious colonies "adopt such Governments . . . as shall best conduce to the Happiness and Safety of their Constituents in particular and America in general," most of them began drafting new constitutions. Not since the English Civil War had Anglophone people tried to frame a republic: a representative government with no king. "We have a government, you know, to form; and God only knows what it will resemble," John Jay wrote from the New York Congress in July 1776. "Our politicians, like some guest at a feast, are perplexed and undetermined which dish to prefer."[1] In the end, however, the state government looked familiar. What New Yorkers created during their year of constitution making was much like the system its royal governors had described for decades to the Board of Trade. Most state framers replicated colonial government, straying here and there to fill the vacuum of royal authority, and even then resorting to English and imperial examples.[2] Framing the state government was novel and exciting, yet the drafters' goal was to confirm what they thought their constitution already was, or what it should have been. Still, much *had* changed: the framers had to imagine a government without a king, royal institutions, or crown officers. They sought to incorporate all that was useful in the old system, discarding what had brought them to rebellion. The new state therefore assumed enormous power. In place of the king were now the people. In place of crown charters and commissions was the state constitution.

The Continental Congress did not use the word "constitution" to describe the governmental plans, and New Yorkers did not apply that term to their efforts until April 1777.[3] "Constitution" did not just signify a written document outlining government; it retained its broader connotation as a vision of a healthy society. The document was only one part of a cluster of institutions and ideas about the rule of law that formed early state constitutionalism. When New York's framers discussed the project of making a new government, they used several familiar verbs: "constitute," with its legal and physiological connotations; "institute," calling to mind foundational laws; "frame" and "establish," old foundational metaphors; and the compound "new model," which conjured the English Civil War.[4]

On 24 May 1776, when New York's revolutionary congress considered the Continental Congress's recommendation, Gouverneur Morris proposed new elections to obtain a mandate for the task. Already, at least one New Yorker viewed "framing" a government as no ordinary task.[5] The Provincial Congress organized a committee to consider how to respond to the recommendation. The committee, which included John Morin Scott and John Jay, reported that the military's "unwarrantable hostilities" against the colonies had "dissolved" the royal government and necessitated "a new and regular form of government and police, the supreme legislative and executive power in which should, for the present, wholly reside and be within this colony, in exclusion of all foreign and external power, authority, dominion, jurisdiction, and pre-eminence whatsoever." But the committee, like Morris, believed that the Provincial Congress had no power to undertake the task. It had been established as a temporary expedient "for the sole purpose of opposing the usurpation of the British Parliament." Reconciliation was now, however, "uncertain." Because "the right of framing, creating, or new modeling civil government, is, and ought to be, in the people," the committee recommended a new election of representatives, which after the Declaration of Independence changed its name to the Provincial Convention. A group of mechanics also demanded that the public ratify the final draft. This was not accepted, but it too suggested the increasingly popular nature of constitution making.[6] The dynamics of sovereignty changed with the repudiation of the British Empire. The king gone, authority came from the people. The body that would draft the constitution was named a "convention," a title recalling extraordinary legislatures throughout English history.[7] It would, however, operate as the province's ordinary legislature too.

In these early days, few considered how the rule of law and the authority of the people would work in practice. Consent and fundamental law had long been complementary concepts in English constitutionalism. Amid war and government making, the ambiguity surrounding key terms such as "law," "people," and "constitution" allowed the various committees, congresses, and conventions to evade the question of which body best represented the people or had the power to declare fundamental law. The convention's relationships to the Continental Congress, the local committees that elected its members, and "the people" referred to in various resolutions were all uncertain. Yet several fundamental principles were clear to prominent New Yorkers. In September 1776, Peter R. Livingston, of the upper manor Livingstons, penned twelve "Maxims, as Fundamentall Principles on which this State ought to be erected." The first was that "all the Authority of a State can of Right be only derived from the People." His second maxim was more radical: "[E]very Member of the state should have a Voice in the Election of Representatives in General Assembly." Freeholders, however, deserved greater representation because "the burthen of supporting Government and defending the State" lay most heavily on them. Another maxim was that legislative, executive, and judicial powers should not be vested in the same people, and he emphasized the importance of independent judges. The right to petition government, the liberty of conscience, and the jury trial should all be protected.[8] Representation, separated powers, and assorted individual rights had long been central to Anglo-American constitutional ideas, and New Yorkers like Livingston made sure that they would be memorialized in the state's first constitution.

Although these "fundamental principles" of the constitution were clear, putting them together in one document took months. Because New York was a central theater of the war, the convention's first priority was to evade the British army. British troops chased it up the Hudson Valley, from New York City to White Plains, Fishkill, Kingston, and finally Poughkeepsie. This was, as historian Allan Nevins called it, "a government on the run."[9] New York's delegates in Philadelphia were alone in not signing the Declaration of Independence, for their instructions did not authorize them to do so. Back home, the Provincial Convention did approve the Declaration, concluding that independence was a "cruel necessity."[10] A month later the convention finally established a committee to draft a "frame of government." Matthew Adgate, a representative from Albany, moved that the committee first "prepare and report a bill of rights; ascertaining and declaring the essential rights and privileges of the good people of this State, as the foundation for such form of government." Gouverneur Morris criticized this proposal, but after some debate the convention decided that the bill of rights ought to be prepared "at the same time" as the "form of government." Implicitly, the two elements — the form of government and the bill of rights — were to be treated as the "foundation" of the government. In the end, however, the convention adopted no separate bill of rights, though many familiar English liberties were incorporated in the body of the constitution.[11]

The committee presented its draft to the convention in March 1777. The sections were read aloud, with emendations suggested orally along the way. Discussion of the plan took place when there was no pressing military business, often at the end of the day, then not again for several days.[12] The convention's journal lists proposed changes and the final votes on each section. Little debate was recorded. The preamble of the final draft consisted of the Continental Congress's resolution advising the colonies to form new governments, the Declaration of Independence, and the Provincial Congress's resolution to draft a new plan of government. It then declared that "all power . . . hath reverted to the people": they in turn authorized the convention "to institute and establish such a government as they shall deem best calculated to secure the rights and liberties of the good people of this state, most conducive of the happiness and safety of their constituents in particular, and America in general."[13] Fifty-two short articles followed. There was no explicit analytical structure, though similar matters were grouped together. The constitution began with the legislature, moved on to the governor and other leading officials, and concluded with a series of articles dealing with the courts and legal procedure — the same order the royal governors followed when they reported to the Board of Trade on the colonial constitution.

Beyond the republican premise that all authority came from the people, there were no striking innovations. Novelty lay in the details. Some of what was new reflected colonial protests against imperial government. But some innovations replaced institutions that were lost with the British Empire. New Yorkers could make do without the crown, but not without English liberties and the structures of empire. Similarly, and despite the resolution that all power resided within the province, the plan was premised on intercolonial union. The drafters referred to the Continental Congress in the preamble, and their assumption seems to have been that most authority would be local but that the province would also act, for limited purposes and voluntarily, in concert with its neighbors. Gradually, the province was shedding its colonial status and becoming a self-governing political unit: a "state."[14]

The Legislature

The first article of the constitution endorsed the principle of popular sovereignty: "[N]o authority shall, on any pretense whatever, be exercised over the people or members of this state, but as shall be derived from and granted by them." The next declared that "the supreme legislative power within this state shall be vested in two separate and distinct bodies of men," an assembly and a senate, each elected by qualified voters.[15] Members of the assembly sat for the fourteen counties. Sparsely populated counties like Richmond (later Staten Island) had only two representatives, while populous ones like New York and Albany had nine and ten, respectively. Senators represented four newly drawn senatorial districts. Election procedures for the lower house immediately sparked controversy. Gouverneur Morris proposed that election "by ballot" be struck from the committee's draft to preserve the colonial method of viva voce voting. Ballot voting would lessen the force of deference, as prominent men would not be able to supervise the voting of those around them. Morris's proposal was initially accepted, but John Jay pushed through a compromise in which the ballot would replace oral voting *after* the war, satisfying those who feared that secret ballots during the war would permit loyalists to undermine the new government. Then, after "a full and fair experiment," if the secret ballot "shall be found less conducive to the safety or interest of the state than the method of voting *viva voce*," the legislature was authorized to switch back on approval by two-thirds of each chamber.[16] The experiment was not reversed. This clause did, however, suggest that amendments normally had to be adopted through another method, such as a constitutional convention.

The senate replaced the colonial council in its capacity as an upper legislative house. The twenty-four senators were apportioned in four senatorial districts. The southern district, which included New York City, had nine senators, the middle and western districts had six apiece, and the eastern district had three. The convention rejected an amendment that would have forbidden the reduction of assembly representatives in a district and instead approved reapportionment of the assembly and senate every seven years to reflect population changes. In short, the convention embraced the principle of proportional representation. Though not mathematically precise and open to manipulation, apportionment would change with future censuses.[17]

The drafting committee initially provided that every male adult who paid taxes and resided in a county or city for one year would have been able to vote in assembly elections. When this draft was circulated privately, some commentators, like loyalist William Smith Jr., complained that this would leave the government "in the Hands of the Peasantry."[18] By the time the committee presented a full draft to the convention, it had added property qualifications for all voters. These were accepted with little change. Among officeholders, senators and governors had to be twenty-pound freeholders; there was no qualification for assemblymen. The convention retained the property qualifications for voting for the assembly: a voter had to pay taxes, reside in his county for at least six months, and possess a twenty-pound freehold, which was half the colonial requirement. The convention accepted Robert R. Livingston's proposal that tenants who rented land worth forty shillings a year receive the franchise. This provision, which tracked a colonial exception, covered long-term tenants like Livingston's own, who did not possess freeholds but had long voted in provincial elections. Similarly, "freemen" of the cities of New York and Albany retained the right to vote whether or not they met the freehold qualification. In contrast to the royal governor and his councillors, who had been appointed by the Privy Council, the governor and senators were elected. To vote for them, however, a man had to possess a freehold of one hundred pounds, a substantial barrier. In the state's early years, only about 10 percent of the adult male population met this requirement.[19] Finally, all voters had to pledge an oath of allegiance to the state.

The legislature had the "full legislative power," and by this the convention meant that the assembly "enjoy[ed] the same privileges, and proceeded in doing business, in like manner as the assemblies of the colony of New York of right formerly did." The assembly retained the power to name the state treasurer, ratifying a colonial development.[20] The assembly also held the power to impeach executive officials, though this required a supermajority of two-thirds.[21] All state officials, other than the chancellor, supreme court judges, and first judge of each county court, held their offices at pleasure until the next election and the recomposition of the appointing power — whether the governor, the assembly (in the case of the treasurer), or the Council of Appointment — or until impeachment.[22] These detailed provisions for the termination of officers resolved another divisive colonial issue.

The Governor

The 1777 constitution made New York's governor one of the strongest in the states. He served a three-year term, as opposed to one year in most other states, and, unlike every other governor except that of the renegade province of Vermont, was elected by voters. The governor had the power to prorogue the assembly and to pardon those convicted of crimes other than murder or treason; pardons for the last two required legislative concurrence. He also had "to inform the legislature, at every session, of the condition of the state" and "recommend such matters to their consideration as shall appear to him to concern its good government, welfare, and prosperity," which regularized the colonial tradition of gubernatorial addresses. In addition to being the chief executive, he was the "commander in chief of the militia, and admiral of the navy, of this state." He also had "to correspond with the Continental Congress, and the other states," one of the few references to intercolonial relations. Here, the governor was to play the role of continental diplomat, informing the legislature of interstate problems and recommending solutions. The role of the state's delegates to Continental Congress — who appointed? who instructed? — went unstated, though the assembly continued to exercise this power. Finally, the governor was to execute the laws faithfully. He had more authority than royal governors, though in sum the executive branch was less powerful than its colonial predecessor, which had included the Privy Council in London. The governor did not hold a legislative veto or power of appointment. These were exercised by two new councils, and the governor was a member of both.[23]

Whitehall to New York: The Councils of Revision and Appointment

The Council of Revision and the Council of Appointment were unique to New York and filled gaps created by the loss of imperial government. The Council of Revision domesticated the Privy Council processes of judicial appeal and legislative review, and the Council of Appointment brought patronage wholly within New York's borders. Because each council comprised at least some elected officials, they were accountable to the people in a way that the Privy Council, no matter how accessible to colonial interests, never was. Yet New Yorkers retained some aspects of the Privy Council, which had on balance treated the province favorably, for example, in boundary disputes with neighbors.[24] New Yorkers, more than people in any other state, embraced conciliar government.

The Council of Revision was not part of the committee draft. Robert R. Livingston Jr. proposed it as a way to review and reject legislation that violated the constitution or "the public good." The convention quickly accepted his proposal.[25] Immediately creole elites like Livingston expressed reservations about the large amount of power held by the legislature and reconstituted something like Privy Council review to check that power. The council comprised the governor, supreme court justices, and the chancellor. It was to review all legislation and return those statutes "inconsistent with the spirit of this Constitution, or with the public good" to the legislature with written objections. These objections were entered in the minutes of each house, which could then reconsider the statutes. Together they could override the veto with a two-thirds vote in each.[26]

Some historians view the Council of Revision as a check on the popular impulses of the Revolution.[27] No doubt some antidemocratic sentiment informed the convention's fear of "hasty and unadvisable" legislation. But most state constitutions provided for some sort of veto, usually in the governor alone, and the striking feature of the New York process is its familiarity. The Council of Revision reviewed legislation to ensure it was not "repugnant" to state law, a standard reminiscent of that applied by the Privy Council in the colonial period. Like the Privy Council, the membership of the Council of Revision changed over time, though the New York council depended on elections and changes in the court personnel.

Neither New York council fitted well into the emergent theory of separated powers. The governor and the senate shared the appointment power in the Council of Appointment. The Council of Revision exercised a veto power that was associated with the executive, yet its members were senators and judges. The standards for review were likewise unclear. The Privy Council had disallowed statutes that it believed violated English law, though whether because of reasons derived from fundamental law or policy it is difficult to say. The New York council too could object for constitutional or political reasons.

But the Council of Revision did have to *give* reasons. Unlike the Privy Council, the New York council had to return written objections to the legislature. These written objections encouraged the development of a jurisprudence of repugnancy. In contrast, the Privy Council's opinions were brief and rarely circulated outside Whitehall. Although the Council of Revision never developed a firm theory of precedent or cited its past opinions, over the years it repeated some objections in almost identical language. To give just one example, the council continually objected to revenue statutes that did not provide standards for tax assessment but rather left such to the discretion of local assessors. It always did so by criticizing "unbounded power" and invoking the principle of no taxation without representation that lay "at the foundation of the late happy Revolution."[28] In addition, and again unlike the

Privy Council, its decisions were not final. The legislature mustered super-majorities to repass almost a third of the bills the council rejected — never an option in the British Empire.[29]

In practice, the Council of Revision approved most laws formulaically, reporting to the legislature that a statute "does not appear improper." When the council did object to a bill, it often provided more than one reason. Sometimes the basis was the constitution; other times it was common law, policy, or fundamental law. An example is the council's rejection of the legislature's first Forfeiture and Confiscation Act in 1779, which targeted loyalist property.[30] The council's objection rested on fundamental law defined in reference to Anglo-American tradition: the act was "repugnant to those plain and immutable laws of justice, which no State can with honor throw off." One of those immutable laws was the trial by jury, which the state constitution protected. The Forfeiture and Confiscation Act, the council concluded, "convicts and punishes the persons named in the bill without affording them an opportunity of availing themselves of a trial by jury." In addition, the statute was "obscure and contradictory." It also entrusted the forfeiture commission with too much discretion, and its "means for carrying it into executions are inadequate to the end." Finally, the council invoked social policy: the act did "not pay proper attention to the circumstances of the less wealthy subjects of the State." Buyers had only one month to pay for the confiscated land. Because "many industrious farmers" would not be able to raise the cash that quickly, the "confiscated property [would] be vested in a few monopolizers and merchants."[31] In short, the council interpreted its mandate broadly and challenged legislation for a variety of reasons. Repugnancy did not mean a direct contradiction with the constitution, absurdity, or impossibility. Rather, it had a looser meaning that covered a range of objections. In this jurisprudence of repugnancy, the constitutional was mixed with the political.

Over the years this power of review drew much criticism that culminated in the abolition of the council in 1821. Some critics complained that the council obstructed legislation, while others objected that its hybrid structure violated the principle of separated powers. Nonetheless, during its forty-four-year existence the council's 165 well-articulated vetoes gave New Yorkers much experience with an institution that reviewed legislation and upheld most statutes while rejecting some. When New York lawyers began to challenge state statutes, they made the same sorts of arguments to courts about the limits of legislative power. While there are few smoking guns connecting the conciliar process and judicial review, discursively at least the Council of

Revision's objections formed a bridge between the imperial review of colonial statutes and judicial review in the new state.

The Council of Appointment inspired more debate because it raised the critical issue of patronage. Gouverneur Morris proposed "that all civil officers not eligible by the people be appointed by the governor and the judges of the supreme court." He soon recanted, asking "[w]hether it would be wise to authorize or permit that the people have a voice in the nomination or appointing of any of the officers." This question led John Jay to propose the Council of Appointment to fill all offices whose mode of appointment was not established by the constitution.[32] The assembly nominated one senator from each of the senatorial districts; these four men formed the council. The governor presided and had "a casting voice, but no other vote, and, with the advice and consent of the said council, shall appoint all of said officers." Like the Council of Revision, this council was unique among the states and domesticated a function of the Privy Council. The goal was to limit the governor's power to appoint executive officers and the power of those officers to select their subordinates. Jay used court clerks as an example to demonstrate the salutary effect of a Council of Appointment. If judges appointed their own clerks, they would be "*tempted* not only to give those appointments to their children, brothers, relations, and favourites, but to continue them in office against the public good." Dependence would breed collusion; all members of the judiciary would combine to conceal "mutual defects or misdemeanours." But if the council appointed clerks, the electoral process could check abuses. If a councillor promoted his "favourites," the appointees would lose their jobs once the patron was "removed from the Council."[33] Council members were elected representatives who would face the public at election time. If they neglected the public's interest, the electorate would punish them. They were more accountable than judges, who Jay could not imagine would ever be elected by the people.

Soon the council did more than simply confirm or deny gubernatorial nominees. In the 1790s, as political tensions mounted, a Republican governor sat with Federalist senators on the council, and the senators claimed that they too had the power to nominate officers. When Governor George Clinton refused to nominate Federalist Egbert Benson to the state supreme court, Benson's supporters on the council nominated him anyway, leaving the governor with only a casting vote, and the senators then outvoted the governor. After the 1795 election, in which Federalist John Jay won the governorship, Republican senators turned the Federalist strategy on its inventors.

They too claimed a concurrent right of nomination, thus frustrating Federalist attempts to reward supporters with patronage. Jay—the council's architect—argued that the drafters had intended for the governor to have the sole right of nomination. He failed to persuade the other members of the council. The controversy culminated in a constitutional convention, the first since 1777, to settle the distribution of power within the council. The convention granted each councillor a concurrent power of nomination, turning the body into a machine for partisan appointment: the party that controlled the senate would control appointments.[34] Parties took the place of patrons, and "favourites" were now called "loyal party members." For two more decades, the council was an instrument of party discipline and the source of endless criticism.

Courts and Common Law

Only two articles in the 1777 constitution mentioned the state judiciary. Article XXIV gave judges good behavior tenure, limited only by a mandatory retirement age of sixty.[35] This altered the prevailing colonial standard, tenure at will. In addition, the office of the chancellor was separated from the governor, which ended the executive's control over equity courts, another source of contention in the colonial period. Article XXXII established the Court of Impeachments and Correction of Errors as the state's highest tribunal. Before the Revolution, there had been two courts of review atop the provincial supreme court. The governor and his council constituted the highest court within the colony, and errors could also be taken to the Privy Council in London. The state constitution replaced them with this single high court that would review errors from the common-law courts and appeals from the chancellor, as well as try impeached officials. Like the royal high courts, this tribunal contained some who were not full-time judges. It included senators, supreme court judges, and the chancellor, though the judges and chancellor were excluded from reviewing their own judgments in the lower courts.[36]

These spare provisions suggest that the framers expected the province's judicial system to continue with little change. From town and county courts to the supreme court, the state judiciary mirrored its colonial predecessor. Several of these courts operated during the war. Those that did not probably could not. The new state supreme court met first in September 1777, Chief Justice John Jay presiding. The minutes reveal that the "usual proclamations were made" for the sheriffs to return writs of process and for all justices of the peace, coroners, and grand jurors to come to court.[37] "Usual," because the court used the same words, titles, and forms as had the colonial supreme court. When it retrieved the official journal from the British after the war, the court made sure that its minutes were transcribed into it, and the clerk left only a few blank pages between the royal court's last session in April 1776 and the state court's first the following year, just as clerks has always done between sessions. The state legislature soon enacted a law "further to organize the Government" in which it instructed that "the Supreme Court of Judicature of this State, and the Inferior Courts of Common Pleas, and the Courts of General or Quarter Sessions of the Peace, in the several Counties within this State, shall be held on, and at such Days and Times, as they were respectively held [before the Revolution]." Paper documents sufficed; parchment was scarce. The seal was new, and writs now ran in the name of the people of New York, not the king. But otherwise procedures continued as before, as best they could and where they could, given the war.[38] This meant that the court exercised jurisdiction only over those counties beyond the reach of the British military. For example, during its brief sitting in September 1777, the supreme court heard only criminal cases from Ulster County, where it sat. It heard only cases from the northern counties when it sat in Albany from 1778 to 1780. The court's docket remained limited during the war and did not draw cases from the whole state until 1782.[39] Otherwise, there was at first little revolution in the courts.

The legal baseline did not change, either. The constitution provided that "such parts of the common law of England, and of the statute law of England and Great Britain, and the acts of the legislature of the colony of New York, as together did form the law of the said colony" in April 1775, when violent resistance began, "shall be and continue the law of this state, subject to such alterations and provisions as the legislature of this state shall, from time to time, make concerning the same."[40] This was not a reception provision but instead "an affirmation that New York would use in the future what it had wrought for itself in the past."[41] The drafting committee had simply stated that "the common law" was the law of New York, but in the convention Robert Yates proposed the limitation of "such parts of the common law" that formed the colony's law and to exclude those parts that had never applied.[42] Which parts applied and which did not created controversy for decades in the future, as in the past. But the New York framers explicitly mentioned core parts of the common law. They preserved trial by jury and prohibited the legislature from creating any new courts except those "as shall proceed according to the common law," two contentious issues during the colonial period.[43] In addition, the constitution gave those indicted for "crimes or misdemeanors" the right to have counsel, an emergent common-law right not widespread in colonial New York and that remained unavailable to defendants in summary actions in the new state.[44] The convention also guaranteed all land and corporate charters granted by the king before 14 October 1775, the date on which Governor William Tryon decided to flee New York City for a naval ship in the harbor.[45] When the king's representative fled, the convention concluded, so went the king's dominion over New York's land. Along with the king, the convention also "rejected" those parts of the common law supporting monarchy and the established Church of England because they were "repugnant to this Constitution."[46] This was part of a larger scheme of religious toleration, which was perhaps the greatest innovation in New York's constitution.

Religious Toleration and the Corporate Charter

The sections of the constitution involving religious toleration were among the most contentious. All in New York's convention agreed to eliminate the partial establishment of the Anglican Church, and most agreed in principle about religious toleration. Debate focused on how far that principle reached and whether it applied to those who were not Protestants. In addition, the debaters asked how far, exactly, the state's power to regulate reached into the private affairs of its citizens. Most members of New York's convention assumed that the state had full sovereignty without stopping to consider how far this logic ran. What, for example, was the status of corporations within the state? Could the state government control them at will? The state convention resolved none of these issues conclusively, but it began to explore the lines between state power and the freedom of voluntary associations, between the public and the private, that would be defined and redefined throughout the nineteenth century.[47]

The final articles about religious worship emerged from a compromise involving three of the most powerful figures in the state: John Jay, an Anglican of Huguenot ancestry; Robert R. Livingston Jr., an Anglican of Scottish, Dutch, and English background; and Gouverneur Morris, similarly mixed but at the time a deist. The result was a liberal provision guaranteeing the freedom of worship. The most remarkable aspect of the controversy was the consensus in the convention that the constitution should forbid the establishment of any denomination and guarantee religious toleration. Such notions had circulated in the province since the King's College controversy two decades earlier and were on most New Yorkers' short list of (as Peter Livingston called them) "fundamental principles." The original draft provided toleration "to all denominations of Christians without preference or distinction and to all Jews, Turks and Infidels, other than to such Christians or others as shall hold and teach true Doctrines [or] principles incompatible with and repugnant to the peace, safety and well being of civil society."[48] Without debate, the Anglican Church lost its privileged position as the established church in southern New York; no longer would it receive tax support from four counties as it had for eighty years. Although the convention deleted the reference to "Jews, Turks and Infidels," it did provide that all Christian denominations would be equal under the law, except for those that were "repugnant to the peace, safety and well being of civil society."[49]

The target of the last clause was Catholicism. Since 1690, instructions to the royal governors had provided that they were "to permit a liberty of conscience to all persons except Papists," and while there were Catholics throughout the province, officially they could not vote or hold office.[50] John Jay spearheaded the effort to continue the exclusion, perhaps inheriting a fear of the Catholic Church from his Huguenot ancestors. He proposed suffrage and office-holding qualifications excluding anyone from a "sect . . . who inculcate and hold for true doctrines, principles inconsistent with the safety of civil society, of and concerning which the Legislature of this State shall from time to time judge and determine." This broad legislative power met with opposition. Jay then narrowed the test oath so that it applied only to Catholics. They, he wrote, "ought not to hold lands in, or be admitted to a participation of the civil rights enjoyed by the members of this State, until such time as the[y] . . . most solemnly swear, that they verily believe in their consciences, that no pope, priest or foreign authority on earth, hath power to absolve the subjects of this State from their allegiance to the same." The oath would have denied Catholics even the right to own property unless they swore allegiance to the state. It also would have forced Catholics to renounce the sacrament of penance, another source of anxiety among Reformed Protestants. The convention rejected Jay's oath.[51]

The day after Jay proposed his oath, Robert R. Livingston Jr. suggested a milder condition: the state would tolerate all religious sects "provided that this toleration shall not extend to justify the professors of any religion in disturbing the peace, or violating the laws of the State." The convention rejected this too but accepted a similar proposal that "the liberty of conscience hereby granted, shall not be construed to encourage licentiousness, or be used in such a manner as to disturb or endanger the safety of the

State."[52] The convention also declared that "civil tyranny" and "spiritual oppression," or "wicked priests and princes," went hand in hand. In a related provision, clergymen were prohibited from civil and military office within the state so that they were not "diverted from the great duties of their function."[53] The goal was to prevent religious oppression in the public sphere *and* to prevent the deflection of ministerial energy from the private. The convention did not, however, build a wall separating religion and government.

Indeed, some ministers wished to have constitutional protection for all denominations, or at least all Protestant ones. In the weeks leading up to the final vote on the state constitution, Robert R. Livingston Jr. and fellow drafters circulated copies among several men not in the legislature.[54] One correspondent was Reverend John Henry Livingston, Robert's second cousin and a minister in the Dutch Reformed Church. Reverend Livingston applauded the proposed guarantee of toleration but warned that it did not do enough to encourage religion. He felt that, although it was unwise to provide public funds for any religious denomination, some legal protection was necessary to help churches support themselves. The minister recommended that the state permit all churches to incorporate on an equal basis. Incorporation would allow congregations to hold property in common and perpetually so that each could become financially secure — or fail through lack of popular support. Incorporation of churches was not a new idea. Throughout the colonial period congregations had applied to the governor and council for church charters, which were almost always granted.[55] John Henry Livingston's next recommendation was new: the constitution should declare that all religious sects were already corporations to save them the expense and hazard of petitioning the legislature for special charters. "Why is not care taken to secure this object without any risk and trouble," the minister asked his cousin, "by weaving the privilege into the very Constitution of Government?" Livingston also assumed that the state government would not have the power to revoke these constitutional charters; rights embedded in the constitution would be beyond the reach of the legislature. The state would be neutral as each sect flourished or perished without tax support on the one hand or discriminatory treatment on the other. "This would be providing for religion," the minister reasoned, "and yet leaving it to the industry and character of each sect to take care of itself."[56] As the New York triumvirate had argued twenty-five years earlier in support of a nonsectarian college charter, government ought not participate in the competition between denominations for popular support.[57]

Robert Livingston objected that constitutionally incorporated churches might become too strong and too rich and compete with the state government for political power. Such fears were ancient; they lay behind the maxim condemning *imperium in imperio*. In addition, each church was already free to hold property without a charter, which only provided "a legal right to what they voluntarily devote to the cause of religion, to the reversion of which the State can have no claim." The state would never have a reversion because corporations lived in perpetuity, keeping their property intact forever. His cousin responded that the state might limit the wealth of a church "to moderate bounds." But this was unnecessary because the property of each denomination would "bear but a small proportion to the property of the State." In addition, John Henry Livingston assumed that churches would be responsible for establishing most of the grammar schools and academies in the state. Accordingly, allowing churches to accumulate property was "perhaps the best way of promoting schools."[58]

Nor was the fear of encouraging "too many little sects" a valid objection to general incorporation. Sectarianism was no concern of government. Denominations always multiplied "in a free country." In contrast "the idea of forcing mankind into an union of Sentiment by any machine of State is altogether preposterous," Reverend Livingston maintained, "and has done more harm to the cause of the gospel than the sword of persecution has ever effected." The problem was not the prospect of too many denominations but rather that an established church would stifle the pursuit of true religion while subsidizing a false one.[59] In other words, a spineless establishment, not an oppressive one, was the great evil. The Reformed minister's target was deism: "foolish Deism is perhaps now as characteristic as Bigotry formerly was; the two extremes come near to each other." To meet this challenge, religious worship required more insulation from state government, and the minister believed that protection should be embedded in the constitution.[60]

For Reverend Livingston as for John Jay, Catholicism was an exception. Catholics deserved the freedom to worship too, but John Henry Livingston wanted them to pledge that they would not submit to any "foreign jurisdiction . . . in things temporal or spiritual whatsoever." The Catholic Church was more than a religion: "[I]t is the most refined combination of spiritual and temporal powers that ever was formed."[61] This distinction between the temporal ambition of the Catholic Church and the spiritual purity of Protestant sects was an old trope from the Reformation. But when linked to disestablishment and liberal incorporation laws, it helped draw a new line between public and private spheres in America. The Catholic Church, the argument proceeded, sought to control government, while Protestant ministers tended to the spiritual needs of their congregants and influenced public policy only indirectly. Protecting the government from a designing church, and shielding churches from a meddling government, was a constitution's purpose.

John Henry Livingston failed to persuade his cousin and the convention to include a clause in the constitution that automatically incorporated churches. However, in 1784 the assembly passed a statute allowing any church to incorporate upon a simple application. It was possibly the first free incorporation law in the Anglophone world and a model for many others in the nineteenth century. The legislature referred to the constitution's guarantee of "the free exercise and enjoyment" of religion and "the duty of all wise, free and virtuous governments, to countenance and encourage virtue and religion." It also criticized "the illiberal and partial distributions of charters of incorporation to religious societies" during the colonial period. Any sect could receive a charter as "a body politic and corporate," hold property collectively to a maximum of twelve hundred pounds income per year, and sue in the courts.[62] Incorporation was no longer the privilege of churches with political clout. The disestablishment-free incorporation nexus (as Akhil Reed Amar calls it) spread among the states, the territories, and finally, by the mid-nineteenth century, everywhere in the Union.[63]

When the convention rejected John Jay's limitation on worship, he sought to achieve the same end of restraining the Catholic Church by restricting naturalization. Before 1789, naturalization was a provincial matter. The colonies had enjoyed the power to naturalize inhabitants within their borders, and so did the new states.[64] The convention accepted Jay's proposal that those seeking naturalization renounce "all allegiance and subjection to all and every foreign king, prince, potentate and state, in all matters ecclesiastical as well as civil." Jay's design was to prevent Catholics from becoming citizens. He immediately realized, however, that the provision could hinder operation of the Dutch Reformed Church, which corresponded with its home church in the Netherlands. He added an exception providing that "nothing herein contained shall be construed to interfere with the connection heretofore subsisting between the Dutch congregations in this State and the classes and synods in Holland." But the Dutch congregants were not the only Protestants who belonged to an international church. Jay then proposed a broader exception for all connections between "non-episcopalian congregations . . . [and] their respective mother churches," as well as that of "the episcopalian churches now in this State, except as involve a foreign subjection." The convention rejected all these qualifications. Jay finally proposed that the legislature be empowered to regulate naturalization, perhaps hoping that it would restrict Catholic immigration. But the convention kept the constitutional naturalization oath, which demanded applicants to "abjure and renounce all allegiance and subjection to all and every foreign king, prince, potentate, and state, in all matters, ecclesiastical as well as civil."[65] In other words, citizenship required renunciation of all loyalty to any European institution. Jay's maneuvers reveal once again the assumption that this convention could bind ordinary legislators. Future legislators could regulate immigration and naturalization, but they could not abolish the constitutionally prescribed oath. The Council of Revision would enforce the limitation, so too the electorate. Otherwise, little was said of enforcement.

English Liberties and New York's Minorities

New York's convention did not pass a separate bill of rights.[66] However, many provisions, like those dealing with religious toleration, affected the rights of individuals and local governments: the right to a jury trial, the prohibition of acts of attainder except for crimes during the war, the religious toleration clauses, the militia clause, the freedom of debate in the legislature, the right of counsel in criminal and impeachment trials, and a clause derived from Magna Carta stating that "no member of this state shall be disenfranchised or deprived of any rights or privileges secured to the subjects of this state by this constitution, unless by the law of the land, or the judgment of his peers." Finally, the convention also enjoined the state government to establish only such courts as allowed by the common law.[67]

In the procedurally oriented world of the eighteenth century, structures that protected rights were themselves rights. Many of these constitutionalized rights were procedural rights defending local decision making and stood as memorials to colonial experience. New Yorkers had fought the Revolution in large part to keep these liberties. And, in traditional manner, some of the rights implied duties. The militia clause, for example, enjoined the state to arm and prepare the militia. It also implied that all adult males must be available for service, excepting Quakers, who paid a fine in lieu of service.[68]

The convention was at least as concerned with shielding localities and the state from external authority as it was with protecting individual rights. When it came to the Continental Congress, the New York framers simply assumed that the state had jurisdiction over all land purchases from Native Americans. Because of the importance of "peace and amity with the Indians" for the state's safety, Jay proposed a section protecting them from fraudulent purchases made during war. No land purchases from the Native Americans were valid unless made with authority of the state government.[69] This put New York on a collision course with the Confederation Congress over Indian diplomacy. The Articles of Confederation, ratified four years later, provided that Congress had the power to regulate "all affairs with the Indians *not members of any of the states*, provided that the legislative right of any state within its own limits be not infringed or violated." Which of the Iroquois were not "members" of New York? James Madison and others reasoned that only those who were not living as members of Indian political societies fell into this category, but a broader interpretation that included all Indians within a state's borders was possible, and the Clinton administration bought land as it pleased.[70] The state did not want settlers and speculators stirring resentment among the Iroquois, most of whom had remained loyal to the British Empire. Neither did the state want to cede control over such land sales to the Continental Congress.[71]

The state constitution also addressed slavery and its abolition. At the time of the Revolution, New York was the largest slave-owning state north of Maryland, and New York City was almost 20 percent unfree. Gouverneur Morris proposed a section committing the state to gradual abolition, invoking natural rights, religion, and Lord Mansfield's recent dictum in *Somerset's Case*:

> WHEREAS a regard to the rights of human nature and the principles of our holy religion, loudly call upon us to dispense the blessings of freedom to all mankind: and inasmuch as it would at present be productive of great dangers to liberate the slaves within this State: It is therefore most earnestly recommended to the future Legislatures of the State of New-York, to take the most effectual measures consistent with the public safety, and the private property of individuals, for abolishing domestic slavery within the same, so that in future ages, every human being who breathes the air of this State, shall enjoy the privileges of a freeman.[72]

Once again, common-law rhetoric was pulled from its context and transformed into constitutional principle.[73] The convention accepted the proposal to commit the state to gradual abolition but added that during the "present situation" it would be "highly inexpedient to proceed to the liberating of slaves."[74] The proposal reflected the optimism of the moment of independence. Yet optimism was tempered by concern for the property rights of slave owners and the fear of disorder that might accompany abolition.

White New Yorkers were not the constitution's only audience. Beginning with Lord Dunmore's proclamation in Virginia in November 1775, the British government offered slaves freedom if they left their American masters and fought for the British. The commandant in New York did not make such an offer until 1779, but all had heard the news from Virginia. When they did, legislators in New York and New Jersey tried to match the offer and passed laws forbidding the arrest of slaves who fled from their masters in royal territory.[75] As for slaves within state-controlled territory, the constitution offered the prospect of freedom sometime in the future if they remained loyal to their owners.

The New York drafters spent little time debating what are now called individual rights. Traditional English liberties, like freehold representation, the jury, and due process in the legal system, figured large in their minds. So too did issues arising from the imperial conditions of New York: slaves and Native Americans were all over New York; its constitution necessarily took account of them. Indeed, in a moment of relative hope, the state's framers imagined a place free of slavery. They also tried to ensure that settlers would not, as in the past, buy land fraudulently from the Native Americans. Whether the state itself would do so remained an open question for years.

Constitutional Politics, 1777–1787: Antiloyalist Legislation, Rutgers v. Waddington, and the Road to Philadelphia

Throughout the war, the relationship between the state and the Continental Congress, and then Confederation government, was unclear. The Articles of Confederation bound the states to congressional requisitions, and New York met most requisitions. Few people, however, analyzed the problem of overlapping jurisdiction.[76] Alexander Hamilton was among the first to assess the limitations of the Confederation. Its inability to raise money directly was its greatest weakness. His desire to bolster the central government's power to tax was as much a matter of practice as principle: there were no Confederation tax collectors to rely on, and state collection was inefficient.[77] From the standpoint of central administration, the situation was worse than before the Revolution. Then, there at least had been imperial tax collectors. This administrative network had contributed to the Revolution, and the states were reluctant to cede the newly won power to control tax collection. New York, in particular, was dependent on the excises it collected in its port. In sum, there was no Confederation administrative infrastructure and no way to legitimate one if it could be built.

Hamilton complained while still serving as Washington's aide that the Continental Congress was at the mercy of states. In a long letter to James

Duane in 1780, he outlined many themes that he developed over the next decade, including criticism of state legislation and a plea for what he called more energetic government. In colonial eyes, an imbalance of power and liberty (or at least *liberties*) had caused the Revolution. The balance now, however, had tilted too far toward liberty. There was "a want of power in Congress," Hamilton complained, and "an excess of the spirit of liberty" in the states. In 1780 the particular problem was that several states refused to meet requisitions, and Congress had no power to levy taxes. Hamilton located the cause where those with imperial vision always had: in the provincial constitutions. "The forms of our state constitutions," he wrote Duane, "make it too difficult to bend them to the pursuit of a common interest." The remedy was to reform central governance — what he called the "empire." Hamilton contrasted two types of empires. The first was "an empire under one simple form of government, distributed into counties provinces or districts, which have no legislatures but merely magistratical bodies to execute the laws of a common sovereign." The danger in these empires was that "the sovereign will have too much power to oppress the parts of which it is composed." He gave no example to Duane, but elsewhere he explained that the Roman Empire had conquered the Grecian republics "by sowing dissensions among them" and argued that the European empires would do the same to the American states. The other type of empire was of "confederated states each with a government completely organised within itself." The examples were the American states, the Greek republics, the Swiss cantons, the Germanic empire, and the United Provinces of the Netherlands. Here the danger was "that the common sovereign will not have power sufficient to unite the different members together, and direct the common forces to the interest and happiness of the whole." The remedy was to retrieve "the power of the purse" and bring "method and energy in the administration." He was ready with one proposal: a national bank like that in England.[78]

Control over tax collection on goods imported into the port of New York was pivotal. Though most New Yorkers supported the first Confederation impost in 1781, peace with Britain increased rivalries among the states. Governor George Clinton and his followers in the assembly repealed the state's approval of the congressional impost, which was supposed to last for twenty-five years, because they hoped to use a state impost to settle New York's large wartime debts. More objectionable than the central impost itself was the appointment of congressional collectors. Men like Abraham Yates considered congressional collectors to be tools of a foreign government. Confederation control of impost collection would destroy the states and "*fuse*" them into a despotic "overgrown Republic." The legislature that agreed to the plan would "*sign the death warrant of American Liberty!*"[79] Hamilton, writing under the pseudonym "Continentalist," had confirmed the first half of Yates's fears: congressional officials would indeed "create in the interior of each state a mass of influence in favor of the federal government." The assembly agreed to give the Confederation Congress part of the imposts but demanded that they be collected by New York officials, who would be subject only to the jurisdiction of New York courts. Congress rejected the compromise, and New York retained all imposts collected in its port for the rest of the decade.[80] It was during this debate that the term "anti-federal" emerged as a label for those who opposed giving the central government more power.[81]

New York's western land claims created a similar tension between the state and the Confederation Congress. On the basis of the Duke of York's 1664 patent and the Stanwix Treaty of 1768, the state government claimed ownership of much of the Ohio Valley.[82] This land claim also involved a dubious interpretation of the 1783 peace treaty. Under the treaty, the British military promised to cede its western forts "with all deliberate speed." Governor George Clinton wanted to negotiate directly with the British to ensure that the forts were handed over to his government, not to the Confederation. Clinton sent a secret emissary to Canada in March 1787, but British governor general Frederick Haldimand refused to meet with the emissary; he would deal only with the Confederation Congress. This fed fears within the state that Congress wished to strip New York of its western land.[83]

With its imposts and western land claims, New York was one of the most obstructionist states in the Confederation. Its policies also polarized people within the state, and consequently New Yorkers were among the first to propose revision of the Articles of Confederation. In 1782, Senator Philip Schuyler, who was Hamilton's father-in-law, proposed a resolution that "the radical Source of most of our Embarrassments is the Want of sufficient Power in Congress." It passed.[84] A year later, just after the signing of the peace treaty, Alexander Hamilton observed to George Washington that "[t]here are two classes of men . . . one attached to state and the other to Continental politics"; the division between them threatened to cause "disunion."[85] For New Yorkers like Schuyler and Hamilton, constitutional reform was necessary to preserve union.

The dispute over congressional power also played a role in the calling of the Philadelphia Convention in 1787. Amid proposals to amend the Articles of Confederation to expand Congress's power in limited ways, such as to regulate commerce among the states, the New York Assembly instructed its congressional delegates to recommend a convention that would consider more radical change. This appears to have been Hamilton's initiative too. Congress rejected the proposal.[86] The Philadelphia Convention, with a limited mandate, met from late May until September. But in writing a new constitution, it followed the spirit of Hamilton's proposal.

Antiloyalist legislation was another source of conflict between the state and the Confederation. Three acts stood out. The first was the Forfeiture and Confiscation Act of 1779, under which the state took loyalist lands and redistributed them to patriots.[87] The second was the Citation Act of 1782, which stopped all debt actions between loyalist creditors and patriot debtors, deferred interest during the war, and allowed repayment in paper currency after the war.[88] Third was the Trespass Act of 1783, which allowed patriots displaced during the war to seek compensation for occupation, damage, or destruction of property by individual loyalists who could not plead a military order as a defense.[89]

This last statute was passed after the war ended but before New York received details of the peace treaty and before the Confederation Congress ratified it. Much of the state's antiloyalist legislation violated Article VI of the treaty, which forbade "future confiscations" along with "any prosecutions commenced against any person or persons for or by reason of the part which he or they may have taken in the present war."[90] Throughout the treaty negotiations, American diplomats refused to restore or indemnify loyalist property, explaining to their British counterparts that much of the confiscation took place "in virtue of the laws of particular States" so that "Congress had no authority to repeal those laws, and therefore could give us none to stipulate for such repeal."[91] This may have been a bargaining ploy, but American negotiators probably doubted Congress's power to bind the states to a treaty; the Articles of Confederation did not grant it such power, and many in the states denied it. Nonetheless, Congress agreed to enforce the treaty "sincerely, strictly and completely."[92] In New York, confiscations actually *increased* after the treaty was signed, forcing out thousands of loyalists.[93] It was as if state officials tried to confiscate as much property as possible, as fast as possible, before Congress devised a way to enforce the treaty.

When those loyalists left, they took their personal property, including money, which is why Hamilton thought that the whole process was as tragic for the states as for the exiles. He joined the New York bar in 1782 and represented many loyalists who stayed and tried to protect their property. It was not so much Hamilton's weakness for the patriciate that made him solicitous toward loyalists. He had this weakness but satisfied it within the ranks of the patriots, and few of his loyalist clients were patrician. The best and the brightest could be replaced — for example, by himself. But as an institution builder, he knew that the next layer of society — modest of talent, large of purse — was just as important. So he lamented the loss of "[m]any merchants of second class, characters of no political consequence, each of whom may carry away eight to ten thousand guineas." These were the men and women (often widows) who, as bondholders, could help float the experiment in independence. But "the popular phrenzy" of punitive legislation was chasing them away.[94] Hamilton's fear that the politics of revenge was draining much needed investment shaped his legal practice.

The defense of loyalists was uncharted territory, a new specialty open to ambitious young attorneys who had served in Washington's army, like Hamilton, Aaron Burr, and Robert Troup. Joining the bar at this time meant passing an oral exam administered by the supreme court judges. During the war, amid a shortage of attorneys, the court reduced the required five-year clerkship to three years and in 1782 briefly eliminated it for war veterans who had studied law before the Revolution. Hamilton obtained a six-month extension of the dispensation and was practicing law the year after he left Washington's command. Most of these officers-turned-lawyers apprenticed briefly with attorneys, read Coke and Blackstone, and mooted legal issues together. Hamilton was unusual in forgoing apprenticeship altogether. He studied on his own and with friends like Troup. It required a "lonely nature," Troup recalled, to master the necessary material in so short a time. Meanwhile, Hamilton took copious notes for future reference, and his study guide for New York's civil procedure seems to have been the source for the first book on the subject.[95]

With courts finally open throughout the state, the postwar period was kind to these lawyers. Hamilton's legal papers make clear that he cut his professional teeth defending loyalists. "[L]egislative folly has afforded so plentiful a harvest to us lawyers," he wrote Gouverneur Morris, "that we have scarcely a moment to spare from the substantial business of reaping it."[96] Private interest and political economy went hand in hand. Hamilton could embark "on the business of making my fortune" while contributing to what he called "the American empire."[97] While litigating cases, he wrote essays criticizing antiloyalist legislation as "industrious efforts to violate the constitution of this state, to trample the rights of the subject, and to chicane or infringe the most solemn obligations of treaty." In late 1783, just as the southern counties rejoined the rest of the state, the legislature passed a bill declaring that all who remained within British lines during the war were aliens and thus could not vote. The Council of Revision disallowed the act, and it was not revived.[98] Nonetheless, it captured the sentiment of many vengeful New Yorkers, a sentiment that fostered other antiloyalist laws. Hamilton maintained that most loyalists were no longer British subjects or aliens. They were American citizens and deserved the full protection of law. Instead, the state treated them as outlaws and tried to "*enact* a civil war." It was no way for New York to begin political independence. "'Tis with governments as individuals," he explained to his readers, "first impressions and early habits give a lasting bias to the temper and character." It was important for America and all "mankind" that the states develop good political practices.[99] Years before James Madison surveyed state laws and analyzed their "political vices," Hamilton was immersed in state politics, criticizing just those vices. By the time Madison wrote of the "multiplicity," "mutability," and "injustice" of state laws in the spring of 1787, Hamilton had long been litigating against them.[100]

The Trespass Act exemplified these postwar retaliations. The act empowered displaced owners of property to collect damages for occupation by loyalist interlopers.[101] The political disposition of these plaintiffs was not always clear. The only requirement was that they had left British-controlled territory during the war and could prove that someone else had occupied their property. The Rutgers family, for example, vacated its New York City brewery and related property in 1778 and returned in 1783. In the interim, the British military had used the property, first as a kitchen for a military hospital and then as a warehouse for naval stores.[102] In the 1784 case of *Rutgers v. Waddington*, Mrs. Rutgers, now widowed, sued in the Mayor's Court for back rent.[103]

The defendants had occupied the brewery first, from 1776 to 1780, under orders from the British commissary general and then, for the next three years, from the commander in chief. Although the law of nations permitted occupants of property vacated during war to raise a military order as a defense, the state statute provided that defendants could not "plead, in Justification, any military Order or Command whatever, of the Enemy."[104] Alexander Hamilton, who along with Brockholst Livingston and Morgan Lewis represented the defendants, claimed that the law of nations and the peace treaty were part of New York law and either supplied the default rules against which the Trespass Act should be interpreted or actually trumped the act.[105] Again, the laws of war, which were part of the law of nations, permitted armies to use abandoned property freely during war, and the 1783 peace treaty promised that the states would not infringe loyalist property rights. While preparing for the case, Hamilton drafted several briefs, one of which cited Sir Edward Coke's proposition in *Bonham's Case* that "[a] statute against Law and reason especially if a private statute is void." A court had the power, Hamilton asserted in these notes, to "render [such an] act Nugatory," an early statement of judicial review.[106] However, Hamilton deemphasized this argument as the case developed and relied instead on strong statutory interpretation. Did the state legislature, he asked, intend to violate the law of nations or the 1783 treaty? "If it was intended the *act is void* [citing *Bonham's Case*] — But let us see whether there are not rules of construction which [render] this extremity unnecessary."[107] It could not, he argued, have been the "intention of [the] wise, honest and well-informed men" in the legislature to violate the law of nations.[108]

The Mayor's Court embraced Hamilton's statutory interpretation and construed the Trespass Act narrowly rather than declare it "void." Yet, given the legislature's clear command that a military order was no justification, the distinction was blurry at best. It did, however, provide the Mayor's Court with a way to work around the statute without claiming the power to nullify legislation. James Duane, mayor of New York from 1784 to 1789, presided over a court comprising himself, the city recorder, and five members of the city's Common Council. Their judgment required the defendants to pay rent for their occupation of the brewery from 1778 to 1780, but not between 1780 and 1783. Only during the latter years did they occupy it under "the *immediate* authority" of the commander in chief. Before that time they operated under the authority of the commissary general, a civilian whose instruction "was an act of usurpation" rather than a military order.[109] Hamilton had distinguished the two officers, perhaps to offer the court a compromise. Commissary generals were civilian employees of the British Treasury, and though they served the military in garrisons, strictly speaking they did not issue military orders.[110]

Though the court accepted this distinction between military and civilian commands, it did not simply follow Hamilton's cue. Mayor Duane was a lawyer, owned a large tract of land upstate, and had been associated with the loyalist DeLancey family before the Revolution.[111] He too had long argued that property rights rested on constitutional principle. While serving in the Continental Congress in 1774, he emphasized the importance of placing "our Rights on a broader & firmer Basis to advance and adhere to some solid and Constitutional Principle which will preserve Us from future Violations — a principle clear & explicit."[112] At that time, the claim was that property was imperiled by a British Parliament that did not represent the colonies. Now, property remained central, and Duane tried to rein in a local legislature that neglected constitutional principle. Representation, in short, was not enough to guarantee good legislation. But Duane's court claimed the power only to make the best sense of statutes, not to set them aside because inconsistent with some other body of law. Duane raised the peace treaty above state law without explicitly holding that the former preempted state authority. Instead, he reconciled the two and located a state source of law that limited state legislation. That source was the law of nations, operative in New York by way of the English common law. He also maintained that the Council of Revision's approval of a statute (it had consented to the Trespass Act) did not mean that a court was required to enforce it. In other words, the council's review did not preclude judicial review in individual cases.[113]

It is a remarkable and discursive opinion. It was also published, which was unusual, because the judges wished to "express our sentiments with more deliberation and correctness; and that nothing to be offered by us, may be misunderstood or misapplied."[114] The court apologized that a case of "national character" arose in a municipal court in front of magistrates "cut off from those studious researches, which great and intricate decisions require." Having excused their art, the judges praised their muses. The lawyers at the bar supplied much "learning," which clarified the issues and demonstrated that the profession had recovered from the Revolution. "We cannot but express the pleasure," the court wrote, "which we have received, in seeing young gentlemen, just called to the bar, from the active and honorable scenes of military life, already so distinguished in an arduous science."[115] The court implied that this litigation was part of the war's aftermath and would help determine its meaning.

The first issue was whether the plaintiff's case was "within the letter and intent" of the Trespass Act. To decide this question, a court should "suppose the lawmaker present, and that you asked him the question — did you intend to comprehend this case? Then you must give yourself such answer as you imagine, he *being an upright and reasonable man*, would have given." The answer was yes, the state legislature had intended to help people like Mrs. Rutgers, a widow driven into exile.[116]

The next issue was "whether the law of nations gives the captors, and the Defendant under them, *rights* which *controul* the operation of the statute, and *bar* the present suit." The court, agreeing with Hamilton, established that the law of nations was part of the law of the "foederal" union of states. This argument had two premises. First, the law of nations was "an indispensable obligation" of every civilized nation and the "chief guardian" of "the rights of human nature." Respect for the law of nations distinguished "the refined and polished nations of Europe from the piratical states of Barbary." In short, it defined civilization.[117] Second, the court maintained that the law of nations was already part of the state's law. "By our excellent constitution, the common law is declared to be part of the law of the land; and the *jus gentium* is a branch of the common law."[118] Prudence played a role too. If the state did not recognize the law of nations, "our *commerce*, and our *persons*, in foreign parts, would be unprotected by the great sanctions, which it has enjoined."[119]

The court understood the desire for vengeance that followed the war. But "[w]hat *we* have suffered cannot alter the common laws of war: they are founded upon reason and humanity, and will prevail as long as reason and humanity are cultivated." Hamilton had argued that the laws of war were obligatory. The court, citing Vattel, distinguished between the "*necessary law of nations*," which was morally binding, and mere usages or customs, from which nations could deviate. The court determined that law of war at issue — the right to use abandoned property without compensating its owner — was not a necessary law of nations. The Confederation, however, had recognized that usage in the peace treaty with Britain. For a single state to violate it now would be "contrary to the very nature of the confederacy, and the evident intention of the articles, by which it is established, as well as dangerous to the union itself."[120] Because the Confederation endorsed the conventional right of armies to use abandoned property during wartime without compensation, individual states should not legislate otherwise. The Confederation could agree to bind the states to the customary law of nations.

The court then analyzed the specific custom at issue: "Whether the capture and occupancy of the city of New-York, is such a conquest as vested the British Commander with the disposal of the rents and profits of real property." The judges surveyed the parties' citations from continental civil-law treatises. Grotius maintained that land and its profits did not vest in the conqueror until after a peace settlement. On the other hand, there was a maxim that "the personal property of those who fly becomes a booty."[121] In short, the authorities conflicted. In preparing for the case, Hamilton first dismissed the problem cavalierly: "Writers differ: And *So do men in every thing*." Later he devised a lawyerly resolution. Grotius spoke of the "usufruct" or "*using the soil*," while Vattel referred to "absolute ownership." The former right belonged to the conqueror immediately, the latter only on perfection of title by peace. Here, the defendant claimed the right only to use Rutgers's property, not to own it.[122] The court followed Hamilton and held that the rental value of the property was incident to its use and need not be repaid to the owner.[123] According to the law of nations, if the British military authorized Waddington's use of Rutgers's property, she could not recover compensation.

But did the law of nation, and the Confederation's endorsement of it, bind the New York legislature? This conflict between Congress's war power and the state's control over its "*internal* police" lay behind the key issue of whether the court "ought to be governed by the *statute*, where it clearly militated against the law of nations." If the statute violated the law of nations under one interpretation, another should be sought. Then came the key move: the court construed the statute to avoid conflict, holding that the legislature did not intend to violate the law of nations. The judges cited Blackstone but seemed to gloss Coke, holding that

> The supremacy of the Legislature need not be called into question; if they think fit positively to enact a law, there is no power which can controul them. When the main óbject of such a law is clearly expressed, and the intention manifest, the Judges are not at liberty, altho' it appears to them unreasonable, to reject it: for this were to set the judicial above the legislative, which would be subversive of all government.
>
> But when a law is expressed in *general words*, and some *collateral matter*, which happens to arise from those general words is *unreasonable*, there the Judges are in decency to conclude, that the consequences were not foreseen by the Legislature; and therefore they are at liberty to expound the statute by *equity*, and only *quoad hoc* to reject it.
>
> When the judicial make these distinctions, they do not controul the Legislature; they endeavour to give their *intention* its proper effect.[124]

Thus, the court tried to sidestep jurisdictional politics. But its stronghanded interpretation muddied the distinction between controlling the legislature and construing legislation. Familiar rules of common-law construction seemed to guide the court. The legislature had not explicitly said that it wished to contravene the law of nations, and it was unreasonable to assume that the statute revoked that law "in *silence*."[125] There is a difference between a court that claims the power to strike down a statute and one that seeks "to explain it by equity." But when equitable interpretation is used to negate the clear command of a statute — here, that defendants could not plead a military order as justification — the legal effect is the same.

Why did the court go further than was "strictly necessary" to decide the claim of Mrs. Rutgers? Because New Yorkers needed to learn the law of nations. "[I]n the infancy of our republic," wrote Duane, "every proper opportunity should be embraced to inculcate a sense of national obligation, and a reverence for institutions, on which the tranquility of mankind, considered as members of different states and communities so essentially depends." The court knew that it was deciding not only widow Rutgers's case; the published opinion would discourage other suitors.[126] It would also "inculcate" the law of nations — of civilized nations — into New Yorkers. As Hamilton had warned in an essay published the same year, "early habits give a lasting bias to the temper and character" of nations as well as individuals.[127]

This legislative effect was noticed immediately. So too the court's questionable claim that it had only interpreted legislation rather than "controlled" the legislature. A group gathered in a New York City tavern to draft a protest. Some of these men soon became leading Antifederalists. Melancton Smith, a farmer, merchant, and lawyer from Dutchess County, headed the group and probably penned the pamphlet. Also present was Anthony Rutgers, son of the plaintiff. The protesters did not wish to rectify just this particular decision. The case could determine others as well because it "may be drawn into precedent, and eventually affect every citizen of this state." Their complaint was that the court exceeded its authority. The legislature had provided that military orders could not be pleaded in justification for trespass; this should have ended the matter. Instead, the court "assumed and exercised a power to set aside an act of the state" and "permitted the *vague and doubtful* custom of nations to be plead[ed] against, and to render abortive, a *clear and positive* statute." The issue was simple and "within the reach of every common understanding":

> Can a Court of Judicature, consistently with our constitution and laws, adjudge contrary to the plain and obvious meaning of a statute?
>
> If these questions are answered in the negative, authorities from Grotius, Puffendorf, Wolfius, Burlamaqui, Vattel, or any other Civilians, are no more to the purpose than so many opinions drawn from the sages of the Six Nations.[128]

Here was an early expression of intellectual nativism, an impulse that gained strength over the next two generations. It was also an argument in favor of equating popular sovereignty with legislative sovereignty: government by the people meant government by their elected representatives. The statute granted relief to patriots forced to flee their homes and recognized no defenses. There was no room for judicial interpretation. The Mayor's Court flouted the clear meaning of the statute and thereby "confound[ed] legislative and judicial powers." A judicial power to "controul the supreme legislative power" was "destructive of liberty, and remove[d] all security of property." The court's exercise of judicial review also undermined the rule of law. "The laws govern where a government is free, and every citizen knows what remedy the laws give him, for every injury"; laws did not govern where a court refused to enforce laws because it deems them "unreasonable." The tavern protesters did not invoke the principle of democracy but rather argued that in a republic legislation was paramount.[129] They also questioned judicial independence. Good behavior tenure was fine if judges restricted their activities to applying the law to individual cases, but not if they possessed the "power to over-rule a plain law." In a republic, judges usurped the people's sovereignty when they declared a statute "unreasonable, because not consonant to the law of nations, or to the opinions of antient or modern civilians and philosophers, for whom they may have a greater veneration than for the solid statutes and supreme legislative power of the state."[130] To these protesters, the Revolution's meaning was clear: the people replaced the crown as sovereign, and the state legislature embodied the people's will.

They made two recommendations, one legal and the other political. First, they advised Mrs. Rutgers to seek a writ of error in the supreme court. If unsuccessful there, she should pursue her remedy in the Court of Errors, the state's highest court. The latter included popularly elected senators. This suggested the second tactic, which was addressed to all voters: "we exhort you to be cautious in your future choice of members [of the senate] that none be elected but those on whom you can rely, as men attached to the liberties of America, and firm friends to our laws and constitution." Here was a venerable tool of popular constitutionalism: exercise of the franchise. The electorate had to choose representatives who would "protect us against judicial tyranny" or else the courts would "leave our Legislature nothing but a name."[131] If the judges started legislating, the legislature must rein in the judges. From the beginning, difficult cases made good electoral politics. British Americans had always lobbied for judges who would protect their interests, but the tavern protesters were unusually blunt.

The protest hit its mark. Mrs. Rutgers soon brought a writ of error in the supreme court, though the case was ultimately settled out of court.[132] In its next session the state assembly excoriated the Mayor's Court for allowing the defendant to plead the military order despite the statute's denial of this justification. An early draft of the resolution observed that the court had found the statute "incompatible with the law of nations."[133] This language was deleted from final resolution, perhaps because the legislature did not want to highlight the conflict between its statute and the law of nations or because the court did not explicitly hold such. Instead, the legislators emphasized the clear meaning of the statute and the subordination of municipalities and their courts to the state legislature. The assembly almost went further to connect law and politics. William Harper, from upstate Montgomery County, introduced a resolution that the Council of Appointment should "appoint such persons to be Mayor and Recorder of the City of New-York, as will govern themselves by the known laws of the land." This direct attack on Mayor Duane was too much for most and was deleted. The assembly finally resolved that the decision was "subversive of all law and good order." If a court could disregard "a plain and known law of the State," then "all our dear bought rights and privileges" would be lost, and the legislature would become "useless."[134]

The state lawmakers invoked the same restrictive interpretation of corporate power against the Mayor's Court that the imperial agents had long used against the province. Localities had to adhere to state law, and courts had to defer to legislatures. The "plain and known law of the state" was supreme above other institutions within the state and those outside its borders. The legislators preferred to think in terms of a hierarchy of lawmakers rather than of abstract bodies of law; within state borders, their will was supreme. They sought to consolidate all authority, drawn up from local sources like municipal corporations and reeled in from external authorities like the Confederation and the law of nations. The state legislature was representative, as the imperial government never had been, and this gave it legitimacy above all competitors. The tavern protesters reminded citizens of their power to enforce their rights by voting for those who would discipline the judges. Parliamentary supremacy was dead; long live the state legislature's supremacy.

By 1784, the fundamental tensions in early American constitutionalism had appeared in New York. Substantively, the *Rutgers* case involved a contest between state legislative power and extraterritorial fundamental law. Procedurally, the Mayor's Court and the protesters disagreed about the mode of enforcing constitutional principle. The judges went out of their way to subject state legislation to external standards. The protesters, in turn, believed that the court had usurped popular power. The legislature *was* the mechanism of implementing the constitution. From their perspective, the Revolution was fought to vindicate representative government. The state constitution established that government; it did not give courts the power to set aside state statutes. Both sides cherished independence and property rights. But they disagreed about the relationship between New York's property regime and external bodies of law. Proto-Federalists like Hamilton and Duane wanted to define property rights by well-known European standards, while the assembly championed its own power to determine who could bring a trespass action. *Rutgers* raised all the leading issues of early national constitutionalism. What were the sources of the American constitution? What were the valid means of enforcing them? How did the people want their constitutional government to function? The state constitution did not answer all these questions. Ambiguity remained about what constituted fundamental law. In that vacuum of authority lawyers like Hamilton laid the groundwork for a new genre of constitutional law.

Postcolonial Constitutionalism
and Transatlantic Legal Culture

*The end of rebellion is liberation, while the
end of revolution is the foundation of freedom.*
Hannah Arendt, *On Revolution* (1963)

W HEN GEORGE WASHINGTON resigned as commander in chief in
1783, he warned that it was "yet to be decided whether the Revolution must
ultimately be considered as a blessing or a curse: a blessing or a curse, not to
the present age alone, for with our fate will the destiny of unborn millions be
involved."[1] After the Philadelphia Convention four years later, Alexander
Hamilton expressed the same anxiety in *Federalist* 1. The question of ratification, he wrote, involved "the fate of an empire, in many respects, the
most interesting in the world."[2] By then most agreed that the Confederation
needed power to make interstate commercial and foreign policy. Some others
wished to go further and empower the central government to restrain the
states from passing populist legislation, such as that relieving debtors and
penalizing loyalists.[3] The question was whether such changes would come at
the expense of revolutionary ideals or were necessary to achieve them. Independence demanded vindication. The founding of new state governments
gave Americans the chance to establish governments based on popular sovereignty, though institutionally they looked quite similar to those of their old
colonies. The Articles of Confederation created a "league of friendship"
among them but did not give Congress the power to pass general laws. It also
left the states as political equals, each more powerful than the whole. This
decentralization permitted states like New York to violate the peace treaty
with Britain, obstruct excise collection, and negotiate land purchases directly
with Native American tribes. To many New Yorkers, these freedoms were

the ends for which the Revolution had been fought. Yet not all agreed. Although the war had ended, the struggle over its meaning continued. The cessation of hostilities forced Americans to make sense of what they had created in the states and what they would do together. The shift from a royal government to a republican one was politically profound. The effect on legal culture — the legal culture of each state and the common legal culture of the Union — was less clear.

In other words, although the colonists had repudiated monarchy and secured their provincial governments, they had not replaced imperial subjecthood with a common citizenship.[4] Most residents of each state were citizens of that state, but what was their legal relationship to people in the other states? Besides the Revolution itself, what did they have in common? Decades of imperial experience. It was the first time a newly independent people re-created their government, and the ratification debate gave them the opportunity to explain to multiple audiences — at home, in Europe, and in posterity — why they had broken from the empire and how their new government was superior to the old.

To this extent, the American founding was a postcolonial moment similar to what was experienced in nations that gained independence from European empires in the twentieth century.[5] Postcolonial studies takes many forms, and the early United States does not fit most of them. The severity and dynamics of imperial rule differ across time and space, and there is something irreducible about each independence movement.[6] It is, however, common for people at the moment of independence to look forward and back, to come to terms with the legacies of imperial rule while charting the future. Even after political liberation, imperial subjects often remain divided between two worlds, at once distancing themselves from their former rulers and evaluating themselves against imperial standards.[7] While political liberations are marked by a signal event — the Declaration of Independence, for example — the process of "decolonising the mind" takes generations.[8] In sum, the current of postcolonial studies that explores the institutional and discursive legacies of imperialism offers insight into the transformation of American legal culture that began with its constitutions.

In the new United States, law was a central site of identity formation for at least two generations after independence. The writing and ratification of the federal Constitution involved a complex reworking of British ideas about government, and for decades legal thinkers built on the founding to create an American law that would preserve the experiment in self-government. The literature the ratifiers wrote to explain the document was postcolonial in that they sought to make sense of the experiment for their readers at home, abroad, and in the future. Their heirs among the lawyers, judges, and treatise writers of the next generation continued their work of using law to forge a commercial union that was supreme within the states and respected across the Atlantic. Their goal was to generate a body of law that would control the states and territories while also offering the American people a way to re-establish their identity in the Atlantic world. This manufacture of a common legal identity *was* a strategy of control.

Two aspects of the early American search for identity distinguish it from more recent examples. First, its primary genre of expression was legal literature. Second, empire had positive rather than negative connotations. In most independence movements that followed, political revolution was a condition precedent to realizing national identity through authentic language, literature, and art. But the American colonies revolted before the high tide of romantic nationalism in the nineteenth century, and for at least a generation language and literature did not much distinguish Americans from Britons.[9] In contrast, early Americans drafted many constitutions and wrote about them often. Constitutions were vehicles of collective self-understanding as well as of self-government, and the federal Constitution soon stood as the paramount expression of the "imagined community" of the American Union.[10] The Constitution, especially as glossed during ratification, embodied a set of principles not restricted to territorial boundaries, one reason that people in the new states called themselves "Americans," a continental signifier at a time when almost every state bordered the Atlantic.[11] Constitutional law doctrines like federalism, the separation of powers, and local and individual rights were designed to travel with Americans as they moved across the continent and through time, even when and where there was no governmental institution to enforce them. A constitution by and for the people also informed them what it meant to be *a* people. It would be self-enforcing or fail — a government of laws, not men.

Some men tried to guide the experiment. After figuring large in the Revolution, lawyers took the lead in framing, explaining, and governing the Union. From Alexander Hamilton and James Duane, who championed the law of nations to protect loyalists and preserve diplomatic relations with Britain, to James Kent and his *Commentaries on American Law* (1826–30), which began with the law of nations, New York lawyers believed that the state's legal culture was enmeshed not only in a federal system but also a larger civilization. These lawyers were used to participating in a legal environment divided into the local, the provincial, and the imperial. They continued to inhabit that stratified, transatlantic world after independence. As American lawyers remixed their legal inheritance to serve new visions of empire, they increasingly saw themselves as members of an international legal culture. Most of their sources remained English. But they drew on continental European ones too and participated in a cosmopolitan Atlantic world with an increasing number of authorities, including their own. In a world of discrete political jurisdictions that shared a repository of law, where was the center? For Federalists and their heirs, it was not a physical place but rather an ideal toward which they aspired: a legal system based on transcendent rules. But universalism was more a remedy for legal federalism than a philosophical premise. Their constitutions, treatises, and statutory revisions helped create a new administrative center in a legal profession bound, they hoped, by a common vision of national law.

This vision of a union bound by law, and of law defined by a learned legal profession, was always controversial and rarely shared by most Americans. There were other visions of union. One recalled the old provincial constitution. Many Antifederalists and their descendants relied on the Union to support commercial connections between the states and defend against foreign threats. Beyond that, they strictly construed federal power. Most power would reside where it always had: in the provinces, now denominated states. The antiauthoritarian impulse that had pervaded colonial New York's marchland and seaports also endured the Revolution. Squatting in the marchland, smuggling in the cities, suspicion of self-proclaimed elites, and popular mobility remained too. Most public men, whether devoted primarily to the Union or to a state, tried to domesticate that popular power, to serve the people's sovereignty while controlling it. All professed loyalty to sovereign people, as before they had to the sovereign crown. Also as before, they sought ways to align the interest of the sovereign with their own interests, to claim its standard and to shape the exercise of its power.

The Imperial *Federalist*

Ratification and the Creation of Constitutional Law

> *No Constitution is the same on Paper*
> *and in Life.*
>
> Gouverneur Morris to
> George Washington, 1787

On 27 OCTOBER 1787, a New York City newspaper published a letter praising the federal Constitution and signed "Publius." Months later the letter was entitled *Federalist* 1, and soon many knew that the author was Alexander Hamilton. His goal was to persuade New York voters to elect Federalists to the state's ratification convention. The task was formidable. Opinion in New York ran against the Constitution. George Clinton, the state's popular governor, opposed it. The state's two Antifederalist delegates had left Philadelphia early in protest against the convention's decision to replace, rather than simply amend, the Articles of Confederation.[1] Hamilton, the third delegate, remained. On returning home, he wrote: "After an unequivocal experience of the inefficacy of the subsisting Foederal Government, you are called upon to deliberate on a new Constitution for the United States of America. The subject speaks its own importance; comprehending in its consequences, nothing less than the existence of the Union, the safety and welfare of the parts of which it is composed, the fate of an empire, in many respects, the most interesting in the world."[2]

The reference to empire was no mere flourish. The term had concrete meaning for Hamilton's readers, who were born in the British Empire. Similarly, "Union," as today it recalls 1861, then brought to mind 1707 and the Act of Union between England and Scotland.[3] The founders remained British Americans, and they spoke the familiar political languages of empire, republic, province, and incorporated locality. This was the narrative context in which Federalists understood the Constitution: it must not only establish new structures for self-government but also empower the Union to participate fully in an Atlantic world dominated by European empires.[4]

These imperial references sound strange today. Many Americans assume that the founding generation repudiated European models and established a democratic society.[5] Historians, on the other hand, have recovered the ideological influences on the founding generation. Recently they have debated whether the framers' constitutionalism was republican and extolled civic virtue or liberal and fostered political individualism. Still, they also view the founding as an unparalleled event in which the framers revised these ideologies to fit new American conditions.[6] The participants in the ratification debate, however, rarely deployed republican or liberal ideas systematically, and the Constitution contained many ideological compromises. In between these visions of democracy and some combination of republicanism and liberalism, a third interpretation of the founding has emerged that emphasizes the framers' commitment to popular sovereignty. Legal scholars like Bruce Ackerman, Akhil Reed Amar, and Larry Kramer have recovered the founders' understanding that, while the new nation was not a direct democracy, the people would continue to participate in constitutional politics after ratification, either in special "moments" of revision or through continuous renegotiation of constitutional meaning.[7] Despite this range of lay and professional interpretations, almost all rely on 1787 as the key date for dividing the modern nation from its colonial past. Consequently, the imperial framework of the constitutional debate is largely forgotten by ordinary Americans and historians alike.[8]

The drafting and ratification of the federal Constitution were remarkable. Rarely have the problems of governance been canvassed so thoroughly. In two short years, a newly independent people redesigned their central government, debated the plan openly, ratified it in representative conventions, and got it up and running. It remains the longest-lived written constitution in the world today. But this achievement has obscured the states' origins as colonies and generated myths of national exceptionalism. Hamilton's original audience was well aware of this imperial context. New Yorkers, because of their strategic position in the old empire and the new Union, were primed to debate the Constitution in terms of empire. From the legislative Charter of Libertyes of 1683 and the petitions demanding restoration of those liberties before the Revolution to the state constitution of 1777, with its preamble recognizing both the Continental Congress and the sovereignty of the people within the state, New Yorkers had expressed their visions of their province in imperial terms.

This experience shaped the way New Yorkers viewed the Union. Consequently, imperial themes pervaded New York's ratification literature. The eighty-five essays that made up *The Federalist Papers*, for example, first appeared in New York newspapers to influence the New York election, and most were written by New Yorkers Alexander Hamilton, who probably wrote fifty-one essays, and John Jay, who wrote five.[9] James Madison, who was in New York to represent Virginia in the Continental Congress, wrote the rest. Although much of what Madison tried to achieve at the Philadelphia Convention and during the ratification debate had been inspired by his experience in the Virginia legislature during the 1780s, he was also influenced by his time in New York. He recognized that New York was well positioned to serve as a headquarters for continental expansion. Madison toured the Mohawk Valley in 1784 and two years later purchased nine hundred acres there with James Monroe because "the vacant land in that part of America opens the surest field of speculation of any in the U.S." The New York speculation was one of "several projects" that he hoped would allow him to "depend as little as possible on the labour of slaves."[10] His plans were sketchy and never amounted to much. But in the mid-1780s his hopes ran up the Hudson and out toward the northwest. Madison, like Hamilton, believed that New York had to ratify the Constitution because the state was central to the Union. So the two men worked in harmony.[11] Each had his own emphases, some that reflected the division of labor (Madison handling congressional power, for example, and Hamilton the executive branch) and others, like Hamilton's cavalier approach to the states, that revealed disagreement about principle and led to antagonism in the 1790s. But in the winter of 1787–88 they shared a vision of the Union and a common goal: to influence an election in New York, not write a treatise on political science.[12] In addition, some of the most insightful Antifederalist criticisms came from New York pens. Robert Yates's "Brutus" letters, Governor George Clinton's "Cato" essays, and the "Letters from a Federal Farmer," now attributed to Melancton Smith, are the best examples.[13] These essays appeared day after day for nine months, an intense volley played for a New York audience.

As campaign material, *The Federalist* failed. Antifederalists won two-thirds of the seats in the state's ratification convention. At the convention, Federalist delegates persuaded enough Antifederalists to support the Constitution in exchange for a promise to consider amendments, which along with similar pledges in other states led eventually to the Bill of Rights. But *The Federalist* contributed little to that compromise. Some Antifederalists capitulated because ten other states had ratified the Constitution before the New York convention voted, exceeding the two-thirds requirement that dissolved the Confederation and made the new government effective in the ratifying states. Another outcome, they feared, might have torn the states apart.[14] Despite interstate communication and republication, *The Federalist* did not affect ratification elsewhere, either.[15] Why, then, do Americans remember *The Federalist* as a success? Because the Constitution succeeded. The ratifiers became the Constitution's original glossators, providing illustrations of its meaning as well as a reasoning style that began with the text but referred to past experience and rested on the premise of full participation in the Atlantic world. This made the terms of debate as important as the elections that the debaters tried to influence. Ratifiers on both sides borrowed freely from each other's writings, generating a stock of ideas that Americans still draw on when interpreting the Constitution. Because of its creative approach to the document, illustrations, and, not least, immediate publication in book form, *The Federalist* in particular became an instruction manual for constitutional interpretation.[16] What originated as political ephemera soon became a source of law, and many early Supreme Court opinions read like continuations of the ratification literature. In addition, nineteenth-century treatise writers such as James Kent and Joseph Story drew heavily, sometimes verbatim, from *The Federalist* when analyzing the Constitution. Before the Civil War, these treatises were at least as important in shaping professional and lay understandings of the Constitution as the few Supreme Court decisions that interpreted the document. When *The Federalist* and similar essays became canonical sources of authority, their imperial orientation was embedded in the nation's constitutional law.

As before the Revolution, people held multiple visions of empire. Both Federalists and Antifederalists used languages and institutions that had circulated throughout the British Atlantic world for decades, and they raised the familiar problem of legal pluralism within an expanding political unit. The debate recalled the long struggle between the imperial agents and the creole elite to control politics and law enforcement in colonial New York. Federalists drew on familiar strategies for controlling wayward provinces and envisioned the new Union as an empire, within and without: superior to the states, equal to the other Atlantic empires, and a model for all the world. Their primary strategy paralleled that of the old imperial agents. They tried to construct a federal administration that would attract the right sort of personnel and possess procedures to carry out their vision of the Union.

Antifederalists, in turn, stressed those parts of the British — or more precisely, *English* — tradition supporting local sovereignty, such as corporate autonomy, local representation, and the jury, much as the provincial elite had for decades.

A secondary, more subtle strategy that both Federalists and Antifederalists used to secure their visions of the Union was to develop substantive definitions and limitations to control constitutional interpretation in the future. Each side sought to inscribe a premise beneath the Constitution that would shape the interpretation of particular clauses. Both sides wanted to avoid the constitutional multiplicity that had fragmented colonial society. Few believed that the key to uniform interpretations of the Constitution was simply that it was written. They knew that constitutional sources, whether written or not, could be marshaled in more than one way. Instead, the key would be the Constitution's unwritten premise, and that is what they concentrated on in the ratification debate. Almost every speech, pamphlet, and argument rested on a vision of what the Constitution was designed to fulfill and exemplified a reasoning style to achieve it.

The debaters viewed their situation — newly independent provinces experimenting with new forms of federation — as unprecedented in the British world. Yet deep continuities marked their debates. They harnessed old materials to generate new constitutional doctrines such as federalism, separated institutional powers, and rights secured from legislative alteration. The new genre of constitutional law served as a vessel for them all. First, the debaters translated the colonial script of provincial corporate autonomy into the new doctrine of federalism. The key move here came when Federalists argued that the central government would better represent the people than the states; at least, it would offer additional representation. Along the way, the corporation was reconceived. No longer the ideal form of political autonomy, it became a mere delegation of power to private parties.

Second, the tension between the ideal of impartial public administration and the practice of local governance reemerged and led to a rethinking of the doctrine of separated powers. Before, the powers subject to separation tracked the old mixed estates of government: the crown was one estate, and it should be separated from the people's estate in the legislature. In addition, the people might be separated within the legislature, one house representing the many and the other representing the few. Now that the people were sovereign, contestants for power drew new lines of separation between the institutions of government. Concern over the social origin of federal administrators led to a reconfiguration of the dramatis personae of constitutional theory, as the triadic model of classical politics gave way to a contest between aristocratic administration and middling democracy. This new binary contributed in the coming decades to competing visions of federal administration, seen sometimes as pursuing the common interest of the people and, at others, wrought by partisanship. Neither vision predominated. Whatever their political orientation, most people alternated uneasily between them. Federalists sought to pursue the public interest through cosmopolitan officials in the executive and judiciary, while Antifederalists, and later Jeffersonian Republicans, preferred instead to repose trust in elected representatives.

Finally, the debate helped distill constitutional law out of the transatlantic legal tradition. Paramount within that tradition was the common law, which was newly distinguished from statute law, creating a three-level legal hierarchy unknown in the colonies or Britain. During the debate over the federal judiciary, Federalists used the fact of legal federalism — the diversity of state common-law regimes — to differentiate common law from fundamental law. In other words, constitutional law began to replace the customary ancient constitution. Federalists also began to position the legal community as guarantors of constitutional law. In response, Antifederalists identified certain rights as fundamental and beyond the reach of the federal government. As the new constitutional genre began to take shape, law was more clearly separated from politics, and then the legal was subdivided into the fundamental and the changeable. In the generation before the Revolution, there had been no clear line between law and politics. Arguments focused on which level of government, or which jurisdiction, had power, not whether some action was irrevocably legal or political. Now, although most of the law was subordinated to politics, and thus changeable by legislation, core bits of the legal inheritance were recast as fundamental, backed by the sovereign people. How the people would enforce that fundamental law — through courts and amendments or the traditional modes of popular constitutionalism like elections, petitions, resistance, and riot — remained uncertain for a long time.[17]

Not everyone agreed about the content of the doctrines or the meaning of their key words, but for decades most Americans agreed to operate within this constitutional culture. Again, the lines between these doctrinal categories remained contested. Still, most of the explosive issues of unity and expansion were cabined within the discourse of constitutionalism. This did not mean that all political questions became legal questions in the sense that they were litigated.[18] Rather, the framers hoped that the central problems of American government would be analyzed with a special discourse designed to contain disagreement, whether those analyses took place in courts, assembly halls, or the streets. The concepts within this discourse — federalism, separated powers, individual rights, and the integrity of constitutional law — derived from colonial political culture and were remixed in light of decades of colonial experience. Yet soon these doctrines were divorced from their historical context and presented as a model for all nations.

The Two Dimensions of American Empire: Enlightenment Science and Colonial Experience

In Hamilton's first *Federalist* essay and throughout the debate, empire had two dimensions. One was abstract and outward looking: the symbolic empire of self-government. The other was concrete and inward looking: a structure for governing extended territories that the founders had experienced firsthand. From one angle, these were the familiar dimensions of empire: internal and external or, in James Harrington's terms, foreign and domestic.[19] There was, however, no distinction between core and periphery. The states *were* the center, and the framers devised a way for the unsettled territories to become states too. In addition, this empire was supposed to be more benevolent than its predecessors, a model of self-government for all the world. This vision of an empire beyond all jurisdiction — of universal liberty — would have been unimaginable for Harrington a century earlier.

Hamilton captured this symbolic empire in his opening paragraph: "[I]t seems to have been reserved to the people of this country, by their conduct and example, to decide the important question, whether societies of men are really capable or not of establishing good government from reflection and choice, or whether they are forever destined to depend, for their political constitutions, on accident and force."[20] This was the empire of conscious government, similar to Thomas Jefferson's "empire of liberty" and Noah Webster's "empire of reason." It rested in part on the universalism creeping into late eighteenth-century thought as well as, paradoxically, on the Dissenting Protestant ideal of a city upon a hill.[21] The hard fact that the Union could barely hold itself together, let alone appear to Europe as a military empire, also informed this image of an exemplary empire. "[T]he whole human race," Hamilton predicted in *Federalist* 9, would be indebted to "the numerous innovations displayed on the American theatre."[22] American government was a didactic spectacle that, if successful, would spread by force of example rather than arms.

Yet Hamilton warned that the prospect of this symbolic empire might not persuade voters to ratify the Constitution. Selfish passions rather than benevolence, he believed, motivated behavior.[23] The trick was to harness those passions for the general good, and this required a keen appreciation of "the true springs by which human conduct is actuated." The central spring was reputation, or fame. Men would do good deeds if they bestowed fame, and fame was possible only in a great empire, not a small republic.[24]

Empire thus also had a more familiar meaning: a set of institutions, languages, and practices that the founding generation had experienced first-hand. While there was concern about the distance between center and periphery, the federal capital and its citizens, much of the ratification debate focused on the relationship between state and federal officials *within* each state. Tension between the imperial agents and provincial settlers had rent the British colonies; the founders wanted to prevent a similar rupture. Because there was no metropolitan capital, this relationship between local inhabitants and federal officials on the ground was even more important. The Confederation government met at that time in New York City and would soon return to Philadelphia. Even when the capital relocated permanently to the District of Columbia in 1800, it would lack the economic and cultural influence that marked a true "seat of empire."[25] Federal agents would have no home — no London to which to write and aspire, no crown to invoke — and would operate everywhere in the Union. Judges would be especially important. They would articulate and enforce the law of the Union. The new empire, even more than the old, would be personified by its agents on the ground. Competing visions of the Union, of course, depended primarily on competing interests and expectations, just as in the British Empire. Yet each vision now contained these two dimensions of experience and ideal.

Early in *Federalist* 1, Hamilton broached the threat of disunion. Ambitious men might calculate greater gains with "the subdivision of the empire into several partial confederacies, than from its union under one government."[26] He and his readers knew that such a "subdivision" was possible: they had just engineered one. Before the Revolution, British imperial agents had made the same charges of parochialism and separatism against the provincial elite and marchland squatters. Hamilton took up these standards and warned of another "civil war."[27] Tumult within the states, like Shays's Rebellion in Massachusetts, were bad omens.[28] Federalists feared that men in the states would do to them what they had done to Great Britain: dissolve ties, ally with enemies, and pursue independence. The Confederation government could do little to stop them.

Along with the criticism of the Confederation, Federalists offered a positive vision of the American empire and a program to achieve it. Hamilton,

Madison, Jay, Washington, and like-minded men had been formulating this program for several years. Hamilton had done so in his "Continentalist" essays of 1781 and 1782. Madison developed his appreciation for a stronger union in his private writings such as the "Vices of the Political Systems of the States."[29] The program included the reestablishment of transatlantic commercial and cultural ties, a national bank, a strong military, a loyal federal administration, well-regulated migration into the western territory, and centralized Indian diplomacy.[30]

Little of the program was contained in the document. The Constitution represented a series of compromises, and Federalists admitted that much of its meaning would depend on practical administration. In Madison's lawyerly terms, its ambiguity would be "liquidated and ascertained by a series of particular discussions and adjudications." Federalists made a virtue of this uncertainty.[31] When Antifederalists championed elements of the ancient constitution, Federalists responded that the states' new situation justified departure from conventional wisdom. But they imagined rather than reported this gap between learning and experience to escape the revolutionary commitment to English forms of local government and republicanism. Federalists drew on inherited learning too, but their sources ranged more widely, from ancient Greece to contemporary Europe, and suggested the variety of solutions available beyond those from English history, civic republicanism, or the state constitutions. It was a battle over the Revolution's legacy as well as to position the Union in relation to Europe and within the trajectory of liberty.

All participants alternated between embracing and recoiling from conventional wisdom, defending precedents and proposing innovations.[32] Hamilton declared that it was the "glory of the people of America" that they had studied the "opinions of former times and other nations" but had not allowed "a blind veneration for antiquity, for custom, or for names, to overcome suggestions of their own good sense, their knowledge of their own situation, and the lessons of their own experience."[33] Noah Webster, the Federalist lawyer who later compiled the first American dictionary, warned that Americans should not "receive indiscriminately the maxims of government, the manners and the literary taste of Europe and make them the ground on which to build our systems in America." Yet just as he did not abandon the English language, he did not jettison English law. There was "a mixture of profound wisdom and consummate folly in the British constitution; a ridiculous compound of freedom and tyranny in their laws." The key was selectivity. Webster, like many Federalists, assumed that Europe's political culture was a museum, the old world an estate auction, and postrevolutionary Americans privileged curators. "It is the business of *Americans* to select the wisdom of all nations," he wrote, "as the basis of her constitutions, — to avoid their errours, — to prevent the introduction of foreign vices and corruptions and check the career of her own, — to promote virtue and patriotism, — to embellish and improve the sciences, — to diffuse a uniformity and purity of *language*, — to add superiour dignity to this infant Empire and to human nature."[34] The search would lead to the best possible constitution because "the wisdom of all ages is collected — the legislators of antiquity are consulted — as well as the opinions and interests of the millions who are concerned." It would be "an *empire of reason*."[35]

Not only were the sources of the ratification literature transatlantic. Frequent references to European perceptions of the American experiment demonstrate that while the founders made and defended their constitutions primarily for voters, they also sought a foreign audience. Fame demanded transatlantic appreciation too. Most of the founders, especially the Federalists, believed that the Constitution should be judged successful only if it persuaded the European empires to accept the United States into the international community.[36]

A remarkable example of an essay written for these dual audiences is Hamilton's *Federalist* 11. He began with a familiar list of the commercial and military benefits of the Union and then analyzed geopolitics in a way that placed the United States in sympathy with all non-European lands while raising it above the others as a benevolent leader.[37] Hamilton drew on the law of nations to divide the world into four parts: Europe, Africa, Asia, and America. "Unhappily for the other three," he wrote, "Europe by her arms and by her negociations, by force and fraud, has, in different degrees, extended her dominion over them all." Knowledge had followed power. European writers claimed that their continent provided the healthiest environment, and so their intellectual culture was superior too. In contrast "all animals," including people, "degenerate in America."[38] Hamilton decried the "arrogant pretensions of the European," declaring that "[i]t belongs to us to vindicate the honor of the human race, and to teach that assuming brother moderation." Ratification would do so, while "[d]isunion will add another victim to his triumphs" because the individual states would become "the instruments of European greatness!"[39] Hamilton placed the Union in league with Africa and Asia. He also appointed it "the Arbiter of Europe in America," which would play the European empires off each other "as our interests may dictate."[40] The Constitution would create "one great American system, superiour to the control or influence, and able to dictate the connection between, the old and the new world!"[41] Hamilton presented the Constitution as a sequel to the Declaration of Independence, expanding its indictment of Britain to all Europe. He did not specify the role of the other European colonies in this "American system"; implicitly they would join the United States or submit to its lead. *Federalist* 11 asked a domestic audience to embrace the Constitution while alerting the world to its symbolic importance.

Some familiar imperial issues were not discussed. The role of the Iroquois is one example. For decades the relationship with the Iroquois was central to New York's political culture. This remained so in the 1780s, as Governor George Clinton's administration purchased vast tracts from the Six Nations. For decades the state sold this land to raise revenue for public improvements rather than impose taxes. Yet there are few references to Native American affairs in the convention journals, *The Federalist*, or elsewhere. Centralization of Indian diplomacy was an electoral loser for Federalists in New York, and Antifederalists too were loath to bring attention to the state's aggressive land purchases.[42] Slavery was another explosive issue of the 1780s, and Jay and Hamilton were founders of New York's Society for Promoting the Manumission of Slaves. Yet slavery was largely absent from the debate. Federalists, an interstate group that included many large slaveholders, avoided the issue and treated it as a state concern. Most Antifederalists could not disagree.[43] Regional tensions, on the other hand, were central to the debate and served as code for distinguishing states dependent on slavery from those that were not.[44] Federalists used regionalism to justify the Constitution's protection of the international slave trade for twenty years. Indian affairs and slavery were living legacies of a colonial system resting on cheap land and coerced labor; Federalists and Antifederalists had reasons for submerging both.

On the other hand, ratification brought new actors into the political culture. The old imperial agents were gone, but a new group of imperial thinkers took their place, some of them also immigrants from the old British provinces. These last, though a minority, were among the most influential Federalists and congregated in the middle Atlantic cities of New York and Philadelphia. There was Hamilton (1755–1804), who was born out of wedlock in the West Indies, worked for a New York mercantile family, and, through its patronage, came to New York for education. Talent and charm won Hamilton his next advantages: marriage into the influential Schuyler family, an advisory position to George Washington, and success at the New York bar.[45] Similar was William Duer (1747–99), born in Devonshire, west England. He assisted Robert Clive in India and managed his father's land in the West Indies before moving to New York in 1768, where he served in the Provincial Convention that drafted the state constitution. Later he worked with Hamilton at the Treasury Department and became one of the new nation's largest land speculators.[46] Another was Robert Morris (1734–1806), who moved to Philadelphia as a factor for a Liverpool tobacco firm, helped finance the Revolutionary War, lobbied for a central bank, and also speculated in frontier land.[47] There was also James Wilson (1742–98), who was born in Scotland and died while serving on the Supreme Court.[48] The first three were instrumental in devising the financial policy of the new federal government; Hamilton and Wilson were preeminent lawyers; and all four married into illustrious creole families, Hamilton and Duer into New York clans. Most Federalist leaders, of course, came from families that had been stalwarts of provincial resistance, and these families increasingly forged interstate alliances.[49] In addition, many loyalists who remained in the states joined the Federalists, among whom a sympathy of vision of the future mattered more than differences a decade earlier.[50] Still, immigrant cosmopolites wielded disproportionate influence, and several of them made New York City their home.

As the old provincial elite became a national elite, replacements emerged within New York, and these state leaders remained provincial in terms of their family background, education, and occupation. Such men had long participated in town and county government, still the site of most public administration, and they championed state sovereignty to protect that local world.[51] Abraham Yates was representative of the type. Yates began his life as an artisan and then apprenticed at law, gained local office, and in the late colonial period served interests of the the Livingston family. After the Revolution, he embraced a new brand of populist localism. For men like him, the Revolution was about more than casting off British rulers. It also undermined deferential politics and gave them an independent base of support.[52] Robert Yates, Abraham's cousin and another a self-educated lawyer from a middling Albany family, was similar. So too Melancton Smith, a self-made lawyer and merchant in Dutchess County. The most successful Antifederalist politician was George Clinton, who governed New York for six straight terms between 1777 and 1795 and then won a seventh term in 1800 before being elected as Thomas Jefferson's vice president in 1804. While national prominence distinguished him from other New York Antifederalists, his beliefs were theirs. Clinton was the son of Charles Clinton, who in 1729 immigrated from Ireland to Little Britain, Ulster County, and became a successful farmer and surveyor. He impressed Cadwallader Colden, who in 1748 arranged for Charles Clinton to be appointed sheriff of New York City, but Charles demurred, preferring country life. While George, a lawyer, rarely turned down an office, he too viewed himself as a yeoman, a defender of men like his father and their neighbors.[53] Throughout his life Clinton supported the Union, but he always placed the state's interests first, and during ratification he opposed the Constitution because he believed it infringed on New York's autonomy. These New Yorkers wrote many of the leading Antifederalist tracts under republican pen names like "Cato," "Sydney," "Brutus," and the "Federal Farmer."

The greatest change in New York's political society was the expansion of popular participation. Ratification itself provided an occasion for this increased participation. When the state legislature instructed localities to hold elections for delegates to the Poughkeepsie convention, it decreed that all adult men, regardless of property holdings, could vote in those elections.[54] Universal white manhood suffrage in ordinary state elections was a generation away, and the full inclusion of racial minorities and women much farther still. But with this small step the New York legislature signaled that the Revolution had elevated the status of common men. Virtual representation no longer sufficed. The vocal but formally voiceless squatters and mechanics began to enter the political sphere, and they did so as members of the state's constitutional community.

Popular forces affected ratification in another, indirect way. An important manifestation of popular constitutionalism was, as before the Revolution, migration beyond existing jurisdictions and into Indian country. Federalists feared that some states or settlers in the western territories would secede, possibly joining with other European empires.[55] On maps that land was now labeled U.S. territory. On the ground it remained a marchland governed by Native Americans, frontier strongmen, and the British military, which retained western forts along the Ohio and Mississippi rivers for another generation.[56] Westward movement was more of a provocation now than before the Revolution because the United States could defend its western borders even less effectively than had the British. Encircled by other empires, containing thousands of aliens it called Indians, and pregnant with unruly migrants, the Confederation lacked the "energy," Federalists warned, to turn boundaries into jurisdiction. These popular forces comprised young men, small families, and land developers luring a stream of immigrants. These migrants spanned the social spectrum, more middling than low and with a fair amount of elite participation.[57] Legal authority had always been weak in North America, a fact that had prompted the imperial agents to reform the legal system in the 1760s, which in turn sparked the Revolution. The situation was little different two decades later. Constitutionalism had to follow, literally, American folkways. Before, during, and after the ratification campaign, settlers voted with their feet. Constitutional law was crafted to shape facts in the future, but the hard fact of mobility conditioned the making of the Constitution.

At the same time that the founders were meeting in Philadelphia to draft the Constitution, the Confederation Congress passed the Northwest Ordinance to guide the process whereby federal territories would become states on an "equal footing" with the original thirteen. The ordinance, which complemented the new Constitution by elaborating its brief section on the admission of new states, established the principle that the new Union, unlike the old empire, would consider those in all its territories as equals who deserved political representation, trial by jury, access to the writ of habeas corpus, and other common-law liberties.[58] Two days before Congress passed the ordinance, George Mason warned the Philadelphia Convention that if new states were not "placed on an equal footing," they would "speedily revolt from the Union." This term "equal footing," a phrase from the law of nations that denoted equal treaty partners, was central to the ordinance; Mason's use of it reveals that the convention delegates communicated with Congress in New York. (Indeed, forty-two of the fifty-three Philadelphia delegates were also congressmen.) The ordinance was partly anti-imperial because it rejected a permanent two-tier hierarchy within the Union. While the territories enjoyed scant autonomy under federal rule, as soon as they had "sixty thousand free inhabitants" they could become states like the others.[59] The ordinance remained, however, an instrument of empire because its drafters assumed that the Union would grow, perhaps even beyond the borders negotiated in the peace treaty with Britain. Settlers would continue to migrate west, and the only question was whether they would remain citizens of the Union when they did.[60] Each side in the ratification debate tried to explain why those settlers should resist the enticements or repel the threats of competitor empires—why "we the people" were *a* people. Each side presented its vision of the Union, hoping to persuade those people to adopt its version of it.

Consent in a Republican Empire

Federalists redefined key concepts of their constitutional culture to persuade their audiences at home, abroad, and in the future that the new Constitution improved on British imperial government. In contrast, Antifederalists spoke the vernacular of traditional English localism, and their horizons did not always extend even to state borders. This localism was a political strength, and although Antifederalists lost the battle of ratification, they succeeded in embedding customs of local control into American constitutionalism.

The primary theme of the ratification debate was simple: Who would rule and where? Historians have long known that a leading issue was whether the great expanse of the United States would frustrate republican government. The Federalists hoped to create a cosmopolitan, interstate governing class, which they thought possible only with strong federal institutions. Antifederalists, on the other hand, wanted to preserve a familiar world of local authority in which many of them figured large. They thought that the states should be held together by affection and trade, not a strong central government. Rather than an abstract discussion of a republic's optimal size, this debate reprised the colonial dispute over the locus of authority in a multi-tiered empire.[61]

Unease about the size of the Union surfaced in the Philadelphia Convention. New York delegates Robert Yates and John Lansing Jr. left Philadelphia in July partly because the convention had exceeded its mandate. But they also worried that concentrating too much authority in a government over so much territory would destroy the "civil liberty of such citizens who could be effectually coerced by it."[62] A large republic, according to orthodox learning, was an oxymoron. When the ratification debate began a few months later, "Cato" (possibly Governor Clinton) cited Montesquieu and other "sensible and approved political authors" for the proposition that faithful representation was impossible in a large republic. Some of the states were already too big to function as republics. Rather than creating a larger "despotic" government, existing states might one day have to subdivide into more manageable jurisdictions. This was no idle speculation. New Yorkers had seen their northeastern counties secede and form Vermont, and they had renounced land claims in the Ohio Valley.[63] While many, including Clinton, had lamented these losses, only force could have prevented them. Similar pressures, "Cato" reported, threatened to fracture Massachusetts and North Carolina. The lesson was clear: if individual states could not keep their territories intact, neither would a large national government—not, at least, without military force.[64]

Antifederalists raised the problem of a large republic often. "Brutus," the pen name of Robert Yates, also invoked Montesquieu to argue that "[i]n a large republic, the public good is sacrificed to a thousand views," while in a small republic it is "easier perceived." The new Union, unlike the Confederation, "will not be a compact entered into by the states in their corporate capacities, but an agreement of the people of the United States, as one great body politic." This meant that its power would "extend to every case for which any government is instituted, whether external or internal." If the Philadelphia plan had simply created "a union of states or bodies corporate," then "the existence of the state governments, might have been secured." The sharp distinction between internal power and external regulation was, as Yates noted, "not a novel one in this country": it derived from arguments to vindicate the corporate integrity of the colonies in the old empire.[65] Antifederalists drew on the language of corporate autonomy to express similar fears that the federal government would suppress provincial law and custom, as well as bypass the state constitutions, and operate directly on individuals. All this was reminiscent of arguments for colonial self-government, except that the apparatus of empire would be pervasive. The seat of the federal government, in its ten-square-mile capital, would be far from some areas of the Union; this was a frequent objection to strong central government. But it would be much closer than London, and its agents would be more involved in local affairs. New Yorkers had already experienced this difference in 1785 when the Confederation Congress, against much opposition, voted to appoint impost collectors on New York piers.[66]

The meaning of the corporate analogy, however, was changing in subtle ways. One example was Antifederalists' frequent use of the word "freeman." In the colonies, this term had usually signified an enfranchised member of a corporation, like the freemen of New York City. Widespread use of the word during the Revolution and in the ratification debate stretched its meaning so that it helped flesh out the new term "citizen." Citizen replaced "subject" as the signifier of membership, and the liberties of freemen defined citizenship. "You may rejoice in the prospects of this vast extended continent becoming filled with freemen," exclaimed Brutus, "who will assert the dignity of human nature."[67] Similarly, the phrase "privileges and immunities," which originated as a trope of corporate power but had slowly escaped into the broader political vernacular, came into its own as a label for constitutional rights.[68] Finally, state-chartered corporations began to proliferate as ways to organize churches, schools, and banks, a trend that began before the Revolution and accelerated rapidly after.[69] How much power each corporation had was unclear, and the boundaries of corporate authority were renegotiated throughout the nineteenth century.

While Antifederalists feared lumping the states with colleges and turnpike companies, Federalists were quick to do so. The Union required "district tribunals," Hamilton declared at the Philadelphia Convention, "corporations for local purposes." The states would fill this administrative role. Yet "even with corporate rights the states will be dangerous to the national government, and ought to be extinguished, new modified, or reduced to a smaller scale."[70] Hamilton's distrust of the states was extreme, but it rested on a common Federalist assumption that the states should be, at best, weak corporations. Several days later, Madison qualified state power with more subtlety. He tried to map the traditional pluralism of British North America onto the modern principle of sovereignty. "The States are not sovereign in the full Extent of the Term," he told the convention. Instead, "there is a gradation from a simple corporation for limited and specified objects, such as an incorporation of a number of mechanicks, up to a full sovereignty as possessed by independent nations whose powers are not limited — the last only are truly sovereign — The States . . . are not in the true meaning of the word sovereigns — They are political associations, or corporations, possessing certain powers — by these they may make some, but not all Laws."[71] This vision of the states as limited corporations was also the premise of the argument that the central and state governments would enjoy "concurrent jurisdiction" over powers like taxation. Concurrence could be admitted, but federal power trumped when the two conflicted.[72]

This belief that the Antifederalists wanted to retain sovereign authority for the states, and thus violate the modern principle of indivisible sovereignty, was a cardinal point among Federalists.[73] Hamilton argued that the "radical vice" in the Confederation was "the principle of Legislation or States or Governments, in their Corporate or Collective Capacities and as contradistinguished from the Individuals of which they consist." He concluded that Antifederalists "still in fine seem to cherish with blind devotion the political monster of an *imperium in imperio*."[74] Federalists were right. Antifederalists held firm to the principle of the ancient constitution that political power should never be absolute. Legal pluralism had long marked the British Empire, but Antifederalists did not theorize about this traditional idea of limited or fragmented power. Instead of a principle they provided a list of traditional safeguards of local authority. With the corporation devalued, they relied especially on the common-law jury and, drawing on the tradition of the mixed constitution, celebrated the "democracy" at the expense of the "aristocracy."[75] These were the terms available to express their fear that a strong union would undermine local control, local law, and local ways of doing social business that seemed to them unchanging, time out of mind. They wanted to preserve the political landscape they knew well and that had been validated in the state constitutions. They used the "state" as a metaphor for that local world. But that term — that jurisdiction — was ill suited to their goals. It was almost as if, by defending state power, they had ceded the localist premise beneath their arguments. Hamilton agreed with Antifederalists that some states were larger than Montesquieu's ideal small republic.[76] New York, for example, had not been able to hold on to Vermont or its western land claims. The state was already too big for the Clintons, Smiths, and Yateses to control, and they were left without an alternative theory that would justify local autonomy *and* unite the states. Behind their defense of state power lay the traditional practices of local authority, along with faith in a common interest that remained underarticulated. As a result, the emerging theory of federalism left little room for local government.[77]

While Federalists ignored local government, they glorified the other end of the spectrum. The Union's imperial potential presented an argument for centralized government that transcended the dialectic of local versus central government. The Union was not only feasible; it represented a new stage in the history of political development. Only next to this bold claim did Antifederalist localism seem unimaginative.[78] The large Republic would not just neutralize factions. It would exceed the sum of its parts — "an empire . . . the most interesting in the world." Hamilton's imperial aspirations shine off everything he wrote, including that first page of *Federalist* 1.[79] In *Federalist* 2, John Jay celebrated the divine destiny of "the people of America" and their continent. Rivers, for example, presented an argument from design: "A succession of navigable waters forms a kind of chain round its borders, as if to bind it together; while the most noble rivers in the world, running at convenient distances, present them with highways for the easy communication of friendly aids, and the mutual transportation and exchange of their various commodities."[80]

Auspicious geography was not the only gift. "Providence," exclaimed this descendant of Huguenot refugees, "g[a]ve this one connected country, to one united people, a people descended from the same ancestors, speaking the same language, professing the same religion, attached to the same principles of government, very similar in their manners and customs, and who, by their joint counsels, arms and efforts, fighting side by side throughout a long and bloody war, have nobly established their general Liberty and Independence." Much of this landscape was imaginary. The "country" had not always been "connected." New Netherland, for example, had separated New England from the southern colonies until 1664. Most but not all of the people were Protestant. Most, if not all, celebrated English law as a guarantor of liberty. But less than half joined the Revolution, and probably only a minority of New Yorkers were descended from the same ancestors if by that Jay meant, strictly, Englishmen. Customs among the new "Americans" also varied greatly. Jay admitted that there were different "orders and denominations among us." Nonetheless "to all general purposes we have uniformly been one people — each individual citizen every where enjoying the same national rights, privileges, and protection." He added that "[t]his intelligent people perceived and regretted th[e] defects" in the Articles of Confederation and, "as with one voice, convened the late Convention at Philadelphia," which was untrue.[81] Jay's history of the colonial period, the civil war that followed, and the Confederation helped construct, rather than simply depicted, the national self-understanding he believed necessary to make the Constitution work. But this "imagined community" did not ring true. There was yet no sense of an American people who shared the same beliefs and a defined space. The term "nation" was too broad for some. The United States was not, thought one Connecticut lawyer, a nation in the "common acceptation of the word" because its people were already "part of one of the oldest Nations in Europe." Culturally and by descent, most Americans were still British. For others, like Hamilton, the term was too narrow to embrace the Union. The Constitution could not rest on a nationalist premise; it would have to create it. The ideal and experience of empire were indispensable to this process of creating a common identity.[82]

Jay's favorite example came from imperial history: the Act of Union of 1707. That act forged Great Britain; two nations became one. Before Madison and Hamilton delved into republics ancient and modern, Jay reminded his readers in *Federalist* 5 that "[t]he history of Great Britain is the one with which we are in general the best acquainted, and it gives us many useful lessons." Two benefits stood out among the many that flowed from what Queen Anne, he recalled, referred to as the "entire and perfect Union." First, it improved defense and gave Britain greater leverage in foreign affairs. Second, it facilitated trade among the British people and increased their wealth. If England, Scotland, Wales, and Ireland were to separate, each would "dwindle into comparative insignificance." He asked the reader to "[a]pply these facts to our own case — Leave America divided into thirteen, or if you please into three or four independent Governments." These regional "confederacies" would suffer commercially and be vulnerable to foreign intrigue.[83] Similarly, Hamilton warned that "*divide et impera*," a corollary of the maxim that *imperium in imperio* was a political solecism, "must be the motto of every nation, that either hates, or fears us."[84] New York's position was especially precarious.

It was "directly exposed" to native and European powers, and it had experienced a rebellion that led to the secession of Vermont.[85] Without the Constitution, the states would be like the British Isles before the Act of Union.

Some Antifederalists dismissed these arguments as beside the point. They too supported a federation. The only question was how centralized its government would be. "The only thing I can understand from [*The Federalist*]," wrote DeWitt Clinton, the young nephew of New York's governor, "is that it is better to be united than divided—that a great many people are stronger than few—and that Scotland is better off since the union with England than before." Clinton exploited the ambiguity of Federalist prescriptions that alternated between celebrations of the old empire and aspirations toward universal liberty. Did Publius intend, Clinton asked, "to persuade us to return back to the old government, and make ourselves as happy as Scotland has by its union, or to accept the new constitution, and get the whole world to join with us, so as to make one large government[?]"[86]

While no one proposed a world government, Federalists did hope to fit the Constitution into the science of politics. Perhaps the best example of the Federalist version of *translatio studii* was James Madison's revision of the conventional wisdom about the optimal size of republics.[87] Because political factionalism was inevitable, he argued, a large republic with many factions would be more stable than a small one with few. Madison was one of the strongest critics of the state governments and advocated federal review of all state legislation on the model of New York's Council of Revision and the Privy Council.[88] His republicanism was built for expansion.

Madison accepted David Hume's iconoclastic claim that large republics were better than small.[89] Hume had derived his appreciation for large republics from the experience of Great Britain. He was born four years after the Act of Union and four before the Jacobite rebellion in 1715. He wrote his seminal essays on republicanism in the 1740s, amid more Jacobite violence. Hume was no Jacobite.[90] But he was a Scot in an Anglo-dominated Great Britain and therefore understood the danger of majority factions. While "Oceana" now covered the Isle of Britain and Ireland too, Scots and Irishmen remained distrusted minorities in the imperial capital.[91] Hume reconstructed the theory of the commonwealth to account for these new religious, ethnic, and economic minorities. In other words, he amended English republicanism to make it British: all of Greater Britain formed a single republic.[92]

Madison found this British republicanism attractive and pushed it further to create what might be called imperial republicanism. The crux of his revision was his assertion that factions were inevitable. In a small republic, a majority faction might oppress minority factions, but in a large republic factions would counterbalance one another, thus neutralizing private interests and allowing the public good to triumph. In addition, the larger area would embrace a greater number of men fit to serve as representatives. In sum, a large republic would help control factions, not (as Hume hoped) prevent factions from forming in the first place.[93] Madison's remedy for factional misrule was to ensure that the federal government could check state legislatures and that the other branches of the federal government could check the House of Representatives.[94] Checks and balances would make imperial republicanism work. Although Madison wrote number 10, like all *The Federalist Papers*, to persuade ratifiers in New York, his reworking of inherited learning would also answer European critics.

Madison's additions also reflected the fact that he was a southern slaveholder. He, like Hume, had conflicting interests in mind when he analyzed republicanism in *Federalist* 10: conflicts between regions and types of property. One group of property owners, such as debtors, should not be permitted to oppress another. Though this essay never mentions slavery, implicit in this factional theory was a warning to holders of slave property.[95] If debtors could control state legislatures and punish creditors, the nascent antislavery movement might someday succeed too. New York was at that time considering its own abolition statute, and southerners feared that the movement for mandatory abolition would spread.[96] In the wake of the Revolution, many slaveholders questioned their reliance on slave labor. Madison, for example, entertained the idea of selling his Virginia plantation and relocating in New York's Mohawk Valley to escape dependence on slavery.[97] He did not, however, want to be *forced* to manumit his slaves. Slave owners, not abolitionist legislators, would decide when and how to end the institution. Most of Madison's audience did not respond to his argument that factions were inevitable and that those in a large republic would neutralize one another.[98] But the theory of diffused representation and elite filtration, and the belief that holders of vested property rights like slave property deserved protection, informed American law for generations.

While British experience was at the root of Federalists' arguments, they also invoked other examples of good and bad empires. Hamilton compared the states to German principalities, whose stifled economy was described in an article entitled "Empire" in Diderot's *Encyclopédie*. "The commerce of the German Empire," Hamilton quoted from the *Encyclopédie*, "is in continual trammels from the multiplicity of the duties which the several Princes and States exact upon the merchandizes passing through their territories; by means of which the fine streams and navigable rivers with which Germany is so happily watered, are rendered almost useless." Surely "the people of this country" had more "genius" than to allow this to happen. If not, "the citizens of each [state]" would find themselves treated as "foreigners and aliens" in neighboring states. The Constitution would facilitate travel and trade and thus establish a common citizenship.[99]

Although the British imperial agents were gone, their arguments for stronger central government resurfaced. Provincial obstruction of customs collection, defense, and diplomacy had been common complaints before the Revolution. Analytical devices persisted too. Cadwallader Colden and Thomas Pownall had drawn on Matthew Hale's *History of the Common Law* to argue that the colonial courts, like local courts in medieval England, were controlled by local elites. Central review in a forum beyond their reach was necessary to protect the crown's interest. Hamilton invoked similar lessons from the "encroachment" of the "great feudal chiefs" on the emperor's power in the Holy Roman Empire and from the Scottish clans before the British Union. The common people were the greatest victims, for "the power of the head of the nation was commonly too weak either to preserve the public peace or to protect the people against the oppressions of their immediate lords."[100] State-based elites posed a similar threat to popular liberty.

Hamilton's analysis of how the "sovereign" united with "the common people" against the "aristocracy" followed an interpretation of medieval history popularized over the previous century. After the Stuart restoration, Tory legal thinkers constructed a triangular sociology of revolt, with the rebellious gentry opposing both the crown and the people. Complementary interests brought the king and people together to end "feudal anarchy." Again, the 1707 Union provided "a cogent example" of how the central government could subdue the "ungovernable spirit" of local clans in Scotland.[101] A counterintuitive argument began to emerge: the federal government might represent the people more truly than the state governments. It was another answer to the charge that Federalists were establishing a unitary, oppressive sovereign. Sovereignty *was* unitary, but the people were the sovereign.

Popular sovereignty was as old a script as the crown's prerogative and other elements of classical politics, but it gained new meaning during the ratification debate. The people delegated part of their sovereignty to the states and part to the federal government. Federal administrators would help ensure that the states remained within their bounds. Federalist celebrations of popular sovereignty were not, however, always what they seemed.[102] In theory, the United States adhered to the spreading European orthodoxy that every polity had a unitary sovereign.[103] Federalists began to identify the people as sovereign only *after* the Philadelphia Convention to answer the Antifederalist charge that the new Constitution centralized all authority. For Federalists, popular sovereignty was a powerful constitutional fiction. While the people possessed all sovereignty, they parceled it out among different institutions and jurisdictions. The largest quantity of that power went to the states, but they gave the highest quality to the federal government. This theory did not, however, identify who would administer government, where, and how.

The Federalists imagined a new empire modeled on the old, but they lacked the institutional leverage of the British imperial agents and the legimating symbol of the crown. Only once established would the federal government provide an institutional home for like-minded men. Yet, paradoxically, the absence of official positions allowed the Federalists to speak broadly for the public interest, or *a* public interest, one they helped create. The absence of a metropolis offered Federalists an opportunity to revise republicanism in more hopeful terms. It was a new map of authority with no invidious distinction between a central capital and peripheral provinces and without fear that expansion would lead to corruption. Indeed, expansion would help *prevent* corruption, as republican ambivalence toward expansion gave way to manifest destiny.[104] In the new Union, there would be a center of personnel and ideas, if not a political capital. Federalists like Hamilton and Madison strove to create that center in the form of like-minded men adhering to similar views of the Union. When in 1785 George Washington called New York City "at present the seat of the empire," some residents might have persuaded themselves that they inhabited London's successor, but most Federalists realized that the center was a sympathy of vision rather than a place.[105] The medium of communication was part of the transformation. Instead of private missives to one another, the Federalists published their arguments for efficient government openly in letters to New York voters and addressed those people as the sovereign. Like the imperial agents, Federalists hoped that their sovereign could be educated, guided, and cajoled. They too hoped that their own interests could be linked to the sovereign's. They also succeeded in generating a public conversation rather than, as among the old imperial agents, a series of private complaints. The new Constitution would, they hoped, create neither a government of men nor one of law but rather one of men governed by a common understanding of law. That understanding of the Constitution's purpose, its unwritten premise, would outlast individual men. If the Federalists successfully persuaded the people to renounce corporate privileges and immunities, they — the Federalists — might be able to determine "the fate of an empire, in many respects, the most interesting in the world."[106]

Between Aristocracy and Democracy:
From Mixed Government to the Separation of Powers

Concern about the social composition of the proposed federal administration was mixed into the debate over the location of authority. Antifederalists feared that the Constitution would engender an elite of government administrators, which they termed an aristocracy. Federalists in turn hoped to establish a cosmopolitan group of federal leaders who shared an imperial vision. One side pictured a democracy of the middling for the middling. The other was moving toward the ideal of a civil service dedicated to the Union and its expansion rather than to the status quo under the state constitutions. Old terms were deployed for a new political world that lacked both a crown and a legal aristocracy. While the social was not quite identical with the political, the mass of white men enjoyed the same legal rights as the social elite and, as suffrage qualifications fell in New York in the 1820s, most political rights too. As the social dimension of constitutionalism collapsed, the new doctrine of separated powers emerged as a strategy to protect interests that could no longer be identified with the classic estates.[107]

Melancton Smith, author of the Antifederalist "Federal Farmer" letters, worried that a strong federal government would homogenize the laws of the demographically and geographically diverse states. "Different laws, customs, and opinions exist in the different states," he protested, "which by a uniform system of laws would be unreasonably invaded." Representation in Congress would be chimerical "if the extreme parts of the society cannot be represented as fully as the central."[108] This Antifederalist picture of the states was quite different from John Jay's providential landscape. Antifederalists feared that representation in the new government would be so diluted that the "extreme parts" — geographic and social — would have little influence.[109] Those elected would become unrepresentative, possibly aristocratic. Thomas Tredwell complained at the ratification convention that the debate was "not between little states and great states" but rather "between little folks and great folks, between patriotism and ambition . . . not so much between navigating states and non-navigating states, as between navigating and non-navigating individuals."[110] Tredwell's metaphor, pitting those who traded on interstate rivers against those who did not, revealed that the battle over state power was at bottom a contest between those satisfied in the states and those who aspired to a grander stage.

Listen to the description of this elite. Smith predicted that federal officeholders would live in a "high" style. "Cato" (again, probably Governor Clinton) feared that "men of opulence" would control Congress, especially the Senate, which was "removed from the people." Another New Yorker warned that ratification would "convert the people of this great country into hewers of wood and drawers of water for the few great ones, into whose hands all power will be thereby unwarily delivered."[111] For Antifederalists, politics was social.

It was also geographic. Antifederalists raised the specter of the federal capital becoming a "court" populated by courtiers. It would become, Thomas Tredwell complained at the ratification convention, a "political hive, where all the drones in the society are to be collected to feed on the honey of the land."[112] The fear was not just that aspiring aristocrats would exclude humble men from the federal government. Honest "middling" men would avoid such positions. The president, "Cato" predicted, would enjoy "the splendor of a prince." The capital, in its own ten-square-mile seat of power, would resemble European royal courts. Unlike state officials, the president and congressmen would enjoy long-term tenures. All inhabitants of the *"federal city"* would view themselves as "the great and mighty of the earth." The capital would be "the asylum of the base, idle, avaricious and ambitious." Senators in particular would "form and pursue interests separate from those who appointed them." Citing Algernon Sidney, the republican thinker, Clinton warned that the new Republic would breed tyranny: "[G]reat power connected with ambition, luxury and flattery, will as readily produce a Caesar, Caligula, Nero and Domitain in America, as the same causes did in the Roman Empire."[113]

The Antifederalists, however, moved beyond the old contrast between court and country. They too employed current European learning. They expressed their fears in terms of the mixed constitution as well as the new sociology of the Scottish Enlightenment. Monarchy was gone. Aristocracy and democracy remained and had to be carefully balanced.[114] The "democracy" in New York, the Antifederalists argued, was composed of modest farmers and merchants—representatives of the new commercial society—while most educated professionals and officeholders represented a regression to a parasitic aristocracy. Antifederalists did not, therefore, cling to the old republican suspicion of commerce. They and the Federalists agreed that agricultural and commercial interests were, in Hamilton's words, "intimately blended and interwoven."[115] The Antifederalists' court-country distinction hinged instead on the character of those who would dominate commerce. Progress lay with the modest and middling.[116]

Melancton Smith was the most articulate critic of the Constitution's social consequences. He referred to "orders," "classes," and "parties" interchangeably, each term conjuring the old mixed constitution. In the end, though, he fixated on the tension between the aristocratic and democratic segments of society, or the many and the few. True, he told the ratification convention, the Constitution established "no legal or hereditary distinctions." Nonetheless, "there are real differences" between men. He feared that the *natural aristocracy* of "birth, education, talents, and wealth," rather than the "middling class," would gain office.[117] "Men of the first class associate more extensively," Smith explained, "have a high sense of honor, possess abilities, ambition, and general knowledge." Below them, second-class men "possess less ambition, and a larger share of honesty: their dependence is principally on middling and small estates, industrious pursuits, and hard labour, while that of the former is principally on the emoluments of large estates, and of the chief offices of government." In addition to these two classical orders, Smith drew on the new economic classifications of merchant, farmer, mechanic, and professional. In this second scheme, the merchants were the pillars of liberty. He then blended the two frameworks to argue that the best *political* group was the "substantial and respectable part of the democracy," which he equated *socially* with middling citizens just "above the majority of the people." Such men "are the most substantial and best informed in the several towns, who occasionally fill the middle grades of offices, &c. who hold not a splendid, but a respectable rank in private concerns."[118] These men were "nearer the mass of the people" and understood "the true commercial interests of a country."[119] In contrast, educated professionals would dominate Congress, and "the schools produce but few advocates for republican forms of government."[120] Smith, an autodidact, had blended classical political theory with emergent sociology to taint those most likely to rule the federal government as relics of an earlier stage of social development.

Smith also innovated on the history of the ancient constitution. In a Whig allegory that was the mirror image of Hamilton's triangular Tory history, Smith portrayed a free England suddenly conquered by a Norman king and "foreign mercenaries." The interlopers "laid arbitrary taxes, and established arbitrary courts, and severely oppress[ed] all orders of people." In response, "the barons and the people" united to retrieve the liberties reflected in the

"Magna Charta, a bill of rights, &c." and secured by legislatures and juries. While refuting Hamilton's story of oppression of the people by a middle order, Smith compared Federalists to the Norman conquerors; the Constitution was their feudal yoke.[121] Federalists were men "of no small talents and of great influence, of consummate cunning, and masters of intrigue, whom the war found poor, or in embarrassed circumstances, and left with princely fortunes, acquired in public employment."[122] It was a picture of ruthless office hunters, as if he had in mind the illegitimate Hamilton, who rose from the tropics, found the war he had sought since age twelve, and insinuated himself into an illustrious family, the confidence of leading men, and high office.[123]

These indictments were paradoxical. Federalists also championed commerce, and management of interstate and foreign trade was the major impetus behind the Philadelphia Convention. Antifederalists did not explain how they reconciled their commitment to localism with the claim to represent the progressive, industrious segment of commercial society. It is possible to imagine a theory that comfortably holds both, such as libertarian political economy, but New York's Antifederalists did not articulate one.[124]

Federalists answered the political sociology of the Antifederalists in three ways. First, some denied that there could be an aristocracy in the United States. The Constitution prohibited titles; there never would be a hereditary nobility. Alternatively, some Federalists equated the term "aristocracy" with the wealthy. Because the Constitution established no property qualifications for voting or office holding, it would not favor the rich.[125] Aristocracy, explained a young lawyer named James Kent, was strictly "a Government of a few permanent Nobles independent of & not chosen by nor amenable to the great body of the People." Any other use of the term was polemical. Kent quipped that if the "Federal Farmer" was correct in designating "men of talents & Property the natural Aristocracy of the Country," then he hoped that he would "always be governed by an aristocracy," a sentiment echoed by state chancellor Robert R. Livingston at the ratification convention and many others for years afterward.[126]

Finally, Hamilton addressed the fear that Congress's distance from its constituents would undermine representative government. New York was again a good example. The state was already too large to allow voters to monitor their representatives directly. "What are the sources of information by which the people in Montgomery county must regulate their judgment of the conduct of their representatives in the state legislature [in New York City]?" Few citizens were "on the spot." The others received political information "from public prints, from correspondences with their representatives, and with other persons who reside at the place of their deliberation." So it would be with federal representation. In addition, and reminiscent of the theory of virtual representation, Hamilton argued that those "who inhabit the country at and near the seat of government, will in all questions that affect the general liberty and prosperity, have the same interest with those who are at a distance." They would alert their fellow citizens to any threats from government.[127] Madison added that roads, canals, and other "new improvements" would decrease the travel time between government and the people.[128]

In any case, Hamilton argued that the Confederation was actually *less* representative of the people than the proposed federal government, for it had not been approved by them directly. Ratification — popular sovereignty in action — would root the federal government more deeply than the Confederation. "The fabric of American Empire ought to rest on the solid basis of The Consent of the People," which he called the "pure original fountain of all legitimate authority." In addition, the proposed House of Representatives would be apportioned by population and thus was more representative than the Confederation Congress, in which each of the states had equal weight. This too appealed to voters in the populous state of New York. Hamilton argued that "every idea of proportion, and every rule of fair representation conspire to condemn a principle, which gives to Rhode-Island an equal weight in the scale of power with Massachusetts, or Connecticut, or New-York. . . . Its operation contradicts that fundamental maxim of republican government, which requires that the sense of the majority should prevail."[129] Distance was no obstacle to effective representation, and the new Congress would better represent New Yorkers than the old. In sum, the United States was neither geographically nor structurally destined to produce an aristocracy.

Yet many Federalists hoped that, in practice, the Constitution would create an aristocracy, if that meant rule by a gifted, cosmopolitan minority. Their ideal was administration in the public rather than local interest, not an aristocracy in opposition to a democracy. "Government will never be respected, and opinion will never give aid to democratical authority," one New York Federalist declared, "when almost every office is in the hands of those who are not distinguished by property, family, education, manners or talents." State government was controlled by "characters who carry every mark of civil inferiority; and who cannot enjoy that confidence and esteem which the world always gives to property and education."[130] "Marcus" added that the new government would benefit all the people, not just farmers and mechanics but also those with "liberal and extensive" educations "because there will be a theatre for the display of talents, which have no influence in State Assemblies, where eloquence is treated with contempt, and reason over-powered by a *silent vote.*" Conversely, the Constitution was "*not* in the Interest of those who enjoy State consequence, which would be lost in the Assemblies of the States. These insects and worms are only seen on their own dunghill. There are minds whose narrow vision can look over the concerns of a State or Town, but cannot extend their short vision to Continental concerns."[131] Noah Webster was more temperate. He explained that Antifederalists simply "think as they have been bred—their education has been rather indifferent—they have been accustomed to think on the small scale."[132] Not for the last time did Federalists attribute opposition to poor breeding and education.

Hamilton famously explained his sociology of politics in a speech to the Philadelphia Convention on 18 June. He argued that there were two classes of people: "the rich and well born" and "the many." The latter deserved representation in "a democratic assembly" but needed to be checked by an upper house serving "during good behavior or life." A permanent senate would provide the moderating ballast that the monarchy gave Britain. Like the king, senators would have "no distinct interest from the public welfare." He concluded that "the British Government was the best in the world" and "doubted whether any thing short of it would do in America."[133] This identification of the governmental elite with the public good was familiar. Before the Revolution, imperial agents like Cadwallader Colden, Thomas Pownall, and William Knox had done the same. A year later in the ratification convention, Hamilton was less laudatory of the rich. The vices of the rich, who were no more virtuous than the poor, were less detrimental because they could be harnessed for the public interest.[134] Hamilton's later denial that the Constitution favored aristocracy may have been disingenuous. Other delegates viewed his 18 June speech as extreme. He was "praised by every gentleman, but supported by no gentleman."[135] Still, Hamilton also may have believed that senators were not a proper aristocracy because, in the final version of the Constitution, they did not serve permanently. Whether he was stung by criticism or changed his views, he no longer celebrated monarchy. Instead, he began to distinguish the people from the states, first doing so three days after his 18 June speech.[136] The sovereign and the states were not the same.

Hamilton also began to search for other institutions to house his cosmopolites. One was the electoral college. James Wilson had proposed the college to break a deadlock between delegates who wanted direct election of the president and those who preferred indirect election by the national legislature. It was a curious body that few embraced as anything other than a compromise. Nonetheless, Hamilton found virtue in it. The college would ensure that the "immediate election" of the president would be made by a special group of men "selected by their fellow citizens from the general mass" and most likely possessing "the information and discernment requisite to so complicated an investigation." Insulated from the heat of politics, the college would calmly elect the president from among those nominated by the states.[137]

More promising was the executive branch. Hamilton had hoped to place executive officers within the states even before the impost controversy of the mid-1780s.[138] Now he argued in several *Federalist* essays that the Constitution structured the executive branch in a way that would promote long-term policy. First, executive authority had to reside in one individual, as in New York, where the governor served without a council. A single executive would be efficient and less corruptible.[139] Hamilton also defended the president's four-year tenure and opposed term limitations. The president represented the people no less than did congressmen. His long tenure would allow him "to act his own opinion with vigor and decision." A permanent salary would safeguard this independence.[140] Yet Hamilton knew that the executive would comprise more than one individual. Most believed that George Washington would be elected the first president, and Hamilton anticipated some office in his administration. He became treasurer, the office made famous (to some, infamous) in Britain by Robert Walpole and the Duke of Newcastle. The imperial agents had attempted to consolidate the executive in the colonial period; Federalists tried to succeed where they failed. Still, much depended on the character of the president and his appointees, and, other than that the president be a natural citizen of at least age thirty-five, there were no qualifications for these offices. There was no guarantee that the right men would staff the executive branch.

Hamilton's hope for institutionalizing a cosmopolitan corps of administrators also lay in an independent federal judiciary. Early in the convention, when justifying the Senate's participation with the president in treaty making, Hamilton dismissed the separation of powers as a "trite topic." Two months later he championed the doctrine as a way to insulate the judiciary from Congress.[141] He knew from colonial experience that the judiciary was a critical part of effective administration. So did the Antifederalists. Consequently, the proposed federal court system generated some of the most innovative and controversial ideas in the debate over the Constitution.

From Fundamental to Constitutional Law:
The Vices of the Judicial Systems of the States

Colonial resistance had rested heavily on common-law constitution-alism, and after independence both Federalists and Antifederalists began to reclaim what they viewed as the essential common law and the enduring principles of the English constitution. But the diversity of the common-law systems among the states, combined with unconstrained legislative power within each state, encouraged an explicitly positivist conception of *the* common law. Although this diversity had long been true, during the colonial period there had been no need to theorize highly about the divergent adaptations of the common law among the colonies.[142] Now, as the states united to form a common constitution, many suddenly apprehended just how much the laws of the states varied. Not only their statutes differed but their common-law systems too.

The diversity of the state common-law regimes encouraged the ratifiers to detach the fundamental-law strands of Anglo-American constitutionalism from the common law. Participants in the constitutional debate began to treat some elements of the common law as fundamental and confined most in a category of malleable "rules of decision," which in turn were distinguished from statute law. In other words, ratification helped refract the eclectic legal resources of the British Empire into schematic categories, preparing the way in the coming decades for the emergence of an instrumental conception of common-law doctrine on the one hand and the equation of constitutional law with fundamental law on the other.

Ratification, therefore, not only resulted in the passage of the Constitution. It also catalyzed a reconception of the nature of constitutions as enforceable against legislatures because decreed by the citizenry in their constitutive role as "the people." Legal scholars have rediscovered popular sovereignty as a polestar for interpreting the founding era.[143] They recognize that the most important development in early American constitutionalism was not that the state and federal constitutions were written but rather that the process of writing them contributed to a new sense that constitutions were the *source* of fundamental law. Soon the identification of fundamental law became a matter of interpreting the Constitution. But who would enforce this fundamental law? And according to what standards? These scholars argue that the judiciary's transformation of fundamental law into "ordinary," or judicially enforceable, law departed from English constitutionalism, which they view as a hybrid of legislative supremacy and popular controls on the legislature. The innovation is attributed to either American creativity or the legal elite's fear of popular sovereignty, an attempt to "tame" the constitution and locate "an aristocratic anchor" to restrain democracy.[144] But comparing the American states with Great Britain creates the optical illusion of discontinuity: the analysis zooms in on two separate legal environments without accounting for the transatlantic empire that had long connected them. Again, while parliamentary supremacy was becoming orthodox in Great Britain, it was never so throughout the British Empire. Most people in the new states remained devoted to the idea that there were fundamental restraints on all government, including legislatures. English-speakers on both sides of the Atlantic had always used the mechanisms of popular constitutionalism, such as petitions, resistance, and mob action; citizens in the new states continued to do so. But the American provincials had also argued — and, more important, *acted* — as though their legal systems could play a large role in curtailing legislation that they viewed as inconsistent with their constitution. That is why they responded so strongly to the imperial agents' attempts to displace colonial judges and juries. In addition, extralegal resistance — of squatters, smugglers, and others — had always been more prevalent and violent in North America. Federalists wanted to eliminate such extralegal behavior from the repertoire of constitutional protest. Teaching disgruntled citizens to enter courts, rather than take to the streets or the disrupt the backcountry, was one goal of legalizing fundamental law. Strong enforcement and interpretation of the Constitution also provided a bridge between high Federalists and ordinary people.

Americans were also accustomed to extraterritorial restraints on provincial legislatures and courts. The Privy Council had reviewed colonial statutes to gauge whether they were "repugnant" to the laws of England and also entertained writs of error from colonial courts. Therefore, when lawyers in the new states spoke of a statute's "repugnancy," they drew not primarily on Sir Edward Coke's cryptic opinion in *Bonham's Case* but rather on the old colonial charter clauses empowering the Privy Council to disallow local legislation that was "repugnant" to English law.[145] New Yorkers appreciated the benefits of this restraint on legislation and included a similar institution, the Council of Revision, in their state constitution. Although neither the Privy Council nor the Council of Revision generated a coherent jurisprudence, they did condition lawyers to think in terms of hierarchies of legal institutions and possibly hierarchies of substantive law.[146] Early state courts, like the

Mayor's Court in *Rutgers v. Waddington*, built on that practice. Federalists and at least some Antifederalists in New York expected the federal judiciary to do so too. There was a menu of remedies available to citizens who believed that government had violated the state or federal constitutions. Judicial review was an increasingly attractive option for Federalists who were skeptical of legislators in the new states and in Congress as well as for Antifederalists who feared an overreaching central government.

Recent scholarship also assumes that law and politics were discrete categories before the 1780s and then Federalists took constitutions out of the political sphere and tried to insulate them within the legal sphere. This rigid distinction between law and politics was, however, not prominent in early modern legal culture. New York's Council of Revision again witnesses the point. State judges and senators together reviewed legislation. Even if they found a statute to be unconstitutional, a supermajority in the legislature could override their decision. This process of review was attractive to several delegates at the Philadelphia Convention, especially James Madison and James Wilson. The latter, for example, feared that the Supremacy Clause alone would not prevent the states from infringing on federal powers. He assumed that judicial review would help, but even the "firmness of Judges is not itself sufficient. Something further is requisite." In turn, opponents of a federal council like George Mason and James Rutledge complained that it would be "worse than making mere corporations of [the states]."[147] Anglo-American constitutionalism had defied the law/politics distinction before and after the Revolution. The ratification debate helped draw the line between law and politics with new clarity, and then federal constitutional law was elevated above both as a hybrid partaking of each.

Consequently, this new legal genre was never treated like "ordinary law." What made constitutional law distinctive was precisely that it combined elements of ordinary law, political ideology, imperial practice, and old notions of fundamental law. Constitutional law created a new discursive "arena of conflict" in which to debate the future of the Union and to impress on people in the states and territories that they were citizens of a larger whole.[148] The makers of constitutional law strove to institutionalize the sort of dialogue that flourished during the ratification debate, and they attempted to ensure that constitutional controversy remained within it. On the one hand, much of the Constitution would remain flexible and subject to debate among the three branches and the people; on the other, the most searing controversies would be negotiated within the legal culture. Judges, politicians, adversaries, and spectators would teach one another what the Constitution meant in practice. But while all could participate, Federalist lawyers strove hard to control the curriculum.

As Federalists imagined it, constitutional law comprised several elements: a professional judiciary; widespread acceptance of some form of judicial review, through which the legal community would play an important role in the construction and interpretation of state and federal constitutions; and an understanding of constitutional law as a new legal genre taught and applied largely by lawyers. Each of these elements took years to crystallize and remained controversial for decades, but Federalists began to lay the groundwork for this orthodoxy during the ratification debate. Within it they embedded an imperial view of a union that was dominant on the North American continent and a full participant in the Atlantic economy. The means to attain this end were not only control over land sales, international diplomacy, and defense but also constitutional protection of property and commerce. For Federalists, this was the context in which the text had be read: a new empire expansive on the continent and exemplary across the sea. Constitutional law did not fulfill all these goals. It did, however, succeed to a greater degree than any previous Anglo-American constitutional strategy for preserving political unity. Lawyers acted much like deputized imperial agents, aligning their interests with that of the Union.

The outlines of this new genre can be traced in the debate over the judiciary. Along with original jurisdiction over cases involving ambassadors, federal officials, and states, Section 2 of Article III provided that the federal courts could hear "all Cases, in Law and Equity, arising under this Constitution, the Laws of the United States, and Treaties" and had appellate jurisdiction over the same cases "both as to Law and Fact." The section also specified that the "Trial of all Crimes, except in cases of Impeachment; shall be by Jury."[149] Antifederalists seized on this expansive jurisdiction over federal questions, the appellate power to find facts, and the limited provision of jury trials to argue that the proposed judiciary violated the liberties of Englishmen for which the Revolution had been fought. They argued that the common law was the guarantor of those liberties; because the federal Constitution did not protect key common-law liberties explicitly, they were in jeopardy. Federalists countered that the first object of the Constitution was fair treatment of citizens throughout the Union. Hamilton, for example, invoked the principle of fairness beneath Sir Edward Coke's opinion *Bonham's Case*: "No man ought certainly to be judge in his own cause, or in any cause in respect to which he has the least interest or bias." He argued that in a host of cases involving state interests, state courts would be "biassed." A federal judiciary was necessary to maintain "that equality of privileges and immunities to which the citizens of the union will be entitled."[150] It would provide uniform interpretations of law affecting the whole Union and a neutral forum for resolving disputes. Here was the post–Norman Conquest, centralizing aspect of common law that Antifederalists denied.

In *Federalist* 22, Hamilton argued that a federal judiciary was necessary to ensure the uniform interpretation of treaties and allow the Union to fulfill its international obligations. The absence of such a forum "crowns the defects of the confederation." Without central review, state courts might render contradictory treaty interpretations. He warned that "if there is in each State, a court of final jurisdiction, there may be as many different final determinations on the same point, as there are courts." The remedy was "one Supreme Tribunal."[151] Since the end of the war, Hamilton had repeatedly criticized the states for breaching treaty obligations and "the true universal principles of liberty" they represented. Earlier he had pointed to the law of nations as the source of these principles.[152] Now he relied on the fundamental law of the Constitution. It would restrain the states and demonstrate to Europe that the Union was a member of the civilized world.

Treaty interpretation was not an isolated case. Uniform interpretation of all national law was necessary. "Thirteen independent courts of final jurisdiction over the same causes, arising upon the same laws," Hamilton warned, "is a hydra in government, from which nothing but contradiction and confusion can proceed." Supreme Court review would provide this uniformity. "Laws are a dead letter," he argued, "without courts to expound and define their true meaning and operation." A federal court of "last resort" would minimize "the bias of local views and prejudices" and declare "uniform rule[s] of civil justice."[153] Federal and state courts would enjoy "concurrent jurisdiction" over many "causes of which the state courts have previous cognizance," including "all cases arising under the laws of the union." What law would guide the courts in such cases? Whatever was relevant. "The judiciary power of every government looks beyond its own local or municipal laws," Hamilton explained, "and in civil cases lays hold of all subjects of litigation between parties within its jurisdiction, though the causes of dispute are relative to the laws of the most distant parts of the globe. Those of Japan not less than of New-York may furnish the objects of legal discussion to our courts."[154] He had greater faith in the cosmopolitanism of federal judges than those in the states. He hoped that state judges would be broad minded too. Still, their judgments had to be subject to federal review or else "the judiciary authority of the union may be eluded at the pleasure of every plaintiff or prosecutor." Such review would "unite and assimilate the principles of national justice and the rules of national decisions."[155] He was beginning to imagine a new federal jurisprudence.

Hamilton used two telling terms in this discussion of federal jurisdiction: "concurrent jurisdiction" and "rules of decision." "Concurrent jurisdiction" was a rare term of art that proliferated in the New York debates. The jurisdiction of many English courts overlapped, and there was a long history of courts wresting business from one another.[156] But within England's pluralist legal system, concurrent jurisdiction connoted equality. More than one common-law court might have jurisdiction over the same cause of action. One might try to prohibit another from deciding the case, but one did not review the other. Here, the federal courts would treat state courts as subordinate. In addition, Hamilton referred to case law in generic terms as "rules of decision" rather than common law. He was recognizing that "common law" could not capture the work product of the different state courts and the federal judiciary because the rules of decision were not common among them.

The Antifederalist "Brutus" argued that, with its broad jurisdiction to decide cases according to common law and equity, as well as its power to interpret the Constitution, the federal judiciary "will operate to effect, in the most certain, but yet silent and imperceptible manner, what is evidently the tendency of the constitution: — I mean, an entire subversion of the legislative, executive and judicial powers of the individual states." Where the federal government had exclusive jurisdiction, its courts would adjudge all state laws touching on such matters "void *ab initio*." Where there was concurrent jurisdiction, federal courts would consider federal law "supreme." The area of overlap would grow as federal judges expanded federal power through a "liberal construction" of the Constitution.[157] The problem was that the judiciary's jurisdiction under Article III was broader than that of Congress under Article I, so the federal courts would trod more on state power than would Congress. Similarly, Melancton Smith compared this elastic federal jurisdiction to that of the courts of King's Bench and Exchequer at Westminster, which used "legal fictions . . . to bring causes within their cognizance" at the expense of local courts.[158] He did not want this chapter of English constitutional history repeated in America. A good constitution would safeguard legal pluralism, not undermine it.

The expansion of federal power, Antifederalists feared, would not stop with the federal judiciary's liberal interpretation of federal legislative power.

Federal courts would also review appeals from state courts. Many Anti-federalists thought that the appeal was a European civil law doctrine, a way to bypass jury determinations. It conjured in their minds capricious European courts, the Star Chamber, and Cadwallader Colden's attempt to review a colonial jury's findings of fact. In contrast, the common law permitted only review of legal determinations. This "good old way of administering justice," wrote "Brutus," brought "justice to every man's door" and followed "the practice of the courts in England, which is almost the only thing I would wish to copy in their government."[159] The jury also protected popular or local representative rights. Along with legislatures, argued Melancton Smith, juries "are the means by which the people are let into the knowledge of public affairs" and safeguard "each others rights."[160] This was the core of the ancient constitution. Antifederalists wanted it to remain intact.

It would not be much better if the federal judiciary used juries in appellate proceedings. In the New England states that allowed appeals of fact, the lower courts had only "nominal" jurisdiction. Juries in these appeals were not drawn locally. Antifederalists believed that jurors, like legislators, represented local constituents. Distant juries would have no firsthand knowledge of the facts or the witnesses. In addition, serial trials were so costly that they were, Brutus claimed, "one of the principal causes" of Shays's Rebellion, in which debt-ridden farmers attacked courthouses in western Massachusetts to prevent the execution of judgments against them. Distant venues also added to the expense of lawsuits, putting them beyond the means of most. Consequently, in cases falling beneath federal jurisdiction "the poorer and middling class of citizens will be under the necessity of submitting to the demands of the rich and the lordly." Regional circuit courts would not reduce costs by much; replacing trial evidence with written depositions would sacrifice face-to-face examinations and the jury's appraisal of witnesses, which Antifederalists thought integral to common-law justice. In sum, federal proceedings would be "little short of a denial of justice."[161]

Juries were guaranteed in criminal trials. But would they be local? Anti-federalists held that it was "essential to the security of life and liberty, that trial of facts be in the vicinity where they happen." Robert Yates wanted each criminal trial to take place in the county of the offense, and he opposed government appeals of unsuccessful prosecutions. Thomas Tredwell complained at the state convention that federal prosecutors might drag a defendant to a "distant county" and try him in front of a "strange jury, ignorant of his character, ignorant of the character of the witnesses, [and] unable to contradict any false testimony brought against him by their own knowledge of facts." These were the same objections that colonists had raised when the imperial agents attempted to try some cases, like violations of the Navigation Acts, in regional courts. Antifederalists listed these concerns in the "declaration of rights" that the state convention attached to its notice of ratification and, later, became parts of the Fifth, Sixth, and Seventh Amendments of the Bill of Rights.[162]

Federalists responded by invoking legal federalism, or the conflict of rules among state legal systems, to justify federal jurisdiction. Typically, it was Antifederalists who argued that the states were too diverse for a close union, for their customs, habits, social systems, and forms of property in had developed individually.[163] By contrast, Federalists emphasized strands of unity like language, religion, and revolution, and they criticized state diversity as a source of "political vice."[164] Now the Federalists borrowed the Antifederalist mainstay, arguing that the states' legal systems were far too diverse to allow the convention to specify which procedures the federal judiciary would follow. Those procedures would be hammered out in Congress and the federal courts.

Hamilton explained that the Constitution's guarantee of jury trials in criminal cases was not exclusive. Juries would be used in most, but not all, civil cases too, as in many states. The absence of a guarantee for the civil jury in the Constitution stemmed from uncertainty about how it would operate, not from hostility toward it. In *Federalist* 83, Hamilton surveyed the state legal systems and found that no two seemed alike. Each reflected its own peculiar evolution. Several states, like New York, contained probate, admiralty, and chancery courts that functioned without juries. Others allowed appeals of fact, not just law, to appellate courts with juries. In short, "there is a material diversity as well in the modification as in the extent of the institution of trial by jury in civil cases in the several states." This examination of the relationship of the jury trial to liberty led Hamilton to grasp what many people knew, but in a profound way that affected his conception of the common law: the federal Union was "a composition of societies whose ideas and institutions in relation to the matter materially vary from each other." Even a basic institution like the jury trial varied among the states. It would not suffice to add an amendment, as the Massachusetts Convention had recommended, requiring juries in all "actions at common law" because this description was "vague and indeterminate." The problem was that the common law was not uniform among the thirteen states. In some states, every cause was "tried in a court of common law," which could mean that "every action may be considered an action at common law." In others, like New York, common-law actions closely tracked those in England. The federal courts would have to alter their procedures when circulating among the states, which struck Hamilton as "capricious." Another solution was to require juries in *all* cases, but Hamilton thought this was unwise. While he agreed that juries in criminal trials helped ensure "the security of liberty," he was not convinced that the civil jury was similarly necessary.[165]

Here Hamilton made the work of the Philadelphia Convention sound more thorough than it was. The issue of civil jury trials arose twice, in the last few days of the convention. When Antifederalist Elbridge Gerry of Massachusetts "urged the necessity of Juries to guard against corrupt Judges," a sympathetic George Mason responded that the convention could not specify when and where to use juries. Instead, Mason believed that a "general principle laid down on this and some other points would suffice." Three days later Gerry tried again, proposing that "trial by jury shall be preserved as usual in civil cases." But fellow Massachusetts delegate and ardent Federalist Nathaniel Gorham objected that "[t]he constitution of Juries is different in different States and the trial itself is *usual* in different cases in different States." Gerry's proposal failed.[166] In the end, the convention thought it best to leave the task of devising a uniform plan to Congress. In *Federalist* 83, Hamilton agreed.[167]

He agreed because he believed "there are many cases in which the trial by jury is an ineligible one." His examples were cases involving diplomats, the law of nations, treaties, prize, and equity. Juries were, for example, not "competent" to decide cases that required a "thorough knowledge" of the law of nations, and mistakes in such sensitive cases might trigger a war. He must also have had in mind conflicts between state antiloyalist legislation and the peace treaty of 1783 of the sort that underlay *Rutgers v. Waddington*. Hamilton added that although juries should "determine matters of fact, yet in *most* cases legal consequences are complicated with fact in such a manner as to render a separation impracticable," which suggested an even larger range of cases from which to exclude juries, such as complex commercial cases.[168] He was proposing to vest federal judges with power over "most" legal issues, not just pure questions of law but also *any* issue that mixed law with fact.

The federal courts' power to decide cases according to equity also made Antifederalists apprehensive. Many Antifederalists viewed equity as a license for federal judges to decide cases as they pleased. At least, equity jurisdiction had to be well defined. Hamilton believed that there was no existing bright line between law and equity. Several of the states either blended the two kinds of law or drew the line between them in different places. Hamilton observed that equity courts handled "special cases," such as those involving "*fraud, accident, trust,* or *hardship*," that demanded departure from "general rules." If law and equity were united, equity principles would overflow into ordinary disputes, meaning that every case might become subject to a "*special* determination." On the other hand, common-law procedures might hamper the operation of equity, and again the jury was the problem: juries might deliberate on equitable issues that were actually "too complicated" for a collection of laymen.[169] The federal courts needed equity jurisdiction to allow them to forgo juries in such cases. Just as the Constitutional Convention could not create a general rule for jury trials in federal cases, it could not define equity consistent with all the state systems. Congress, in partnership with the federal courts, would define the judiciary's jurisdiction.

Madison had come to a similar understanding of "felonies on the high seas" and other crimes against the law of nations over which the federal courts would have jurisdiction. Federal definition of these crimes was necessary because the states had defined them inconsistently, and within each state they "varie[d] in each with every revision of its criminal laws."[170] State legislative freedom, the first boon of the Revolution, had led to disparate and changeable laws. For the most part, this was fine. Some legal definitions, however, had to be uniform. Free from any single definition of the common law, Congress could determine when juries were necessary and define key terms like "felonies on the high seas." Uniformity was crucial. Federalist Charles Pinckney argued that the federal judiciary was "the keystone of the arch, the means of connecting and binding the whole together, of preserving uniformity in all the judicial proceedings of the Union." The judiciary would have more "energy and integrity" than the other branches, and it would not only "decide all national questions which should arise within in the Union, but [also] control and keep the state judicials within their proper limits."[171] From the outset, Federalists depended on the judiciary to be the "keystone" of the Union.

Hamilton also rejected the call for an amendment adopting the whole of the common law. New York's constitution, like several others, had such a clause.[172] But the common law and statutes adopted were explicitly subject to legislative alteration. Consequently, Hamilton argued, the provision "can be considered no part of a declaration of rights, which under our constitutions must be intended as limitations of the power of the government itself."[173] Indeed, these changes to the common law offered additional proof that the common law did not provide uniformity. Not only did common law vary among the states, but it also changed over time within each state. "The Common law," James Madison explained to George Washington,

> is nothing more than the unwritten law, and is left by all the Constitutions [state and federal] equally liable to legislative alterations. . . . If [the delegates to the Philadelphia Convention] had in general terms declared the Common law to be in force, they would have broken in upon the legal Code of every State in the most material points: they wd. have done more, they would have brought from G.B. a thousand heterogeneous & antirepublican doctrines, and even the *ecclesiastical Hierarchy itself*, for that is a part of the Common law. If they had undertaken a discrimination, they must have formed a digest of laws, instead of a Constitution.[174]

Before the Revolution, no one had ever equated the common law with Anglo-American fundamental law. But no one had sharply distinguished the two either. The common law, Federalists suddenly concluded, was an eclectic resource from which to help build American law. It was not a fixed body of law binding on the new states or nation. The political charge of state individuation had alternated, from an obstacle to centralization to a reason for its necessity. When analyzing the jury, Hamilton wrapped legal pluralism in the Antifederalists' own rhetoric of state differentiation and called not just for centralized decision making, up from local juries and toward federal judges, but also for uniform doctrine in areas of federal concern.

Federalist attempts to reduce local influence over law enforcement embodied a familiar imperial strategy. What was new was the plan for a freestanding federal jurisprudence. While viewing the common law in positivist terms — changeable and divergent among the states — Federalists did not repudiate fundamental law. They now equated fundamental law not with common law or other sources from Anglo-American constitutionalism but rather with a separate body of law, the law of the Constitution. When combined with federal prescriptions for cosmopolitan judges and legal education, the creation of constitutional law was more threatening to local rule than any prerevolutionary British plan.

Central to this creation of constitutional law was the elaboration of what became known as judicial review. In *Federalist* 78, Hamilton maintained that judges were under a duty "to declare all acts contrary to the manifest tenor of the constitution void." He portrayed the judiciary as "an intermediate body between the people and the legislature" that would vindicate "the intention of the people" against "the intention of their agents," the Constitution against legislation. Here he was imagining horizontal judicial review, a federal court reviewing congressional legislation. Others, like James Wilson, made it clear that judicial review would also operate vertically and allow federal courts to strike down state legislation that conflicted with the Constitution. As Hamilton put it, an unconstitutional statute was one "repugnant" to the Constitution, which was what the Privy Council had called colonial statutes that were inconsistent with English law.[175] Although Hamilton's explanation of judicial review played little role in ratification, it became a resource for generations of lawyers and judges who supported the judiciary's power to nullify state and federal statutes. It is not clear what standard of review Hamilton had in mind. He could not have imagined what now is called "judicial supremacy," whereby the Supreme Court claims the power to determine the Constitution's meaning such that few constitutional issues are settled until litigated before the Court. Yet neither did he imply that the Court had merely a coordinate power, along with the other branches, to decide the constitutional issues arising before it.[176] Nor was Hamilton describing a mechanical exercise of laying a statute alongside the Constitution and measuring whether the former fit within the latter.

Instead, Hamilton argued that the Supreme Court had to ascertain the "manifest tenor of constitution," which might lead it to uphold an act or strike it down. The convention had rejected Madison's proposed federal council of revision to review congressional statutes as well as his plan for congressional review of state statutes. No institution replaced the Privy Council. There was, however, a federal Supreme Court. Issues requiring the interpretation of federal law, including whether legislation conflicted with the Constitution, would come to the federal courts through their original or appellate jurisdiction. A government with a "limited constitution" meant that there were "exceptions to the legislative authority," and these, Hamilton declared, could be "preserved in practice no other way than through the medium of the courts of justice; whose duty it must be to declare all acts contrary to the manifest tenor of the constitution void." This practice, he asserted, was consistent with that in many of "the American [state] constitutions." Thinking of *Rutgers* and similar cases, he added that "the benefits of the integrity and moderation of the judiciary have already been felt in more states than one." Judges deserved this role of policing repugnancy because they excelled at legal interpretation, and the Constitution was another type of law, albeit the "fundamental law."[177]

When he described some of the rules of construction that a court would use when interpreting the Constitution, Hamilton relied again on common-law legal culture—its educational tradition, literature, and interpretive techniques. Hamilton also referred to the necessity of courts to issue writs of habeas corpus, and he assumed that the Constitution gave the judges that power. But it nowhere did so explicitly. That power can be derived from the suspension clause in Article I, enjoining Congress not to suspend the writ "unless when in Cases of Rebellion or Invasion the public Safety may require it."[178] In *Federalist* 84, Hamilton pointed to this clause to rebut accusations that the Constitution did not protect traditional common-law liberties. He assumed that the power to issue the writ was implicit in "the judicial power," perhaps implicit in any Anglo-American court's jurisdiction.[179] The point is that Hamilton, at least, imagined that the federal courts would exercise extensive jurisdiction, which they would help define through aggressive interpretation of Article III. He believed that the federal courts could play the role of peaceful intermediary between the federal government and the people: the "least dangerous" branch compared with the other candidates.[180] In part, the Federalists made a virtue of necessity: congressional review of state law was unpopular in Philadelphia. But they also believed that the federal courts could manufacture uniform law in a relatively uncontroversial way.

Hamilton made clear who would staff this least dangerous branch: professional judges. He invoked the doctrine of separated powers to exclude those untrained in the law from interpreting legislation. Well-educated judges would not wield "arbitrary discretion" but instead adhere to "strict rules and precedents." These precedents would grow to "very considerable bulk and must demand long and laborious study to acquire a competent knowledge of them." The role of judge was a specialized task for which few were qualified, and, "making the proper deductions for the ordinary depravity of human nature, the number must be still smaller of those who unite the requisite integrity with the requisite knowledge."[181] The necessity of assigning the task of reviewing legislation to "fit characters" also militated against a federal council of revision. His objection here was not that such a council violated the separation of powers. Rather, the legislators serving on it "will rarely be chosen with a view to those qualifications which fit men for the stations of judges." They would suffer from "defective information" and vote along the lines of "party divisions." Professional training, on the other hand, would ensure that judges would be more learned and virtuous than legislators.[182] Once again, a healthy legal culture was necessary to make the Constitution work.

Hamilton did recognize the importance of structural safeguards. Good behavior tenure and permanent salaries were necessary to secure the "steady, upright and impartial administration of the laws." The colonists had sought to obtain these guarantees from the crown to ensure that judges were not dependent on the monarchy. Judicial independence was just as necessary in a republic to prevent "the encroachments and oppressions of the representative body."[183] He was describing a new kind of judge who would understand the purpose of the Constitution, devise rules to further it, and adhere to such rules once laid down.

Some Antifederalists feared this insular judiciary. In England, good behavior tenure protected judges from an overreaching monarch. Still, their decisions could be reviewed in the House of Lords, which "Brutus" equated with review by a representative legislature. This popular check was missing in the federal Constitution. In addition, English judges "consider themselves bound to decide according to the existing laws of the land, and never undertake to controul them by adjudging that they are inconsistent with the constitution — much less are they vested with the power of giv[ing] an *equitable* construction to the constitution." Under the proposed Constitution, by contrast, "the judges are supreme — and no law, explanatory of the constitution, will be binding on them." The judges would use rules of statutory construction to explicate the Constitution. These rules, as Blackstone described them, gave courts much "latitude." In particular, federal judges will "decide the meaning of the constitution" not just "according to the natural and ob[vious] meaning of the words, but also according to the spirit and intention of it." Judges, not the people, would have the final say about the Constitution. Through the accretion of precedents, "with which the public will not be generally acquainted," federal power would expand at the expense of the states.[184]

Some Antifederalists opposed judicial review on principle. New York Antifederalists could recall *Rutgers v. Waddington*, for example, in which the Mayor's Court negated the plain meaning of a state statute. But not all Antifederalists opposed judicial review. "Brutus," for example, took it for granted that federal judges would construe federal statutes strongly because state courts did the same with state statutes. Citing a Rhode Island case that nullified a state paper money scheme, he approved strong judicial interpretation "in opposition to the words of [a] Statute" in order to preserve the "fundamental maxims" of the state constitution. "In this way," he observed, "have our courts, I will not say evaded the law, but so limited it in its operation as to work the least possible injustice."[185] The problem was not that judges would interpret the constitution. They would and should. The issue was *which* judges would do so. "Brutus" wanted to give primary responsibility for such interpretation to *state* rather than federal judges.

Federalists embraced a positivist, noncustomary conception of the common law after examining its diversity in the states, and Antifederalists came to a similar conclusion about *most* of the common law after predicting the effects of the federal government in the future. In short, they too reexamined custom to distinguish immutable from mutable rights and arranged law in their own hierarchy. Federal review of state legislation made Antifederalists fear that all state law was vulnerable. In response, they began to view certain aspects of English common law as fundamental. Here again they drew on the old to sharpen perception of the new. Federalists had suddenly embraced legal federalism to justify investing the federal courts with broad jurisdiction.

However, when it came to "fundamental rights" like the jury trial, Antifederalists denied that there was such a great difference among the states. Melancton Smith "confess[ed]" that he "never thought the people of these states differ so essentially in these respects; they having all derived these rights, from one common source, the British systems." If the delegates disagreed so much about jury trials that they could not agree on the wording of a clause protecting them, or to "establish many other [fundamental] rights," then the Union rested on "no solid basis whatever."[186] Another Antifederalist complained in an open letter to the New York and Virginia conventions that even "[t]he most blind admirer of this Constitution must in his heart confess that it is as far inferior to the British Constitution, of which it is an imperfect imitation, as darkness is to light." In the latter, "the rights of men, the primary objects of the social Compact—are fixed on an immoveable foundation & clearly defined & ascertained by their Magna Charta, their Petition of Rights & Bill of Rights, & their Effective administration by Ostensible Ministers, secures Responsability."[187] The new Constitution did not protect these ancient liberties.

Melancton Smith sought to ensure that the new Constitution protected such rights. He delineated three kinds of rights: natural, constitutional, and legal rights. He did not enumerate the first, except in the familiar British terms of life, liberty, and property. He spent most of his effort distinguishing "constitutional" and "legal" rights:

[S]ome are natural and inalienable, of which even the people cannot deprive individuals: Some are constitutional or fundamental; these cannot be altered or abolished by the ordinary laws; but the people, by express acts, may alter or abolish them—These, such as the trial by jury, the benefits of the writ of habeas corpus, &c. individuals claim under the solemn compacts of the people, as constitutions, or at least under laws so strengthened by long usage as not to be repealable by the ordinary legislature—and some are common or mere legal rights, that is, such as individuals claim under laws which the ordinary legislature may alter or abolish at pleasure.[188]

Smith elaborated his customary theory of constitutional rights by contrasting them with natural and legal rights. Constitutional rights were hard won, and preserving them required constant vigilance. "Men, in some countries do not remain free, merely because they are entitled to natural and unalienable rights; men in all countries are entitled to them, not because their ancestors once got together and enumerated them on paper, but because, by repeated negociations and declarations, all parties are brought to realize them, and of course believe them to be sacred."[189] Over time, a people would agree that certain rights were constitutional. He gave several examples: the civil and criminal jury trial, indictment by grand jury, the writ of habeas corpus, security against ex post facto laws and unreasonable searches, due process, the right to confront witnesses, the freedom of the press, among others. Most of these, Smith pointed out, were "but a part of those estimable rights the people of the United States are entitled to . . . by the course of the common law." These rights should have been expressly included in the Constitution. Since they were not, Antifederalists listed them as recommended amendments, which, along with similar lists from other states, formed the basis for the federal Bill of Rights. Although ratification was not formally conditioned on procuring a bill of rights, in practice many Antifederalists thought it was. A bill of rights, Smith wrote, was just one means among several for "constantly keeping in view . . . the particular principles on which our freedom must always depend." Others were "addresses" and "newspapers."[190] Publicity and lifelong education would preserve these rights.

Federalists were dismayed by the demand for a bill of rights. In a representative government, they asked, against whom was a bill of rights directed? Declarations of liberties were traditionally aimed at the crown, to curb the prerogative. They were unnecessary in a republic.[191] Others thought that bills of rights were appropriate only at the state level, where most government took place. But gradually some Federalists began to see the advantages of a bill of rights. Such a list would encourage Congress not to tread on certain liberties. This shift was part of a larger reimagining of corruption. Increasingly corruption was defined in terms of public encroachment on the private sphere, rather than of the executive branch encroaching on the legislature or the center on the periphery. For men like Madison, a primary function of this liberty was to protect private property from a corrupt legislature. A declaration of rights might help bolster those rights against legislative invasion. He originally called the state bill of rights "parchment barriers"; but he came to believe that continued education of the people about the importance of such rights, along with judicial enforcement, would help fix those rights permanently.[192]

Although there never was the second constitutional convention that New York Antifederalists hoped for, within four years Congress and the states had approved ten constitutional amendments that incorporated many of the common-law rights that Antifederalists thought were vulnerable under the Constitution. At least a few Antifederalists believed that these restraints against Congress would be enforced by the courts. Patrick Henry declared in the Virginia ratification convention that it was "the highest encomium of this country, that the acts of the legislature, if unconstitutional, are liable to be opposed by the judiciary." He complimented his state's judiciary for having the "firmness to counteract the legislature in some cases." But he questioned whether the federal courts would have the "fortitude" to exercise horizontal review of congressional legislation, for there was no reason to believe that those courts would be "independent of the other branches."[193] Consequently, for reasons quite different from those of the Federalists, some Antifederalists also supported judicial review to protect fundamental, constitutional rights from overreaching federal and state legislatures. To some Antifederalists, judicial review was a legitimate but *insufficient* means of enforcing the Constitution. It was one of several tools in the constellation of constitutional resistance, most of which revolved around politics in or near legislatures. It was not the center of their constitutionalism, just as it was not yet the center of Federalist constitutionalism either. For Federalists, however, judicial review was part of a more circumscribed repertoire of ways to define the Constitution, most of which would be controlled by leaders of the legal culture.

Constitution Law and Constitutional Politics in the 1790s

The founding has long occupied a central place in American constitutional mythology, and increasingly its meanings are invoked as sources of constitutional law.[194] Yet the modern understanding of the founding is incomplete because it does not take into account the imperial context in which the Constitution was drafted and debated. Federalists in particular believed that while independence required freedom from the British Empire, only its replacement by a new American empire would ensure the success of the Revolution. In fits and starts, the ratifiers began to create a new legal glue to bind the states. They innovated on inherited scripts of republicanism, corporate power, and the mixed constitution to create the new doctrines of federalism and separated powers. They also identified those ancient liberties of Englishmen that deserved special protection. These became memorialized in the Bill of Rights. Together these became the core of constitutional law, which was neither just like ordinary law nor a matter of ordinary politics. Instead, it was a new substantive legal genre with its own vocabulary, style of reasoning, emotional atmosphere, and interpretive institutions. The process of creation was gradual. But already by 1793 John Jay, as chief justice of the U.S. Supreme Court, could use the new term "constitutional law" and assume that his readers understood what he meant.[195]

In that case, *Chisholm v. Georgia*, the executor for the estate of a South Carolina merchant sued the state of Georgia in federal court for a debt incurred when the merchant supplied clothing to the state during the Revolution. Georgia invoked sovereign immunity, claiming that Article III's grant of federal jurisdiction to cases between "a State and Citizens of another State" extended only to those in which the state brought the action, not in which it was a defendant. The Supreme Court held in a four-to-one decision that the creditor could sue the state in federal court. The styles and methodologies of the opinions in this case are quite unlike most early modern judicial opinions, so much so that legal historian Julius Goebel Jr., who called *Chisholm* the Court's "first great case," dismissed most of the opinions as "fuss[y]," "fanciful," and "decorated . . . with all the furbelows of learning."[196]

The opinions were elaborate. It was one of the first cases that the Court decided on the merits. Each justice was a veteran of the ratification debate. None passed up the opportunity to explain the relationship between individual rights, state government, and the Union.[197] Justice James Iredell alone held that the Constitution did not automatically vest jurisdiction in the federal courts to hear a suit against a state. Whether or not Congress *could* extend that jurisdiction was, for Iredell, a close question. Thus far, it had not tried. The reason was that the sovereign was immune from lawsuits under the common law, and the states had inherited the crown's sovereignty. He rejected Attorney General Edmund Randolph's argument that the states were mere corporations. Besides, "the word 'corporation' . . . has a more extensive meaning than people generally are aware of." Indeed, "*any* body politic" was a corporation. The states were sovereign corporations and deserved the immunity that was a perquisite of sovereignty.[198]

Justice William Cushing agreed that "all States whatever are corporations or bodies politics. The only question is, what are their powers?" The corporation no longer connoted self-government; it was now defined by the American constitutions. Federal jurisdiction did not trespass onto the states' rights because the people had established the Court as "a common umpire" to hear disputes involving the states, which might otherwise lead to war. "That an object of this kind was had in view of the framers of the Constitution," Cushing maintained, "I have no doubt, when I consider the clashing interfering laws which were made in the neighboring States, before the adoption of the Constitution."[199]

The other justices also denied that the states were sovereign. Justice James Wilson reasoned that popular sovereignty made the doctrine of immunity inapplicable. Even in "free" nations, "the *state* has assumed a supercilious preeminence above the *people*, who have *formed* it: Hence the haughty notions of *state independence, state sovereignty and state supremacy*." But in the United States the people were sovereign, and they had agreed in the Constitution to allow people in one state to sue another state's government. It was all a matter of whether "the people of the *United States* form a Nation." He answered affirmatively.[200] Law was the medium through which this new nationality was imagined.[201] Chief Justice John Jay, who had proclaimed in *Federalist* 2 that Americans formed a nation, here argued similarly that the Constitution was "a compact made by the people" rather than the states. Accordingly, "fellow citizens and joint sovereigns cannot be degraded by appearing with each other in their own Courts to have their controversies determined." The people had established a neutral forum for just such a purpose. Finally, the people had "reason to prize and rejoice" in the privilege of suing their state governments, "and they ought not to forget, that nothing but the free course of Constitutional law and Government can ensure the continuance and enjoyment of them."[202]

The Court's decision in *Chisholm* provoked outrage in many states. The Georgia legislature, for example, passed a law that made service of an order from the Supreme Court a felony carrying the penalty of death.[203] Other states protested too. Two years later, the states ratified the Eleventh Amendment, which protected them from being sued without their consent. The main point is not just that the states lost power in *Chisholm* and then won it back with a new instrument of popular constitutionalism—the amendment process. The other novelty was the way the justices explained their decision.

These were the same people using the same style of reasoning to organize the same sources to make the same argument they had in the ratification debate: the states were corporations subordinate to the people, who expected judges to prevent those governments from infringing on individual rights of contract and property. The justices did not need to cite the ratification literature because they had written it. Their repetition and borrowing were familiar, as were their organizing concepts: corporations, popular sovereignty, and the idea that the federal courts represented the people against the states. But now this political argumentation was becoming *law*, formalized in courts but not quite like ordinary law. Ancient constitutional devices were funneled into professional doctrine. Those doctrines were themselves privileges of the nation and were protected, in Jay's words, by "the free course of constitutional law and government." Goebel was right: this sort of language was new *in* the courts, but it was familiar in the traditional venues of constitutional debate, such as British and American legislatures, colonial petitions, the revolutionary and ratification pamphlets, and in the streets. When congressmen introduced the Eleventh Amendment, they too spoke the language of empire that was becoming the language of national citizenship. The process of amendment did not undermine the Supreme Court's construction of the Constitution; it merely assured the people that they retained the ultimate power to define their Constitution. This legalization of fundamental law did not end disagreement over the constitution of the Union, but it disciplined that debate and gave it new form. Although the content of constitutional law always remained contested, the form itself was increasingly accepted.

Judicial enforcement of constitutional law was gradually accepted, but the courts were not its only medium of definition.[204] The most powerful vehicle for disseminating and inculcating constitutional law was legal literature. Prominent examples were *The Federalist Papers* and Federalist-inspired treatises in the next generation such as James Kent's *Commentaries on American Law*. Judicial opinions written to explain administrative outcomes and collected in reports — a new form of literature themselves — were only one subset of this literature, and for a long time not the most important. Those early opinions were written in a new way to fit the decisions they represented into a doctrinal framework, unlike all but a few decisions in the common-law world at the time. They were instead like *The Federalist* and similar essays: learned, self-consciously cosmopolitan, experimental. They were written by ratifiers like Jay, Wilson, and John Marshall, who wrote not just to settle cases between litigants but also to persuade citizens at large. Even when the judges failed in that larger didactic purpose, they did reach lawyers and law students.

The members of this legal community — as practitioners, officeholders, and citizens — played a leading role in "liquidating" constitutional meaning in the coming years.

The creation of constitutional law also entailed a rethinking of constitutional history. Antifederalists at first used history to identify immutable rights, but gradually they began to exchange the customary basis of constitutions for a consensual one: constitutions became more source than memorial. And for Federalists, antiquity was never proof of virtue. The past was a laboratory in which to test institutions. Herein lies a paradox in the remixing of ancient constitutionalism into constitutional law. Federalists devalued custom because it hampered their attempt to create a functioning empire. But the alternative they made to allow experimentation did so among relative experts: those who could master the ever more refined doctrines of constitutional law. The funneling of most constitutional discussion into constitutional law was thus a double-edged sword. On one side, the discipline of a legal genre, with its specialized terminology and partial insulation from politics, tended to make constitutional debate less accessible to average citizens. On the other, it offered a more effective weapon against governmental abuse because its doctrine allowed more precise identification of grievances and offenders as compared with the popular remedies of petition, resistance, and riot. At the least, constitutional law provided a remedy to *some* aggrieved citizens and dissuaded them from resorting to more drastic alternatives.

Thus some scholars like Sylvia Snowiss, Gordon Wood, and Larry Kramer argue that the Federalists "legalized" and "tamed" the Constitution, meaning that they treated the Constitution like "ordinary law."[205] But Federalists never treated the Constitution just like "ordinary law" because they rested it on the political premise that the Constitution was an engine for imperial development, which made constitutional law a hybrid of law and politics. Antifederalists also did not treat the Constitution like "ordinary law" because they believed that unchangeable rights should be at its core. Both Antifederalists and Federalists recognized that a constitution that was too malleable would endanger their visions of the Union, whether based on substantial state autonomy or on a strong central administration. Both sides sought to create doctrines of limitation that became known as constitutional law. The new genre was supposed to contain the productive tension between experimentation and fundamentality. Of course, the new genre was not fully created in the ratification debate, but the ratifiers began to perform within it.

Therefore, although constitutional law was never fully determinative of constitutional meanings, it did help cabin those meanings by marking some

boundaries while allowing competition within them. Constitutional pluralism was formalized into doctrines of structural relations. Federalism allowed
vertical differentiation between the states and the federal government, as well
as horizontal variation among the states. Separated powers, or checks and
balances, gave each of the three branches much freedom to construe its
own power, along with some mechanisms to limit the powers of the other
branches. In other words, the framers and ratifiers created institutional space
for pluralism, and they left much of the Constitution's construction to normal politics. Consequently, there were institutional pockets in which multiple understandings of the Constitution could develop at any given time and
that gave ample room for changes in those understandings over time.

"Taming" is also a misleading term because the new Constitution was
more powerful than older versions, both as a sword for public authority and
as a shield for private rights. In most of the early cases in which the Supreme Court exercised judicial review, it upheld congressional legislation
that exceeded the powers granted in the bare text but was consistent with its
"spirit," a spirit emanating from the unwritten premise that the Union was
an empire — unwritten in the Constitution but written all over the ratification debate. Supreme Court opinions for the next generation, such as those
by John Jay, James Wilson, and especially John Marshall, rested on that
premise.[206] Chief Justice Marshall, for example, referred to the United States
as "our wide-spreading empire," "this newly created empire," and a "rising empire."[207] That this new jurisprudence was not primarily negative, or
nullifying, is clear from the work of his Court. It was to this imperial premise
that Marshall implicitly referred when he declared, while upholding the
national bank in *McCulloch v. Maryland*, that "we must never forget that it is a
constitution we are expounding."[208]

In this new empire, colonization was not just of land and Native Americans but also of those people who tried to escape it, who made plans for
splinter confederacies and deals with competing empires. The project, again,
was to generate a body of law that would control the states and territories
while also offering the people a way of reestablishing their identity in the
Atlantic world. Federalists and their legatees strove to transform the imperial
"center" from a metropolis that imposed law on the periphery into a new
kind of legality based on transcendent rules. This was their answer to the
long quest in North America for a binding imperial law. Because this answer
involved the creation of a juristic elite, it was not accepted by state leaders
who were expanding political access and making political parties the center of
civic identity. So the quest continued.

Empire State

Constitutional Politics and the Convention of 1821

> *[T]he friends of rational liberty in all quarters of the globe have their attention fastened upon independent, confederated America; in the front rank of this confederacy, in the most conspicuous station, stands the great state of New-York, and the result of the Convention will decide her fate, perhaps for ever.*
> Elisha Williams (1821)

B ETWEEN THE RATIFICATION of the federal Constitution and the Civil War, the states controlled most government administration. They were more powerful in the new Union than the colonies had been in the British Empire because they absorbed power from two directions: down from imperial institutions and up from local ones, like towns, counties, and juries, that had played such a large role in colonial affairs. State preeminence was not precisely what Antifederalists had tried to secure during the ratification debate. Most had more local authority in mind. But the Antifederalist specter of an omnipotent central government remained just that: a specter. The federal government did not become the behemoth Antifederalists feared because most citizens did not want it to. As voting requirements fell in the early nineteenth century and the class of the truly sovereign expanded, state power became even more preeminent. Constitutionally, the emphasis in the United States was on the *states*. The primary instrument of popular constitutionalism was the state convention, and New Yorkers held a series of state constitutional conventions in the first half of the nineteenth century.

Popular Sovereignty and State Power

After the Revolution, each state was nearly omnipotent within its borders. This authority manifested itself in many ways. In New York, the state was the primary lawmaker, the source of most patronage, and the largest property owner. Through legislation, public offices, and land grants, the government interacted with ordinary people everyday. This power, however, also made it the target of popular grievances. Petitions and resistance were most often directed at the state government, and this ensured that it, rather than the federal government, was the site of most constitutional change in the first half of the nineteenth century.

Most of these constitutional changes actually *weakened* state government.[1] Within a generation after the Revolution, popular support grew for divesting the state of much of the power it took from the British Empire in 1777 and retained under the Constitution of 1787. The most significant changes were the enfranchisement of almost all white males; clearer separations between the executive, legislature, and judiciary, which increased competition between the branches and made state government as a whole less effective; and an increase in the number of elective, rather than appointive, offices. In short, state power declined. Yet the Antifederalist animus remained intact, for these initiatives did not redound to the benefit of the federal government. Instead, the reforms transferred much authority back to local institutions, where many Antifederalists had wanted it to be. The story of state constitutionalism in the early Republic is one of resurgent localism and the devolution of power, a trend that continued through the antebellum period and ended only with the Civil War and its constitutional aftermath.[2]

Most states had several constitutional conventions during the nineteenth century. New York had five, about one every generation. These conventions often added, rather than replaced, articles, so that the state constitution grew in length and detail. When U.S. Supreme Court chief justice John Marshall contrasted the "great outlines" of a constitution with "the prolixity of a legal code," he was speaking of the federal Constitution, not the state constitutions.[3] One reason the federal Constitution remained spare was that for so long so little of it impinged on everyday life. The opposite was true of the state constitutions, which the people revised to reflect changing notions of how government should function each day on the ground. It would be wrong, however, to conclude that state constitutions became simply superstatutes that detailed the framework of government. They contained more than the nuts and bolts of administration. Each constitution also conveyed a vision of how the government related to its citizens and expressed the rights and duties of the people. That is why New Yorkers convened noisily once a generation to rewrite their constitution.

One consequence of making the state constitution the battleground for the leading issues of early nineteenth-century politics — patronage, suffrage requirements, canal funding, taxes, and so on — was that state constitutionalism remained much like that in the colonies. In comparison with the federal Constitution, its raw materials were varied, its participants diverse, and its direction less predictable. Such diversity and malleability were familiar. State government was now the site of struggles that had earlier occurred in London and at the local level, as well as in the provincial government. Within its borders New York's state government had, in legal theory, no competitors.[4]

In the late eighteenth and early nineteenth centuries, New York's government was as contentious as ever and more involved in the everyday life of its citizens.[5] Increasingly, however, political maneuvers implicated the constitution. This was in part the legacy of endless constitutional attacks on royal government in the colony and in part because of the people's new power to remake their constitution. Suddenly every controversial governmental activity was liable to constitutional redefinition. The state's administration was constitutional, or not, in the eyes of whichever group happened to be out of power at the moment.

This highly charged constitutional environment contributed to the growth of political parties, which organized themselves around competing interpretations of the state constitution. As their influence grew, parties in turn accelerated the constitutionalization of politics. Groups lobbying for advantage in the state capital needed electoral support. To get it, they had to persuade voters to join their cause. As the electorate grew, the causes had to be more compelling to attract a majority, and legitimizing policies in terms of the state's constitution was an effective way to appeal to the people. Yet for two generations after the Revolution, parties themselves remained constitutionally suspect. Many viewed parties in traditional republican terms: as factions that threatened to corrupt politics and undermine the public interest.[6] This too fueled the constitutionalization of politics as parties sought to identify their causes with the constitution. Placing a party program beyond constitutional reproach enabled voters to follow a party standard without fear of participating in corruption. Opponents of organized parties also found it advantageous to appeal to the constitution. Those out of power and unable to get back in could go beyond electoral politics and rally the people for a convention. Conventions were more pure than the legislature, in part because all could vote for delegates at a time when many could not vote in elections for legislators or the governor. Limitations on suffrage became associated with corrupt parties, and so they fell away as parties struggled to gain an advantage over each other, claiming to be parties of the people rather than of politicians.[7]

New Yorkers held a limited convention in 1801 to settle whether the governor enjoyed the sole power of nomination in the Council of Appointment or shared that power with the senators on the council. The convention passed an amendment giving each member the power to nominate state officers. The Council of Appointment, which by then had become a strong instrument of party politics, was again the proximate cause for the next state convention, in 1821. This time, however, the party out of power— Republicans under the leadership of Martin Van Buren—demanded far-reaching reforms, including the elimination of both the Council of Appointment and the Council of Revision as well as the expansion of the suffrage. The Van Burenites hoped that a larger electorate would enable them to defeat Governor DeWitt Clinton, a former Republican who claimed to be above parties but was increasingly allied with Federalists. The Clintonians and their allies on the Council of Revision tried to prevent the convention by disallowing the statute that called for it on the grounds that such a step required popular approval in a referendum. They succeeded only in delaying the convention: New Yorkers voted overwhelmingly to hold a convention with an unlimited mandate.[8]

Expanding the Electorate:
The Constitutional Politics of Suffrage Reform

When the state constitutional convention opened in August 1821, the reduction and equalization of suffrage qualifications already had broad support. There was no need for separate classes of voters, most believed, because America did not have separate legal estates. Thus, suffrage qualifications for gubernatorial and senatorial elections should be equal to those for assembly elections. "Here," one delegate exclaimed, "there is but one estate—the people."[9] In addition, there was support for reducing all those qualifications. The drafters took their cue from the elections to select delegates to the federal ratification convention back in 1788; that act had empowered all men who paid taxes or worked on the state's roads to vote for delegates to the Poughkeepsie convention. A similar standard was used for electing delegates to the 1821 convention.[10] Now this standard was extended to all elections. Yet not everyone wanted to eliminate all requirements, and some wished to *increase* them for some state citizens: African Americans.

Those wary of suffrage expansion recurred to the traditional republican principle that a man who did not hold enough land to support himself lacked the independence to participate in politics. Concern centered on wage laborers. Would urban workers simply follow the instructions of their employers? "That man who holds in his hands the subsistence of another," Chief Justice Ambrose Spencer warned the convention, "will always be able to control his will." Some saw New York City as swarming with laborers who were dependent on their masters, and they invoked Thomas Jefferson's criticism of cities. Spencer called cities "sores" on the "body politics," and Chancellor James Kent referred to New York City as "the future London of America," destined to be a home of "pauperism."[11] To prevent urban laborers from becoming an important factor in state politics, Spencer proposed retaining property qualifications at least for elections to the state senate. Kent agreed. "Society is an association for the protection of property as well as of life," he declared, "and the individual who contributes only one cent to the common stock, ought not to have the same power and influence in directing the property concerns of the partnership, as he who contributes his thousands." It was not, as John Jay had said a generation earlier, that the people who owned New York ought to govern it.[12] Property ownership was a proxy for responsibility. Property was also, Kent believed, "a sheet anchor amidst the future factions and storms of the republic."[13] It was an antidote to party. In addition, men of property supported civic institutions like churches, schools, and hospitals. To them, Spencer claimed, "we owe all the embellishments and the comforts and blessings of life." Delegates from the rural counties had another reason for preserving the property requirement: it favored their constituents. Property qualifications fostered rather than inhibited democracy, believed Abraham Van Vechten of Albany County, because they protected "common farmers — the stable pillars of the state." In contrast, free suffrage would empower transient urban workers, who did not take democracy seriously.[14]

These traditional arguments could not hold back the tide of suffrage liberalization. All men, claimed delegate John Cramer, were dependent. "The rich man is as dependent on the poor man for his labour, as the poor man is on the rich man for his wages." Then Cramer added an analogy aimed directly at Chief Justice Spencer and Chancellor Kent, attacking their conservatism while acknowledging that, as judges, they represented the ideal of independence: "I know of no men who are more dependent on others for their bread and raiment, than the judges of your supreme court are upon the legislature, and who will pretend that this destroys their independence."[15] David Buel argued that the fear of landless mobs was misplaced. America was not Europe; there was no legal distinction between those who owned land and those who did not. Primogeniture had been abolished, entail prohibited, and "an entire revolution has taken place in regard to real property." Most men held some property. All had the opportunity to do so. In this society, the key to independent judgment was education, not property. The common schools would ensure that citizens safeguarded their freedom.[16] In the meantime, the vote itself was the primary way to protect rights.[17] Property was no longer the best measure of public merit or independence. Property was becoming a private affair, a notion that was formalized in legal doctrine and had ramifications for the rest of the century.

Other evidence besides land ownership could indicate independence. Paying taxes was one. Serving in the militia was another. Working on public projects was a third. Each sort of public participation gave the individual a stake in society similar to a freehold. Samuel Young spoke for the drafting committee when he declared that "all who sustain public burdens, either by money, or personal services, should be entitled to vote."[18] These substitute requirements would also exclude many African American males. General Erastus Root thought that black men could be excluded because they were not called on to serve in the militia. He also feared that black voters, many of whom lived in New York City, would skew elections so that "the whole state would be controlled by a few hundred of this species of population." Root assumed that African Americans would vote as a bloc, and others agreed. John Z. Ross, a delegate from western Genesee County, believed that the push for racial equality was nothing but a partisan maneuver by those who "expect to control their votes."[19]

Those who opposed racial discrimination, like Peter A. Jay and James Kent, were leading Federalists. Their party did enjoy the support of most black voters and did not want to lose it.[20] However, their opposition to state-enforced discrimination cannot be reduced to party politics. They also appealed to legal and equitable arguments. Jay, the son of John Jay, pointed out that many black men who could vote under the original constitution would be excluded under the new one and thus stripped of a vested right. Such discrimination would "stain the constitution" in a state that had long ago "taken the high ground against slavery." Kent suggested that such discrimination might violate the privileges and immunities clause of the federal Constitution.[21] The bid to raise property qualifications was not merely partisan.

Racism spread across the convention floor too. Samuel Young of Saratoga declared that African Americans were "not competent" to vote and would sell their votes.[22] In the end, the convention eliminated property qualifications for white men but increased those for black men, who now had to possess a $250 freehold. Under the new constitution, 90 percent of white men could vote, but only a small fraction of black men met the discriminatory property qualification.[23]

From Conciliar to Executive Government

The drafters of the 1777 constitution had internalized most of mechanisms of imperial governance within the state in two new councils. One was the Council of Appointment, which appointed most executive officers. The other was the Council of Revision, which reviewed all legislation and had a qualified power to veto it. They proved controversial for two related reasons. First, the councils mixed executive, legislative, and judicial officers, which was increasingly viewed with suspicion. The coalescing wisdom was that members of each branch should remain within their own sphere and check the ambitions of the other branches, not combine in hybrid institutions. It was at the state level that the doctrine of separated powers was refined. During the colonial period, the powers to be balanced were the royal executive and the colonial legislature. The states domesticated the executive and experimented with ways to redefine the balance between it and the legislature.[24] Second, parties used the separation-of-powers doctrine as a political weapon, invoking it when threatened by another party's dominance in one institution of government, especially the Council of Appointment. So, while the state constitution shaped New York's tumultuous political culture, politics in turn generated pressure for constitutional amendment.[25]

These two councils, of Appointment and Revision, were catalysts for constitutional change. The constitution of 1777 vested the power to appoint almost every civil and militia officer in the Council of Appointment, drawing that power down from the British Empire and up from local jurisdictions. The governor and four senators, selected by all senators, formed the council. Every legal transaction involved a state officer, making the appointment power a pervasive force in the life of the ordinary citizen. The convention of 1801 was designed to weaken the governor's power to nominate executive officers throughout the state. The 1821 convention abolished the council and distributed the power of appointment among the governor, the legislature, and the people in local elections.

In 1801, Federalist governor John Jay found himself with a Council of Appointment in which Republicans were a majority. To increase his power in the council, Jay claimed that the governor had the sole power to nominate public officials; after nomination, the full council could vote to confirm or reject the appointment. But the other councillors claimed an equal power of nomination, not just an equal vote to confirm. If they succeeded, the Republicans would nominate and then confirm only Republican officers and frustrate the governor's ability to appoint Federalists. To settle the dispute, Jay sought declaratory opinions from the legislature and the state judiciary. Both declined.[26] The legislature then called a limited constitutional convention to resolve the question, and after a short two weeks of work, the convention sustained the Republican interpretation. Under the 1801 amendment, each member of the council could nominate officeholders, and then each member had an equal vote to select among those nominated. This convention also reapportioned the legislature and reduced the number of representatives in each house.[27] Giving each member — senators as well as the governor — the power to nominate executive officers helped transform the council into a patronage machine. The party that controlled the senate would control most appointments within the state, which raised the stakes in legislative elections. Those who fared poorly in elections railed against the council. Thus, opposition to it shifted after each election.

The convention of 1821 abolished the council and gave the governor the power to appoint superior court judges as well as militia officers. The legislative houses had the power to appoint the secretary of state, comptroller, treasurer, attorney general, surveyor general, and commissary general. The courts appointed their own clerks. County supervisors and the county courts nominated justices of the peace. And sheriffs were elected at the county level.[28]

The abolition of the Council of Appointment was not controversial. But giving the governor the power to appoint most executive positions was. Democrats associated with Martin Van Buren moved to make almost all positions appointive. Several delegates feared, however, that vesting all appointments in one person would make the governor too powerful: a new governor, at the head of a party, would sweep clean all offices. On this score, the appointment of justices of the peace was particularly contentious and gave rise to an unusual alliance between radical Democrats, who favored making most offices elective, and high Federalists, who feared that the judiciary would become a patronage mill. Federalists may also have feared losing their control over the courts.

Chancellor Kent took the lead in opposing gubernatorial appointment of justices of the peace. That would exacerbate "faction or corruption" in the selection of officers who, more than any others, were supposed to be detached from party spirit. He cited Sir Edward Coke for the proposition that the English had once elected justices of the peace, which was "evidence of the popular genius of the ancient English constitution."[29] Ancient constitutionalism could still be invoked as a bulwark against central control, even within a republican state. Central appointment, on the other hand, would generate abuse. "The great value of these local appointments," Kent argued, "is that they weaken by dividing the force of party. They will break down the scheme of one great, uniform, organized system of party domination throughout the state, and they will give to the minor party in each county, some chance for some participation in the local affairs of the county. . . . The future happiness, and, I might almost say, the future destiny of the people of this state, turn upon such an arrangement."[30]

Kent supported popular election as a way to oppose partisan appointment. Others saw positive benefits in local election. Peter Jay warned that courts dependent on the governor would "crush the minority" by persecuting political opponents. Local elections would be free of these designs. Indeed, they would help insulate local interests from state oppression. Jay analogized the state-local relationship to that between the federal government and the state. The "great secret" of the federal Constitution's success "consists in the numerous partitions of power which it makes, and its distribution to the various members which compose it, of the right to regulate all their local concerns."[31] The same partitions and distributions of power that marked federalism were needed within the state. Federalists like Kent and Jay saw local influence as one of the last bastions of their party's power. Peter Van Ness, who was more sympathetic to democracy than Jay or Kent, had faith in the people rather than in party managers associated with governors. He justified popular participation in the legal system by analogizing it to the jury: if the people could render verdicts in courts, they could select the judges too. The people would show good judgment, favor men they knew personally, and elect "peacemakers."[32]

Against this pressure, Van Buren claimed that he opposed local election not because he distrusted the people but rather because he feared that elected judges would be biased against their political opponents. That, not central appointment, would politicize legal administration.[33] He supported a compromise in which county boards of supervisors would nominate a list of justices of the peace, and each court of common pleas would nominate a list;

if the lists were not identical, the governor would select names from the two lists. This method of appointment was finally accepted. In practice, it gave the appointment power to the governor. Opposition to this procedure soon emerged on the grounds that it gave the governor and his party too much power to control local administration. In 1826, an amendment passed that made the justices elective by the towns.[34]

Once let loose in the 1821 convention, the principle of electing local officials, especially electing judges, was hard to cabin. Amid the debate on justices of the peace, one delegate proposed electing sheriffs. Van Buren voted against it, presumably because it decentralized the appointment of executive officers. High Federalists like Kent opposed it too, which made for another curious alliance. The Federalists feared that sheriffs would become vengeful office seekers. Justices of the peace were, presumably, trained to be impartial. Sheriffs were not. Local election of these powerful officers would only excite the "party feelings" that the constitution should mitigate. "[P]etty intrigue would be made the order of the day," predicted Nathan Williams, "and every county in the state would be thrown into convulsions." A sheriff could be expected to "visit upon his unfortunate enemies with a most cruel and destructive vengeance" while excusing his friends, so that "no monies would be collected from them, except through rules and attachments almost without end."[35] In addition, the plan would weaken the governor and turn the state into "a confederacy of counties" much like the confederation of states before the federal Constitution. Rufus King analogized the sheriffs in the counties to the federal marshals in states; one was a state official, the other a federal official. No one would allow state election of federal marshals, so why permit local county election of state sheriffs? The sheriff was one official who had to be a gubernatorial appointee.[36]

Erastus Root and other democratic Republicans rejected the analogy between the state and the federal government, and they denied that a sheriff should be a "tool in the hands of the executive." The election of sheriffs was a way of returning power to citizens, "to give to the people some of the wheat — not the chaff only."[37] These arguments won the day, and much of the future too. Under the 1821 constitution, sheriffs were chosen in county elections, a precedent expanded to justices of the peace and city officials under an amendment in 1826 and all state judges two decades later.[38]

The Council of Revision was almost as controversial as the Council of Appointment. It comprised the governor, Supreme Court judges, and the chancellor. By the second decade of the nineteenth century, the council seemed to many to violate the separation of powers. But what would take its place? Most delegates at the 1821 convention believed that a gubernatorial veto offered enough protection against unwise legislation. But some thought that even this veto was unnecessary. Should there be any veto? Or should all bills passed by both houses instantly become law?

The problem with the council, thought Republican Daniel Tompkins, was that it had not limited itself to constitutional objections; it also rejected statutes on the basis of policy.[39] He knew this to be true because he had sat on the council for thirteen years as a governor and then as a supreme court judge. His premise was that constitutional and political disallowance involved two qualitatively different standards. The assumption that constitutionality was a special determination pervaded the debate. Accordingly, the nature of the judiciary became pivotal in the discussion of what would replace the Council of Revision.

Most agreed that the governor should hold a legislative veto, subject to legislative override, but remained concerned that this was not a sufficient check on the legislative process, especially when one party dominated state government. Delegates spanning the political spectrum agreed that the judiciary offered at least some protection against bad legislation. Unlike in some states, such as Kentucky, judicial review had broad support among New Yorkers.[40] Peter R. Livingston argued that a veto was unnecessary because judges and juries would nullify statutes that interfered with the people's liberties. "If the judicial department but do their duty," he told the convention, "all laws in violation of the Constitution are but as blank paper."[41] The institutions of judicial review and jury nullification were more effective than the Council of Revision, which defied the separation of powers. Judicial review offered a better check on dangerous legislation than the council or the governor, and it separated judges from mere policy decisions. Putting judges on a political body like the Council of Revision risked contaminating the legal process with politics. "God forbid the time should ever arrive," declared John Duer, "when suitors shall be anxious to inquire into the political sentiments of the judge by whom their causes are to be heard."[42] Ezekiel Bacon, of Oneida County, supported the gubernatorial veto, but even without it an unconstitutional law would have a short life. A statute that was "clearly unconstitutional" would be tested in the courts, where it would be "annulled, the great principles of the constitution preserved, and the sacredness of private rights effectively maintained."[43] If the governor had a sole veto, the anomalous council would be gone, and judges would be insulated from the legislative process. The judges' role would be limited to reviewing the constitutionality of those statutes in individual cases. New Yorkers saw judicial integrity and judicial review as antidotes to partisan law making. Almost all delegates, regardless of party, embraced the ideal of judicial independence and the institution of judicial review. Courts offered ballast against partisan legislatures, and judges were supposed to "annul" statutes that were "clearly unconstitutional" — but *only* such statutes.

Martin Van Buren leveled one last charge against the Council of Revision: its published opinions had become fodder for partisan politics. One example was during the War of 1812. Chancellor Kent had objected to a few of the state's military measures, particularly the Conscription Act. His opinions "were industriously circulated throughout the state to foment the elements of faction. . . . The object of those objections was to impress the public mind with a belief that their representatives were treading under foot the laws and constitution of their country." The problem was that the council objected on *political* rather than *constitutional* grounds. In addition, council members sometimes released their opinions even when they were outvoted and the council as a whole approved legislation. In this instance, Kent's objections had not persuaded the council, but nonetheless he sent his opinions to the newspapers. Years later in his *Autobiography*, Van Buren complained that Kent ignored the overwhelming legislative majorities that had passed the acts and did not limit himself to "constitutional grounds, expressed with moderation," but also invoked political grounds. Van Buren also believed that Kent's additional public statements implied that the state government was in the hands of a cabal.[44] Elimination of the Council of Revision would remove judges from politics — and take away a platform that Federalist judges had used to criticize Republican administrations.

The removal of politically motivated judges would have the same effect. If all delegates seemed to agree that judges had the power to determine the constitutionality of legislation, they disagreed about whether the sitting judges were capable of the task. Some of the Republican animus against the judges derived from their political affiliation. Therefore, in addition to eliminating the council, the convention terminated all five judges on the Supreme Court. Three of the Supreme Court's judges — Chief Justice Ambrose Spencer and Associate Justices William Van Ness and Jonas Platt — were in the convention. Spencer, who rarely hid his political inclinations, was in particular a lightening rod. The politics of the issue were apparent to all. "[W]e are about to make a constitutional provision which has no other object than that of pulling from our bench of our supreme court certain individuals who have become odious to a portion of the community," complained David Buel. "It will be a disgrace to us."[45] Most of his colleagues disagreed. The justices were dismissed when the new constitution took effect, and the governor had sole power to appoint replacements.[46]

Popular Sovereignty and the Rule of Law

The convention of 1821 demonstrated how much had changed in New York's political culture a generation after the ratification debate. The federal Constitution was not a brooding omnipresence in the convention. Instead of fear of a strong central government, there was new worry of a powerful partisan *state* government. Here, the federal Constitution provided a model of how to divide and limit power. If the debate in 1787 and 1788 had been about the extent of the state's reserved powers, the debate in 1821 explored how to discipline that power to prevent a single party from dominating the state. The new state constitution represented an attempt to devolve authority back to local governments and constitutionalize the practical authority they had long enjoyed. Institutional remnants of the British Empire that eroded local power, namely, the councils of Revision and Appointment, were eliminated. A streamlined executive received a new veto and the sole power to appoint most top officials. A majority of the legislature was free to pass any legislation so long as it could get the governor to sign. The exception was any law granting a corporate charter or appropriating money for a local or private purpose, which now required a two-thirds supermajority. This limitation on legislative power started a trend that became more restrictive in state constitutions written during the rest of the nineteenth century. The state's chartering of banks and its financing of the Erie Canal, which opened in 1825, led to large public debts and concern about whether the government was financially prudent or corrupt. Supermajority requirements were supposed to ensure that such projects were in the public interest. They also diminished the legislature's power, creating space for other nodes of authority—such as the legal elite on and off the bench.[47]

The convention agreed that two important checks on state power remained. One was that of the voters. The other was the ability of private actors to test the constitutionality of legislation in the courts. Political parties tried to harness the first check; legal mandarins like James Kent tried to control the second by defining the constitutional protection of private rights. Neither check was absolute, and popular support for each varied over time.[48] But both received formal elaboration in New York, where they served as models for much of the rest of the nation. The party system's definition of constitutional meaning, through electoral politics, and the elite bar's attempt to control constitutional interpretation in treatises, schools, and courts were complementary rather than antagonistic. Founders of the party system and leaders of the legal culture each claimed to represent the rule of law and the people. One opened access to politics for many ordinary men, and the other retained mastery of an increasingly complex legal science. They did not always coexist peacefully, but most of the time they did. When they did not, there was always the threat of a new state constitutional convention that might, like the one in 1821, terminate the judges and start anew.

Even the individuals who helped build these institutions could work together effectively. No politician in the early nineteenth century more personified the promise and limits of parties as vehicles of popular sovereignty than Martin Van Buren. No judge better embodied the ideal of law as a check on legislative excess than James Kent. A generation earlier, men like this might have found more than one occasion to scorn, criticize, and perhaps slander each other. Because they held such divergent views of the state's political culture, it is not inconceivable that they could have found themselves at the far end of politics, in a duel.[49] Neither man was temperamentally suited to such conduct. Indeed, they enjoyed amicable relations. But more was at work than personality. Civility was the new coin of the constitutional realm. Good faith opinions in politics and disinterested judgment in the courts were common denominators between men like Van Buren and Kent. After Kent objected to the state's war measures in 1814, he refrained from public comment on politics while on the bench. Van Buren praised him for this; Republicans only wanted to see judges "*devote their time to the studies and duties of their office.*" This master of party politics claimed that disinterested judgment, rather than policy outcome, was the key to good judging. "I do not believe," Van Buren said of Kent, "that he ever, in his long and honorable career, did an act whatever may have been its error, that he did not at least conscientiously think to be right."[50] All agreed that Kent was a studious judge; Republicans just did not want him to be a political participant too. Van Buren reported that Thomas Addis Emmet, an Irish immigrant lawyer, called Kent "a learned and able judge—but a poor Jury-man" because he had so little experience "with the world."[51] Law and politics required different skills.

Kent might have agreed with much of this. According to Van Buren, Kent returned the compliment to the politician, praising him years later as a "very good President" who did "nothing of which either of us has any reason to be ashamed" and apologizing for opposition in the past.[52] After the War of 1812, which marked the end of the Federalist Party as a force in politics, Kent concentrated on the law. But law for him was no dry science, detached from the way people lived every day and from their visions of how they wished to live in the future. Included in his role as a judge and chancellor was state constitution making, which is why he felt no reluctance to participate in the 1821 convention. Kent never lost his keen sense of the legal culture's power to guide the people in the exercise of their political power.

An Empire of Law

All former empires rose, the work of guilt,
On conquest, blood, or usurpation built:
But we, taught wisdom by their woes and crimes,
Fraught with their lore, and born to better times;
Our constitutions form'd on freedom's base,
Which all the blessings of all lands embrace;
Embrace humanity's extended cause,
A world of our empire, for a world of our laws. . . .

David Humphreys (1786)

I N AN EARLY PAMPHLET calling for revision of the Articles of Confederation, Noah Webster warned the state governments that "selfishness" led to "self-ruin, and that *provincial interest* is inseparable from *national interest*."[1] Webster is best remembered for his *American Dictionary of the English Language*, published in 1828 and the culmination of his long search for an American lexicon. That effort began a half century earlier when Webster published *A Grammatical Institute of the English Language* (1783), in which he argued that it was the "duty" of the new Americans "to attend to the *arts of peace*, and particularly the interests of *literature*; to see if there be not some errours to be corrected, some defects to be supplied, and some improvements to be introduced into our systems of education, as well as into those of our civil policy."[2] In the 1780s, some thought it "strange" that Webster and others were already demanding a new American literature, "but a little while agone twas almost bold to suppose it would not tarnish the Alphabet of Europe to wrap it around an American Idea."[3] The Revolution proved otherwise. Now a new literature was needed to express those new American ideas. As with literature, so too law. The projects were not just parallel; they involved the same people. Lawyers were often writers and promoters of a national literature, like Webster himself.[4]

Language and law were both central to national identity in early modern Europe and in postrevolutionary America. The German philosopher Johann Gottfried Herder and other late eighteenth-century counter-Enlightenment thinkers explored the tension between universal principles and national cultures. Their efforts helped generate the idea that different environments bred different cultures.[5] Webster read Herder and other romantic theorists and sympathized with their celebration of cultural distinctions. Law and language suffered from similar conditions. Webster's earliest concern was uniform pronunciation. He believed that dialects undermined cultural nationalism. Here Webster put aside his celebration of cultural diversity: within a national jurisdiction, variety was detrimental. Pronunciation was a prime example. "Every county in England, every State in America and almost every town in each State," he complained just after the Revolution, "has some peculiarities in pronunciation which are equally erroneous and disagreeable to its neighbours." The reason was that grammatical instruction was left to "parents and nurses—to ignorance and caprice—to custom, accident or nothing." All of this prevented national uniformity.[6] The remedy in linguistics was a standard manual and, ultimately, an American dictionary. An expert like Webster, believing that he had the public interest at heart, would instruct the young how to pronounce and spell their nation's language. The remedy in law was stronger government, laid out in a new constitution. The postcolonial projects of creating national language and law both involved an interplay of popular participation and elite persuasion. All this was part of the Federalist attempt to forge what historian John L. Brooke calls a "consensual and unitary public sphere": a didactic elite would lead the way, and the people would choose to follow.[7]

A few years later, Webster supported the federal Constitution as an instance of his cultural theory at work. The framers excelled at adjusting the wisdom of tradition to the special environment of America. Alongside "the fabled demi-gods of antiquity" would lie the "names of those men who have digested a system of constitutions for the American empire." He converted common-law customary theory into an American mode of improvement. The past provided numerous constitutional resources; the new Americans could select the best to improve their own. "In the formation of our constitution, the wisdom of all ages is collected—the legislators of antiquity are consulted—as well as the opinions and interests of the millions who are concerned. In short, it is an *empire of reason*."[8]

Tradition, wise selection, and the consent of millions: these provided the perfect balance between experience and innovation. It was "the *duty* of every citizen to examine the principles of [the Constitution], to compare them with the principles of other governments, with a constant eye to our particular situation and circumstances." In practice, this meant comparing the Constitution with "the two *best constitutions* that ever existed in Europe, the *Roman* and the *British*." Intelligent observers would aid the people in this process. Point by point, Webster maintained that the federal Constitution marked "an *improvement* on the *best* constitutions that the world ever saw." If it was ratified, those citizens would "enjoy the blessings, which heaven has lavished, in rich profusion, upon the this western world."[9] Webster concluded that the Constitution embodied his ideal of cosmopolitan adaptation and nationalistic innovation.

In 1828 Webster at last completed his *American Dictionary*. It was necessary because the English language was not the same in the United States as it was in England. "[A]lthough the body of language is the same as in England, and it is desirable to perpetuate that sameness, yet some differences must exist." Different lands required different words to describe those lands. Topography and environment, for example, varied across the globe. "But the principal differences between the people of this country and of all others," Webster maintained, "arise from different forms of government, different laws, institutions, and customs." Some English laws were irrelevant in the United States, those regulating hunting, hawking, and heraldry, for example. "On the other hand, the institutions in this country which are new and peculiar, give rise to new terms or to new applications of old and which will not be inserted in their dictionaries, unless copied from ours." These institutional differences were subtle but important. One example was the noun "justice," or judge. English dictionaries defined it as "one deputed by the *King* to do right by way of judgement—he is a *Lord* by his office." But in America this monarchical definition made no sense. Similarly, "*Constitutionally* is defined by Todd or Chalmer, [as] *legally*, but in this country the distinction between *constitution* and *law* requires a very different definition."[10] An American dictionary would explain differences of meaning hidden behind a common vocabulary.

With new connotations came a distinctive "idiom" whose premier stylists, Webster believed, included "the authors of the Federalist," his old acquaintance Chancellor Kent, and the legal reports coming from federal and "some" state judges. This flourishing of national legal literature encouraged him. Webster's goal was to "purify" the language, by which he meant "giving it more regularity and consistency in its forms, both of words and sentences; and in this manner to furnish a standard of our vernacular tongue, which we shall not be ashamed to bequeath to *three hundred millions of people*, who are destined to occupy, and I hope, adorn the vast territory within our jurisdiction."[11] At the same time, jurists were also attempting to define that vast territory and the millions destined to occupy it. The goal was to make the territory and its people citizens of a single jurisdiction rather than several.

James Kent's Cosmopolitan Law for America

James Kent provided the legal complement to Webster's *Dictionary* in his *Commentaries on American Law*, published in four volumes between 1826 and 1830.[12] Yet Kent was less concerned with separating America from Britain than with making the United States a single jurisdiction while at the same time keeping it within the pale of European civilization. When Kent was completing the *Commentaries*, a young law student asked him about the condition of American law when he became a state judge in 1798. "We had no law of our own," Kent replied, "and nobody knew what it was."[13] This was misleading. Kent was referring to the lack of published judicial reports, not the absence of a legal system or profession.[14] But it was the sort of thing this former state chief justice, chancellor, and legal writer might have begun to believe when he compared his own education in English and European sources of law with the growing American literature available in the late 1820s. "We" were citizens of the United States, newly independent at the time that Kent had secluded himself to study law when Yale College suspended classes in the middle of 1779. The "law" was learned through Sir William Blackstone's *Commentaries on the Laws of England*, English reports and histories, procedural handbooks, and continental European treatises.[15] Even more important was the apprenticeship, the practical education that immersed the clerk in the oral tradition of the common law and taught him how to interpret the profession's literature. This law comprised common law, some English statutes, and state statutes. There was no sense of *an* American law.

A generation later, Kent implied, there was an American law, and it could be found in many state and federal reports and in his *Commentaries*.[16] American law was no longer colonial law, and the most important aspect of this transformation was that English common law was becoming simply *the* common law: a transatlantic body of principles as well as a way of reasoning about law, not the procedures and rules of decision in the jurisdictionally limited English royal courts. To be sure, many of the procedures and rules invoked in day-to-day litigation in New York were the same in 1798, and 1828, as they had been in, say, 1768. Some of the lawyers practicing in 1798 had practiced in the colonial period. Most had been trained by colonial lawyers. Law was a conservative business. The working knowledge of its practitioners depended heavily on three sources: student education, the continuous training obtained while practicing, and the profession's reference literature. For law to change, one or more of these institutions of legal culture had to change.

Federalist lawyers and their heirs restructured each of these institutions. They did not—or could not—do so directly through legislation. Federalist influence was never strong in most state legislatures, including New York's, and it weakened after the election of 1800, in which Thomas Jefferson and his Republicans swept most of the country. Instead, Federalists turned to the nonlegislative dimensions of law and legal training, the areas of legal culture that were beyond the reach of electoral politics. They established new law lectureships and schools to educate aspirants to the bar.[17] They formed professional associations and literary clubs to educate one another in law and related arts. They published a new professional literature. They did something else too: they added a new layer of theory to English law. In daily transactions and litigation, most legal rules remained the same as they had long been: the conventions of their courts. But increasingly these conventions were seen as *rules*: abstract mandates detached from the jurisdictional apparatus that enforced them. Many participated in this transformation, but it was primarily Federalist lawyers who reshaped the law into bodies of doctrine not rooted in any single jurisdiction.

The object was legal uniformity, but this was a means to the further end of political unity. Uniform substantive law would help bind the original states and provide a prefabricated legal infrastructure for new ones out west. The purpose of Kent's *Commentaries*, as the author told a friend, was "to discuss the law as known and received at Boston, New York, Philadelphia, Baltimore, Charleston, &c. and as proved by the judicial decisions in those respective states." He focused on the Atlantic trading ports and confessed that he did "not much care what the law is in Vermont or Delaware or Rhode Island, or many other states. Can we not assume American common law to be what is declared in the federal courts and in the courts of the states I have mentioned in some others, without troubling ourselves with every local peculiarity? I shall *assume* what I have to say, to be the law of every state, where an exception is not shown, because I mean to deal in *general Principles* and those positive regulations, legislative and judicial, which constitute the basis of all American jurisprudence."[18] Kent assumed that judges in these leading cities would generate the best, most consistent law. Provincial variation was an "exception" to these "general principles."

The project of legal unification began during the ratification debate with constitutional law and soon spread to other areas of law, helping to give shape to those areas *as* substantive fields of law. Rules, and therefore the rights they defined, preceded remedy.[19] Personnel and procedure remained important. Federalists were concerned about the quality of federal administrators. They continued to question the relevance of localist institutions like the jury, defended an independent judiciary, and helped engineer judicial review. In the long run, however, they failed to control the state and public judiciaries. But if they could not control decision making directly, they could try to control the raw material on which decisions were made: the reports, treatises, handbooks, and educational institutions that inculcated law's purpose. In place of an administrative empire, of great leaders surrounded by gifted advisers, emerged an empire of law: of painstaking acculturation of lawyers and judges in a supposedly nonpartisan legal culture. This was the vision of lawyers like Kent and Joseph Story who came of age during and just after the ratification debate and revered the founders. It was the vision of the commentators who followed the glossators.

Federalists and their heirs defined their new law primarily in terms of coherent maxims and principles, printed it in books, and fitted it within the newly clarified hierarchy of American law. Constitutional law was atop this hierarchy, statutes next, and common law at the bottom. Yet the newly clarified substance of the common law helped define both constitutions and statutes, a cross-fertilization that belied the strict lines between the three. Whether or not there would be a pyramid of sovereign institutions, there would be a hierarchy of legal genres. Packed in books such as *The Federalist Papers*, court reports, jurisprudential treatises like Kent's *Commentaries* and others — so many of them conceived in the imperial context of New York — the law became portable in a way the old British imperial agents had only begun to imagine. Law conceptualized as substantive fields of doctrine proved a more effective mechanism of constraint against popular resistance and political dissolution in a large empire than procedure and personnel alone. Inculcated in students, practitioners, and judges alike, rather than enforced by government administrators from above, these books did much to define American law. Since for so long so little else of American culture differed from British, this law helped define Americans as well. Soon judges, lawyers, and juries in far-flung outposts pored over those new legal sources with little regard for the spatial, social, or political distance separating author and reader as Federalist law traveled far beyond its matrix. When they applied this American law, they defined themselves as American citizens. They performed the abstract ideal of union on the ground in Cincinnati, Indianapolis, and beyond.

Some books were new, but the old ones remained. And much in the new was not new. Many of the sources that James Kent used to elaborate American law were European. His *Commentaries* were part of an early modern tradition of national institutes that were written as new nation-states released themselves from the grip of the Holy Roman Empire and its *ius commune*. An institutionalist had two objectives: to unify national law and distinguish it from an international body of law. Blackstone's *Commentaries* fitted the model, and from this angle all Kent did was domesticate the institutionalist structure, drawing a baseline for further nationalist experimentation. To the historian of legal literature, Kent's law appears Anglo-European in form.[20]

As an institutionalist, Kent wanted first to present the law as uniform across the United States. This required subjecting the primary law-making bodies, state legislatures and state courts, to external standards, both federal and international. But American legal federalism changed the institutionalist mission. While many European institutionalists had grappled with the problem of internal legal diversity and viewed their institutes as projects of unification, their primary goal was to distinguish national law from continental *ius commune*, and the provinces they dealt with in their kingdoms did not have constitutional protection. Overcoming state jurisdictional boundaries proved more difficult than overcoming what one early modern French institutionalist dismissed as "the very diffuse and often stupidly varying customs of this Kingdom."[21] Similarly, in Europe there was often a reciprocal influence between institutes and codes. Nationalist jurists wrote institutes, and national legislatures drafted codes.[22] But Kent and other Federalist heirs resisted most codification efforts because they arose at the *state* rather than the national level. The federal government lacked the power to enact a private-law code.[23] Federal control over state law was limited to areas of its constitutional jurisdiction, and even here some doubt remained about congressional power to define that jurisdiction and that of federal judges to strike down state law. Consequently, Federalists turned to other institutions to minimize the effects of legal federalism. Kent's *Commentaries* were fundamental to that project. In them he publicized high Federalist conceptions of the Constitution and of the common law.

If there were a national code, Kent believed it should be "the immense code of the common law" that judges identified by applying "the dictates of natural justice, and of cultivated reason, to particular cases."[24] The first purpose of this national common law was to reduce differences among the states, not to distinguish them all from other nations. Rather than emphasize national distinctiveness, Kent strove to prevent too much deviation from what he called the "the civilized nations of Europe."[25] The United States was no longer part of Britain, and it had its own legal culture. But its law derived from Europe.

This was Kent's major contribution to American legal culture: he clarified the separation between "constitutional jurisprudence" and the "municipal law" of statutes and judge-administered law, a separation that Federalists had limned in the ratification debate. He mapped an American private law too. To accomplish the latter, he presented the states' municipal laws as systematic and principled, along the lines of constitutional law, rather than merely as frameworks for dispute resolution. That, at least, that was his goal. Kent began the project at Columbia College in the mid-1790s in some of the first university lecture classes in the United States. He owed the position to Federalist patronage, and he repaid the favor by inscribing Federalist principles into American law.[26] In the second year of the lectures, Kent drew only two students, and the college did not renew the lectureship. According to one of Kent's friends, the city's "principal lawyers" did not advise their clerks to attend, fearing that the young men would quit the office for the lecture hall. For the rest of the century there was tension between the apprenticeship system and academic instruction, and Kent's friend was probably right that practitioners preferred to have clerks pay fees and copy files rather than learn the "science" of the law.[27]

Three decades later, after the state constitution's age limitation forced Kent from the bench, Columbia renewed the lectures. Kent soon published them as the *Commentaries*, the first volume of which demonstrates that its structure differed from that of Blackstone's *Commentaries* or of other European institutes. Blackstone had begun with a brief treatment of natural law and then moved quickly to municipal law and the dominance within it of parliamentary legislation. After a brisk one hundred pages on the "nature of English law," containing only superficial reference to the British Empire, Blackstone turned to the substantive law affecting persons, following the institutionalist division of the law into persons, things, and actions derived from Justinian's sixth-century *Institutes of Roman Law*.[28] Kent borrowed this scheme for three of his four volumes, and he acknowledged Justinian's *Institutes* as an influence on all European and American law.[29] But the preliminary treatment of the layers of law required its own volume.

That first volume is a monument to the transformation of American public law because it rested on a theory of legal genres developed out of the experience of leaving one empire and constituting another. Volume 1 has three parts: the law of nations, American constitutional law, and the sources of municipal law. Unlike Blackstone, Kent did not include status law in his first volume. In the new republican society, status was not supposed to be central, though the law in action reflected the continued importance of status categories better than the law in the books. Indeed, the removal of status law from the beginning of his *Commentaries* served Kent's argument that the states' laws were similar to one another and compared favorably with European law. In particular, it allowed him to marginalize the law of slavery, which in his age of northern abolition cut against the argument that American law was uniform.[30] Instead, Kent began by mapping jurisdictional rather than personal relationships.

He began with the law of nations. This was unusual in an institutionalist work, but it placed the United States within European civilization. In addition, knowledge of the law of nations would help American merchants preserve neutrality on the seas and avoid "the vortex of European contests."[31] Finally, the law of nations offered an intriguing example of a body of law that existed outside conventional jurisdictions. No institution enforced the law of nations, and many disagreed about whether its sources lay in positive agreement, custom, or natural law. Yet no one denied its importance. According to Kent, Grotius gave the law of nations rational form and thus its persuasive force. "He arose like a splendid luminary," Kent wrote of Grotius, "dispelling darkness and confusion, and imparting light and security to the intercourse of nations."[32]

Like the law of nations among European kingdoms, federal constitutional law and national common law lacked effective enforcement within the states. Perhaps they too could gain respect, and power, by persuasive force of their doctrine. The law of nations attracted several American jurists in the early Republic. James Wilson, for example, taught the law of nations in his earliest lectures at the College of Philadelphia in 1791.[33] At Columbia a few years later, the law of nations was the subject of Kent's third lecture, after one on the history of civil governments and another surveying "the history of the American union." But when he revised his lectures thirty years later, the law of nations came first.[34] "When the United States ceased to be a part of the

British empire, and assumed the character of an independent nation," Kent declared on the first page of his *Commentaries*, "they became subject to that system of rules which reason, morality, and custom had established among the civilized nations of Europe, as their public law." Much of that European law was "instituted or positive law, founded on usage, consent, and agreement." Nonetheless, "it would be improper to separate this law entirely from natural jurisprudence, and not to consider it as deriving much of its force, and dignity, and sanction, from the same principles of right reason, and the same view of nature and constitution of man, from which the science of morality is deduced." Consequently, "knowledge of international law is highly necessary, not only to lawyers practising in our commercial ports, but to every gentleman who is animated by liberal views, and a generous ambition to assume stations of high public trust."[35] While training in the law of nations was necessary for commercial lawyers on the east coast, it also exposed all students to moral reasoning and might influence legal decision making and public administration across the Union.

Another cosmopolitan resource was Roman private law. When discussing private-law doctrines, Kent cited continental civil-law sources alongside English ones wherever possible, even when he had not read or fully understood them.[36] Kent believed that these citations made his private-law rules unassailable. His respect for things Roman did not, however, extend to public law. "In every thing which concerns civil and political liberty," he observed, Roman law "cannot be compared with the free spirit of the English and American common law."[37] Finally, much of Kent's American law, especially its public law, came from the experience of revolution and reconstitution. He was able to weave these many sources together to present a compelling case that there was *an* American law. Kent made eclecticism seem systematic, and when he approached American law in interimperial and intraimperial ways, he was less an American Blackstone than an American Grotius, imagining a body of customary law that bound the states together as a nation and also linked them to a transatlantic civilization.

For Kent, as for many legal thinkers in the early United States, it was impossible to think of law without thinking first of constitutions.[38] Their conceptualization of constitutional law as a substantive body of law, which controlled all courts and legislatures, influenced the way they thought about other legal genres. This is how Kent justified his references to English law. For him, the common law was not simply the law of the English central courts but rather a collection of rules that functioned as the default setting for municipal law in all the states. It was "a collection of principles, to be found in the opinions of sages or deduced from universal and immemorial usage, and receiving progressively the sanction of the courts."[39] Statutes could trump this customary law, but judges used that law to make sense of statutes and even constitutions.[40] It was also transatlantic, and its rules flowed east back to Britain. New political borders made lawyers on both sides of the Atlantic more self-conscious about their separate legal environments, and each side learned from the other's attempts to hold their remnant empires together. There were personal encounters and epistolary correspondence; but legal reports and treatises were the most important medium of influence, as English lawyers read and cited some leading American treatises. In short, Kent's common law was an extension of the unifying principle of constitutional law to other areas of law. The founders, especially Federalists, had created constitutional law to help control the interpretation of the federal Constitution; their heirs continued to define that new genre *and* sought to create a national private law too. Like a central crystal, constitutional law began to reshape other areas of law surrounding it.

Who was he, America's first influential law professor and treatise writer? He was a mediocre lawyer and not an especially original thinker. His talents were synthetic thinking and graceful advocacy. He was also a tireless worker, proud in his old age that he began his career as an industrious clerk in the law office of Egbert Benson, the Federalist state attorney general. "My fellow students who were more gay and gallant, thought me very odd and dull in my taste," Kent recalled four decades later, "but out of five of them four died in middle life as drunkards. I was free from all dissipations, and chaste as pure virgin snow. I never danced, played cards, or sported with a gun, or drank anything but water."[41] Here was an old man lecturing youth. But it was true.

He worked hard not because he loved the law. "Law, I must frankly confess, is a field which is uninteresting and boundless," he wrote a fellow student in 1782. "The study is so encumbered with voluminous rubbish and the baggage of folios that it requires uncommon assiduity and patience to manage so unwieldy a work." Why endure the labor? "[I]t leads forward to the first stations in the State."[42] A legal career led to power if one was diligent and patient. Kent was both. As a middle-aged state judge, Kent suffered various ailments while riding circuit, which at the time meant riding on horseback through the state's western reaches. He frequently exhausted what his brother Moss called his "battered constitution" and suffered from the family curse of a "desponding Imagination." The remedy was always the same: more work. "Industry," he maintained, "is the Panacea of most human anxieties."[43]

Another relief was classical literature. Edward Livingston reintroduced Kent to Latin in 1786 while both were trying cases on the state circuit. This "opened to me a world of learning, of happiness and of fame," he recalled, "and I flattered myself I had discovered the true mine of my most solid happiness and honour." From then on Kent complained when legal work kept him "from my old classical companions such as Cicero, Homer & Voltaire." This list, and especially the last name, suggests what was clear to Kent's contemporaries but is less so two centuries later: he was a witty, warm companion who kept up with the latest literature and supported his friends' writing too. Scholarly reading was an independent good, beyond what it taught him about the law. "[N]ext to my wife," he wrote in 1828, "my library has been the solace of my greatest pleasure & devoted attachment."[44] In return, Kent hoped to contribute a lasting work to the nation's library. He did.

An additional mainstay was Federalist politics. In the summer of 1788, while practicing his new craft in Poughkeepsie, Kent attended New York's ratification convention. He was awed by Hamilton's performance, became a disciple, and cherished *The Federalist Papers*.[45] Soon he became involved in Federalist politics, wrote pamphlets with Noah Webster defending the Jay Treaty and its rapprochement with Britain against Republican criticism, became a master in chancery under John Jay's patronage, and then received the lectureship at Columbia.[46]

This environment — New York's strong Federalist culture on the one hand and intellectual cosmopolitanism on the other — shaped Kent's lectures and the ensuing *Commentaries*. The former influence was more important. His mentors were high Federalists: Hamilton, Jay, and Benson. In addition, he moved in Federalist literary circles. In the 1790s there was the "Friendly Club," which included Kent, Dr. Elihu Hubbard Smith, dramatist William Dunlap, doctor and historian Samuel Latham Mitchell, William Woolsey, novelist Charles Brockden Brown, law reporter William Johnson, and Noah Webster. The club met regularly, shared books, published the *New York Magazine*, supported Webster's *American Minerva*, and pursued other political and cultural activities.[47] In the 1820s, Kent was a member of the Bread and Cheese Club, which comprised many of the old "Friends" plus writers like James Fenimore Cooper and William Cullen Bryant, as well as artists Thomas Cole and Asher B. Durand.[48] Most of these men were new New Yorkers and part of the postrevolutionary New England migration to the city.[49] New York's articulate and imperialist cultural elites were once again immigrants. And lawyers. The law they practiced, like the literature they wrote, was simultaneously postcolonial, as they sought independence from Britain, and imperial, for they created a pattern of American legal culture that would spread throughout the states and across the continent.

Like generations of common lawyers, Kent believed that the key to law was reason, though not intuitive reason. Rather, it was the reason embedded in foundational legal principles. A learned profession, schooled by magnificent treatises, derived and applied these principles. This celebration of the artificial reason of the jurists was familiar in Anglo-American law at least since the days of Sir Edward Coke, but Kent added a cosmopolitanism evident when he began his *Commentaries* with the law of nations. Without endorsing a specific theory of natural law, he tried to find some concordance between it and the law of nations.[50] Consequently, the first part of his *Commentaries* is a substitute for, or an empirical investigation of, natural law.

It was also a gambit for authority. Knowledge of continental civil law was, as Perry Miller quipped, "a badge of cultivation."[51] Some historians conclude that Federalist lawyers used European citations to mystify their opponents and restrain parochial legislatures. Those sources were more useful to leverage authority *within* the legal community. Most codifiers did not intend to leave legal reform to the unschooled legislators. Instead, the legislature would delegate the task to legal specialists, whether members of their assemblies or not.[52] While on the New York bench, Kent recalled, "I made much use of the *Corpus Juris*, & as the Judges (Livingston excepted) knew nothing of French or civil law I had immense advantage over them. I could generally put my Brethren to rout & carry my point by my mysterious wan[d] of French and civil law." It took little persuasion because many of his colleagues "were republicans & very kindly disposed to everything that was French, & this enabled me without exciting any alarm or jealousy, to make free use of such authorities & thereby enrich our commercial law."[53] His political opponents' transatlantic ideals enabled Kent to enforce his own.

Kent's attempt to create an American common law reveals that second-generation Federalists did not believe that constitutional law alone was enough to bind the states. Between the election of 1800 and the Hartford Convention of 1815, Federalists lost almost all their political power. In New York, Federalists retained political influence by allying with erstwhile Republicans, like DeWitt Clinton.[54] Their dominance of the judiciary was waning over time, and while those courts were rendering decisions that shaped constitutional law for generations, most legal disputes involved private law rather than constitutions. So Federalists like Kent began to forge new, sturdy interpretations of common-law doctrine that would determine cases or at least restrain juries from returning general verdicts in whatever manner they pleased. The goal was to create a uniform American private law, the same in one state as in the others. There were many reasons for this Federalist focus on private law. One was the fear of Republican domination of the federal government, the flip side of the Jeffersonian attack on the Federalist-dominated courts.[55] Another was the wave of state constitutional revisions that democratized and weakened state government, like the one in New York in 1821. State constitutional delegates intended to transfer power to localities and private parties. Lawyers quickly helped fill this vacuum of authority.[56] Finally, judicial review had limited effect on unifying national law because it depended on episodic adjudication.

This quest for legal uniformity precipitated a debate about whether the federal courts were empowered to apply the common law and whether they should use English common-law standards to define constitutional guarantees.[57] Unlike many state constitutions, the federal Constitution did not declare that the common law was the default law of its courts. In Section 34 of the Judiciary Act of 1789, Congress provided that "the laws of the several states except where the Constitution, treaties or statutes or the United States shall otherwise require or provide, shall be regarded as rules of decision in trials at common law, in the courts of the United States, in cases where they apply." It was clear to all that the "laws of the several states" included statutory law. But did it encompass state common law too?[58] If so, to the extent that state common law varied, then federal courts hearing cases pursuant to diversity jurisdiction would have to decide cases differently as they received them from different states. The same federal court might decide one case one way and the next day decide a similar one, originating in another state, differently.

The debate over federal common law signaled another step in the fundamental shift in the conception of the common law. Traditionally, the common law functioned as a procedural apparatus that resolved disputes. Increasingly in the early Republic, Americans conceived of it as a series of interlocking substantive doctrines. This shift was part of the legacy of ancient constitutionalism that detached many common-law liberties from that apparatus. Now, this process of disentangling substance from procedure spread beyond traditional constitutional liberties like the jury, freehold tenure, and judicial independence. The advocates of a federal common law knew they could not simply invoke *the* common law, for there were many mutated common-law systems in the states. The ideal of a federal common law — a truly *common* law — was based on the hope that there could be agreement on some principles affecting all the states. As a result, the common law began to take on an interstate, even transnational, identity: a set of rules and principles for which English or American decisions were only evidence.[59] Federalists began to embrace this ideal of a uniform common law in the 1790s, although at the time of ratification they had argued that the common law varied among the states. By contrast, those protective of state sovereignty, like the old Antifederalists and new Jeffersonian Republicans, now doubted whether the common law had the coherence and integrity necessary to serve as a federal standard.[60] They also questioned the independence of Federalist-appointed judges and started new debates over the legitimacy of judicial discretion.[61]

This search for a uniform common law affected the controversy over the Sedition Act. The Adams administration passed the act to silence dissent over its foreign policy toward France. Jeffersonian Republicans were outraged. The constitutional issue raised under the act was whether truth was a defense to sedition. Under the common law it was not. Federalists suddenly turned to English law to interpret the American Bill of Rights. Jeffersonians disagreed; truth should be a defense.[62] The debate is often viewed as one of many instances in which Federalists tried to impose the common law on the United States. What it really demonstrates is the extent to which the common law became a political football. During the ratification debate a decade earlier, Antifederalists had championed common-law liberties to oppose the federal Constitution, while Federalists like Alexander Hamilton and James Wilson had pointed out the inadequacy of the common law, at least as adapted in the states, as a source for national standards. Common-law court procedures, writs, and professional barriers still varied from state to state.[63] But now many Federalists embraced common-law doctrine as defining the First Amendment's command that Congress make no law abridging the freedom of speech and press. The Republicans, on the other hand, embraced the old Antifederalist mainstay: juries should have the power to nullify federal law.[64] What was the common law: the jury? the strong judge? inflexible doctrine? The answer depended on the identity of the respondent. Federalists, at least, began to see the political utility of strong common-law doctrine.

Their grip on judicial procedure and personnel loosening, Federalist legal thinkers turned to substance. Rather than complex and variable procedural devices, as well as the dense learning surrounding those procedures, that law might be seen as a collection of fundamental and transcendent principles. The distillation of constitutional law provided a model for thinking of law in substantive terms. Jurists asked whether common-law doctrines, like constitutional ones, served the good of all the states. Union — the promotion of commercial ties between the states, which in turn would generate a sense of common citizenship—was the measure of substantive fitness. Throughout the first half of the nineteenth century that unionist pattern was impressed on successive areas of private law by means of specialized treatises, well-organized statutory codes, and judicial opinions that presented the common law as a rational science. If there could not be Federalist judges throughout the Union, perhaps there could be Federalist private law—Federalist doctrines instead of the king's writ, a Federalist library in place of the Inns of Court. By the mid-nineteenth century, lawyers began to think of the common law in terms of its separate branches: contract, tort, and property. These discrete doctrinal fields resulted from a complex process of intellectual, professional, and political struggle.[65] Nonetheless, most jurists used these legal doctrines to promote the Union and common citizenship. The old English common-law handbooks that fostered colonial Anglicization remained, and to these Federalists added new guides, treatises, and reports. The focus was on those areas of law that affected all states or that the federal judiciary could define, in part or whole. These included commercial law, admiralty law, the conflict of laws, and, to a lesser degree, equity.

Commercial and admiralty law are the best examples. Strands of continental jurisprudence that had been current in British America before the Revolution became more prominent after. Sometimes the use of these sources was an instrument of cultural politics, an attempt by Federalists to extract deference to their decisions. But to conclude that learned citations were window dressing misses the cultural significance of oceanic trade in the early nineteenth century. Commerce was not simply business; it was the leading indicator of civilization. The rules of etiquette for this international society lay in treatises on commercial law. Accordingly, in areas of law affecting trade, such as commercial and maritime law, lawyers and judges in America as well as in Britain sought guidance in the older resources of Europe.[66] Chief Justice Lord Mansfield led the way for incorporating *lex mercatoria* into English law.[67] American jurists followed his lead, but they had the additional task of getting federal jurisdiction over commercial cases. A large chapter of this story involved the federalization of commercial law and the extension of admiralty jurisdiction, both its subject matter and territorial ambit, including to all inland rivers that were navigable-in-fact. These antebellum trends culminated in the judicial and scholarly work of Supreme Court justice Joseph Story, but again Hamilton sketched the outline in *The Federalist*, and Kent laid the foundation in his courts and *Commentaries*.[68]

Kent cited civilian sources on *lex mercatoria* often and praised Mansfield for introducing that tradition into the Anglo-American legal world. "When Lord Mansfield mentioned the law merchant as being a branch of public law," Kent wrote in his *Commentaries*, "it was because that law did not rest essentially for its character and authority on the positive institutions and local customs of any particular country, but consisted of certain principles of equity and usages of trade, which general convenience and a common sense of justice had established, to regulate the dealings of merchants and mariners in all the commercial countries of the civilized world."[69] Here Kent invoked the core ideas of Federalist jurisprudence: Mansfield as a conduit of European law; the cosmopolitan, even natural, character of commercial law; the ideal of a civilized world linked by commerce; and the inexact use of "public law" to lend gravity to a legal genre. His *Commentaries* are full of such paeans. He never passed up an opportunity to cite Justinian, civilian commentators, and the French Code. Consequently, Kent's pages sometimes read more like an annotated bibliography than legal analysis. That was just the point. If Mansfield brought commercial law into the common-law world, Hamilton and Kent introduced it into the United States if by no other means than providing a learned bibliography.

> The reports of judicial decisions in the several states . . . evince great attention to maritime questions; and they contain abundant proofs that our courts have been dealing largely with the business of an enterprising and commercial people. . . . If we take the reports of New York in chronological order, we shall find that the first five volumes occupy the period when Alexander Hamilton was a leading advocate at our bar. That accomplished lawyer . . . showed, by his precepts and practice, the value to be placed on the decisions of Lord Mansfield. He was well acquainted with the productions of Valin and Emerigon; and if he be not truly one of the founders of commercial law of this state, he may at least be considered as among the earliest of those jurists who recommended those authors to the notice of the profession, and rendered the study and citation of them popular and familiar.[70]

Published reports would carry the innovations of Hamilton and Mansfield far beyond their sites of origin. So would Kent's *Commentaries*. Until law schools became the primary institutions of legal education, his work was the standard introduction to American law. Although most of his citations came from Europe and the New York courts, his book traveled far into the continent.

A related adaptation of European sources involved the conflict of laws. In a section of his chapter on divorce law entitled "Diversity of the Law in the United States," Kent warned that "[t]he *conflictus legum* is the most perplexing and difficult title of any in the jurisprudence of public law."[71] *Conflictus legum*, or the conflict of laws, was a branch of the law of nations that guided judges in one nation when interpreting and applying the law of another. Kent analogized the United States to European nation-states, which recognized the doctrine of *lex loci*: a contract valid where made ought to be valid everywhere. Kent believed that the states should recognize the same doctrine. It had an exception: "[T]he acts of parties, valid where made, should be recognized in other countries, provided they be not contrary to good morals, nor repugnant to the policy and positive institutions of the state." Kent showed that it was not just a doctrine for international law, for it had helped parties negotiate the legal pluralism between England and Scotland in Great Britain. The American federal system, Kent observed, also generated conflicting sources of law. Consequently, American judges needed principles to guide them when applying the law of other domestic jurisdictions. He never resolved this problem of conflicting state law. But he did refer to the "principle of public law, requisite for the safe intercourse and commerce of mankind, that acts valid by the law of the place where they arise, are valid everywhere." He also qualified it: "[T]his principle relates only to civil acts founded on the volition of the parties, and not to such as proceed from the sovereign power," which was the germ of American choice of law jurisprudence.[72] Joseph Story credited Kent as his "Master" when he developed the doctrine of comity a decade later. "To no part of the world is it of more interest and importance than to the United States," Story wrote, "since the union of a national government with that of twenty-four distinct, and in some respects independent states, necessarily creates very complicated relations and rights between the citizens of those states, which calls for the constant administration of extra-municipal principles."[73] The principle of comity gave cosmopolitan state and federal judges the discretion to avoid peculiar local rules when deciding issues of state law and fashion a national commercial law, though it also gave state judges license to ignore such doctrines too. Story bolstered this principle with citations from the law of nations and fashioned a doctrine of intranational choice of law. In turn, his principle influenced British jurists addressing jurisdictional pluralism within their empire.[74]

Finally, Kent and Story were the most influential craftsmen of equity in the nineteenth century. Kent self-consciously published his equity cases to set a standard that other judges could follow. His reports were especially important in jurisdictions that had no separate equity courts, as in New

England, and thus no local learning on which to draw. "I am glad to see American Chancery Reports," Story wrote to William Johnson, who served as Kent's reporter. These reports "cannot but be useful & instructive, since our local institutions & habits must require many applications of principle & practice. In my own circuit [New England] they will be double useful, since . . . there is no tribunal exercising an equity jurisdiction. . . . [T]he reports with which you have honored the profession will not suffer in comparison with those of the highest age of the British Empire."[75] When Story wrote his own treatise on equity jurisprudence in the 1830s, he lamented that in America it was only lately studied as "a system of enlightened and exact principles." Even in New York, "whose rank in jurisprudence has never been second to that of any State in the Union," equity was undeveloped until Kent applied it with his "extraordinary learning, unconquerable diligence, and brilliant talents."[76] While the Supreme Court claimed for the federal courts an independent power to invoke equitable remedies, the states retained control over most of what fell under the rubric of equity, and state judges increasingly learned what equity meant from Kent and Story.[77]

For Kent, Story, and other nationalists, there was no legislative shortcut for unifying private law. Codes were inadequate substitutes for the common law as expounded in opinions and treatises. In the United States, codification was a state movement designed to organize state statutes and, more controversial, simplify and reformulate the common law. Because they were state initiatives, codes would only aggravate legal federalism. In addition, Kent believed that the common law should not be simplified. Its "complex science," he maintained, was "a tax we pay for freedom, wealth, and refinement." Anyone who studied medieval English legal sources like the treatises of Glanvill and Bracton would see that the common law,

so humble in its origin, . . . has become so beneficial in its expansion, [and] will naturally feel his mind kindling and enlarging, like that of a traveler who ascends to the feeble sources of some mighty river, stealing obscurely from the deep recesses of the mountains, and widening and deepening as it flows, nourishing in its early career rude industry and infant settlements, but becoming in its lengthening course subservient to commerce, sustaining villages, towns and cities on its banks, and, finally, by its rich products, distributing wealth, plenty and happiness to distant nations.[78]

It is an image worthy of his friends in the Hudson River school of painting. The figure of ancient, sublime origins fitted law like other versions of the course of empire because law was a natural resource of civilization, helping to move it from "rude industry" to international commerce.[79]

Like all sources of law, Federalist law books and doctrines could be marshaled to serve local purposes. But although Federalists could not fully control the legal environment of the states, they did confine it. Settlers in the territories did lambaste lawyers, a cultural tension James Fenimore Cooper captured in the contest between Natty Bumppo and Judge Marmaduke Temple in *The Pioneers*.[80] There were, however, other ways for Federalist jurists to influence legal administration besides controlling courts directly.[81] When those seeking authority in the West invoked law, they needed a script. Eastern law books provided one. "May we not also look to the publication of the reports [of cases in federal courts]," asked one lawyer in the Federalist *North American Review*, "for the making of the Common Law of our country more regular and uniform in its character, than it has been hitherto?" State courts were "separate and independent," their decisions "often at variance and sometimes diametrically opposite." The federal courts were different. They were "powerfully associated" and respected one another's decisions.

> They go moreover into every part of the Union, and gather intelligence from the most gifted and eminent counsel of our country, and come together annually for the purpose of hearing, and conferring, and disposing of litigated rights, under circumstances peculiarly favorable to the clear and correct settlement of the law. No party feelings nor sectional views can sway them. . . . By a judiciary thus composed of the ablest judges, and acting under such advantages, the true principles of justice must be reached, if they are within the reach of human genius.[82]

Those judges would put the common law "on a more steady and regular foundation" and rescue it "from that inconsistency and variance for which it has been so long and so deservedly reproached."[83]

Judicial reports were not enough. Peter DuPonceau, a French immigrant lawyer, saw more clearly than most the weakness of national law in United States. England, for example, had "one great judicature, sitting at Westminster," and "[a]lthough divided into different tribunals, the same spirit pervades them all." Above them was the House of Lords, ruling with finality. "[W]e have, on the contrary," DuPonceau observed, "twenty-four different supreme judicatures, with a countless number of inferior tribunals, dispersed over an immense extent of territory. Beyond them is no authority whose decisions are binding in all cases." The Supreme Court had limited jurisdiction, and state judges ignored its decisions except on matters of federal law. Sometimes they ignored them on matters of federal law too. As a result, there was nothing "to prevent our national law from falling into that state of confusion which will inevitability follow from the discordant judgments of so many co-ordinate judicial authorities." In place of authoritative decision makers, DuPonceau urged the legal community to impress a uniform understanding of the "sound principles" of law upon its students. The study of "general jurisprudence and . . . the eternal immutable principles of right and wrong" was the only way to foster a "uniformity of jurisprudence in this widely extended union." Principles of legal "science" had to come first; "statutes and judicial decisions will gradually take their colour from them." How? Through "learned treatises and free discussions." He advised legal writers that "mere compilations" were not enough. Well-reasoned arguments were necessary. "In short, jurisprudence ought to be treated as a philosophical science."[84]

These nationalist sources of law — treatises, reports, and addresses — could not guarantee uniformity. Still, they were less malleable than the old common-law culture of the colonies and early states. There were, finally, handbooks for governance and dispute resolution in America. Even if the Federalists, who had made themselves into new corps of imperial agents, lost office and their early dominance in the judiciary, there would remain an imperial program, a relatively autonomous operating system for American law.[85] The literature they wrote in the early Republic was rigorous and demanded respect. Natty Bumppo might flee Judge Temple's eastern jurisdiction, not laugh in his face. And while Temple stayed put, the new legal scripture followed.

The influence of Federalist legal literature can be traced through judicial citation, law student curricula, and republication in the first half of the nineteenth century. It is more difficult to demonstrate that this literature informed the average American's sense of citizenship. One way to gauge the success of the Federalist project is to ask whether western settlers did in fact remain loyal or whether they resisted, rebelled, and seceded. There were several attempts to divide territories from the Union, but before 1861 these attempts failed.[86] The territorial governments embraced the common and statute laws of selected original states, evidence that at least their governing men found the prospect of joining the Union on an equal footing more attractive than going it alone or joining another European empire.[87] Without presuming to understand the minds of individual settlers, it is fair to conclude that many accepted the Union. They accepted federalism, but there was no agreement about the precise relationship between the states and the federal government. They accepted separated powers, and again this did not mean that there was a fixed definition of the relationship between the legislature, executive, and judiciary. They accepted the language of constitutional rights, which meant guarding their own and respecting those of others, with little institutional enforcement of either. They learned these doctrines when they adopted eastern laws and read the leading books on the meaning of American law: *The Federalist*, a growing number of reports, Kent's *Commentaries*, and treatises like those by Justice Story.

Transatlantic Radicals and State Codification

But what of those who had a different experience with the English common law? Imagine a group of English-speaking lawyers who rebelled against London's governance, characterizing it as corrupt in the same terms used by the American revolutionaries. Imagine that these lawyers, like American lawyers, "knew what [their country] had been, and they knew what she was, and they looked forward to what she might be — elevated to her proper rank in the scale of empires, a broad representative system of government in full operation."[88] Imagine also that they lost their revolution and were indicted for treason and sentenced to death. Finally, imagine that the prosecutors offered to spare the rebels' lives and exile them in exchange for a full account of the conspiracy, including details of their alliance with the French. It would be as if the civil war in North America had been suppressed and the Privy Council offered John Jay freedom in a foreign country if he revealed the states' diplomacy, then queried Hamilton about plans for a new government. Instead of *The Federalist Papers*, there would be an interrogation report. How would such men, exiles abroad, feel about the English constitutional legacy?

Such men existed in the United Irish movement, and several lived out their exile in New York.[89] Their revolution of 1798 collapsed dramatically: spies, torture, confessions, death sentences, and exile. Their politics was a mix of parliamentary reform, home rule, and religious toleration. Most of the radicals paid homage to Tom Paine, most of the Protestants were Dissenters, and many were middle-class professionals.[90] The main problem with Ireland, they believed, was the corrupt informal constitution of the Irish Parliament. "[T]wo thirds of it," one rebel complained, was "the property of individuals in the pay of the British cabinet." Reform seemed hopeless without independence. Significantly, the Irish reformers claimed that the American Revolution, not the French, was their model.[91] Their ideal was to be an "independent republic" like America, envisioned as a land of free trade and no religious establishment yet retaining an "intimate connexion" with Britain. When the rebellion failed, many exiles tried to immigrate to the United States, where they had friends and opportunities, especially among sympathetic Republicans. But Federalists, who feared that "hordes of wild Irishmen" would "disturb our domestic tranquillity," and also vote for Republicans, lengthened the process of naturalization in 1798.[92] After the Jeffersonian Republicans won national office in 1800, they revised the naturalization laws, and soon Irish exiles arrived in New York in great numbers.

The leading Irish refugees gained prominence in their new home. In New York, lawyers such as William Sampson and Thomas Addis Emmet became influential members of the state and federal bar.[93] Sampson, an Anglican from Derry, was trained at Trinity College and Lincoln's Inn. After eight years of imprisonment, first in Dublin and then in France, Sampson arrived in New York on 4 July 1806. Sampson's sympathy with his new home was immediate, and in his memoirs, published a year after his arrival, he compared the American and Irish revolutions. Their constitutional narratives were, he claimed, the same. Sampson referred to the governing "faction" in Ireland and the English oligarchy that acted "in the name of a constitution" while destroying it.[94] Invoking commonwealth ideology, he accused the colonial administrators in Dublin of "corruption" because they bought and sold their offices like commodities. By contrast, "the American Revolution had reduced the theories of the great philosophers of England, France and other countries, into practice."[95] The story of Ireland was that of America, except that in the northeastern Atlantic the epic of liberty turned tragic.[96] Sampson was charged with treason for defending the right of a printer to report the rebels' protests. Sentenced to exile, he concluded that English liberty was a charade.

> Until these times, if the British constitution had not been practised in Ireland, it had been at least professed, particularly since its nominal independence had been guaranteed by the king and parliament. I need not tell you, that the essence of that constitution is, that men should be tried by juries of their fellow-citizens, their peers; and by the law of the land; and in no arbitrary manner deprived of life, liberty or property. If it be not this, it is nothing but a shadow or a sound. But by this revolutionary act [i.e., the Insurrection Act], proclamations were to stand for laws. And justices of the peace, often foreign mercenary soldiers, were to take the place of

juries, and had the power of proclaiming counties and districts *out of the king's peace.*[97]

All this was familiar to Sampson's American readers. Later in his memoirs he related the English invasion of Ireland. Glossing the legend of the Norman Yoke, Sampson argued that before this conquest, the Irish had enjoyed their own system of law and a written code.[98] Sampson carried the myth of this ancient code with him to America and invoked it in judicial arguments, public addresses, and historical writings. The content of this code was unknowable, "for with the other interesting monuments of that nation's antiquity, it was trodden under the hoof of the satyr that invaded her."[99] This reverence for a lost body of law was a version of ancient constitutionalism long familiar in the English-speaking world. And when advocating a "National Code," Sampson was no orthodox disciple of Jeremy Bentham. Rather, he joined the old tradition of customary law with the new cause of written codes.[100]

In 1823, after two decades of success at the New York bar, Sampson delivered a screed against the "superstitions" of the common law at the New-York Historical Society. His nominal target was Blackstone. But his audience was awaiting Kent's *Commentaries* and was eager to name him the American Blackstone. An attack on Blackstone was an attack on Kent. The English legal writer, Sampson declared, poured forth "bombastic encomiums upon the common law." The common law might fit a monarchy, where "the king is law," but not a young republic that should be a "model of judicial polity equal to that already exhibited in our political institutions." Legal reform had not kept up with political change. American politics was open and democratic; common law was monarchical and mystifying. In America, "the people know that their law is the creature of their own power, the work of their own hands, and that if it is not good it is to their own shame."[101] But their lawyers still worshiped the "pagan idol" of the common law: "Taken in many senses, it had truly none. It was oral tradition opposed to written law; it was written law, but presuming the writing to be lost; it was that of whose origin there was no record or memory, but of which he evidence was both in books and records. It was opposed to statute law, to civil law, to maritime and mercantile law, to the law of nations; but most frequently contrasted with equity itself. It was common sense, but of an artificial kind, such as is not the sense of any common man; it was the perfection of reason, but that meant artificial reason."[102]

The common law, Sampson concluded, was a cloak for a tyranny of lawyers and judges. The remedy was "a judicial code, substituted in the place of antiquated legends, usages, and customs."[103] The Irish rebellion convinced him that the rights of Englishmen were insubstantial. He carried to New York a new skepticism about the common law and related liberties. In New York, as in most of the original states, there was little opposition to the common law until these refugees arrived from the common-law revolution that failed.

Yet Kent and Sampson agreed on one thing: law was too variable among the states. Sampson wanted a *national* code, not many state codes. He appreciated the role of doctrinal treatises in reducing the law to reasoned science, but they were not enough. After praising New Yorker Gulian Verplanck's treatise on contracts, Sampson urged the author, who also served in Congress, to build a federal code along with federal roads. Contract law was "not the only branch of our jurisprudence that requires reform. . . . Whilst others are focusing toward the great objects of national improvement I ask you as one of your constituents why you do not in your place as a national representative make your voice heard and challenge 'wiser heads' to join with you in settling what is so important to settle — the doubts uncertainties and discrepancies which still perplex the administration of justice in our land."[104]

There never was a national code of private law. The states did not adopt comprehensive codes, either. But the call by Sampson and other radicals for codes did resonate among state legislators, who could not easily navigate their own statute law.[105] New York was the first state to codify its statute law according to analytical principles. In 1825, Governor DeWitt Clinton asked the legislature to do more than simply revise the laws. Revision was a familiar project that weeded out defunct statutes and listed those that remained chronologically. Clinton called instead for a "complete code founded on the salutary principles of the common law, adapted to the interests of commerce and the useful arts, the state of society and the nature of our government, and embracing those improvements which are enjoined by enlightened experience." An analytically organized code would also "destroy judicial legislation, which is fundamentally at war with the genius of republican government."[106] The assembly appointed James Kent, Erastus Root, and Benjamin Butler as revisers. Kent, who was ambivalent about codification, declined and was replaced by William Duer, who had clerked with Alexander Hamilton. Root and Butler were part of Martin Van Buren's wing of the Republican Party, the "Albany Regency."[107] Root was replaced first by Henry Wheaton, who went on to become America's foremost scholar of the law of nations, and then by

John C. Spencer. The revisers followed the institutionalist outline and organized the state's statutes under the headings of persons, property, civil courts and actions, and criminal law. Substantively, the revisers abolished feudal tenures and declared all land to be allodial. But they preserved existing, long-term leases, so the revision had little impact on the manorial leases on the old Hudson Valley patents, which were a persistent cause of trouble and sparked riots again in the 1840s.[108] The revisers also rewrote many statutes in plain language.[109] Butler's son maintained that "it was the first attempt to create and establish for any commonwealth governed by the English Common Law . . . a body of written law, systematically arranged, based on the principles of the law as a science, regulating the exercise of public and private rights, establishing domestic, property and contract relations, and covering the administration of every department of the Government, without touching the integrity of the unwritten law, or transcending the proper bounds of legislative control."[110]

Twenty years later, New York adopted David Dudley Field's code of civil procedure, which was part of a two-generation shift in the focus of a lawsuit from the pleadings to the doctrinal rules. With the decline of the general verdict and the rise of rationalized doctrine, the role of the judge expanded, and that of the jury shrank.[111] Even the codes, which some radicals thought would be made by the people for the people, tended to reduce the role of the people in day-to-day legal administration, for in practice the codification controversy was a conflict between two groups of lawyers: those who wanted to unify American law through treatises and legal education, and those who wanted to do so as delegates of state legislatures.[112] Both groups were professional, but the first justified its treatises on the basis of its expertise in legal science, whereas the second sought legitimation from the legislature. From a distance, the conflict does not seem to warrant the heated rhetoric it generated at the time, with cries of aristocracy on one side and laments for the fate of the Union on the other. But in the 1820s, much political debate was still carried out in terms of aristocracy versus democracy. This binary had framed much of the federal ratification debate a generation earlier and remained a popular idiom in the state constitutional conventions of the early nineteenth century.

The politics of those conventions also revealed that chants of democracy were not always what they seemed. Neither were calls for aristocracy. There were, for example, no demands for special legal privileges. More common was the identification of lawyers as special guardians of political stability and ballast against popular politics. Yet this identification was as much prescriptive as descriptive, and whether it was in any meaningful sense true remained long in dispute.

Democracy in America?

On the morning of 11 May 1831, the steamship *The President* entered New York's harbor from Newport. It arrived twice a week, bringing travelers from New England over the Long Island Sound. This day the ship brought two Frenchmen who made New York their first destination in a ten-month excursion through the states to survey the country's new penitentiaries for the French government. But the men, both in their twenties, had larger ambitions. The United States, they thought, offered an example not just in the design and operation of its prisons. There the progress of democracy and equality had reached farthest fastest, but all nations were headed in the same direction. The two were ambivalent about this mechanical law of progress. They were liberals, and yet they were also lesser nobles, and one of them, Alexis Charles Henri Clerel de Tocqueville, knew that progress carried costs. His maternal grandparents had been executed during the Reign of Terror, and his parents spent ten months in prison awaiting the same fate until Robespierre lost power. More tumult came just the previous year, when the monarchy fell again, making life as a Parisian magistrate uncomfortable for Tocqueville. While he believed that equality was not just inevitable but also good, he remained anxious about the future and wondered if the law of progress could be shaped to fit his nation's circumstances. The American present might provide a lesson for France's future.[113]

Even before Tocqueville and his friend, Gustave Beaumont, had sailed, they planned a thorough study of American society. "We are leaving," Tocqueville wrote on the eve of his journey, "with the intention of examining, in detail and as scientifically as possible, all the mechanism (*resorts*) of that vast American society which everyone talks of and no one knows."[114] The travelers spent six weeks in New York City and another three upstate, sailing up the Hudson to Albany and then traveling overland to Lake Erie. Letters they wrote during these first two months in America support the conclusion of historians George Pierson and Thomas Bender that Tocqueville outlined his analysis of American society quickly.[115] *Democracy in America*, intended as a guidebook to Europe's future and the repository of nagging epigrams about American culture, crystallized in New York.

Immediately Tocqueville made observations destined to become clichés.

On the boat to America, he met a New Yorker who was unembarrassed by his nation's commercial ethos. The neat shops and diligence of those Tocqueville met confirmed the stereotype: here was a commercial people. There was equality of appearance and treatment but also petty social distinctions. There were relaxed gender relations; plentiful natural resources; separation of church and state; social glue composed not of virtue but rather of enlightened self-interest and associations; faith in education to control democratic excess; mediocre art; and weak government. Quickly Tocqueville concluded that the United States was exceptional—"another world"—because of its environment, and many of its features were ill suited to Europe.[116] This environmental interpretation reassured Tocqueville that democracy would not transform France into America.

He came an apprehensive republican looking for virtue. Instead he found self-interest. "Picture yourself if you can," he wrote a friend in France from New York City, "a society formed of all the nations of the earth . . . a society without roots, without memories, without prejudices, without habits, without common ideas, without national character; a hundred times happier than ours; more virtuous? I doubt it. There's the starting point. What serves as a tie to these diverse elements? What makes of them a people? *L'interet*. That's the secret. Individual *interet* which sticks through at each instant, *l'interet* which, moreover, comes out in the open and calls itself a social theory."[117] Tocqueville's limited insight is revealed in this passage. Interest was a glue, but not the only one. He was wrong, and has led countless students of American civilization astray, in his assertion that postcolonial Americans were "without memories" and "common ideas." Although Americans might still have lacked a *national* character, their legal culture was providing one. Yet these became the first and often last words about nineteenth-century America.

Another thing Tocqueville did not see was government. He did meet many New York lawyers, including James Kent, who gave him a copy of his *Commentaries* to teach him about American law and government. Tocqueville carried these four volumes, along with *The Federalist Papers*, with him throughout his travels and back to France, consulting them often while penning his work. The legal literature of high Federalism was his Baedeker to the American democracy.[118] And so his observation about lawyers was almost inevitable and easily misunderstood: "In America there are no nobles or literary men, and the people are apt to distrust the wealthy; lawyers consequently form the highest political class and the most cultivated portion of society. . . . If I were asked where I place the American aristocracy, I should reply without hesitation that it is not among the rich, who are united by no common tie, but that it occupies the judicial bench and the bar."[119]

Recall the context. Tocqueville arrived in New York City and saw no government. What held it all together? Where were the imposing buildings? Where were the government officers, magistrates like himself? There were few. They must be located in the state capital. So he went to Albany. The same there, even more deserted. He was mystified by the physical absence of government. Even the governor slept in a boardinghouse. "It's useless to torment the spirit seeking for the government," Tocqueville concluded after four months in the states; "it is nowhere to be perceived, and the truth is that it does not, so to speak, exist."[120] It was a conclusion that he famously modified: there were juries, habits, public opinion. These generated law, often oppressive law. Yet he never found the familiar embodiments of authority: men like him, dressed in the black or the red.

But lawyers were everywhere, and he saw that they had books, like *The Federalist*, Kent's and Story's *Commentaries*, and common-law manuals.[121] Lawyers, judges, and handbooks: there was government and law. He concluded that the legal community was America's governing class. Tocqueville did not recognize that this configuration was rooted in English legal culture, and he could not have known that two generations earlier the British imperial agents had tried to transform it to make their empire work. Where those imperial reformers failed, the Federalists and their heirs had more success. Encapsulated in legal literature, their laws of union traveled from one coast to another even before the political borders did.

As the circle closed, another opened. This continuous legal innovation, far from being exceptional or purely nationalistic, begins to resolve the paradox of constitutional development on the margins. U.S. legal thinkers, prominent among them New Yorkers, formalized constitutional law in response to their own situation. They wrote their books and taught their law to fill the vacuum of authority that had long frustrated imperially minded people in North America and that threatened to become even larger as national boundaries expanded and state power declined. Their work influenced jurists within the Union and also abroad: north in Canada, south in Latin America, and east in Europe.[122] Not just for Tocqueville were they the guides to the modern constitution.

Conclusion

W HEN THIS PROJECT BEGAN a decade ago, "empire" was not a common concern in the academy. Democracy was spreading in Eastern Europe, and in the United States there were speculations on a "peace dividend." It seems a long time ago. Among other changes, many commentators now refer to "the American empire," a term intended to capture either U.S. military ventures, American corporate expansion, or both.[1] These are not the empires analyzed in this book. Deep research, on a variety of issues and across different eras, is necessary before anyone can conclude that other episodes in American history illuminate the curiously reciprocal relationship between imperial expansion and constitutional liberty. The focus here has been on two or three generations of British North Americans living in one province. This book has sought to identify the constitutional resources that structured the way New Yorkers viewed their position on the edge of the British Atlantic world and how they reworked those resources when breaking with the British Empire and creating a new union. There might be a continuous dialectic between received ideas and changing practices in every legal culture. In eighteenth-century New York, the result was particularly transformative. The most creative product — constitutional law — still affects American citizens, and others, every day.

Those who settled colonial New York did not intend to transform constitutionalism. Initially, they were simply participating in one of many episodes of imperial expansion. The typical image of an empire is a state that expands outward, all migration and energy flowing from the center, the map gradually being redenominated in the terms of the conqueror. But the British Empire was never such a well-planned endeavor and, indeed, was not fully comprehended as an "empire" in the modern sense until the eighteenth century. Only in moments of crisis did participants articulate what they were doing together and what each sought from the others. In those crises, English legal terms dominated, but in North America they carried some new and strange meanings. From the beginning, colonial authority was a contest between metropolitan officials, imperial agents, settlers, their creole descendants, and Native Americans, often in shifting alliances. Initially, the English constitution and common law defined the English nation in opposition to the other royal territories, distinguishing realm from dominions. But substantive elements of this constitutionalism escaped England as settlers demanded English liberties and the imperial agents conceded some of them. This English constitutional currency circulated throughout the empire, integrative at first and disintegrative later, when settlers used it to distinguish their colonies from a supposedly corrupting metropolis — the mirror image of English fears at the dawn of overseas colonization.

If the first British Empire began as a series of experiments, it ended when its central government no longer found it feasible to hold on to half of its North American colonies, the thirteen in which many people viewed themselves as most entitled to ancient English liberties and where some were willing to resort to violent resistance to secure those liberties. On the east side of the Atlantic, the Revolution resulted in imperial contraction, though only temporarily. On the west side, it was unclear whether the Confederation would contract, expand, or stagnate. It cannot be known how long the states would have survived in a loose confederation. But some men, New Yorkers prominent among them, had greater ambitions for the Union and for themselves. They expressed this ambition in traditional Anglo-American ways: in terms of an empire whose constitution preserved liberty and conveyed it to new lands too. The debate between Federalists and Antifederalists in the linchpin state of New York helped create new bonds between the states, the people in the states, and the people who emigrated west into the territories. Equality among all citizens and jurisdictions — on an "equal footing" — was a cardinal principle of this Union, not a protest from the marchland. With a movable constitutional border between core and periphery, continental conquest would appear as the spread of self-government. Constitutional law took decades to construct and always remained under revision, but by the third decade of the nineteenth century few doubted that it helped bind the Union, in part by creating a peaceful discursive space in which all citizens could debate the meaning of that Union.

In terms of holding together their respective empires, the difference between the imperial agents before the Revolution and the Federalists after is the degree of success: failure for the former, qualified success for the latter. With power divided between the states and the federal government, and among various institutions with each, no institution alone determined the Constitution's meaning or that of citizenship within it. At the time of the framing, most concerns centered on the extent of state power, congressional power, and that of the federal executive. A few Antifederalists expressed concerns about the federal courts. Even fewer mentioned the role of the legal profession. The last — lawyers — were unmentioned in the document but gained great influence in defining the Constitution in the courts and outside them, as advocates, legislators, and writers. Although Tocqueville remarked on the importance of lawyers and observed that government was spare, he did not put the two observations together: the legal profession helped make the expansive Union work despite the lack of extensive administration. Lawyers functioned as the new imperial agents, acting out a vision of union expressed in early literature like *The Federalist* and refined in nineteenth-century legal treatises that doubled as civics manuals. That achievement — the creation of a portable legal culture not mentioned in any written American constitution but crucial for the function of them all — is what made the Union a new kind of empire. Lawyers and legal culture alone could not hold it together. But the Union had no chance without them.

As the states democratized their constitutions, part of what continued to hold them all together was the dephysicalization of sovereignty. Power no longer resided in a central capital; neither did it reside in multiple state capitals. The emergent theory of democracy was that all the people — or, in practice, white men — had sovereignty and delegated it to various centers, near and far. The Federalists tried to use this idea of popular sovereignty for their own purposes, such as to bolster the judiciary. The Democrats established a national party wary of embracing substantive principles so that each state organization could develop its own policies to fit local electoral needs. But the narrative of the independent United States would be much easier to write if it involved simply relating the master plans of elites. Instead, the historian can trace the outlines of plans that failed, that succeeded in part, that did shape, without determining, the meaning of the Union.

In the end, legal culture did provide a glue of union, and those who fought to preserve it in the 1860s recurred endlessly to the Constitution and the two dimensions of empire laid out in *Federalist* 1. There was the empire of self-government, to which secession had always been a sign of failure, and there was the empire of functional government expanding across space. The story of this devotion to the Union in the mid-nineteenth century goes well beyond that of constituting empire in the eighteenth century. But the fate of that Union cannot be comprehended without understanding how people in early New York helped reconfigure constitutionalism on the edge of the Atlantic world.

NOTES

ABBREVIATIONS

DHNY

Edmund B. O'Callaghan, ed. *Documentary History of New York*. 4 vols. Albany, N.Y.: Weed, Parsons, 1849–51.

DHRC

Merrill Jensen et al., eds. *The Documentary History of the Ratification of the Constitution*. 31 vols. to date. Madison: State Historical Society of Wisconsin, 1976– .

Federalist Papers

Alexander Hamilton, John Jay, and James Madison. *The Federalist Papers*. Edited by Jacob E. Cooke. Middletown, Conn.: 1961.

General Assembly Journal, 1691–1765

New York General Assembly. *Journal of the Votes and Proceedings of the General Assembly of the Colony of New York. Began the 9th day of April, 1691; and ended the [23d of December, 1765]*. 2 vols. New York, 1766.

General Assembly Journal, 1766–1776

New York General Assembly. *Journal of the Votes and Proceedings of the General Assembly of the Colony of New York, from 1766 to 1776, Inclusive*. 9 vols. in 1. Albany, N.Y., 1820.

Hamilton Papers

Alexander Hamilton. *The Papers of Alexander Hamilton*. Edited by Harold C. Syrett et al. 27 vols. New York: Columbia University Press, 1961–87.

HR

Hall of Records, Surrogate's Court Building, New York City.

Johnson Papers

William Johnson. *The Papers of Sir William Johnson*. Edited by James Sullivan and Alexander C. Flick. 14 vols. Albany: University of the State of New York, 1921–65.

KP

James Kent Papers, photocopy of microfilm, Law School Library, Yale University. Originals in the Library of Congress, Washington, D.C.

LPAH

Alexander Hamilton. *The Law Practice of Alexander Hamilton: Documents and Commentary*. Edited by Julius Goebel Jr. et al. 5 vols. New York: Columbia University Press, 1969–81.

Madison Papers

James Madison. *The Papers of James Madison*. Edited by William T. Hutchinson et al. 17 vols. Chicago: University of Chicago Press, 1962–91.

NYCD
> John Romeyn Brodhead and E. B. O'Callaghan, eds. *Documents Relative to the Colonial History of the State of New-York: Procured in Holland, England, and France.* 15 vols. Albany, N.Y.: Weed, Parsons, 1853–87.

NYHS
> New-York Historical Society, New York City.

NYHS Coll.
> *Collections of the New-York Historical Society.*

NYPL
> New York Public Library, New York City.

NYSA
> New York State Archives, Albany, New York.

State-Trials
> *Cobbett's Complete Collection of State-Trials and Proceedings for High Treason and Other Crimes and Misdemeanors from the Earliest Period to the Present Time.* Compiled by T. B. Howell and Thomas J. Howell. 34 vols. London, 1816–28.

WMQ
> *William and Mary Quarterly*, 3d ser.

INTRODUCTION

1. The Earl of Bellomont to the Board of Trade, 17 Apr. 1699, *NYCD*, 4:505.

2. Adams, *The Hudson*, 14; Boyle, *Hudson River*, 20–40; Carmer, *The Hudson*, 3–25. After the English conquest, the legend grew that Hudson had actually discovered the region in 1608, only to be forced to sell his right to the Dutch the following year, which made the English conquest a reclamation. Smith, *History of the Province of New-York*, 1:10.

3. [Kennedy], *Serious Advice to the Inhabitants of the Northern Colonies*, 17.

4. [William Smith Jr.], "A brief Consideration of *New-York*, with respect to its natural Advantages: Its Superiority in several Instances, over some of the neighbouring Colonies," 18 Jan. 1753, in Klein, *Independent Reflector*, 104; [William Smith Jr.], "The Consideration of the natural Advantages of *New-York* . . . ," 22 Nov. 1753, in Klein, *Independent Reflector*, 434. See also Smith, *History of the Province of New-York*, 2:228, and Albion, *Rise of New York Port*, 16–22.

5. On the slave population in New York City and throughout the colony, see Davis, "New York's Long Black Line."

6. For Massachusetts, see Bailyn, *Ordeal of Thomas Hutchinson*. For Georgia, see Bellot, *William Knox*, 17–41.

7. George Washington to the Mayor, Aldermen, and Commonalty of New York City, 10 Apr. 1785, in Washington, *Papers of George Washington*, 2:487.

8. George Washington to James Duane, 10 Apr. 1785, in Washington, *Papers of George Washington*, 2:485–86.

9. Hamilton, *Federalist* 1, 27 Oct. 1787, *Federalist Papers*, 3. All *Federalist* essays cited in the notes are from *Federalist Papers*.

10. For a recent example of living constitutionalism, see Strauss, "Irrelevance of Constitutional Amendments." For historical examples, see Kammen, *Machine That Would Go of Itself*, 156–76. For a nonoriginalist search for historical limits on constitutional interpretation, see Horwitz, "Foreword: The Constitution of Change." Rakove usefully distinguishes between original meaning, intent, and understanding in *Original Meanings*, 7–11. See also Clifford Geertz, "After the Revolution: The Fate of Nationalism in the New States," in *Interpretation of Cultures*, 250–51 (explaining culture as "at once the product and a determinant of social interaction" because symbols of meaning exist in a dialectic with social process).

11. Cf. Arendt, *On Revolution*, 179–214. See also Daniel T. Rodgers, "Exceptionalism," in Molho and Wood, *Imagined Histories*, 21–40.

12. Primus, *American Language of Rights*, 62–65, 78–126 (describing the "oppositionality" and "reactive pattern" of the founders' political discourse); Kenyon, "Men of Little Faith"; Moglen, "American Federalisms."

13. But see Williams, *Roots of Modern American Empire*; Kaplan and Pease, *Cultures of United States Imperialism*; Sharpe, "Is the United States Postcolonial?"; and, most recently, Ferguson, *Colossus*. On the distorting effect of Europe's nineteenth-century empires on early modern historiography, see Jack P. Greene, "Negotiated Authorities: The Problem of Governance in the Extended Polities of the Early Modern Atlantic World," in *Negotiated Authorities*, 2–4.

14. See, e.g., Andrews, *Colonial Period of American History*; Andrews, *Colonial Background of the American Revolution*; and Labaree, *Royal Government in America*. These imperial historians were reacting against earlier nationalist historians, like George Bancroft, who charted the rise of American democracy.

15. See Bailyn, *History and the Creative Imagination*, 19.

16. See Novick, *That Noble Dream*, 332–48.

17. For one warning, see Bailyn, *Ordeal of Thomas Hutchinson*.

18. See, e.g., Urofsky and Finkelman, *March of Liberty*.

19. See, e.g., Bailyn, "Idea of Atlantic History"; Bailyn and Morgan, *Strangers within the Realm*; Greene, *Peripheries and Center*; Pocock, "British History"; Pocock, "Limits and Divisions of British History"; Meinig, *Atlantic America*; and Robbins, "Core and Periphery in Modern British History." See also Armitage, *Theories of Empire*. On the lack of attention to "the legal structure of the empire," see Stanley N. Katz, "The Problem of a Colonial Legal History," in Greene and Pole, *Colonial British America*, 461.

20. The concept of integration comes from the exemplary works of Atlantic history. See Bailyn, "Idea of Atlantic History"; J. Godechot and R. R. Palmer, "Le probleme de l'Atlantique du XVIIIeme au XXeme siecle"; and Hancock, *Citizens of the World*.

21. See, e.g, Burke, *Account of the European Settlements in America*, 2:288. Cf. Gordon, *Controlling the State*, which contrasts hierarchical theories of government premised on a unitary sovereign with theories of "countervailing" power.

22. Katz, "Problem of a Colonial Legal History," 463. See also Friedman, "American Legal History," 569, 576.

23. Bailyn, *Ideological Origins of the American Revolution*, 67.

24. Ibid., 67–69, 175–84; Wood, *Creation of the American Republic*, 260–61, 307. See also Gerald Stourzh, "*Constitution*: Changing Meanings of the Term from the Early Seventeenth Century to the Late Eighteenth Century," in Ball and Pocock, *Conceptual Change and the Constitution*, 47. Bailyn and Wood advert to the lineage of fundamental law, in medieval theory and in seventeenth-century oppositional thought, but both believe it was anachronistic in eighteenth-century England. The seminal idea about this shift in constitutional meaning may lie in the work of Charles H. McIlwain, as interpreted by Oscar and Mary Handlin. Handlin and Handlin, *Dimensions of Liberty*, 32, 55; McIlwain, *Constitutionalism*. See also Sherry, "Founders' Unwritten Constitution," 1154–55.

25. Reid elsewhere calls them "two conceptions of the British constitution" and "two constitutional traditions." Reid, *In Defiance of the Law*, 32, 33, 34. See also Reid, *Constitutional History of the American Revolution*, 4 vols. (1986–93); Black, "Constitution of Empire"; Greene, "From the Perspective of Law"; Greene, *Peripheries and Center*, 129–50; Greene, "Negotiated Authorities" and "The Colonial Origins of American Constitutionalism," in *Negotiated Authorities*, 1–42; and Leder, *Liberty and Authority*, 85–86. Some historians suggest that research should now focus on the "actual practices" of constitutional governance in the colonies, rather than on "authoritative statements" claiming to define the constitution of the empire. Hartog, review of *Peripheries and Center* in *WMQ*; Bliss, "Review Essay" in *Journal of American Studies*.

26. The gradual acceptance of resistance as legal is a key theme in Burgess, *Absolute Monarchy*. See also Donald R. Kelley, "Kingship and Resistance," in Davis, *Origins of Modern Freedom in the West*, 235–68. For the centrality of the English constitution in early modern England, see Pocock, *Ancient Constitution*; Glenn Burgess, *Politics of the Ancient Constitution*; and Smith, *Gothic Bequest*.

27. Helpful discussions include Llewellyn, "Constitution as an Institution"; Wormuth, *Origins of Modern Constitutionalism*; Hendrik Hartog, "The Constitution of Aspiration and 'The Rights That Belong to Us All,'" in Thelen, *Constitution and American Life*, 353–74; Gordon, "Critical Legal Histories"; Levinson, *Constitutional Faith*; and Maine, *Ancient Law*, 226. Conceiving constitutions as projects rather than objects focuses attention on the way historical actors used legal resources to interpret, and remake, their world. For this style of intellectual history, see Skinner, *Foundations of Modern Political Thought*, 1:xii–xiii, and Thomas, *Colonialism's Culture*, 58, 60. See also Bourdieu, "Force of Law."

28. See Adams, *First American Constitutions*, 301–14.

29. Cf. Hart and Stimson, *Writing a National Identity*.

30. See Bourdieu, "Force of Law." For an older discussion of the practices undergirding constitutions, see Holdsworth, "Conventions of the Eighteenth-Century Constitution."

31. On political languages, see Pocock, *Politics, Language, and Time*; Skinner, "Meaning and Understanding in the History of Ideas"; and Pole, "English Law and the Republican Concept of the State."

32. The conventional wisdom is captured in a recent Supreme Court opinion:

"Federalism was our Nation's own discovery. The Framers split the atom of sovereignty. It was the genius of their idea that our citizens would have two political capacities, one state and one federal, each protected from incursion by the other." *U.S. Term Limits, Inc. v. Thornton*, 514 U.S. 779, 838 (1997) (Kennedy, J., concurring). Cf. Rakove, "Making a Hash of Sovereignty."

33. Bruce Ackerman usefully distinguishes ordinary politics and constitutional politics, although I disagree with his schematic version of their alternation in American history. See Ackerman, "Constitutional Law/Constitutional Politics."

34. Harold A. Innis's thesis that printed media travel well across space but lose integrity through time whereas just the opposite is true for oral tradition is suggestive here. Innis, *Empire and Communications*.

35. See Hulsebosch, "*Imperia in Imperio*," and Morgan, *American Slavery, American Freedom*.

36. Thompson, *Customs in Common*.

37. On popular constitutionalism in the founding era and after, see Kramer, *People Themselves*, and Cornell, *Other Founders*. See generally Waldstreicher, *In the Midst of Perpetual Fetes*, and Gilje, *Road to Mobocracy*.

38. For a suggestive discussion of legal and constitutional behaviorism, or of signaling attachment through action rather than words, see Reid, "Some Lessons of Western History," and Levinson, *Constitutional Faith*, 127–35. In *Jefferson's Empire*, Onuf has written that the language of empire informed the character of American nationalism.

39. See Powell, *Community Built on Words*, 212–13; Genovese, *Roll, Jordan, Roll*, 25–43; and Hannah Arendt, "Reflections on Violence," in Silvers and Epstein, *Anthology*, 35–76.

PART ONE

1. See generally Helgerson, *Forms of Nationhood*, and Pocock, *Ancient Constitution*. On the reciprocal relationship between nation building and empire building, see Elizabeth Mancke, "Empire and State," in Armitage and Braddick, *British Atlantic World*, 175–95.

2. The classic exposition is Julius Goebel Jr., "The Matrix of Empire," introduction to Smith, *Appeals to the Privy Council*, xiii–lxi.

CHAPTER ONE

1. On "keywords" that unlock cultural meaning, see Williams, *Keywords*. See also Pocock, *Politics, Language, and Time* and "The Concept of Language and the Metier d'Historien: Some Considerations on Practice," in Pagden, *Languages of Political Theory in Early Modern Europe*, 19–38.

2. See Seeley, *Expansion of England*, 13, 242. The rule of law is not, of course, a peculiarly English idea. See, e.g., Skinner, *Foundations of Modern Political Thought*, 2:113–84, and Gierke, *Development of Political Theory*, 299–361. But the constitutionalist version of the rule of law was and remains marked by Anglo-American

characteristics. See Marshall, "Empire and Authority in the Late Eighteenth Century"; Bayly, *Imperial Meridian*, 14; and Greenberg et al., *Constitutionalism and Democracy*.

3. Armitage, *Ideological Origins of the British Empire*, 31.

4. See Ullmann, " 'This Realm of England Is an Empire' "; Charles H. McIlwain, "Some Illustrations of the Influence of Unchanged Names for Changing Institutions," in Sayre, *Interpretations of Modern Legal Philosophies*, 486; and Adams, "On the Term 'British Empire.' " For the intellectual history of empire, see Armitage, *Ideological Origins of the British Empire*; Koebner, *Empire*; Muldoon, *Empire and Order*; Yates, *Astraea*, 38–59; Pagden, *Lords of All the World*; and Armitage, *Theories of Empire*.

5. Armitage, *Ideological Origins of the British Empire*, 37.

6. See Firth, " 'The British Empire' "; J. G. A. Pocock, "States, Republics, and Empires: The American Founding in Early Modern Perspective," in Ball and Pocock, *Conceptual Change and the Constitution*, 68–69; and Armitage, "Making the Empire British."

7. See Osgood, "Corporation as a Form of Colonial Government."

8. Francis Bacon, "Of Empire" and "Of the True Greatness of Kingdoms and Estates," in Whately, *Bacon's Essays with Annotations*, 200–204, 309. See also Bacon, *De Augmentis Scientiarum*, bk. 8, chap. 3, in Bacon, *Works of Francis Bacon*, 5:78–88, and Koebner, *Empire*, 57–59.

9. Harrington, *Commonwealth of Oceana; and, A System of Politics*, 11, 16–17, 217–28; Fukuda, *Sovereignty and the Sword*, 154–61; J. G. A. Pocock, introduction to Harrington, *Political Works*, 48, 71–72. On the radical republicans, see Robbins, *Eighteenth-Century Commonwealthman*, 40. The Cromwellian Navigation Acts, which distinguished between "this Commonwealth of England" and "the English Plantations," may have influenced Harrington's distinction between the "nation" and its provinces. See An Act for Increase of Shipping, and Encouragement of the Navigation of this Nation, in Firth and Rait, *Acts and Ordinances of the Interregnum*, 2:559–62.

10. See Armitage, *Ideological Origins of the British Empire*, 125–45, and, generally, Pocock, *Machiavellian Moment*.

11. See, e.g., Edmund Burke, Speech of 31 May 1774, in Cavendish, *Debates of the House of Commons*, 89–90.

12. Armitage, *Ideological Origins of the British Empire*, 8. For the overlap between the imperial and national ideologies, compare Helgerson, *Forms of Nationhood*, with Armitage, *Ideological Origins of the British Empire*.

13. See Galloway, *Union of Scotland and England*; Levack, *Formation of the British State*; and Robertson, *Union for Empire*.

14. Kettner, *Development of American Citizenship*, 16–28; Price, "Natural Law and Birthright Citizenship."

15. *State-Trials*, 2:564.

16. For this form of polity, see Elliott, "Europe of Composite Monarchies," and H. G. Koenigsberger, "*Dominium Regale or Dominium Politicum et Regale*: Monarchies and Parliaments in Early Modern Europe," in *Politicians and Virtuosi*, 1–25.

On the distinction between dynastic realms and nations, see Anderson, *Imagined Communities*.

17. For similar fears in Britain during the nineteenth century, see Taylor, "Radical Critique of Empire." Sir Thomas Gresham founded the Royal Exchange in the sixteenth century.

18. Compare Maitland, *English Law and the Renaissance*, with J. H. Baker, "English Law and the Renaissance," in *Legal Profession and the Common Law*, 461–76. See also Brian Levack, "The Civil Law, Theories of Absolutism, and Political Conflict in Late Sixteenth- and Early Seventeenth-Century England," in Schochet, *Law, Literature, and the Settlement of Regimes*, 29–48.

19. Helgerson, *Forms of Nationhood*, 66–67.

20. Craven, *Dissolution of the Virginia Company*, 37; Morgan, *American Slavery/American Freedom*, 79–80. At home, the crown's use of martial law on civilians led to a grievance in the 1628 Petition of Right. Kenyon, *Stuart Constitution*, 83–84. By that time, however, martial law had been abandoned in Virginia. Craven, *Dissolution of the Virginia Company*, 70.

21. On the pervasiveness of the chain of being in early modern culture, see Lovejoy, *Great Chain of Being*.

22. See Judson, *Crisis of the Constitution*. On jurisdictional politics within pluralist legal systems, see Benton, *Law and Colonial Cultures*, 7–12.

23. An exception existed for the "necessary habitation" by an "alien friend" to encourage "trade and traffick, which is the life of every island." *State-Trials*, 2:638.

24. Ibid., 624. The classic study is Kantorowicz, *King's Two Bodies*.

25. *State-Trials*, 2:44–45.

26. The exception was Ireland. The English court of King's Bench had the power to hear cases, brought by writ of error, that came from the Irish court of King's Bench, though this power was controverted in Ireland. Flaherty, "Empire Strikes Back."

27. *State-Trials*, 2:643.

28. The example Coke used was "the kings' writ to command any of his subjects, residing in any foreign country, to return into any of the king's own dominions." Ibid. See also John Vaughan, "Process into Wales," 124 Eng. Rep. 1130, 1132 (1706), and Max Radin, "The Rivalry of Common-Law and Civil Law Ideas in the American Colonies," in Reppy, *Law*, 2:410.

29. Though Coke did not use this term himself. See Pocock, *Ancient Constitution*, 261 n. 8.

30. Coke, preface to *Le tierce part des reportes del Edward Coke*, unpaginated. This analysis also suggests why Coke borrowed the continental distinction between conquered lands belonging to Christians and those belonging to infidels: Christians, such as the eleventh-century Anglo-Saxons, retained their law; infidels did not. In the eighteenth century Lord Mansfield rejected the distinction as "absurd" and a product of "the mad enthusiasm of the crusades." *Campbell v. Hall*, 98 Eng. Rep. 1045, reprinted in *State-Trials*, 20:323 (K.B. 1774). For the continental distinction, see Pagden, *Lords of All the World*, 91–94.

31. John Selden, preface to *Jani Anglorum Facies Altera* (1610), translated as

"The Reverse or Back-face of the English Janus. To-wit, All that is Met with in Story Concerning the Common and Statute Law of English Britanny," in Westcot, *Tracts Written by John Selden*, unpaginated.

32. Milsom, *Historical Foundations*, 11.

33. Compare Maitland, *English Law and the Renaissance*, with Baker, "English Law and the Renaissance."

34. See Frederick Madden, "Some Origins and Purposes in the Formation of British Colonial Government," in Robinson and Madden, *Essays in Imperial Government*, 10. It remained the starting point for conceptualizing the empire into the twentieth century. See, e.g., Keith, *Dominions as Sovereign States*, 111.

35. Berman, "Origins of Historical Jurisprudence."

36. *State-Trials*, 2:641. See also ibid., 612 (claiming that the advocates "told no strange histories, cited no foreign laws, produced no alien precedents").

37. Lord Chancellor Ellesmere criticized Coke's reasoning in his own opinion. Ibid., 659–96. See generally A. F. McC. Madden, "1066, 1776, and All That: The Relevance of the English Medieval Experience of 'Empire' to Later Constitutional Issues," in Flint and Williams, *Perspectives of Empire*, 9–26, and Goebel, "Matrix of Empire."

38. Coke, proeme to *Fourth Part of the Institutes*, unpaginated. This volume was published posthumously. For recent use of the cartographic metaphor, see Tomlins, *Legal Cartography*.

39. Coke, proeme to *Fourth Part of the Institutes*.

40. See Sutherland, "Conquest and Law."

41. *State-Trials*, 2:638–39.

42. Ibid., 638. Coke adhered to a harsher version of dispossession than that advocated by the Spanish jurist Francisco de Vitoria. See Anthony Pagden, "Dispossessing the Barbarian: The Language of Spanish Thomism and the Debate over Property Rights of the American Indians," in *Languages of Political Theory in Early Modern Europe*, 79–98. See also Sutherland, "Conquest and Law," 47–48.

43. See, e.g., James Wilson, "Considerations on the Nature and Extent of the Legislative Authority of the British Parliament," in *Works of James Wilson*, 2:721–46, and John Adams, "Novanglus," 27 Mar. 1775, in Adams, *Novanglus and Massachusettensis*, 111–12. See also Kettner, *Development of American Citizenship*, 131–72.

44. See Schuyler, *Parliament and the British Empire*, 1–39; Goebel, review of *Parliament and the British Empire* in *Columbia Law Review*.

45. Black, "Constitution of Empire"; McIlwain, *American Revolution*.

46. Black, "Constitution of Empire," 1181. See also Greene, *Peripheries and Center*, 23–24.

47. Ireland, for example, had its own Parliament but was also subject to the English Parliament when named in its statutes. Between 1494 and 1782, Irish parliamentary legislation had to be preapproved by the king under Poynings' Law, an institution unique to Ireland. Poynings' Law, 1485, 10 Hen. VII, c. 4 (repealed 1781, 21 & 22 Geo. III, c. 47). See Beckett, *Making of Modern Ireland*, 51, 225. The "naming" doctrine was generally accepted, especially in the metropole, but occasionally rejected by Irish legal thinkers. See Jacqueline Hill, "Ireland without

Union: Molyneux and His Legacy," in Robertson, *Union for Empire*, 271–96, and Flaherty, "Empire Strikes Back."

48. Consensus among historians now is that Parliament could legislate on external, but not internal, aspects of the overseas territories, and there is nothing in Coke to dispute this — though not enough to support it fully, either. Reid, *Constitutional History of the American Revolution*, vol. 3, *The Authority to Legislate* (1991), 32 (hereafter cited as Reid, *Authority to Legislate*); Reid, *Constitutional History of the American Revolution*, vol. 2, *The Authority to Tax* (1987), 42 (hereafter cited as Reid, *Authority to Tax*); Bailyn, *Ideological Origins of the American Revolution*, 213 n. 55; Greene, *Peripheries and Center*, 88.

49. For these domestic struggles in the years preceding the American Revolution, see Spector, *American Department of the British Government*.

50. See chapter 2.

51. See Wheeler, "Calvin's Case (1608) and the McIlwain-Schuyler Debate," 589.

52. *State-Trials*, 2:639. Coke probably imagined that these would be English emigrants, but he did not restrict these rights to them alone.

53. Ibid., 643.

54. For the nature of colonial appeals, in which it was "customary" to review the whole record and both law and fact, see Smith, *Appeals to the Privy Council*, 109–11.

55. See John M. Murrin, "The Legal Transformation: The Bench and Bar of Eighteenth-Century Massachusetts," in Katz and Murrin, *Colonial America*, 540–72, and Moglen, "Settling the Law."

56. For the continuation of this process in the early nineteenth century, see Hulsebosch, "Writs to Rights," and Milsom, "Nature of Blackstone's Achievement," 4.

57. Advowson, for example, which gave a property holder the right to nominate a clergyman to fill the chapel on his property.

58. J. H. Baker, "Personal Liberty under the Common Law of England," in Davis, *Origins of Modern Freedom in the West*, 178–202.

59. Pollock and Maitland, *History of English Law*, 1:384. See also ibid., 571–84, and [Rastall], *Les Termes de la Ley*, 232, 280.

60. Baker, "Personal Liberty under the Common Law of England," 201.

61. See, e.g., *Darcy v. Allen*, 77 Eng. Rep. 1260 (K.B. 1602), and Thorne, *Sir Edward Coke*, 10–11.

62. Pollock and Maitland, *History of English Law*, 1:176. See generally Bellomo, *Common Legal Past of Europe*.

63. McIlwain, *Constitutionalism*, 54–63; McIlwain, "Magna Carta and Common Law," in *Constitutionalism and the Changing World*, 138; Milsom, *Historical Foundations*, 11–36 (describing the common law as "the by-product of an administrative triumph"); Schechter, "Popular Law and Common Law in Medieval England." A debate remains over whether the centralization was *intended* to minimize the power of local feudal lords. Milsom believes not. For the opposite position, see Pollock and Maitland, *History of English Law*, 1:136–38, 144–48, 149–51, 2:44–62.

64. See A. W. B. Simpson, "The Common Law and Legal Theory," in *Legal*

Theory and Legal History, 381, and David T. Konig, "Colonization and the Common Law in Ireland and Virginia, 1569–1634," in Henretta, Kammen, and Katz, *Transformation of Early American History*, 92.

65. Maine, *Dissertations on Early Law and Custom*, 389. See generally Plucknett, *Concise History of the Common Law*, 353–418, and Maitland, *Forms of Action at Common Law*.

66. See Plucknett, "Genesis of Coke's Reports" (concluding that Coke was less interested than previous reporters in pleadings and more in judicial "statements of general principle, making little distinction between those which were the basis of the decision and those which were only obiter").

67. John P. Reid, "The Jurisprudence of Liberty: The Ancient Constitution in the Legal Historiography of the Seventeenth and Eighteenth Centuries," in Sandoz, *Roots of Liberty*, 147–231; Corinne C. Weston, "England: Ancient Constitution and Common Law," in Burns, *Cambridge History of Political Thought*, 374–411.

68. Coke, *Second Part of the Institutes*, 179; Coke, preface to *Reports of Sir Edward Coke*, pt. 3, pp. iii–ix; Coke, preface to *Reports of Sir Edward Coke*, pt. 9, p. xxxviii; *Prohibitions del Roy*, 77 Eng. Rep. 1342–43 (K.B. 1608). On the dual meaning of custom — continuity and evolution — see Burgess, *Politics of the Ancient Constitution*, 6–7, 13–15, 20–78, and Pocock, *Ancient Constitution*, 36–55, 270–76, 339.

69. Coke, preface to *Reports of Sir Edward Coke*, pt. 10, p. xxviii.

70. Coke, *Reports of Sir Edward Coke*, pt. 5, p. v. On the publication of the common law, see Ross, "Commoning of the Common Law."

71. Johnson et al., *Commons Debates, 1628*, 2:357–58.

72. See also Reid, *Constitutional History of the American Revolution*, vol. 1, *The Authority of Rights* (1986), 103–13 (hereafter cited as Reid, *Authority of Rights*), and Rakove, *Declaring Rights*, 20.

73. *Darcy v. Allen*, 77 Eng. Rep. 1260 (K.B. 1602). See Corré, "Argument, Decision, and Reports of Darcy v. Allen."

74. *Bonham's Case*, 77 Eng. Rep. 646 (C.P. 1610).

75. "The censors cannot be judges, ministers and parties: judges to give sentence or judgment; ministers to make summons; and parties to have the moiety of their forfeiture." Ibid., 77 Eng. Rep. 646, 652.

76. Ibid., 77 Eng. Rep. 652.

77. Compare Thorne, "Dr. Bonham's Case," with Gray, "Bonham's Case Reviewed"; Plucknett, "Bonham's Case and Judicial Review"; and Baker, *Introduction to English Legal History*, 210–11.

78. On the process whereby the meaning of a case outgrows its holding, see Goodhart, "Ratio Decidendi of a Case." For similar abstraction in the history of ideas, see Skinner, "Meaning and Understanding in the History of Ideas."

79. Coke, *First Part of the Institutes*, 11b.

80. Ibid. See also Davies, *Question Concerning Impositions, Tonnage, Poundages*, 2–3. See also Judson, *Crisis of the Constitution*, 246, and Knafla, *Law and Politics in Jacobean England*, 164–67.

81. Mr. Selden's Argument, *State-Trials*, 3:153. See also Speech of Edward Lit-

tleton, 7 Apr. 1628, Johnson et al., *Commons Debates, 1628*, 2:335b–336b. Selden had been imprisoned between 1629 and 1631 for his parliamentary activity. Judson, *Crisis of the Constitution*, 247.

82. Davies, preface to *Les primer reports des cases*, unpaginated.

83. See also Hale, *History of the Common Law of England*, 17–19.

84. For Coke's parliamentary career, see White, *Sir Edward Coke and "The Grievances of the Commonwealth."*

85. See Burgess, *Absolute Monarchy*, 180; Cook, "Against Common Right and Reason"; Lewis, "Sir Edward Coke (1552–1633)"; MacKay, "Coke — Parliamentary Sovereignty or the Supremacy of the Law?"; and Arthur von Mehren, "The Judicial Conception of Legislation in Tudor England," in Sayre, *Interpretations of Modern Legal Philosophies*, 751–66. See also Kishlansky, *Parliamentary Selection.* Cf. Hinton, "Decline of Parliamentary Government under Elizabeth I and the Early Stuarts," 124, 127–29.

86. White, *Sir Edward Coke and the "Grievances of the Commonwealth,"* 222.

87. Reid, "Ordeal by Law of Thomas Hutchinson," 602; Reid, "In Accordance with Usage," 339–40.

88. Coke, preface to *Reports of Sir Edward Coke*, pt. 9, p. iv; Coke, *First Part of the Institutes*, 81a; Coke, proeme to *Second Part of the Institutes*, unpaginated; Coke, *Third Part of the Institutes*, 1797), 111. Pocock now concedes "that the term 'constitution,' as used throughout this book, has not been systematically cleared of anachronism." Pocock, *Ancient Constitution*, 261 n. 8. See also Burgess, *Absolute Monarchy*, 129–41.

89. One older meaning of the word derived from Roman law, in which *constitutio* denoted an imperial decree; constitution still signified a regulation or ordinance in English ecclesiastical law. This legal environment was not, however, the direct source for the broader connotation. Stourzh, *"Constitution,"* 43–44; McIlwain, "Some Illustrations of the Influence of Unchanged Names," 489–90.

90. Montesquieu, *Spirit of the Laws*, 156–66. It soon appeared in the work of civilians like Vattel, which, in a curious pattern of cross-reference, eighteenth-century British colonists cited to confirm their understanding of the English constitution.

91. Forset, *Comparative Discourse of the Bodies Natural and Politique*, 10–11, 29, 78, 3–4. On Forset (also spelled Forsett), see Greenleaf, *Order, Empiricism and Politics*, 68–79, and *Dictionary of National Biography*, s.v. "Forsett, Edward." See also Fulbecke, *Pandectes of the Law of Nations*, and Stourzh, *"Constitution,"* 38–43. On the rise and reception of "sovereignty," see Franklin, *Bodin and the Rise of Absolutist Theory*, 23–40, and Mark Francis and John Morrow, "After the Ancient Constitution: Political Theory and English Constitutional Writings, 1760–1832," in Schochet, *Empire and Revolutions*, 351–77.

92. Quoted in *Prohibitions del Roy*, 12; Coke, *Reports of Sir Edward Coke*, 63, 65.

93. Fortescue, *Governance of England.*

94. See Hinton, "Decline of Parliamentary Government under Elizabeth I and the Early Stuarts"; Judson, *Crisis of the Constitution*; Wormuth, *Origins of Modern Constitutionalism*, 37–40; and McIlwain, *Constitutionalism*, 79, 93–122. Cf. Bur-

gess, *Politics of the Ancient Constitution*, and Burgess, *Absolute Monarchy*. For the distinction between absolute and limited monarchy elsewhere in Europe, see H. G. Koenigsberger, "*Dominium Regale or Dominium Politicum et Regale*: Monarchies and Parliaments in Early Modern Europe," in *Politicians and Virtuosi*, 1–25; Kelley, "Kingship and Resistance," 235–68; and Smith, "Idea of the Rule of Law in England and France in the Seventeenth Century."

95. Weston, *English Constitutional Theory and the House of Lords*, 26–28, 99–123; Weston and Greenberg, *Subjects and Sovereigns*, 35–123; Wormuth, *Origins of Modern Constitutionalism*, 51–55.

96. Mendle, *Dangerous Positions*; Fukuda, *Sovereignty and the Sword*. Theorists of absolute sovereignty, like Hobbes and Filmer, never accepted the redefinition. Wormuth, *Origins of Modern Constitutionalism*, 54–55; Weston, "England," 394–95; Gordon, *Controlling the State*, 237–69.

97. For an early example equating the constitution with fundamental law, see *Case of Impositions, State-Trials*, 2:481, and McIlwain, "Some Illustrations of the Influence of Unchanged Names," 490. For examples of consent-based theories of government, see Hopfl and Thompson, "History of Contract as a Motif in Political Thought."

98. Thompson, "History of Fundamental Law in Political Thought"; Reid, *Authority of Rights*, 74–77; McIlwain, *American Revolution*, 159–67. See also Burgess, *Absolute Monarchy*, 134–35, 192, and Gough, *Fundamental Law*, 30.

99. See Bacon, *Elements of the Common Lawes of England*, [iii]; Coke, proeme to *Second Part of the Institutes*; and Blackstone, *Commentaries*, 1:238.

100. See Goebel, "Constitutional History and Constitutional Law," 558–59, 562, 567; Goebel, "The Common Law and the Constitution," in Jones, *Chief Justice John Marshall*, 103; and McIlwain, *Constitutionalism*, 48–49, 63. Cf. McIlwain, "English Common Law, Barrier against Absolutism"; McIlwain, "Magna Carta and Common Law," 176–77; Mark DeWolfe Howe, "The Sources and Nature of Law in Colonial Massachusetts," in Billias, *Law and Authority in Colonial America*, 15; Ernest Baker, "Blackstone on the British Constitution," in *Essays on Government*, 141; Cairns, "Blackstone, an English Institutist," 347; Burgess, *Absolute Monarchy*, 129–47; and Howell A. Lloyd, "Constitutionalism," in Burns, *Cambridge History of Political Thought*, 271.

101. Care, *English Liberties, or the Free-Born Subject's Inheritance*. On Care, see Schwoerer, *Ingenious Mr. Care*. For another representative list, see Blackstone, *Commentaries*, 1:123–25. See also Lois G. Schwoerer, "The Contributions of the Declaration of Rights to Anglo-American Radicalism," in Jacob and Jacob, *Origins of Anglo-American Radicalism*, 105–24.

102. See Richard Tuck, " 'The Ancient Law of Freedom': John Selden and the Civil War," in Morrill, *Reactions to the English Civil War*, 146–47, and Morrill, *Revolt of the Provinces*.

103. See David Wootton, "Leveller Democracy and the Puritan Constitution," in Burns, *Cambridge History of Political Thought*, 426–34; Seaberg, "Norman Conquest and the Common Law"; Veall, *Popular Movement for Law Reform*; and Wormuth, *Origins of Modern Constitutionalism*, 43–159.

104. Tuck, "'Ancient Law of Freedom.'"

105. In addition, the Agreements of the People never functioned as plans of government, and the Instrument of Government was proclaimed by Cromwell. The Humble Petition did receive legislative consent but was operative for only one month.

106. An Act for Increase of Shipping, and Encouragement of the Navigation of this Nation.

107. Schuyler, *Parliament and the British Empire*, 102–16.

108. See, e.g., Atwood, *Fundamental Constitution of the English Government*. See also John Miller, "Crown, Parliament, and People," in Jones, *Liberty Secured?*, 53–87.

109. Hale, *History of the Common Law of England*, 40. Harold Berman identifies Selden as the bridge between Coke's theory of ancient law and Hale's evolutionary theory. Berman, "Origins of Historical Jurisprudence," 1695, 1702–03. See also J. G. A. Pocock, "Burke and the Ancient Constitution: A Problem in the History of Ideas," in *Politics, Language and Time*, 215–22; Peter Goodrich and Yofat Hachamovitch, "Time Out of Mind: An Introduction to the Semiotics of Common Law," in Fitzpatrick, *Dangerous Supplements*, 164; Clanchy, *From Memory to Written Record*; Donald Kelley, "Civil Science in the Renaissance: The Problem of Interpretation," in Pagden, *Languages of Political Theory in Early Modern Europe*, 71–72; and Howard Nenner, "Liberty, Law, and Property: The Constitution in Retrospect from 1689," in Jones, *Liberty Secured?*, 88–121.

110. Hale, *Prerogatives of the King*, 14–15; Matthew Hale, "Reflections by the Lrd. Cheife Justice Hale on Mr. Hobbes His Dialogue of the Lawe," in Holdsworth, *History of English Law*, 5:507–8; Burgess, *Absolute Monarchy*, 138–40; Nenner, "Liberty, Law, and Property," 105–7.

111. See Jack P. Greene, "The Glorious Revolution and the British Empire, 1688–1783," in *Negotiated Authorities*, 78–92.

112. Viscount Bolingbroke, "A Dissertation on Parties," in *Works of Lord Bolingbroke*, 2:88–89. See also Burns, "Bolingbroke and the Concept of Constitutional Government," and Quentin Skinner, "The Principle and Practice of Opposition: The Case of Bolingbroke versus Walpole," in McKendrick, *Historical Perspectives in English Thought and Society*, 93–128. For a different interpretation of this passage, see Wood, *Creation of the American Republic*, 261. Cf. Bailyn, *Ideological Origins of the American Revolution*, 68 n. 12.

113. Bolingbroke, "Dissertation on Parties," 2:7.

114. Hume, *History of England from the Invasion of Julius Caesar*, 4:345–47 and 345 n*. See also Pocock, *Ancient Constitution*, 375–76; Eugene F. Miller, "Hume on Liberty in the Successive English Constitutions," in Capaldi and Livingston, *Liberty in Hume's History of England*, 53–103; Duncan Forbes, introduction to Hume, *History of Great Britain*, 24–38; Forbes, *Hume's Philosophical Politics*, 233–307; Burgess, *Politics of the Ancient Constitution*, 131–32; and Donald W. Livingston, "Hume, English Barbarism and American Independence," in Sher and Smitten, *Scotland and America in the Age of the Enlightenment*, 136.

115. On the Court Whigs, see Browning, *Political and Constitutional Ideas of the Court Whigs.*

116. Blackstone, *Commentaries*, 1:49–53, 156–57, 122–23. For his reservations about legislative policy, see ibid., 10, 63, 86, 89, 4:436, and Lieberman, *Province of Legislation Determined*, 14, 26, 59–61, 200, 205. He approved instead the partial reform undertaken by judges, best represented by Mansfield's incorporation into the common law of the law merchant while serving on King's Bench. Blackstone, *Commentaries*, 3:267–68.

117. Blackstone, *Commentaries*, 1:54.

118. Ibid., 91. See generally Lieberman, *Province of Legislation Determined*, 56–67.

119. Blackstone, *Commentaries*, 1:206, 51–52, 149, 151, 325–26. On the last, see Holdsworth, "Conventions of the Eighteenth-Century Constitution"; Namier, *Structure of Politics*; Namier, *England in the Age of the American Revolution*; Plumb, *Growth of Political Stability*; Bailyn, *Origins of American Politics*; Katz, *Newcastle's New York*; and Henretta, "*Salutary Neglect.*"

120. Blackstone did not use the term "constitutional law" in his *Commentaries.* Dicey, *Introduction to the Study of Law of the Constitution*, 6–7; Cairns, "Blackstone, an English Institutist," 347. On the eve of the Revolution, Lord Mansfield, chief justice of King's Bench, did employ the term in *Campbell v. Hall*, 98 Eng. Rep. 1045 (K.B. 1774). That case involved a Grenadian colonist's objection to a royal tax levied without any legislative consent. The argument was that, once the king introduced English law by proclamation, the grant was irrevocable and he could not again resort to prerogative rule. Mansfield, vindicating the plaintiff's objection, transformed (and altered) Coke's dictum concerning conquest in *Calvin's Case* into a "maxim of constitutional law," perhaps borrowing the term from the plaintiff's counsel. *State-Trials*, 20:290, 327.

CHAPTER TWO

1. Murrin, "Legal Transformation," 540–72. Earlier Puritan colonists, in other colonies, had been more ambivalent about English law. Haskins, *Law and Authority in Early Massachusetts.*

2. See Reid, *Constitutional History of the American Revolution*, 4 vols. (1986–93); Adams, *Political Ideas of the American Revolution*, 123–32; Goebel, "Constitutional History and Constitutional Law," 563–64; Julius Goebel Jr., "The Courts and the Law," in Flick, *History of the State of New York*, 3:32–33; Hamlin, *Legal Education in Colonial New York*, 65–66; and Stoner, *Common Law and Liberal Theory*, 13. Cf. Bailyn, *Ideological Origins of the American Revolution*, 179.

3. This institutional localism was the constitutional complement to the local law that many colonists brought to America. On the latter, see Goebel, "King's Law and Local Custom in Seventeenth Century New England." On the "centrifugal tendencies" in the early modern empires, including the British, see Greene, "Negotiated Authorities," 1–24.

4. John Dryden, "Annus Mirabilis" (1667), in *Poetical Works*, 29.

5. For the patroonships and New Netherland generally, see Rink, *Holland on the Hudson*; Condon, *New York Beginnings*; and Nissenson, *Patroon's Domain*.

6. The war was not a total loss for the Dutch. In exchange for their poorly performing American colony they secured Surinam in South America and Pulo-Run in Indonesia. Carter, *Neutrality or Commitment*, 5–6. A third Dutch war followed in which the Dutch briefly regained control of New York for fifteen months in 1673–74. Ritchie, *Duke's Province*, 85–93.

7. Grant of New Netherland, &c., to the Duke of York, 16 Mar. 1664, *NYCD*, 2:295–98, also printed in *Colonial Laws of New York*, 1:1–5.

8. Osgood, *American Colonies in the Seventeenth Century*, 2:169–99; Barnes, *Dominion of New England*, 33–34. See generally Schwarz, *Jarring Interests*.

9. Barnes, *Dominion of New England*, 34. He also transferred the Maine territory and Atlantic islands to Massachusetts.

10. *Colonial Laws Of New York*, 1:2. See also Ritchie, *Duke's Province*, 9–20.

11. *NYCD*, 2:296. The East Greenwich clause was commonly used in the sixteenth and seventeenth centuries because its liberal terms attracted patentees. Hurstfield, "Greenwich Tenures of the Reign of Edward VI"; McPherson, "Revisiting the Manor of East Greenwich." Cf. Cheyney, "Manor of East Greenwich in the County of Kent." On proprietary patents, see Osgood, *American Colonies in the Seventeenth Century*, 2:3–57.

12. *NYCD*, 2:296; Smith, *Appeals to the Privy Council*, 51–53; Goebel, "Matrix of Empire." Smith suggests that the appellate power had been implicit in the earliest charters by analogy to trading companies and the Channel Islands. Smith, *Appeals to the Privy Council*, 6–45. Nonetheless, early Massachusetts governors had denied that there was a right of appeal beyond their courts to London. Mary S. Bilder, "Salamanders and Sons of God: The Culture of Appeal in Early America," in Tomlins and Mann, *Many Legalities of Early America*, 75–76. This may have compelled the Privy Council to make the right of appeal explicit in Restoration-era charters. Later, amount-at-issue and other jurisdictional restrictions were added. On the significance of the nonrepugnancy clause, see Goebel and Naughton, *Law Enforcement in Colonial New York*, xxi–xxii, 3–6, 13, and Keith, *Constitutional History of the First British Empire*, 305. The duke instructed his governors to make all judicial writs run in the king's name, which meant that the proprietary courts were royal courts even before James's investiture. *NYCD*, 3:219.

13. Only three of the nine New York judgments were reversed. Appeals were more frequent from a handful of colonies, notably Jamaica, Barbados, Rhode Island, the Leeward Islands, and Virginia. See appendix A in Smith, *Appeals to the Privy Council*, 667–71.

14. *NYCD*, 2:297; An Act for Increase of Shipping, and Encouragement of the Navigation of this Nation; Keith, *Constitutional History of the First British Empire*, 7, 51–52.

15. On the corporate quality of the North American colonies, see Hurst, *Legitimacy of the Business Corporation in the Law of the United States*, 4; Williston, "History of the Law of Business Corporations before 1800," 106–11; Cheyney, "Some English Conditions Surrounding the Settlement in Virginia," 511–12; Andrews,

Trade, Plunder and Settlement, 16–17; Osgood, "Corporation as a Form of Colonial Government"; and Greene, *Peripheries and Center,* 75, 83–97, 206–7. For the tradition of local autonomy in America and England, see Hartog, *Public Property and Private Power*; Goebel, "Courts and the Law," 3:10–11; Goebel, "King's Law and Local Custom in Seventeenth Century New England"; Allen, *In English Ways,* 47–54, 208–9; Reid, *Authority of Rights,* 72–73, 138, 237; Greene, *Peripheries and Center,* 11–12, 141; Bliss, *Revolution and Empire,* 24; and Kishlansky, "Community and Continuity," 140, 146.

16. For the Stuarts' feudal ideal, see Palumbo, "Imperial Fantasies," and Viola F. Barnes, "Land Tenures in English Charters of the Seventeenth Century," in *Essays in Colonial History Presented to Charles McLean Andrews by His Students,* 4–40. Some argue that manors in the marchlands along the Scottish and Welsh borders provided the model for the colonies. Goebel, *Some Legal and Political Aspects,* 5–6; Allen, *In English Ways,* 47–54.

17. See Governor Dongan's Report to the Committee of Trade on the Province of New York, 22 Feb. 1687, *DHNY,* 1:186; U.S. Bureau of the Census, *Historical Statistics of the United States: Colonial Times to 1970,* 2:1168. There were at least six significant ethnic groups in early New York: Dutch, German, English, French, Portuguese-Jewish, and African. Archdeacon, *New York City,* 33; Cohen, "How Dutch Were the Dutch of New Netherland?"; Bosher, "Huguenot Merchants and the Protestant International in the Seventeenth Century."

18. Articles of Capitulation on the Reduction of New Netherland, 27 Aug. 1664/5, *NYCD,* 2:250–53.

19. Commission of 27 Jan. 1662, *Calendar of State Papers, Colonial Series,* 5:79; Commission to Colonel Richard Nicolls, 1664, app. to Brodhead, *History of the State of New York,* 2:653. The duke's grant permitted absentee governance. *NYCD,* 2:296–97.

20. So were his successors, Edmund Andros and Thomas Dongan. Webb, "'Brave Men and Servants to His Royal Highness,'" 61, 73; Webb, "Data and Theory of Restoration Empire," 448.

21. See, e.g., Instructions for Governor Dongan, 27 Jan. 1682/3, *NYCD,* 3:331. For alternative models for the council — the House of Lords when meeting without the governor as a legislative council, the Privy Council when sitting as an executive council with the governor — see Smith, *History of the Province of New-York,* 1:254–55, and Smith, *Historical Memoirs,* 1:40–41, 181, 201. The practical power of the council is much disputed. See Labaree, *Royal Government in America,* 100, 135–71, 403, 407–9; Jessica Kross, "'Patronage Most Ardently Sought': The New York Council, 1665–1775," in Daniels, *Power and Status,* 205–31; Varga, "New York Government and Politics during the Mid-Eighteenth Century," 240–49; Tully, *Forming American Politics,* 316; and Main, *Upper House in Revolutionary America,* 55. Councillors were occasionally dismissed for political reasons. Bonomi, *Factious People,* 89–90.

22. Quoted in Barnes, *Dominion of New England,* 40 n. 47. See also Jopp, "'Kingly Government,'" 64–92. English-speaking towns on Long Island and in Westchester petitioned for a legislature early on but were ignored for years. See,

e.g., Order on Petitions, and Nicolls' Answer, 1669, *NYCD*, 14:631–32, and Duke of York to Governor Andros, 6 Apr. 1675 and 28 Jan. 1676, *NYCD*, 3:230, 235.

23. *Colonial Laws of New York*, 1:6–93.

24. The town-based structure characterized the New England colonies more than it did England. Goebel, *Some Legal and Political Aspects*, 19–21.

25. On the Duke's Laws, see Goebel and Naughton, *Law Enforcement in Colonial New York*, 16–19, and Moglen, "Settling the Law," 29–34. Nicolls thought the Duke's Laws "not much different" from those in Connecticut. Quoted in Moglen, "Settling the Law," 30.

26. See Freedoms and Exemptions Granted by the West India Company to All Patroons, Masters, or Private Persons Who Will Plant Colonies in New Netherland, 7 June 1629, expanded 1640, *Laws and Ordinances of New Netherland*, 1–10, and *NYCD*, 1:119–23.

27. Hale, *Prerogatives of the King*, 242; Goebel, *Some Legal and Political Aspects*, 9–10; Barnes, "Land Tenures in English Charters of the Seventeenth Century," 34, 38–39.

28. The literature on the New York manors is extensive and lately deemphasizes the legal and political power of the lords qua lords. See, e.g., Kim, *Landlord and Tenant in Colonial New York*; Moglen, "Settling the Law," 109–54; Goebel, *Some Legal and Political Aspects*; and Edward F. DeLancey, "The Origin and History of Manors in New York, and in the County of Westchester," in Scharf, *History of Westchester County, New York*, 31–160. On the decline of the manorial courts in England, see Cheyney, *European Background of American History*, 292–93.

29. See, e.g., Journal of New Netherland, *NYCD*, 1:181; Ordinance of the Director and Council of New Netherland establishing a Board of Nine Men in New Amsterdam, 25 Sept. 1647, *Laws and Ordinances of New Netherland*, 75–78; Report of the Committee of the States General on the Affairs of New Netherland, [1650], *NYCD*, 1:391; Fernow, *Records of New Amsterdam*, 1:49; West India Company to the States-General, 24 Oct. 1664, *NYCD*, 2:272; O'Callaghan, *History of New Netherland*, 2:192; and Osgood, *American Colonies in the Seventeenth Century*, 2:106–9. On the tradition of political decentralization in the United Provinces, see Price, *Holland and the Dutch Republic in the Seventeenth Century*.

30. Governor Andros's Commission to New York City, 1675, in New York City, *Minutes of the Common Council of the City of New York, 1675–1776*, 1:1; Petition of the Mayor and Common Council of New York for a New Charter, 9 Nov. 1683, *NYCD*, 1:337–39. Dongan Charters of the City of New York and Albany, 20 Apr. 1686, *Colonial Laws of New York*, 1:181–95, 195–216. See also Marcus Benjamin, "Thomas Dongan and the Granting of the New York City Charter, 1682–1686," in Wilson, *Memorial History of the City of New York*, 1:399–446.

31. *NYCD*, 3:287–89, 318–21; *NYHS Coll.* (1912), 8–12; *Acts of the Privy Council*, 2:24–25; Ritchie, *Duke's Province*, 155–59; Osgood, *American Colonies in the Seventeenth Century*, 2:162–64; Goebel and Naughton, *Law Enforcement in Colonial New York*, 334–36; Hamlin and Baker, *Supreme Court of Judicature*, 33. Osgood noted that much of the earliest opposition to taxes arose in New England–oriented towns on Long Island.

32. Petition of the Court of Assizes for an Assembly, 29 July 1681, in Brodhead, *History of the State of New York*, 2:658.

33. Instructions for Governor Dongan, 27 Jan. 1682/3, *NYCD*, 3:331–33; Ritchie, *Duke's Province*, 155–79. See generally Kammen, *Deputyes and Libertyes*.

34. *NYCD*, 14:770–71; Smith, *History of the Province of New-York*, 1:55; Benjamin, "Thomas Dongan and the Granting of the New York City Charter," 1:405–6; A Bill for the Regulating of Elections of Representatives in General Assembly, 16 May 1699, *Colonial Laws of New York*, 1:405–8. In 1701, those paying forty shillings in rent annually were also allowed to vote. Probably about half the white adult male population met the property qualification. Before 1689, the Stuarts had commanded toleration of Catholics. Instructions issued after the Glorious Revolution granted toleration for all "except Papists" and required "Oaths of allegiance and Supremacy and the Test" of all provincial officeholders. *NYCD*, 3:689; An Act for the More Regular Proceedings in the Elections of Representatives, 18 Oct. 1701, *Colonial Laws of New York*, 1:452–54. A generation later amid factional warfare, the assembly also excluded Jews from provincial elections. *NYCD*, 6:56n; Smith, *History of the Province of New-York*, 2:33–35. See also Paul Finkelman, "The Soul and the State: Religious Freedom in New York and the Origins of the First Amendment," in Schechter and Bernstein, *New York and the Union*, 78–105; Klein, "Democracy and Politics in Colonial New York"; and Varga, "Election Procedures in Colonial New York."

35. Cf. Reid, *Authority to Legislate*, 172–79.

36. *Colonial Laws of New York*, 1:111–16. See also Lincoln, *Constitutional History of New York*, 1:429–34; Lovejoy, "Equality and Empire"; Ritchie, *Duke's Province*, 170–79; Moglen, "Settling the Law," 43–49; and Lustig, *Privilege and Prerogative*, 6.

37. For Leisler's Rebellion, see Bonomi, *Factious People*, 75–81; Reich, *Leisler's Rebellion*; Ritchie, *Duke's Province*, 198–231; John M. Murrin, "English Rights as Ethnic Aggression: The English Conquest, the Charter of Liberties of 1683, and Leisler's Rebellion in New York," in Pencak and Wright, *Authority and Resistance in Early New York*, 56–94; and Leder, "Politics of Upheaval in New York."

38. An Act to Divide this Province and Dependencies, into Shires and Counties, 1 Nov. 1783, reenacted 1 Oct. 1691, *Colonial Laws of New York*, 1:121–23, 267–68; An Act to Settle Courts of Justice, 1 Nov. 1683, *Colonial Laws of New York*, 1:125–28; An Act for the Establishing Courts . . . , 6 May 1691, *Colonial Laws of New York*, 1:226–31. While the quotation is from Moglen's analysis of the 1683 act, it is even more true of the 1691 regime, as his treatment demonstrates. Moglen, "Settling the Law," 50, 60–62; Hamlin and Baker, *Supreme Court of Judicature*, 1, 56–57, 67–77. See also Nicholas Varga, "The Development and Structure of Local Government in Colonial New York," in Daniels, *Town and Country*, 194; Herbert Alan Johnson, "The Advent of Common Law in Colonial New York," in Billias, *Law and Authority in Colonial America*, 74–91; Budd, "Law in Colonial New York," 1757–72; Howe, "Sources and Nature of Law in Colonial Massachusetts," 1–16; and Goebel and Naughton, *Law Enforcement in Colonial New York*, 19–20, 24–27.

39. A point I owe to John M. Murrin.

40. Some of the large counties were subdivided into precincts for more practical management, and such commissions operated at the precinct rather than county level. Bonomi, *Factious People*, 34–35.

41. See, e.g., Fox, *Minutes of the Court of Sessions*; *Transcriptions of Early County Records of New York State: Minutes of the Board of Supervisors of Ulster County*; and *Transcriptions of Early County Records of New York State: Records of the Road Commissioners of Ulster County*. For an overview of local tax collection and poor relief in colonial New York, see Fairlie, *Centralization of Administration in New York State*, 78–80, 148–57.

42. Desan, "Constitutional Commitment to Legislative Adjudication in the Early American Tradition"; Desan, "Remaking Constitutional Tradition at the Margins of the Empire"; Mark, "Vestigial Constitution."

43. See Bailyn, *Ideological Origins of the American Revolution*, 161–75, and Kammen, *Deputyes and Libertyes*.

44. Smith, *History of the Province of New-York*, 1:259; Bonomi, *Factious People*, 39. On factionalism and the role of government in colonial society, see Bailyn, *Origins of American Politics*, 100–104. I have found no records of the assembly committees that administered petitions; many of the petitions were lost in the Albany capitol building fire of 1911. Some petitions to local government are available. See, e.g., New York City Common Council Papers, 1670–1831, Municipal Archives, HR.

45. See Werner, *Civil List and Constitutional History*, 269–434, passim. The small size of the assembly ensured that it was somewhat more oligarchical than the local institutions. See Bonomi, *Factious People*, 8–9, 31–32, 37–39; Patricia U. Bonomi, "Local Government in Colonial New York: A Base for Republicanism," in Judd and Polishook, *Aspects of Early New York Society and Politics*, 29–50; Wright, "Local Government in Colonial New York"; Wright, "Local Government and Central Authority in New Netherland"; Varga, "Development and Structure of Local Government in Colonial New York," 203; Hartog, "Public Law of a County Court"; and Adams, *Defence of the Constitutions*, 3:112. More cautious is Countryman, *People in Revolution*, 31–33. Martin Bruegel argues that the manor lords constituted a quasi-feudal oligarchy in "Unrest," which, revealingly, focuses on one manor.

46. The assembly legislated a per diem rate of six shillings. An Act for Allowance to the Representatives, 18 Oct. 1701, *Colonial Laws of New York*, 1:466–67. For distant counties, it raised the allowance. See, e.g., An Act for Fixing the Allowance to the Representatives of the Counties of Tryon and Cumberland, 8 Mar. 1773, *Colonial Laws of New York*, 5:591–92. However, this was not always paid. Occasionally a representative or the executor of his estate petitioned the assembly to help obtain reimbursement. The assembly would oblige by passing a law requiring the county to pay the amount owed under threat of criminal prosecution. See, e.g., *Colonial Laws of New York*, 1:929–30. See also Smith, *History of the Province of New-York*, 1:256–57; Osgood, *American Colonies in the Seventeenth Century*, 2:365; and Petitions to the New York City Common Council, Common Council Papers, 1670–1831, Municipal Archives, HR. A 1710 statute in Britain established substantial real property qualifications for members of Parliament, mooting the issue

of compensation until wages were instituted in the nineteenth century. Before the eighteenth century, members were compensated under writs *de levandis expensis* or other local arrangements, much as colonial legislators still did. Plucknett, *Taswell-Langmead's English Constitutional History*, 204–5, 578–80; Rush and Shaw, *House of Commons*, 162.

47. See Fletcher, *Reform in the Provinces*, and Russell, *Causes of the English Civil War*.

48. Greene, "Political Mimesis"; Lincoln, *Constitutional History of New York*, 1:447–49. See also Bliss, *Revolution and Empire*, 242–47, and Savelle, *Seeds of Liberty*, 305–18. For rejection of the analogy, see Board of Trade to Governor Lord Cornbury, *NYCD*, 4:1171–72. While parliamentary analogies became more frequent, both models coexisted throughout the remainder of the colonial period, each available for deployment as circumstances demanded. Even at home there were those who kept alive the analogy between Parliament and a corporation. Philips, *Long Parliament Revived*, 7:478; [John Trenchard and Thomas Gordon], "All Government Proved To Be Instituted by Men . . . ," 6 Jan. 1721, in Hamowy, *Cato's Letters*, 2:418–19. Despite this eclecticism of theory and practice, sometimes these institutional models were seen as exclusive. Compare [Kennedy], *Essay on the Government of the Colonies*, with Smith, *History of the Province of New-York*, 1:256–57. For the "diffusion and localization of authority" after the Glorious Revolution, at home and abroad, see Jennifer Carter, "The Revolution and the Constitution," in Holmes, *Britain after the Glorious Revolution*, 53–54, and Greene, "Colonial Origins of American Constitutionalism," 36–38.

49. Board of Trade Recommendation on the Charter of Liberties and Privileges, 3 Mar. 1684–5, *NYCD*, 3:357; Observations on the Charter of the Province of New York, 3 Mar. 1684–85, *NYCD*, 3:357–59. See also Moglen, "Settling the Law," 47, 52; Spencer, *Phases of Royal Government in New York*, 58–59, 91; Colvin, "Bicameral Principle in New York Legislature," 26–28; and Lovejoy, "Equality and Empire."

50. See generally Barnes, *Dominion of New England*.

51. In a 1686 commission, the king gave the full legislative power to Governor Thomas Dongan. *NYCD*, 3:378. On commissions, instructions, and subsidiary "instruments of royal authority," see Labaree, *Royal Government in America*, 6–36, 85–91, and Goebel and Naughton, *Law Enforcement in Colonial New York*, 6–12.

52. See chapter 1.

53. See Webb, *Lord Churchill's Coup*. For a contemporary theoretical discussion of the legislative power, see Locke, *Two Treatises of Government*, bk. II, secs. 211–43.

54. There is a voluminous literature on the provincial tumult, known as "Leisler's Rebellion," coincidental to the English revolt, and many causes have been identified, from political to social and religious. See, e.g., Reich, *Leisler's Rebellion*; Mason, "Aspects of the New York Revolt of 1689"; Bonomi, *Factious People*, 75–81; John M. Murrin, "The Menacing Shadow of Louis XIV and the Rage of Jacob Leisler: The Constitutional Ordeal of Seventeenth-Century New

York," in Schechter and Bernstein, *New York and the Union*, 29–71; and Voorhees, "'Fervent Zeale' of Jacob Leisler."

55. *Colonial Laws of New York*, 1:244–48. In the 1691 act, the assembly provided for annual rather than triennial elections, expressly defined a freeholder as a man possessing a forty-shilling freehold, and disenfranchised Roman Catholics.

56. Report of the Board of Trade against the Act Declaratory of the Rights, &c., of the People of New-York, 11 May 1697, *NYCD*, 4:263–65; Instruction no. 299, May 1697, Labaree, *Royal Instructions to British Colonial Governors*, 1:201.

57. Budd, "Law in Colonial New York," 1760–61.

58. See, e.g., The Humble Petition and Representation . . . to the King, 18 Oct. 1764, *General Assembly Journal, 1691–1765*, 2:766–72. Some metropolitan jurists thought that, once granted, a colonial legislature could not be revoked. Lord Mansfield so concluded — but not until 1774. *Campbell v. Hall*, 98 Eng. Rep. 1045 (K.B. 1774). Goebel argued that the "rule of indefeasible delegation" of jurisdiction was "a very ancient rule of law and was certainly known to colonial lawyers." Goebel and Naughton, *Law Enforcement in Colonial New York*, 9.

59. Smith, *History of the Province of New-York*, 1:257; Kent, *Charter of the City of New-York, with Notes Thereon*, 4, 108. The counties were Albany (including the city of Albany), Westchester, Suffolk, Queen's, King's, Ulster, Richmond, Dutchess, and Orange. Rensselaerswyck, the only surviving Dutch manor, received an assembly seat; Livingston and Van Cortlandt Manors were added early in the English period. The manors soon were required to hold freehold elections as if they were counties. An Act for Regulating the Choice of Representatives for the Manor of Cortlandt, 22 June 1734, *Colonial Laws of New York*, 2:835–37. The principle of apportionment was just entering English political culture. See, e.g., Locke, *Two Treatises of Government*, bk. II, chap. 13, sec. 158.

60. Originally the governor sat and voted with the council when considering assembly bills. Later the Board of Trade recommended that the council convene separately in its legislative capacity, as opposed to its executive function. The journal of the "Legislative Council" shows that the council met separately and then invited the governor to join to confirm bills into law. There were often joint conferences of the council and assembly that negotiated the final form of bills. Board of Trade to King, 6 Feb. 1736, *NYCD*, 6:40–41; E. B. O'Callaghan, introduction to New York Council, *Journal of the Legislative Council*, xxvi–xxvii and passim.

61. Early on the governor, council, and assembly gathered for ceremonial publication, but the journals suggest that often the governor signed bills in the presence of the council and the speaker of the assembly and then had the acts posted outside City Hall. See New York Council, *Journal of the Legislative Council*, 10, 143. See also Smith, *History of the Province of New-York*, 1:256.

62. See, e.g., Bradford, *Laws and Acts of the General Assembly of Their Majesties Province of New-York*.

63. An Act to Revise, Digest, & Print the Laws of this Colony, 27 Nov. 1741 and 24 Dec. 1750, *Colonial Laws of New York*, 3:192–94, 832–35; Livingston and Smith,

Laws of New-York from the Year 1691 to 1751, quotations at i–ii; Livingston and Smith, *Laws of New-York, from the 11th Nov. 1742, to 22d May 1762*. The session laws created a record for lawyers' practice and the Privy Council's review. Both they and the journals were printed in chronological order, with limited cross-references, many mistakes, and no system for recording those statutes disallowed, repealed, or expired, making the volumes awkard reference tools. There were partial revisions earlier in the eighteenth century. Preface to *Colonial Laws of New York*, v; *Bulletin of the New York Public Library* 7 (1903): 143–46. Daniel Horsmanden, commissioned to revise the laws in 1741, never completed the task. "Revisers of the Laws," List of Officials, E. B. O'Callaghan Papers, NYHS.

64. A private act of the English Parliament was not printed in the "sessional statute" at the end of each sitting, meaning that "in litigation, it could not be pleaded generally but had to be produced in an exemplification under the great seal or a copy formally certified by the clerk of Parliament if the court was to take notice of it." Elton, *Parliament of England*, 44.

65. Peter Van Schaack, preface to Van Schaack, *Laws of New-York, from the Year 1691, to 1773, Inclusive*, iv.

66. Smith, *History of the Province of New-York*, 1:254–56; Lincoln, *Constitutional History of New York*, 443. For the colonial legislative process, see Labaree, *Royal Government in America*, 172–268. The Privy Council distinguished between nullification (rare) and disallowance (frequent). Certain laws were declared null and void from the time of their initial passage in the province; most were deemed of no effect in the future, from the time of disallowance. See Smith, *Appeals to the Privy Council*, and Smith, "Administrative Control of the Courts of the American Plantations."

67. On these local officials, see Fletcher, *Reform in the Provinces*; Thomson, *Lords Lieutenants in the Sixteenth Century*; and Landau, *Justices of the Peace*.

68. See, e.g., Governor George Clinton's Commission, 3 July 1741, *NYCD*, 6:190–95. The governor signed a septennial act in 1743; this was approved in London, though an earlier triennial act had been disallowed. An Act for Limiting the Continuance of the General Assemblys of this Colony, 17 Dec. 1743, *Colonial Laws of New York*, 3:295–96; Keith, *Constitutional History of the First British Empire*, 237. On the governor and council as the provincial court of last resort, see Goebel and Naughton, *Law Enforcement in Colonial New York*, 10–12.

69. Bailyn, *Origins of American Politics*, 66–69. On the subjection of the prerogative to legal limitation in the sixteenth and seventeenth centuries, see Judson, *Crisis of the Constitution*, 275–348, 355, 376, 386, and Nenner, *By Colour of Law*, 53–57, 61–75.

70. See, e.g., Cadwallader Colden to Gov. George Clinton, 4 Feb. 1752, *NYHS Coll.* (1920), 309–10.

71. Bailyn, *Origins of American Politics*, 96.

72. Governor Robert Hunter to Secretary St. John, 12 Sept. 1711, *NYCD*, 5:255–56; Harrington, *Commonwealth of Oceana; and, A System of Politics*, 11, 16–17. William Lambarde referred to the Privy Council as the "Great Councell," while the Houses of Parliament were the "Common Councell." Lambarde, *Archeion*, 58–61.

73. On Hunter, see Lustig, *Robert Hunter*.

74. *Blankard v. Galdy*, 2 Salk. 411, 412, 91 Eng. Rep. 356 (K.B. 1693). For the doctrine of settlement, see Hulsebosch, "Ancient Constitution and the Expanding Empire," 470–75. Cf. Moglen, "Settling the Law," vi–xiii.

75. Haffenden, "Crown and the Colonial Charters"; Smith, *Appeals to the Privy Council*, 65, 72, 132–34. The Privy Council created the Lords Council (after 1675, Committee) of Trade and Foreign Plantations and replaced that with the Lords Commissioners for Trade and Plantations (the Board of Trade) in 1696. A similar policy of rechartering occurred at home. For contemporary commentary, see Sacret, "Restoration Government and Municipal Corporations," and Levin, *Charter Controversy in the City of London*.

76. *Smith v. Brown*, 2 Salk. 666, 91 Eng. Rep. 566 (K.B. 1705 [1702]).

77. *Campbell v. Hall*, 98 Eng. Rep. 1045 (1774), in *State-Trials*, 20:304.

78. He added that "the Common Law of England, is the Common Law of the Plantations, and all statutes in affirmance of the Common Law passed in England, antecedent to the settlement of a colony, are in force there, unless there is some private Act to the contrary." Mr. West's Opinion, in Chalmers, *Opinions of Eminent Lawyers*, 206. For a more modest statement, see Privy Council Memorandum, 2 Peere Williams 75, 24 Eng. Rep. 646 (P.C. 1722).

79. John Randolph to Captain Pearse, ca. 1734, quoted in Smith, *History of the Province of New-York*, 1:266n.

80. See Moglen, "Settling the Law," 62.

81. Goebel, "Common Law and the Constitution," 102.

82. What today is called the choice of law question. For a rare and incisive treatment of this problem in early America, see William E. Nelson, "The American Revolution and the Emergence of Modern Doctrines of Federalism and Conflict of Laws," in Coquillette, *Law in Colonial Massachusetts*, 419–67.

83. For a skeptical view, see Levy, "Did the Zenger Case Really Matter?" See generally Bonomi, *Factious People*, 103–39.

84. Stanley N. Katz, introduction to Alexander, *Brief Narrative*, 3.

85. Governor Cosby to the Board of Trade, 18 Dec. 1732, *NYCD*, 5:937; Governor Cosby to the Duke of Newcastle, 3 May 1733, *NYCD*, 5:942–50; Council of New York to the Duke of Newcastle, *NYCD*, 17 Dec. 1733, 5:981; Governor Cosby to the Lords of Trade, 19 June 1734, *NYCD*, 6:4–5.

86. For DeLancey, see Katz, *Newcastle's New York*, 207–12 and passim.

87. Governor Cosby to the Board of Trade, 19 June 1734, *NYCD*, 6:4–7; Articles of Complaint against Governor Cosby by Rip Van Dam, 17 Dec. 1733, *NYCD*, 6:977. See also Katz, introduction to Alexander, *Brief Narrative*, 1–35, and Moglen, "Considering *Zenger*."

88. On the struggle to enforce quitrents and the role of chancery courts in the process, see Bond, *Quit-Rent System*.

89. The early governors ordered towns to renew their patents, and the new ones required quitrents. Reich, *Leisler's Rebellion*, 13.

90. See Bryson, *Equity Side of the Exchequer*.

91. Katz, "Politics of Law in Colonial America." See also Bond, *Quit-Rent*

System, 268–69; "On the Delays in Chancery," 7 June 1753, in Klein, *Independent Reflector*, 253; Goebel and Naughton, *Law Enforcement in Colonial New York*, 27 n. 135.

92. Bond, *Quit-Rent System*, 273–76. For the statute, see An Act for the More Easy Collecting of His Majesty's Quit Rents, 5 July 1755, *Laws of Colonial New York*, 3:1107–21.

93. Bond, *Quit-Rent System*, 25–28, 110–13.

94. Ibid., 29–30, 271–75.

95. Ibid., 33–34; Bonomi, *Factious People*, 208.

96. See, e.g., Cadwallader Colden to Governor Cosby, Report on the State of the Lands in New York, 1732, *DHNY*, 1:377–89.

97. Bond, *Quit-Rent System*, 266.

98. *NYCD*, 5:731.

99. Katz, introduction to Alexander, *Brief Narrative*, 5; Katz, *Newcastle's New York*, 63–68.

100. Katz, introduction to Alexander, *Brief Narrative*, 2.

101. "A Song Made upon the Foregoing Occasion," *New-York Weekly Journal*, quoted in Alexander, *Brief Narrative*, 111.

102. DeLancey, *Charge of the Honourable James DeLancey Esq.*, 3–4; [Morris], *Some Observations on the Charge Given by the Honourable* James DeLancey, 9–10. Morris also "took the unfamiliar and therefore drastic step of publishing his opinion" in the case. Moglen, "Settling the Law," 80; Morris, "Opinion and Argument of Lewis Morris to Governor William Cosby." See also Smith, *History of the Province of New-York*, 1:259. For earlier disputes over the governor's power to erect new courts, see New York Council, *Journal of the Legislative Council*, 1:563, 568–71, and Earl of Bellomont to the Board of Trade, 13 May 1699, *NYCD*, 5:515–17.

103. Smith, *Mr. Smith's Opinion Humbly Offered to the General Assembly*, 1, 33–34; Murray, *Mr. Murray's Opinion Relating to the Courts of Justice*, 4, 2, 15. Provincial lawyers had advised a previous governor that "the King cannot by law establish Courts of Justice of his own Authority" without an act of assembly. Earl of Bellomont to Board of Trade, 13 May 1699, *NYCD*, 4:515.

104. Andrew J. O'Shaughnessy captures the importance of West Indian slavery to metropolitan society in *Empire Divided*, 3–33.

105. "Treaty of Aix-la-Chappelle," 18 Oct. 1748, art. IV.

106. Wiecek, "Statutory Law of Slavery and Race," 263.

107. For remnant papers on this case, most of which were lost in the Albany capitol fire of 1911, see New York Colonial Mss., box 113, vol. 83, pp. 74–115, NYSA. There were a few similar cases in the late seventeenth and early eighteenth centuries. McManus, *History of Negro Slavery in New York*, 87–90.

108. Clinton to the Duke of Bedford, 12 June 1750, *NYCD*, 6:575; Colden to Clinton, 19 June 1750, *NYHS Coll.* (1920), 223–25.

109. McCusker and Menard, *Economy of British America*, 72n, 77–78.

110. John Ayscough to Colden, 9 May 1749, *NYHS Coll.* (1920), 110; Colden to George Clinton, Nov. 1749, *NYHS Coll.* (1920), 154; *Dictionary of American Biography*, s.v. "Clinton, George."

111. For the details of this incident, see *NYCD*, 6:571–76, 583–85; *NYHS Coll.* (1920), 213–18, 222–25, 242; and *New York Post-Boy*, 11 June 1750, 13 Aug. 1750.

112. Captain Roddam to James DeLancey, 8 June 1750, *NYCD*, 6:572; Clinton to the Duke of Bedford, 12 June 1750, *NYCD*, 6:574; Goebel and Naughton, *Law Enforcement in Colonial New York*, 304 n. 84; DeLancey to Roddam, 9 June 1750, *NYCD*, 6:572.

113. Roddam to DeLancey, 8 June 1750, *NYCD*, 6:572.

114. Clinton to the Duke of Newcastle, 10 May 1747 and 5 Nov. 1747, *NYCD*, 6:341–42, 351. The assembly complained that this mode of financing was not legal. "A Letter from some of the Representatives in the late General Assembly to the Governor," 15 June 1747, *General Assembly Journal, 1691–1765*, 2:206–21. Clinton went to Albany in an attempt to quell mutiny in late June. "Abstract of Evidence," *NYCD*, 6:665; Clinton to Board of Trade, 22 June 1747, *NYCD*, 6:352.

115. The clause first appeared in the commission of Governor John Montgomerie, 4 Oct. 1727, *NYCD*, 5:838–39, and was repeated in Clinton's commission, 3 July 1741, *NYCD*, 6:193.

116. Kent, *Charter of the City of New-York, with Notes Thereon*, 37. The Common Council had requested a new charter to expand its regulatory authority over the port of New York to increase trade. New York City, *Minutes of the Common Council of the City of New York, 1675–1776*, 4:19–20. As Montgomerie's successor pointed out, the corporation received control over the entire shoreline of Manhattan and islands in the rivers, so that "his Majesty's prerogative & interest may be in danger of suffering, and his ships stationed here under a necessity of becoming petitioners to the Corporation for a convenient place to careen or refitt." Cosby to Board of Trade, 29 Aug. 1733, *NYCD*, 5:956.

117. DeLancey to Roddam, 12 June 1750, *NYCD*, 6:572–73. See also Roddam to DeLancey, 9 June 1750, *NYCD*, 6:573, and DeLancey to Roddam, 12 June 1750, *NYCD*, 6:573.

118. On DeLancey, see Bonomi, *Factious People*, 140–49, 171–78, and Katz, *Newcastle's New York*, 207–12.

119. Clinton to Duke of Bedford, 12 June 1750, *NYCD*, 6:574; *New-York Gazette, Revived in the Weekly Post-Boy*, 11 June 1750.

120. Crown agents continually wrote home to complain about the loyalties of the attorney general and others associated with the provincial judiciary. See, e.g., Clinton to Board of Trade, 24 Oct. 1752, *NYCD*, 6:766.

121. Richard Bradley to Roddam, 23 July 1750, *NYCD*, 6:583–84.

122. Roddam to Clinton, 26 July 1750, *NYCD*, 6:584–85; Clinton to Roddam, 27 July 1750, *NYCD*, 6:585.

123. Clinton to the Duke of Bedford, "Observations on the Chief Justice's Behaviour, on account of a late unhappy accident, humbly submitted to Your Grace," 12 June 1750, *NYCD*, 6:575–76.

124. Colden to Clinton, 19 June 1750, *NYHS Coll.* (1920), 223–25.

125. Goebel and Naughton, *Law Enforcement in Colonial New York*, 554–55, 557–58, 573–74.

126. John Ayscough to Colden, 8 Aug. 1750, *NYHS Coll.* (1920), 222–23.

127. *New York Post-Boy*, 1 Aug. 1750.

128. John Ayscough to Colden, 18 June 1750, *NYHS Coll.* (1920), 213.

129. John Ayscough to Colden, 11 June 1750, *NYHS Coll.* (1920), 242.

130. Goebel and Naughton, *Law Enforcement in Colonial New York*, 306.

131. See Chalmers, *Opinions of Eminent Lawyers*, 206–32. See also Black, "Constitution of Empire," 1200–1201; Keith, *Constitutional History of the First British Empire*, 182–86; and Smith, *Appeals to the Privy Council*, 464–643.

132. A contemporary assessment is Smith, *History of the Province of New-York*, 1:266–67. See also Goebel, "Constitutional History and Constitutional Law," 565. On the "right to isonomy," or equal enjoyment of English rights, see Reid, *Authority of Rights*, 82–86. The Act of Settlement was designed to confirm the succession of the Hanoverians after the death of William and Anne without issue. 12 & 13 William III, c. 2, reprinted in Williams, *Eighteenth-Century Constitution*, 56–60.

133. The late colonial boycotts provide the most famous example. See Dickerson, *Navigation Acts and the American Revolution*. Just as important was persistent law avoidance, especially the flouting of trade regulations.

134. See generally Brown, *British Statutes in American Law*, 1–22; Goebel, review of *Parliament and the British Empire* in *Columbia Law Review*; Smith, *Appeals to the Privy Council*, 486–87, 520–22; and Greene, *Peripheries and Center*, 25–28.

135. An Act to Declare the Extension of Several Acts of Parliament Made since the Establishment of a Legislation in this Colony: and Not Declared in the Said Act to Extend to the Plantations, 24 Dec. 1767, *Colonial Laws of New York*, 4:953–56; *Acts of the Privy Council*, 5:284–85.

136. Meaning the British Parliament. Blackstone, *Commentaries*, 1:105–6. A few years later, Blackstone elaborated the restrictions on the operation of English law in discovered provinces, stressing Parliament's power to "new-model" all colonial constitutions. Blackstone, *Commentaries*, 1:4, supplement, ii–iii.

137. Burke, *Works of the Right Honourable Edmund Burke*, 1:500–501. See generally Hoffman, *Edmund Burke, New York Agent*.

138. Stokes, *View of the Constitution of the British Colonies*, i, 4, 30.

139. Report of His Excellency William Tryon Esquire, 11 June 1774, *DHNY*, 1:754.

PART TWO

1. Mr. Clarke's Answers to Queries of the Board of Trade, 2 June 1738, *NYCD*, 6:120.

2. Answer to the Several Queries from the Board of Trade by the Honorable George Clinton Esq Governour of New York, 23 May 1749, *NYCD*, 6:508–9. On Colden's relationship to Clinton, see Clinton to Under Secretary Andrew Stone, 24 July 1747, *NYCD*, 6:377, and Smith, *History of the Province of New-York*, 2:138.

3. Colden, Observations on the Balance of Power in Government, [1744–45], *NYHS Coll.* (1935), 251, 253. This is evidently a draft answer prepared for Clinton. For Colden's drafting of Clinton's letters and speeches, see, e.g., Colden to Clinton, 29 Jan. 1747/8, *NYHS Coll.* (1920), 6–7; Clinton to Colden, 31 Jan. 1747,

NYHS Coll. (1920), 10; and Colden to Clinton, 9 Feb. 1748/9, *NYHS Coll.* (1920), 93–94.

4. Board of Trade, Report on the Province of New York, 2 April 1751, *NYCD*, 6:616, 636–37. See also *Acts of the Privy Council*, 4:209, 246–47. The recommendation for independent salaries was incorporated into the controversial thirty-ninth article of the next governor's commission, which enjoined him to seek "a permanent salary settled by law upon a solid foundation for defraying the necessary charges of government," including salaries for the governor, supreme court judges, and other "necessary officers and ministers of government," as well as support for defense and Indian affairs. Instruction no. 290, 1753–55, in Labaree, *Royal Instructions to British Colonial Governors*, 1:190–93.

5. See, e.g., Charles W. Spencer, "The Rise of the Assembly, 1691–1760," in Flick, *History of the State of New York*, 2:153–99. On the practical operation of the eighteenth-century English constitution, by which many accepted the unofficial influence of the crown and interest groups, see Holdsworth, "Conventions of the Eighteenth-Century Constitution"; Namier, *Structure of Politics*; Plumb, *Growth of Political Stability*; and Bailyn, *Origins of American Politics*, 59–105.

6. Reid, *Authority of Rights*, 227–37; Black, "Constitution of Empire"; Greene, "From the Perspective of Law"; Greene, *Peripheries and Center*, 129–50; Johnson, "'Parliamentary Egoisms.'" Cf. Leder, *Liberty and Authority*, 85–86.

7. Greene, "Negotiated Authorities," 17; Greene, *Quest for Power*.

8. Reid, *In Defiance of the Law*, 32, 33, 34.

9. Reviewers of Greene and Reid suggest that historians shift focus from "authoritative statements" claiming to define the constitution of the empire to the "actual practices" of constitutional governance. Hartog, review of *Peripheries and Center* in *WMQ*; Bliss, "Review Essay" in *Journal of American Studies*.

CHAPTER THREE

1. For shifting political alliances in New York, see Bailyn, *Origins of American Politics*, 107–14, and Katz, *Newcastle's New York*. This idea that there were competing interpretations of the constitution, amounting in effect to multiple constitutions, is rooted in the work of several scholars. See Horwitz, "Foreword: The Constitution of Change"; Cover, "Foreword: *Nomos* and Narrative"; Llewellyn, "Constitution as an Institution"; and the histories of political languages, such as Pocock, *Politics, Language, and Time*. See also Hartog, "Pigs and Positivism"; Peter Onuf, introduction to *Maryland and the Empire*, 3–13, 34–39; and Sugarman, "English Constitution." Jack Greene posits that there were separate constitutions for Great Britain, the colonies and dominions, and the empire as a whole. Greene, *Peripheries and Center*, xi, 67. The argument here is that New Yorkers divided among themselves in their perceptions of the province's constitution. Suggestive in this regard is McAnear, "Politics in Provincial New York," 971, 977, 990–91, and Shannon, "Crossroads of Empire," 15–113.

2. Here as elsewhere, "lawlessness" was an expression of opprobrium, not a term of legal precision. Cf. Hartog, "Pigs and Positivism." "Marchland" first sig-

nified the land "anciently claimed by the kings of both realms" between England and Scotland and between England and Wales. Hale, *Prerogatives of the King*, 20; Francis Bacon, "The Jurisdiction of the Marches" (1608), in *Works of Francis Bacon*, 7:567–611. William Johnson referred to the land west of the Appalachians as "Marches & Frontiers." William Johnson to the Earl of Shelburne, 3 Dec. 1767, *NYCD*, 7:1001.

3. [Kennedy], *Essay on the Government of the Colonies*, 16, 15. Kennedy's statement that colonists enjoyed English common and statute law was unusual; it was designed to bolster the status of the Church of England in the colonies. See [Kennedy], *Speech Said to Have Been Delivered Some Time Before the Close of the Last Sessions*, 6. On royal government, see generally Labaree, *Royal Government in America*. Max Savelle wrongly dismissed imperial officeholders in North America and mischaracterized their politics as a mixture of "feudalism and Robert Filmer." Savelle, *Seeds of Liberty*, 292–305.

4. Colden, "An Account of Governor Clinton's Administration," n.d., Cadwallader Colden Papers, NYHS; [Kennedy], *Essay on the Government of the Colonies*, 34.

5. Parliamentary sovereignty became metropolitan dogma only late in the eighteenth century. See chapter 4.

6. Barrow, *Trade and Empire*, 1–2; Knorr, *British Colonial Theories*.

7. Knox, *Extra-Official State Papers Addressed to the Right Hon. Lord Rawdon*, 2:11.

8. Beverly McAnear contrasts the rotating governors with lesser officials who remained in the provinces at length. McAnear, *Income of the Colonial Governors*, 132–33.

9. It is possible that Colden was born in Ireland while his mother was visiting Scots-Irish relatives. Useful sources on Colden include Keys, *Cadwallader Colden*; Shammas, "Cadwallader Colden and the Role of the King's Prerogative"; and Steacy, "Cadwallader Colden."

10. Cadwallader Colden, "History of William Cosby's Administration as Governor of the Province of New-York and of Lieutenant Governor George Clarke's Administration Through 1737," *NYHS Coll.* (1935), 283–355.

11. Lewis Morris to the Marquis of Lothian, 26 Mar. 1735, *NYHS Coll.* (1918), 124–25.

12. Colden, *The History of the Five Indian Nations of Canada, Which are Dependent on the Province of New-York in America*. The two volumes of this work were first published under separate titles in New York in the 1720s, and a third part remained unpublished until the twentieth century. Colden, "Continuation of Colden's History of the Five Nations, for the Years 1707 through 1720," *NYHS Coll.* (1935), 359–434.

13. See Milton M. Klein, "Archibald Kennedy," in Leder, *Colonial Legacy*, 2:75–105.

14. Will of Archibald Kennedy, *NYHS Coll.* (1897), 285–87. Kennedy's death, like that of many colonial officeholders, set off a patronage feeding frenzy. See, e.g., Goldsborough Banyar to Governor Monckton, 14 June 1763, and Oliver DeLancey to Monckton, June 1763, George Chalmers Collection, NYPL. The victor was fellow Scot Andrew Elliot. Ernst, "Andrew Elliot."

15. MacBean, *Biographical Register of Saint Andrew's Society*, 1:7. On the type, see Price, "One Family's Empire."

16. [Kennedy], *Essay on the Government of the Colonies*; [Kennedy], *Serious Advice to the Inhabitants of the Northern Colonies*, 15, 5.

17. See Stanley M. Pargellis, "The Four Independent Companies of New York," in *Essays in Colonial History Presented to Charles McLean Andrews*, 96–123.

18. [Kennedy], *Serious Considerations on the Present State of Affairs*; Colden to Gov. George Clinton, 8 Aug. 1751, *NYHS Coll.* (1920), 271–87; Klein, "Archibald Kennedy: Colonial Pamphleteer," 77–81. All the leading imperial agents lobbied for Johnson's appointment. Johnson to Governor George Clinton, 2 Dec. 1754, *Johnson Papers*, 9:146–50; Richard Shuckbrugh to William Johnson, 14 May 1751, *Johnson Papers*, 1:332; Peter Wraxall, "Some Thoughts upon the British Indian Interest in North America . . . ," 9 Jan. 1755[6], *NYCD*, 7:15–31; Cadwallader Colden, "An Account of the Indian Trade and Its Importance," n.d., Cadwallader Colden Papers, Misc. Mss., NYHS; Andrew Elliot to [Sir Gilbert Elliot], [May or June 1755], Andrew Elliot Papers, NYHS; Alden, "Albany Congress," 206–7.

19. On Johnson, see Hamilton, *Sir William Johnson*; Flexner, *Lord of the Mohawks*; and Guzzardo, "Sir William Johnson's Official Family." On Warren, see Gwyn, *Enterprising Admiral*.

20. Johnson first became instrumental as a military contractor during King George's War (George Clinton to Johnson, 27 Aug. 1746, *Johnson Papers*, 1:59–60) and after that remained busy with imperial diplomacy. Peter Wraxall claimed that the Iroquois "looked upon [Johnson] as their Chief, their Patron & their Brother they acted under his Command & were almost wholly directed by him." McIlwain, *Abridgment of the Indian Affairs*, 248n.

21. The Albany Congress proposed a "General Government" of the colonies that would regulate Indian relations. The colonial assemblies did not support the proposal. See Shannon, "Crossroads of Empire," 212–20; McAnear, "Politics in Provincial New York," 853–60; and Alden, "Albany Congress."

22. For the commission, see *Johnson Papers*, 2:434–35, and *NYCD*, 7:76, 458–59.

23. Bailyn, *Voyagers to the West*, 576–82. Johnson's Mohawk Valley approximated the "middle ground" discussed in White, *Middle Ground*.

24. On Molly and Joseph Brant, see Johnston, "Molly Brant," and Kelsey, *Joseph Brant*.

25. See, e.g., Johnson to the Board of Trade, 30 Oct. 1764, *NYCD*, 7:672; Johnson to Arthur Lee, 28 Feb. 1771, *DHNY*, 4:430–37; Johnson to Lee, 28 Mar. 1772, *Johnson Papers*, 12:950–55. See also Hamilton, "Sir William Johnson."

26. Colden, *History of the Five Indian Nations*; [Kennedy], *Importance of Gaining and Preserving the Friendship of the Indians*.

27. Johnson to William Smith (of Philadelphia), 10 Apr. 1767, *Johnson Papers*, 5:530–31. This included religious conversion: Johnson's son-in-law edited a translation of the Book of Common Prayer for the Iroquois. *NYCD*, 8:815.

28. Wainwright, *George Croghan, Wilderness Diplomat*; Ernst, "Andrew Elliot, Forgotten Loyalist"; Katz, *Newcastle's New York*, 139–63 (on George Clarke);

Goldsborough Banyar Papers, NYHS; Schutz, *Thomas Pownall, British Defender of American Liberty*; Gipson, *Lewis Evans*; Bridenbaugh, *Mitre and Sceptre* (on the SPG); Gage, *Correspondence*. Imperial administration before the Revolution was not "garrison government." For instance, although New York City was its continental headquarters, the royal military in New York was neglected by British ministers for most of the century. Pargellis, "Four Independent Companies of New York," 96–123. But I agree with Stephen S. Webb's general thesis that the British Empire tried repeatedly to impose imperial control on the provinces. See Webb, *The Governors-General* and *Lord Churchill's Coup*. Patricia U. Bonomi has recently questioned the commonplace assumption that there was no court faction in the British colonies, or at least in New York. Bonomi, *Lord Cornbury Scandal*, 9–10.

29. For social interaction, including a regular "club," see James Alexander to Cadwallader Colden, 10 Dec. 1750, *NYHS Coll.* (1920), 240; George Clinton to Cadwallader Colden, 6 Jan. 1752, *NYHS Coll.* (1920), 307; and William Johnson to Goldsborough Banyar, [2 Apr. 1762], *Johnson Papers*, 13:225.

30. The letters of Andrew Elliot illuminate the patronage process. For a decade Elliot implored his family help him gain a lucrative colonial post, writing to his father, brother, sister, and mother. See, e.g., Andrew Elliot to Lord Minto, 15 Feb. 1757; Elliot to Gilbert Elliot, 27 Feb. 1757, 27 Oct. 1757, and 16 Aug. 1761; Elliot to Mother, 24 Nov. 1761; and Elliot to Sister, 24 Nov. 1761 and 25 June 1762, all in the Andrew Elliot Papers, NYHS. He succeeded in 1763, when he became customs collector and receiver general after Kennedy's death.

31. Cf. Ned Landsman, "The Legacy of the British Union for the North American Colonies: Provincial Elites and the Problem of Imperial Union," in Robertson, *Union for Empire*, 298.

32. "The cultivating & improvement of the Land is the great Design of settling Colonies in America by which only they can be usefull to their Mother Country & prosper." Cadwallader Colden, "Comments on Government in General," n.d., Cadwallader Colden Papers, Misc. Mss., NYHS.

33. Most of the agents, both Anglicans and Dissenters, supported the Church of England as the colony's official church not because of theology but rather out of annoyance with local "nibbling at the Prerogative of the Crown." [Kennedy], *Speech Said to Have Been Delivered Some Time Before the Close of the Last Sessions*, 5. Kennedy was Presbyterian.

34. On the absence of coherent imperial strategy at home, see Jacob M. Price, "Who Cared about the Colonies? The Impact of the Thirteen Colonies on British Society and Politics, circa 1714–1775," in Bailyn and Morgan, *Strangers within the Realm*, 395–436; Katz, *Newcastle's New York*, 10–20; Henretta, *"Salutary Neglect"*; Sosin, *Whitehall and the Wilderness*; and, for contemporary insight, Smith, *History of the Province of New-York*, 1:5. This was the point of J. R. Seeley's comment that the empire was created "in a fit of absence of mind" — at home. Seeley, *Expansion of England*, 12. Kathleen Wilson and David Armitage prove that there was an imperial ideology in England, but not a coherent strategy for maintaining colonies. See Wilson, *Sense of the People*, and Armitage, *Ideological Origins of the British Empire*.

Closer to the point are recent works exploring the construction of "Great Britain" and "Briton." Pocock, "Limits and Divisions of British History"; Colley, *Britons*, 130. In particular, Linda Colley observes about many Scottish colonists that "[a] British imperium . . . enabled Scots to feel themselves peers of the English in a way still denied to them in an island kingdom." Colley, *Britons*, 130. See also Colley, "Britishness and Otherness"; Ned C. Landsman, "The Provinces and the Empire: Scotland, the American Colonies, and the Development of British Provincial Identity," in Stone, *Imperial State at War*, 258–87; Landsman, "Legacy of the British Union for the North American Colonies," 297–317; Kammen, *Colonial New York*, 178–79; and Levack, *Formation of the British State*, 62, 206–7. Allowing for differences in emphasis, this holds too for the Irish as well as other self-conscious provincials within the empire. See also Bailyn and Clive, "England's Cultural Provinces"; Syme, *Colonial Elites*, 4; Robert K. Merton, "Patterns of Influence: Local and Cosmopolitan Influentials," in Merton, *Social Theory and Social Structure*, 387–420; and Edward Shils, "Center and Periphery," in Shils, *Constitution of Society*, 93–109. Cf. Robbins, " 'When It Is That Colonies May Turn Independent,' " 230.

35. Hancock, *Citizens of the World*.

36. For different attempts to relate commerce to empire, compare Johnson, "Imperial Webb," and Bruce P. Lenman, " 'Garrison Government'? Governor Alexander Spotswood and Empire," in Simpson, *Scottish Soldier Abroad*, 67–80, with Webb, "Data and Theory of Restoration Empire," 431–59.

37. [Kennedy], *Serious Advice to the Inhabitants of the Northern Colonies*, 17.

38. See, e.g., [Kennedy], *Observations on the Importance of the Northern Colonies*.

39. Colden, *History of the Five Indian Nations*. Colden's map, like the rest of his *History*, was indebted to earlier French efforts. See DeL'Isle, *Carte de Louisiane et du cours du Mississipi*, and Lieutenant Governor George Clarke to the Board of Trade, 24 May 1739, *NYCD*, 6:143.

40. Colden, *History of the Five Indian Nations*, 2:36–37, 43–46. The province's rivers would link the Atlantic and the Mississippi, "by which means an Inland Navigation may be made to the Bay of Mexico." Colden to Lieutenant Governor George Clarke, 14 Feb. 1738, *NYCD*, 6:122. See also Lord Adam Gordon, "Journal of an Officer," [1765–66], in Mereness, *Travels in the American Colonies*, 419.

41. He returned home to help suppress the Jacobite rebellion of 1715 and marry. Keys, *Cadwallader Colden*, 107, 323. See generally Steele, *English Atlantic*.

42. A few historians have recognized the importance of secondary figures in the formation of imperial policy. See Wickwire, *British Subministers and Colonial America*, 50–85; Clark, *Rise of the British Treasury*; Spector, *American Department of the British Government*; Plumb, *Growth of Political Stability*, 10–14; and Syme, *Colonial Elites*, 3.

43. On these interest groups and their decline in the mid-eighteenth century, see Katz, *Newcastle's New York*, and Olson, *Making the Empire Work*.

44. Examples can be found in Colden's letter book, Kennedy's overlapping pamphlets, and Johnson's extensive correspondence. Even those agents who did not maintain letter books had key ideas and phrases indelibly printed in their mind. Cf. Roger Chartier, "Introduction: An Ordinary Kind of Writing: Model

Letters and Letter-Writing in Ancien Regime France," in Chartier, Boureau, and Dauphin, *Correspondence*, 20.

45. Andrew Elliot to his father, Lord Minto, 18 Nov. 1750, Andrew Elliot Papers, NYHS. "Country" was originally synonymous with "county." Zagorin, "Court and the Country." In the colonies, it was usually synonymous with "province." Wilson, "My Country Is My Colony"; Fitch, "American Nationalism and the Revolution," 51–64. For the similar complaint that most came to the colony for "the improvement of their Purses," not "Conversation or any of the Liberal Arts," see Cadwallader Colden, "Comments on Government in General," n.d., Cadwallader Colden Papers, Misc. Mss., NYHS.

46. See, e.g., Governor Clinton's Report on the Province, 23 May 1749, *NYCD*, 6:508–9.

47. See Brathwaite, *Development of Creole Society in Jamaica*, xiv–xv. See also Richard N. Adams, "On the Relation between Plantation and 'Creole Cultures,'" in *Plantation Systems of the New World*, 73–79. On the creolization of culture, see Greene, *Pursuits of Happiness*, 171–206; Hoffer, *Law and People in Colonial America*, 14; Pagden and Canny, *Colonial Identity in the Atlantic World*; and Warner, *Letters of the Republic*.

48. See, e.g., Eleazar Wheelock to William Johnson, 28 Mar. 1765, *DHNY*, 4:355 (describing Native Americans as "lazy savages" and "bad tenants" of God), and William Smith Jr. to General Horatio Gates, 22 Nov. 1763, box 1, microfilm, Horatio Gates Papers, NYHS (referring to them as "Barbarians" and "Demons").

49. On multiple or "stacked loyalties," see Steele, "Empire and Provincial Elites," 19, and Colley, "Britishness and Otherness," 315–16. See also John M. Murrin, "A Roof without Walls: The Dilemma of American National Identity," in Beeman, Botein, and Carter, *Beyond Confederation*, 333–48. The work of postcolonial studies is also helpful for rethinking creolization. See Homi K. Bhabha, "Of Mimicry and Men," in *Location of Culture*, 85–92, and Lawson, "Comparative Studies and Post-Colonial Settler Cultures," 153–59.

50. J. H. Plumb, "The Acceptance of Modernity," in McKendrick, Brewer, and Plumb, *Birth of Consumer Society*, 316–34. See also Borsay, *English Urban Renaissance*, and Andrew Hook, "Philadelphia, Edinburgh and the Scottish Enlightenment," in Sher and Smitten, *Scotland and America in the Age of the Enlightenment*, 133–41. Jack P. Greene notes the pervasiveness of "improvement" in colonial society, though he stresses its connection with "individual happiness" and finds it especially predominant in the southern colonies. Greene, *Pursuits of Happiness*, 5, 197–98, 205.

51. Colden to William Douglass, [1728], *NYHS Coll.* (1917), 271–72. See also Keys, *Cadwallader Colden*, 1–26, and Hoermann, "Cadwallader Colden, a Savant in the Wilderness." On associations among eighteenth-century intellectuals, see Schlereth, *Cosmopolitan Ideal in Enlightenment Thought*.

52. See Haley, "Voluntary Organizations"; Kammen, *Colonial New York*, 242–77; Bender, *New York Intellect*, 9–40; Klein, "Cultural Tyros of Colonial New York"; and Milton M. Klein, introduction to Klein, *Independent Reflector*, 33.

53. "On Our Defect of Public Spirit: Its Beneficial Influence in *Philadelphia*," in

Klein, *Independent Reflector*, 444. The message of this uncompleted article appeared in various published issues of the *Independent Reflector*.

54. Compare Kammen, *People of Paradox*, 184–86, 222, and Greene, "Search for Identity," with Murrin, "Anglicizing an American Colony," and McAnear, "Politics in Provincial New York," 540–46.

55. Cf. Bhabha, *Location of Culture*, 87.

56. For the trading contacts of one mercantile family, see White, *Beekman Mercantile Papers*. See also Harrington, *New York Merchant on the Eve of the Revolution*.

57. See, e.g., John Watts to Sir William Baker, 24 Sept. 1765, *NYHS Coll.* (1928), 388. See generally Pares, *Yankees and Creoles*.

58. Haley suggest that the voluntary associations "familiarized the populace with alternatives to official authority, and they produced men capable of taking the initiative once normal channels were blocked." Haley, "Voluntary Organizations," 40, 209. New Yorkers were not always the first to establish such institutions, but the number and energy of their organizations in the last quarter century before independence were unmatched in the colonies.

59. [Smith], "Brief Consideration of *New-York*," 104, and "Consideration of the natural Advantages of *New-York*," 433–39. See also Smith, *History of the Province of New-York*, 2:228, and Albion, *Rise of New York Port*, 16–22.

60. See, e.g., Klein, "From Community to Status"; Keep, *History of the New York Society Library*; Bard, *Discourse on the Duties of a Physician*; MacBean, *Biographical Register of Saint Andrew's Society*; Bowring et al., *History of St. George's Society*; Stevens, *Colonial Records of the New York Chamber of Commerce*; Osgood, "Society of Dissenters"; and Haley, "Voluntary Organizations."

61. A sense of the tight genetic world of colonial New York can be had in O'Callaghan, *Names of Persons for Whom Marriage Licenses Were Issued*. See also Becker, *History of Political Parties*, 12–14. Some New Yorkers went to Britain for education, a cosmopolitan seasoning that made them no less provincial, though marginally more likely to remain loyal after 1775. On the example of the De-Lanceys, a few more of whom were educated and maintained family connections in England than Livingstons, see Launitz-Schurer, *Loyal Whigs and Revolutionaries*, and Katz, *Newcastle's New York*, 54–55.

62. "There are in this Province two ancient and respectable families," it was claimed in 1770, "viz. the DeL——n——y and the L——n, who are the only competitors for power." *New York Journal*, 15 Apr. 1770. But the two families were on the same side of many issues. On the limitations of the familial interpretation of politics, see Varga, "New York Government and Politics during the Mid-Eighteenth Century," 156 n. 2; Klein, "Politics and Personalities in Colonial New York"; and Tully, *Forming American Politics*, 254–56. See also Bonomi, *Factious People*.

63. See Haskins, *Law and Authority in Early Massachusetts*. The quest for autonomy by prominent New Yorkers involved a search for identity and was as well an attempt to project themselves as social elites. See Haley, "Voluntary Organizations," 197. For eighteenth-century social structure and elite formation, see Bernard Bailyn, "Politics and Social Structure in Virginia," in Katz and Murrin, *Colo-*

nial America, 207–30; Bridenbaugh, *Cities in the Wilderness*; Main, *Social Structure of Revolutionary America*; Jaher, *Urban Establishment*; Isaac, *Transformation of Virginia*; Bushman, *Refinement of America*; Jack P. Greene, "The Growth of Political Stability: An Interpretation of Political Development in the Anglo-American Colonies, 1660–1760," in *Negotiated Authorities*, 148–50; and Wilkenfeld, *Social and Economic Structure of the City of New York*.

64. Smith, *History of the Province of New-York*, 1:2–3, 6 n+, 5, title page (quoting Thomson, *Liberty* [London, 1735–36]).

65. Williston, "History of the Law of Business Corporations before 1800," 114; Pollock and Maitland, *History of English Law*, 1:486–511; Baldwin, *Modern Political Institutions*, 141–95; Davis, *Corporations*, 223–27; Walter Ullmann, "Mediaeval Theory of Legal and Illegal Organizations." Some claimed that the corporation was not a common-law device, but by the eighteenth century it was treated as such. Compare Davies, *Question Concerning Impositions, Tonnage, Poundages*, 34, with Blackstone, *Commentaries*, 1:455–73.

66. This dynamic ambiguity between sovereign and grantee pervades the history of Anglo-American law. See, e.g., Blackstone, *Commentaries*, 2:50; Milsom, *Historical Foundations*, 15–36; and Goebel, review of *Parliament and the British Empire* in *Columbia Law Review*.

67. Pollock and Maitland, *History of English Law*, 1:486–511.

68. See, e.g., [Viscount Bolingbroke], *Country Journal, or the Craftsman*, no. 172, 18 Oct. 1729; Blackstone, *Commentaries*, 4:114; [Ramsay], *Essay on the Constitution*, 49; [Alexander Hamilton], "The Farmer Refuted," in *Hamilton Papers*, 1:164; Bailyn, *Ideological Origins of the American Revolution*, 206–7; and Wood, *Creation of the American Republic*, 344–54. The phrase originated as a criticism of church government within the Holy Roman Empire. See generally Tierney, *Crisis of Church and State*.

69. [Kennedy], *Essay on the Government of the Colonies*, 14. Kennedy's argument resembled royalist treatments of the Commons and chartered cities in the seventeenth century. See, e.g., Brady, *Historical Treatise on Cities, and Burghs or Boroughs*.

70. William Smith Jr. called Kennedy's analysis "accurate and bright" but also claimed that the assembly took "the practice of the British House of Commons for their model," precisely what Kennedy denied. Smith, *History of the Province of New-York*, 1:257 n*, 256. The triumvirate planned but did not complete an issue of the *Independent Reflector* criticizing Kennedy's devaluation of the provincial legislature, not his metaphor. "The Slavish and Pestilent Principles Contained in a Pamphlet, entitled *An Essay on the Government of the Colonies . . .* ," in Klein, *Independent Reflector*, 443.

71. On the "probative, evidentiary significance" of charters, see Reid, *Authority of Rights*, 164–68. See also Reid, "In Accordance with Usage."

72. See, e.g., Davis, *Essays in the Earlier History of American Corporations*, 1:11, 76, 84, 86, 101, 102. Most of New York's individual churches received charters; some of these were drafted by lawyers. New York Council, *Calendar of Council Minutes*; Draft of Charters to the Lutheran Church of the City of New York, [1758], and the Reformed Church of the Township of Orange, [1761–63?], box 2,

lot 196, William Smith Jr. Papers, NYPL. A notable exception was the Presbyterian Church of New York City. The Privy Council rejected its petition for a charter in 1767 in part because of the Presbyterian Church's conflicts with the Church of England. Report of the Lords of Trade against the Petition of the Presbyterian Church of New York, 10 July 1767, *NYCD*, 7:943–44. For quasi-corporate bodies, see, e.g., Haley, "Voluntary Organizations," and Bayles, *Old Taverns of New York*.

73. "The Advantages of Education," 8 Nov. 1753, in Klein, *Independent Reflector*, 419–20. See generally Humphrey, *From King's College to Columbia*.

74. "A Farther Prosecution of the Same Subject," 12 Apr. 1753, in Klein, *Independent Reflector*, 191.

75. Ibid., 196. On Livingston and the movement for a nonsectarian college, see Klein, *American Whig*, 263–350.

76. Blackstone, *Commentaries*, 1:460; Davis, *Essays in the Earlier History of American Corporations*, 1:5. There were a few exceptions to these rules.

77. "Farther Prosecution of the Same Subject," 191–97. "The Watch Tower," mostly the work of William Livingston, ran in the *New-York Mercury* for about one year beginning in November 1754. All three attended Yale. Smith married a Livingston. Livingston and Smith studied law with William Smith Sr., the provincial supreme court justice who earlier had helped defend John Peter Zenger. See Dillon, *New York Triumvirate*.

78. *John Englishman*. After the Revolution, Seabury claimed authorship of the responses to the "The Watch Tower," by which he must have meant the *John Englishman* series. Memorial of Samuel Seabury, 20 Oct. 1783, American Loyalists, 1783–1790: Transcript of Manuscript Books and Papers of the Commission of Enquiry into the Losses and Services of the American Loyalists, 76 vols., 41:560, NYPL.

79. *John Englishman*, VII, 7 June 1755; ibid., IV, 2 May 1755; ibid., IX, June 21, 1755; ibid., I, 11 Apr. 1755; ibid., III, 25 Apr. 1755. See also Jones, *History of New-York during the Revolutionary War*, 1:6. For emphasis on the religious aspects of the controversy, see Gerardi, "The King's College Controversy."

80. See Humphrey, *From King's College to Columbia*, 67–78, 278.

81. See, e.g., Reid, *In Defiance of the Law*, 32–49. See also Mullett, *Fundamental Law and the American Revolution*, 50.

82. *New-York Evening Post*, 7 July 1747.

83. Henry Beekman to Loving Cousin, 7 Jan. 1744/5, box 1, Beekman Papers, NYHS. It is unclear to which law Beekman referred.

84. Governor George Clinton, Address to the Assembly, 13 Oct. 1747, *NYCD*, 6:634.

85. Governor Benjamin Fletcher to the Assembly, 1 Apr. 1693 and 12 Sept. 1693, New York Council, *Journal of the Legislative Council*, 1:39, 42.

86. Governor Bellomont to the Assembly, 21 Mar. 1698, New York Council, *Journal of the Legislative Council*, 1:119.

87. Address of George Clarke, 3 Oct. 1739, New York Council, *Journal of the Legislative Council*, 1:736.

88. Minutes of 24 Mar. and 3 Mar. 1775, *General Assembly Journal*, 1766–1776,

1755:92–33, 53, 56. This distinction was lost in the McIlwain-Schuyler debate. Reid, *Authority to Tax*, 42; Reid, *Authority to Legislate*, 247, 305–10; Bailyn, *Ideological Origins of the American Revolution*, 213 n. 55; Greene, *Peripheries and Center*, 79–104.

89. Petition to the House of Lords, 11 Dec. 1765, *General Assembly Journal, 1691–1765*, 2:799. See also *General Assembly Journal, 1766–1776*, 1776: 70–71 (31 Dec. 1768).

90. Watts to Monckton, 26 Feb. 1765, *NYHS Coll.* (1928), 336.

91. Parliament originally set the molasses tax in the Molasses Act of 1733. The new Revenue Act, also known as the Molasses and Sugar Act, prohibited the import of foreign rum, increased the documentation ships had to carry, increased the number of enumerated goods covered by the Navigation Acts, required that all duties and fines be paid in sterling, and placed the burden of proof in enforcement actions on defendants. Greene and Pole, *Blackwell Encyclopedia of the American Revolution*, 164.

92. The Representation and Petition of the General-Assembly of New-York, 18 Oct. 1764, *General Assembly Journal, 1691–1765*, 2:779. For attribution, see Smith, *Historical Memoirs*, 1:24; Smith to Governor Monckton, 5 Nov. 1764, George Chalmers Collection, NYPL; and Dillon, *New York Triumvirate*, 87 n. 8. For an earlier invocation of English rights, see the Assembly to Governor Cornbury, 9 June 1704, New York Council, *Journal of the Legislative Council*, 1:217.

93. To the Lords Spiritual and Temporal in Parliament Assembled, 18 Oct. 1764, *General Assembly Journal, 1691–1765*, 2:774.

94. Ibid., 2:773–74.

95. The Humble Petition and Representation of the Representatives of Your Majesty's Loyal Colony of New-York, to the King, 18 Oct. 1764, *General Assembly Journal, 1691–1765*, 2:769–72.

96. See, e.g., The Petition of the General Assembly of the Colony of *New-York*, 11 Dec. 1765, *General Assembly Journal, 1691–1765*, 2:797; Petition to the King, 31 Dec. 1768, *General Assembly Journal, 1766–1776*, 1769: 11–13 (7 Apr. 1769); Petition to the House of Lords, *General Assembly Journal, 1766–1776*, 1769: 13–15; and Petitions to the King, Lords, and Commons, 25 Mar. 1775, *General Assembly Journal, 1766–1776*, 1775: 121–31. For the drafting of these later representations, see [Smith], "Draft Petition from New York in 1769," box 2, lot 197, William Smith Jr. Papers, NYPL; [William Smith], "To the Right Honourable the Lords Spiritual and Temporal . . . ," March 1775, copy in box 1, lot 180, William Smith Jr. Papers, NYPL; and Smith, *Historical Memoirs*, 1:214, 228–28c.

97. Smith, *Historical Memoirs*, 1:272–73.

98. Petitions to the King, Lords, and Commons, 25 Mar. 1775, *General Assembly Journal, 1766–1776*, 121–31.

99. See Upton, *Loyal Whig*.

100. Smith, "Notes for Mr. Hamilton on the American Dispute," Nov. 1775, box 1, lot 194, William Smith Jr. Papers, NYPL (emphasis added).

101. See also Greene, *Peripheries and Center*, and Bailyn, *Ideological Origins of the American Revolution*, 203–4.

102. Reid, *Authority to Legislate*, 17–33. See also Kramer, *People Themselves*, 24–29.

103. Compare Reid, *Constitutional History of the American Revolution*, abridged ed., 101, with McLaughlin, "Background of American Federalism," and Green, *Peripheries and Center*, 172–74. See also Bailyn, *Ideological Origins of the American Revolution*, 224–29.

104. William Livingston to Catherine Macaulay, 21 Sept. 1769, Livingston Papers, Pierpont Morgan Library, New York City.

105. [William Livingston], "The American Whig V," *New-York Gazette and Weekly Mercury*, 11 Apr. 1768. The essay is sometimes attributed to William Smith Jr., and it resonates with Smith's favorite themes. See, e.g., Smith to Jonathan Trumbull, 12 June 1773, quoted in Michael Kammen, introduction to Smith, *History of the Province of New-York*, xxxv ("It is easy to foresee, that a Foundation is laid for a vast Empire in this western World"). Because the two often shared their work, it may have been jointly authored. Though Livingston denied a desire for independence, some readers, like Anglican minister Samuel Seabury, saw the essay as "the immediate forerunner" of the Revolution. Memorial of Samuel Seabury, 20 Oct. 1783, Loyalist Transcripts, 41:561, NYPL; Norbert Kilian, "New Wine in Old Skins? American Definitions of Empire and the Emergence of a New Concept," in Angermann, Frings, and Wellenreuther, *New Wine in Old Skins*, 137–45; Egnal, *Mighty Empire*; Koebner, *Empire*, 170–73. George Berkeley proclaimed that "[w]estward the course of empire takes its way." Berkeley, "Verses on the Prospect of Planting Arts and Learning in America" (London, 1752), in *Works of George Berkeley*, 4:366.

106. Even the tenants on the Hudson River valley estates saw the value of improvements to their land and sold them to their landlords. Kim, *Landlord and Tenant in Colonial New York*, 179–80, 221–26, 243–44, 250–70, 278.

107. On the sailors' protests for free trade and against impressment, see Lemisch, *Jack Tar vs. John Bull*; Linebaugh and Rediker, *Many-Headed Hydra*, 143–73; and Gilje, *Liberty on the Waterfront*.

108. Historians have noted the importance of the enclosure movement and its related "improvements" throughout the British Isles in generating a supply of immigrants to the colonies. Many urban immigrants also came originally from those enclosed fields. See, e.g., Bailyn, *Voyagers to the West*, 44, 45, 291–92, 376, 606, and Bailyn, "Introduction: Europeans on the Move, 1500–1800," in Canny, *Europeans on the Move*, 2. There is a substantial literature on the enclosure movement in the British Isles. See, e.g., E. P. Thompson, "Custom, Law and Common Right," in *Customs in Common*, 97–184. On midcentury immigrants "swarming to the north" in New York, see Bailyn, *Voyagers to the West*, 573–637; Handlin, "Eastern Frontier of New York"; and McGregor, "Settlement Variations and Cultural Adaptation."

109. Anthropologists have reminded us that the activity of historical actors speaks volumes about their intellectual premises. See, e.g., Geertz, *Interpretation of Cultures*.

110. For the "rules and rituals of mob behavior" in eighteenth-century New

York, see Gilje, *Road to Mobocracy*, 16–25, and Maier, *From Resistance to Revolution*. On inducing legal norms from popular behavior, see Reid, "Some Lessons of Western History," and De Soto, *Mystery of Capital*, 106–51. On the difficulty of measuring backcountry politicization, see Nobles, "Breaking the Backcountry." Historians of religion offer examples of how to recapture the "lived experience" of complicated doctrine. Hall, *Lived Religion in America*.

111. See Rich, "Population of Elizabethan England." For conflicting British opinions about the individual right of "loco-motion" and governmental power to restrain migration, see Bailyn, *Voyagers to the West*, 52–57, and Graham, *Colonists from Scotland*, 90–104.

112. Bailyn, *Peopling of British North America*, 16–17, 60–86; Wycoff, *Developer's Frontier*.

113. Taylor, review of *The Developer's Frontier* in *WMQ*.

114. Cf. Savelle, *Seeds of Liberty*, 318–26 (discussing "the embryonic ideal of democracy" in frontier communities).

115. "In the Middle Ages," wrote the English legal historian Frederic W. Maitland, "land law was the basis of all public law." Maitland, *Constitutional History of England*, 38. Political theorists confirmed that this was still the case in the seventeenth century. See, e.g., Harrington, *Commonwealth of Oceana; and, A System of Politics*. William Blackstone informed his eighteenth-century students that the whole edifice of English law rested on land law. Blackstone, *Commentaries*, 2:44.

116. Only the manor of Rensselaerswyck survived the English takeover, and its privileges were designed to induce immigration. Freedoms and Exemptions Granted by the West India Company to All Patroons, Masters, or Private Persons Who Will Plant Colonies in New Netherland, 7 June 1629, *Laws and Ordinances of New Netherland*, 1–10.

117. See, e.g., Libby, *Geographical Distribution of the Vote of the Thirteen States*, 21–26; Becker, *History of Political Parties*, 8–10; Spaulding, *New York in the Critical Period*, 45, 77–80; and Mark, *Agrarian Conflicts in Colonial New York*. See also Higgins, *Expansion in New York*, 22–32, and Christenson, "Administration of Land Policy in Colonial New York," 18–68. The manors may have slowed development of the Hudson Valley. See Earl of Bellomont to the Board of Trade, 1700, *NYCD*, 4:791; Bellomont to Board of Trade, 1698, *NYCD*, 4:397; Colden to Governor William Shirley, 25 July 1749, *NYHS Coll.* (1920), 124; "Representations of Cadwallader Colden . . . against the Bill for Facilitating the Partition of Lands in Joint Tenancy, November, 1721," *NYHS Coll.* (1934), 160–64; Colden to Governor Cosby, Report on the State of the Lands in New York, 1732, *DHNY*, 1:377–89; and Colden to the Board of Trade, 20 Sept. 1764, *NYCD*, 7:654–55. High official fees also hindered subdivision and settlement of land. La Potin, "Minisink Grant." However, such fees provided much of the imperial agents' compensation when the assembly would not grant them salaries.

118. Kim, *Landlord and Tenant in Colonial New York*; Kim, "New Look at the Great Landlords of Eighteenth-Century New York"; Bonomi, *Factious People*, 5–7, 20; Smith, *History of the Province of New-York*, 1:215. But see Smith, *History of the*

Province of New-York, 1:225. See also Colden to the Board of Trade, 1 Mar. 1762, *NYCD*, 7:492; Abraham Lott to Rutger Bleecker, 21 Apr. 1770 and 23 May 1770, box 2, Bleecker, Collins, and Abeel Papers, NYPL; and Memorial of John Watts for Frederick Philipse, American Loyalist Transcripts, 41:627–28, NYPL.

119. For the growth of the manorial counties, see Countryman, *People in Revolution*, 42. Livingston and Governor Hunter attempted to use Palatine immigrants to extract naval stores from Livingston Manor, but most of the Germans fled for the Mohawk and Delaware valleys. See Instruction No. 623, 23 Jan. 1710, in Labaree, *Royal Instructions to British Colonial Governors*, 2:623; Higgins, *Expansion in New York*, 47–55; and Fingerhut, "Assimilation of Immigrants on the Frontier of New York," 2–3.

120. [Smith], "Consideration of the natural Advantages of *New-York*," 437–38. See also "On the Importation of *Mendicant* Foreigners," 28 Dec. 1752, in Klein, *Independent Reflector*, 83–85; "Of the Transportation of Felons," 15 Mar. 1753, in Klein, *Independent Reflector*, 164–69; and Livingston, *Letter to the Right Reverend Father in God, John Lord Bishop of Llandaff*.

121. For promotion of immigration, see Bailyn, *Voyagers to the West*, 573–637. New York's population trebled during the thirty years before the Revolution, a faster rate of growth than that of all of its contiguous neighbors except New Hampshire, which had a similar rate. Pennsylvania grew at a slightly slower rate. The populations of Massachusetts, Connecticut, and New Jersey doubled. U.S. Bureau of the Census, *Historical Statistics of the United States: Colonial Times to 1970*, 2:1168. On the census, see Locke, *Two Treatises of Government*, bk. I, p. 200, para. 33, and Henry Steele Commager, "America and the Enlightenment," in Barlow, Levy, and Masugi, *American Founding*, 268–71.

122. This is in contrast to his precise description of New York's eastern boundaries with other colonies. Smith, *History of the Province of New-York*, 1:222, 197–201. Colden also lamented that there were "no regulations for determining the boundaries between New York and Canada." Colden to the Board of Trade, 14 Feb. 1738, *NYCD*, 6:121–25.

123. See Additional Instruction to Gov. Moore, 5 July 1769, *NYCD*, 8:175; Smith, *Historical Memoirs*, 1:108; Lord Dartmouth to Governor Tryon, 3 Mar. 1772, *DHNY*, 1:578–79; Board of Trade to the Privy Council, 13 Feb. 1776, *DHNY*, 1:585–86; and Hoffman, *Edmund Burke, New York Agent*, 112–16, 218–20, 229. French claimants renounced their titles during the Revolution in the hope of regaining Canada. Macdonald, *Seigneurie of Alainville on Lake Champlain*, 29.

124. For New Jersey, see Smith, *History of the Province of New-York*, 1:216. The New Hampshire grant controversy can be traced in *DHNY*, 4:539–1034. See also Bellesiles, *Revolutionary Outlaws*; Jones, *Vermont in the Making*; and Schwarz, *Jarring Interests*, 168–74.

125. See Schwarz, *Jarring Interests*.

126. Historians estimate the Iroquois population at fifteen thousand in the mid-seventeenth century and about the same a century later, losses to disease and war offset in part by the absorption of the Tuscaroras (the Sixth Nation) in 1722. Hurley, "Children or Brethren," 16; Aquila, *Iroquois Restoration*, 30. On the Iro-

quois and imperial strategy, see Jennings, *Ambiguous Iroquois Empire*; Dennis, *Cultivating a Landscape of Peace*; Richter, *Ordeal of the Longhouse*; and Nammack, *Fraud, Politics, and the Dispossession of the Indians*.

127. On the decline of native-colonist relations in the eighteenth century, see Salisbury, "Indians' Old World," 458, and White, *Middle Ground*.

128. See John Tabor Kempe, draft response to Board of Trade, box 10, Goldsborough Banyar Papers, NYHS; Cadwallader Colden to the Board of Trade, 1 Mar. 1762, *NYCD*, 7:490–94; and Higgins, *Expansion in New York*, 30–32. For the arguments of Samuel Wharton and others that purchase from Native Americans did confer title, see Williams, "Jefferson, the Norman Yoke, and American Indian Lands," 183–86.

129. Edward Countryman nicely describes Johnson as "a cork blocking the only low-altitude access westward between the St. Lawrence and Georgia." Countryman, "Indians, the Social Order, and the Social Significance of the American Revolution," 348.

130. Bailyn, *Voyagers to the West*, 89–125.

131. [Kennedy], *Observations on the Importance of the Northern Colonies*, 10.

132. Greenberg, *Crime and Law Enforcement*, 71, 87–88. See generally Maier, *From Resistance to Revolution*, 16–26.

133. Jacob Van Schaack to Colden, 31 Dec. 1760, *NYHS Coll.* (1921), 383.

134. Greenberg, *Crime and Law Enforcement*, 158, 172–74. The papers of Attorney General John Tabor Kempe at the New-York Historical Society are replete with examples of violent resistance to authority.

135. Greenberg, *Crime and Law Enforcement*, 178–79; Moglen, "Settling the Law," 186.

136. Robert Livingston Jr. to Abraham Yates Jr., 3 Mar. 1755, Abraham Yates Jr. Papers, NYPL. I have found no record of this proclamation. On Massachusetts's support of the encroaching settlers, see Kim, *Landlord and Tenant in Colonial New York*, 281–345.

137. Livingston to Yates, 15 Dec. 1756 and 15 May 1757, Abraham Yates Jr. Papers, NYPL. Livingston also could not compel Yates to select his candidate for jailer; Cadwallader Colden's nominee got the post. Livingston to Yates, 21 Oct. 1754 and 31 Jan. 1755, Abraham Yates Jr. Papers, NYPL.

138. Livingston to Yates, 18 May 1757, Abraham Yates Jr. Papers, NYPL. The tenants, whom Livingston called "John Van Gelden" and sons and the council called "The Indians Johannes Vangelden and son," were released "upon advice of Lord Loudoun," commander in chief of the British military. New York Council, *Calendar of Council Minutes*, 433.

139. Countryman, *People in Revolution*, 47–55; Moglen, "Settling the Law," 148–49, 188–90; Kim, *Landlord and Tenant in Colonial New York*, 346–415.

140. Earl of Shelburne to Governor Moore, 11 Dec. 1766, *NYCD*, 7:879.

141. See Kim, *Landlord and Tenant in Colonial New York*, 415. For discussion of whether leniency in eighteenth-century British criminal law was a strategy to extract deference or a necessity caused by insufficient enforcement, see Langbein, "*Albion's* Fatal Flaw."

142. Hugh Wallace to William Johnson, 14 July 1772, *Johnson Papers*, 8:543–44.

143. There was nothing new in this blend of biblical and common law in the British world. See Haskins, *Law and Authority in Early Massachusetts*, 141–62, and Nenner, *By Colour of Law*, 6–13.

144. Typical was Ethan Allen's reaction to news of Governor William Tryon's proclamation that land west of the Connecticut River belonged to New York: "[H]ave we not always overcome them[?] . . . [I]f they shall ever come again we shall Drive them two hundred miles and send them to hell. . . . So your name is Tryon, tri on and be Damn he shall have his match if he comes here." Information of Benjamin Buck, 24 Jan. 1772, *DHNY*, 4:764. For quick resort to arms when legal argument failed, see Sheriff Robert Yates to John Tabor Kempe and James Duane, 20 July 1771, copy, Bancroft Collection, 35:577–89, NYPL. For the bounties on Kempe and James Duane, see Peter Yates to James Duane, 7 Apr. 1772, copy, Bancroft Collection, 35:619–21, NYPL.

145. Petition of Benjamin Hough to Colden, 9 Mar. 1775, *DHNY*, 4:891–93. Cf. Burke, *Popular Culture in Early Modern Europe*, 123–24. For penal whipping and banishment, see Goebel and Naughton, *Law Enforcement in Colonial New York*, 298–99, 690–91, 704–5. For legalistic arguments vindicating the New Hampshire grants, see Allen, *Brief Narrative of the Proceedings of the Government of New-York*, and [Young], *Some Reflections on the Disputes*. For popular appropriation of custom, "some part of the constitutionalist rhetoric of his rulers," and other legal claims of the "free-born Englishman" in eighteenth-century England, see E. P. Thompson, "Custom and Culture" and "The Patricians and the Plebs," in *Customs in Common*, 6, 74. See also Pencak, Dennis, and Newman, *Riot and Revelry in Early America*; Taylor, " 'Kind of Warr' "; Richard M. Brown, "Violence and the American Revolution," in Kurtz and Hutson, *Essays on the American Revolution*, 81–120; Moore, *Injustice*, 18; and Rudé, *Crowd in History*.

146. *Colonial Laws of New York*, 5:647–55; *Proceedings of the Convention of the Representatives of the New-Hampshire Settlers*, 16. The act bypassed grand jury indictments. It expired without effect; the new state government discharged all "offences" under the statute in 1778. Goebel and Naughton, *Law Enforcement in Colonial New York*, 445–47; *Laws of the State of New York*, 1:20–21. Importantly, some of these settlers were also land developers.

CHAPTER FOUR

1. Hamilton, *Sir William Johnson*, 312. A London pamphlet recounted Johnson's role in the colonies: *An Account of the Conferences held, and Treaties Made, between Major-General Sir William Johnson, Bart. and the Chief Sachems and Warriours.* On naming the land, see Michael Zuckerman, "Identity in British America: Unease in Eden," in Canny and Pagden, *Colonial Identity in the Atlantic World*, 128, and Seed, "Taking Possession and Reading Texts."

2. Johnson to the Board of Trade, Including Sentiments, Remarks and Additions Humbly Offered to the Lords Commissioners of Trade and Plantations, on

Their Plan for the Future Management of Indian Affairs, 8 Oct. 1764, *NYCD*, 7:657–66; Board of Trade to Johnson, Including the Plan for the Future Management of Indian Affairs, 10 July 1764, *NYCD*, 7:634–41. Following Francis Parkman, some historians have noted the revolutionary effect of the westward migration after 1763. See, e.g., Gipson, "American Revolution as an Aftermath of the Great War for Empire"; Peckham, "Speculations on the Colonial Wars"; Sosin, *Revolutionary Frontier*; and Abernethy, *Western Lands and the American Revolution*.

3. The Royal Proclamation of 7 Oct. 1763, in Jensen, *English Historical Documents*, 642–43; "Mr. Pownall's Sketch of a Report," appendix to Humphreys, "Lord Shelburne and the Proclamation of 1763," 259. The ministry's sources of information — the reports of the imperial agents — reveal that Johnson helped lay the groundwork for the proclamation in his correspondence to the Board of Trade throughout the Seven Years' War, and the board actively sought his advice while drafting it and the complementary "Plan for the Future Management of Indian Affairs," which followed in 1764. Order of the King in Council on a Report of the Lords of Trade, 23 Nov. 1761, *NYCD*, 7:472–76; Lords of Trade to the King, 2 Dec. 1761, *NYCD*, 7:477–79; Johnson to the Board of Trade, 17 May 1759, *DHNY*, 2:781–85; Johnson to Richard Peters, 30 Mar. 1763, *Johnson Papers*, 4:76; Board of Trade to Johnson, 5 Aug. 1763, *NYCD*, 7:535–36; Johnson to the Board of Trade, 13 Nov. 1763, *NYCD*, 7:578; Johnson to Gage, 23 Dec. 1763, *Johnson Papers*, 4:272; Board of Trade to Johnson, 10 July 1764, *NYCD*, 7:634–41; Johnson to the Board of Trade, 8 Oct. 1764, *Johnson Papers*, 4:556–63; Johnson to Colden, 9 Oct. 1764, *Johnson Papers*, 4:565–67. See also Colden to the Board of Trade, 12 Oct. 1764, *NYCD*, 7:667–70. For similar skepticism about London's role in generating western policy, see Sosin, *Whitehall and the Wilderness*, 46–78.

4. Johnson to the Board of Trade, 20 Aug. 1766, *NYCD*, 7:853.

5. Johnson to Secretary Conway, 28 June 1766, *NYCD*, 7:834–36.

6. Johnson to the Earl of Shelburne, 16 Dec. 1766, *NYCD*, 7:880–82. See generally Higgins, *Expansion in New York*, 83–99.

7. *NYCD*, 7:881.

8. Johnson to Colden, 20 Feb. 1761, *Johnson Papers*, 3:338–41; Johnson to Colden, 20 Mar. 1762, *Johnson Papers*, 3:652–53; Colden to Johnson, 7 Mar. 1761 and 27 Dec. 1761, *NYHS Coll.* (1876), 70–71, 143–44; Johnson to Colden, 25 July 1763, *Johnson Papers*, 4:176–77; Johnson to Amherst, [5 Feb. 1762], *Johnson Papers*, 3:618–20; A Meeting with Canajoharies, 10 Mar. 1763, *Johnson Papers*, 4:50–61.

9. Johnson to Clinton, 7 May 1747, *NYCD*, 6:362.

10. George Klock Jr. to Mr. Bleecker, Son of John Bleecker, 23 Nov. 1769, box 2, Bleecker, Collins, and Abeel Papers, NYPL.

11. Johnson to Colden, 20 Feb. 1761, *Johnson Papers*, 3:339; Colden to Johnson, 7 Mar. 1761, *NYHS Coll.* (1876), 70. See also Calendar of Letter, 29 Dec. 1763, *Johnson Papers*, 4:280.

12. Johnson to Shelburne, 16 Dec. 1766, *NYCD*, 7:883. In desperation, General Thomas Gage applauded an assembly bill proposing capital punishment for those who illegally settled on Indian lands unless they moved within thirty days of warn-

ing. Gage to William Johnson, 31 Jan. 1768, *Johnson Papers*, 6:86. It never became law.

13. [Young], *Some Reflections on the Disputes*, 14. The titles at issue were from Massachusetts and New Hampshire governors. On Young, see Maier, "Reason and Revolution."

14. [John Henry Lydius], "Considerations, which may be improved to induce his Majesty to erect a new & distinct Colony, a certain Tract of Country in North America, scituate, & may be bounded by or near the lines hereafter described," [ca. 1764], Henry Lydius Misc., NYHS.

15. For background, see the Board of Trade to Hardy, 19 Mar. 1756, *NYCD*, 7:77, and *General Assembly Journal, 1766–1776*, 2:497, 510, 525, 764–65. See also Higgins, *Expansion in New York*, 27–29, 83–85, and Nammack, *Fraud, Politics, and the Dispossession of the Indians*, 53–69.

16. [Young], *Some Reflections on the Disputes*, 19; *General Assembly Journal, 1691–1765*, 2:764 (4 Oct. 1764). On the importance of title recordation in early New York, see Moglen, "Settling the Law," 119–20, and Nissenson, "Development of a Land Registration System in New York."

17. Johnson to Colden, 27 Feb. 1765, *Johnson Papers*, 4:653, 654.

18. Colden to Johnson, 15 Mar. 1765, *Johnson Papers*, 4:681–82.

19. Johnson to Colden, 21 Mar. 1765, *Johnson Papers*, 4:694. A scire facias was the writ used to revoke letters patent.

20. John Tabor Kempe to Johnson, 12 Aug. 1765, *Johnson Papers*, 4:817–19. Several years later, Kempe argued the same in a report to the Board of Trade: "Purchases from the Indian Natives as of their aboriginal Right have never been held to be a legal Title in this Province, the Maxim obtaining here as well as in England that the King is the Fountain of all real Property and that from this Source all Titles are to be derived." Kempe to Board of Trade, [1773], draft, box 10, Goldsborough Banyar Papers, NYHS.

21. Commissions were letters patent issued under the great seal of England, the king's highest instrument of delegation, while instructions were issued under a lesser seal. Labaree, *Royal Government in America*, 6–7; Keith, *Constitutional History of the First British Empire*, 180–81. On early modern notions of the king's interest in property, see Aylmer, " 'Property' in Seventeenth-Century England." Kempe's interpretation of aboriginal title was similar to Chief Justice John Marshall's sixty years later. *Johnson v. McIntosh*, 21 U.S. 543 (1823).

22. See Freedoms and Exemptions Granted by the West India Company to All Patroons . . . , 7 June 1629, *Laws and Ordinances of New Netherland*, 9, and Smith, *History of the Province of New-York*, 1:260.

23. Johnson to Kempe, 6 Nov. 1765, *Johnson Papers*, 4:862–64. See also Johnson to Kempe, 5 Sept. 1765, *Johnson Papers*, 11:923–27, and Kempe to Johnson, 23 Sept. 1765, *Johnson Papers*, 11:948–51.

24. Johnson to Colden, 25 July 1763, *Johnson Papers*, 4:177.

25. Johnson to Kempe, 1 Oct. 1762, *Johnson Papers*, 10:541–42.

26. Johnson to Kempe, 6 Nov. 1765, *Johnson Papers*, 4:862–64; Johnson, "A

Review of the Progressive State of the Trade, Politics and Proceedings of the Indians in the Northern District . . . ," [Sept. 1767?], *NYCD*, 7:972. See also Johnson to the Board of Trade, 10 Oct. 1764, *NYCD*, 7:673, and Moore to the Earl of Shelburne, 8 Nov. 1766, *NYCD*, 7:876–77. Johnson negotiated a settlement in 1768 in which the Mohawks relinquished title to the eastern part of their claim in return for a cash payment. John Morin Scott et al. to Johnson, 13 July 1768, *Johnson Papers*, 6:273–74; Johnson to the Earl of Hillsborough, 17 Aug. 1768, *NYCD*, 8:94; Higgins, *Expansion in New York*, 84–85.

27. Johnson to the Board of Trade, 30 Oct. 1764, *NYCD*, 7:672. See also Cronon, *Changes in the Land*, 54–81.

28. Johnson to John Pownall, 18 Apr. 1763, *Johnson Papers*, 4:90–91; George Croghan to Johnson, 14 Apr. 1764, *Johnson Papers*, 4:396–99; Colden to the Board of Trade, 31 May 1765, *NYCD*, 7:741–43; Johnson to Richard Peters, 30 Jan. 1766, *Johnson Papers*, 5:20–22; Johnson to John Johnson, 26 Jan. 1767, *Johnson Papers*, 5:475–78; Adam Gordon to Johnson, 17 May 1767, *Johnson Papers*, 12:316–17; John Pownall to John Johnson, 12 June 1767, *Johnson Papers*, 5:564; Order in Council, 22 May 1769, *Johnson Papers*, 6:770–73; Johnson to Thomas Penn, 15 Sept. 1769, *Johnson Papers*, 7:176–78; Instruction on Purchase of Lands from Indians, 1755, in Labaree, *Royal Instructions to British Colonial Governors*, 2:467–68; Hamilton, "American Knight in Britain," 121, 127. Many imperial agents in the colonies viewed land grants as their primary compensation. See, e.g., Kempe to Johnson, 23 May 1766, *Johnson Papers*, 12:92–93, and Crary, "American Dream." Johnson's grant was unusual only in its size.

29. Johnson to General Jeffrey Amherst, 30 July 1763, *NYCD*, 7:534; Johnson to Amherst, 25 Aug. 1763, *NYCD*, 7:542–44; Johnson to the Board of Trade, 25 Sept. 1763, *NYCD*, 7:559–62; Johnson to Colden, 20 Dec. 1763, *Johnson Papers*, 4:282.

30. Johnson to Thomas Gage, 23 Dec. 1771, *Johnson Papers*, 8:348–49.

31. Johnson to Lord Hillsborough, 27 June 1772, *NYCD*, 8:300–301.

32. For the Stanwix Treaty journal and deed, see *NYCD*, 8:111–37. Contemporary criticisms of Johnson include Lord Hillsborough to Johnson, 14 Jan. 1769, *NYCD*, 8:144–45, and Lords of Trade to the King, 25 Apr. 1769, *NYCD*, 8:158–63. For acceptance of the Iroquois cession by the Privy Council while disallowing grants to Croghan and other Johnson associates, see Lord Hillsborough to Johnson, 13 May 1769, *NYCD*, 8:165–66. See also Sosin, *Whitehall and the Wilderness*, 165–80; White, *Middle Ground*, 353; Marshall, "Sir William Johnson and the Treaty of Fort Stanwix"; Billington, "Fort Stanwix Treaty of 1768"; Alvord, *Mississippi Valley in British Politics*, 2:72–76; and Halsey, *Old New York Frontier*, 103–5. For Johnson's belief that the Native Americans might remain hunters for another century, and also that this would not prevent them from being "Civilized Member[s] of Society," see Johnson to William Smith (of Philadelphia), 10 Apr. 1767, *Johnson Papers*, 5:530.

33. Johnson to the Earl of Dartmouth, 4 Nov. 1772, *NYCD*, 8:314–17. Other shareholders in the new colony included George Croghan and Benjamin Franklin. On the Stanwix Treaty and debate over new colonies, see Representations of the

Board of Trade on the State of Indian Affairs, 7 Mar. 1768, *NYCD*, 8:19–31; Alvord, *Mississippi Valley in British Politics*, 2:119–48; Alden, *John Stuart*, 246–60; Gipson, *British Empire before the American Revolution*, 11:471–78; Sosin, *Whitehall and the Wilderness*, 181–210; Volwiler, *George Croghan and the Westward Movement*, 261–77; and Hinderaker, *Elusive Empires*, 166–75.

34. 14 Geo. III, c. 83.

35. While condemning quitrents, Vermonters declared "private property . . . subservient to public uses," adding that the state must compensate for property so taken. Vermont Constitution, 1777, preamble, chap. 1, art. XVII and art. II. The right to emigrate was part of some continental natural-law theories but not the common law. Reid, *Authority of Rights*, 82–86, 119–20. See also Chafee, *Three Human Rights in the Constitution of 1787*, 163–67, 171–84. Thomas Jefferson's *A Summary View of the Rights of British America*, written three years earlier, may have provided some of the language for the Vermont provision on the right to emigrate. The Virginia legislature did not accept his provision. Thomas Jefferson, "Draft Instructions to the Virginia Delegates in the Continental Congress (MS Text of *A Summary View, &c.*)," [July 1774], *Papers of Thomas Jefferson*, 1:121–37; Virginia Convention, "Instructions by the Virginia Convention to Their Delegates in Congress," August 1774, in Jefferson, *Papers of Thomas Jefferson*, 1:141–44. Cf. Konig, "Contingency and Constitutionalism in Colonial New York," 383.

36. [William Livingston], "The Watch Tower," *New-York Gazette, Revived in the Weekly Post-Boy*, 27 Jan. 1752. On the jury in early America, see Greenberg, *Crime and Law Enforcement*, 172, 175–76; Goebel and Naughton, *Law Enforcement in Colonial New York*, 603–10; Nelson, *Americanization of the Common Law*; and Stimson, *American Revolution in the Law*.

37. *New-York Gazette, Revived in the Weekly Post-Boy*, 27 Jan. 1752. Livingston cited seventeenth-century antiquarian Henry Spelman, "the principal architect" of the periodization of English history into prefeudal, feudal, and postfeudal. Pocock, *Ancient Constitution*, 119.

38. Moglen, "Taking the Fifth," 1105–11; Goebel and Naughton, *Law Enforcement in Colonial New York*, 379–83. Summary criminal jurisdiction survived the Revolution. See *Jackson ex dem. Wood v. Wood*, 2 Cow. 819 (N.Y. 1824).

39. John Tabor Kempe to Benjamin Strong, Selah Strong, and Richard Wood-hull, 3 Mar. 1769 and 9 June 1769 (photocopy), box 1, John Tabor Kempe Papers, NYHS. See also Moglen, "Settling the Law," 162–63, and Goebel and Naughton, *Law Enforcement in Colonial New York*, 379–83, 606–7.

40. Johnson to the Earl of Dartmouth, 4 Nov. 1772, *NYCD*, 8:317, 316. There is no evidence that Native Americans served on New York juries. There were no stated racial or religious qualifications, but a juror had to own a sixty-pound free-hold or earn the same in rent every year. An Act for Returning of Able & Sufficient Juries, 27 Nov. 1741 (made permanent 6 Dec. 1746), *Colonial Laws of New York*, 3:185–92, 599. For Native American participation in other colonies' courts, see Kawashima, *Puritan Justice and the Indian*, 127–33; Ramirez, "Mixed Jury and the Ancient Custom of Trial by Jury De Medietate Linguae," 789–96; Hoffer, *Law and People in Colonial America*, 31–32; and Katherine Hermes, " 'Justice Will Be Done

Us': Algonquin Demands for Reciprocity in the Courts of European Settlers," in Tomlins and Mann, *Many Legalities of Early America*, 123–49.

41. Colden to the Board of Trade, 12 Oct. 1764, *NYCD*, 7:668; Colden to Governor George Clinton, 8 Aug. 1751, *NYCD*, 6:741. See also Johnson to Kempe, 6 Nov. 1765, *Johnson Papers*, 4:862–64, and Johnson, "A Review of the Progressive State of the Trade, Politics and Proceedings of the Indians . . . ," [Sept. 1767?], *NYCD*, 7:972, 976. It is ironic that the Iroquois appeared "ambulatory" to Colden, who moved from Scotland to London, then to Philadelphia and on to New York. Compared with other North American Indians they were sedentary agriculturalists, a source of their strength. Wessel, "Agriculture and Iroquois Hegemony in New York."

42. Proclamation of 1763, in Jensen, *English Historical Documents*, 643.

43. Wiener, *Civilians under Military Justice*, 66–68. The 1765 Mutiny Act is better known as the Quartering Act. On the extension of military command after 1763, see Carter, "Military Office in America."

44. Board of Trade to Johnson, Along with Plan for the Future Management of Indian Affairs, 10 July 1764, *NYCD*, 7:757–66; *Journal of the Commissioners for Trade and Plantations*, 70–71; Johnson to the Board of Trade, including Sentiments, Remarks and Additions Humbly Offered to the Lords Commissioners of Trade and Plantations, on Their Plan for the Future Management of Indian Affairs, 7 Oct. 1764, *NYCD*, 7:661–66 (for an unedited version, see Alvord and Carter, *Critical Period*, 327–42); Johnson to Shelburne, 3 Dec. 1767, *NYCD*, 7:100. For Johnson's lobbying for the plan, which included the personal efforts of his deputy in London, see George Croghan to Johnson, 24 Feb. 1764, *Johnson Papers*, 4:339–42, and Croghan to Johnson, 10 Mar. 1764, *Johnson Papers*, 4:362–63. The commissary system never developed to meet all of Johnson's expectations, but he did implement parts of it. For discussion of commissary selection and appointment, see Johnson to Croghan, 15 Mar. 1766, *Johnson Papers*, 5:76–77, and Johnson to General Gage, [15 Mar. 1766], *Johnson Papers*, 5:80–81; for a sample commission, see Warrant and Instructions to Alexander McKee, [24 Mar. 1766], *Johnson Papers*, 12:49–52. The best scholarly treatment of the 1764 plan is Marshall, "Colonial Protest and Imperial Retrenchment."

45. Johnson to John Brown, 31 Oct. 1766, *Johnson Papers*, 5:404–5.

46. Johnson to John Brown, 31 Oct. 1766, *Johnson Papers*, 5:404–5; Benjamin Roberts to Johnson, 30 Sept. 1767, *Johnson Papers*, 5:710–17; Jehu Hay to George Croghan, 15 Oct. 1767, *Johnson Papers*, 5:728–31.

47. Johnson to General Thomas Gage, 24 Nov. 1767, *DHNY*, 2:885–88; Board of Trade to the King, 7 Mar. 1768, *NYCD*, 8:19–31; Johnson to Henry Moore, 24 Nov. 1768, *Johnson Papers*, 6:493–96. For partial treatment of the commissary plan of 1764, see Gipson, *British Empire before the American Revolution*, 11:431–37, and Alden, *John Stuart*, 142–55. Peter Marshall concludes that "[c]olonial unrest, personal prudence, political instability in England, proved of greater importance in contributing to the failure of imperial regulation than did the financial cost of control." Marshall, "Colonial Protest and Imperial Retrenchment," 17.

48. For these contacts, see, e.g., Robert Calendar to William Edgar, 31 Dec.

1763, William Edgar Papers, vol. 1, NYPL; Lord Shelburne to General Thomas Gage, 11 Dec. 1766, in Gage, *Correspondence*, 2:47–51; and Humphreys, "Notes and Documents." See generally Katz, *Newcastle's New York*, and Olson, *Making the Empire Work*.

49. Even some traders lamented that they were "amongst a parcel of rascals, who mock at authority and government." William Maxwell to William Edgar, 3 Sept. 1767, William Edgar Papers, vol. 1, NYPL; Frederick Hambach to Edgar, 23 Mar. 1767, William Edgar Papers, vol. 1, NYPL.

50. See Leder, *Robert Livingston*, 250–52.

51. Johnson to Kempe, 26 Dec. 1766, *Johnson Papers*, 12:233. The Schermerhorns were a family of Dutch extraction based in Schenectady, founded by fur traders to evade the traditional Albany monopoly. See Guzzardo, "Sir William Johnson's Official Family," 7–8; Monroe, *Schenectady*, 43–44. See also Norton, *Fur Trade in Colonial New York*, esp. 43–59, and Charles H. McIlwain, introduction to *Abridgment of the Indian Affairs*, xxxv–lxxv.

52. Johnson to Amherst, 30 July 1763, *NYCD*, 7:534; Johnson to Amherst, 25 Aug. 1763, *NYCD*, 7:542–44.

53. Johnson to the Board of Trade, 13 Nov. 1763, *NYCD*, 579–80. For the imperial agents' inflation of the "Iroquois Empire" (which paralleled their inflation of the British), see Jones, *License for Empire*, 34, 61–62; Jennings, *Ambiguous Iroquois Empire*, 13–16, 162, 212, 373–74; Richard L. Haan, "Covenant and Consensus: Iroquois and English, 1676–1760," in Richter and Merrell, *Beyond the Covenant Chain*, 56; Richter, *Ordeal of the Longhouse*, 136–37, 190, 275–76; and Hinderaker, "'Four Indian Kings' and the Imaginative Construction of the First British Empire."

54. In addition to fifteen hundred pounds for damages, the jury awarded seventy-six pounds for Forsey's legal expenses. *Forsey v. Cunningham*, Supreme Court of Colonial New York, Writ of Execution, 27 Oct. 1765, file P-186-K-8, HR.

55. Colden to Board of Trade, 7 Nov. 1764, *NYCD*, 7:676–78; Smith, *Historical Memoirs*, 1:24–32; Smith, *Appeals to the Privy Council*, 383–416; Johnson, "George Harison's Protest." See also *Report of an Action of Assault, Battery, and Wounding*.

56. William Smith Jr. to Governor Monckton, 5 Nov. 1764, and Smith to Monckton, 25 Jan. 1765, in Smith, *Historical Memoirs*, 1:26–28.

57. Horsmanden to Monckton, 8 Dec. 1764 and 10 Sept. 1767, George Chalmers Collection, NYPL.

58. Smith, *Historical Memoirs*, 1:24; *Report of an Action of Assault, Battery, and Wounding*, 43–45; Watts to General Monckton, 10 Dec. 1764, *NYHS Coll.* (1928), 313; Report of the Attorney and Solicitor Generals on Appeals in New-York, 2 Nov. 1765, *NYCD*, 7:815–16. Little is known about Colden's knowledge of Scottish law, so it is difficult to measure the sincerity and opportunism in his remark to Watts.

59. Colden's Opinion on Appeals, [Jan. 1765], *NYHS Coll.* (1923), 1–7; Colden to the Board of Trade, 22 Jan. 1765, *NYCD*, 7:695–700.

60. Colden's Opinion on Appeals, [Jan. 1765], *NYHS Coll.* (1923), 1–7; Colden to the Board of Trade, 22 Jan. 1765, *NYCD*, 7:695–700. On the assembly's

power of nomination, see Colden, Observations on the Balance of Power in Government, [1744–45], *NYHS Coll.* (1935), 257. See also John Tabor Kempe to Colden, 31 Oct. 1764, *NYHS Coll.* (1923), 368–71, and Kempe to Colden, 16 Nov. 1764, *NYHS Coll.* (1923), 378. Thomas Pownall drew the same lesson from Hale in a pamphlet published in London a few months earlier, but Colden must have arrived at his conclusions independently: his quotations are more accurate. Pownall, *Administration of the Colonies* (1764), 55; Hale, *History of the Common Law of England*, 90.

61. This in addition to "Appeales . . . in Case of Error" involving upwards of twenty pounds. Judicature Act, 6 May 1691, *Colonial Laws of New York*, 1:229–31; Moglen, "Settling the Law," 168–70. For provincial criticism of local courts, see Smith, *History of the Province of New-York*, 1:260–61.

62. *The Conduct of Cadwallader Colden, Esquire* (London, 1767), in *NYHS Coll.* (1877), 429–67; Colden to Earl of Shelburne, 28 Nov. 1767, *NYCD*, 7:994–97; Colden to Lord Mansfield, 22 Jan. 1768, *NYHS Coll.* (1877), 146–50; Colden to Mansfield, 29 Jan. 1768, *NYHS Coll.* (1877), 154–57. Livingston's multiple offices became controversial in the late 1760s. Livingston, *Address of Mr. Livingston to the House of Assembly*; *General Assembly Journal, 1766–1776*, 1769–70: 46 (21 Dec. 1769); *General Assembly Journal, 1766–1776*, 1770–71: 52 (25 Jan. 1771); Hoffman, *Edmund Burke, New York Agent*, 103–4, 194–98.

63. Smith, *History of the Province of New-York*, 1:230.

64. "Note of Recognizances . . . ," [1762], box C–F, Kempe Legal Papers, NYHS. This and related documents implicate Waddel Cunningham, Jacob Walton, George Harison, William Kennedy, Thomas Livingston, Abraham Lott, John Fox, Thomas White, William Paulding, Jacob Wendel, Samuel Van Horne, Jacobus Van Zandt, and William Moore, among others. They dealt directly with merchants in France and traded everything from meat to naval stores. An early governor estimated that illegal trade accounted for a quarter of all imports. Earl of Bellomont to the Board of Trade, 13 May 1799, *NYCD*, 5:516. For contemporary admission of the illegal trade by one New York family, see White, *Beekman Mercantile Papers*, 1:124, 185, 188, 283, 503, 2:686–94, 3:1323. Insurance was even available in London to cover confiscation. Beekman to Joseph Scott, 12 Apr. 1754, in White, *Beekman Mercantile Papers*, 1:211.

65. Beekman to Joseph Scott (London), 12 Apr. 1754, in White, *Beekman Mercantile Papers*, 1:211.

66. Quoted in Smith, *Historical Memoirs*, 1:161.

67. Smith, *History of the Province of New-York*, 1:230.

68. See *NYCD*, 6:571–76, and chapter 2, pp. 64–68.

69. *Archibald Kennedy qui tam v. Thirty Two Barrels of Gunpowder* (1754), in Hough, *Reports of Cases in the Vice Admiralty*, 82–83; *George Spencer qui tam v. William Richardson et al.* (1760), in *Reports of Cases in the Vice Admiralty*, 181–83; Smith, *Appeals to the Privy Council*, 515–17. See also Goebel and Naughton, *Law Enforcement in Colonial New York*, 235–38, 300–302. The vice admiralty judges, Lewis Morris Jr. and then his son Richard, acceded to the diminution of their jurisdiction. Prize, not smuggling, cases formed the core of their caseload.

70. See, e.g., The Petition of George Spencer to Governor Robert Monckton, 2 Aug. 1763, George Chalmers Collection, NYPL.

71. See Lovejoy, "Rights Imply Equality," and Ubbelohde, *Vice-Admiralty Courts and the American Revolution*.

72. Burke, "Speech on Conciliation," in *Works of the Right Honourable Edmund Burke*, 2:124–25. See also Klein, "New York Lawyers and the Coming of the American Revolution."

73. Colden to Halifax, 22 Feb. 1765, *NYCD*, 7:705–6; Colden to the Board of Trade, 22 Jan. 1765, *NYCD*, 7:699; Colden to the Board of Trade, 9 Nov. 1765, *NYCD*, 7:774; Colden to Secretary Conway, 14 Jan. 1766, *NYCD*, 7:805. For the Stamp Act riots in New York, see Nash, *Urban Crucible*, 184–99.

74. Johnson to Colden, 13 Sept. 1765, *NYHS Coll.* (1923), 76.

75. Johnson to General Thomas Gage, 17 May 1766, *Johnson Papers*, 5:216.

76. Gage to Secretary Conway, 21 Dec. 1765, in Gage, *Correspondence*, 1:79; Gage to Conway, 8 Nov. 1765, in Gage, *Correspondence*, 72–73. See also Gage to Johnson, 5 May 1766, *Johnson Papers*, 5:201. For a different view of the seamen, see Lemisch, "Jack Tar in the Streets."

77. Johnson to Colden, 20 Feb. 1761, *Johnson Papers*, 3:338–41; Johnson to Colden, 20 Mar. 1762, *Johnson Papers*, 3:652–53; Colden to Johnson, 7 Mar. 1761, *NYHS Coll.* (1922), 70–71; Colden to Johnson, 27 Dec. 1761, *NYHS Coll.* (1876), 143–44; Johnson to Colden, 25 July 1763, *NYHS Coll.* (1922), 228–31; Rudolph Shoemaker to Johnson, 11 Apr. 1772, *Johnson Papers*, 8:442; Johnson to Colden, 19 Mar. 1761, *NYHS Coll.* (1922), 18. On the influx of Irish and Scots, see Bailyn, *Voyagers to the West*, 573–637. For analogous alliances between imperial officials and indigenous leaders in Britain's later colonies, see Cannadine, *Ornamentalism*, 58–70.

78. Frey, *Minute Book of the Committee of Safety of Tryon County*. The remaining Johnsons fought for the crown and then fled to Canada. It is in this context of frustration that one must interpret the claim that Johnson ruled Tryon County "completely." Countryman, *People in Revolution*, 33; Guzzardo, "Democracy along the Mohawk."

79. Colden to Governor William Shirley, 25 July 1749, *NYHS Coll.* (1920), 124–25; Colden to John Catherwood, 21 Nov. 1749, *NYHS Coll.* (1920), 163. See generally Klein, "Prelude to Revolution in New York."

80. Colden to John Pownall, 12 Jan. 1762, *NYHS Coll.* (1876), 154. In addition, Prat was an Anglican and married the sister of Samuel Auchmuty, rector of New York's Trinity Church.

81. Prat to the Board of Trade, 24 May 1762, *NYCD*, 7:501–2. Prat's dependence on external patronage brought on New Yorkers' hostility. Robert Livingston Jr. to Abraham Yates Jr., 8 Dec. 1761, Abraham Yates Jr. Papers, NYPL.

82. Colden to the Earl of Egremont, 14 Sept. 1763, *NYCD*, 7:549. See also Colden to the Board of Trade, 6 Dec. 1765, *NYCD*, 7:795–800.

83. Colden to the Board of Trade, 7 Nov. 1764, *NYCD*, 7:677.

84. Colden to the Board of Trade, 6 Dec. 1765, *NYCD* 7:795–800. See also Colden to Governor William Cosby, 1732, *DHNY*, 1:377–89. On eighteenth-

century sociology, see Meek, *Social Science and the Ignoble Savage*, and Verburg, *Two Faces of Interest*.

85. Colden, "Comments on Government in General," [n.d.], Cadwallader Colden Papers, Misc. Mss., NYHS. See also Shammas, "Cadwallader Colden and the Role of the King's Prerogative." Colden's handwriting is unclear; he may have written "20,000" acres rather than "10,000."

86. "The Dougliad, no. 1," *New-York Gazette and Weekly Mercury*, 23 Apr. 1770. For the reasonable conclusion that Duane was the author, see Alexander, *Revolutionary Conservative*, 96 n. 14. See also James Duane to Robert Livingston Jr., 19 Feb. 1770, Livingston Family Papers, Gilder Lehrman Collection, Pierpont Morgan Library, New York City.

87. "Dougliad, no. 8," *New-York Gazette and Weekly Mercury*, 28 May 1770. The act provided that "a sum be granted unto his Majesty for furnishing the troops quartered in this colony with necessaries." An Act for Making a Further Provision of [two thousand] pounds for Furnishing His Majesty's Troops Quartered in This Colony with Necessaries for One Year, 5 Jan. 1770, *Colonial Laws of New York*, 5:23–24. The remaining "Dougliad" essays argued that there was precedent for the assembly's appropriation and that there was consent for this particular instance. For the Restraining Act, which threatened suspension of the New York Assembly, see Kammen, *Colonial New York*, 356.

88. *General Assembly Journal, 1766–1776*, 1769–70: 39–42; *General Assembly Journal, 1766–1776*, 1770–71: 7–8; Alexander Colden to Anthony Todd, 11 July 1770, *NYCD*, 8:220; Norman MacLeod to Johnson, 12 Mar. 1770, *Johnson Papers*, 7:483. For the elections of 1768 and 1769, see Champagne, "Family Politics versus Constitutional Principles"; Bonomi, *Factious People*, 246–78; and Friedman, "New York Assembly Elections of 1768 and 1769."

89. Jack P. Greene and Richard Jellison, "The Currency Act of 1764 in Metropolitan-Colonial Relations, 1764–76," in Greene, *Negotiated Authorities*, 456–58.

90. "The Dougliad, no. 7," *New-York Gazette and Weekly Mercury*, 21 May 1770. The separation of the three functional powers under the English constitution, in which the judges' role is "*jus dicere et non jus dare*," is discussed in "The Dougliad, no. 6," *New-York Gazette and Weekly Mercury*, 14 May 1770.

91. Cadwallader Colden, "The Rise & Progress of the Publick Dissentions of New York" (n.d., ca. 1750), Cadwallader Colden Papers, Misc. Mss., NYHS.

92. Memorial of Daniel Horsmanden to Governor Monckton, 4 June 1763, George Chalmers Collection, NYPL; Smith, *History of the Province of New-York*, 2:270–71; Chalmers, *Opinions of Eminent Lawyers*, 491. Good behavior tenure in the English courts was established in the aftermath of the Glorious Revolution. Havighurst, "James II and the Twelve Men in Scarlet."

93. Colden to the Board of Trade, 5 Apr. 1761, *NYCD*, 7:461; Colden to Board of Trade, 2 June 1761, *NYCD*, 7:467; Board of Trade to Privy Council, 18 Nov. 1761, *NYCD*, 7:471–72; Board of Trade to the King, 2 Dec. 1761, *NYCD*, 7:479; Order of the King in Council, 23 Nov. 1761, *NYCD*, 7:474–75.

94. See Smith, *History of the Province of New-York*, 1:267; New York City Bar Agreement, 26 Nov. 1756, in Hamlin, *Legal Education in Colonial New York*, 162; and Law Society Agreement, July 1764, box 2, lot 201, William Smith Jr. Papers, NYPL. Criticism of the legal system for "Excessive fees and dilatoriness of the Courts of Law" was common, but some provincials suspected that Colden's innovations were not designed to reform these problems. Robert Livingston Jr. to Abraham Yates Jr., 8 Dec. 1761, Abraham Yates Jr. Papers, NYPL.

95. Baker, *Introduction to English Legal History*, 162–65. On "legal literates" who dominated practice before the formation of bar associations, see Bilder, "Lost Lawyers."

96. Eben Moglen describes this process as one of "localization," arguing that by the mid-eighteenth century the bar was increasingly born and educated in the colonies, where before it had relied on personnel from and training in England. Moglen, "Settling the Law," 65–108. See also Hamlin, *Legal Education in Colonial New York*, 4; Klein, "From Community to Status"; and Murrin, "Legal Transformation," 540–72.

97. See An Act to Revise, Digest, & Print the Laws of this Colony, 24 Dec. 1750, *Colonial Laws of New York*, 3:832–35, and Livingston and Smith, *Laws of New-York from the Year 1691 to 1751*. A second volume of the revised statutes was published in 1762.

98. Law Society Agreement, July 1764, box 2, lot 201, William Smith Jr. Papers, NYPL.

99. John Watts to Sir Willam Baker, 22 Jan. 1762, *NYHS Coll.* (1928), 3. On the Inns of Court and their decline, see Holdsworth, "Elizabethan Age in English Legal History and Its Results," 333, and Hamlin, *Legal Education in Colonial New York*, 14–17.

100. "Of Abuses in the Practice of the *LAW*," 26 July 1753, in Klein, *Independent Reflector*, 299–304. Cf. "The Importance of the Office of the Justice of the Peace, with Qualifications Necessary for Its Due Discharge," 13 Sept. 1753, in Klein, *Independent Reflector*, 352–57.

101. Law Society Agreement. See also "Of Abuses in the Practice of the *LAW*," 26 July 1753, in Klein, *Independent Reflector*, 299–304, and "The Importance of the Office of the Justice of the Peace, with Qualifications Necessary for Its Due Discharge," 13 Sept. 1753, in Klein, *Independent Reflector*, 352–57.

102. Minutes of the Moot Club, 1770–75, NYHS.

103. Letter to the Council, 23 Jan. 1758, New York Council, *Journal of the Legislative Council*, 2:1324.

104. Watts to Colonel Isaac Barré, 28 Feb. 1762, *NYHS Coll.* (1928), 27. Watts did observe that "the differences between a man eminent in his profession & a low, dirty worthless, groveling petty fogger is as great as the distance from earth to Heaven." Watts to John Watts Jr., 1 Apr. 1772, John Watts Papers, NYHS.

105. Robert R. Livingston to Robert Livingston, 18 Sept. 1767, copy, Bancroft Collection, vol. 275, NYPL.

106. Horsmanden immigrated to New York from England before 1730. For his

ambiguous position in provincial society, see Smith, *History of the Province of New-York*, 2:100–101, 270–71. His court sat last in April 1776. Minutes of the Supreme Court of Judicature, 1775–81 (engrossed), HR.

107. The imperial agents did not oppose good behavior tenure in all offices, just those they could not control. A decade later Colden tried to secure good behavior tenure for his son as surveyor general, the office he held for more than fifty years. When William Smith Jr., who had followed his father onto the council, mentioned the earlier contrary instruction, David Colden argued there was "no Instruction, & at length reminded me that the Book of Instructions *was burnt last Winter*"! Smith, *Historical Memoirs*, 1:204–6.

108. Brewer, *Sinews of Power*; John Brewer, "The Eighteenth-Century British State: Contexts and Issues," in Stone, *Imperial State at War*, 60; Thomas Ertman, "*The Sinews of Power* and European State-Building Theory," in Stone, *Imperial State at War*, 33–51.

109. See, e.g., Aylmer, "From Office-holding to Civil Service"; Stokes, "Bureaucracy and Ideology"; and Rubinstein, "End of the 'Old Corruption' in Britain."

110. The eleven volumes of Colden papers published by the New-York Historical Society are a monument to his habit.

111. Douglass, *Summary, Historical and Political*, 1:242, 243, 257.

112. Thomas Pownall, *Administration of the Colonies*, 4th ed. (1768), xv, 21, 31, 34, 35.

113. Pownall, Speech of 19 Apr. 1769, copy, Bancroft Collection, vol. 326, NYPL.

114. Pownall to Dr. S. Cooper, 14 July 1770, copy, Bancroft Collection, vol. 326, NYPL.

115. Bellot, *William Knox*.

116. Knox, *Extra-Official State Papers*, 15–17.

117. Stokes, *View of the Constitution of the British Colonies*.

118. See Baker, *Introduction to English Legal History*, 177–99.

119. Lord Mansfield to George Grenville, 24 Dec. 1764, in Smith, *Grenville Papers*, 2:476–78. The Quebec Act was largely the work of William Knox, undersecretary of state in the American Department. Bellot, *William Knox*, 122, 126–27. For the deportation of the Acadians, see Anderson, *Crucible of War*, 113–14.

120. See David Milobar, "Quebec Reform, the British Constitution and the Atlantic Empire: 1774–1775," in Lawson, *Parliament and the Atlantic Empire*, 65–88; Marshall, "Empire and Authority in the Late Eighteenth Century."

121. Alexander Wedderburn, Speech of 26 May 1774, in Cavendish, *Debates of the House of Commons*, 58; Edmund Burke, speech of 31 May 1774, in Cavendish, *Debates of the House of Commons*, 89–90.

122. Alexander Hamilton, "Remarks on the Quebec Bill: Part Two," 22 June 1775, in *Hamilton Papers*, 1:175. For other protests against the Quebec Act, see Petition to the Commons, 25 Mar. 1775, *General Assembly Journal, 1766–1776*, 1775: 130; Continental Congress, *Journals*, 1:66–67, 70–71, 72; Burnett, *Letters of the Members of the Continental Congress*, 1:77–79; and Livingston, *Other Side of the Question*, 25–27.

123. See Price, "Who Cared about the Colonies?," 395–436.

124. Brewer, *Party Ideology and Popular Politics*, 44, 200.

125. See Namier, "Monarchy and the Party System," in *Personalities and Power*, 25, 37–38; Namier and Brooke, introduction to *House of Commons, 1754–1790*, 1:62; Namier, *Structure of Politics*, 16–17; Plumb, *Growth of Political Stability*, xviii, 2, 188; Brewer, *Party Ideology and Popular Politics*, 58–59. See also Morgan, "American Revolution," 8.

126. Henry Mearchant to Ezra Stiles, 5 Sept. 1771, copy, Bancroft Collection, 35:593, NYPL.

127. Henretta, "*Salutary Neglect*," 105; Andrews, *Colonial Period of American History*, 4:404–8; Greene, *Peripheries and Center*, 73–76; Katz, *Newcastle's New York*, 10–20; Sosin, *Whitehall and the Wilderness*, 52–78; Clark, *Rise of the British Treasury*. For the urban renaissance outside London, see Borsay, *English Urban Renaissance*.

128. Barrow, *Trade and Empire*; Plumb, *Growth of Political Stability*, 72–75; Henretta, "*Salutary Neglect*," 46–47, 259.

129. Commission for the Board of Trade, 15 May 1696, *NYCD*, 4:145–48.

130. Basye, *Lords Commissioners of Trade*, 49–56, 79–80. Basye notes that administrative details hindered even the formulation of trade policy.

131. Andrews, *Colonial Period of American History*, 4:300; Labaree, *Royal Government in America*, 427–28, 66; Katz, *Newcastle's New York*, 13–17; Basye, *Lords Commissioners of Trade*, 218.

132. Walpole, *Memoirs of King George II*, 2:16.

133. *NYCD*, 4:757; Basye, *Lords Commissioners of Trade*, 66–82.

134. Instruction of 14 Apr. 1752, in Labaree, *Royal Instructions to British Colonial Governors*, 2:748–49.

135. Basye, *Lords Commissioners of Trade*, 92–105; Spector, *American Department of the British Government*, 13–14.

136. Russell, *Review of American Colonial Legislation*, 47–48.

137. Lord Mansfield, House of Lords Debate, 7 Feb. 1775, in Hansard, *Parliamentary History of England*, vol. 18, col. 269. See also Lord Mansfield, House of Lords Debate, 10 Feb. 1766, in Hansard, *Parliamentary History of England*, vol. 16, col. 174.

138. See, e.g., Atwood, *Fundamental Constitution of the English Government*.

139. See Basye, *Lords Commissioners of Trade*, 24–31; Henretta, "*Salutary Neglect*," 337–47; Katz, *Newcastle's New York*, 243; Olson, "Board of Trade and London-American Interest Groups in the Eighteenth-Century," 45; and Walpole, *Memoirs of King George II*, 2:16–17. On the contemporary uncertainty about the meaning of 1689, see Nenner, *By Colour of Law*, 195–96, 198–99, and Greene, "Colonial Origins of American Constitutionalism," 36–38.

140. Spector, *American Department of the British Government*, 11–21.

141. See Olson, *Making the Empire Work*.

142. Andrew Elliot to [Sir Gilbert Elliot], 10 Nov. 1765 and 23 Aug. 1767, Andrew Elliot Papers, NYHS.

143. Robert R. Livingston to Robert Livingston, 19 Oct. 1765, copy, Bancroft Collection, vol. 275, NYPL. On the Congress, see Weslager, *Stamp Act Congress*.

144. Robert R. Livingston to John Sargent, 20 Dec. 1765, copy, Bancroft Collection, vol. 275, NYPL.

145. Robert R. Livingston to Monckton, 8 Nov. 1765, The Aspinwall Papers, in *Massachusetts Historical Society Collections*, 10:559–67.

146. To the Honorable Cadwallader Colden, [1 Nov. 1765], *NYHS Coll.* (1923), 84–85; To the Honorable Cadwallader Colden, [3 Nov. 1765], *NYHS Coll.* (1923), 88; Declaration of Colden, 2 Nov. 1765, George Chalmers Collection, NYPL; Colden to Lord Mansfield, 27 Jan. 1768, *NYHS Coll.* (1877), 156. See also John Watts to James Napier, 7 Nov. 1765, *NYHS Coll.* (1928), 398.

147. Colden to Shelburne, 23 Nov. 1767, *NYCD*, 7:996; Moore to Shelburne, 21 Aug. 1767, 5 Oct. 1767, and 29 Dec. 1767, *DHNY*, 7:949, 980, 1006; Kammen, *Colonial New York*, 349–50, 355–56; Varga, "New York Restraining Act."

148. John Watts to Monckton, 9 Nov. 1765, *NYHS Coll.* (1928), 400–401; Watts to Moses Franks, 22 Dec. 1765, *NYHS Coll.* (1928), 406–7. See also Smith, *Historical Memoirs*, 2:272–73.

149. See Smith, *Historical Memoirs*, 1:44, 49–50, 147, 190, 224–25, 243–47. See also William Smith Jr., "Thoughts on the Dispute between Great Britain and Her Colonies," reprinted in Calhoon, "William Smith Jr.'s Alternative to the American Revolution"; Smith, "Draft Penned after Conversing with My Brother," Dec. 1775, box 1, lot 194, William Smith Jr. Papers, NYPL; and Smith, "Observations on the Loss of the American Provinces," [1785?], box 2, lot 205, William Smith Jr. Papers, NYPL, reprinted partially in Zeichner, "William Smith's 'Observations on America.'" For similar plans outside New York, see Jack P. Greene, "The Origins of the American Revolution: A Constitutional Interpretation," in Levy and Mahoney, *Framing and Ratification of the Constitution*, 36–53.

150. Gouverneur Morris to Penn, 20 May 1774, cited in Sparks, *Life of Gouverneur Morris*, 1:23–26. For use of "levellers," see, e.g., Smith, *Historical Memoirs*, 1:295–96.

151. On the patterns of crowd behavior, see Rudé, *Crowd in History*, and Thompson, *Customs in Common*.

PART THREE

1. Jones, *History of New-York*, 2:115.
2. Cf. Barrow, "American Revolution as a Colonial War for Independence."
3. See Goebel, "*Ex Parte* Clio," 462–72.

CHAPTER FIVE

1. William Smith Jr. to Governor Monckton, 3 Nov. 1765, George Chalmers Collection, NYPL.
2. Smith, *Historical Memoirs*, 1:156.

3. Lord George Germain to [Lord Suffolk], [16 or 17 June 1775], *Historical Manuscripts Commission: Report on the Manuscripts of Mrs. Stopford-Sackville*, 2:3.

4. On the battle for New York City, see Schechter, *Battle for New York*. On the borderlands, see Kim, "Limits of Politicization in the American Revolution"; Catherine S. Crary, "Guerrilla Activities of James DeLancey's Cowboys in Westchester County: Conventional Warfare or Self-Interested Freebooting?," in East and Judd, *Loyalist Americans*, 14–24. See also Van Buskirk, *Generous Enemies*.

5. New York Constitution, 1777, art. I.

6. Continental Congress, 23 May 1774, in Force, *American Archives*, 1:295–98. The subcommittee that wrote the proposal included John Jay, James Duane, Alexander MacDougall, and Isaac Low. Becker, *History of Political Parties*, 117–19; Morris, *John Jay*, 132; Van Schaack, *Life of Peter Van Schaack*, 16–17. One historian identifies John Jay as the main author of the circular letter proposing the Continental Congress. Alexander, *Political History of the State of New York*, 1:7. On the successive committees, see Adams, *First American Constitutions*, 27–48; Jones, *History of New-York*, 1:438–67, 477–89; Becker, *History of Political Parties*, 112–92; Tiedemann, *Reluctant Revolutionaries*, 186–206, 216–29; Mason, *Road to Independence*, 62–99; and Barck, *New York City*, 39–46.

7. The continental colonies of Georgia, Nova Scotia, Newfoundland, Quebec (which together had a European population of about 117,000 in 1770, though much of it French), and the two Floridas did not participate. Neither did the Caribbean colonies of Barbados, Jamaica, and the Leeward Islands, which had a population of 45,000 European whites in 1770. See McCusker and Menard, *Economy of British America*, 112, 154. For the Revolution's effect in the Caribbean, see O'Shaughnessy, *Empire Divided*.

8. "Letter from the New-York Committee to the counties, requesting to elect Delegates to a Provincial Congress," 28 Apr. 1775, in *Journals of the Provincial Congress*, 1:4; Colden to the Earl of Dartmouth, 1 June 1774, *NYCD*, 8:433. The term "elections" must be used advisedly. In some counties committee and then Provincial Congress representatives were chosen by broad elections, but in others they were appointed by small groups of men in the local committees. This same uneven pattern of provincial elections persisted until after the Revolution. Becker, *History of Political Parties*, 201–2, 229–37, 252; Mason, *Road to Independence*, 88–90, 113–17, 179; Frey, *Minute Book of the Committee of Safety of Tryon County*, 27, 77, 89–90.

9. Colden to the Earl of Dartmouth, 1 June 1774, *NYCD*, 8:433–34. On the distinction between legal and constitutional, see Reid, *Authority of Rights*, 7–8, and Reid, *Constitutional History of the American Revolution*, abridged ed. (1995), xviii–xix.

10. Livingston, *Other Side of the Question*, 28.

11. "A General Association, agreed to, and subscribed by the freeholders, Freemen and Inhabitants of the city and county of New-York," 29 Apr. 1775, in *Journals of the Provincial Congress*, 5. Local committees, usually organized along town or county lines, varied greatly, in both composition and attachment to the empire. Countryman, *People in Revolution*, 124–30, 179–84. For the loyalty and moderation

of many who participated in the early committees and congresses, see Colden to the Earl of Dartmouth, 6 July 1774, *NYCD*, 8:469–70; Colden to Dartmouth, 2 Aug. 1774, *NYCD*, 8:485–86; Colden to Dartmouth, 7 Sept. 1774, *NYCD*, 8:488; Colden to Dartmouth, 6 Oct. 1774, *NYCD*, 8:493; Colden to Dartmouth, 7 Dec. 1774, *NYCD*, 8:512–14; Memorial of Isaac Low, American Loyalists, 1783–1790: Transcripts of the Manuscript Books and Papers of the Commission of Enquiry, 43:159, NYPL; and Ashton, "Loyalist Experience, New York," 51–70.

12. Bruegel, "Unrest." The classic treatment is Fox, *Decline of Aristocracy*.

13. *Journals of the Provincial Congress*, 1:59, 58. This was one of many similar plans of accommodation that circulated between 1774 and 1776.

14. Ibid.; 2:16, 1:218, 1:219. The delegates at this point were Philip Livingston, John Jay, James Duane, John Alsop, and Isaac Sears. Sometimes New York was too cautious, even for its own delegates. "I confess," John Jay wrote the Provincial Congress, "I am not a little jealous of the honour of the Province, and am persuaded that its reputation can not be maintained without some little spirit being mingled with its prudence." Ibid., 1:218.

15. The president was elected by the Congress itself. Low later remained loyal to the empire.

16. *Journals of the Provincial Congress*, 1:8, 11; Mason, *Road to Independence*, 206. See also Resolutions of 14 October 1774, Continental Congress, *Journals*, 1:63–73. On the pragmatic of the Continental Congress, see Rakove, *Beginnings of National Politics*.

17. See, e.g., Robert R. Livingston to James Duane, 16 Feb. 1776; Bancroft Collection, vol. 276, NYPL; James Duane's Propositions before the Committee on Rights, [7–22 Sept. 1774]; and Smith, *Letters of Delegates to Congress*, 1:38–44. On the polarizing effect of the British military's actions, see Mason, *Road to Independence*, 62–99.

18. *Journals of the Provincial Congress*, 1:336, 379. Lee persistently questioned the loyalties of New Yorkers and proposed burning the city on evacuation, a suggestion that was carried out, though at whose hands is unclear.

19. See, e.g., ibid., 1:50, 97–98, 116, 129, 165.

20. Ibid., 1:364–66.

21. Ibid., 1:503–5. See also ibid., 1:491, 507–12, 516–17.

22. Ibid., 1:203.

23. Ibid., 1:240, 236.

24. Ibid., 1:778. On the problem of interstate relations, see Onuf, *Origins of the Federal Republic*, and Rakove, *Beginnings of National Politics*.

25. Trumbull protested that the leader of the "whole transaction" was New Yorker Isaac Sears. *Journals of the Provincial Congress*, 1:214, 491–92.

26. John Adams, Notes of Debates in the Continental Congress, 6 Sept. 1774, in *Diary and Autobiography of John Adams*, 2:124–26.

27. Adams, *First American Constitutions*, 42–51; Onuf, *Origins of the Federal Republic* 32; Hugh M. Flick, "The Rise of the Revolutionary Committee System," in Flick, *History of the State of New York*, 3:241; Becker, *History of Political Parties*, 255; Mason, *Road to Independence*, 191–97.

28. *Journals of the Provincial Congress*, 1:178.

29. [John Jay], "A Hint to the Legislature of the State of New York," [15 Jan.–2 Apr. 1778], in Morris, *John Jay*, 461–63.

30. *Journals of the Provincial Congress*, 1:255. See also ibid., 1:301, 323. On the English practice of compensating for expropriation, see Treanor, "Original Understanding of the Takings Clause and the Political Process."

31. *Journals of the Provincial Congress*, 1:414–15.

32. Ibid., 1:403–4.

33. See, e.g., ibid., 1:429.

34. Ibid., 1:471–72, 473, 478.

35. Ibid., 1:476–77.

36. An Act for the Forfeiture and Sale of the Estates of Persons who have adhered to the Enemies of this State, and for declaring the Sovereignty of the People of this State in Respect to all Property, 22 Oct. 1779, 3rd sess., chap. 25 (1779), *Laws of the State of New York*, 1:173–84 (amended several times).

37. For the list, see Flick, *Loyalism in New York*, 147.

38. *Journals of the Provincial Congress*, 1:500–501.

39. *Journals of the Provincial Congress*, 1:450, 459–60, 461.

40. See Paltsits, *Minutes of the Commissioners for Detecting and Defeating Conspiracies in the State of New York*, and *Minutes of the Committee and of the First Commission for Detecting and Defeating Conspiracies in the State of New York, December 11, 1776–September 23, 1778*, in *NYHS Coll.* (1924–25). For court-martials by the militia, see, e.g., Clinton, *Public Papers of George Clinton*, 1:749–62, 764–82. See generally Flick, *Loyalism in New York*, 58–94, 116–60.

41. Rakove, *Beginnings of National Politics*, 136–62; Greene, *Peripheries and Center*, 154–57.

42. John Jay to Alexander MacDougall, 11 Apr. 1776, Jay, *John Jay*, 1:254; James Madison, "Vices of the Political System of the United States," in *Madison Papers*, 9:345–58.

43. New York Constitution, 1777, preamble; Continental Congress, *Journals*, 3:342, 357–58. The 10 May resolution recommended that the colonies "adopt such Governments . . . as shall best conduce to the Happiness and Safety of their Constituents in particular and America in general." Continental Congress, *Journals*, 3:342. On 15 May Congress added a preamble that "every kind of authority under the said crown should be totally suppressed, and all the powers of government exerted, under the authority of the people of the colonies." Continental Congress, *Journals*, 3:357–58. See also Jay, *John Jay*, 1:266, 268–69. Only Connecticut and Rhode Island did not draft new constitutions during the Revolution.

44. Adams, *Diary and Autobiography of John Adams*, 3:386; Adams, *First American Constitutions*, 61.

45. An exception was Goldsborough Banyar, formerly the royal secretary of the colony, who took a loyalty oath to the state of New York on 16 Sept. 1778. Banyar Loyalty Oath, copy, Bancroft Collection, 37:273, NYPL.

46. Champagne, "Family Politics versus Constitutional Principles"; Bonomi, *Factious People*, 246–78.

47. Launitz-Schurer, *Loyal Whigs and Revolutionaries*; Stanley N. Katz, "Between Scylla and Charybdis: James DeLancey and American Politics in Early Eighteenth-Century New York," in Olson and Brown, *Anglo-American Political Relations*, 92–108; Countryman, "Uses of Capital in Revolutionary America"; Esmond Wright, "The New York Loyalists: A Cross-Section of Colonial Society," in East and Judd, *Loyalist Americans*, 74–94.

48. For the example of the Morris family, see Ashton, "Loyalist Experience, New York," 122–23. See also Becker, "John Jay and Peter Van Schaack," in *Everyman His Own Historian*, 284–98; Potter, *Liberty We Seek*; Ranlet, *New York Loyalists*; Brown, *King's Friends*, 75–107; Ashton, "Loyalist Experience, New York"; Hoffer, Hull, and Allen, "Choosing Sides"; and East and Judd, *Loyalist Americans*.

49. Graymont, *Iroquois in the American Revolution*; Francis Jennings, "Tribal Loyalty and Tribal Dependence," in Wright, *Red, White, and True Blue*, 19–31.

50. Williamson, *Vermont in Quandary*, 67–164.

51. Kim, "Impact of Class Relations and Warfare in the American Revolution." On tenant loyalism, compare Staughton Lynd, "The Tenant Rising at Livingston Manor, May 1777," in *Narratives of the Revolution in New York*, 170–82, with Brown, *King's Friends*, 104.

52. Countryman, *People in Revolution*, 162–65; Lemisch, *Jack Tar vs. John Bull*.

53. For example, the royal supreme court's last term was in April 1776. Minutes of the Supreme Court of Judicature, 1775–1781 (engrossed), p. 99, HR.

54. 16 Geo. III, c. 5. The act reciprocated the embargo ordered by the Continental Congress. Barck, *New York City*, 49. The first peace commissioners were empowered to restore "any colony or province or any county, town, port, district or place within any of the said colonies or provinces, to be at our peace" and free to trade in the empire. Instructions to Peace Commissioners, 6 May 1776, in Davies, *Documents of the American Revolution*, 2:120–25.

55. See Wiener, *Civilians under Military Justice*, esp. 95–140.

56. The Charter of Libertyes and Priviledges, 30 Oct. 1683, *Colonial Laws of New York*, 1:114. No royal instruction permitted governors to exercise martial law over civilians. Cf. Labaree, *Royal Instructions to British Colonial Governors*, 1:397 (instructing governors "to forbear in time of peace" from instituting martial law over soldiers).

57. Wiener, *Civilians under Military Justice*, 68–69, 92–93, 187–88.

58. Charles Gould to Sir William Howe, 20 June 1777, reprinted in Wiener, *Civilians under Military Justice*, 265. The Articles of War consisted of about three dozen commands concerning the behavior of sailors on military ships, including privateers and ships granted letters of marque. *Articles of War*, [1756], Broadside Collection, NYHS.

59. In this, provincial lawyers repeated a venerable, though debatable, common-law interpretation of military justice. Blackstone, *Commentaries*, 1:400. See also Johnson et al., *Commons Debates, 1628*, 2:362–63, 368–69, 463, and Boynton, "Martial Law and the Petition of Right."

60. Jones, *History of New-York*, 2:117–19, 2:436–53. A similar petition followed two years later. *Address of the Inhabitants of the City of New-York*. See also R. W. G.

Vail, "The Loyalists Declaration of Dependence," in *Narratives of the Revolution in New York*, 32–35.

61. Commissioners to Germain, 30 Nov. 1776, in Davies, *Documents of the American Revolution*, 12:257–58.

62. Peace Commissioners Lord Carlisle, Sir Henry Clinton, and William Eden to Secretary Lord George Germain, 16 Nov. 1778, in Stevens, *B. F. Stevens's Facsimiles*, facs. 1216; Carlisle and Eden to Germain, 27 Nov. 1778, in Stevens, *B. F. Stevens's Facsimiles*, facs. 1227; Carlisle and Eden to Germain, 8 Mar. 1779, in Stevens, *B. F. Stevens's Facsimiles*, facs. 1269; Henry Clinton to Germain, 9 Mar. 1781, in Davies, *Documents of the American Revolution*, 20:80–82; K. G. Davies, "The Restoration of Civil Government by the British in the American Revolution," in Wright, *Red, White, and True Blue*, 111–33.

63. On the southern strategy, see Furlong, "Civilian-Military Conflict"; John Shy, "British Strategy for Pacifying the Southern Colonies, 1778–1781," in Crow and Tise, *Southern Experience in the American Revolution*, 155–73; and Mackesy, *Could the British Have Won the War of Independence?*

64. Jones, *History of New-York*, 2:22–25, 175–76. The military advantages of restoration in Georgia were ambiguous. Shy, "British Strategy for Pacifying the Southern Colonies."

65. For military strategy in New York, see Klein, "Why Did the British Fail to Win the Hearts and Minds of New Yorkers?"; Klein, "Experiment That Failed"; and Tiedemann, "Patriots by Default."

66. *NYCD*, 8:685–86.

67. Tryon to Germain, 1 Mar. 1779, *NYCD*, 8:759. Other cases, such as piracy cases, were sent to London. Smith, *Historical Memoirs*, 3:250.

68. Jones, *History of New-York*, 2:107.

69. *Dictionary of American Biography*, s.v. "Jones, Thomas"; Edward F. De-Lancey, introduction to Jones, *History of New-York*.

70. Jones, *History of New-York*, 2:27.

71. Ibid., 51–52, 135–36. See also Smith, *Historical Memoirs*, 3:263.

72. Jones, *History of New-York*, 2:139.

73. Ibid., 113. Jones's case against the miliary regime is laid out in ibid., 98–142.

74. Report of the Magistrates of Police, [1781], box 3, Andrew Elliot Papers, NYSA; Memorandum Book, 22–29, 43–44, box 7, Andrew Elliot Papers, NYSA; Barck, *New York City*, 54–55, 85–86, 90–93. For references to the chamber, see, e.g., Stephen P. Adye to Isaac Low, 1 Aug. 1780, *NYHS Coll.* (1875), 221–22; Major General James Pattison to Low, 12 Aug. 1780, *NYHS Coll.* (1875), 422–23, 426; and Stevens, *Colonial Records of the New York Chamber of Commerce*, 204, 215, 219, 223, 237, 247–48, 261–67, 270, 275–77, 287–88.

75. See, e.g., "Proclamation by Lieutenant General Knyphausen," *New-York Gazette and Weekly Mercury*, 24 Apr. 1780. Knyphausen was in charge of the Hessian forces. This proclamation and others were published along with German translations.

76. Lord George Germain to Governor Tryon, 1 Apr. 1779, *NYCD*, 8:761: Germain to Governor Robertson, 9 July 1779, *NYCD*, 8:767–68; Germain to

Robertson, 3 Sept. 1779, *NYCD*, 8:773; Governor Robertson to Secretary Robinson, 4 Aug. 1780, *NYCD*, 8:798.

77. Proclamation by Governor Robertson, 15 Apr. 1780, in Klein and Howard, *Twilight of British Rule*, 91–94. In practice, the post was advisory: the royal supreme court last sat in April 1776.

78. Robertson to Germain, 1 July 1780, *NYCD*, 8:794.

79. Jones, *History of New-York*, 1:426.

80. Robertson to Germain, 1 Sept. 1780, *NYCD*, 8:799–800; Germain to Robertson, 5 July 1780, *NYCD*, 8:796; Germain to Robertson, 6 Sept. 1780, *NYCD*, 8:802.

81. Jones, *History of New-York*, 2:12, 14–15, 66–68, 103, 104n, 121, 126, 164; Robertson to Lord George Germain, 1 Sept. 780, *NYCD*, 8:801. For a sympathetic portrait of Robertson, see Klein, "Experiment That Failed," and Klein and Howard, introduction to *Twilight of British Rule*, 1–63.

82. Smith, *Historical Memoirs*, 3:399, 401, 412, 415, 419–21, 476.

83. Jones, *History of New-York*, 2:78–79, 45.

84. See ibid., 42–46.

85. Ibid., 84–85.

86. On runaway slaves who served in the British army, see Graham R. Hodges, "Black Revolt in New York City and the Neutral Zone: 1775–1783," in Gilje and Pencak, *New York in the Age of the Constitution*, 20–47; Hodges, *Root and Branch*, 139–61; and Frey, *Water from the Rock*. British transportation of New York slaves out of the province was a grievance under the peace treaty and an excuse, for some, to violate it. Thomas Jefferson to George Hammond, 29 May 1792, in Jefferson, *Papers of Thomas Jefferson*, 23:571; Alexander Hamilton, "Second Letter from Phocion," [April 1784], in *Hamilton Papers*, 3:540.

87. Smith, *Historical Memoirs*, 3:73–74; Barck, *New York City*, 114–15.

88. Adye, *Treatise on the Courts-Martial*. Adye's treatise was also printed in London the same year and reprinted in Philadelphia during the Revolution. Eldon R. James, "A List of Legal Treatises Printed in the British Colonies and the American States Before 1801," in Campbell, *Harvard Legal Essays*, 170, 180. Shortly after its publication, the manual became "the principal authority on courts martial and the theory of military law" in Britain and the United States. Steppler, "British Military Law," 861; Nicholson, "Courts-Martial in the Legion Army," 81–82.

89. Adye, *Treatise on the Courts-Martial*, 7n. On the conflicting interpretations of the Articles of War, see Wiener, *Civilians under Military Justice*, 14–16, 24–29, 186–88.

90. Adye, *Treatise on the Courts-Martial*, iii–iv; *Dictionary of National Biography*, s.v. "Adye, Stephen Payne." Actually, there was a 1682 handbook, and other books had touched on courts-martial. Holdsworth, *History of English Law*, 6:612, 699, 12:347; Steppler, "British Military Law," 861 n. 3.

91. Adye, *Treatise on the Courts-Martial*, 19–24, 35.

92. These numbers are derived from "Trials of Civilians by British General Courts-Martial during the War of American Independence," app. 2, in Wiener, *Civilians under Military Justice*, 277–300.

93. Correspondence in Klein and Howard, *Twilight of British Rule*: Robertson to Clinton, 29 Mar. 1780, 88–89; Robertson to Clinton, 3 May 1780, 96–97; Robertson to Clinton, 27 June 1780, 123; Robertson to Amherst, 1 July 1780, 131; Robertson to Germain, 28 Jan. 1781, 176; and Robertson to the Earl of Shelburne, 9 May 1782, 245–47; Smith, *Historical Memoirs*, 3:281, 289, 292–94, 296–98, 471–72.

94. Smith to William Eden, 14 Dec. 1778, in Stevens, *B. F. Stevens's Facsimiles*, facs. 1229. See also Smith to Eden, 2 Nov. 1779, in Stevens, *B. F. Stevens's Facsimiles*, facs. 1204 (revolt is "the genuine Offspring of that unmixed Democracy prevalent in the Plantations").

95. Smith, *Historical Memoirs*, 3:177–78, 485, 486, 490–92; Calendar of Council Minutes, 1 Mar. 1782, in Davies, *Documents of the American Revolution*, 19:273–74; correspondence in Klein and Howard, *Twilight of British Rule*: Robertson to Germain, 22 Mar. 1782, 238–40; Robertson to the Earl of Shelburne, 9 May 1782, 245–47; Robertson to Amherst, 22 Mar. 1782, 241–42; and Robertson to Amherst, 12 May 1782, 249–51; Clinton, *American Rebellion*, 353, 398, 593–94; Davies, "Restoration of Civil Government," 132–33.

96. Smith, *Historical Memoirs*, 3:508, 509, 511, 517; William Smith Jr. to Carleton, 31 May 1782, box 6, folder 4, Andrew Elliot Papers, NYSA; F. Smyth to Carleton, 31 May 1782, box 6, folder 4, Andrew Elliot Papers, NYSA; John Tabor Kempe to Carleton, 2 June 1782, box 6, folder 4, Andrew Elliot Papers, NYSA. For the informal advisory council of Smith, Smyth, and Kempe, see Smith, *Historical Memoirs*, 3:511–15. I have found no evidence that the royal Court of Errors was established.

97. Smith, *Historical Memoirs*, 3:491.

98. Smith, Memorandum on Reviving Civil Authority, [1782], box 6, folder 4, Andrew Elliot Papers, 4, NYSA; Notes on Sir Guy Carleton's Proposal, 27 May 1782, box 2, lot 194, William Smith Jr. Papers, NYPL; Smith, *Historical Memoirs*, 3:511–15. For Smith's concern that councillors might be "liable to [an] action at Westminster," see Smith, *Historical Memoirs*, 3:471.

99. Smith, Memorandum on Reviving Civil Authority; Smith, *Historical Memoirs*, 3:521.

100. Smith to Sir Guy Carleton, 10 Sept. 1782, box 3, lot 208, William Smith Jr. Papers, NYPL.

101. William Smith Jr. to Evan Nepean, 17 Aug. 1785, copy, Bancroft Collection, 32:279, NYPL; Smith to Nepean, 1 June 1789, copy, Bancroft Collection, 33:375, NYPL. Smith never sold his New York lands, which continued to generate income for his family into the nineteenth century. Account Books, Smith Misc. Mss., NYHS.

102. See Bayly, *Imperial Meridian*, 100–132, and Gould, *Persistence of Empire*, 181–214.

CHAPTER SIX

1. Continental Congress, *Journals*, 4:342, 357–58; John Jay to Edward Rutledge, 6 July 1776, in Jay, *John Jay*, 1:68.

2. Donald S. Lutz, "The First American Constitutions," in Levy and Mahoney, *Framing and Ratification of the Constitution*, 69–81; Benjamin F. Wright, "The Early History of Written Constitutions in America," in Wittke, *Essays in History and Political Theory*, 344–71. Connecticut and Rhode Island were alone in retaining their colonial charters.

3. The first use of "constitution" in the convention journals was on 20 Apr. 1777, the day of the final vote on it. *Journals of the Provincial Congress*, 1:892.

4. For "institute," see Luig, "Institutes of National Law"; for "frame and establish," see Thompson, "History of Fundamental Law in Political Thought"; and for "new model," see Kishlansky, *Rise of the New Model Army*.

5. On the early recognition of the popular basis of constitution making in the states, see Kruman, *Between Authority and Liberty*.

6. *Journals of the Provincial Congress*, 1:460, 462–63, 468–69. See also Douglass, *Rebels and Democrats*, 61.

7. On the significance of conventions, see Wood, *Creation of the American Republic*, 310–43.

8. Peter R. Livingston, "Maxims, as Fundamentall Principles on which the Constitution of this State ought to be erected," Sept. 1776, box 2, lot 197, William Smith Papers, NYPL.

9. Nevins, *American States during and after the Revolution*, 158.

10. Robert R. Livingston Jr. to the Provincial Convention, 8 June 1776, Bancroft Collection, vol. 276, NYPL; New York Congress to Their Delegates in Continental Congress, 11 June 1776, in Force, *American Archives*, 6:814 (reply of the Provincial Convention); Resolution of 9 July 1776, *Journals of the Provincial Congress*, 1:518.

11. *Journals of the Provincial Congress*, 1:552; Galie, *Ordered Liberty*, 48–49. For a survey of state protection of traditional liberties, see Kruman, *Between Authority and Liberty*, 35–53. John Jay played the leading role in writing the state constitution, though it was a collective effort. Editorial note, in Jay, *John Jay*, 1:389–95.

12. See Mason, *Road to Independence*, 130–31.

13. New York Constitution (1777), preamble.

14. On the contemporary ambiguity of "state," see Pole, "Politics of the Word 'State.'"

15. New York Constitution (1777), arts. I, II. A related article (art. XXXI) specified that all statutes and writs should run in the name of the people, not the king.

16. *Journals of the Provincial Congress*, 1:836, 866–67; New York Constitution (1777), arts. I, II, VI.

17. *Journals of the Provincial Congress*, 1:867–68; New York Constitution (1777), arts. V, XII. New York was the "first to provide both for districts with equal numbers of people and periodic redistricting." Lutz, *Popular Consent and Popular Control*, 109. On the emergence of proportional representation, see Pole, *Political Representation in England*, 172–89.

18. Smith, *Historical Memoirs*, 2:18, 20.

19. New York Constitution (1777), arts. VII, VIII, X, XII, XVII. By 1821,

almost 80 percent of free men could vote for the assembly, while not quite 40 percent could vote for the senate and governor. Williamson, *American Suffrage*, 197.

20. New York Constitution (1777), arts. IX, XXII.

21. Ibid., art. XXXIII; *Journals of the Provincial Congress*, 1:878.

22. New York Constitution (1777), arts. XXIV.

23. New York Constitution (1777), arts. XVII–XIX. Alexander Hamilton was in the minority in seeing "a want of vigor in the executive." Hamilton to Gouverneur Morris, 19 May 1777, in *Hamilton Papers*, 1:255.

24. Schwarz, *Jarring Interests*.

25. *Journals of the Provincial Congress*, 1:860, 862.

26. New York Constitution (1777), art. III.

27. See, e.g., Vile, *Constitutionalism and the Separation of Powers*, 134, 144, 148, 150.

28. See, e.g., Street, *Council of Revision*, 215–16, 231–32, 311–12, 317.

29. The legislature repassed 51 of the 169 bills rejected by the council during its existence (1777–1821). Ibid., 7, 481–515.

30. An Act for the Forfeiture and Sale of the Estates of Persons who have adhered to the Enemies of this State, and for declaring the Sovereignty of the People of this State in Respect to all Property, 22 Oct. 1779, 3rd sess., chap. 25, *Laws of the State of New York*, 1:173–84 (amended several times).

31. Street, *Council of Revision*, 219–26; New York Assembly, *Journal of the Assembly of the State of New York, 1779* (Albany, 1779), 103, 106. Speculators did in fact buy much of the land, though much was resold to small farmers. Lynd, "Who Should Rule at Home?"; Lynd, *Anti-Federalism in Dutchess County*, 74–75; Crary, "Forfeited Loyalist Lands in the Western District of New York"; Yoshpe, *Disposition of Loyalist Estates*.

32. *Journals of the Provincial Congress*, 1:873–75; New York Constitution (1777), art. XXII. Jay developed the idea in conversation with Morris and Robert R. Livingston Jr. Jay to Morris and Livingston, 29 Apr. 1777, in Jay, *John Jay*, 1:128–36; Lincoln, *Constitutional History of New York*, 1:534.

33. New York Constitution (1777), art. XXIII; *Journals of the Provincial Congress*, 875; Jay to Morris and Livingston, 29 Apr. 1777, in Jay, *John Jay*, 1:131–32.

34. New York Constitutional Amendments of 1801, art. V. On the council, see Gitterman, "Council of Appointment in New York," and Flick, "Council of Appointment of New York State." See also Hamilton, *Federalist* 77, 2 Apr. 1788, *Federalist Papers*, 517–18.

35. This unusual restriction applied only to the supreme court judges and the chancellor. The state framers may have had in mind Cadwallader Colden, who served on the council (which had judicial power) until his death at eighty-seven, or Chief Justice Daniel Horsmanden, who held his post until he died at eighty-four.

36. New York Constitution (1777), art. XXXII.

37. Minutes of the Supreme Court of Judicature, 1775–1781 (engrossed), 10 Sept. 1777, p. 107, HR. Notations make clear that these minutes were not entered into the official minute book until 1788.

38. An Act Further to Organize the Government of this State, 16 Mar. 1778, 1st sess. 1778, chap. 12, *Laws of the State of New York*, 1:21–24; New York Constitution (1777), art. XXXI. Charlotte County remained refractory, as always. An Act for Holding Courts of Common Pleas, and of General Sessions of the Peace, in the County of Charlotte, 23 Oct. 1779, 2nd sess. 1779, chap. 12, *Laws of the State of New York*, 1:192–93.

39. Compare Minutes of the Supreme Court of Judicature, 1775–1781 (engrossed), HR, with Minutes of the Supreme Court of Judicature, 31 July 1781–1 Nov. 1783 (engrossed), HR.

40. New York Constitution (1777), art. XXXV.

41. Julius Goebel Jr., "Law Enforcement in Colonial New York: An Introduction," in Flaherty, *Essays in the History of Early American Law*, 368.

42. Lincoln, *Constitutional History of New York*, 1:541.

43. New York Constitution (1777), art. XLI. The convention also rejected a proposal to allow conviction with less than unanimous verdict.

44. New York Constitution (1777), art. XXXIV. Under the common law, criminal defendants did not have a right to representation, but by the eighteenth century legislation was eroding the prohibition. Blackstone, *Commentaries*, 4:349–50; Langbein, *Origins of Adversary Criminal Trial*; Moglen, "Taking the Fifth."

45. New York Constitution (1777), art. XXXVI. Governor Tryon asked Mayor Hicks for a pledge of security for his person and property, and he left when he did not receive it. See Governor Tryon to Mayor Hicks, 10 Oct. 1775, *NYCD*, 8:638; Tryon to Hicks, 14 Oct. 1775, *NYCD*, 8:639; and Tryon to Hicks, 19 Oct. 1775, *NYCD*, 8:641.

46. New York Constitution (1777), art. XXXV.

47. Cf. Wood, "Origins of Vested Rights."

48. Lincoln, *Constitutional History of New York*, 1:542.

49. New York Constitution (1777), art. XXXVIII.

50. Instruction on Religious Liberty, 1690, in Labaree, *Royal Instructions to British Colonial Governors*, 2:494.

51. *Journals of the Provincial Congress*, 1:844. On Jay's religious convictions, see Bonomi, "John Jay, Religion, and the State."

52. *Journals of the Provincial Congress*, 1:845–46. See also Lincoln, *Constitutional History of New York*, 1:540–46.

53. New York Constitution (1777), art. XXXIX. On the relationship between religion and state in early America, see Hamburger, *Separation of Church and State*, 1–189.

54. Other readers included John Wheelock in Hanover, New Hampshire, and the loyalist William Smith Jr. John Wheelock to Robert R. Livingston, 19 Mar. 1777, microfilm reel 1, Robert R. Livingston Papers, NYHS; Smith, *Historical Memoirs*, 2:18–20, 26.

55. One exception was the Presbyterian Church of New York City. After failing three times to obtain a charter from the governor, the church petitioned the Privy Council directly in 1766. The refusal the next year was interpreted as punishment

for the Presbyterian community's opposition to imperial regulation and an American bishop. Klein, *American Whig*, 477.

56. John Henry Livingston to Robert R. Livingston, 28 Feb. 1777, microfilm reel 1, Robert R. Livingston Papers, NYHS.

57. For the college controversy, see chapter 3.

58. John Henry Livingston to Robert R. Livingston, 17 Mar. 1777, microfilm reel 1, Robert R. Livingston Papers, NYHS. James Madison later expressed similar fears that incorporated churches would gain too much power. Hamburger, *Separation of Church and State*, 181–84.

59. John Henry Livingston to Robert R. Livingston, 17 Mar. 1777, microfilm reel 1, Robert R. Livingston Papers, NYHS.

60. Ibid.

61. John Henry Livingston to Robert R. Livingston, 8 Apr. 1777, microfilm reel 1, Robert R. Livingston Papers, NYHS.

62. An Act to Enable All the Religious Denominations in this State to Appoint Trustees Who Shall Be a Body Corporate, 6 Apr. 1784, 7th sess. 1784, chap. 18, *Laws of the State of New York*, 1:613–18. See also Seavoy, *Origins of the American Business Corporation*, 9. Later statutes completed the disestablishment of the Anglican Church and protected Catholic priests from prosecution under the constitutional provision. Pauline Maier argues that Massachusetts was first to develop "laws strikingly like later general acts of incorporation" as early as 1753. Maier, "Revolutionary Origins of the American Corporation," 56–57. The 1753 act was designed to facilitate the alienation and development of any commons that lay beyond town limits by granting *proprietors* the right to organize and decide how to dispose of the jointly owned land. Akagi, *Town Proprietors of the New England Colonies*, 60, 79, 71, 157. It was more of a private bill than a free incorporation statute.

63. Amar, *Bill of Rights*, 246–57.

64. Though each colony's act of naturalization was effective only within its borders. See generally Kettner, *Development of American Citizenship*.

65. *Journals of the Provincial Congress*, 1:846, 852–52; New York Constitution (1777), art. XLII.

66. Seven of the early state constitutions had separate bills of rights. Adams, *First American Constitutions*, 147.

67. New York Constitution (1777), arts. XLI, XL, IX, XXXIV, XXIX, XIII. On the individual and collective significance of such rights, see Amar, *Bill of Rights*.

68. New York Constitution (1777), art. XL.

69. *Journals of the Provincial Congress*, 1:880–81; New York Constitution (1777), art. XXXVII.

70. Graymont, *Iroquois in the American Revolution*, 266–70 (emphasis added).

71. See ibid.; Jack Campisi, "From Stanwix to Canandaigua: National Policy, States' Rights and Indian Land," in Vescey and Starna, *Iroquois Land Claims*, 49–65.

72. *Journals of the Provincial Congress*, 1:887.

73. On *Somerset's Case*, see Oldham, *Mansfield Manuscripts*, 2:1221–44.

74. *Journals of the Provincial Congress*, 889. New York passed a gradual abolition statute in 1799.

75. Van Buskirk, *Generous Enemies*, 129–54.

76. For growing dissatisfaction with the Confederation, see Rakove, *Beginnings of National Politics*, and Rakove, "The Collapse of the Articles of Confederation," in Barlow, Levy, and Masugi, *American Founding*, 225–45.

77. Cochran, *New York in the Confederation*, 55, 156–57; De Pauw, *Eleventh Pillar*, 10. For opposition to direct taxes, see Slaughter, *Whiskey Rebellion*, 11–27.

78. Hamilton to James Duane, 3 Sept. 1780, in *Hamilton Papers*, 2:400–418. For the Roman analogy, see Hamilton, "Remarks in the New York Assembly on an Act Granting to Congress Certain Imposts and Duties," [15 Feb. 1787], in *Hamilton Papers*, 4:92.

79. [Yates], *Political Papers*, 13, 19; Yates, "Address to the People," in Ford, *Pamphlets on the Constitution of the United States*, 104–5; New York Senate, *Journal of the Senate of the State of New-York*, 7th sess. (New York, 1784), 39. For a discussion of Clinton's changing attitude toward the Confederation impost, see Kaminski, *George Clinton*, 60–61, 89–96, 155, and Spaulding, *His Excellency George Clinton*, 168–69.

80. See Hamilton, Remarks in the New York Assembly on an Act Granting to Congress Certain Imposts and Duties, [15 Feb. 1787], in Hamilton, *Papers of Alexander Hamilton*, 4:71–92. See generally De Pauw, *Eleventh Pillar*, 31–43, and Cochran, *New York in the Confederation*, 142–50, 163, 172–79. Fear of "continental collectors" continued through the constitutional debate. See Elliot, *Debates*, 2:330–34.

81. See *DHRC*, 17:202–5. One critic called New York an "*anti-federal sister*." "Acirema," *New York Daily Advertiser*, 11 May 1786, in *DHRC*, 17:203. Later opponents of the federal Constitution rejected the negative term "Antifederalist." See, e.g., [DeWitt Clinton], "A Countryman II," 13 Dec. 1787, in Storing and Dry, *Complete Anti-Federalist*, 6:76.

82. See, e.g., Charles DeWitt to Gov. George Clinton, 14 June 1784, in Burnett, *Letters of the Members of the Continental Congress*, 7:545.

83. Kaminski, *George Clinton*, 84–89.

84. It is "generally assumed" that Hamilton, Schuyler's son-in-law, authored the resolution. Resolutions of the New York Legislature Calling for a Convention of the States to Revise and Amend the Articles of Convention, [20 July 1782], *Hamilton Papers*, 3:110–13; De Pauw, *Eleventh Pillar*, 44.

85. Hamilton to Washington, 9 Apr. 1783, in Burnett, *Letters of the Members of the Continental Congress*, 7:129.

86. The proposal passed by one vote in the state legislature. *DHRC*, 1:186–87; *Hamilton Papers*, 4:93; James Madison, "Notes of Debates in Congress," 21 Feb. 1787, in *DHRC*, 1:188–89. See also Hamilton, Unsubmitted Resolution Calling for a Convention to Amend the Articles of Confederation, [July 1783], in *Hamilton Papers*, 3:420–26. James Madison believed that the proposal's further requirement that the states hold new elections for delegates, to legitimize the

broader mandate, was designed to sabotage the idea. Given the ambivalence toward the Confederation within New York, it is possible that *both* interpretations are correct.

87. Forfeiture and Confiscation Act, *Laws of the State of New York*, 1:173–84. The act divided loyalists into two categories: fifty-nine named leaders, mostly royal officeholders, who were attainted; and other loyalists convicted in a "patterned in some particulars on the proceedings used in cases of felony but stripped of traditional safeguards." Editorial note, *LPAH*, 1:198.

88. An Act Relative to Debts Due to Persons within the Enemy Lines, 12 July 1782, 6th sess. 1782, chap. 1, *Laws of the State of New York*, 1:499–501.

89. An Act for Granting a More Effectual Relief in Cases of Certain Trespasses, 17 Mar. 1783, 6th sess. 1783, chap. 31, *Laws of the State of New York*, 1:552.

90. *LPAH*, 1:210–11.

91. Benjamin Franklin to Robert R. Livingston, 14 Oct. 1782, in Wharton, *Revolutionary Diplomatic Correspondence of the United States*, 5:811. See also Bemis, *Diplomacy of the American Revolution*, 231–33, 235–38, 241.

92. The provisional Articles of Peace were signed on 30 November 1782 and ratified on 15 April 1783; the "definitive" treaty was ratified in Congress on 14 January 1784. Continental Congress, *Journals*, 26:29–30.

93. See editorial note, *LPAH*, 1:210–16. See also Van Tyne, *Loyalists in the American Revolution*, 190–242, 268–85.

94. Alexander Hamilton to Robert R. Livingston, 13 Aug. 1783, in *Hamilton Papers*, 3:431. See also Adair, *Fame and the Founding Fathers*, 3–26; Stourzh, *Alexander Hamilton*, 71–75, 101–04; Elkins and McKitrick, *Age of Federalism*, 107–13, 258–63; and Kenyon, "Alexander Hamilton." On loyalist women, see Kerber, *Women of the Republic*, 119–36, and Kerber, *No Constitutional Right to Be Ladies*, 3–33.

95. Minutes of the Supreme Court of Judicature, 1781–83 (engrossed minutes), 18 Jan. 1782, 26 Apr. 1782, 26 Oct. 1782, pp. 92–93, 153, 289, HR; *LPAH*, 1:39–41, 46–49; Tripp, "Robert Troup," 68–75; Robert Troup to Richard Varick, 14 June 1783, box 4, Varick Papers, NYHS; Wyche, *Treatise on the Practice of the Supreme Court of Judicature*.

96. Hamilton to Gouverneur Morris, 21 Feb. 1784, in *Hamilton Papers*, 4:512. In three years, Hamilton "handled forty-five Trespass Act suits besides some twenty other suits under common law actions, the Confiscation Act, and the Citation Act." Editorial note, *LPAH*, 1:525. Burr and Troup also appeared frequently in such actions, though Hamilton seems to have represented more loyalist defendants than they.

97. Hamilton to Major General Nathanael Greene, 10 June 1783, *Hamilton Papers*, 3:376; Hamilton to George Washington, 3 July 1787, *Hamilton Papers*, 4:224.

98. See *Hamilton Papers*, 5:483 n. 1, 542 n. 1.

99. [Alexander Hamilton], "A Letter from Phocion to the Considerate Citizens of New York," [Jan. 1784], *Hamilton Papers*, 3:483–97; [Hamilton], "Second Letter from Phocion," 3:530–58.

100. The thesis that state abuses, rather than Confederation weakness, was the primary force behind the Philadelphia Convention is argued by Rakove, *Original Meanings*, 35–56; Wood, *Creation of the American Republic*, 393–429; and editorial note, in *Madison Papers*, 9:346–48.

101. Trespass Act, *Laws of the State of New York*, 1:552. Some owners also brought separate common-law debt actions to collect back rent. *McDougall v. Leonard* (N.Y. Sup. Ct., 1785–86), noted in *LPAH*, 1:421, 456.

102. Stephen P. Adye to Brigadier General Frederick von Hackenberg, 29 July 1779, *NYHS Coll.* (1875), 233. On British use of rebel property during the war, see Barck, *New York City*, 55, 85–86, 91–92, 224–26.

103. Papers relating to this 1784 case are reprinted in *LPAH*, 1:282–419. See also Morris, *Select Cases from the Mayor's Court of New York City*, 302–27.

104. The statute is excerpted in *LPAH*, 1:201.

105. Brockholst Livingston (1757–1823), son of William Livingston, served as an aide to General Philip Schuyler during the war and as secretary to brother-in-law John Jay in Spain. He became a state and, later, federal Supreme Court justice. *LPAH*, 1:293 n. 31. Lewis (1754–1844) clerked under John Jay and served as chief of staff to General Horatio Gates during the war. He later became attorney general, the state's chief justice, and governor. *LPAH*, 1:293 n. 32.

106. *LPAH*, 1:357, 358.

107. *LPAH*, 1:382. This last quotation comes from Hamilton's sixth brief; it may represent his most cautious line of argument, and it was one adopted by the court.

108. *LPAH*, 1:357, 336. Hamilton and other lawyers first raised the Confederation's peace treaty as a defense in cases arising under New York's Confiscation Act. Hamilton, John Lawrence, Morgan Lewis, and Richard Varick to the President of Congress, 10 Dec. 1782, in *Hamilton Papers*, 3:478–79; editorial note, *LPAH*, 1:297.

109. *LPAH*, 1:411.

110. Editorial note, *LPAH*, 1:289.

111. For Duane's legal career and ambitious land speculations, see Alexander, *Revolutionary Conservative*. A friend to loyalists, Duane lobbied in the state senate to allow John Watts Jr. to purchase land that the state had confiscated from his father. New York Senate, *Journal of the Senate of the State of New-York*, 7th sess. (New York, 1784), 106 (20 Apr. 1784).

112. James Duane to [?], 11 Aug. 1774, in Smith, *Letters of Delegates to Congress*, 1:52–53.

113. *LPAH*, 1:413–16. This and other cases foreshadowing judicial review are surveyed in Sosin, *Aristocracy of the Long Robe*, 203–26.

114. Opinion of the Mayor's Court, *LPAH*, 1:392, 393. The Mayor's Court did not issue reports until it was transformed into the Court of Common Pleas for the City and County of New York in 1821. Morris, introduction to *Select Cases from the Mayor's Court of New York City*, 49.

115. *LPAH*, 1:393.

116. *LPAH*, 1:394, 396, 397.

117. *LPAH*, 1:399–400.

118. *LPAH*, 1:402. Duane declared that Hamilton's citations to Coke, Blackstone, and Chief Justice Mansfield were "full and conclusive." Ibid.

119. *LPAH*, 1:402.

120. *LPAH*, 1:402–6.

121. *LPAH*, 1:409–10.

122. *LPAH*, 1:346, 370–71.

123. *LPAH*, 1:411.

124. *LPAH*, 1:415.

125. *LPAH*, 1:417–18.

126. *LPAH*, 1:418–19. It seems to have worked: some cases were settled soon after, most likely because of the court's strong ruling. *LPAH*, 1:426. However, it is difficult to trace the precedential effect of early modern decisions because full paper trails exist for only a few cases. Goebel speculates that plaintiffs began opting for the state supreme court rather than New York's Mayor's Court in the wake of *Rutgers*. *LPAH*, 1:507–20, 523.

127. [Hamilton], "Letter from Phocion to the Considerate Citizens of New York," 3:483–97; [Hamilton], "Second Letter from Phocion," 3:530–58.

128. Smith et al., *Address from the Committee*, 15, 13, 6–7.

129. Ibid., 6–7, 8, 10, 11.

130. Ibid., 12.

131. Ibid., 13–14 (emphasis added).

132. Hamilton to Thomas Jefferson, 19 Apr. 1792, in *Hamilton Papers*, 11:317.

133. New York Assembly, *Journal of the Assembly of the State of New York, 1785* (New York, 1785), 22.

134. Resolution of 2 Nov. 1784, New York Assembly, *Journal of the Assembly of the State of New York, 1785*, (New York, 1785), 32–34.

PART FOUR

1. George Washington, "Circular to the States," June 1783, in *Writings of George Washington*, 26:486.

2. Hamilton, *Federalist 1*, 27 Oct. 1787, *Federalist Papers*, 3.

3. Compare Jensen, *Articles of Confederation*, with Wood, *Creation of the American Republic*.

4. See Murrin, "Roof without Walls," 333–48.

5. "Postcolonial" has temporal and existential meaning. It can signify what occurs after colonialism; it also connotes the cultural domination and resistance that colonized people experience during as well as after imperial rule. The latter meaning lies beneath the field of postcolonial studies. Ashcroft, Griffiths, and Tiffin, *Empire Writes Back*, 2; Ashcroft, Griffiths, and Tiffin, introduction to *Post-Colonial Studies Reader*, 1. See also Said, *Culture and Imperialism*, xxv.

6. The most closely related experiences were those of white settlers in the British dominions: Canada, Australia, and New Zealand. Like them, the new Americans were simultaneously "imperialised and colonising," freeing themselves from

one empire and then creating another. Ashcroft, Griffiths, and Tiffin, *Empire Writes Back*, 2, 19, 133–45; Lawson, "Comparative Studies"; Lawson, "Cultural Paradigm for the Second World," 68; Anna Johnston and Alan Lawson, "Settler Colonies," in Schwartz and Ray, *Companion to Postcolonial Studies*, 369; Slemon, "Unsettling the Empire"; Hulme, "Including America." Some call the Commonwealth nations "second world" because they are "forever caught between *two* First Worlds, the originating world of Europe as Imperial centre and the First World of the (ab)original peoples." Lawson, "Comparative Studies." Cf. Michael Warner, "What's Colonial about Colonial America?," in St. George, *Possible Pasts*, 49–70 (arguing that British Americans were not "anticolonial" because they did not reject "the colonial project"). It would be unhelpful, if not obtuse, to compare the American Revolution to twentieth-century independence movements in Asia, Africa, the Middle East, or the Caribbean.

7. Literary scholars in particular have analyzed the "postcolonial anxiety" that writers in new nations express in their concerns about language, audience, symbolic reference, and authenticity. Lawrence Buell, "Postcolonial Anxiety in Classic U.S. Literature," in Singh and Schmidt, *Postcolonial Theory and the United States*, 196–219. Buell rightly warns that the United States' original postcoloniality should not be invoked to "evade the fact of present imperium" (197). Indeed, the way early Americans reworked their imperial legacy — by envisioning the United States as an "empire of liberty" — might help explain why the United States has always been reluctant to view itself, as some others do, as a more ambiguous empire. For similar caution, see Chaplin, "Expansion and Exceptionalism in Early American History," 1453–54.

8. Thiong'o, *Decolonising the Mind*; Helen Tiffin, "Post-colonial Literatures and Counter-discourse," in Ashcroft, Griffiths, and Tiffin, *Post-Colonial Studies Reader*, 95. See generally Said, *Orientalism*, and Viswanathan, *Masks of Conquest*.

9. See Lepore, *A Is for American*; Ellis, *After Revolution*; Warner, *Letters of the Republic*; Ziff, *Literary Democracy*; Davidson, *Revolution and the Word*.

10. On nationalism as resting on "imagined community," see Anderson, *Imagined Communities*.

11. This convention still irks many from elsewhere in North and South America and beyond. Peter Hulme, "Postcolonial Theory and Early America: An Approach from the Caribbean," in St. George, *Possible Pasts*, 35.

CHAPTER SEVEN

1. Compare Spaulding, *His Excellency George Clinton*, 172–73, with Kaminski, *George Clinton*, 121.

2. Hamilton, *Federalist* 1, 27 Oct. 1787, 3. All *Federalist* essays cited in the notes are from *Federalist Papers*. The preface to the collected essays published in March 1788 declared that they concerned "the very existence of this new Empire." *DHRC*, 16:469.

3. See Robertson, *Union for Empire*.

4. Hamilton used "empire" and imperial examples (usually favorably) in thir-

teen *Federalist* essays, compared with his reference (often derogatory) in ten essays to republics and republican government. The imperial theme was ever present in his mind. See, e.g., Hamilton to George Washington, 3 July 1787, in *Hamilton Papers*, 4:224 (referring to the Philadelphia Convention as "the golden opportunity to rescue the American empire from disunion anarchy and misery"). A brief consideration of Hamilton's imperial thought is Stourzh, *Alexander Hamilton*, 196–99. See also Kilian, "New Wine in Old Skins?," 145–48; Pocock, introduction to Harrington, *Political Works*, 150–51; and J. G. A. Pocock, "1776: The Revolution against Parliament," in *Three British Revolutions*, 16. Cf. Rose, "Ancient Constitution vs. the Federalist Empire." For the ways in which interpretive commitments shape legal meaning, see Cover, "Foreword: *Nomos* and Narrative."

5. See Hartz, *Liberal Tradition in America*, 35–66.

6. Compare Wood, *Creation of the American Republic*, with Appleby, *Republicanism and Liberalism in the Historical Imagination*; Cornell, *Other Founders*; and Wilentz, *Chants Democratic*. See also Flaherty, "History 'Lite' in Modern American Constitutionalism."

7. See, e.g., Ackerman, *We the People*; Amar, *Bill of Rights*; Kramer, *People Themselves*; and Kramer, "Foreword: We the Court."

8. An important exception is Greene, *Peripheries and Center*.

9. Hamilton first arranged to have New Yorker Gouverneur Morris participate in this new *"Triumvirate"* (George Washington to Alexander Hamilton, 28 Aug. 1788, *DHRC*, 18:352), but Morris wrote too slowly. Another choice, William Duer, was not a gifted essayist. Hamilton then enlisted James Madison. See Jensen et al., editor's note, *DHRC*, 13:486–87; Adair, "Authorship of the Disputed Federalist," in *Fame and the Founding Fathers*, 58–59; and Jacob E. Cooke, introduction to *Federalist Papers*, xi–xxx. Five hundred copies of the first volume containing thirty-six essays were published in New York City in March 1788. They, and the second volume published two months later, were sold in several states and abroad, with several volumes circulating in Virginia, largely through Madison's efforts. But the vast majority were sold within New York, and many copies remained unsold. In sum, publication was limited outside New York City or in other states. Crane, "Publius in the Provinces"; Jensen et al., editor's note, *DHRC*, 16:466–69.

10. James Madison to James Monroe, 14 Mar. 1786, in *Madison Papers*, 8:497; Madison to Edmund Randolph, 26 July 1785, *Madison Papers*, 8:328. See also Drew R. McCoy, "James Madison and Visions of American Nationality in the Confederation Period: A Regional Perspective," in Beeman, Botein, and Carter, *Beyond Confederation*, 239–43.

11. It is possible that they collaborated on a few essays. Cooke, introduction to *Federalist Papers*, xxvii. Their working relationship during the winter of 1787–88 has never been fully reconstructed. A good treatment is Adair, "Authorship of the Disputed Federalist Papers," 49–74. See also Elkins and McKitrick, *Age of Federalism*, 102–14. Cf. Mason, "Federalist—A Split Personality."

12. See Adair, "Authorship of the Disputed Federalist Papers," 28, 58; Furtwangler, *Authority of Publius*, 32–43; Moglen, "Incompleat Burkean," 543–45; and Primus, *American Language of Rights*, 84–91. Historians of political thought have

cautioned against confusing "the coherence of a work or body of political writing" with "its character as a historical phenomenon." J. G. A. Pocock, "Languages and Their Implications: The Transformation of the Study of Political Thought," in *Politics, Language and Time*, 5–6; Skinner, "Limits of Historical Explanation"; Skinner, "Meaning and Understanding in the History of Ideas." See also Rakove, *Original Meanings*, 3–22, and Bernard Bailyn, "The Ideological Fulfillment of the American Revolution: A Commentary on the Constitution," in *Faces of Revolution*, 246–47.

13. Federalists elsewhere considered New York the fount of Antifederalism. "A Landholder VIII," *Connecticut Courant*, 24 Dec. 1787, *DHRC*, 15:76, 78. See also St. John de Crevecoeur to Comte de la Luzerne, New York, 16 May 1788, *DHRC*, 18:16; Antoine de la Forest to Comte de Montmorin, 15 Dec. 1787, *DHRC*, 14:446–47; and George Washington to James Duane, 10 Apr. 1785, in Washington, *Papers of George Washington*, 485–86.

14. Article VII of the Constitution provided that ratification by nine states would make it effective in those states; on 2 July, New Hampshire became the ninth state to ratify. New York ratified the Constitution on 26 July. "Act of Continental Congress Putting Constitution into Effect," in Kurland and Lerner, *Founders' Constitution*, 4:669–70. A rumor circulating before the ratification convention was that the Antifederalists predicted they would lose but would insist on amendments. Samuel A. Otis to Benjamin Lincoln, 8 May 1788, *DHRC*, 17:395. For attempted interstate cooperation between Antifederalists from New York and those of other states to secure amendments, see *DHRC*, 17:395–98, 18:32–61. For the machinations at the Poughkeepsie convention, see De Pauw, *Eleventh Pillar*, esp. 113–17, 193–95, 241–54; Spaulding, *New York in the Critical Period*, 203–31; Riker, *Strategy of Rhetoric*, 229–40; and Brooks, "Alexander Hamilton, Melancton Smith and the Ratification of the Constitution in New York."

15. See Crane, "Publius in the Provinces," and editorial note, *DHRC*, 13:490–92.

16. See Rakove, *Original Meanings*, 149–50, and Philip Bobbitt, "The Constitutional Canon," in Balkin and Levinson, *Legal Canons*, 338. On the founding generation's struggle with the concept of authorship, see Fliegelman, *Declaring Independence*, 164–89.

17. For the vitality of popular constitutionalism in the early Republic, see Kramer, *People Themselves*.

18. Cf. Tocqueville, *Democracy in America*, trans. Reeve, 1:280.

19. Harrington, *Commonwealth of Oceana; and, A System of Politics*, 11.

20. Hamilton, *Federalist* 1, 27 Oct. 1787, 3.

21. See Onuf, *Jefferson's Empire*, 1–17; Boyd, "Thomas Jefferson's 'Empire of Liberty' "; Stephanson, *Manifest Destiny*; Tuveson, *Redeemer Nation*, 91–136; and Amar, "Some New World Lessons for the Old World."

22. Hamilton, *Federalist* 9, 21 Nov. 1787, 51.

23. He warned that "particular interests" and "local institutions" might overcome "the public good." Hamilton, *Federalist* 1, 27 Oct. 1787, 4. See also Noah Webster, *Examination into the Leading Principles of the Federal Constitution Proposed*

by the Late Convention Held at Philadelphia (1787), in Ford, *Pamphlets on the Constitution of the United States*, 29. For the Scottish realism behind these sentiments, see White, *Philosophy, the Federalist, and the Constitution*, 113–28.

24. Hamilton, *Federalist* 15, 1 Dec. 1787, 72–73; Stourzh, *Alexander Hamilton*, 95–106, 201–5; Adair, *Fame and the Founding Fathers*, 23–25; White, *Philosophy, the Federalist, and the Constitution*, 85–101. See generally Hirschman, *Passions and the Interests*.

25. Elkins and McKitrick, *Age of Federalism*, 163–93.

26. Hamilton, *Federalist* 1, 27 Oct. 1787, 4.

27. Hamilton, *Federalist* 23, 18 Dec. 1787, 115. A survey of such plots is Slaughter, *Whiskey Rebellion*, 28–60. See also Andrew R. L. Cayton, " 'When Shall We Cease to Have Judases?' The Blount Conspiracy and the Limits of the 'Extended Republic,' " in Hoffman and Albert, *Launching the "Extended Republic,"* 156–89.

28. Hamilton, *Federalist* 21, 12 Dec. 1787, 100. See also Hamilton, *Federalist* 16, 4 Dec. 1787, 75, 79.

29. Hamilton wrote six "Continentalist" letters from July 1781 to July 1782. *Hamilton Papers*, 2:649–52, 654–57, 660–65, 669–74, 3:75–82, 99–106. For Madison's outline, see "Vices of the Political System of the United States," *Madison Papers*, 9:345–58.

30. On the bank, see Janet A. Riesman, "Money, Credit, and Federalist Political Economy," in Beeman, Botein, and Carter, *Beyond Confederation*, 128–61. On the military establishment, see George Washington, "Sentiments on a Peace Establishment," 2 May 1783, in *Writings of George Washington*, 26:374–98, and Prucha, *Sword of the Republic*. On administration, see White, *Federalists*, 478, 507–8. On territorial and Native American policy, see Onuf, *Origins of the Federal Republic*, 160–85; and Prucha, *American Indian Policy in the Formative Years*. See generally Jack N. Rakove, "From One Agenda to Another: The Condition of American Federalism, 1783–1787," in *American Revolution*, 80–103.

31. Madison, *Federalist* 37, 11 Jan. 1788, 236. See also Hamilton, *Federalist* 78, 28 May 1788, 525–26, and *Federalist* 82, 28 May 1788, 553.

32. See Bailyn, *Faces of Revolution*, 236, 239, and Rakove, *Original Meanings*, 149–60. In their relationship to European authority, the ratifiers exhibited what Lawrence Buell calls a "resistance-deference syndrome." Buell, "Postcolonial Anxiety," 204.

33. Hamilton, *Federalist* 15, 1 Dec. 1787, 66–67.

34. Webster, *Grammatical Institute*, pt. I, 3, 15.

35. Webster, *Examination into the Leading Principles of the Federal Constitution*, 29.

36. See Onuf and Onuf, *Federal Union, Modern World*; Armitage, "Declaration of Independence and International Law"; and Helfman, "Law of Nations in *The Federalist Papers*."

37. Hamilton, *Federalist* 11, 24 Nov. 1787, 65–73.

38. Hamilton's example was Cornelius de Pauw, *Recherches Philosophiques sur les Americains* (Berlin, 1770). Hamilton, *Federalist* 11, 24 Nov. 1787, 72n*. It was to answer Buffon's similar analysis that Thomas Jefferson wrote that other monument of American postcolonial literature, *Notes on the State of Virginia*. For the quadra-

section of the globe in the law of nations, see Gould, "Zones of Law, Zones of Violence," 479.

39. Hamilton, *Federalist* 11, 24 Nov. 1787, 72–73.

40. Ibid., 68.

41. Ibid., 73.

42. For the tension between the state and Confederation Indian policy, see Graymont, *Iroquois in the American Revolution*, 259–91; Graymont, "New York State Indian Policy after the Revolution"; Jack Campisi, "From Stanwix to Canandaigua: National Policy, States' Rights and Indian Land," in Vescey and Starna, *Iroquois Land Claims*, 49–65; Lehman, "End of the Iroquois Mystique"; and Higgins, *Expansion in New York*, 100–114.

43. Only a few Antifederalists, including some freeholders in New York, criticized the slave trade and slavery itself as hypocritical among people who revolted in the name of liberty. See, e.g., "Letter from Countryman in Dutchess County, V," 22 Jan. 1788, in Storing and Dry, *Complete Anti-Federalist*, 6:62. See also Finkelman, "Book Review," 202–6, and Finkelman, "Founders and Slavery." The Manumission Society, founded in 1785, ran a school for the children of slaves to prepare them for freedom. Richard B. Morris, "John Jay and the New York State Constitution and Courts after Two Hundred Years," in *Essays on the Genesis of the Empire State*, 8; James E. Cronin, introduction to *Diary of Elihu Hubbard Smith*, 13–14. Jay was the society's first president and Hamilton its first secretary.

44. When discussing representation and the three-fifths clause, for example, Madison asked New Yorkers to imagine the situation of those in slave-dependent states, but he did not defend slavery in the abstract. Madison, *Federalist* 54, 12 Feb. 1788, 367–70. He also praised the slave trade clause for putting the nation on the path toward ending that traffic. Madison, *Federalist* 42, 22 Jan. 1788, 281–82.

45. There are many biographies of Hamilton. See, e.g., Cooke, *Alexander Hamilton*, and Chernow, *Alexander Hamilton*.

46. Jones, *"The King of the Alley."*

47. Ver Steeg, *Robert Morris*.

48. Smith, *James Wilson, Founding Father*. Again, similar configurations might be found in other states, but they did not produce the same political literature.

49. See Wood, *Creation of the American Republic*, 471–518.

50. Despite antiloyalist legislation in New York and elsewhere, Peter Van Schaak maintained that most loyalists could resume their normal lives after the peace treaty. Van Schaack, *Life of Peter Van Schaack*, 322. For suggestive accounts on the reintegration of loyalists, see Benton, *Whig-Loyalism*, 190–213, and Mass, *Return of the Massachusetts Loyalists*.

51. New York Antifederalists were central to what Saul Cornell calls "middling" Antifederalism. Cornell, *Other Founders*, 81–106, 119–20. See also Lynd, *Anti-Federalism in Dutchess County*, esp. 26–31. Many Antifederalists were involved in state and local government, making it difficult to characterize them as libertarian. But see Wood, *Creation of the American Republic*, 519–24.

52. Bielinski, *Abraham Yates, Jr.*; Countryman, *People in Revolution*, 222–24.

53. Kaminski, *George Clinton*, 12.

54. De Pauw, *Eleventh Pillar*, 159.

55. A good treatment of many of these conflicts is Onuf, *Origins of the Federal Republic*.

56. See White, *Middle Ground*, 413–517; Hinderaker, *Elusive Empires*, 185–270.

57. See Taylor, *William Cooper's Town*, and Wycoff, *Developer's Frontier*.

58. U.S. Constitution, art. VI, § 3. See also Eblen, *First and Second American Empires*; Duffey, "Northwest Ordinance as a Constitutional Document"; Onuf, *Statehood and Union*; and Levinson, "Why the Canon Should Be Expanded."

59. Farrand, *Records*, 1:578–79. Mason was not a member of the Confederation Congress, but his use of the phrase "equal footing" indicates that he had read or heard about the ordinance, which uses the same phrase. Northwest Ordinance (1787), §14, art. V. See also Adams, *Defence of the Constitutions*, 505–6. Gouverneur Morris was one of the very few who disagreed with the equality principle. Farrand, *Records*, 1:571, 583. See generally Gordon S. Wood, "Launching the 'Extended Republic,'" in Hoffman and Albert, *Launching the "Extended Republic*," 22; Robert F. Berkhofer Jr., "The Northwest Ordinance and the Principle of Territorial Evolution," in Bloom, *American Territorial System*, 45–55; and Wilson, *Imperial Republic*, 60–61.

60. See Hinderaker, *Elusive Empires*, 236–70.

61. See, e.g., Wood, *Creation of the American Republic*, 499–518; Cecelia M. Kenyon, "Introduction: The Political Thought of the Antifederalists," in *The Antifederalists*, xxxix–xlviii; and Terence Ball, "'A Republic—If You Can Keep It,'" in *Conceptual* Ball and Pocock, *Change and the Constitution*, 137–64.

62. Robert Yates and John Lansing to Governor George Clinton, 21 Dec. 1787, *New York Daily Advertiser*, 14 Jan. 1788, DHRC, 15:366–70. See also Farrand, *Records*, 1:249–50, 336–38. On the ambiguous motives of Yates and Lansing, see De Pauw, *Eleventh Pillar*, 62–64.

63. Onuf, *Origins of the Federal Republic*, 91, 97–98, 124–25.

64. "Cato I," *New York Journal*, 26 Sept. 1787, DHRC, 13:255–57 (all "Cato" essays cited in the notes are from the *New York Journal*); "Cato III," 25 Oct. 1787, DHRC, 13:473–77. For Clinton's attempts as governor to hold on to these lands, going so far as to negotiate secretly with the British in an attempt to obtain their western forts, see Kaminksi, *George Clinton*, 63–77, 81–89. While most historians have identified Clinton as the author of the "Cato" letters, Linda Grant De Pauw argues that "Cato" was Abraham Yates. De Pauw, *Eleventh Pillar*, 283–92.

65. "Brutus XII," *New York Journal*, 7 Feb. 1788, DHRC, 16:74 (all "Brutus" essays cited in the notes are from the *New York Journal*); "Brutus I," 18 Oct. 1787, DHRC, 13:417–18; "Brutus XII," 7 Feb. 1788, DHRC, 16:74.

66. Most New York Antifederalists supported the Confederation impost but wanted it collected by local officials, not "continental collectors." Elliot, *Debates*, 2:330–34, 359–60; Melancton Smith, "An Address to the People of the State of New-York: Showing the Necessity of Making Amendments to the Constitution," New York, 1788, DHRC, 17:158–60. Federalists like Hamilton answered that local officials would frustrate collection. Hamilton, "Remarks in the New York Assembly on an Act Granting to Congress Certain Imposts and Duties," [15 Feb. 1787],

in *Hamilton Papers*, 4:71–92; Elliot, *Debates*, 3:361. See De Pauw, *Eleventh Pillar*, 31–43, and, for an economic interpretation for Antifederalist opposition to the federal impost, Cochran, *New York in the Confederation*. The impost debate paralleled the writs of assistance controversy of a generation earlier.

67. "Brutus I," 18 Oct. 1787, *DHRC*, 13:413. See also Melancton Smith, in Elliot, *Debates*, 2:328; New York's Declaration of Rights, *Poughkeepsie Country Journal*, 29 July 1788, *DHRC*, 18:299; and Thomas Tredwell, in Elliot, *Debates*, 2:403. The title of an Antifederalist newspaper in Pennsylvania was the *Freeman's Journal*, and Federalist Tench Coxe wrote a series of essays under the pseudonym "Freeman."

68. See, e.g., Hamilton, *Federalist* 80, 28 May 1788, 537, and Thomas Tredwell, in Elliot, *Debates*, 2:404.

69. On the proliferation of corporations, see Davis, *Essays in the Earlier History of American Corporations*; Seavoy, *Origins of the American Business Corporation*; Teaford, *Municipal Revolution in America*; Whitehead, *Separation of College and State*; Tewksbury, *Founding of American Colleges and Universities*; Hammond, *Banks and Politics in America*; Handlin and Handlin, "Origins of American Business Corporations," 22–23, and *Commonwealth*; Maier, "Revolutionary Origins of the American Corporation"; and Hall, *Organization of American Culture*. Throughout this era of proliferation, debates raged about corporate immunity from state and federal legislation.

70. Hamilton, 19 June 1787, in Farrand, *Records*, 1:287, 328. For criticism of the corporate argument by an imperial agent, see [Kennedy], *Essay on the Government of the Colonies*, 14.

71. Madison, 29 June 1787, in Farrand, *Records*, 1:463–64. See also Madison, 29 June 1787, in Farrand, *Records*, 1:471; "West-Chester Farmer," 3 June 1787, *DHRC*, 13:128–30. These positions were reversible. A generation later, Federalist legatees championed corporate power to oppose state regulation. See, e.g., *Dartmouth College v. Woodward*, 17 U.S. 518 (1819).

72. There were numerous objections to concurrent jurisdiction. Antifederalists argued that Congress's right to tax the states, in conjunction with the clause granting that body all authority "necessary and proper" to carry out its enumerated functions, would strip the states' power to raise revenue. Without the full power to tax, a state would perish: "There cannot be a greater solecism in politics than to talk of power in a government, without the command of any revenue. It is absurd as to talk of an animal without blood, or the subsistence of one without food." "Brutus V," 13 Dec. 1787, *DHRC*, 14:425–26; Melancton Smith, in Elliot, *Debates*, 2:340–41. See also Hamilton, Robert R. Livingston, and Gilbert Livingston, in Elliot, *Debates*, 2:355–56, 361–63, 385, 387. "Brutus" conceded that the federal government should have some revenue base; but the proposed federal power of taxation, when combined with the necessary and proper clause, might lead to preemption of the states' right to collect any revenue. "Brutus VI," 27 Dec. 1787, *DHRC*, 15:110–17. The first use of the term in the Federalist context was by John Jay in a memorandum on state violations of treaties, particularly state laws infringing loyalist property rights. Jay denied that the states had "concurrent jurisdiction"

over matters covered by treaties and other "general and national purposes." John Jay to Congress, 12 Oct. 1786, *Secret Journals of the Acts and Proceedings of Congress*, 4:185–287.

73. For the theory of sovereignty in Britain, see Francis and Morrow, "After the Ancient Constitution," 351–77.

74. Hamilton, *Federalist* 15, 1 Dec. 1787, 93. See also Madison with Hamilton, *Federalist* 20, 11 Dec. 1787, 128–29; Madison to Thomas Jefferson, 24 Oct. and 1 Nov. 1787 (excerpts), *DHRC*, 13:445; and "A Well Wisher to the United States of America, who came lately from London to New-York," in *Observations on the Articles of Confederation*. Cf. Rakove, *Original Meanings*, 188–91.

75. After Federalists downgraded the corporate metaphor, Antifederalists began to fret that the states would be left, in the words of New Yorker Robert Lansing, with "only corporate rights." Elliot, *Debates*, 2:376. See also "A Citizen of Philadelphia" and "Remarks on the Address of Sixteen Members," 18 Oct. 1787, *DHRC*, 13:301; Thomas Tudor Tucker to St. George Tucker, 28 Dec. 1787 (excerpt), *DHRC*, 15:144; Elbridge Gerry, in Farrand, *Records*, 1:474; and John Rutledge, in Farrand, *Records*, 2:391.

76. Hamilton, *Federalist* 9, 21 Nov. 1787, 52. See also Hamilton, in Elliot, *Debates*, 1:473; Hamilton, in Elliot, *Debates*, 2:343.

77. On the constitutional position of local government after the Revolution, see Hartog, *Public Property and Private Power*.

78. Cf. Kenyon, "Men of Little Faith," and Elkins and McKitrick, "Founding Fathers."

79. Hamilton, *Federalist* 1, 27 Oct. 1787, 3. See also [Hamilton], "The Continentalist VI," [4 July 1782], *Hamilton Papers*, 3:106.

80. Jay, *Federalist* 2, 31 Oct. 1787, 9. John D. Seelye explicates the riverine theme in the early American culture in *Beautiful Machine*.

81. Jay, *Federalist* 2, 31 Oct. 1787, 9–10. See also Ferguson, "Forgotten Publius."

82. John Cotton to James Kent, 25 Jan. 1783, KP. See also Murrin, "Roof without Walls." For Federalist attempts to create a national identity, see Waldstreicher, *In the Midst of Perpetual Fetes*, 53–107. For Jeffersonian attempts, see Onuf, *Jefferson's Empire*.

83. Jay, *Federalist* 5, 10 Nov. 1787, 23–27; Jay, *Federalist* 4, 7 Nov. 1787, 21–22. See also [John Jay], "An Address to the People of the State of New-York . . . The 17th of September, 1787," New York, 1788, *DHRC*, 17:118; Hamilton, *Federalist* 17, 5 Dec. 1787, 109; and Madison, *Federalist* 56, 19 Feb. 1788, 382. For a particularly centralist interpretation of the British Union and its lesson for the American states, proposing among other measures something like Poynings' Law to give Congress power to review state legislation, see "A Well Wisher to the United States of America," 3–4, 7. See also *Pennsylvania Gazette*, 29 Aug. 1787, *DHRC*, 13:191–92.

84. Hamilton, *Federalist* 7, 17 Nov. 1787, 43. See also Jay, *Federalist* 4, 7 Nov. 1787, 19–20; Hamilton, *Federalist* 7, 17 Nov. 1787, 41; Hamilton, *Federalist* 11, 24 Nov. 1787, 69–70; Hamilton, *Federalist* 24, 19 Dec. 1787, 156; Hamilton,

Federalist 25, 21 Dec. 1787, 158; Madison, *Federalist* 14, 30 Nov. 1787, 87; and [Jay], *Address to People of the State of New-York, DHRC*, 17:109–10.

85. Hamilton, *Federalist* 25, 21 Dec. 1787, 158–59. See also Madison, *Federalist* 41, 19 Jan. 1787, 274–75, and *DHRC*, 15:423.

86. [DeWitt Clinton], "Countryman," *New York Journal*, 10 Jan. 1788.

87. Buell, "Postcolonial Anxiety," 203.

88. Madison, "Vices of the Political System of the United States"; Madison to Caleb Wallace, 23 Aug. 1785, 9:351; Madison to Edmund Randolph, 8 Apr. 1787, 9:370; Madison to George Washington, 16 Apr. 1787, 9:383; Madison, Address at the Philadelphia Convention, 21 July 1787, 10:109–10, all in *Madison Papers*. See also Rakove, *Original Meanings*, xvi, 35–56, and Hobson, "Negative on State Laws."

89. The similarity between Madison's analysis of factions in *Federalist* 10 and that in Hume's essays demonstrates the influence of the Scot on the Virginian. Adair, " 'That Politics May Be Reduced to a Science.' "

90. See Hume, "Of the Parties of Great Britain," in *Essays Moral, Political and Literary*, 73, n. 1. Cf. Adair, " 'That Politics May Be Reduced to a Science,' " 357.

91. Hume included Ireland within Great Britain. Hume, "Idea of a Perfect Commonwealth," in *Essays Moral, Political and Literary*, 502.

92. See Robbins, *Eighteenth-Century Commonwealthman*, 9; Robbins, " 'When It Is That Colonies May Turn Independent.' "

93. Madison, *Federalist* 10, 22 Nov. 1787, 64; Morgan, "Safety in Numbers." See also Madison, "Vices of the Political System of the United States," in *Madison Papers*, 9:357.

94. Rakove, "The Madisonian Moment," in *Original Meanings*, 35–56.

95. Elsewhere Madison described slaves as having "the mixt character of persons and of property." Madison, *Federalist* 54, 12 Feb. 1788, 368.

96. One New York assemblyman, during what one horrified Briton referred to as the "liberating frenzy" of the late 1780s, proposed a bill that would have allowed freed slaves to hold high office. A colleague objected that most slaves could not read, which inspired the introduction of another bill requiring slave owners to educate their slaves in preparation for freedom. Sir George Yonge to [unnamed], 6 Jan. 1789, copy, Bancroft Collection, NYPL, 30:210. New York passed a less radical gradual emancipation statute a decade later, in 1799. See generally Zilversmit, *First Emancipation*.

97. Madison to Edmund Randolph, 26 July 1785, *Madison Papers*, 8:328.

98. See Kramer, "Madison's Audience."

99. Hamilton, *Federalist* 22, 14 Dec. 1787, 137. Hamilton cited *"Encyclopedie,* article *empire,"* in his analysis of the German kingdoms. Diderot and d'Alembert, *Encyclopédie*, 5:582–83. The translation was apparently his own. For comparisons with other empires, positive and negative, see, e.g., Hamilton to James Duane, 3 Sept. 1780, *Hamilton Papers*, 2:403; [Hamilton], "The Continentalist II," [19 July 1781], *Hamilton Papers*, 2:656; Hamilton, "The Continentalist III," [9 Aug. 1781], *Hamilton Papers*, 2:661; James Madison to Thomas Jefferson, 24 Oct. 1787, *Madison Papers*, 10: 205–20; and Hamilton, *Federalist* 30, 28 Dec. 1787, 188.

100. Hamilton, *Federalist* 17, 5 Dec. 1787, 108. See also Hamilton, in Elliot, *Debates*, 2:353–54, and Hamilton, in Farrand, *Records*, 1:285.

101. Hamilton, *Federalist* 17, 5 Dec. 1787, 109. For a British version of this story, see [Ramsay], *Essay on the Constitution*, 14–15. This dynamic variation on the Polybian estates model probably derives from James Harrington. See Harrington, *Political Works*, 408, 436, 606–9; J. G. A. Pocock, introduction to *Political Works*, 10–12; and Wormuth, *Origins of Modern Constitutionalism*, 129–34. David Hume popularized it in the eighteenth century. Hume, "Of Refinement in the Arts," in *Essays Moral, Political and Literary*, 284; Forbes, *Hume's Philosophical Politics*, 176–80, 279–82, 300. The idea that the king enjoyed complementary interests with the mass of people was an older rationalization of expansive royal power. See Pocock, *Ancient Constitution*, 117–23, 148–70, 182–228. For an early articulation of the triangular justification of royal power in an imperial context, see Davies, *Discovery of the True Causes*, 265. Davies may have influenced Harrington. See Harrington, *Political Works*, 71, 159.

102. Compare Morgan, *Inventing the People*, 280–83; Hartz, *Economic Policy and Democratic Thought*, 25–26; and Griffin, *American Constitutionalism*, 19–26, with Greene, *Peripheries and Center*, 202–7; Wood, *Creation of the American Republic*, 344–89; and *U.S. Term Limits, Inc. v. Thornton*, 514 U.S. 779, 838 (1995) (Kennedy, J., concurring) (commending the framers for "split[ting] the atom of sovereignty"). See also Weston and Greenberg, *Subjects and Sovereigns*; Ullmann, *Principles of Government and Politics in the Middle Ages*, 19–26; and Gierke, *Development of Political Theory*, 143–240.

103. See Blackstone, *Commentaries*, 1:49.

104. On manifest destiny, see Stephanson, *Manifest Destiny*.

105. See George Washington to the Mayor, Aldermen, & Commonalty of New York City, 10 Apr. 1785, in Washington, *Papers of George Washington*, 2:487.

106. Hamilton, *Federalist* 1, 27 Oct. 1787, 3. This attempt to forge a common understanding of the Constitution was not, however, the same as creating a pervasive "governmentality." Though substantive conceptions of constitutional law set boundaries for acceptable constitutional interpretations, they did not determine the way individual Americans thought and acted. Cf. Michel Foucault, "On Governmentality," in *Foucault Effect*, and Hardt and Negri, *Empire*, 22–27, 87–90.

107. See Wood, *Creation of the American Republic*, 450, 453, 553–62, 602–8.

108. "Federal Farmer I," 8 Nov. 1787, *DHRC*, 14:25; "Federal Farmer II," 8 Nov. 1787, *DHRC*, 14:26–27. On representation, see Kenyon, "Introduction: Political Thought of the Antifederalists," xlvix–lxi, and Wood, *Creation of the American Republic*, esp. 596–600. See also Lutz, *Popular Consent and Popular Control*. Paul L. Ford identified Richard Henry Lee as the author of the "Federal Farmer" letters, but I agree with those who conclude that it was Melancton Smith. Webking, "Melancton Smith and the *Letters from the Federal Farmer*"; Rakove, *Original Meanings*, 228–29.

109. Smith complained that the capital might be eight hundred miles away, perhaps thinking of the distance between New York and South Carolina. Elliot, *Debates*, 2:265, 335.

110. Ibid., 396.

111. Ibid., 246; "Cato VI," 13 Dec. 1787, *DHRC*, 14:431; "Timeleon," *New York Journal*, extra ed., 1 Nov. 1787, *DHRC*, 13:638. See also Kenyon, "Introduction: Political Thought of the Antifederalists," lii, lviii.

112. Elliot, *Debates*, 2:402.

113. "Cato IV," 8 Nov. 1787, *DHRC*, 14:9–10; "Cato V," 22 Nov. 1787, *DHRC*, 14:183–84; "Brutus XVI," 10 Apr. 1788, *DHRC*, 17:67. See also "Cato VI," 13 Dec. 1787, *DHRC*, 14:428–32; "Cato VII," 3 Jan. 1788, *DHRC*, 15:240–43; "Federal Farmer XVIII," 2 May 1788, *DHRC*, 17:366–70; Gilbert Livingston, in Elliot, *Debates*, 2:287–88; and [Abraham Yates], "Sydney I," 13 June 1788, in Ford, *Essays on the Constitution of the United States*, 306. See generally Hutson, "Country, Court, and Constitution," and John M. Murrin, "The Great Inversion, or, Court versus Country: A Comparison of the Revolution Settlements in England (1688–1721) and America (1776–1816)," in Pocock, *Three British Revolutions*, 368–453.

114. The reduction of the orders to be balanced in the mixed constitution from three to two is evident throughout Antifederalist writing. See, e.g., "Federal Farmer I," 8 Nov. 1787, *DHRC*, 14:23; Smith, in Elliot, *Debates*, 2:246; and "Cato VI," 13 Dec. 1787, *DHRC*, 14:431. For the emergence of the stadial theory of social evolution (hunting, pastoral, agricultural, and commercial), see Meek, *Social Science and the Ignoble Savage*.

115. Hamilton, *Federalist* 12, 22 Nov. 1787, 55. Hamilton added, however, that the two interest groups still might differ over policy matters. See Hamilton, *Federalist* 35, 5 Jan. 1788, 217–18. Cf. Lance Banning, "Political Economy and the Creation of the Federal Republic," in Konig, *Devising Liberty*, 11–49.

116. For agrarian interpretations of Antifederalism, see Main, *Antifederalists*; Main, *Political Parties before the Constitution*; Benson, *Turner and Beard*, 216–23; Hutson, "Country, Court, and Constitution," 365–67; Bruegel, "Unrest"; Lynd, *Anti-Federalism in Dutchess County*; and Spaulding, *New York in the Critical Period*. See generally Libby, *Geographical Distribution of the Vote of the Thirteen States*, 69. See also Jensen, *New Nation*. Others view the Antifederalists as capitalists and the Federalists as backward-looking protectors of virtue. Gordon S. Wood, "Interest and Disinterestedness in the Making of the Constitution," in Beeman, Botein, and Carter, *Beyond Confederation*, 69–109; Saul Cornell, "Politics of the Middling Sort: The Bourgeois Radicalism of Melancton Smith and Abraham Yates, and the New York Antifederalists," in Gilje and Pencak, *New York in the Age of the Constitution*, 151–75.

117. "A substantial yeoman, of sense and discernment, will hardly ever be chosen." Elliot, *Debates*, 2:245–46. Smith derived his notion of the "natural aristocracy" from Adams's *Defence of the Constitution*. Smith, in Elliot, *Debates*, 2:281. See also the remarks of Governor Clinton, in Elliot, *Debates*, 2:261–62. On the availability of binary, hierarchical, and triadic models of class in early modern British culture, see Cannadine, *Rise and Fall of Class in Britain*.

118. "Federal Farmer IX," 2 May 1788, *DHRC*, 17:289.

119. Elliot, *Debates*, 2:245–46; "Federal Farmer IX," 2 May 1788, *DHRC*, 17:289.

120. "Federal Farmer VII," 2 May 1788, *DHRC*, 17:279–81. Cf. Wood, "Interest and Disinterestedness in the Making of the Constitution," 69–109, and Cornell, "Politics of the Middling Sort" (describing the Antifederalists as liberal new men). Robert Yates was more blunt. The new Constitution would usher in "a swarm of revenue and excise officers to prey upon the honest and industrious part of the community, eat up their substance, and riot on the spoils of the country." Not even the church and the "bed-chamber" were sacred. "Brutus V," 13 Dec. 1787, *DHRC*, 14:425; "Brutus VI," 27 Dec. 1787, *DHRC*, 15:113–14. Antifederalist delegate John Williams quoted "Brutus" at the ratification convention. Elliot, *Debates*, 2:330–31.

121. "Federal Farmer VIII," 2 May 1788, *DHRC*, 17:283–84. Smith cited the popular account by the Swiss commentator Jean L. DeLolme, *The Constitution of England; or, An Account of the English Government*, first published in French in 1771 and in English in 1784. For the Whig history of the conquest, see Pocock, *Ancient Constitution*, 30–55, and Christopher Hill, "The Norman Yoke," in *Puritanism and Revolution*, 5–122.

122. "Brutus Junior," 8 Nov. 1787, *DHRC*, 14:4–5.

123. For Hamilton's early equation of war with opportunity, see Alexander Hamilton to Edward Stevens, 11 Nov. 1769, *Hamilton Papers*, 1:4.

124. For Antifederalist political economy, see Foner, *Tom Paine and Revolutionary America*, 145–82, and Cornell, *Other Founders*, 174–87.

125. See, e.g., Hamilton, in Elliot, *Debates*, 2:256.

126. James Kent to Nathaniel Lawrence, 9 Nov. 1787, *DHRC*, 14:75; Robert R. Livingston, in Elliot, *Debates*, 2:277–78.

127. Hamilton, *Federalist* 84, 28 May 1788, 439–40. Montgomery County, in the Mohawk Valley, was formerly Tryon County, which William Johnson had carved out of Albany County in 1772.

128. Madison, *Federalist* 14, 30 Nov. 1787, 87.

129. Hamilton, *Federalist* 22, 14 Dec. 1787, 111, 104–05.

130. "Americanus," *New York Daily Advertiser*, 1 Aug. 1787, *DHRC*, 13:183–84. Lance Banning argues that Hamilton wanted to create "a monied and office-holding class directly dependent on [the federal] government for the promotion of its economic interests," an idea that begins well but concludes too narrowly. Banning, "Political Economy and the Creation of the Federal Republic," 19.

131. "Marcus," *New York Daily Advertiser*, 15 Oct. 1787, *DHRC*, 13:383–84. See also Gouverneur Morris to George Washington, 30 Oct. 1787, *DHRC*, 13:513.

132. *Connecticut Courant*, 20 Nov. 1786, *DHRC*, MFM: Conn. 3.

133. Hamilton, Speech of 18 June 1787, in Farrand, *Records*, 1:288–89, 299, 309–10. See also Hamilton, in Elliot, *Debates*, 2:305; Hamilton, *Federalist* 75, 26 Mar. 1788, 506. Native New Yorker Gouverneur Morris echoed these sentiments in the Philadelphia Convention. Farrand, *Records*, 1:512–14, 533, 545, 567, 571, 2:202, 207. On Madison's hope that the Senate would preserve nationalist interests and his appreciation of the crown's neutrality, see Rakove, *Original Meanings*, 78–79; *Madison Papers*, 9:384, 370; and Wood, "Interests and Disinterestedness in the Making of the Constitution," 92. See generally Swift, *Making of an American Senate*.

134. Elliot, *Debates*, 2:257. On Hamilton's desire to exploit the vices of the wealthy for public advantage, see Stourzh, *Alexander Hamilton*, 95–106. See generally Hirschman, *Passions and the Interests*.

135. Farrand, *Records*, 1:366.

136. Ibid., 374. Hamilton's prediction about the Senate was correct. Jack N. Rakove, "The Structure of Politics at the Accession of George Washington," in Beeman, Botein, and Carter, *Beyond Confederation*, 261–94.

137. Hamilton, *Federalist* 68, 12 Mar. 1788, 458.

138. Hamilton, "Remarks in the New York Assembly on an Act Granting to Congress Certain Imposts and Duties," [15 Feb. 1787], *Hamilton Papers*, 4:71–92.

139. Hamilton, *Federalist* 76, 1 Apr. 1788, 511, 513. See also Hamilton, *Federalist* 69, 14 Mar. 1788, 462–70, and *Federalist* 70, 15 Mar. 1788, 471–80. On whether the executive was to be controlled by the president or the cabinet as a whole, see Banning, "Republican Ideology and the Triumph of the Constitution," 169.

140. Hamilton, *Federalist* 71, 17 Mar. 1788, 483, and *Federalist* 73, 21 Mar. 1788, 488. Jay had similar ideas about the diplomatic corps. Jay, "Address to the People"; Monaghan, *John Jay*, 244–77.

141. Compare Hamilton, *Federalist* 75, 26 Mar. 1788, 503, with Hamilton, *Federalist* 78, 28 May 1788, 522–23.

142. See, e.g., [Morris], *Some Observations on the Charge Given by the Honourable James Delancey*, 9–10.

143. See, e.g., Ackerman, *We the People*; Amar, *Bill of Rights*; Primus, *American Language of Rights*; Kramer, *People Themselves*; and Wilf, "First Republican Revival."

144. Kramer, "Foreword: We the Court," 74–128; Hartz, *Liberal Tradition in America*, 102–3. Sylvia Snowiss calls the process by which the Constitution became enforceable in courts the "legalization of fundamental law": where before constitutions had been political devices, now they were narrowly conceived as "ordinary law." Snowiss, *Judicial Review and the Law of the Constitution*, 13–16, 64.

145. Cf. Stoner, *Common Law and Liberal Theory*.

146. See Smith, *Appeals to the Privy Council*, esp. 51–53; Goebel and Naughton, *Law Enforcement in Colonial New York*, xxi–xxii, 3–6, 13; and Bilder, *Transatlantic Constitution*, 186–96.

147. Farrand, *Records*, 1:164–69, 2:27–29, 73–80, 390–91. See also Hobson, "Negative on State Laws."

148. For similar interpretations of the founders' conception of constitutional law as a hybrid of law and political theory, see Eisgruber, "Marbury, Marshall, and the Politics of Constitutional Judgment"; Eisgruber, "John Marshall's Judicial Rhetoric"; White, *Marshall Court*, 195–200; and Powell, *Community Built on Words*. For law as an "arena of conflict," see Hartog, "Pigs and Positivism." See also Gustafson, *Representative Words*, 37–65.

149. Article III established "one supreme Court" and left the construction of "inferior Courts" to the discretion of Congress. The Judiciary Act of 1789 established lower courts and made some of the Supreme Court's original jurisdiction

exclusive and some concurrent with the lower federal and state courts. See Ritz, *Rewriting the History of the Judiciary Act of 1789*.

150. Hamilton, *Federalist* 80, 28 May 1788, 538.

151. Hamilton, *Federalist* 22, 14 Dec. 1787, 143. See also Hamilton, *Federalist* 16, 4 Dec. 1787, 102, and Madison, *Federalist* 39, 16 Jan. 1788, 256–57.

152. [Hamilton], "Letter from Phocion to the Considerate Citizens of New York," 3:483–96; Table on the Briefs in *Rutgers v. Waddington, LPAH,* 1:336–37. Cf. Helfman, "Law of Nations in *The Federalist Papers*," 112–14.

153. Hamilton, *Federalist* 80, 28 May 1788, 535, and *Federalist* 22, 14 Dec. 1787, 143–44.

154. Hamilton, *Federalist* 82, 28 May 1788, 555.

155. Ibid., 555–56.

156. Blackstone, for example, discussed the "concurrent jurisdiction" of the ecclesiastical courts and chancery over actions to recover legacies. Blackstone, *Commentaries,* 2:513.

157. "Brutus XI," 31 Jan. 1788, *DHRC,* 15:515; "Brutus XII," 14 Feb. 1788, *DHRC,* 16:122. See also "Brutus XIII," 21 Feb. 1788, *DHRC,* 16:172. See also Wills, *Explaining America,* 130–31.

158. "Federal Farmer XVIII," 2 May 1788, *DHRC,* 17:368–69.

159. "Brutus XIV," 28 Feb. 1788, 6 Mar. 1788 (2 parts), *DHRC,* 16:256–58, 328–30; Thomas Tredwell, in Elliot, *Debates,* 2:400. Here the Antifederalists paraphrased Blackstone's paean to the multitude of local courts provided in "our antient constitution." Blackstone, *Commentaries,* 3:30. For examples of the criticism of the federal judiciary, see Elbridge Gerry, in Farrand, *Records,* 2:631–33; "Cincinnatus I: To James Wilson, Esquire," *New York Journal,* 1 Nov. 1787, *DHRC,* 13:532–33; "Cincinnatus II: To James Wilson, Esquire," *New York Journal,* 8 Nov. 1787, *DHRC,* 14:12–14; "Cincinnatus III: To James Wilson, Esquire," *New York Journal,* 15 Nov. 1787, *DHRC,* 14:126–27; "An Old Whig, III," *Philadelphia Independent Gazetteer,* 20 Oct. 1787 (reprinted in the *New York Journal,* 1 Dec. 1787), *DHRC,* 13:428; and "Centinel II," *Philadelphia Freeman's Journal,* 24 Oct. 1787, *DHRC,* 13:463. Brutus lifted the line about bringing "justice to every man's door" from Blackstone; but the latter was referring to the variety of courts in England, not the jury. Blackstone, *Commentaries,* 3:30.

160. "Federal Farmer XV," 2 May 1788, *DHRC,* 17:338–39. See also "Timeleon," *New York Journal,* extra ed., 1 Nov. 1787, *DHRC,* 13:636–38.

161. "Brutus XIV" (pt. 2), 6 Mar. 1788, *DHRC,* 16:328–30; "Federal Farmer II," 8 Nov. 1787, *DHRC,* 14:26–27. See also "Federal Farmer XVIII," 2 May 1788, *DHRC,* 17:365–66. Yates was one of the few outside New England who seemed to be aware of the appellate process in Massachusetts and Rhode Island. More typical was Luther Martin's complaint that appeal of factual determinations in addition to questions of law was "very different from what our court of appeals, or any court of appeals in the United States or in England enjoys." Martin, "Address No. II," *Maryland Journal,* 21 Mar. 1788, *DHRC,* 16:453.

162. "Brutus II," 1 Oct. 1787, *DHRC,* 13:527; Thomas Tredwell, in Elliot,

Debates, 2:400; Declaration of Rights and Form of Ratification, *Poughkeepsie Country Journal*, 29 July 1788, *DHRC*, 18:298, 299. Cf. Krauss, "Original Understanding of the Seventh Amendment Right to Jury Trial."

163. The "Brutus" essays offer many examples.

164. See, e.g., Jay, *Federalist* 2, 31 Oct. 1787, 9–10, and Madison, "Vices of the Political System of the United States," *Madison Papers*, 9:345–58.

165. Hamilton, *Federalist* 83, 28 May 1788, 558–74. See also Hamilton, *Federalist* 81, 28 May 1788, 541–52. James Wilson made a similar point just after the convention. Wilson, "Speech at a Public Meeting in Philadelphia," *DHRC*, 13:340–41; Wilson, in Elliot, *Debates*, 2:488. Other framers made the same point in the ratification conventions. Elliot, *Debates*, 2:114 (Dawes in Massachusetts), 3:534–35 (Madison in Virginia), 4:144–45, 165–66 (Spaight and Iredell in North Carolina), 2:260 (Pinckney in South Carolina).

166. Elbridge Gerry, in Farrand, *Records*, 2:587, 628.

167. Hamilton, *Federalist* 83, 28 May 1788, 566–67, 573.

168. Ibid., 568 (emphasis added). Cf. Wolfram, "Constitutional History of the Seventh Amendment"; James Oldham, "Reconsidering the Seventh Amendment Right to Jury Trial in Light of English Practice of the Late Eighteenth Century," in O'Donovan and Rubin, *Human Rights and Legal History*, 225–53.

169. Hamilton, *Federalist* 81, 28 May 1788, 539–40, and *Federalist* 83, 28 May 1788, 569–71.

170. Madison, *Federalist* 42, 22 Jan. 1788, 281.

171. Pinckney's Comments, in Elliot, *Debates*, 4:258.

172. N.Y. Constitution, art. XXXV (1777).

173. Hamilton, *Federalist* 84, 28 May 1788, 578.

174. Madison to Washington, 18 Oct. 1787, *DHRC*, 13:409. This was in response to George Mason's objection that the Constitution infringed common-law rights. Ten years later, amid the Alien and Sedition Act controversy, Madison projected this interpretation back into the colonial period and argued that the English common law then "was unknown . . . as a law pervading and operating through the whole as one society." Madison, Report on the [Virginia] Resolutions, [10 Jan. 1799], *Writings of James Madison*, ed. Hunt, 6:373.

175. Hamilton, *Federalist* 78, 28 May 1788, 521–30; James Wilson, in Elliot, *Debates*, 2:489–90. See also Hamilton, *Federalist* 81, 28 May 1788, 543.

176. For analysis of these two versions of judicial review — "judicial supremacy" and the departmental model — in the early Republic, see Kramer, *People Themselves*, 93–144.

177. Hamilton, *Federalist* 78, 28 May 1788, 524–30. See also Corwin, "Progress of Constitutional Theory." Cf. Snowiss, *Judicial Review and the Law of the Constitution*, 45–89.

178. U.S. Constitution, art. 1, § 9.

179. Hamilton, *Federalist* 84, 28 May 1788, 576, 577. See also Hamilton, *Federalist* 83, 28 May 1788, 562; and Freedman, *Habeas Corpus*, 15–16.

180. Hamilton, *Federalist* 78, 28 May 1788, 521–30.

181. Ibid., 528–30.

182. Hamilton, *Federalist* 81, 28 May 1788, 544.

183. Hamilton, *Federalist* 78, 28 May 1788, 522; Hamilton, *Federalist* 79, 28 May 1788, 531–33.

184. "Brutus XV," 20 Mar. 1788, *DHRC*, 16:431–35; "Brutus XI," 31 Jan. 1788, *DHRC*, 15:513–14.

185. "Brutus XIV" (pt. 2), 6 Mar. 1788, *DHRC*, 16:330.

186. "Federal Farmer II," 8 Nov. 1787, *DHRC*, 14:27.

187. [John F. Mercer?], "Address to the Members of the New York and Virginia Conventions," 30 Apr. 1788, *DHRC*, 17:260–61.

188. "Federal Farmer VI," 2 May 1788, *DHRC*, 17:273. For examples of common-law rights that were reconceptualized as a constitutional rights, see Moglen, "Taking the Fifth," and Treanor, "Original Understanding of the Takings Clause and the Political Process."

189. "Federal Farmer XVI," 2 May 1788, *DHRC*, 17:344. For similar vagueness about the legal status of natural rights, see Blackstone, *Commentaries*, 1:125. Natural rights and natural law were not considered supplements to the civil legal order but rather were guides for how to interpret constitutions. See Hamburger, "Natural Rights, Natural Law, and American Constitutions."

190. "Federal Farmer XVI," 2 May 1788, *DHRC*, 17:344–50. For New York's version, see New York's "Instrument of Ratification," in De Pauw, *Eleventh Pillar*, 293–302.

191. See Hamilton, *Federalist* 84, 28 May 1788, 575–80; [Noah Webster], "To the Dissenting Members of the Late Convention of Pennsylvania," *New York Daily Advertiser*, 31 Dec. 1787, *DHRC*, 15:199–200. See also Wood, *Creation of the American Republic*, 536–43.

192. For a critical exchange between James Madison and Thomas Jefferson, see Rakove, *Declaring Rights*, 157–66. See also Finkelman, "James Madison and the Bill of Rights."

193. Patrick Henry, in Elliot, *Debates*, 3:325. See also Elliot, *Debates*, 3:567; Kenyon, "Introduction: Political Thought of the Antifederalists," lxxxvii–lxxxviii. Some leading Antifederalists, like George Mason and Luther Martin, also endorsed federal judicial review of state legislation that conflicted with the federal Constitution. Farrand, *Records*, 2:76–77, 78.

194. Compare Rakove, *Original Meanings*, with Barnett, "Original Meaning of the Commerce Clause." See also *United States v. Lopez*, 514 U.S. 549, 585 (1995) (Thomas, J., concurring) (invoking the framers' understanding of "commerce" to interpret the scope of Congress's commerce power).

195. *Chisholm v. Georgia*, 2 U.S. 419, 479 (1793). See also Powell, *Community Built on Words*, 31–37.

196. He was referring to the opinions of Wilson and Jay in particular. Goebel, *Antecedents and Beginnings to 1801*, 728, 731–32.

197. All were Federalist appointees of President Washington. Justice John Blair, a Virginian, was at the Philadelphia Convention and the Virginia ratification convention. Justice William Cushing was a delegate to the Massachusetts ratification convention. Justice James Iredell was a delegate to the North Carolina convention.

Chief Justice John Jay was a contributor to *The Federalist*. Justice James Wilson was at the Philadelphia Convention and served in the Pennsylvania convention.

198. *Chisholm*, 2 U.S. at 447–48 (emphasis added).

199. Ibid., 468–69.

200. Ibid., 453, 461, 462.

201. See generally Anderson, *Imagined Communities*.

202. *Chisholm*, 2 U.S. at 471, 474, 479.

203. Phillips, *Georgia and State Rights*, 27–28.

204. Recent scholarship reveals that judicial review was not widely accepted until the mid-nineteenth century. Kramer, *People Themselves*; Whittington, *Constitutional Construction*; Friedman, "History of the Countermajoritarian Difficulty, Part 1." Cf. White, "Constitutional Journey of *Marbury v. Madison*."

205. Snowiss, *Judicial Review and the Law of the Constitution*, 13–16 and passim; Kramer, "Foreword: We the Court," 74–128; Wood, "Origins of Judicial Review Revisited, or How the Marshall Court Made More Out of Less."

206. President George Washington, for example, used fidelity to this Constitution as something of a "litmus test for Supreme Court nominations." Casto, *Supreme Court in the Early Republic*, 65–70.

207. Quoted in Faulkner, *Jurisprudence of John Marshall*, 39. See also ibid., 38–44, and Wilson, *Imperial Republic*, 147–85.

208. *McCulloch v. Maryland*, 17 U.S. 316, 407 (1819). Christopher L. Eisgruber emphasizes this positive function of judicial review in "John Marshall's Judicial Rhetoric," 444. See also Black, *People and the Court*, 34–86.

CHAPTER EIGHT

1. For a survey of state constitutional revisions in the early nineteenth century, see Coit, "Diffusion of Democracy." See also Peterson, *Democracy, Liberty and Property*; Green, *Constitutional Development in the South Atlantic States*; and Moss, "Democracy, Citizenship and Constitution-Making in New York."

2. On the decline of local power after the Civil War, see Hartog, *Public Property and Private Power*, and Novak, *People's Welfare*.

3. *McCulloch v. Maryland*, 17 U.S. 316, 407 (1819). See Tarr, *Understanding State Constitutions*, 6–11.

4. This story of how the states absorbed power from above and below has not been told in full. For New York City's relationship to state government in the early Republic, see Hartog, *Public Property and Private Power*.

5. Bonomi, *Factious People*, and Benson, *Concept of Jacksonian Democracy*, 4.

6. For a recent analysis of the persistence of this negative view of parties, see Leonard, *Invention of Party Politics*.

7. For such party dynamics in New York, see Benson, *Concept of Jacksonian Democracy*, and Russo, "Political Process in New York State."

8. Fox, *Decline of Aristocracy*, 230–37.

9. Ogden Edwards, in Carter and Stone, *Debates of the Convention of 1821*, 178.

10. Williamson, *American Suffrage*, 201.

11. Ambrose Spencer, in Carter and Stone, *Debates of the Convention*, 197, 253; James Kent, in Carter and Stone, *Debates of the Convention*, 221.

12. Monaghan, *John Jay*, 323.

13. James Kent, in Carter and Stone, *Debates of the Convention*, 220–21; Ambrose Spencer, in Carter and Stone, *Debates of the Convention*, 218.

14. Abraham Van Vechten, in Carter and Stone, *Debates of the Convention*, 229, 230–31.

15. John Cramer, in Carter and Stone, *Debates of the Convention*, 239.

16. David Buel, in Carter and Stone, *Debates of the Convention*, 241–42.

17. On the shift from property to suffrage as a protection for rights, see Coit, "Diffusion of Democracy," 357–58.

18. Samuel Young, in Carter and Stone, *Debates of the Convention*, 274.

19. Erastus Root, in Carter and Stone, *Debates of the Convention*, 185–86; John Z. Ross, in Carter and Stone, *Debates of the Convention*, 180–81.

20. See Fox, "Negro Vote in Old New York."

21. Peter A. Jay, in Carter and Stone, *Debates of the Convention*, 184; Kent, in Carter and Stone, *Debates of the Convention*, 191. Samuel Young responded to Kent's argument by citing one of Kent's own judicial decisions holding that the privileges and immunities clause protected only people from other states, not people within the state. Lincoln, *Constitutional History of New York*, 1:662.

22. Samuel Young, in Carter and Stone, *Debates of the Convention*, 191.

23. N.Y. Constitution (1821), art. II, § 1. The 90 percent figure is from Williamson, *American Suffrage*, 204.

24. Suggestive here is Wright, "Origins of the Separation of Powers in America." See generally Gwyn, *Meaning of the Separation of Powers*.

25. New York's 1777 constitution contained no provision for amendment, but everyone assumed that it could be amended in another convention.

26. See Moss, "Democracy, Citizenship and Constitution-Making in New York," 21–22.

27. Lincoln, *Constitutional History of New York*, 1:596–612.

28. N.Y. Constitution (1821), art. IV.

29. James Kent, in Carter and Stone, *Debates of the Convention*, 318–19, 355.

30. Ibid., 319.

31. Peter Jay, in Carter and Stone, *Debates of the Convention*, 345, 347–48.

32. Van Ness, in Carter and Stone, *Debates of the Convention*, 334–38.

33. Van Buren, in Carter and Stone, *Debates of the Convention*, 340, 342.

34. Lincoln, *Constitutional History of New York*, 2:5–6.

35. Nathan Williams, in Carter and Stone, *Debates of the Convention*, 385. The vote is recorded in Carter and Stone, *Debates of the Convention*, 388–89.

36. Nathan Williams, in Carter and Stone, *Debates of the Convention*, 386; Rufus King, in Carter and Stone, *Debates of the Convention*, 387.

37. Erastus Root, in Carter and Stone, *Debates of the Convention*, 384, 388.

38. For sheriffs, see N.Y. Constitution (1821), art. IV, § 8. For the amendment that made justices of the peace elective, see Lincoln, *Constitutional History of New*

York, 1:222–23. All state judges became elective in 1846. N.Y. Constitution (1846), art. VI.

39. Daniel Tompkins, in Carter and Stone, *Debates of the Convention*, 79.

40. For opposition in Kentucky, see Ruger, "'Question Which Convulses a Nation.'"

41. Peter R. Livingston, in Carter and Stone, *Debates of the Convention*, 51.

42. John Duer, in Carter and Stone, *Debates of the Convention*, 107–8.

43. Ezekiel Bacon, in Carter and Stone, *Debates of the Convention*, 118.

44. Martin Van Buren, in Carter and Stone, *Debates of the Convention*, 72; Van Buren, *Autobiography*, 60.

45. David Buel, quoted in Lincoln, *Constitutional History of New York*, 1:682.

46. N.Y. Constitution (1821), art. IV, § 7, art. V, § 4, art. IX, § 1. The new governor permitted Kent to remain as chancellor until he reached the mandatory retirement age of sixty.

47. N.Y. Constitution (1821), art. VII, § 9; Gunn, *Decline of Authority*, 170–97.

48. For the fortunes of parties and judicial review in the nineteenth century, see Kramer, *People Themselves*. On the nineteenth-century United States as a nation of courts and parties, see Skowroneck, *Building a New American State*.

49. For the political function of dueling, see Freeman, *Affairs of Honor*.

50. Van Buren, *Autobiography*, 62.

51. Ibid., 63.

52. Ibid.

CHAPTER NINE

1. Webster, *Sketches of American Policy*, 48. Webster was born in Connecticut and schooled at Yale, but he pursued his early careers in law and journalism in New York, where he wrote much of his cultural and political analysis.

2. Webster, *Grammatical Institute*, pt. I, 4. On Webster's linguistic projects, see Lepore, *A Is for American*, 15–41; V. P. Bynack, "Noah Webster's Linguistic Thought and the Idea of an American National Culture," in Shuffleton, *American Enlightenment*, 353–68; and Ellis, *After the Revolution*, 161–212.

3. Simeon Baldwin to James Kent, 16 Jan. 1785, KP.

4. See generally Ferguson, *Law and Letters in American Culture*.

5. Herder, *On the Origin of Language*, 87–166; Herder, *Against Pure Reason*. Montesquieu prefigured the environmental thesis, but his observations of local variation were subordinated to his universalist premise. Webster was also influenced by the French philosopher Condillac, who developed a theory of linguistic relativity holding that "[a]s government influences the character of a people, so the character of a people influences that of language." Kramer, review of *The Autobiographies of Noah Webster*, in *New England Quarterly*, 150.

6. Webster, *Grammatical Institute*, pt. I, 5. Webster did not mention the *actual* multiplicity of languages in America. There were vibrant German- and Dutch-speaking communities in New York and elsewhere, as well as numerous Native American dialects.

7. John L. Brooke, "Ancient Lodges and Self-Created Societies: Voluntary Association and the Public Sphere in the Early Republic," in Hoffman and Albert, *Launching the "Extended Republic,"* 283–359. See also Grasso, *Speaking Aristocracy;* Warner, *Republic of Letters;* Jordan, " 'Old Words' in 'New Circumstances' "; Gustafson, *Representative Words;* Fliegelman, *Declaring Independence;* and Van Anglen, *New England Milton.* Webster started to publish his works only after encouragement from "a few Gentlemen of eminence," but he did not want "to use the authority of respectable names to impose a worthless production upon his countrymen." Webster, *Grammatical Institute,* pt. I, 14.

8. Webster, *Examination into the Leading Principles of the Federal Constitution,* 29.

9. Webster, *Examination into the Leading Principles of the Federal Constitution,* 30, 35, 64, 65.

10. Noah Webster, "Preface to the *American Dictionary*" (1828), in *Autobiographies of Noah Webster,* 105–6.

11. Ibid., 106–7.

12. Kent, *Commentaries.*

13. James Kent to Thomas Washington, 6 Oct. 1828, in *Select Essays in Anglo-American Legal History,* 1:843.

14. A distinction he made clear in Kent, *Address Delivered before the Law Association.*

15. See Kent, *Memoirs and Letters,* 18–19. Good discussions of Kent's career include Horton, *James Kent,* and George Goldberg, "James Kent, the American Blackstone: The Early Years," in Harding, *Law-Making and Law-Makers in British History,* 157–94.

16. On the growth of an indigenous legal literature in the early Republic, see Warren, *History of the American Bar,* 325–40, and Bauer, *Commentaries on the Constitution.*

17. See Carrington, "Revolutionary Idea of University Legal Education," and Siegel, " 'To Learn and Make Respectable Hereafter.' "

18. James Kent to Peter DuPonceau, 29 Dec. 1826, DuPonceau Papers, quoted in Bloomfield, *American Lawyers in a Changing Society,* 361 n. 55.

19. See Hulsebosch, "Writs to Rights," and Goebel, "Common Law and the Constitution," 107–113.

20. Langbein, "Chancellor Kent and the History of Legal Literature." See also Cairns, "Blackstone, an English Institutist"; Cairns, "Institutional Writings in Scotland Reconsidered"; Luig, "Institutes of National Law"; and Bellomo, *Common Legal Past of Europe.*

21. Charles Dumoulin, quoted in Watson, *Roman and Comparative Law,* 150.

22. Luig, "Institutes of National Law," 200–203.

23. The few proposals for a national private law code, such as Jeremy Bentham's "pannomian," received little support. See Jeremy Bentham to President James Madison, Oct. 1811, in Bentham, *Works,* 4:453–67, and Madison to Bentham, 8 May 1816, in Bentham, *Works,* 4:467–68. See also Bentham's open letters to the citizens of the United States, July 1817, in Bentham, *Works,* 4:478–507.

24. Kent, *Commentaries,* 1:472.

25. Ibid., 1.

26. Kent admitted that "[i]t was the character I had insensibly acquired as a scholar and a Federalist and a presumed (though it was not true) well-read lawyer that . . . I was appointed a Professor." Kent, *Memoirs and Letters*, 58. Some of the lectures were published. Kent, *Introductory Lecture to a Course of Law Lectures*; Kent, *Dissertations*. On university legal education in the early Republic, see Carrington, "Revolutionary Idea of University Legal Education."

27. Elihu Hubbard Smith to John Allen, 24 Jan. 1796, in Cronin, *Diary of Elihu Hubbard Smith*, 126–27.

28. Cairns, "Blackstone, an English Institutist." See also Chambers, *Course of Lectures on the English Law*, 1:268–92. Chambers's lectures ("composed in association with Samuel Johnson") were not published until 1986.

29. For Kent's treatment of European civil law, see Kent, *Commentaries*, 1:526–48.

30. For Kent's discussions of slavery, which was "the foundation of large masses of property in the southern parts," see Kent, *Commentaries*, 1:191–200, 2:248–58. The decline or transformation of status categories in American law has not received comprehensive treatment. On particular areas, see Tomlins, *Law, Labor, and Ideology in Early America* (master and servant), and Hartog, *Man and Wife in America* (marital status).

31. Kent, *Commentaries*, 1:115.

32. Ibid., 15. See Grotius, *Rights of War and Peace*. Kent implicitly embraced Protestant rather than Catholic origins of the law of nations. See generally Muldoon, "Contribution of the Medieval Canon Lawyers to the Formation of International Law."

33. James Wilson, "Lectures on Law," in *Works of James Wilson*, 1:148–67; Onuf and Onuf, *Federal Union, Modern World*; Lenner, "Separate Spheres," 253–58.

34. Kent, *Dissertations*; Kent, "A Lecture, Introductory to a Course of Law Lectures" (1824), in Miller, *Legal Mind in America*, 95–105.

35. Kent, *Commentaries*, 1:1–2, 20. See also Kent, "Lecture, Introductory to a Course of Law Lectures," 99–103.

36. See Alan Watson, "Chancellor Kent's Use of Foreign Law," in Reimann, *Reception of Continental Ideas in the Common Law World*, 45–62; Hoeflich, "Roman Law in American Legal Culture," 1735.

37. Kent, *Commentaries*, 1:547–48.

38. Professor Langbein admits that "Volume One of Kent's book will throw you off the scent slightly if you are looking for the institutionalist tradition," but he concludes that "Kent's decision to cover the Constitution in an institutionalist work for the United States was clever, because it allowed him to root his *Commentaries* in a topic that was unmistakably American," and this survey of federal law helped "offset" his "determined reliance on English law." Langbein, "Chancellor Kent and the History of Legal Literature," 592. James Wilson also included the American constitutions in his 1791 lectures at the College of Philadelphia. Wilson, *Lectures on Law*, in Wilson, *Works of James Wilson*, 1:399–440, 2:441–93.

39. Kent, *Commentaries*, 1:471.

40. On the Federalists' "extra-constitutional principles," see Lenner, "Tale of Two Constitutions," and White, *Marshall Court*, 674–76.

41. Kent to Thomas Washington, in *Select Essays in Anglo-American Legal History*, 1:838.

42. Kent to Simeon Baldwin, 10 Oct. 1782, KP.

43. Moss Kent to James Kent, 26 July 1817, KP; James Kent to Moss Kent, 2 Oct. 1793 and 10 Feb. 1797, KP.

44. James Kent, "Memoranda of My Life," May 1799, KP; James Kent to Moss Kent, 22 June 1796, KP; Kent to Thomas Washington, in *Select Essays in Anglo-American Legal History*, 1:837–38. Still, James warned Moss not "devote too much time to classical Literature & neglect the more *useful* tho less inviting object of *Business* & litigation." James Kent to Moss Kent, 4 June 1790, KP.

45. "I had commenced in 1786 to be a zealous Federalist & read everything on politics. I got the Federalist almost by heart, and became intimate with Hamilton." Kent to Thomas Washington, in *Select Essays in Anglo-American Legal History*, 1:841. See also Kent to Nathaniel Lawrence, 8 Dec. 1787 and 21 Dec. 1787, DHRC, 14:390, and Kent to Elizabeth Hamilton, 10 Dec. 1832, in Kent, *Memoirs and Letters*, 302–3.

46. Kent and Webster's essays ("Vindication of the Jay Treaty") were originally published in the *American Minerva*, a New York Federalist newspaper, and are reprinted in Webster, *Collection of Papers*.

47. See Cronin, *Diary of Elihu Hubbard Smith*, and Bender, *New York Intellect*, 27–36. See also Roche, "Uranian Society." Hamilton and King offered Webster a loan to move to New York City and publish a newspaper, the *Minerva*, supporting Washington's administration. Five years later, Hamilton, angered by Webster's refusal to support his branch of the Federalist Party, set up a rival newspaper, and Webster soon retired to work on his dictionary. Ellis, *After the Revolution*, 198, 207.

48. Bender, *New York Intellect*, 34–35.

49. Albion, *Rise of New York Port*, 241–54. See generally Fox, *Yankees and Yorkers*.

50. See Bailey, "Early Legal Education in the United States," 328.

51. Miller, *Life of the Mind in America*, 166–69. See also Watson, "Chancellor Kent's Use of Foreign Law"; Hoeflich, "Roman Law in American Legal Culture"; and Charles A. Donahue, "*Animalia Ferae Naturae*: Rome, Bologna, Leyden, Oxford and Queen's County, N.Y.," in Bagnall and Harris, *Studies in Roman Law*, 39–63.

52. On codification, compare Miller, *Life of the Mind in America*, 239–65, and Cook, *American Codification Movement*, with Gordon, review of *The American Codification Movement*, in *Vanderbilt Law Review*.

53. Kent to Thomas Washington, in *Select Essays in Anglo-American Legal History*, 1:843.

54. On the decline of the Federalist Party, see Banner, *To the Hartford Convention*. On Clinton's appeal to the Federalists, see Cornog, *Birth of Empire*, 137.

55. Ellis, *Jeffersonian Crisis*.

56. Gunn, *Decline of Authority*; Henretta, "Rise and Decline of 'Democratic Republicanism.'"

57. Horwitz, *Transformation of American Law*, 9–16; Palmer, "Federal Common Law of Crime"; Preyer, "Jurisdiction to Punish."

58. Warren, "New Light on the Federal Judiciary Act of 1789," 85–88.

59. See Goebel, "Common Law and the Constitution," 114–23. On the use of federal general common law in diversity actions to subsidize commercial expansion in the late nineteenth century, see Purcell, *Litigation and Inequality*.

60. See, e.g., James Madison, "Notes on the Common Law," [ca. Sept. 1799], *Madison Papers*, 17:261–69; St. George Tucker, *Examination of the Question*. These positions continued to flip, and there were great debates over which rules represented the true common law. A good example is the prosecution of New York Federalist editor Harry Croswell in 1803 for libeling President Thomas Jefferson, which turned on the question of whether truth constituted a valid defense. *LPAH*, 1:775–848.

61. For the Republican criticism of the judiciary, see Ellis, *Jeffersonian Crisis*.

62. See Goebel, *Antecedents and Beginnings to 1801*, 633–51, and Elkins and McKitrick, *Age of Federalism*, 695–726.

63. See Warren, *History of the American Bar*, 292–324.

64. The power of juries to find law in early America is controverted. See Krauss, "Inquiry into the Right of Criminal Juries to Determine the Law."

65. See, e.g., Horwitz, *Transformation of American Law*; Nelson, *Americanization of the Common Law*, 164–74; Friedman, *Contract Law in America*; White, *Tort Law in America*; and Fisher, "Law of the Land."

66. Helmholz, "Use of the Civil Law in Post-Revolutionary American Jurisprudence"; Stein, "Attraction of the Civil Law in Post-Revolutionary America"; Hoeflich, "Translation and the Reception of Foreign Law"; Hoeflich, *Roman and Civil Law*. See also Max Radin, "The Rivalry of Common-Law and Civil Law Ideas in the American Colonies," in Reppy, *Law*, 2:404–31.

67. Oldham, *Mansfield Manuscripts*, 1:596–635. See also Johnson, *Law Merchant and Negotiable Instruments*.

68. *De Lovio v. Boit*, 7 Fed. Cas. 418 (C.C.D. Mass. 1815); *Swift v. Tyson*, 41 U.S. 1 (1842); Hamilton, *Federalist* 81, 28 May 1788, 568–70. See also White, *Marshall Court*, 427–84; Freyer, *Harmony and Dissonance*; and Note, "*Swift v. Tyson* Exhumed." For a recent discussion of the legal innovation required to create a national market, see Henretta, " 'Market' in the Early Republic."

69. Kent, *Commentaries*, 3:2.

70. Ibid., 20.

71. Ibid., 2:109–10.

72. Ibid., 116–19, 454–63. A fellow law student raised this problem with Kent during ratification. Simeon Baldwin to James Kent, 8 Mar. 1788, DHRC, 16:350–51.

73. Story, *Commentaries on the Conflict of Laws*, iii–iv, v, 9. See generally Newmyer, *Supreme Court Justice Joseph Story*, 295–300. Cf. Watson, *Joseph Story and the Comity of Errors*.

74. See Burge, *Commentaries on Colonial and Foreign Laws*, 1:x–xi.

75. Quoted in William Johnson to James Kent, 16 Nov. 1816, KP. See also Moss Kent to James Kent, 1 Feb. 1817, KP.

76. Story, *Commentaries on Equity Jurisprudence*, 47–48.

77. *Robinson v. Campbell*, 16 U.S. 212, 222–23 (U.S. 1818). Peter C. Hoffer observes that there were few federal equity cases in the nineteenth century. Hoffer, *Law's Conscience*, 103–5.

78. Kent, *Address Delivered before the Law Association*, 7, 12.

79. G. Edward White argues that American jurists repudiated the cyclical theory and embraced continuous progress in his *The Marshall Court*. Cole completed his allegorical painting *The Course of Empire* in 1836, the same year Kent delivered his address to the New York bar association.

80. Perry Miller explored the legal reform movement, and the struggle between Bumppo and Temple, in *Life of the Mind in America*, 99–116.

81. Robert Darnton notes that while interpretations of written texts may vary, "texts shape the response of readers, however active they may be." Darnton, "What Is the History of Books?," 78–80. See also Ferguson, "Ideology and the Framing of the Constitution," and Ferguson, "'We Hold These Truths': Strategies of Control in the Literature of the Founders," in Bercovitch, *Reconstructing American Literary History*, 1–29 (discussing the founding generation's "faith in the text to stabilize the uncertain world in which they live" and to "forg[e] artificial unities amidst active competitors and a contentious, far-flung populace"). John P. Reid documents the transfer of eastern common law to the west in *Law for the Elephant*.

82. James M. Porter, "Review of *Reports of Cases Argued and Determined in the Circuit Court of the United States for the Second Circuit* by Elijah Paine Jr.," *North American Review* 60 (July 1828), in Miller, *Legal Mind in America*, 174.

83. Ibid., 175.

84. Peter DuPonceau, *Dissertation on the Nature, and Extent of the Courts of the United States . . .* (Phildelphia, 1824), in Miller, *Legal Mind in America*, 114–16. For striking examples of state avoidance of Supreme Court decisions during the Marshall Court, see the discussion of *Green v. Biddle*, 8 Wheat. 1 (1823), and *Worcester v. Georgia*, 6 Pet. 515 (1832), in White, *Marshall Court*, 641–48, 716–40.

85. See Balkin, *Cultural Software*.

86. A good survey of such plots in the 1790s is Slaughter, *Whiskey Rebellion*. Cf. Kenneth N. Owens, "Patterns in Territorial Politics," in Bloom, *American Territorial System*, 161–79 (arguing that "territorial party managers helped fix politically a form of internal colonialism upon frontier societies whose representatives they claimed to be").

87. For the adoption of the common and statute laws of the eastern states in the western territories, see Brown, *British Statutes in American Law*, 157–200.

88. Haines, *Memoir of Thomas Addis Emmet*, 51–52.

89. John P. Reid argues that there were different "conditions of law" in the two British colonies of Ireland and Massachusetts. In Massachusetts there was stronger local control over legal institutions; consequently, the empire could more easily

impose its will on Ireland, and its revolution failed. Reid, *In a Defiant Stance*, 1–6, 11–13, 135–42, 152–58. Cf. Greene, "From the Perspective of Law," 62.

90. Durey, *Transatlantic Radicals*.

91. "The Examination of William James MacNeven, before the Secret Committee of the House of Lords," 7 Aug. 1798, in Emmet, MacNeven, and O'Connor, *Origin and Progress of the Irish Union*, 28, 21, 23, 24; "Substance of Thomas Addis Emmet's Examination, before the Secret Committee of the House of Lords," 10 Aug. 1798, in Emmet, MacNeven, and O'Connor, *Origin and Progress of the Irish Union*, 33, 37; "The Examination of Thomas Addis Emmet, before the Secret Committee of the House of Commons," 14 Aug. 1798, in Emmet, MacNeven, and O'Connor, *Origin and Progress of the Irish Union*, 42. Michael Durey comments that the Irish rebels' identification with only America and not France "must be taken with a grain of salt." Durey, *Transatlantic Radicals*, 163–67. See also Bonwick, *English Radicals and the American Revolution*, 260, 265–66.

92. Carter, " 'Wild Irishman' under Every Federalist's Bed"; Smith, *Freedom's Fetters*, 22–34. On the transatlantic network of middle-class Dissenters and radicals in the late eighteenth century, see Durey, *Transatlantic Radicals*; Twomey, *Jacobins and Jeffersonians*; and Isaac Kramnick, "Religion and Radicalism: The Political Theory of Dissent," in *Republicanism and Bourgeois Radicalism*, 43–70.

93. Emmet argued for the Livingston-Fulton monopoly in *Gibbons v. Ogden*, 22 U.S. 1 (1824), for example, and Sampson participated in several high-profile labor and free-press cases. On Sampson's career, see Bloomfield, *American Lawyers in a Changing Society*, 59–90.

94. Sampson, *Memoirs*, 64.

95. Ibid., 338, 339, 353.

96. Ibid., iv.

97. Ibid., 92, 30.

98. Ibid., 288.

99. Sampson, *Journeymen Cordwainers of the City of New-York, Defendants*, 65.

100. In a European parallel, James Q. Whitman describes Anton Friedrich Justus Thibaut's attempt to blend codification and gothic legalism in early nineteenth-century Germany. Whitman, *Legacy of the Roman Law in the German Romantic Era*, 104–5.

101. Sampson, *Anniversary Discourse*, 13, 67, 15.

102. Ibid., 17–18.

103. Ibid., 61.

104. William Sampson to Gulian Verplanck, July 1826, box 7, Verplanck Mss., NYHS.

105. Cook, *American Codification Movement*, 210. See also Miller, *Life of the Mind in America*, 239–65.

106. DeWitt Clinton, Annual Message to the Legislature, 4 Jan. 1825, in Lincoln, *State of New York*, 90.

107. For Kent's ambivalence, see Kent, *Commentaries*, 4:345–47.

108. On the antirent movement, see Huston, *Land and Freedom*, and McCurdy, *Anti-Rent Era in New York Law and Politics*.

109. *Revised Statutes of the State of New-York*; *Report from the Commissioners Appointed to Revise the Laws of the State of New York*. The third volume was filled with all statutes that did not fit under the four headings in the first two. The vast majority of these were private acts. For an appraisal of the revision's effect on property law, see Alexander, *Commodity and Propriety*, 107–26.

110. Butler, *Revision of the Statutes*, 22–23.

111. See Nelson, *Americanization of the Common Law*; Stimson, *American Revolution in the Law*; and Hulsebosch, "Writs to Rights." On the Field code, see Alison Reppy, "The Field Codification Concept," in *David Dudley Field Centenary Essays*, 17–54, and Widmer, *Young America*, 155–84.

112. Suggestive here is Gordon, review of *The American Codification Movement* in *Vanderbilt Law Review*.

113. Pierson, *Tocqueville and Beaumont*, 14–15, 23, 58.

114. Ibid., 32.

115. Ibid., 149–67; Bender, introduction to Tocqueville, *Democracy in America*, xxiii.

116. Pierson, *Tocqueville and Beaumont*, 81, 150, 159–62.

117. Ibid., 129.

118. Ibid., 136, 602–7, 727, 734–35. Tocqueville took extensive notes on both works. Tocqueville, *Journey to America*, 228–33, 245–57, 298; Schleifer, *Making of Tocqueville's Democracy in America*, 87–111, 195–99. Joseph Story concluded that Tocqueville copied much of his book from *The Federalist*, Kent's *Commentaries*, and Story's own work. Schleifer, *Making of Tocqueville's Democracy in America*, 99. He also met John C. Spencer, the statutory reviser who published the first American edition of *Democracy in America*. Pierson, *Tocqueville and Beaumont*, 216–17.

119. Tocqueville, *Democracy in America*, 1:278.

120. Pierson, *Tocqueville and Beaumont*, 185–88, 403.

121. For consultation of manuals, see Tocqueville, *Journey to America*, 291.

122. A brief survey is George A. Billias, "American Constitutionalism and Europe, 1776–1848," in *American Constitutionalism Abroad*, 13–39. For recent ruminations, see Ackerman, "Essay."

CONCLUSION

1. Among many treatments, see especially Ferguson, *Colossus*, and Hardt and Negri, *Empire*.

Primary Sources

MANUSCRIPTS

Albany, N.Y.
   New York State Archives
      Corporation Register
      Andrew Elliot Papers
      Historical Manuscripts, English
      Quit Rent Register
Boston, Mass.
   Massachusetts Historical Society
      William Livingston Papers
      Sedgewick Papers
New Haven, Conn.
   Yale University, Law School Library
      James Kent Papers, photocopy of microfilm (originals in the Library of
         Congress, Washington, D.C.)
New York, N.Y.
   Columbia University, Rare Books and Manuscripts Room
      Van Schaack Papers
   Hall of Records, Surrogate's Court Building
      Municipal Archives
         New York City Common Council Papers, 1670–1831
      County Clerk's Office of Old Records
         Supreme Court of Judicature, Minutes, 1775–1790
   Museum of the City of New York
      DeLancey Family Papers
   New-York Historical Society
      Goldsborough Banyar Papers
      Broadside Collection
      DeWitt Clinton Miscellaneous Manuscripts
      Cadwallader Colden Papers
      Debating Club Minutes
      Andrew Elliot Papers
      Horatio Gates Papers
      John Tabor Kempe Papers: Letters and Legal Papers
      Robert R. Livingston Papers
      John Henry Lydius Miscellaneous Manuscripts
      Moot Club Minutes
      E. B. O'Callaghan Papers

Rutherford Collection
Samuel Shoemaker Diary
William Smith Jr. Miscellaneous Manuscripts
Peter Van Schaack Papers
Varick Papers
John Watts Papers
New York Public Library
William Alexander Papers
American Loyalists, 1783–1790: Transcripts of the Manuscript Books and
    Papers of the Commission of Enquiry into the Losses and Services of the
    American Loyalists
Bancroft Collection, vols. 30–37, 156, 168, 178, 221–22, 275–77, 298, 326,
    347, 359
Belles Lettres Club Minutes
Bleecker, Collins, and Abeel Papers
Chalmers Collection
DeWitt Clinton Papers
James DeLancey Manuscripts
William Edgar Papers
Gansevoort-Lansing Collection
Jones Family Papers
Livingston Family Papers
New York City Miscellaneous Manuscripts
New York State Miscellaneous Manuscripts
Philip Schuyler Papers
William Smith Jr. Papers
Van Rensselaer–Fort Papers
Abraham Yates Jr. Papers

BOOKS AND PAMPHLETS

*An Account of the Conferences held, and Treaties Made, between Major-General Sir
    William Johnson, Bart. and the Chief Sachems and Warriours.* London, 1756.
Adair, James. *The History of the American Indians.* London, 1775.
Adams, John. *A Defence of the Constitutions of Government of the United States of
    America.* 3 vols. Philadelphia, 1787.
Adams, John, and Jonathan Sewall. *Novanglus and Massachusettensis.* Boston: Hews
    & Goss, 1819.
The Address of the Inhabitants of the City of New York . . . . New York, 1778.
Adye, Stephen P. *A Treatise on the Courts-Martial.* New York, 1769.
Alexander, James. *A Brief Narrative of the Case and Trial of John Peter Zenger.*
    Edited by Stanley N. Katz. Cambridge, Mass., 1963.
Allen, Ethan. *A Brief Narrative of the Proceedings of the Government of New-York. . . .*
    Hartford, 1774.
Atwood, William. *The Fundamental Constitution of the English Government, Proving*

King William and Queen Mary Our Lawful and Rightful King and Queen. London, 1690.

Bacon, Francis. *The Elements of the Common Lawes of England . . . Contayning a Collection of Some Principall Rules and Maximes of the Common Law.* 1630. Reprint, New York, 1997.

Bard, Samuel. *A Discourse on the Duties of a Physician with some Sentiments, on the Usefulness and Necessity of a Public Hospital. . . .* New York, 1769.

Blackstone, William. *Commentaries on the Laws of England.* 4 vols. 1765–69. Reprint, Chicago, 1979.

Brady, Robert. *Historical Treatise on Cities, and Burghs or Boroughs.* London, 1690.

Burge, William. *Commentaries on Colonial and Foreign Laws Generally, and in Their Conflict with Each Other, and the Law of England.* 4 vols. London, 1836.

Burke, Edmund. *An Account of the European Settlements in America.* London, 1757.

B[urton], R[obert]. *The English Empire in America; Or, A View of the Dominions of the Crown of England in the West-Indies.* London, 1685.

Care, Henry. *English Liberties, or the Free-Born Subject's Inheritance, Containing Magna Charta, The Petition of Right, the Habeas Corpus Act, and Divers Other Most Useful Statutes.* 5th ed. Boston, 1722.

Child, Josiah. *A New Discourse on Trade.* London, 1693.

Clinton, DeWitt. *Account of the Salmo Otsego, or the Otsego Basse.* New York, 1822.

———. *Discourse Delivered before the New-York Historical Society. . . .* New York, 1812.

———. *An Introductory Discourse, Delivered before the Literary and Philosophical Society of New-York, on the Fourth of May, 1814.* New York, 1815.

———. *Remarks on the Fishes of the Western Waters of the State of New-York.* New York, 1815.

Coke, Edward. *The First Part of the Institutes of the Laws of England; or, A Commentary upon Littleton.* Edited by Charles Butler. 19th ed., corrected. 2 vols. London, 1832.

———. *The Fourth Part of the Institutes of the Laws of England: Concerning the Jurisdiction of Courts.* 1644. Reprint, London, 1817.

———. *Le tierce part des reportes del Edward Coke.* London, 1602.

———. *The Reports of Sir Edward Coke.* Edited by John H. Thomas and John F. Fraser. New ed. 13 pts. in 6 vols. London, 1826.

———. *The Second Part of the Institutes of the Laws of England: Containing the Exposition of Many Ancient, and Other Statutes.* 4th ed. London, 1671.

———. *The Third Part of the Institutes of the Laws of England: Concerning High Treason, and other Pleas of the Crown, and Criminal Causes. . . .* London, 1797.

Colden, Cadwallader. *The History of the Five Indian Nations Depending on the Province of New-York in America.* 2 vols. London, 1747.

Cowell, John. *The Institutes of the Lawes of England.* Translated by W. G. London, 1651.

Davies, John. *A Discovery of the True Causes Why Ireland Was Never Entirely Subdued, and Brought under Obedience of the Crowne of England, untill the Beginning of His Maiesties Happy Raigne.* London, 1612.

——. *Les primer reports des cases et matters en ley resolues & adiudges en les courts del roy en Ireland*. 1615. Reprint, London, 1628.

——. *The Question Concerning Impositions, Tonnage, Poundages . . . Fully Stated and Argued from Reason, Law and Policy*. London, 1656.

DeLancey, James. *The Charge of the Honourable James DeLancey Esq. . . .* New York, 1734.

DeLolme, Jean L. *The Constitution of England; or, An Account of the English Government*. London, 1853.

De Pauw, Cornelius. *Recherches philosophiques sur les Americains*. Berlin, 1770.

Douglass, William. *A Summary, Historical and Political, of the First Planting, Progressive Improvements, and Present State of the British Settlements in North America*. London, 1750.

Forset, Edward. *A Comparative Discourse of the Bodies Natural and Politique*. 2 vols. London, 1606.

Fortescue, Sir John. *The Governance of England, Otherwise Called The Difference Between an Absolute and a Limited Monarchy*. [1471–76?]. Reprint, London, 1876.

Fulbecke, William, comp. *The Pandectes of the Law of Nations: Contayning Severall Discourses of the Questions, Points and Matters of Law, Wherein the Nations of the World Doe Consent and Accord*. London, 1602.

Gibbon, Edward. *The History of the Decline and Fall of the Roman Empire*. 6 vols. London, 1776–88.

Grotius, Hugo. *The Rights of War and Peace*. Translated by A. C. Campbell. 1625. Reprint, Washington, D.C., 1901.

Hale, Matthew. *The History of the Common Law of England*. Chicago: University of Chicago Press, 1971.

——. *The Prerogatives of the King*. Edited by D. E. C. Yale. London: Selden Society, 1976.

Hamilton, Alexander, John Jay, and James Madison. *The Federalist Papers*. Edited by Jacob E. Cooke. Middletown, Conn., 1961.

Harrington, James. *The Commonwealth of Oceana; and, A System of Politics*. Edited by J. G. A. Pocock. Cambridge, England, 1992.

[Hawles, John]. *The English-man's Right: A Dialogue between a Barrister at Law, and a Jury-Man*. London, 1680.

Hopkins, Stephen. *The Rights of Colonies Examined*. Providence, 1765.

Hulme, Obadiah. *An Historical Essay on the English Constitution; or, An Impartial Inquiry into the Elective Power of the People, from the First Establishment of the Saxons in This Kingdom*. London, 1771.

Hume, David. *Essays Moral, Political and Literary*. Oxford, 1963.

——. *The History of England from the Invasion of Julius Caesar to the Abdication of James the Second, 1688*. New ed. 6 vols. Boston, 1854.

——. *History of Great Britain: The Reigns of James I and Charles I*. Edited by Duncan Forbes. London, 1970.

Humphreys, David. *A Poem, On the Happiness of America: Addressed to the Citizens of America*. Hartford, 1786.

Jefferson, Thomas. *Notes on the State of Virginia*. Edited by William Peden. Chapel Hill: University of North Carolina Press, 1954.

John Englishman, in Defence of the English Constitution. 10 issues. New York, 1755.

Johnson, Samuel. *Taxation no Tyranny; an Answer to the Resolutions of the American Congress*. London, 1775.

[Kennedy, Archibald]. *An Essay on the Government of the Colonies*. New York, 1752.

[———]. *The Importance of Gaining and Preserving the Friendship of the Indians to the British Interest, Considered*. New York, 1751.

[———]. *Observations on the Importance of the Northern Colonies under Proper Regulations*. New York, 1750.

[———]. *Serious Advice to the Inhabitants of the Northern Colonies, on the Present Situation of Affairs*. New York, 1755.

[———]. *Serious Considerations on the Present State of Affairs of the Northern Colonies*. New York, 1754.

[———]. *A Speech Said to Have Been Delivered Some Time Before the Close of the Last Sessions, by a Member Dissenting from the Church*. New York. 1755.

Kent, James. *An Address Delivered before the Law Association of the City of New-York, October 21, 1836*. New York, 1836.

———. *The Charter of the City of New-York, with Notes Thereon*. New York, 1836.

———. *Commentaries on American Law*. 4 vols. New York, 1826–30.

———. *Dissertations: Being the Preliminary Part of a Course of Law Lectures*. New York, 1795.

———. *An Introductory Lecture to a Course of Law Lectures, delivered November 17, 1794*. New York, 1794.

Knox, William. *Extra-Official State Papers, Addressed to the Right Hon. Lord Rawdon, and the Other Members of the Two Houses of Parliament, Associated for the Preservation of the Constitution and Promoting the Prosperity of the British Empire*. London, 1789.

[———]. *The Justice and Policy of the Late Act of Parliament for Making More Effectual Provision for the Government of the Province of Quebec. . . .* London, 1774.

Lambarde, William. *Archeion; or, A Discourse upon the High Courts of Justice in England*. Edited by Charles H. McIlwain and Paul L. Ward. Cambridge, Mass., 1957.

Livingston, Philip. *The Other Side of the Question; or, A Defence of the Liberties of North-America*. New York, 1774.

Livingston, Robert R. *The Address of Mr. Livingston to the House of Assembly, In Support of His Right to a Seat*. New York, 1769.

Livingston, William. *A Letter to the Right Reverend Father in God, John Lord Bishop of Llandaff. . . .* New York, 1768.

[———]. *A Review of the Military Operations in North-America*. London, 1757.

Locke, John. *Two Treatises of Government*. Edited by Peter Laslett. Rev. ed. Cambridge, England, 1963.

Madox, Thomas. *Firma Burgi, or an Historical Essay Concerning the Cities, Towns, and Boroughs of England*. London, 1726.

Maine, Henry. *Ancient Law*. New York, 1888.

———. *Dissertations on Early Law and Custom*. London, 1883.

Mather, Increase. *A Brief Account Concerning Several of the Agents of New-England, Their Negotiation at the Court of England: With Some Remarks on the New Charter Granted to the Colony of Massachusetts*. . . . London, 1691.

McIlwain, Charles H., ed. *An Abridgment of the Indian Affairs, Contained in Four Folio Volumes, Transacted in the Colony of New York, from the Year 1678 to the Year 1751*. Cambridge, Mass., 1915.

Montesquieu, Charles. *The Spirit of the Laws*. Translated and edited by Anne M. Cohler, Basia Carolyn Miller, and Harold Samuel Stone. Cambridge, England, 1989.

[Morris, Lewis]. *Some Observations on the Charge Given by the Honourable* James DeLancey. . . . New York, 1734.

Moyle, J. B., trans. *The Institutes of Justinian*. 5th ed. Oxford: Clarendon Press, 1937.

Murray, Joseph. *Mr. Murray's Opinion Relating to the Courts of Justice in the Colony of New-York*. New York, 1734.

Observations on the Articles of Confederation of the Thirteen States of America. New York, [1787].

Oldmixon, John. *The British Empire in America*. Rev. ed. London, 1741.

Paley, William. *The Principles of Moral and Political Philosophy*. London, 1785.

Pownall, Thomas. *The Administration of the Colonies*. London, 1764.

———. *The Administration of the Colonies*. 4th ed. London, 1768.

The Proceedings of the Convention of the Representatives of the New-Hampshire Settlers. Hartford, 1775.

[Ramsay, Allan]. *Essay on the Constitution*. 2d ed. London, 1766.

[Rastall, John]. *Les Termes de la Ley; or, Certain Difficult and Obscure Words and Terms of the Common and Statute Law of England*. London, 1721.

The Report of an Action of Assault, Battery, and Wounding . . . between Thomas Forsey, Plaintiff, and Waddel Cunningham, Defendant. New York, 1764.

Sampson, William. *An Anniversary Discourse, Delivered before the Historical Society of New York, on Saturday, December 6, 1823; Showing the Origin, Progress, Antiquities, Curiosities, and Nature of the Common Law*. New York: E. Bliss & E. White, 1824.

———. *Journeymen Cordwainers of the City of New-York, Defendants*. New York, 1810.

Smith, Adam. *An Inquiry into the Nature and Causes of the Wealth of Nations*. Edited by Edwin Canaan. 2 vols. in 1. Chicago, 1976.

Smith, Melancton, et al. *An Address from the Committee Appointed at Mrs. Vandewater's on the 13th day of September, 1784*. New York, 1784.

Smith, Page. *James Wilson, Founding Father, 1742–1798*. Chapel Hill, N.C., 1956.

Smith, Thomas. *De Republica Anglorum*. Edited by Mary Dewar. Cambridge, England, 1982.

Smith, William. *Mr. Smith's Opinion Humbly Offered to the General Assembly of the*

Colony of New-York, on the Seventh of June, 1734 at Their Request. New York, 1734.

Smith, William, Jr. History of the Province of New-York. Edited by Michael Kammen. 2 vols. Cambridge, Mass., 1972.

Starkey, Thomas. A Dialogue between Pole and Lupset. Edited by T. F. Mayer. London, 1989.

Stokes, Anthony. A View of the Constitution of the British Colonies in North America and the West Indies, at the Time the Civil War Broke Out on the Continent of America. 1783. Reprint, London, 1969.

Story, Joseph. Commentaries on Equity Jurisprudence As Administered in England and America. 10th ed. Edited by Issac F. Redfield. 2 vols. Boston, 1870.

———. Commentaries on the Conflict of Laws, Foreign and Domestic: In Regard to Contracts, Rights, and Remedies, and Especially in Regard to Marriages, Divorces, Wills, Successions, and Judgments. Boston, 1834.

Tocqueville, Alexis de. Democracy in America. Translated and edited by Henry Reeve, Francis Bowen, and Philip Bradley. 2 vols. New York, 1945.

———. Democracy in America. Edited by Thomas Bender. Modern Library ed. New York, 1981.

———. Journey to America. Edited by J. P. Mayer. Translated by George Lawrence. New Haven, Conn., 1960.

Tucker, St. George. Examination of the Question, "How Far the Common Law of England Is the Law of the Federal Government of the United States?" Richmond, Va., [1818].

Webster, Noah. A Collection of Papers on Political, Literary and Moral Subjects. New York, 1843.

———. A Grammatical Institute of the English Language. Hartford, 1783.

———. Sketches of American Policy. Hartford, 1785.

Westcot, Redman, trans. Tracts Written by John Selden of the Inner Temple, Esquire. London, 1683.

Wyche, William. A Treatise on the Practice of the Supreme Court of Judicature of the State of New-York in Civil Actions. New York, 1794.

[Yates, Abraham]. Political Papers, Addressed to the Advocates for a Congressional Revenue. New York, 1786.

[Young, Thomas]. Some Reflections on the Disputes between New-York, New-Hampshire, and Col. John Henry Lydius of Albany. New Haven, Conn., 1764.

LEGISLATIVE AND ADMINISTRATIVE MATERIAL

New York, Colony

Bradford, William, comp. The Laws and Acts of the General Assembly of Their Majesties Province of New-York. New York, 1694.

The Colonial Laws of New York from the Year 1664 to the Revolution. 5 vols. Albany, N.Y., 1894–96.

Fox, Dixon R., ed. The Minutes of the Court of Sessions (1657–1696), Westchester

County, New York. Publications of the Westchester Historical Association. White Plains, N.Y., 1924.

Hough, Charles M., ed. *Reports of Cases in the Vice Admiralty of the Province of New York and in the Court of Admiralty of the State of New York, 1715–1788*. New Haven, Conn., 1925.

Laws and Ordinances of New Netherland, 1623–1674. Edited by E. B. O'Callaghan. Albany, N.Y., 1868.

Livingston, William, and William Smith Jr., comps. *Laws of New-York, from the 11th Nov. 1742, to 22d May 1762*. New York, 1762.

——. *Laws of New-York from the Year 1691 to 1751, Inclusive*. New York, 1752.

Morris, Richard B., ed. *Select Cases from the Mayor's Court of New York City, 1674–1784*. Washington, D.C., 1935.

New York City. *Minutes of the Common Council of the City of New York, 1675–1776*. 8 vols. New York, 1905.

New York Council. *Calendar of Council Minutes, 1668–1783*. Compiled by Berthold Fernow. 1902. Reprint, Harrison, N.Y., 1987.

——. *Journal of the Legislative Council of the Colony of New York, 1691–1775*. Edited by E. B. O'Callaghan. 2 vols. Albany, N.Y., 1861.

New York General Assembly. *Journal of the Votes and Proceedings of the General Assembly of the Colony of New York. Began the 9th day of April, 1691; and ended the [23d of December, 1765]*. 2 vols. New York, 1766.

——. *Journal of the Votes and Proceedings of the General Assembly of the Colony of New York, from 1766 to 1776, Inclusive*. 9 vols. in 1. Albany, N.Y., 1820.

Transcriptions of Early County Records of New York State: Minutes of the Board of Supervisors of Ulster County, 1710/11–1730/31. Albany, N.Y., 1939.

Transcriptions of Early County Records of New York State: Records of the Road Commissioners of Ulster County. 2 vols. Albany, N.Y., 1940.

Van Schaack, Peter, comp. *Laws of New-York, from the Year 1691, to 1773, Inclusive*. New York, 1773.

New York, State

Journals of the Provincial Congress, Provincial Convention, Committee of Safety and Council of Safety of the State of New-York, 1775–1776–1778. 2 vols. Albany, N.Y., 1842.

Laws of the State of New York . . . 1777–1801. 5 vols. Albany, N.Y., 1886.

New York Assembly. *Journal of the Assembly of the State of New York, 1777–1792*. New York and Albany, N.Y., 1777–92.

New York City. *Minutes of the Common Council of the City of New York, 1784–1831*. 19 vols. New York, 1917.

New York Senate. *Journal of the Senate of the State of New-York*. New York and Albany, N.Y., 1777–90.

Paltsits, Victor H., ed. *Minutes of the Commissioners for Detecting and Defeating Conspiracies in the State of New York: Albany County Sessions, 1778–1781*. 3 vols. Albany, N.Y., 1909–10.

Report from the Commissioners Appointed to Revise the Laws of the State of New York. Albany, N.Y., 1826.

The Revised Statutes of the State of New-York, Passed during the Years 1827–1828. 3 vols. Albany, N.Y., 1829.

United States

Continental Congress. *Journals of the Continental Congress, 1774–1789.* Edited by Worthington C. Ford and Galliard Hunt. 34 vols. Washington, D.C., 1904–37.

Thorpe, Francis N., ed. *The Federal and State Constitutions, Colonial Charters, and Other Organic laws of . . . the United States of America.* 7 vols. Washington, D.C., 1909.

U.S. Bureau of the Census. *Historical Statistics of the United States: Colonial Times to 1970.* 2 vols. Washington, D.C.: U.S. Dept. of Commerce, Bureau of the Census, 1975.

Great Britain

Acts of the Privy Council of England, Colonial Series. 6 vols. 1908–12. Reprint, Nendeln, Liechtenstein, 1966.

Calendar of State Papers, Colonial Series (1661–1668). Edited by W. Noel Sainsbury et al. 45 vols. to date. London, 1860–1994.

Cobbett's Parliamentary History of England. Vol. 2. London, 1808.

Complete Collection of State-Trials and Proceedings for High Treason and Other Crimes and Misdemeanors from the Earliest Period to the Present Time. Compiled by T. B. Howell and Thomas J. Howell. 34 vols. London, 1816–28.

Firth, C. H., and R. S. Rait, eds. *Acts and Ordinances of the Interregnum, 1649–1660.* 3 vols. London, 1911.

Hansard, T. C., comp. *The Parliamentary History of England, from the Earliest Period to the Year 1803.* Vol. 18. London, 1813.

Johnson, Robert C., et al., eds. *Commons Debates, 1628.* 6 vols. New Haven, Conn., 1977–83.

Journal of the Commissioners for Trade and Plantations from January 1764 to December 1767. London, 1936.

Richardson, H. G., and G. O. Sayles, eds. *Rotuli Parliammentorum Anglie, MCCLXXIX–MCCLXXIII.* London, 1935.

Simmons, R. C., and P. D. G. Thomas, eds. *Proceedings and Debates of the British Parliament Respecting North America, 1754–1783.* 6 vols. Millwood, N.Y., 1982–87.

NEWSPAPERS

The Country Journal, or the Craftsman
New York Daily Advertiser
New-York Evening Post

New-York Gazette, Revived in the Weekly Post-Boy
New-York Gazette and Weekly Mercury
New York Journal
New-York Mercury
New York Post-Boy

PUBLISHED PRIMARY SOURCE COLLECTIONS

Adams, John. *Diary and Autobiography of John Adams.* Edited by L. H. Butterfield et al. 4 vols. Cambridge, Mass.: Harvard University Press, Belknap Press, 1961.

———. *The Works of John Adams.* Edited by Charles F. Adams. 10 vols. Boston: Little, Brown, 1850–56.

The Aspinwall Papers. In *Massachusetts Historical Society Collections.* 4th ser. Vols. 9 and 10. Boston: Massachusetts Historical Society, 1871.

Bacon, Francis. *The Works of Francis Bacon.* Edited by James Spedding, Robert L. Ellis, and Douglas D. Health. 14 vols. London: Longman, 1861–79.

Bailyn, Bernard, ed. *The Debate on the Constitution: Federalist and Antifederalist Speeches, Articles, and Letters during the Struggle over Ratification.* 2 vols. New York: Library of America, 1993.

Bentham, Jeremy. *The Works of Jeremy Bentham.* Compiled by John Bowring. 11 vols. New York: Russell & Russell, 1962.

Berkeley, George. *The Works of George Berkeley.* Edited by Alexander C. Fraser. 4 vols. Oxford: Clarendon Press, 1901.

Bolingbroke, Viscount. *The Works of Lord Bolingbroke.* 4 vols. Philadelphia: Carey & Hart, 1841.

Brodhead, John Romeyn, and E. B. O'Callaghan, eds. *Documents Relative to the Colonial History of the State of New-York: Procured in Holland, England, and France.* 15 vols. Albany, N.Y.: Weed, Parsons, 1853–87.

Browning, Andrew, ed. *English Historical Documents, 1660–1714.* London: Eyre & Spottiswoode, 1953.

Burke, Edmund. *The Works of the Right Honourable Edmund Burke.* 6 vols. London: Henry G. Bohn, 1854–56.

———. *The Works of the Right Honorable Edmund Burke.* Rev. ed. 12 vols. Boston: Little, Brown, 1865.

Burnett, Edmund C., ed. *Letters of the Members of the Continental Congress.* 8 vols. Washington, D.C.: Carnegie Institute of Washington, 1921–36.

Carter, Nathaniel H., and William L. Stone, eds. *Reports of the Proceedings and Debates of the Convention of 1821, Assembled for the Purpose of Amending the Constitution of the State of New York.* Albany, N.Y.: E & E Hosford, 1821.

Cavendish, Sir Henry, comp. *Debates of the House of Commons in the Year 1774, on the Bill for Making More Effectual Provision for the Government of the Province of Quebec.* London: Ridgway, 1839.

Chalmers, George, ed. *Opinions of Eminent Lawyers on Various Points of English Jurisprudence.* Burlington, Vt.: Goodrich & Co., 1858.

Chambers, Sir Robert. *A Course of Lectures on the English Law Delivered at the University of Oxford, 1767–1773*. Edited by Thomas M. Curley. 2 vols. Madison: University of Wisconsin Press, 1986.

Clinton, George. *Public Papers of George Clinton, First Governor of New York, 1777–1795, 1801–1804*. Edited by Hugh Hastings. 10 vols. Albany: State of New York, 1899–1914.

Clinton, Henry. *The American Rebellion: Sir Henry Clinton's Narrative of His Campaigns, 1775–1782, with an Appendix of Original Documents*. Edited by William Willcox. New Haven, Conn.: Yale University Press, 1954.

Collections of the New-York Historical Society. New York: Printed for the Society, 1868–.

Crevecoeur, Hector St. John. *Letters from an American Farmer*. New York: Oxford University Press, 1997.

Davies, John. *The Poems of Sir John Davies*. Edited by Robert Kreuger. Oxford: Clarendon Press, 1975.

Davies, K. G., ed. *Documents of the American Revolution, 1770–1783*. 21 vols. Shannon: Irish University Press, 1972.

DeL'isle, Guillaume. *Carte de Louisiane et du cours du Mississipi*. Paris, 1718.

Dryden, John. *The Poetical Works of John Dryden*. Boston: Houghton Mifflin, 1909.

Elliot, Jonathan, ed. *The Debates in the Several State Conventions on the Adoption of the Federal Constitution*. 3 vols. Philadelphia: J. B. Lippincott, 1876.

Emmet, Thomas Addis, W. J. MacNeven, and A. O'Connor, *The Origin and Progress of the Irish Union*. Belfast: Athol Books, 1974.

Farrand, Max, ed. *The Records of the Federal Convention of 1787*. 4 vols. New Haven, Conn.: Yale University Press, 1911–37.

Fernow, Berthold, ed. *The Records of New Amsterdam, from 1653–1674 A.D.* 7 vols. New York: Knickerbocker Press, 1897.

Force, Peter, comp. *American Archives*. 6th series. Washington, D.C.: M. St. Clair Clarke and Peter Force, 1837–53.

Ford, Paul L., ed. *Essays on the Constitution of the United States Published during Its Discussion by the People, 1787–1788*. Brooklyn N.Y.: Historical Printing Club, 1892.

——, ed. *Pamphlets on the Constitution of the United States Published during Its Discussion by the People, 1787–1788*. Brooklyn, N.Y.: n.p., 1888.

Frey, Samuel L., ed. *The Minute Book of the Committee of Safety of Tryon County*. New York: Dodd, Mead, 1905.

Gage, Thomas. *The Correspondence of General Thomas Gage*. Edited by Clarence E. Carter. 2 vols. New Haven, Conn.: Yale University Press, 1931–33.

Haines, Charles G. *Memoir of Thomas Addis Emmet*. New York: G. & C. & H. Carvill, 1829.

Hamilton, Alexander. *The Law Practice of Alexander Hamilton: Documents and Commentary*. Edited by Julius Goebel Jr. et al. 5 vols. New York: Columbia University Press, 1964–81.

——. *The Papers of Alexander Hamilton*. Edited by Harold C. Syrett et al. 27 vols. New York: Columbia University Press, 1961–87.

Hamlin, Paul M., and Charles E. Baker, ed. *Supreme Court of Judicature of the Province of New York, 1691–1704: Introduction.* New York: New-York Historical Society, 1952.

Hamowy, Ronald, ed. *Cato's Letters: Or, Essays on Liberty, Civil and Religious, and Other Important Subjects.* 2 vols. Indianapolis, Ind.: Liberty Fund, 1995.

Harrington, James. *The Political Works of James Harrington.* Edited by J. G. A. Pocock. Cambridge: Cambridge University Press, 1977.

Historical Manuscripts Commission: Report on the Manuscripts of Mrs. Stopford-Sackville, of Drayton House, Northamptonshire. 2 vols. London: n.p., 1904–10.

Jameson, J. Franklin, ed. *Narratives of New Netherland, 1609–1664.* New York: Scribner's, 1909.

Jay, John. *John Jay: Unpublished Papers, 1745–1784.* Edited by Richard B. Morris et al. 2 vols. New York: Harper & Row, 1975.

Jefferson, Thomas. *The Papers of Thomas Jefferson.* Edited by Julian P. Boyd. 31 vols. to date. Princeton, N.J.: Princeton University Press, 1950.

Jensen, Merrill, ed. *English Historical Documents: American Colonial Documents to 1776.* London: Eyre & Spottiswoode, 1955.

Jensen, Merrill, et al., eds. *The Documentary History of the Ratification of the Constitution.* 20 vols. to date. Madison: State Historical Society of Wisconsin, 1976–.

Johnson, William. *The Papers of Sir William Johnson.* Edited by James Sullivan and Alexander C. Flick. 14 vols. Albany: University of the State of New York, 1921–65.

Kent, William. *Memoirs and Letters of James Kent, LL.D.* Boston: Little, Brown, 1898.

Kenyon, J. P., ed. *The Stuart Constitution, 1603–1688: Documents and Commentary.* 2d ed. Cambridge: Cambridge University Press, 1986.

Klein, Milton M., ed. *The Independent Reflector, or Weekly Essays on Sundry Important Subjects More Particularly Adapted to the Province of New-York.* Cambridge, Mass.: Harvard University Press, Belknap Press, 1963.

Klein, Milton M., and Ronald W. Howard, eds. *The Twilight of British Rule in Revolutionary America: The New York Letter Book of General James Robertson, 1780–1783.* Cooperstown, N.Y.: New York State Historical Association, 1983.

Labaree, Leonard W., ed. *Royal Instructions to British Colonial Governors, 1670–1776.* 2 vols. New York: D. Appleton-Century, 1935.

Lincoln, Charles Z., ed. *State of New York: Messages from the Governors.* Vol. 3. Albany, N.Y.: J. B. Lyon Co., 1909.

Madison, James. *Letters and Other Writings of James Madison.* 4 vols. Philadelphia: J. B. Lippincott, 1865.

——. *Notes of Debates in the Federal Convention of 1787 Reported by James Madison.* Edited by Adrienne Koch. New York: Norton, 1969.

——. *The Papers of James Madison.* Edited by William T. Hutchinson et al. 17 vols. Chicago: University of Chicago Press, 1962–91.

——. *The Writings of James Madison.* Edited by Galliard Hunt. 9 vols. New York: G. P. Putnam's Sons, 1900–1910.

Mereness, Newton D., ed. *Travels in the American Colonies*. New York: Macmillan, 1916.

Miller, Perry, ed. *The Legal Mind in America from Independence to the Civil War*. Garden City, N.Y.: Doubleday, 1962.

O'Callaghan, Edmund B., ed. *Calendar of Historical Manuscripts in the Office of the Secretary of State*. 2 vols. Albany, N.Y.: Weed, Parsons, 1865.

———, ed. *Documentary History of New York*. 4 vols. Albany, N.Y.: Weed, Parsons, 1849–51.

———, comp. *Names of Persons for Whom Marriage Licenses Were Issued by the Secretary of the Province of New-York*. Albany, N.Y.: Weed, Parsons, 1860.

Oldham, James. *The Mansfield Manuscripts and the Growth of English Law in the Eighteenth Century*. 2 vols. Chapel Hill: University of North Carolina Press, 1992.

Onuf, Peter S., ed. *Maryland and the Empire, 1773: The Antilon-First Citizen Letters*. Baltimore: Johns Hopkins University Press, 1974.

Peterson, Merrill D., ed. *Democracy, Liberty and Property: The State Constitutional Conventions of the 1820s*. Indianapolis, Ind.: Bobbs-Merrill, 1966.

Philips, Thomas. *The Long Parliament Revived. . . . 1661*. In *The Somers Collection of Tracts*, vol. 7, edited by Walter Scott. 2d ed. London: n.p., 1812.

Sampson, William. *Memoirs of William Sampson*. 2d ed. Leesburg, Va.: Samuel B. T. Caldwell, 1817.

Secret Journals of the Acts and Proceedings of Congress. 4 vols. Boston: Thomas B. Wait, 1820–21.

Smith, Paul H., ed. *Letters of Delegates to Congress: 1774–1789*. 26 vols. Washington, D.C.: Library of Congress, 1976–2000.

Smith, W. J., ed. *The Grenville Papers*. 4 vols. London: J. Murray, 1852–53.

Smith, William, Jr. *Historical Memoirs of William Smith, Historian of the Province of New York, Member of the Governor's Council and Last Chief Justice of That Province under the Crown, Chief Justice of Quebec*. Edited by William H. W. Sabine. 3 vols. New York: New York Times, 1956–71.

Stevens, Benjamin F., comp. *B. F. Stevens's Facsimiles of Manuscripts in European Archives Relating to America, 1773–1783*. 12 vols. London: Whittingham, 1892.

Stevens, John A., ed. *The Colonial Records of the New York Chamber of Commerce, 1768–1784*. 1867. Reprint, New York: B. Franklin, 1971.

Van Buren, Martin. *The Autobiography of Martin Van Buren*. Edited by John C. Fitzpatrick. Washington, D.C.: Government Printing Office, 1920.

Walpole, Horace. *Memoirs of King George II*. Edited by John Brooke. 3 vols. New Haven, Conn.: Yale University Press, 1985.

Washington, George. *The Papers of George Washington: Confederation Series*. Vol. 2. Charlottesville: University Press of Virginia, 1992.

———. *The Writings of George Washington from the Original Manuscript Sources, 1745–1799*. Edited by John C. Fitzpatrick. 39 vols. Washington, D.C.: Government Printing Office, 1931–44.

Webster, Noah. *The Autobiographies of Noah Webster: From the Letters and Essays,*

Memoir, and Diary. Edited by Richard M. Rollins. Columbia: University of South Carolina Press, 1989.

Wharton, Francis, ed. *The Revolutionary Diplomatic Correspondence of the United States.* 6 vols. Washington, D.C.: Government Printing Office, 1889.

Whately, Richard, ed. *Bacon's Essays with Annotations.* Boston: Lee & Shepard, 1879.

White, Philip L., ed. *The Beekman Mercantile Papers, 1746–1799.* 3 vols. New York: New-York Historical Society, 1956.

Williams, C. H., ed. *English Historical Documents, 1485–1558.* London: Eyre & Spottiswoode, 1967.

Williams, E. Neville, ed. *The Eighteenth-Century Constitution, 1688–1815: Documents and Commentary.* Cambridge: Cambridge University Press, 1960.

Wilson, James. *The Works of James Wilson.* Edited by Robert G. McCloskey. 2 vols. Cambridge, Mass.: Harvard University Press, Belknap Press, 1967.

Secondary Sources

BOOKS AND COLLECTED ESSAYS

Abernethy, Thomas P. *Western Lands and the American Revolution.* New York: Russell & Russell, 1959.

Ackerman, Bruce A. *We the People.* 2 vols. Cambridge, Mass.: Harvard University Press, Belknap Press, 1991, 1998.

Adair, Douglass. *Fame and the Founding Fathers: Essays by Douglass Adair.* Edited by Trevor Colbourn. New York: Norton, 1974.

Adams, Arthur G. *The Hudson: A Guidebook to the River.* Albany: State University of New York Press, 1981.

Adams, George B. *The Constitutional History of England.* New York: H. Holt, 1921.

Adams, Randolph G. *Political Ideas of the American Revolution: Britannic-American Contribution to the Problem of Imperial Organization, 1765–1775.* Durham, N.C.: Trinity College Press, 1922.

Adams, Willi Paul. *The First American Constitutions: Republican Ideology and the Making of the State Constitutions in the Revolutionary Era.* Translated by Rita and Robert Kimber. Chapel Hill: University of North Carolina Press, 1980.

Akagi, Roy H. *The Town Proprietors of the New England Colonies: A Study of Their Development, Organization, Activities and Controversies, 1620–1770.* Philadelphia: Press of the University of Pennsylvania, 1924.

Albion, Robert G. *The Rise of New York Port.* New York: Scribner's, 1939.

Alden, John. *John Stuart and the Southern Colonial Frontier.* Ann Arbor: University of Michigan Press, 1944.

Alexander, DeAlva S. *A Political History of the State of New York.* 3 vols. 1909. Reprint, Port Washington, N.Y.: I. J. Friedman, 1969.

Alexander, Edward P. *A Revolutionary Conservative: James Duane of New York.* New York: Columbia University Press, 1938.

Alexander, Gregory S. *Commodity and Propriety: Competing Visions of Property in American Legal Thought, 1776–1970.* Chicago: University of Chicago Press, 1997.

Allen, David G. *In English Ways: The Movement of Societies and the Transferal of English Local Law and Custom to Massachusetts Bay in the Seventeenth Century.* Chapel Hill: University of North Carolina Press, 1981.

Alvord, Clarence W. *The Genesis of the Proclamation of 1763.* N.p., 1900.

———. *The Mississippi Valley in British Politics.* 2 vols. New York: Russel & Russell, 1959.

Alvord, Clarence W., and Clarence E. Carter, eds. *The Critical Period, 1763–1765.* Collections of the Illinois State Historical Library. Vol. 10. Springfield, Ill.: Trustees of the Illinois State Historical Library, 1915.

Amar, Akhil R. *The Bill of Rights: Creation and Reconstruction.* New Haven, Conn.: Yale University Press, 1998.

Anderson, Benedict. *Imagined Communities: Reflections on the Origin and Spread of Nationalism.* Rev. ed. London: Verso, 1991.

Anderson, Fred. *Crucible of War: The Seven Years' War and the Fate of the Empire in British North America, 1754–1766.* New York: Knopf, Distributed by Random House, 2000.

Andrews, Charles M. *The Colonial Background of the American Revolution.* New Haven, Conn.: Yale University Press, 1924.

———. *The Colonial Period of American History.* 4 vols. New Haven, Conn.: Yale University Press, 1934–38.

———. *Colonial Self-Government, 1652–1689.* New York: Harper & Brothers, 1904.

Andrews, Kenneth R. *Trade, Plunder and Settlement: Maritime Enterprise and the Genesis of the British Empire, 1480–1630.* Cambridge: Cambridge University Press, 1984.

Angermann, Erich, Marie-Louise Frings, and Hermann Wellenreuther, eds. *New Wine in Old Skins: A Comparative View of Socio-political Structures and Values Affecting the American Revolution.* Stuttgart, Germany: Klett, 1976.

Appleby, Joyce. *Republicanism and Liberalism in the Historical Imagination.* Cambridge, Mass.: Harvard University Press, 1992.

Aquila, Richard. *The Iroquois Restoration: Iroquois Diplomacy on the Colonial Frontier, 1701–1754.* Detroit, Mich.: Wayne State University Press, 1983.

Archdeacon, Thomas J. *New York City, 1664–1710: Conquest and Change.* Ithaca, N.Y.: Cornell University Press, 1976.

Arendt, Hannah. *On Revolution.* New York: Viking Press, 1965.

Aristotle. *Aristotle: Selections.* Edited and translated by Terence Irwin and Gail Fine. Indianapolis, Ind.: Hackett, 1995.

———. *The Basic Works of Aristotle.* Edited by Richard McKeon. Translated by Benjamin Jowitt. New York: Random House, 1941.

Armitage, David. *The Ideological Origins of the British Empire.* Cambridge: Cambridge University Press, 2000.

———, ed. *Theories of Empire, 1450–1800.* London: Ashgate, 1998.

Armitage, David, and Michael J. Braddick, eds. *The British Atlantic World, 1500–1800*. New York: Palgrave Macmillan, 2002.

Ashcroft, Bill, Gareth Griffiths, and Helen Tiffin, eds. *The Empire Writes Back: Theory and Practice in Post-Colonial Literatures*. New York: Routledge, 1989.

———, eds. *The Post-Colonial Studies Reader*. New York: Routledge, 1995.

Bagehot, Walter. *The English Constitution*. New York: D. Appleton & Co., 1924.

Bagnall, Roger S., and William V. Harris, eds. *Studies in Roman Law in Memory of A. Arthur Schiller*. Leiden, Netherlands: Brill, 1986.

Bailyn, Bernard. *Faces of Revolution: Personalities and Themes in the Struggle for American Independence*. New York: Knopf, Distributed by Random House, 1990.

———. *History and the Creative Imagination*. St. Louis, Mo.: Washington University, 1985.

———. *The Ideological Origins of the American Revolution*. Cambridge, Mass.: Harvard University Press, Belknap Press, 1967.

———. *New England Merchants in the Seventeenth Century*. Cambridge, Mass.: Harvard University Press, 1955.

———. *The Ordeal of Thomas Hutchinson*. Cambridge, Mass.: Harvard University Press, Belknap Press, 1974.

———. *The Origins of American Politics*. New York: Knopf, 1968.

———. *The Peopling of British North America: An Introduction*. New York: Knopf, 1986.

———. *Voyagers to the West: A Passage in the Peopling of America on the Eve of the Revolution*. New York: Knopf, Distributed by Random House, 1986.

Bailyn, Bernard, and Philip D. Morgan, eds. *Strangers within the Realm: Cultural Margins of the First British Empire*. Chapel Hill: University of North Carolina Press, 1991.

Baker, Ernest. *Essays on Government*. Oxford: Clarendon Press, 1945.

Baker, J. H. *An Introduction to English Legal History*. 4th ed. London: Butterworths, 2002.

———. *The Legal Profession and the Common Law: Historical Essays*. London: Hambledon Press, 1986.

Baldwin, Simeon E. *Modern Political Institutions*. Boston: Little, Brown, 1908.

Balkin, J. M. *Cultural Software: A Theory of Ideology*. New Haven, Conn.: Yale University Press, 1998.

Balkin, J. M., and Sanford Levinson, eds. *Legal Canons*. New York: New York University Press, 2000.

Ball, Terence, James Farr, and Russell L. Hanson, eds. *Political Innovation and Conceptual Change*. New York: Cambridge University Press, 1989.

Ball, Terence, and J. G. A. Pocock, eds. *Conceptual Change and the Constitution*. Lawrence: University Press of Kansas, 1988.

Bancroft, George. *History of the United States of America: From the Discovery of the Continent*. 6 vols. Rev. ed. Boston: Little, Brown, 1878.

Banner, James M., Jr. *To the Hartford Convention: The Federalists and the Origins of Party Politics in Massachusetts, 1789–1815*. New York: Knopf, 1970.

Banning, Lance. *The Sacred Fire of Liberty: James Madison and the Founding of the Federal Republic*. Ithaca, N.Y.: Cornell University Press, 1995.

Barck, Oscar T. *New York City during the War for Independence*. New York: Columbia University Press, 1931.

Barlow, J. Jackson, Leonard W. Levy, and Ken Masugi, eds. *The American Founding: Essays on the Formation of the Constitution*. New York: Greenwood Press, 1988.

Barnes, Thomas G. *Somerset, 1625–1640: A County's Government during the "Personal Rule."* Cambridge, Mass.: Harvard University Press, 1961.

Barnes, Viola. *The Dominion of New England: A Study in British Colonial Policy*. New Haven, Conn.: Yale University Press, 1923.

Barrow, Thomas C. *Trade and Empire: The British Customs Service in Colonial America, 1660–1775*. Cambridge, Mass.: Harvard University Press, 1967.

Basye, Arthur H. *The Lords Commissioners of Trade and Plantations, Commonly Known as the Board of Trade, 1748–1782*. New Haven, Conn.: Yale University Press, 1925.

Bauer, Elizabeth Kelley. *Commentaries on the Constitution, 1790–1860*. New York: Columbia University Press, 1952.

Baxter, William T. *The House of Hancock: Business in Boston, 1724–1775*. Cambridge, Mass.: Harvard University Press, 1945.

Bayles, W. Harrison. *Old Taverns of New York*. New York: Frank Alleben Genealogical Co., 1915.

Bayly, C. A. *Imperial Meridian: The British Empire and the World, 1780–1830*. London: Longman, 1989.

Becker, Carl L. *Everyman His Own Historian*. New York: F. S. Crofts & Co., 1935.

———. *The History of Political Parties in the Province of New York, 1760–1776*. Madison: University of Wisconsin, 1909.

Beckett, J. C. *The Making of Modern Ireland, 1603–1923*. London: Faber & Faber, 1981.

Beeman, Richard, Stephen Botein, and Edward C. Carter II, eds. *Beyond Confederation: Origins of the Constitution and American National Identity*. Chapel Hill: University of North Carolina Press, 1987.

Bellesiles, Michael A. *Revolutionary Outlaws: Ethan Allen and the Struggle for Independence on the Early American Frontier*. Charlottesville: University Press of Virginia, 1993.

Bellomo, Manlio. *The Common Legal Past of Europe, 1000–1800*. Translated by Lydia G. Cochrane. Washington, D.C.: Catholic University of America Press, 1995.

Bellot, Leland J. *William Knox: The Life and Thought of an Eighteenth-Century Imperialist*. Austin: University of Texas Press, 1977.

Bemis, Samuel F. *The Diplomacy of the American Revolution*. Bloomington: Indiana University Press, 1957.

Bender, Thomas. *New York Intellect: A History of Intellectual Life in New York City, from 1750 to the Beginnings of Our Own Time*. New York: Knopf, Distributed by Random House, 1987.

Benson, Lee. *The Concept of Jacksonian Democracy: New York as a Test Case.* Princeton, N.J.: Princeton University Press, 1961.

———. *Turner and Beard: American Historical Writing Reconsidered.* New York: Free Press, 1965.

Benton, Lauren. *Law and Colonial Cultures: Legal Regimes in World History, 1400–1900.* New York: Cambridge University Press, 2002.

Benton, William A. *Whig-Loyalism: An Aspect of Political Ideology in the American Revolutionary Era.* Rutherford, N.J.: Farleigh Dickenson University Press, 1969.

Bercovitch, Sacvan. *Reconstructing American Literary History.* Cambridge, Mass.: Harvard University Press, 1986.

Bhabha, Homi K. *The Location of Culture.* London: Routledge, 1994.

Bielinski, Stefan. *Abraham Yates, Jr., and the New Political Order in Revolutionary New York.* Albany: New York State American Revolution Bicentennial Commission, 1975.

Biemer, Linda Briggs. *Women and Property in Colonial New York: The Transition from Dutch to English Law, 1643–1727.* Ann Arbor, Mich.: UMI Research Press, 1983.

Bilder, Mary Sarah. *The Transatlantic Constitution: Colonial Legal Culture and the Empire.* Cambridge, Mass.: Harvard University Press, 2004.

Billias, George A., ed. *American Constitutionalism Abroad: Selected Essays in Comparative Constitutional History.* New York: Greenwood Press, 1990.

———, ed. *Law and Authority in Colonial America: Selected Essays.* Barre, Mass.: Barre Publishers, 1965.

Black, Charles L., Jr. *The People and the Court: Judicial Review in a Democracy.* Englewood Cliffs, N.J.: Prentice Hall, 1960.

Black's Law Dictionary. 5th ed. St. Paul, Minn.: West, 1979.

Bliss, R. M. *Revolution and Empire: English Politics and the American Colonies in the Seventeenth Century.* Manchester, England: Manchester University Press, 1990.

Bloom, John P., ed. *The American Territorial System.* Athens: Ohio University Press, 1973.

Bloomfield, Maxwell H. *American Lawyers in a Changing Society.* Cambridge, Mass.: Harvard University Press, 1976.

Bond, Beverly W., Jr. *The Quit-Rent System in the American Colonies.* New Haven, Conn.: Yale University Press, 1919.

Bonomi, Patricia U. *A Factious People: Politics and Society in Colonial New York.* New York: Columbia University Press, 1971.

———. *The Lord Cornbury Scandal: The Politics of Reputation in British America.* Chapel Hill: University of North Carolina Press, 1998.

Bonwick, Colin. *English Radicals and the American Revolution.* Chapel Hill: University of North Carolina Press, 1977.

Borsay, Peter. *The English Urban Renaissance: Culture and Society in the Provincial Town, 1660–1770.* Oxford: Clarendon Press, 1989.

Bourguignon, Henry J. *The First Federal Court: The Federal Appellate Prize Court of the American Revolution.* Philadelphia: American Philosophical Society, 1977.

Bowring, Charles W., et al. *A History of St. George's Society of New York from 1770–1913.* New York: Federal Printing Co., 1913.

Boyle, Robert H. *The Hudson River: A Natural and Unnatural History.* New York: Norton, 1969.

Bradley, James E. *Popular Politics and the American Revolution in England: Petitions, the Crown, and Public Opinion.* Macon, Ga.: Mercer, 1986.

Brant, Irving. *James Madison: The Nationalist, 1780–1787.* Indianapolis, Ind.: Bobbs-Merrill, 1948.

Brathwaite, Edward. *The Development of Creole Society in Jamaica, 1770–1820.* Oxford: Clarendon Press, 1971.

Brewer, John. *Party Ideology and Popular Politics at the Accession of George III.* New York: Cambridge University Press, 1976.

———. *The Sinews of Power: War, Money and the English State, 1688–1783.* New York: Knopf, 1989.

Bridenbaugh, Carl. *Cities in the Wilderness.* New York: Ronald Press Co., 1938.

———. *Mitre and Sceptre: Transatlantic Faiths, Ideas, Personalities, and Politics, 1689–1775.* New York: Oxford University Press, 1962.

Brodhead, John R. *History of the State of New York.* 2 vols. New York: Harper & Brothers, 1853–71.

Brown, Elizabeth B. *British Statutes in American Law, 1776–1836.* Ann Arbor: University of Michigan Law School, 1964.

Brown, Wallace. *The King's Friends: The Composition and Motives of the American Loyalist Claimants.* Providence, R.I.: Brown University Press, 1965.

Browning, Reed. *The Political and Constitutional Ideas of the Court Whigs.* Baton Rouge: Louisiana State University Press, 1982.

Bryson, William H. *The Equity Side of the Exchequer: Its Jurisdiction, Administration, Procedures and Records.* Cambridge: Cambridge University Press, 1975.

Burchell, R. A., ed. *The End of Anglo-America: Historical Essays in the Study of Cultural Divergence.* Manchester, England: Manchester University Press, 1991.

Burgess, Glenn. *Absolute Monarchy and the Stuart Constitution.* New Haven, Conn.: Yale University Press, 1996.

———. *The Politics of the Ancient Constitution: An Introduction to English Political Thought, 1603–1642.* Basingstoke, England: Macmillan, 1992.

Burke, Peter. *Popular Culture in Early Modern Europe.* Rev. ed. Aldershot, England: Scolar Press 1994.

Burns, J. H. *The Cambridge History of Political Thought, 1450–1770.* Cambridge: Cambridge University Press, 1991.

Bushman, Richard. *The Refinement of America.* New York: Knopf, Distributed by Random House, 1992.

Butler, William A. *The Revision of the Statutes of the State of New York and the Revisers.* New York: Banks & Brothers, 1889.

Cam, Helen. *Law-Finders and Law-Makers in Medieval England*. London: Merlin Press, 1962.

Campbell, Morton Carlisle. *Harvard Legal Essays Written in Honor of and Presented to Joseph Henry Beale and Samuel Williston*. Cambridge, Mass.: Harvard University Press, 1934.

Cannadine, David. *Ornamentalism: How the British Saw Their Empire*. New York: Oxford University Press, 2001.

———. *The Rise and Fall of Class in Britain*. New York: Columbia University Press, 1999.

Cannon, Garland. *Oriental Jones: A Biography of Sir William Jones (1746–1794)*. New York: Asia Publishing House, 1964.

Canny, Nicholas P. *The Elizabethan Conquest of Ireland: A Pattern Established, 1565–76*. Hassocks, England: Harvester Press, 1976.

———, ed. *Europeans on the Move: Studies on European Migration*. Oxford: Clarendon Press, 1994.

———. *Kingdom and Colony: Ireland in the Atlantic World, 1560–1800*. Baltimore: Johns Hopkins University Press, 1988.

Canny, Nicholas P., and Anthony Pagden, eds. *Colonial Identity in the Atlantic World, 1500–1800*. Princeton, N.J.: Princeton University Press, 1987.

Capaldi, Nicholas, and Donald W. Livingston, eds. *Liberty in Hume's History of England*. Boston: Kluwer Academic, 1990.

Carmer, Carl. *The Hudson*. New York: Holt, Rinehart, & Winston, 1939.

Carter, Alice C. *Neutrality or Commitment: The Evolution of Dutch Foreign Policy, 1667–1795*. London: Edward Arnold, 1975.

Carter, Paul. *The Road to Botany Bay: An Exploration of Landscape and History*. New York: Knopf, 1988.

Casto, William R. *The Supreme Court in the Early Republic: The Chief Justiceships of John Jay and Oliver Ellsworth*. Columbia: University of South Carolina Press, 1995.

Chafee, Zechariah. *Three Human Rights in the Constitution of 1787*. Lawrence: University of Kansas Press, 1956.

Channing, Edward. *Town and County Government in the English Colonies of North America*. Baltimore: N. Murray, publication agent, Johns Hopkins University, 1884.

Chartier, Roger, Alain Boureau, and Cecile Dauphin, eds. *Correspondence: Models of Letter-Writing from the Middle Ages to the Nineteenth Century*. Translated by Chistopher Woodall. Princeton, N.J.: Princeton University Press, 1997.

Chernow, Ron. *Alexander Hamilton*. New York: Penguin Press, 2004.

Cheyney, Edward P. *European Background of American History, 1300–1600*. 1904. Reprint, New York: F. Ungar, 1966.

Chrimes, S. B. *English Constitutional Ideas in the Fifteenth Century*. New York: AMS Press, 1936.

Clanchy, M. T. *From Memory to Written Record: England, 1066–1307*. 2d ed. Oxford: Blackwell, 1993.

Clark, Dora Mae. *The Rise of the British Treasury: Colonial Administration in the Eighteenth Century*. New Haven, Conn.: Yale University Press, 1960.

Clark, J. C. D. *The Language of Liberty, 1660–1832: Political Discourse and Social Dynamics in the Anglo-American World*. Cambridge: Cambridge University Press, 1994.

Cobb, Sanford H. *The Rise of Religious Liberty in America*. New York: Macmillan, 1902.

Cochran, Thomas C. *New York in the Confederation: An Economic Study*. Philadelphia: University of Pennsylvania Press, 1932.

Cohn, Bernard. *Colonialism and Its Forms of Knowledge: The British in India*. Princeton, N.J.: Princeton University Press, 1996.

Colbourn, H. Trevor. *The Lamp of Experience: Whig History and the Intellectual Origins of the American Revolution*. Chapel Hill: University of North Carolina Press, 1965.

Colley, Linda. *Britons: Forging the Nation, 1707–1837*. New Haven, Conn.: Yale University Press, 1992.

Condon, Thomas J. *New York Beginnings: The Commercial Origins of New Netherland*. New York: New York University Press, 1968.

Cook, Charles M. *The American Codification Movement: A Study of Antebellum Legal Reform*. Westport, Conn.: Greenwood Press, 1981.

Cooke, Jacob E. *Alexander Hamilton*. New York: Scribner's, 1982.

Coquillette, Daniel, ed. *Law in Colonial Massachusetts, 1630–1800*. Boston: Colonial Society of Massachusetts, 1984.

Cornell, Saul. *The Other Founders: Anti-Federalism and the Dissenting Tradition in America, 1788–1828*. Chapel Hill: University of North Carolina Press, 1999.

Cornog, Evan. *The Birth of Empire: DeWitt Clinton and the American Experience, 1769–1828*. Oxford: Oxford University Press, 1998.

Corwin, Edward S. *The "Higher Law" Background of American Constitutional Law*. Ithaca, N.Y.: Cornell University Press, 1955.

Countryman, Edward. *A People in Revolution: The American Revolution and Political Society in New York, 1760–1790*. New York: Norton, 1989.

Craven, Wesley F. *Dissolution of the Virginia Company: The Failure of a Colonial Experiment*. New York: Oxford University Press, 1932.

Crawford, Michael J., and Christine F. Hughes. *The Reestablishment of the Navy, 1787–1801*. Washington, D.C.: Naval Historical Center, Department of the Navy, 1995.

Cronin, James E., ed. *The Diary of Elihu Hubbard Smith (1771–1798)*. Philadelphia: American Philosophical Society, 1973.

Cronon, William. *Changes in the Land: Indians, Colonists, and the Ecology of New England*. New York: Hill & Wang, 1983.

Cross, Claire, David Loades, and J. J. Scarisbrick, eds. *Law and Government under the Tudors*. Cambridge: Cambridge University Press, 1988.

Crow, Jeffrey J., and Larry E. Tise, eds. *The Southern Experience in the American Revolution*. Chapel Hill: University of North Carolina Press, 1978.

Daniels, Bruce C., ed. *Power and Status: Officeholding in Colonial America.* Middletown, Conn.: Wesleyan University Press, 1986.

———, ed. *Town and Country: Essays on the Structure of Local Government in the American Colonies.* Middletown, Conn.: Wesleyan University Press, 1978.

Davidson, Cathy. *Revolution and the Word: The Rise of the Novel in America.* New York: Oxford University Press, 1986.

Davis, John P. *Corporations: A Study of the Origin and Development of Great Business Corporations and Their Relation to the Authority of the State.* New York: Capricorn Books, 1961.

Davis, Joseph S. *Essays in the Earlier History of American Corporations.* 2 vols. Cambridge, Mass.: Harvard University Press, 1917.

Davis, R. W., ed. *The Origins of Modern Freedom in the West.* Stanford, Calif.: Stanford University Press, 1995.

Dawson, John P. *A History of Lay Judges.* Cambridge, Mass.: Harvard University Press, 1960.

Dennis, Matthew. *Cultivating a Landscape of Peace: Iroquois-European Encounters in Seventeenth-Century America.* Ithaca, N.Y.: Cornell University Press, 1993.

De Pauw, Linda Grant. *The Eleventh Pillar: New York State and the Federal Constitution.* Ithaca, N.Y.: Cornell University Press, 1966.

De Soto, Hernando. *The Mystery of Capital: Why Capitalism Triumphs in the West and Fails Everywhere Else.* New York: Basic Books, 2000.

Diament, Lincoln. *Chaining the Hudson: The Fight for the River in the American Revolution.* New York: Carol Publishing Group, 1989.

Dicey, Albert V. *Introduction to the Study of Law of the Constitution.* 7th ed. London: Macmillan, 1908.

———. *The Privy Council.* 1887. Reprint, Westport, Conn.: Hyperion Press, 1979.

Dicey, Albert V., and Robert S. Rait. *Thoughts on the Union between England and Scotland.* London: Macmillan, 1920.

Dickerson, Oliver M. *The Navigation Acts and the American Revolution.* Philadelphia: University of Pennsylvania Press, 1951.

Dillon, Dorothy R. *The New York Triumvirate.* New York: Columbia University Press, 1949.

Douglass, Elisha P. *Rebels and Democrats: The Struggle for Equal Political Rights and Majority Rule during the American Revolution.* Chapel Hill: University of North Carolina Press, 1955.

Durey, Michael. *Transatlantic Radicals and the Early American Republic.* Lawrence: University Press of Kansas, 1997.

Dworkin, Ronald. *Law's Empire.* Cambridge, Mass.: Harvard University Press, Belknap Press, 1986.

East, Robert A. *Business Enterprise in the American Revolutionary Era.* New York: Columbia University Press, 1938.

East, Robert A., and Jacob Judd, eds. *The Loyalist Americans: A Focus on Greater New York.* Tarrytown, N.Y.: Sleepy Hollow Restorations, 1975.

Eblen, Jack E. *The First and Second United States Empires: Governors and Territorial Government, 1784–1912.* Pittsburgh, Pa.: University of Pittsburgh Press, 1968.

Egnal, Marc. *A Mighty Empire: The Origins of the American Revolution.* Ithaca, N.Y.: Cornell University Press, 1988.

Elkins, Stanley, and Eric McKitrick. *The Age of Federalism.* New York: Oxford University Press, 1993.

Ellis, Joseph J. *After the Revolution: Profiles of Early American Culture.* New York: Norton, 1979.

Ellis, Richard E. *The Jeffersonian Crisis: Courts and Politics in the Young Republic.* New York: Oxford University Press, 1971.

Elton, G. R. *The Parliament of England, 1559–1581.* Cambridge: Cambridge University Press, 1986.

———. *The Tudor Revolution in Government: Administrative Changes in the Reign of Henry VIII.* Cambridge: Cambridge University Press, 1953.

Essays in Colonial History Presented to Charles McLean Andrews by His Students. New Haven, Conn.: Yale University Press, 1931.

Everitt, Alan. *The Community of Kent and the Great Rebellion, 1640–1660.* Leicester, England: Leicester University Press, 1971.

Fabend, Firth Haring. *A Dutch Family in the Middle Colonies, 1660–1800.* New Brunswick, N.J.: Rutgers University Press, 1991.

Fairlie, John A. *The Centralization of Administration in New York State.* New York: Columbia University, 1898.

Faulkner, Robert K. *The Jurisprudence of John Marshall.* Princeton, N.J.: Princeton University Press, 1968.

Ferguson, Arthur B. *The Articulate Citizen and the English Renaissance.* Durham, N.C.: Duke University Press, 1965.

Ferguson, Niall. *Colossus: The Price of America's Empire.* New York: Penguin Press, 2004.

Ferguson, Robert A. *Law and Letters in American Culture.* Cambridge, Mass.: Harvard University Press, 1984.

Fitzpatrick, Peter, ed. *Dangerous Supplements: Resistance and Renewal in Jurisprudence.* Durham, N.C.: Duke University Press, 1991.

Flaherty, David H., ed. *Essays in the History of Early American Law.* Chapel Hill: University of North Carolina Press, 1969.

Fletcher, Anthony. *Reform in the Provinces: The Government of Stuart England.* New Haven, Conn.: Yale University Press, 1986.

Flexner, James T. *Lord of the Mohawks: A Biography of Sir William Johnson.* New York: Little, Brown, 1979.

Flick, Alexander, ed. *The American Revolution in New York: Its Political, Social and Economic Significance.* Albany: University of the State of New York, 1926.

———, ed. *History of the State of New York.* 10 vols. New York: Columbia University Press, 1933–37.

———. *Loyalism in New York during the American Revolution.* New York: Arno Press, 1969.

Fliegelman, Jay. *Declaring Independence: Jefferson, Natural Language, and the Culture of Performance.* Stanford, Calif.: Stanford University Press, 1993.

Flint, John E., and Glyndwr Williams, eds. *Perspectives of Empire: Essays Presented to Gerald S. Graham*. London: Longman, 1973.

Foner, Eric. *Tom Paine and Revolutionary America*. New York: Oxford University Press, 1976.

Forbes, Duncan. *Hume's Philosophical Politics*. Cambridge: Cambridge University Press, 1975.

Foucault, Michel. *The Foucault Effect: Studies in Governmentality*. Chicago: University of Chicago Press, 1991.

Fox, Dixon R. *The Decline of Aristocracy in the Politics of New York, 1801–1840*. New York: Columbia University, 1919.

———. *Yankees and Yorkers*. New York: New York University Press, 1940.

Fox, Edith M. *Land Speculation in the Mohawk Country*. Ithaca, N.Y.: Cornell University Press, 1949.

Franklin, Julian H. *Bodin and the Rise of Absolutist Theory*. Cambridge: Cambridge University Press, 1973.

Freedman, Eric M. *Habeas Corpus: Rethinking the Great Writ of Liberty*. New York: New York University Press, 2001.

Freeman, Joanne B. *Affairs of Honor: National Politics in the New Republic*. New Haven, Conn.: Yale University Press, 2001.

Frey, Sylvia R. *Water from the Rock: Black Resistance in a Revolutionary Age*. Princeton, N.J.: Princeton University Press, 1991.

Freyer, Tony. *Harmony and Dissonance: The* Swift *and* Erie *Cases in American Federalism*. New York: New York University Press, 1981.

Friedman, Lawrence M. *Contract Law in America: A Social and Economic Case Study*. Madison: University of Wisconsin Press, 1965.

Friedrich, Carl J. *Constitutional Government and Democracy*. 4th ed. Waltham, Mass.: Blaisdell, 1968.

Fukuda, Arihiro. *Sovereignty and the Sword: Harrington, Hobbes, and Mixed Government in the English Civil Wars*. Oxford: Clarendon Press, 1997.

Furtwangler, Albert. *The Authority of Publius: A Reading of the Federalist Papers*. Ithaca, N.Y.: Cornell University Press, 1984.

Galie, Peter J. *Ordered Liberty: A Constitutional History of New York*. New York: Fordham University Press, 1996.

Galloway, Bruce R. *The Union of England and Scotland, 1603–1608*. Edinburgh: J. Donald, 1986.

Gaustad, Edwin S. *A Religious History of America*. New York: Harper & Row, 1966.

Geertz, Clifford. *The Interpretation of Cultures*. New York: Basic Books, 1973.

Gellner, Ernest. *Nations and Nationalism*. Oxford: Blackwell, 1983.

Genovese, Eugene D. *Roll, Jordan, Roll: The World the Slaves Made*. New York: Pantheon Books, 1974.

Gibb, Andrew D. *Law from over the Border: A Short Account of a Strange Jurisdiction*. Edinburgh: W. Green, 1950.

Gierke, Otto von. *The Development of Political Theory*. Translated by Bernard Freyd. New York: Norton, 1939.

Gilje, Paul A. *Liberty on the Waterfront: American Maritime Culture in the Age of Revolution*. Philadelphia: University of Pennsylvania Press, 2004.

———. *The Road to Mobocracy: Popular Disorder in New York City, 1763–1834*. Chapel Hill: University of North Carolina Press, 1987.

Gilje, Paul A., and William Pencak, eds. *New York in the Age of the Constitution, 1775–1800*. Rutherford, N.J.: Fairleigh Dickenson University Press, 1992.

Gipson, Lawrence H. *The British Empire before the American Revolution*. 15 vols. New York: Knopf, 1936–70.

———. *Lewis Evans, to Which Is Added Evans' "A Brief Account of Pennsylvania."* Philadelphia: Historical Society of Pennsylvania, 1939.

Goebel, Julius, Jr. *Antecedents and Beginnings to 1801*. Vol. 1 of *History of the Supreme Court of the United States*. New York: Macmillan, 1971.

———. *Some Legal and Political Aspects of the Manors in New York*. Baltimore: The Order of Colonial Lords of Manors in America, 1928.

Goebel, Julius, Jr., and T. Raymond Naughton. *Law Enforcement in Colonial New York: A Study in Criminal Procedure (1664–1776)*. Montclair, N.J.: Patterson Smith, 1970.

Goodfriend, Joyce D. *Before the Melting Pot: Society and Culture in Colonial New York City, 1664–1730*. Princeton, N.J.: Princeton University Press, 1992.

Gordon, Scott. *Controlling the State: Constitutionalism from Ancient Athens to Today*. Cambridge, Mass.: Harvard University Press, 1999.

Gough, J. W. *Fundamental Law in English Constitutional History*. Rev. ed. Oxford: Clarendon Press, 1961.

Gould, Elijah H. *The Persistence of Empire: British Political Culture in the Age of the American Revolution*. Chapel Hill: University of North Carolina Press, 2000.

Graham, Ian C. C. *Colonists from Scotland: Emigration to North America, 1707–1783*. Ithaca, N.Y.: Cornell University Press, 1956.

Grasso, Christopher. *A Speaking Aristocracy: Transforming Public Discourse in Eighteenth-Century Connecticut*. Chapel Hill: University of North Carolina Press, 1999.

Graymont, Barbara. *The Iroquois in the American Revolution*. Syracuse, N.Y.: Syracuse University Press, 1972.

Green, Fletcher M. *Constitutional Development in the South Atlantic States, 1776–1860: A Study in the Evolution of Democracy*. Chapel Hill: University of North Carolina Press, 1930.

Green, Thomas A. *Verdict According to Conscience: Perspectives on the English Criminal Trial Jury, 1200–1800*. Chicago: University of Chicago Press, 1985.

Greenberg, Douglas. *Crime and Law Enforcement in the Colony of New York, 1691–1776*. Ithaca, N.Y.: Cornell University Press, 1976.

Greenberg, Douglas, et al., eds. *Constitutionalism and Democracy: Transitions in the Contemporary World*. New York: Oxford University Press, 1993.

Greene, Evarts B., and Virginia D. Harrington. *American Population before the Federal Census of 1790*. New York: Columbia University Press, 1932.

Greene, Jack P., ed. *The American Revolution: Its Character and Limits*. New York: New York University Press, 1987.

———, ed. *Negotiated Authorities: Essays in Colonial Political and Constitutional History*. Charlottesville: University Press of Virginia, 1994.

———. *Peripheries and Center: Constitutional Development in the Extended Polities of the British Empire and the United States*. Athens: University of Georgia Press, 1986.

———. *Pursuits of Happiness: The Social Development of Early Modern British Colonies and the Formation of American Culture*. Chapel Hill: University of North Carolina Press, 1988.

———. *The Quest for Power: The Lower Houses of Assembly in the Southern Royal Colonies, 1689–1776*. Chapel Hill: University of North Carolina Press, 1963.

Greene, Jack P., and J. R. Pole, eds. *The Blackwell Encyclopedia of the American Revolution*. London: Blackwell, 1991.

———, eds. *Colonial British America: Essays in the New History of the Early Modern Era*. Baltimore: Johns Hopkins University Press, 1984.

Greenleaf, W. H. *Order, Empiricism and Politics: Two Traditions of English Political Thought, 1500–1700*. London: Oxford University Press, 1964.

Griffin, Stephen M. *American Constitutionalism: From Theory to Politics*. Princeton, N.J.: Princeton University Press, 1996.

Griffith, Ernest S. *History of American City Government: The Colonial Period*. New York: Oxford University Press, 1938.

Gross, Hanns. *Empire and Sovereignty: A History of the Public Law Literature in the Holy Roman Empire, 1599–1804*. Chicago: University of Chicago Press, 1973.

Gunn, L. Ray. *The Decline of Authority: Public Economic Policy and Political Development in New York State, 1800–1860*. Ithaca, N.Y.: Cornell University Press, 1988.

Gustafson, Thomas. *Representative Words: Politics, Literature, and the American Language, 1776–1865*. Cambridge: Cambridge University Press, 1992.

Gwyn, Julian. *The Enterprising Admiral: The Personal Fortune of Admiral Sir Peter Warren*. Montreal: McGill-Queens University Press, 1974.

Gwyn, William B. *The Meaning of the Separation of Powers: An Analysis of the Doctrine from Its Origins to the Adoption of the United States Constitution*. New Orleans: Tulane University, 1965.

Hall, David D., ed. *Lived Religion in America: Toward a History of Practice*. Princeton, N.J.: Princeton University Press, 1997.

———. *Worlds of Wonder, Days of Judgment: Popular Religious Belief in Early New England*. New York: Knopf, 1989.

Hall, Peter D. *The Organization of American Culture, 1700–1900: Private Institutions, Elites, and the Origins of American Nationality*. New York: New York University Press, 1982.

Halsey, Francis W. *The Old New York Frontier*. New York: Scribner's, 1901.

Hamburger, Philip. *Separation of Church and State*. Cambridge, Mass.: Harvard University Press, 2002.

Hamilton, Milton W. *Sir William Johnson: Colonial American, 1715–63*. Port Washington, N.Y.: Kennikat Press, 1976.

Hamlin, Paul M. *Legal Education in Colonial New York*. New York: New York University Law Quarterly Review, 1939.

Hammond, Bray. *Banks and Politics in America: From the Revolution to the Civil War*. Princeton, N.Y.: Princeton University Press, 1957.

Hancock, David. *Citizens of the World: London Merchants and the Integration of the British American Community, 1735–1785*. New York: Cambridge University Press, 1995.

Handlin, Oscar, and Mary Flug Handlin. *Commonwealth: A Study of the Role of Government in the American Economy, Massachusetts, 1774–1861*. Rev. ed. Cambridge, Mass.: Harvard University Press, Belknap Press, 1969.

———. *The Dimensions of Liberty*. Cambridge, Mass.: Harvard University Press, Belknap Press, 1961.

Harding, Alan, ed. *Law-Making and Law-Makers in British History*. London: Royal Historical Society, 1980.

Hardt, Michael, and Antonio Negri. *Empire*. Cambridge, Mass.: Harvard University Press, 2000.

Harrington, Virginia D. *The New York Merchant on the Eve of the Revolution*. New York: Columbia University Press, 1935.

Hart, Vivien, and Stimson, Shannon C., eds. *Writing a National Identity: Political, Economic, and Cultural Perspectives on the Written Constitution*. Manchester, England: Manchester University Press, 1993.

Hartog, Hendrik B., ed. *Law in the American Revolution and the Revolution in the Law*. New York: New York University Press, 1981.

———. *Man and Wife in America: A History*. Cambridge, Mass.: Harvard University Press, 2000.

———. *Public Property and Private Power: The Corporation of the City of New York in American Law, 1730–1860*. Chapel Hill: University of North Carolina Press, 1983.

Hartz, Louis. *Economic Policy and Democratic Thought: Pennsylvania, 1776–1860*. Cambridge, Mass.: Harvard University Press, 1948.

———. *The Liberal Tradition in America*. New York: Harcourt, 1955.

Haskins, George L. *Law and Authority in Early Massachusetts: A Study in Tradition and Design*. New York: Macmillan, 1960.

Hay, D., Peter Linebaugh, and E. P. Thompson, eds. *Albion's Fatal Tree: Crime and Society in Eighteenth-Century England*. New York: Pantheon Books, 1975.

Helgerson, Richard. *Forms of Nationhood: The Elizabethan Writing of England*. Chicago: University of Chicago Press, 1992.

Henretta, James. *"Salutary Neglect": Colonial Administration under the Duke of Newcastle*. Princeton, N.J.: Princeton University Press, 1972.

Henretta, James, Michael Kammen, and Stanley N. Katz, eds. *The Transformation of Early American History: Society, Authority, and Ideology*. New York: Knopf, 1991.

Herder, Johann G. *Against Pure Reason: Writings on Religion, Language, and History*. Translated by Marcia Bunge. Minneapolis, Minn.: Fortress Press, 1993.

———. *On the Origin of Language*. Translated by John H. Moran and Alexander
  Gode. Chicago: University of Chicago Press, 1966.
Higgins, Ruth L. *Expansion in New York, with Especial Reference to the Eighteenth
  Century*. Columbus: Ohio State University, 1931.
Hill, Christopher. *Puritanism and Revolution: Studies in Interpretation of the English
  Revolution in the 17th Century*. London: Secker & Warburg, 1958.
Hinderaker, Eric. *Elusive Empires: Constructing Colonialism in the Ohio Valley,
  1673–1800*. New York: Cambridge University Press, 1997.
Hirsch, E. D., Jr. *Validity in Interpretation*. New Haven, Conn.: Yale University
  Press, 1967.
Hirschman, Albert O. *The Passions and the Interests: Political Arguments for
  Capitalism before Its Triumphs*. Princeton, N.J.: Princeton University Press,
  1977.
Hodges, Graham R. *Root and Branch: African Americans in New York and East
  Jersey, 1613–1863*. Chapel Hill: University of North Carolina Press, 1999.
Hoeflich, M. H. *Roman and Civil Law and the Development of Anglo-American
  Jurisprudence in the Nineteenth Century*. Athens: University of Georgia Press,
  1997.
Hoffer, Peter C. *Law and People in Colonial America*. Baltimore: Johns Hopkins
  University Press, 1992.
———. *The Law's Conscience: Equitable Constitutionalism in America*. Chapel Hill:
  University of North Carolina Press, 1990.
Hoffman, Ronald D., and Peter J. Albert, eds. *Launching the "Extended Republic":
  The Federalist Era*. Charlottesville: University Press of Virginia, 1996.
Hoffman, Ross J. S. *Edmund Burke, New York Agent*. Philadelphia: American
  Philosophical Society, 1956.
Holdsworth, William S. *A History of English Law*. 17 vols. London: Methuen,
  1903–72.
Holmes, Geoffrey, ed. *Britain after the Glorious Revolution, 1689–1715*. New York:
  St. Martin's Press, 1969.
Horton, James T. *James Kent: A Study in Conservatism, 1763–1847*. New York:
  D. Appleton-Century, 1939.
Horwitz, Morton J. *The Transformation of American Law, 1780–1860*. Cambridge,
  Mass.: Harvard University Press, 1977.
Humphrey, David C. *From King's College to Columbia, 1746–1800*. New York:
  Columbia University Press, 1976.
Hurst, J. Willard. *The Legitimacy of the Business Corporation in the Law of the United
  States, 1780–1970*. Charlottesville: University Press of Virginia, 1970.
Huston, Reeve. *Land and Freedom: Rural Society, Popular Protest, and Party Politics
  in Antebellum New York*. New York: Oxford University Press, 2000.
Innis, Harold A. *Empire and Communications*. Rev. ed. Toronto: University of
  Toronto Press, 1972.
Isaac, Rhys. *The Transformation of Virginia, 1740–1790*. Chapel Hill: University
  of North Carolina Press, 1982.

Ives, E. W., ed. *The English Revolution, 1600–1660*. New York: Barnes & Noble, 1968.

Jacob, Margaret C., and James Jacob, eds. *Origins of Anglo-American Radicalism*. Boston: Allen & Unwin, 1984.

Jaher, Frederic C. *The Urban Establishment: Upper Strata in Boston, New York, Charleston, Chicago, and Los Angeles*. Urbana: University of Illinois Press, 1982.

Jennings, Francis. *The Ambiguous Iroquois Empire*. New York: Norton, 1984.

Jensen, Merrill. *The Articles of Confederation: An Interpretation of the Socio-Constitutional History of the American Revolution, 1774–1781*. Madison: University of Wisconsin Press, 1966.

———. *The New Nation: A History of the United States during the Confederation, 1781–1789*. 1950. Reprint, Boston: Northeastern University Press, 1981.

Johnson, Herbert A. *The Law Merchant and Negotiable Instruments in Colonial New York, 1664–1730*. Chicago: Loyola University Press, 1963.

Jones, Dorothy V. *License for Empire: Colonization by Treaty in Early America*. Chicago: University of Chicago Press, 1983.

Jones, J. R., ed. *Liberty Secured? Britain before and after 1688*. Stanford, Calif.: Stanford University Press, 1992.

Jones, Matt B. *Vermont in the Making, 1750–1777*. Cambridge, Mass.: Harvard University Press, 1939.

Jones, Robert F. *"The King of the Alley": William Duer, Politician, Entrepreneur, and Speculator, 1768–1799*. Philadelphia: American Philosophical Society, 1992.

Jones, Thomas. *History of New-York during the Revolutionary War*. Edited by Edward F. DeLancey. 2 vols. New York: New-York Historical Society, 1879.

Jones, W. Melville, ed. *Chief Justice John Marshall: A Reappraisal*. Ithaca, N.Y.: Cornell University Press, 1956.

Judd, Jacob, and Irwin H. Polishook, eds. *Aspects of Early New York Society and Politics*. Tarrytown, N.Y.: Sleepy Hollow Restorations, 1974.

Judson, Margaret A. *The Crisis of the Constitution: An Essay in Constitutional and Political Thought in England, 1603–1645*. New Brunswick, N.J.: Rutgers University Press, 1949.

Kaminski, John P. *George Clinton: Yeoman Politician of the New Republic*. Madison, Wis.: Madison House, 1993.

Kammen, Michael G. *Colonial New York: A History*. New York: Scribner's, 1975.

———. *Deputyes and Libertyes: The Origins of Representative Government in Colonial America*. New York: Knopf, 1969.

———. *A Machine That Would Go of Itself: The Constitution in American Culture*. New York: Knopf, 1986.

———. *People of Paradox: An Inquiry Concerning the Origins of American Civilization*. New York: Knopf, 1972.

———. *A Rope of Sand: The Colonial Agents, British Politics, and the American Revolution*. Ithaca, N.Y.: Cornell University Press, 1968.

Kantorowicz, Ernst H. *The King's Two Bodies: A Study in Mediaeval Political Theology*. Princeton, N.J.: Princeton University Press, 1957.

Kaplan, Amy, and Donald E. Pease, eds. *Cultures of United States Imperialism.* Durham, N.C.: Duke University Press, 1993.

Katz, Stanley N. *Newcastle's New York: Anglo-American Politics, 1732–1753.* Cambridge, Mass.: Harvard University Press, Belknap Press, 1968.

Katz, Stanley N., and John M. Murrin, eds. *Colonial America: Essays in Politics and Social Development.* 3d ed. New York: Knopf, 1983.

Kawashima, Yasuhide. *Puritan Justice and the Indian: White Man's Law in Massachusetts, 1630–1763.* Middletown, Conn.: Wesleyan University Press, 1986.

Keep, Austin B. *History of the New York Society Library.* New York: De Vinne Press, 1908.

Keith, Arthur Berriedale. *Constitutional History of the First British Empire.* Oxford: Clarendon Press, 1930.

———. *The Dominions as Sovereign States: Their Constitutions and Governments.* London: Macmillan, 1938.

Kelsey, Isabel T. *Joseph Brant, 1743–1807: Man of Two Worlds.* Syracuse, N.Y.: Syracuse University Press, 1984.

Kenyon, Cecelia M. *The Antifederalists.* Boston: Northeastern University Press, 1985.

Kerber, Linda K. *No Constitutional Right to Be Ladies: Women and the Obligations of Citizenship.* New York: Hill & Wang, 1998.

———. *Women of the Republic: Intellect and Ideology in Revolutionary America.* Chapel Hill: University of North Carolina Press, 1980.

Kettner, James H. *The Development of American Citizenship, 1608–1870.* Chapel Hill: University of North Carolina Press, 1978.

Keys, Alice M. *Cadwallader Colden: A Representative Eighteenth Century Official.* New York: Columbia University Press, 1906.

Kierner, Cynthia A. *Traders and Gentlefolk: The Livingstons of New York, 1675–1790.* Ithaca, N.Y.: Cornell University Press, 1992.

Kim, Sung Bok. *Landlord and Tenant in Colonial New York: Manorial Society, 1664–1775.* Chapel Hill: University of North Carolina Press, 1978.

Kishlansky, Mark A. *Parliamentary Selection: Social and Political Choice in Early Modern England.* Cambridge: Cambridge University Press, 1986.

———. *The Rise of the New Model Army.* Cambridge: Cambridge University Press, 1979.

Klein, Milton M. *The American Whig: William Livingston of New York.* New York: Garland, 1993.

Knafla, Louis. *Law and Politics in Jacobean England: The Tracts of Lord Chancellor Ellesmere.* Cambridge: Cambridge University Press, 1977.

Knorr, Klaus E. *British Colonial Theories, 1570–1850.* Toronto: University of Toronto Press, 1944.

Koebner, Richard. *Empire.* Cambridge: Cambridge University Press, 1961.

Koenigsberger, H. G. *Politicians and Virtuosi: Essays in Early Modern History.* London: Hambledon Press, 1986.

Konig, David T., ed. *Devising Liberty: Preserving and Creating Freedom in the New American Republic*. Stanford, Calif.: Stanford University Press, 1995.

Kramer, Larry D. *The People Themselves: Popular Constitutionalism and Judicial Review*. New York: Oxford University Press, 2004.

Kramer, Michael P. *Imagining Language in America, from the Revolution to the Civil War*. Princeton, N.J.: Princeton University Press, 1992.

Kramnick, Isaac. *Republicanism and Bourgeois Radicalism: Political Ideology in Late Eighteenth-Century England and America*. Ithaca, N.Y.: Cornell University Press, 1990.

Kraus, Michael. *Intercolonial Aspects of American Culture on the Eve of the Revolution*. 1928. Reprint, New York: Octagon Books, 1972.

Kruman, Marc W. *Between Authority and Liberty: State Constitution Making in Revolutionary America*. Chapel Hill: University of North Carolina Press, 1997.

Kupperman, Karen O., ed. *America in European Consciousness, 1493–1750*. Chapel Hill: University of North Carolina Press, 1995.

Kurland, Philip B., and Ralph Lerner, eds. *The Founders' Constitution*. 5 vols. Chicago: University of Chicago Press, 1987.

Kurtz, Stephen J., and James H. Hutson, eds. *Essays on the American Revolution*. Chapel Hill: University of North Carolina Press, 1973.

Labaree, Leonard W. *Royal Government in America: A Study of the British Colonial System before 1783*. New Haven, Conn.: Yale University Press, 1930.

Landau, Norma. *The Justices of the Peace, 1679–1760*. Berkeley: University of California Press, 1984.

Landsman, Ned C. *Scotland and Its First American Colony: A Transatlantic Examination of Ethnicity and Social Development in Lowland Scotland and Central New Jersey, 1693–1765*. Princeton, N.J.: Princeton University Press, 1985.

Langbein, John H. *The Origins of Adversary Criminal Trial*. New York: Oxford University Press, 2003.

Launitz-Schurer, Leopold S. *Loyal Whigs and Revolutionaries: The Making of the Revolution in New York, 1765–1776*. New York: New York University Press, 1980.

Lawson, Philip, ed. *Parliament and the Atlantic Empire*. Edinburgh: Edinburgh University Press, 1995.

Leder, Lawrence H., ed. *The Colonial Legacy*. Vol. 2, *Some Eighteenth-Century Commentators*. New York: Harper & Row, 1971.

———. *Liberty and Authority: Early American Political Ideology, 1689–1763*. Chicago: Quadrangle Books, 1968.

———. *Robert Livingston, 1654–1728, and the Politics of Colonial New York*. Chapel Hill: University of North Carolina Press, 1961.

Lemisch, Jesse. *Jack Tar vs. John Bull: The Role of New York's Seamen in Precipitating the American Revolution*. New York: Garland, 1997.

Leonard, Gerald. *The Invention of Party Politics: Federalism, Popular Sovereignty, and Constitutional Development in Jacksonian Illinois*. Chapel Hill: University of North Carolina Press, 2002.

Lepore, Jill. *A Is for American: Letters and Other Characters in the Newly United States*. New York: Knopf, 2002.

Levack, Brian P. *The Formation of the British State: England, Scotland, and the Union, 1603–1707*. Oxford: Clarendon Press, 1987.

Levin, Jennifer. *The Charter Controversy in the City of London, 1660–1688, and Its Consequences*. London: Athlone, 1969.

Levinson, Sanford. *Constitutional Faith*. Princeton, N.J.: Princeton University Press, 1988.

Levy, Leonard W. *Legacy of Suppression: Freedom of Speech and Press in Early American History*. Cambridge, Mass.: Harvard University Press, Belknap Press, 1960.

Levy, Leonard W., and Dennis J. Mahoney, eds. *The Framing and Ratification of the Constitution*. New York: Macmillan, 1987.

Libby, Orin G. *The Geographical Distribution of the Vote of the Thirteen States on the Federal Constitution, 1787–1788*. Madison: University of Wisconsin, 1894.

Lieberman, David. *The Province of Legislation Determined: Legal Theory in Eighteenth-Century Britain*. Cambridge: Cambridge University Press, 1989.

Lilly, Edward P. *The Colonial Agents of New York and New Jersey*. Washington, D.C.: Catholic University of America, 1936.

Lincoln, Charles Z. *The Constitutional History of New York*. 5 vols. Rochester, N.Y.: Lawyers Co-operative Publishing Co., 1906.

Linebaugh, Peter, and Marcus Rediker. *The Many-Headed Hydra: Sailors, Slaves, Commoners and the Hidden History of the Revolutionary Atlantic*. Boston: Beacon Press, 2000.

Lovejoy, Arthur O. *The Great Chain of Being: A Study in the History of an Idea*. Cambridge, Mass.: Harvard University Press, 1936.

Lustig, Mary Lou. *Privilege and Prerogative: New York's Provincial Elite, 1710–1776*. Madison, N.J.: Fairleigh Dickenson University Press, 1995.

———. *Robert Hunter, 1666–1734, New York's Augustan Statesman*. Syracuse, N.Y.: Syracuse University Press, 1983.

Lutz, Donald S. *Popular Consent and Popular Control: Whig Political Theory in the Early State Constitutions*. Baton Rouge: Louisiana State University Press, 1980.

Lynd, Staughton. *Anti-Federalism in Dutchess County, New York: A Study of Democracy and Class Conflict in the Revolutionary Era*. Chicago: Loyola University Press, 1962.

Maas, David E. *The Return of the Massachusetts Loyalists*. New York: Garland, 1989.

MacBean, William M. *Biographical Register of Saint Andrew's Society of the State of New York*. 2 vols. New York: St. Andrew's Society of the State of New York, 1922–25.

Macdonald, A. de Lery. *The Seigneurie of Alainville on Lake Champlain*. Baltimore: The Order of Colonial Lords of Manors in America, 1929.

Mackesy, Piers. *Could the British Have Won the War of Independence?* Worcester, Mass.: Clark University Press, 1976.

Maier, Pauline. *From Resistance to Revolution: Colonial Radicals and the Development of American Opposition to Britain, 1765–1776.* New York: Knopf, 1972.

Main, Jackson Turner. *The Antifederalists: Critics of the Constitution, 1781–1788.* Chapel Hill: University of North Carolina Press, 1961.

———. *Political Parties before the Constitution.* Chapel Hill: University of North Carolina Press, 1973.

———. *The Social Structure of Revolutionary America.* Princeton, N.J.: Princeton University Press, 1965.

———. *The Upper House in Revolutionary America, 1763–1788.* Madison: University of Wisconsin Press, 1967.

Maitland, Frederic W., *The Constitutional History of England.* Cambridge: Cambridge University Press, 1920.

———. *English Law and the Renaissance.* Cambridge: Cambridge University Press, 1901.

———. *The Forms of Action at Common Law.* Edited by A. H. Chaytor and W. J. Whittaker. Cambridge: Cambridge University Press, 1963.

Maitland, Frederic W., and Francis C. Montague. *A Sketch of English Legal History.* New York: AMS Press, 1978.

Mark, Irving. *Agrarian Conflicts in Colonial New York, 1711–1775.* New York: Columbia University Press, 1940.

Martin, James K., and Mark E. Edward. *A Respectable Army: The Military Origins of the Republic, 1763–1789.* Arlington Heights, Ill.: H. Davidson, 1982.

Mason, Bernard. *The Road to Independence: The Revolutionary Movement in New York, 1773–1777.* Lexington: University of Kentucky Press, 1966.

McAnear, Beverly. *The Income of the Colonial Governors of British North America.* New York: Pageant Press, 1967.

McBain, Howard L. *DeWitt Clinton and the Origins of the Spoils System in New York.* New York: Columbia University Press, 1907.

McCoy, Drew R. *The Last of the Fathers: James Madison and the Republican Legacy.* New York: Cambridge University Press, 1989.

McCurdy, Charles W. *The Anti-Rent Era in New York Law and Politics, 1839–1865.* Chapel Hill: University of North Carolina Press, 2001.

McCusker, John J., and Russell Menard. *The Economy of British America, 1607–1789.* Chapel Hill: University of North Carolina Press, 1991.

McIlwain, Charles H. *The American Revolution: A Constitutional Interpretation.* New York: Macmillan, 1924.

———. *Constitutionalism: Ancient and Modern.* Rev. ed. Ithaca, N.Y.: Cornell University Press, 1947.

———. *Constitutionalism and the Changing World.* Cambridge: Cambridge University Press, 1939.

———. *The High Court of Parliament and Its Supremacy: An Historical Essay on the Boundaries between Legislation and Adjudication in England.* New Haven, Conn.: Yale University Press, 1910.

McKendrick, Neil, ed. *Historical Perspectives: Studies in English Thought and Society in Honour of J. H. Plumb.* London: Europa, 1974.

McKendrick, Neil, John Brewer, and J. H. Plumb, eds. *The Birth of Consumer Society*. London: Europa, 1982.

McManus, Edgar. *A History of Negro Slavery in New York*. Syracuse, N.Y.: Syracuse University Press, 1966.

Meek, Ronald L. *Social Science and the Ignoble Savage*. Cambridge: Cambridge University Press, 1976.

Meinig, D. W. *Atlantic America, 1492–1800*. New Haven, Conn.: Yale University Press, 1986.

Mendle, Michael. *Dangerous Positions: Mixed Government, the Estates of the Realm, and the Making of the* Answer to the XIX Propositions. Tuscaloosa: University of Alabama Press, 1985.

Merrell, James H. *The Indians' New World: Catawbas and Their Neighbors from European Contact through the Era of Removal*. Chapel Hill: University of North Carolina Press, 1989.

Merritt, Richard L. *Symbols of American Community, 1735–1775*. New Haven, Conn.: Yale University Press, 1966.

Merton, Robert K. *Social Theory and Social Structure*. Rev. ed. Glencoe, Ill.: Free Press, 1957.

Miller, Nathan. *Enterprise of a Free People: Aspects of Economic Development of New York during the Canal Period, 1792–1838*. Ithaca, N.Y.: Cornell University Press, 1962.

Miller, Perry. *The Life of the Mind in America from the Revolution to the Civil War* New York: Harcourt, Brace, and World, 1965.

Milsom, S. F. C. *Historical Foundations of the Common Law*. 2d ed. London: Butterworths, 1981.

Molho, Anthony, and Gordon Wood, eds. *Imagined Histories: American Historians Interpret the Past*. Princeton, N.J.: Princeton University Press, 1998.

Monaghan, Frank. *John Jay: Defender of Liberty against Kings*. New York: Bobbs-Merrill, 1935.

Monroe, Joel H. *Schenectady: Ancient and Modern*. Geneva, N.Y.: W. F. Humphrey, 1914.

Moore, Barrington, Jr. *Injustice: The Social Bases of Obedience and Revolt*. White Plains, N.Y.: M. E. Sharpe, 1978.

Morgan, Edmund S. *American Slavery, American Freedom: The Ordeal of Colonial Virginia*. New York: Norton, 1975.

———. *Inventing the People: The Rise of Popular Sovereignty in England and America*. New York: Norton, 1988.

Morrill, J. S., ed. *Reactions to the English Civil War, 1642–1649*. New York: St. Martin's Press, 1982.

———. *The Revolt of the Provinces: Conservatives and Radicals in the English Civil War, 1630–1650*. London: Allen & Unwin, 1976.

Morris, Richard B., ed. *Essays on the Genesis of the Empire State*. Albany: New York State Bicentennial Commission, 1979.

Muldoon, James. *Empire and Order: The Concept of Empire, 800–1800*. New York: St. Martin's Press, 1999.

Mullett, Charles F. *Fundamental Law and the American Revolution, 1760–1776.* New York: Columbia University Press, 1933.

Namier, Lewis B. *England in the Age of the American Revolution.* 2d ed. London: Macmillan, 1961.

——. *Personalities and Powers.* London: H. Hamilton, 1955.

——. *The Structure of Politics at the Accession of George III.* 2d ed. London: Macmillan, 1963.

Namier, Lewis B., and John Brooke. *The House of Commons, 1754–1790.* 3 vols. London: Her Majesty's Stationery Office, 1964.

Nammack, Georgiana C. *Fraud, Politics, and the Dispossession of the Indians: The Iroquois Land Frontier in the Colonial Period.* Norman: University of Oklahoma Press, 1969.

Narratives of the Revolution in New York: A Collection of Articles from The New-York Historical Society Quarterly. New York: New-York Historical Society, 1975.

Narrett, David E. *Inheritance and Family Life in Colonial New York City.* Ithaca, N.Y.: Cornell University Press, 1992.

Nash, Gary. *The Urban Crucible: Social Change, Urban Consciousness, and the Origins of the American Revolution.* Cambridge, Mass.: Harvard University Press, 1979.

Nelson, William E. *Americanization of the Common Law: The Impact of Legal Change on Massachusetts Society, 1760–1830.* Cambridge, Mass.: Harvard University Press, 1975.

Nenner, Howard. *By Colour of Law: Legal and Constitutional Politics in England, 1660–1689.* Chicago: University of Chicago Press, 1977.

Nevins, Allen. *The American States during and after the Revolution, 1775–1789.* New York: Macmillan, 1924.

Newcomb, Benjamin H. *Political Partisanship in the American Middle Colonies, 1700–1776.* Baton Rouge: Louisiana State University Press, 1995.

Newmyer, R. Kent. *Supreme Court Justice Joseph Story: Statesman of the Old Republic.* Chapel Hill: University of North Carolina Press, 1985.

Nissenson, Samuel G. *The Patroon's Domain.* New York: Columbia University Press, 1937.

Norton, Thomas E. *The Fur Trade in Colonial New York, 1686–1776.* Madison: University of Wisconsin Press, 1974.

Notestein, Wallace. *The Winning of the Initiative by the House of Commons.* London: H. Milford, Oxford University Press, 1924.

Novak, William J. *The People's Welfare: Law and Regulation in Nineteenth-Century America.* Chapel Hill: University of North Carolina Press, 1996.

Novick, Peter. *That Noble Dream: The "Objectivity Question" and the American Historical Profession.* New York: Cambridge University Press, 1988.

O'Callaghan, E. B. *History of New Netherland.* 2 vols. New York: G. S. Appleton, 1848.

O'Donovan, Katherine, and Gerry R. Rubin, eds. *Human Rights and Legal History: Essays in Honour of Brian Simpson.* New York: Oxford University Press, 2000.

Olson, Alison Gilbert. *Making the Empire Work: London and American Interest Groups, 1690–1790.* Cambridge, Mass.: Harvard University Press, 1992.

Olson, Alison Gilbert, and Richard M. Brown, eds. *Anglo-American Political Relations, 1675–1775*. New Brunswick, N.J.: Rutgers University Press, 1970.

Onuf, Peter S. *Jefferson's Empire: The Language of American Nationhood*. Charlottesville: University Press of Virginia, 2000.

———. *The Origins of the Federal Republic: Jurisdictional Controversies in the United States, 1775–1783*. Philadelphia: University of Pennsylvania Press, 1983.

———. *Statehood and Union: A History of the Northwest Ordinance*. Bloomington: University of Indiana Press, 1987.

Onuf, Peter S., and Nicholas Onuf. *Federal Union, Modern World: The Law of Nations in an Age of Revolutions, 1776–1814*. Madison, Wis.: Madison House, 1993.

Osgood, Herbert L. *The American Colonies in the Seventeenth Century*. 3 vols. New York: Macmillan, 1904–7.

O'Shaughnessy, Andrew J. *An Empire Divided: The American Revolution and the British Caribbean*. Philadelphia: University of Pennsylvania Press, 2000.

Pagden, Anthony, ed. *The Languages of Political Theory in Early Modern Europe*. Cambridge: Cambridge University Press, 1987.

———. *Lords of All the World: Ideologies of Empire in Spain, Britain, and France, c.1500–c.1800*. New Haven, Conn.: Yale University Press, 1995.

Pagden, Anthony, and Nicholas Canny, eds. *Colonial Identity in the Atlantic World, 1500–1800*. Princeton, N.J.: Princeton University Press, 1987.

Palmer, Robert R. *The Age of the Democratic Revolution: A Political History of Europe and America, 1760–1800*. 2 vols. Princeton, N.J.: Princeton University Press, 1959.

Pares, Richard. *Yankees and Creoles: The Trade between North America and the West Indies before the American Revolution*. Cambridge, Mass.: Harvard University Press, 1956.

Parker, John, and Carol Urness, eds. *The American Revolution: A Heritage of Change*. Minneapolis, Minn.: Associates of the James Ford Bell Library, 1975.

Pawlisch, Hans S. *Sir John Davies and the Conquest of Ireland: A Study in Legal Imperialism*. Cambridge: Cambridge University Press, 1985.

Peltonen, Markku. *Classical Humanism and Republicanism in English Political Thought, 1570–1640*. Cambridge: Cambridge University Press, 1995.

Pencak, William, Matthew Dennis, and Simon P. Newman, eds. *Riot and Revelry in Early America*. University Park: Pennsylvania State University Press, 2002.

Pencak, William, and Conrad E. Wright, eds. *Authority and Resistance in Early New York*. New York: New-York Historical Society, 1988.

———, eds. *New York and the Rise of American Capitalism: Economic Development and the Social and Political History of an American State, 1780–1890*. New York: New-York Historical Society, 1989.

Peterson, Arthur Everett, and George William Edwards. *New York as an Eighteenth-Century Municipality, 1731–1776*. New York: Columbia University Press, 1917.

Phillips, Ulrich B. *Georgia and State Rights*. Yellow Springs, Ohio: Antioch Press, 1968.

Pierson, George W. *Tocqueville and Beaumont in America.* New York: Oxford University Press, 1938.

Plantation Systems of the New World. Social Science Monographs 7. Washington, D.C.: Pan American Union, 1959.

Plucknett, Theodore F. T. *A Concise History of the Common Law.* 5th ed. Boston: Little, Brown, 1956.

———. *Statutes and Their Interpretation in the First Half of the Fourteenth Century.* Cambridge: Cambridge University Press, 1922.

———. *Taswell-Langmead's English Constitutional History: From the Teutonic Conquest to the Present Time.* 11th ed. London: Sweet & Maxwell, 1960.

Plumb, J. H. *The Growth of Political Stability in England, 1675–1725.* London: Macmillan, 1967.

Pocock, J. G. A. *The Ancient Constitution and the Feudal Law: A Study of English Historical Thought in the Seventeenth Century: A Reissue with a Retrospect.* Cambridge: Cambridge University Press, 1987.

———. *The Machiavellian Moment: Florentine Political Thought and the Atlantic Republican Tradition.* Princeton, N.J.: Princeton University Press, 1975.

———. *Politics, Language, and Time: Essays on Political Thought and History.* New York: Atheneum, 1973.

———, ed. *Three British Revolutions, 1641, 1688, 1776.* Princeton, N.J.: Princeton University Press, 1980.

Pole, J. R. *Political Representation in England and the Origins of the American Republic.* Berkeley: University of California Press, 1966.

Pollock, Frederick, and Frederic W. Maitland. *The History of English Law before the Time of Edward I.* 2d ed. 2 vols. Cambridge: Cambridge University Press, 1952.

Potter, Janice. *The Liberty We Seek: Loyalist Ideology in Colonial New York and Massachusetts.* Cambridge, Mass.: Harvard University Press, 1983.

Powell, H. Jefferson. *A Community Built on Words: The Constitution in History and Politics.* Chicago: University of Chicago Press, 2002.

Price, J. L. *Holland and the Dutch Republic in the Seventeenth Century: The Politics of Particularism.* Oxford: Clarendon Press, 1994.

Primus, Richard A. *The American Language of Rights.* New York: Cambridge University Press, 1999.

Prucha, Francis P. *American Indian Policy in the Formative Years: The Indian Trade and Intercourse Acts, 1790–1834.* Cambridge, Mass.: Harvard University Press, 1962.

———. *The Sword of the Republic: The United States Army on the Frontier, 1783–1846.* Lincoln: University of Nebraska Press, 1969.

Purcell, Edward, Jr. *Litigation and Inequality: Federal Diversity Jurisdiction in Industrial America, 1870–1958.* New York: Oxford University Press, 1992.

Rakove, Jack N. *The Beginnings of National Politics: An Interpretive History of the Continental Congress.* New York: Knopf, 1979.

———. *Declaring Rights: A Brief History with Documents.* Boston: Bedford Books, 1998.

———. *Original Meanings: Politics and the Ideas in the Making of the Constitution.* New York: Knopf, 1996.

Ranlet, Philip. *The New York Loyalists.* Knoxville: University of Tennessee Press, 1986.

Reich, Jerome R. *Leisler's Rebellion: A Study of Democracy in New York, 1664–1720.* Chicago: University of Chicago Press, 1953.

Reid, John P. *The Constitutional History of the American Revolution.* 4 vols. Madison: University of Wisconsin Press, 1986–93.

———. *The Constitutional History of the American Revolution.* Abridged ed. Madison: University of Wisconsin Press, 1995.

———. *Controlling the Law: Legal Politics in Early National New Hampshire.* DeKalb: Northern Illinois University Press, 2004.

———. *In a Defiant Stance: The Conditions of Law in Massachusetts Bay, the Irish Comparison, and the Coming of the American Revolution.* University Park: Pennsylvania State University Press, 1977.

———. *In Defiance of the Law: The Standing-Army Controversy, the Two Constitutions, and the Coming of the American Revolution.* Chapel Hill: University of North Carolina Press, 1981.

———. *Law for the Elephant: Property and Social Behavior on the Overland Trail.* San Marino, Calif.: Huntington Library, 1980.

Reimann, Mathias, ed. *The Reception of Continental Ideas in the Common Law World, 1820–1920.* Berlin: Duncker & Humblot, 1993.

Reppy, Allison, ed. *David Dudley Field: Centenary Essays.* New York: New York University, 1949.

———, ed. *Law: A Century of Progress, 1835–1935.* 3 vols. New York: New York University Press, 1937.

Richter, Daniel K. *The Ordeal of the Longhouse: The Peoples of the Iroquois League in the Era of European Colonization.* Chapel Hill: University of North Carolina Press, 1992.

Richter, Daniel K., and James H. Merrell, eds. *Beyond the Covenant Chain: The Iroquois and Their Neighbors in Indian North America, 1600–1800.* Syracuse, N.Y.: Syracuse University Press, 1987.

Riker, William H. *The Strategy of Rhetoric: Campaigning for the American Constitution.* Edited by Randall L. Calvert, John Mueller, and Rick K. Wilson. New Haven, Conn.: Yale University Press, 1996.

Rink, Oliver A. *Holland on the Hudson: An Economic and Social History of Dutch New York.* Ithaca, N.Y.: Cornell University Press, 1986.

Ritchie, Robert C. *The Duke's Province: A Study of New York Politics and Society, 1664–1691.* Chapel Hill: University of North Carolina Press, 1977.

Ritz, Wilfred J. *Rewriting the History of the Judiciary Act of 1789: Exposing Myths, Challenging Premises, and Using New Evidence.* Edited by Wythe Holt. Norman: University of Oklahoma Press, 1990.

Robbins, Caroline. *The Eighteenth-Century Commonwealthman: Studies in the Transmission, Development and Circumstance of English Liberal Thought from the*

Restoration of Charles II until the War with the Thirteen Colonies. Cambridge, Mass.: Harvard University Press, 1959.

Robertson, John, ed. *A Union for Empire: Political Thought and the British Union of 1707*. Cambridge: Cambridge University Press, 1995.

Robinson, Kenneth, and Frederick Madden, eds. *Essays in Imperial Government Presented to Margery Perham*. Oxford: Blackwell, 1963.

Rudé, George. *The Crowd in History: A Study of Popular Disturbances in France and England, 1730–1848*. New York: Wiley, 1964.

Rush, Michael, and Malcolm Shaw. *The House of Commons: Services and Facilities*. London: Allen & Unwin, 1974.

Russell, Conrad. *The Causes of the English Civil War*. Oxford: Clarendon Press, 1990.

———. *Parliaments and English Politics, 1621–1629*. Oxford: Clarendon Press, 1979.

Russell, Elmer B. *The Review of American Colonial Legislation by the King in Council*. New York: Columbia University, 1915.

Said, Edward. *Culture and Imperialism*. New York: Knopf, 1993.

———. *Orientalism*. New York: Pantheon Books, 1978.

Sainsbury, John. *Disaffected Patriots: London Supporters of Revolutionary America, 1769–1782*. Kingston, Ontario: McGill-Queen's University Press, 1987.

Sandel, Michael J. *Liberalism and the Limits of Justice*. New York: Cambridge University Press, 1982.

Sandoz, Ellis, ed. *The Roots of Liberty: Magna Carta, Ancient Constitution, and the Anglo-American Tradition of Rule of Law*. Columbia: University of Missouri Press, 1993.

Savelle, Max. *Seeds of Liberty: Genesis of the American Mind*. New York: Knopf, 1948.

Sayre, Paul, ed. *Interpretations of Modern Legal Philosophies: Essays in Honor of Roscoe Pound*. New York: Oxford University Press, 1947.

Scharf, J. Thomas, ed. *History of Westchester County, New York*. 2 vols. Philadelphia: L. E. Preston & Co., 1886.

Schechter, Barnet. *The Battle for New York: The City at the Heart of the American Revolution*. New York: Walker & Co., 2002.

Schechter, Stephen L., and Richard B. Bernstein, eds. *New York and the Union*. Albany: New York State Commission on the Bicentennial of the United States Constitution, 1990.

Schlatter, Richard. *Private Property: The History of an Idea*. New Brunswick, N.J.: Rutgers University Press, 1951.

Schleifer, James T. *The Making of Tocqueville's* Democracy in America. Chapel Hill: University of North Carolina Press, 1980.

Schlereth, Thomas J. *The Cosmopolitan Ideal in Enlightenment Thought: Its Form and Function in the Ideas of Franklin, Hume, and Voltaire, 1694–1790*. Notre Dame, Ind.: University of Notre Dame Press, 1977.

Schmitt, Albert R. *Herder und Amerika*. The Hague: Mouton, 1967.

Schochet, Gordon J., ed. *Empire and Revolutions: Papers Presented at the Folger Institute Seminar "Political Thought in the English-Speaking Atlantic, 1760–1800."* Washington, D.C.: Folger Institute, Folger Shakespeare Library, 1993.

———, ed. *Law, Literature, and the Settlement of Regimes: Papers Presented at the Folger Institute Seminar "Political Thought in the Elizabethan Age, 1558–1603."* Washington, D.C.: Folger Institute, Folger Shakespeare Library, 1990.

Schutz, John A. *Thomas Pownall, British Defender of American Liberty: A Study of Anglo-American Relations in the Eighteenth Century.* Glendale, Calif.: A. H. Clark Co., 1951.

Schuyler, Robert L. *Parliament and the British Empire: Some Constitutional Controversies Concerning Imperial Legislative Jurisdiction.* New York: Columbia University Press, 1929.

Schwartz, Henry, and Sangeeta Ray, eds. *A Companion to Postcolonial Studies.* Malden, Mass.: Blackwell, 2000.

Schwarz, Philip J. *The Jarring Interests: New York's Boundary Makers, 1664–1776.* Albany: State University of New York Press, 1979.

Schwoerer, Lois G. *The Ingenious Mr. Henry Care, Restoration Publicist.* Baltimore: Johns Hopkins University Press, 2001.

Seavoy, Ronald E. *The Origins of the American Business Corporation, 1784–1855.* Westport, Conn.: Greenwood Press, 1982.

Seed, Patricia. *Ceremonies of Possession in Europe's Conquest of the New World, 1492–1640.* New York: Cambridge University Press, 1995.

Seeley, J. R. *The Expansion of England.* 1881. Reprint, Chicago: University of Chicago Press, 1971.

Seelye, John D. *Beautiful Machine: Rivers and the Republican Plan, 1775–1825.* New York: Oxford University Press, 1991.

———. *Prophetic Waters: The River in Early American Life and Literature.* New York: Oxford University Press, 1977.

Select Essays in Anglo-American Legal History. 3 vols. Boston: Little, Brown, 1907–9.

Seton-Watson, R. W., ed. *Tudor Studies.* London: Longmans, Green & Co., 1924.

Sher, Richard B., and Jeffrey R. Smitten, eds. *Scotland and America in the Age of the Enlightenment.* Edinburgh: Edinburgh University Press, 1990.

Shields, David S. *Civil Tongues and Polite Letters in British America.* Chapel Hill: University of North Carolina Press, 1997.

———. *Oracles of Empire: Poetry, Politics, and Commerce in America, 1690–1750.* Chicago: University of Chicago Press, 1990.

Shils, Edward A. *The Constitution of Society.* Chicago: University of Chicago Press, 1982.

Shuffleton, Frank, ed. *The American Enlightenment.* Rochester, N.Y.: University of Rochester Press, 1993.

Silverberg, Robert. *The Mound Builders.* Athens: Ohio University Press, 1986.

Silvers, Robert B., and Barbara Epstein, eds. *Anthology: Selected Essays from the First Thirty Years of the New York Review of Books.* New York: New York Review of Books, 2001.

Simpson, A. W. B. *Legal Theory and Legal History: Essays on the Common Law*. London: Hambledon Press, 1987.

Simpson, Grant G., ed. *The Scottish Soldier Abroad, 1247–1967*. Edinburgh: John Donald Publishers, 1992.

Singh, Amritjit, and Peter Schmidt, eds. *Postcolonial Theory and the United States: Race, Ethnicity, and Literature*. Jackson: University Press of Mississippi, 2000.

Siry, Steven E. *DeWitt Clinton and the American Political Economy: Sectionalism, Politics, and Republican Ideology, 1787–1828*. New York: P. Lang, 1990.

Skinner, Quentin. *The Foundations of Modern Political Thought*. 2 vols. Cambridge: Cambridge University Press, 1978.

Skowroneck, Stephen. *Building a New American State: The Expansion of National Administrative Capacities, 1877–1920*. New York: Cambridge University Press, 1982.

Slaughter, Thomas P. *The Whiskey Rebellion: Frontier Epilogue to the American Revolution*. New York: Oxford University Press, 1986.

Smith, A. Hassell. *County and Court: Government and Politics in Norfolk, 1558–1603*. Oxford: Clarendon Press, 1974.

Smith, James M. *Freedom's Fetters: The Alien and Sedition Laws and American Civil Liberties*. Ithaca, N.Y.: Cornell University Press, 1956.

———. ed. *Seventeenth Century America: Essays in Colonial History*. Chapel Hill: University of North Carolina Press, 1959.

Smith, Joseph H. *Appeals to the Privy Council from the American Plantations*. New York: Columbia University Press, 1950.

Smith, Joseph H., and Thomas G. Barnes. *The English Legal System: Carryover to the Colonies*. Los Angeles: William Andrews Clark Memorial Library, University of California, 1975.

Smith, Page. *James Wilson, Founding Father, 1742–1798*. Chapel Hill: University of North Carolina Press, 1956.

Smith, R. J. *The Gothic Bequest: Medieval Institutions in British Thought, 1688–1863*. Cambridge: Cambridge University Press, 1987.

Snowiss, Sylvia. *Judicial Review and the Law of the Constitution*. New Haven, Conn.: Yale University Press, 1990.

Snyder, K. Alan. *Defining Noah Webster: Mind and Morals in the Early Republic*. Lanham, Md.: University Press of America, 1990.

Sosin, Jack M. *The Aristocracy of the Long Robe: The Origins of Judicial Review in America*. New York: Greenwood Press, 1989.

———. *The Revolutionary Frontier, 1763–1783*. New York: Holt, Rinehart, & Winston, 1967.

———. *Whitehall and the Wilderness: The Middle West in British Colonial Policy, 1760–1775*. Lincoln: University of Nebraska Press, 1961.

Sparks, Jared. *The Life of Gouverneur Morris*. 3 vols. Boston: Gray & Bowen, 1832.

Spaulding, E. Wilder. *His Excellency George Clinton: Critic of the Constitution*. New York: Macmillan, 1938.

———. *New York in the Critical Period, 1783–1789*. New York: Columbia University Press, 1932.

Spector, Margaret M. *The American Department of the British Government, 1768–1782*. New York: Columbia University Press, 1940.

Spencer, Charles W. *Phases of Royal Government in New York, 1691–1719*. Columbus: Press of F. J. Heer, 1905.

Steele, Ian K. *The English Atlantic, 1675–1740: An Exploration of Communication and Community*. New York: Oxford University Press, 1986.

Stephanson, Anders. *Manifest Destiny: American Expansion and the Empire of Right*. New York: Hill & Wang, 1995.

St. George, Robert Blair, ed. *Possible Pasts: Becoming Colonial in Early America*. Ithaca, N.Y.: Cornell University Press, 2000.

Stimson, Shannon C. *The American Revolution in the Law: Anglo-American Jurisprudence before John Marshall*. Princeton, N.J.: Princeton University Press, 1990.

Stone, Lawrence, ed. *An Imperial State at War: Britain from 1689 to 1815*. London: Routledge, 1994.

Stoner, James R. *Common Law and Liberal Theory: Coke, Hobbes, and the Origins of American Constitutionalism*. Lawrence: University Press of Kansas, 1992.

Storing, Herbert J. *What the Anti-Federalists Were For: The Political Thought of the Opponents of the Constitution*. Chicago: University of Chicago Press, 1981.

Storing, Herbert J., and Murray Dry, eds. *The Complete Anti-Federalist*. 7 vols. Chicago: University of Chicago Press, 1981.

Stourzh, Gerald. *Alexander Hamilton and the Idea of Republican Government*. Stanford, Calif.: Stanford University Press, 1970.

Street, Alfred B. *The Council of Revision of the State of New York: Its History, a History of the Courts with Which Its Members Were Connected; Biographical Sketches of Its Members; and Its Votes*. Albany, N.Y.: W. Gould, 1859.

Swift, Elaine K. *The Making of an American Senate: Reconstitutive Change in Congress, 1787–1841*. Ann Arbor: University of Michigan Press, 1996.

Syme, Ronald. *Colonial Elites: Rome, Spain, and the Americas*. London: Oxford University Press, 1958.

Tarr, G. Alan. *Understanding State Constitutions*. Princeton, N.J.: Princeton University Press, 1998.

Taylor, Alan. *William Cooper's Town: A Story of Power and Persuasion on the Frontier of the Early American Republic*. New York: Knopf, 1995.

Teaford, John. *The Municipal Revolution in America: Origins of Modern Urban Government, 1650–1825*. Chicago: University of Chicago Press, 1975.

Tewksbury, Donald G. *The Founding of American Colleges and Universities before the Civil War*. New York: Teachers College, Columbia University, 1932.

Thelen, David, ed. *The Constitution and American Life*. Ithaca, N.Y.: Cornell University Press, 1988.

Thiong'o, Ngugi wa. *Decolonising the Mind: The Politics of Language in African Literature*. London: J. Currey, 1986.

Thomas, Nicholas. *Colonialism's Culture: Anthropology, Travel and Government*. Princeton, N.J.: Princeton University Press, 1994.

Thompson, E. P. *Customs in Common: Studies in Traditional Popular Culture*. New York: New Press, 1991.

——. *Whigs and Hunters*. New York: Pantheon Books, 1975.

Thomson, Gladys S. *Lords Lieutenants in the Sixteenth Century: A Study in Tudor Local Administration*. London: Longmans, Green & Co., 1923.

Thorne, Samuel E. *A Discourse upon the Exposicion and Understandinge of Statutes with Sir Thomas Egerton's Additions*. San Marino, Calif.: Huntington Library, 1942.

——. *Essays in English Legal History*. London: Hambledon Press, 1985.

——. *Sir Edward Coke, 1552–1952*. London: Quaritch, 1957.

Tiedemann, Joseph S. *Reluctant Revolutionaries: New York City and the Road to Independence, 1763–1776*. Ithaca, N.Y.: Cornell University Press, 1997.

Tierney, Brian, ed. *The Crisis of Church and State, 1050–1300*. Englewood Cliffs, N.J.: Prentice Hall, 1964.

Tomlins, Christopher L. *Law, Labor, and Ideology in Early America*. New York: Cambridge University Press, 1993.

——. *The Legal Cartography of Colonial English Intrusions on the American Mainland in the Seventeenth Century*. American Bar Foundation Working Paper #9816. Chicago: American Bar Association, 1999.

Tomlins, Christopher L., and Bruce Mann, eds. *The Many Legalities of Early America*. Chapel Hill: University of North Carolina Press, 2001.

Tucker, Robert W., and David C. Hendrickson. *The Fall of the First British Empire: Origins of the War for American Independence*. Baltimore: Johns Hopkins University Press, 1982.

Tully, Alan. *Forming American Politics: Ideals, Interests, and Institutions in Colonial New York and Pennsylvania*. Baltimore: Johns Hopkins University Press, 1994.

Turner, Frederick Jackson. *The Frontier in American History*. New York: H. Holt, 1920.

Turner, Victor W. *Dramas, Fields, and Metaphors: Symbolic Action in Human Society*. Ithaca, N.Y.: Cornell University Press, 1974.

Tuveson, Ernest L. *Redeemer Nation: The Idea of America's Millennial Role*. Chicago: University of Chicago Press, 1968.

Twomey, Richard J. *Jacobins and Jeffersonians: Anglo-American Radicals in the United States, 1790–1820*. New York: Garland, 1989.

Ubbelohde, Carl. *The Vice-Admiralty Courts and the American Revolution*. Chapel Hill: University of North Carolina Press, 1960.

Ullmann, Walter. *Principles of Government and Politics in the Middle Ages*. 3d ed. London: Methuen, 1974.

Upton, Leslie F. S. *The Loyal Whig: William Smith of New York and Quebec*. Toronto: University of Toronto Press, 1969.

Urofsky, Melvin I., and Finkelman, Paul. *A March of Liberty: A Constitutional History of the United States*. 2d ed. New York: Oxford University Press, 2002.

Van Anglen, Kevin. *The New England Milton: Literary Reception and Cultural Authority in the Early Republic*. University Park: Pennsylvania State University Press, 1993.

Van Buskirk, Judith L. *Generous Enemies: Patriots and Loyalists in Revolutionary New York*. Philadelphia: University of Pennsylvania Press, 2002.

Van Schaack, Henry C. *The Life of Peter Van Schaack, LL.D.* New York: D. Appleton & Co., 1842.

——. *Memoirs of the Life of Henry Van Schaack . . . during the American Revolution*. Chicago: A. C. McClurg, 1892.

Van Tyne, Claude H. *The Loyalists in the American Revolution*. 1902. Reprint, New York: P. Smith, 1929.

Vaughan, Alden T., and George A. Billias. *Perspectives on Early American History: Essays in Honor of Richard B. Morris*. New York: Harper & Row, 1973.

Veall, Donald. *The Popular Movement for Law Reform, 1640–1660*. Oxford: Clarendon Press, 1970.

Verburg, R. M. *The Two Faces of Interest: The Problem of Order and the Origins of Political Economy and Sociology as Distinctive Fields of Inquiry in the Scottish Enlightenment*. Amsterdam: Thesis Publishers, 1991.

Ver Steeg, Clarence L. *Robert Morris: Revolutionary Financier*. Philadelphia: University of Pennsylvania Press, 1954.

Vescey, Christopher, and Starna, William A., eds. *Iroquois Land Claims*. Syracuse, N.Y.: Syracuse University Press, 1988.

Vile, M. J. C. *Constitutionalism and the Separation of Powers*. Oxford: Clarendon Press, 1967.

Vinogradoff, Paul. *Outlines of Historical Jurisprudence*. New York: Oxford University Press, 1922.

Viswanathan, Guari. *Masks of Conquest: Literary Study and British Rule in India*. New York: Oxford University Press, 1998.

Volwiler, Albert T. *George Croghan and the Westward Movement, 1741–1782*. Cleveland: Arthur H. Clark Co., 1926.

Wainwright, Nicholas B. *George Croghan, Wilderness Diplomat*. Chapel Hill: University of North Carolina Press, 1959.

Waldstreicher, David. *In the Midst of Perpetual Fetes: The Making of Perpetual Nationalism*. Chapel Hill: University of North Carolina Press, 1997.

Warner, Michael. *Letters of the Republic: Publication and the Public Sphere in Eighteenth-Century America*. Cambridge, Mass.: Harvard University Press, 1990.

Warren, Charles. *History of the American Bar*. Boston: Little, Brown, 1911.

Watson, Alan. *Joseph Story and the Comity of Errors: A Case Study in the Conflict of Laws*. Athens: University of Georgia Press, 1992.

——. *Roman Law and Comparative Law*. Athens: University of Georgia Press, 1991.

Watts, Edward. *Writing and Postcolonialism in the Early Republic*. Charlottesville: University Press of Virginia, 1998.

Webb, Sidney, and Beatrice Webb. *The Development of English Local Government, 1689–1835*. London: Oxford University Press, 1963.

Webb, Stephen S. *The Governors-General: The English Army and the Definition of the Empire, 1569–1681*. Chapel Hill: University of North Carolina Press, 1979.

———. *Lord Churchill's Coup: The Anglo-American Empire and the Glorious Revolution Reconsidered.* New York: Knopf, 1995.

Werner, Edgar A. *Civil List and Constitutional History of the Colony and State of New York.* New York: Weed, Parsons, 1883.

Weslager, C. A. *The Stamp Act Congress: With an Exact Copy of the Complete Journal.* Newark: University of Delaware Press, 1976.

Weston, Corrine C. *English Constitutional Theory and the House of Lords, 1556–1832.* New York: Columbia University Press, 1965.

Weston, Corrine C., and Janelle R. Greenberg. *Subjects and Sovereigns: The Grand Controversy over Legal Sovereignty in Stuart England.* Cambridge: Cambridge University Press, 1981.

White, G. Edward. *The Marshall Court and Cultural Change, 1815–1835.* Abridged ed. New York: Oxford University Press, 1991.

———. *Tort Law in America: An Intellectual History.* New York: Oxford University Press, 1980.

White, Leonard D. *The Federalists: A Study in Administrative History.* New York: Macmillan, 1948.

White, Morton. *Philosophy, The Federalist, and the Constitution.* New York: Oxford University Press, 1987.

White, Richard. *The Middle Ground: Indians, Empires, and Republics in the Great Lakes Region, 1650–1815.* New York: Cambridge University Press, 1991.

White, Stephen D. *Sir Edward Coke and "The Grievances of the Commonwealth," 1621–1628.* Chapel Hill: University of North Carolina Press, 1979.

Whitehead, John S. *The Separation of College and State: Columbia, Dartmouth, Harvard, and Yale, 1776–1876.* New Haven, Conn.: Yale University Press, 1973.

Whitman, James Q. *The Legacy of Roman Law in the German Romantic Era: Historical Vision and Legal Change.* Princeton, N.J.: Princeton University Press, 1990.

Whittington, Keith E. *Constitutional Construction: Divided Powers and Constitutional Meaning.* Cambridge, Mass.: Harvard University Press, 1999.

Wickwire, Franklin B. *British Subministers and Colonial America, 1763–1783.* Princeton, N.J.: Princeton University Press, 1966.

Widmer, Edward L. *Young America: The Flowering of Democracy in New York City.* New York: Oxford University Press, 1999.

Wiener, Frederick B. *Civilians under Military Justice: The British Practice since 1689, Especially in North America.* Chicago: University of Chicago Press, 1967.

Wilentz, Sean. *Chants Democratic: New York City and the Rise of the American Working Class, 1788–1850.* New York: Oxford University Press, 1984.

Wilkenfeld, Bruce. *The Social and Economic Structure of the City of New York, 1695–1796.* New York: Arno Press, 1978.

Williams, Raymond. *Keywords: A Vocabulary of Culture and Society.* New York: Oxford University Press, 1976.

Williams, William A. *The Roots of Modern American Empire: A Study of the Growth* and Shaping of Social Consciousness in a Marketplace Society. New York: Random House, 1969.

Williamson, Chilton. American Suffrage: From Property to Democracy, 1760–1860. Princeton, N.J.: Princeton University Press, 1960.

———. Vermont in Quandary, 1763–1825. Montpelier: Vermont Historical Society, 1949.

Wills, Gary. Explaining America: The Federalist. Garden City, N.Y.: Doubleday, 1981.

Wilson, James G. The Imperial Republic: A Structural History of American Constitutionalism from the Colonial Era to the Beginning of the Twentieth Century. London: Ashgate, 2002.

———, ed. Memorial History of the City of New York. New York: New York Historical Co., 1892.

Wilson, Kathleen. The Sense of the People: Politics, Culture and Imperialism in England, 1715–1785. Cambridge: Cambridge University Press, 1995.

Wittke, Carl, ed. Essays in History and Political Theory in Honor of Charles H. McIlwain. Cambridge, Mass.: Harvard University Press, 1936.

Wood, Gordon S. The Creation of the American Republic, 1776–1787. New York: Norton, 1969.

———. The Radicalism of the American Revolution. New York: Vintage Books, 1991.

Wormuth, Francis D. The Origins of Modern Constitutionalism. New York: Harper, 1949.

Wright, Esmond, ed. Red, White, and True Blue: The Loyalists in the Revolution. New York: AMS Press, 1976.

Wycoff, William. The Developer's Frontier: The Making of the Western New York Landscape. New Haven, Conn.: Yale University Press, 1988.

Yates, Frances. Astraea: The Imperial Theme in the Sixteenth Century. London: Routledge & Kegan Paul, 1975.

Yoshpe, Harry B. The Disposition of Loyalist Estates in the Southern District of the State of New York. New York: Columbia University Press, 1939.

Ziff, Larzer. Literary Democracy: The Declaration of Cultural Independence in America. New York: Viking Press, 1981.

Zilversmit, Arthur. The First Emancipation: The Abolition of Slavery in the North. Chicago: University of Chicago Press, 1967.

ARTICLES

Ackerman, Bruce A. "Constitutional Law/Constitutional Politics." Yale Law Journal 99 (1985): 453–513.

———. "Essay: The Rise of World Constitutionalism." Virginia Law Review 83 (1997): 771–97.

Adair, Douglass. " 'That Politics May Be Reduced to a Science': David Hume, James Madison, and the Tenth Federalist." Huntington Library Quarterly 20 (1957): 343–60.

Adams, James T. "On the Term 'British Empire.'" *American Historical Review* 27 (1922): 485–89.

Alden, John. "The Albany Congress and the Creation of the Indian Superintendencies." *Mississippi Valley Historical Review* 27 (1940): 193–210.

Amar, Akhil R. "Some New World Lessons for the Old World." *University of Chicago Law Review* 58 (1993): 483–510.

Armitage, David. "The Cromwellian Protectorate and the Languages of Empire." *Historical Journal* 35 (1992): 531–55.

———. "The Declaration of Independence and International Law." *William and Mary Quarterly*, 3d ser., 59 (2002): 3–38.

———. "Making the Empire British: Scotland in the Atlantic World, 1542–1707." *Past and Present*, no. 155 (1997): 34–63.

Aylmer, G. E. "From Office-holding to Civil Service: The Genesis of Modern Bureaucracy." *Transactions of the Royal Historical Society*, 5th ser., 30 (1980): 91–109.

———. "'Property' in Seventeenth-Century England." *Past and Present*, no. 86 (1980): 87–97.

Bailey, Mark Warren. "Early Legal Education in the United States: Natural Law Theory and Law as a Moral Science." *Journal of Legal Education* 48 (1998): 311–28.

Bailyn, Bernard. "The Beekmans of New York: Trade, Politics, and Families: A Review Article." *William and Mary Quarterly*, 3d ser., 14 (1957): 598–608.

———. "Communication and Trade: The Atlantic in the Seventeenth Century." *Journal of Economic History* 13 (1953): 381–82.

Bailyn, Bernard, and John Clive. "England's Cultural Provinces: Scotland and America." *William and Mary Quarterly*, 3d ser., 11 (1954): 200–213.

Banning, Lance. "Republican Ideology and the Triumph of the Constitution, 1789 to 1793." *William and Mary Quarterly*, 3d ser., 31 (1974): 167–88.

Barnett, Randy E. "The Original Meaning of the Commerce Clause." *University of Chicago Law Review* 68 (2001): 101–47.

Barrow, Thomas C. "The American Revolution as a Colonial War for Independence." *William and Mary Quarterly*, 3d ser., 25 (1968): 452–64.

Berman, Harold J. "Origins of Historical Jurisprudence: Coke, Selden, Hale." *Yale Law Journal* 103 (1994): 1651–1738.

Bilder, Mary S. "The Lost Lawyers: Early American Legal Literates and Transatlantic Legal Culture." *Yale Journal of Law and the Humanities* 11 (1999): 47–117.

———. "The Origin of the Appeal in America." *Hastings Law Journal* 48 (1997): 913–68.

Billington, Ray A. "The Fort Stanwix Treaty of 1768." *New York History* 25 (1944): 182–94.

Black, Barbara A. "The Constitution of Empire: The Case for the Colonists." *University of Pennsylvania Law Review* 124 (1976): 1157–1211.

Bliss, R. M. "Review Essay: The British Empire and the American Constitution." *Journal of American Studies* 21 (1987): 431–35.

Bodle, Wayne. "Themes and Directions in Middle Colonies Historiography, 1980–1994." *William and Mary Quarterly*, 3d ser., 50 (1994): 355–88.

Bonomi, Patricia U. "John Jay, Religion, and the State." *New York History* 81 (2000): 9–18.

———. "New York: The Royal Colony." *New York History* 82 (2001): 5–24.

Bosher, J. F. "Huguenot Merchants and the Protestant International in the Seventeenth Century." *William and Mary Quarterly*, 3d ser., 52 (1995): 77–102.

Bourdieu, Pierre. "The Force of Law: Toward a Sociology of the Juridical Field." *Hastings Law Journal* 38 (1987): 805–53.

Boyd, Julian P. "Thomas Jefferson's 'Empire of Liberty.'" *Virginia Quarterly Review* 24 (1948): 538–54.

Boynton, Lindsay. "Martial Law and the Petition of Right." *English Historical Review* 79 (1964): 255–84.

Brooks, Robin. "Alexander Hamilton, Melancton Smith and the Ratification of the Constitution in New York." *William and Mary Quarterly*, 3d ser., 24 (1967): 339–58.

Bruegel, Martin. "Unrest: Manorial Society and the Market in the Hudson Valley, 1780–1850." *Journal of American History* 62 (1996): 1393–1424.

Budd, Martin L. "Law in Colonial New York: The Legal System of 1691." *Harvard Law Review* 80 (1967): 1752–72.

Buell, Lawrence. "Melville and the Question of American Decolonization." *American Literature* 64 (1992): 215–37.

Burns, J. H. "Bolingbroke and the Concept of Constitutional Government." *Political Studies* 10 (1962): 264–76.

Burrows, Edwin G., and Michael Wallace. "The American Revolution: The Ideology and Psychology of National Liberation." *Perspectives in American History* 6 (1972): 167–306.

Cairns, John W. "Blackstone, an English Institutist: Legal Literature and the Rise of the Nation State." *Oxford Journal of Legal Studies* 4 (1984): 316–60.

———. "Institutional Writings in Scotland Reconsidered." *Journal of Legal History* 4 (1983): 76–117.

Calhoon, Robert M. "William Smith Jr.'s Alternative to the American Revolution." *William and Mary Quarterly*, 3d ser., 22 (1965): 105–18.

Carrington, Paul. "The Revolutionary Idea of University Legal Education." *William and Mary Law Review* 31 (1990): 527–74.

Carter, Clarence E. "The Military Office in America, 1763–1775." *American Historical Review* 28 (1923): 475–88.

Carter, Edward C., II. "A 'Wild Irishman' under Every Federalist's Bed: Naturalization in Philadelphia, 1789–1806." *Pennsylvania Magazine of History and Biography* 94 (1970): 331–46.

Champagne, Roger. "Family Politics versus Constitutional Principles: The New York Assembly Elections of 1768 and 1769." *William and Mary Quarterly*, 3d ser., 20 (1963): 57–79.

Chaplin, Joyce. "Expansion and Exceptionalism in Early American History." *Journal of American History* 89 (2003): 1431–55.

Cheyney, Edward P. "The Manor of East Greenwich in the County of Kent." *American Historical Review* 11 (1905–6): 29–35.

———. "Some English Conditions Surrounding the Settlement in Virginia." *American Historical Review* 12 (1907): 507–28.

Cohen, David S. "How Dutch Were the Dutch of New Netherland?" *New York History* 62 (1981): 42–60.

Colley, Linda. "Britishness and Otherness: An Argument." *Journal of British Studies* 31 (1992): 309–29.

Cook, Harold J. "Against Common Right and Reason: The College of Physicians versus Dr. Thomas Bonham." *American Journal of Legal History* 29 (1985): 301–22.

Coquillette, Daniel R. "Legal Ideology and Incorporation." 3 pts. *Boston University Law Review* 61 (1981): 1–89, 315–71; 67 (1987): 289–361.

Corré, Jacob I. "The Argument, Decision, and Reports of Darcy v. Allen." *Emory Law Journal* 45 (1996): 1261–1327.

Corwin, Edward S. "The Progress of Constitutional Theory between the Declaration of Independence and the Meeting of the Philadelphia Convention." *American Historical Review* 30 (1925): 511–36.

Countryman, Edward. "Indians, the Social Order, and the Social Significance of the American Revolution." *William and Mary Quarterly*, 3d ser., 53 (1996): 343–62.

———. "The Uses of Capital in Revolutionary America: The Case of the New York Loyalist Merchants." *William and Mary Quarterly*, 3d ser., 49 (1992): 3–28.

Cover, Robert M. "Foreword: *Nomos* and Narrative." *Harvard Law Review* 97 (1983): 4–68.

Crane, Elaine F. "Publius in the Provinces: Where Was *The Federalist* Reprinted outside New York City?" *William and Mary Quarterly*, 3d ser., 21 (1964): 589–92.

Crary, Catherine Snell. "The American Dream: John Tabor Kempe's Rise from Poverty to Riches." *William and Mary Quarterly*, 3d ser., 14 (1957): 176–95.

———. "Forfeited Loyalist Lands in the Western District of New York — Albany and Tryon Counties." *New York History* 35 (1954): 239–58.

Cust, Richard, and Peter G. Lake. "Sir Richard Grosvenor and the Rhetoric of Magistracy." *Bulletin of the Institute of Historical Research* 54 (1981): 40–53.

Darnton, Robert. "What Is the History of Books?" *Daedelus* 111 (Summer 1982): 65–83.

Davis, Thomas J. "New York's Long Black Line: A Note on the Growing Slave Population, 1626–1790." *Afro-Americans in New York Life and History* 2 (1978): 41–59.

Desan, Christine A. "The Constitutional Commitment to Legislative Adjudication in the Early American Tradition." *Harvard Law Review* 111 (1998): 1381–1503.

———. "Remaking Constitutional Tradition at the Margins of the Empire: The

Creation of Legislative Adjudication in Colonial New York." *Law and History Review* 16 (1998): 257–317.

Duffey, Denis P. "The Northwest Ordinance as a Constitutional Document." *Columbia Law Review* 95 (1995): 929–68.

East, Robert. "The Business Entrepreneur in a Changing Colonial Economy, 1763–1795." *Journal of Economic History* 6 (1946): 16–27.

Eisgruber, Christopher L. "John Marshall's Judicial Rhetoric." *Supreme Court Review* 1996 (1996): 439-81.

———. "Marbury, Marshall, and the Politics of Constitutional Judgment." *Virginia Law Review* 89 (2003): 1203–34.

Elkins, Stanley, and Eric McKitrick. "The Founding Fathers: Young Men of the Revolution." *Political Science Quarterly* 76 (1961): 181–216.

Elliott, J. H. "A Europe of Composite Monarchies." *Past and Present*, no. 137 (1992): 48–72.

Elton, G. R. Review of *Clio Unbound: Perception of the Social and Cultural Past in Renaissance England*, by Arthur B. Ferguson. *History and Theory* 20 (1981): 92–100.

Ernst, Robert. "Andrew Elliot, Forgotten Loyalist of Occupied New York." *New York History* 57 (1976): 285–320.

Ferguson, Robert A. "The Forgotten Publius: John Jay and the Aesthetics of Ratification." *Early American Literature* 34 (1999): 223–40.

———. "Ideology and the Framing of the Constitution." *Early American Literature* 22 (1987): 157–65.

Finkelman, Paul. "Book Review: Herbert Storing, *The Complete Anti-Federalist*." *Cornell Law Review* 70 (1984–85): 182–207.

———. "The Founders and Slavery: Little Ventured, Little Gained." *Yale Journal of Law and the Humanities* 13 (2001): 413–49.

———. "James Madison and the Bill of Rights: A Reluctant Paternity." *Supreme Court Review* (1990): 301–47.

Firth, C. H. " 'The British Empire.' " *Scottish Historical Review* 15 (1918): 185–89.

Flaherty, Martin S. "The Empire Strikes Back: *Annesley v. Sherlock* and the Triumph of Imperial Parliamentary Supremacy." *Columbia Law Review* 87 (1987): 593–622.

———. "History 'Lite' in Modern American Constitutionalism." *Columbia Law Review* 95 (1995): 523–90.

Flick, Hugh M. "The Council of Appointment of New York State: The First Attempt to Regulate Political Patronage, 1777–1822." *New York History* 15 (1934): 253–80.

Fox, Dixon R. "The Negro Vote in Old New York." *Political Science Quarterly* 22 (1917): 252–75.

Friedman, Barry. "The History of the Countermajoritarian Difficulty, Part 1: The Road to Judicial Supremacy." *New York University Law Review* 73 (1998): 333–433.

Friedman, Bernard. "The New York Assembly Elections of 1768 and 1769: The Disruption of Family Politics." *New York History* 46 (1965): 3–24.

Friedman, Lawrence M. "American Legal History: Past and Present." *Journal of Legal Education* 34 (1984): 563–76.

Furlong, Patrick J. "Civilian-Military Conflict and the Restoration of the Royal Province of Georgia, 1778–1782." *Journal of Southern History* 38 (1972): 415–42.

Gerardi, Donald. "The King's College Controversy, 1753–1756, and the Ideological Roots of Toryism in New York." *Perspectives in American History* 11 (1977–78): 147–96.

Gipson, Lawrence H. "The American Revolution as an Aftermath of the Great War for Empire." *Political Science Quarterly* 65 (1950–51): 86–104.

Gitterman, J. M. "The Council of Appointment in New York." *Political Science Quarterly* 7 (1892): 80–115.

Godechot, J., and R. R. Palmer. "Le probleme de l'Atlantique du XVIIIeme au XXeme siecle." *Storia Contemporanea: Relezioni del X Congresso Internazionale di Scienze Storiche* 5 (1955): 175–239.

Goebel, Julius, Jr. "Constitutional History and Constitutional Law." *Columbia Law Review* 38 (1938): 555–77.

———. "*Ex Parte Clio.*" *Columbia Law Review* 54 (1954): 450–83.

———. "King's Law and Local Custom in Seventeenth Century New England." *Columbia Law Review* 31 (1931): 416–48.

———. Review of *Parliament and the British Empire*, by Robert L. Schuyler. *Columbia Law Review* 30 (1930): 273–76.

Goodhart, A. L. "The Ratio Decidendi of a Case." *Modern Law Review* 22 (1959): 117–24.

Gordon, Robert W. "Critical Legal Histories." *Stanford Law Review* 36 (1984): 57–125.

———. Review of *The American Codification Movement*, by Charles Cook. *Vanderbilt Law Review* 36 (1983): 431–58.

Gould, Elijah. "Zones of Law, Zones of Violence: The Legal Geography of the British Atlanta circa 1772." *William and Mary Quarterly*, 3d ser., 60 (2003): 471–510.

Gray, Charles M. "Bonham's Case Reviewed." *Proceedings of the American Philosophical Society* 116 (1972): 35–58.

Graymont, Barbara. "New York State Indian Policy after the Revolution." *New York History* 57 (1976): 438–74.

Greene, Jack P. "From the Perspective of Law: Context and Legitimacy in the Origins of the American Revolution." *South Atlantic Quarterly* 85 (1986): 56–77.

———. "Political Mimesis: A Consideration of the Historical and Cultural Roots of Legislative Behavior in the British Colonies in the Eighteenth Century." *American Historical Review* 75 (1969): 337–60.

———. "Search for Identity: An Interpretation of the Meaning of Selected

Patterns of Social Response in Eighteenth-Century America." *Journal of Social History* 3 (1970): 189–220.

Grey, Thomas C. "The Origin of the Unwritten Constitution: Fundamental Law in American Revolutionary Thought." *Stanford Law Review* 30 (1978): 843–93.

Griffiths, J. A. G. "The Brave New World of Sir John Laws." *Modern Law Review* 63 (2000): 159–76.

Guzzardo, John C. "Democracy along the Mohawk: An Election Return, 1773." *New York History* 57 (1976): 30–52.

Haffenden, Philip S. "The Crown and the Colonial Charters, 1675–1688." *William and Mary Quarterly*, 3d ser., 15 (1958): 297–311, 452–66.

Hamburger, Philip A. "The Constitution's Accommodation of Social Change." *Michigan Law Review* 88 (1989): 239–327.

———. "Natural Rights, Natural Law, and American Constitutions." *Yale Law Journal* 102 (1993): 907–60.

Hamilton, Milton W. "An American Knight in Britain: Sir John Johnson's Tour, 1765–1767." *New York History* 42 (1961): 119–44.

———. "Sir William Johnson: Interpreter of the Iroquois." *Ethnohistory* 10 (1963): 270–86.

Handlin, Oscar. "The Eastern Frontier of New York." *New York History* 18 (1937): 50–75.

Handlin, Oscar, and Mary Flug Handlin. "Origins of American Business Corporations." *Journal of Economic History* 5 (1945): 1–23.

Handlin, Oscar, and Mark Irving, eds. "Chief Daniel Nimham v. Roger Morris, Beverly Robinson, and Philip Philipse — An Indian Land Case in Colonial New York, 1765–1767." *Ethnohistory* 11 (1964): 193–246.

Hanyan, Craig R. "DeWitt Clinton and Partisanship: The Development of Clintonianism." *New-York Historical Society Quarterly* 56 (1972): 109–31.

Hartog, Hendrik. "Pigs and Positivism." *Wisconsin Law Review* 1985 (1985): 899–935.

———. "The Public Law of a County Court: Judicial Government in Eighteenth Century Massachusetts." *American Journal of Legal History* 20 (1976): 282–329.

———. Review of *Peripheries and Center*, by Jack P. Greene. *William and Mary Quarterly*, 3d ser., 45 (1988): 773–75.

Havighurst, Alfred F. "James II and the Twelve Men in Scarlet." *Law Quarterly Review* 69 (1953): 522–46.

Helfman, Tara. "The Law of Nations in *The Federalist Papers*." *Legal History* 23 (2002): 107–28.

Helmholz, Richard. "Use of the Civil Law in Post-Revolutionary American Jurisprudence." *Tulane Law Review* 66 (1992): 1649–84.

Henretta, James A. "The 'Market' in the Early Republic." *Journal of the Early Republic* 18 (1998): 289–304.

———. "The Rise and Decline of 'Democratic Republicanism': New York and the Several States." *Albany Law Review* 53 (1989): 357–401.

Hinderaker, Eric. "The 'Four Indian Kings' and the Imaginative Construction of the First British Empire." *William and Mary Quarterly*, 3d ser., 53 (1996): 487–526.

Hinton, R. W. K. "The Decline of Parliamentary Government under Elizabeth I and the Early Stuarts." *Cambridge Historical Journal* 13 (1957): 116–32.

Hobson, Charles F. "The Negative on State Laws: James Madison, the Constitution, and the Crisis of Republican Government." *William and Mary Quarterly*, 3d ser., 36 (1979): 215–36.

Hoeflich, Michael. "Roman Law in American Legal Culture." *Tulane Law Review* 66 (1992): 1723–43.

———. "Translation and the Reception of Foreign Law in the Antebellum United States." *American Journal of Comparative Law* 50 (2002): 753–75.

Hoermann, Alfred. "Cadwallader Colden, a Savant in the Wilderness." *New-York Historical Society Quarterly* 62 (1978): 271–88.

Hoffer, Peter C., N. E. H. Hull, and Steven L. Allen. "Choosing Sides: A Quantitative Study of the Personality Determinants of Loyalist and Revolutionary Political Affiliation in New York." *Journal of American History* 65 (1978): 344–66.

Holdsworth, William. "The Conventions of the Eighteenth-Century Constitution." *Iowa Law Review* 17 (1931–32): 161–80.

———. "The Elizabethan Age in English Legal History and Its Results." *Iowa Law Review* 12 (1927): 321–35.

Hopfl, Harro, and Martyn P. Thompson. "The History of Contract as a Motif in Political Thought." *American Historical Review* 84 (1979): 919–40.

Horton, James T. "The Western Eyres of Judge Kent." *New York History* 18 (1937): 152–66.

Horwitz, Morton J. "Foreword: The Constitution of Change: Legal Fundamentality without Fundamentalism." *Harvard Law Review* 107 (1993): 30–117.

Hulme, Peter. "Including America." *Ariel* 26 (1995): 117–23.

Hulsebosch, Daniel J. "The Ancient Constitution and the Expanding Empire: Sir Edward Coke's British Jurisprudence." *Law and History Review* 21 (2003): 439–82.

———. "The Constitution in the Glass Case and the Constitution in Action." *Law and History Review* 16 (1998): 397–401.

———. "*Imperia in Imperio*: The Multiple Constitutions of Empire in New York, 1750–1777." *Law and History Review* 16 (1998): 319–79.

———. "Writs to Rights: 'Navigability' and the Transformation of the Common Law in the Nineteenth Century." *Cardozo Law Review* 23 (2002): 1049–1106.

Humphreys, R. A. "Lord Shelburne and the Proclamation of 1763." *English Historical Review* 49 (1934): 241–64.

———. "Notes and Documents: Governor Murray's View of the Plan of 1764 for the Management of Indian Affairs." *Canadian Historical Review* 16 (1935): 162–69.

Hurstfield, Joel. "The Greenwich Tenures of the Reign of Edward VI." *Law Quarterly Review* 65 (1949): 72–81.

Hutson, James H. "Country, Court, and Constitution: Antifederalists and the Historians." *William and Mary Quarterly*, 3d ser., 38 (1981): 337–68.

Johnson, Herbert A. "George Harison's Protest: New Light on Forsey versus Cunningham." *New York History* 50 (1969): 61–82.

Johnson, Richard R. "The Imperial Webb: The Thesis of Garrison Government in Early America Considered." *William and Mary Quarterly*, 3d ser., 43 (1986): 408–30.

——. " 'Parliamentary Egoisms': The Clash of Legislatures in the Making of the American Revolution." *Journal of American History* 74 (1987): 338–62.

Johnston, Jean. "Molly Brant: Mohawk Matron." *Ontario History* 56 (1964): 105–24.

Jordan, Cynthia S. " 'Old Words' in 'New Circumstances': Language and Leadership in Post-Revolutionary America." *American Quarterly* 40 (1988): 491–513.

Katz, Stanley N. "The Politics of Law in Colonial America: Controversies over Chancery Courts and Equity Law in the Eighteenth Century." *Perspectives in American History* 5 (1971): 257–84.

Kenyon, Cecelia M. "Alexander Hamilton: Rousseau of the Right." *Political Science Quarterly* 73 (1958): 161–78.

——. "Men of Little Faith: The Antifederalists on the Nature of Representative Government." *William and Mary Quarterly*, 3d ser., 12 (1955): 3–43.

Kim, Sung Bok, "Impact of Class Relations and Warfare in the American Revolution: The New York Experience." *Journal of American History* 69 (1982): 326–46.

——. "The Limits of Politicization in the American Revolution: The Experience of Westchester County, New York." *Journal of American History* 80 (1993): 868–89.

——. "A New Look at the Great Landlords of Eighteenth-Century New York." *William and Mary Quarterly*, 3d ser., 27 (1970): 581–614.

Kishlansky, Mark A. "Community and Continuity: A Review of Selected Works on English Local History." *William and Mary Quarterly*, 3d ser., 37 (1980): 139–46.

Klein, Milton M. "The Cultural Tyros of Colonial New York." *South Atlantic Quarterly* 66 (1967): 218–32.

——. "Democracy and Politics in Colonial New York." *New York History* 40 (1959): 221–46.

——. "An Experiment That Failed: General James Robertson and Civil Government in British New York, 1779–1783." *New York History* 61 (1980): 230–54.

——. "From Community to Status: The Development of the Legal Profession in Colonial New York." *New York History* 60 (1979): 133–56.

——. "New York in the American Colonies: A New Look." *New York History* 53 (1972): 132–56.

——. "New York Lawyers and the Coming of the American Revolution." *New York History* 55 (1974): 383–407.

———. "Politics and Personalities in Colonial New York." *New York History* 47 (1966): 3–16.

———. "Prelude to Revolution in New York: Jury Trials and Judicial Tenure." *William and Mary Quarterly*, 3d ser., 17 (1960): 439–62.

———. "Why Did the British Fail to Win the Hearts and Minds of New Yorkers?" *New York History* 64 (1983): 357–75.

Koebner, Richard. "The Emergence of the Concept of Imperialism." *Cambridge Journal* 5 (1952): 726–41.

Koenigsberger, H. G. "Composite States, Representative Institutions and the American Revolution." *Historical Research* 62 (1989): 135–53.

Konig, David T. "Contingency and Constitutionalism in Colonial New York." *Law and History Review* 16 (1998): 381–85.

———. "A Summary of the Law of British America." *William and Mary Quarterly*, 3d ser., 50 (1993): 42–50.

Kramer, Larry D. "Madison's Audience." *Harvard Law Review* 115 (1999): 611–79.

———. "Foreword: We the Court." *Harvard Law Review* 115 (2001): 4–79.

Kramer, Michael P. Review of *The Autobiographies of Noah Webster*. *New England Quarterly* 64 (1991): 148–51.

Krauss, Stanton D. "An Inquiry into the Right of Criminal Juries to Determine the Law in Colonial America." *Journal of Criminal Law and Criminology* 89 (1998): 111–214.

———. "The Original Understanding of the Seventh Amendment Right to Jury Trial." *University of Richmond Law Review* 33 (1999): 407–83.

Langbein, John H. "*Albion's* Fatal Flaw." *Past and Present*, no. 98 (1983): 96–120.

———. "Chancellor Kent and the History of Legal Literature." *Columbia Law Review* 93 (1993): 547–94.

———. "The Historical Origins of the Privilege against Self-Incrimination at Common Law." *Michigan Law Review* 92 (1994): 1066–71.

La Potin, Armand. "The Minisink Grant: Partnerships, Patents, and Processing Fees in Eighteenth Century New York." *New York History* 56 (1975): 29–50.

Lawson, Alan. "Comparative Studies and Post-Colonial Settler Cultures." *Australian-Canadian Studies* 10 (1992): 153–59.

———. "A Cultural Paradigm for the Second World." *Australian-Canadian Studies* 9 (1991): 67–78.

Leder, Lawrence H. "The Politics of Upheaval in New York, 1689–1709." *New-York Historical Society Quarterly* 44 (1960): 413–27.

Lehman, David J. "The End of the Iroquois Mystique: The Oneida Land Cession Treaties of the 1780s." *William and Mary Quarterly*, 3d ser., 47 (1990): 523–47.

Lemisch, L. Jesse. "Jack Tar in the Streets: Merchant Seamen in the Politics of Revolutionary America." *William and Mary Quarterly*, 3d ser., 25 (1968): 371–407.

———. "New York's Petitions and Resolves of December 1765: Liberals vs. Radicals." *New-York Historical Society Quarterly* 49 (1965): 313–26.

Lenner, Andrew. "Separate Spheres: Republican Constitutionalism in the Federalist Era." *American Journal of Legal History* 41 (1997): 250–81.

———. "A Tale of Two Constitutions: Nationalism and the Federalist Era." *American Journal of Legal History* 40 (1996): 72–105.

Levinson, Sanford. "Why the Canon Should Be Expanded to Include the Insular Cases and the Saga of American Expansionism." *Constitutional Commentary* 17 (2000): 241–66.

Levy, Leonard W. "Did the Zenger Case Really Matter? Freedom of the Press in Colonial New York." *William and Mary Quarterly*, 3d ser., 17 (1960): 35–50.

Lewis, John U. "Sir Edward Coke (1552–1633): His Theory of 'Artificial Reason' as a Context for Modern Basic Legal Theory." *Law Quarterly Review* 84 (1968): 330–42.

Llewellyn, Karl. "The Constitution as an Institution." *Columbia Law Review* 34 (1934): 1–40.

Lovejoy, David S. "Equality and Empire: The New York Charter of Libertyes, 1683." *William and Mary Quarterly*, 3d ser., 21 (1964): 493–515.

———. "Rights Imply Equality: The Case against Admiralty Jurisdiction in America, 1764–1776." *William and Mary Quarterly*, 3d ser., 16 (1959): 459–84.

Luig, Klaus. "The Institutes of National Law in the Seventeenth and Eighteenth Centuries." *Juridical Review* 17 (1972): 193–226.

Lynd, Staughton. "Who Should Rule at Home? Dutchess County, New York, in the American Revolution." *William and Mary Quarterly*, 3d ser., 18 (1961): 330–59.

MacKay, R. A. "Coke — Parliamentary Sovereignty or the Supremacy of the Law?" *Michigan Law Review* 22 (1924): 215–47.

Maier, Pauline. "Reason and Revolution: The Radicalism of Dr. Thomas Young." *American Quarterly* 28 (1976): 229–49.

———. "The Revolutionary Origins of the American Corporation." *William and Mary Quarterly*, 3d ser., 50 (1993): 51–84.

Maitland, F. W. "The Crown as Corporation." *Law Quarterly Review* 17 (1901): 131–46.

Mark, Gregory A. "The Vestigial Constitution: The History and Significance of the Right to Petition." *Fordham Law Review* 66 (1998): 2153–2231.

Marshall, P. J. "Empire and Authority in the Late Eighteenth Century." *Journal of Imperial and Commonwealth History* 15 (1987): 105–22.

Marshall, Peter. "Colonial Protest and Imperial Retrenchment: Indian Policy, 1764–1768." *Journal of American Studies* 5 (1971): 1–17.

———. "Sir William Johnson and the Treaty of Fort Stanwix, 1768." *Journal of American Studies* 1 (1967): 149–79.

Mason, Alpheus T. "The Federalist — A Split Personality." *American Historical Review* 57 (1952): 625–51.

Mason, Bernard. "Aspects of the New York Revolt of 1689." *New York History* 30 (1949): 165–80.

McGregor, Robert K. "Settlement Variations and Cultural Adaptation in the

Immigration History of Colonial New York." *New York History* 73 (1992): 193–212.

McIlwain, Charles H. "The English Common Law, Barrier against Absolutism." *American Historical Review* 49 (1943): 23–31.

McLaughlin, Andrew C. "The Background of American Federalism." *American Political Science Review* 12 (1918): 215–40.

McPherson, B. H. "Revisiting the Manor of East Greenwich." *American Journal of Legal History* 42 (1998): 35–56.

Milsom, S. F. C. "The Nature of Blackstone's Achievement." *Oxford Journal of Legal Studies* 1 (1981): 1–12.

Moglen, Eben. "Considering *Zenger*: Partisan Politics and the Legal Profession in Provincial New York." *Columbia Law Review* 94 (1994): 1495–1524.

———. "The Incompleat Burkean: Bruce Ackerman's Foundation for Constitutional History." *Yale Journal of Law and the Humanities* 5 (1993): 531–52.

———. "Taking the Fifth: Reconsidering the Origins of the Constitutional Privilege against Self-Incrimination." *Michigan Law Review* 92 (1994): 1086–1130.

Morgan, Edmund S. "The American Revolution: Revisions in Need of Revising." *William and Mary Quarterly*, 3d ser., 14 (1957): 3–15.

———. "Safety in Numbers: Madison, Hume and the Tenth *Federalist*." *Huntington Library Quarterly* 49 (1986): 95–112.

Morris, Lewis. "The Opinion and Argument of Lewis Morris to Governor William Cosby, 1733." *Proceedings of the New Jersey Historical Society* 55 (1937): 87–116.

Muldoon, James. "The Contribution of the Medieval Canon Lawyers to the Formation of International Law." *Traditio* 28 (1972): 483–97.

Nicholson, Bradley J. "Courts-Martial in the Legion Army: American Military Law in the Early Republic, 1792–1796." *Military Law Review* 144 (1994): 77–109.

Nissenson, Samuel G. "The Development of a Land Registration System in New York." *New York History* 20 (1939): 16–42.

Nobles, Gregory H. "Breaking the Backcountry: New Approaches to the Early American Frontier, 1750–1800." *William and Mary Quarterly*, 3d ser., 46 (1989): 641–70.

Note. "*Swift v. Tyson* Exhumed." *Yale Law Journal* 79 (1970): 284–310.

Olson, Alison Gilbert. "The Board of Trade and London-American Interest Groups in the Eighteenth-Century." *Journal of Imperial and Commonwealth History* 8 (1980): 33–50.

Osgood, Herbert L. "The Corporation as a Form of Colonial Government." *Political Science Quarterly* 11 (1896): 259–77, 502–33.

———, ed. "The Society of Dissenters Founded at New York in 1769." *American Historical Review* 6 (1901): 498–507.

Palmer, Robert C. "The Federal Common Law of Crime." *Law and History Review* 4 (1986): 267–323.

Pawlisch, Hans S. "Sir John Davies, the Ancient Constitution, and Civil Law." *Historical Journal* 23 (1980): 689–702.

Peckham, Howard H. "Speculations on the Colonial Wars." *William and Mary Quarterly*, 3d ser., 17 (1960): 463–72.

Plucknett, T. F. T. "Bonham's Case and Judicial Review." *Harvard Law Review* 40 (1926): 30–70.

———. "The Genesis of Coke's Reports." *Cornell Law Quarterly* 27 (1942): 190–213

Pocock, J. G. A. "Between Gog and Magog: The Republican Thesis and the *Ideologia Americana*." *Journal of the History of Ideas* 48 (1987): 325–46.

———. "British History: A Plea for New Subject." *Journal of Modern History* 47 (1975): 601–28.

———. "The Limits and Divisions of British History: In Search of an Unknown Subject." *American Historical Review* 87 (1982): 311–36.

Pole, J. R. "The Politics of the Word 'State' and Its Relation to American Sovereignty." *Parliaments, Estates and Representation* 8 (1988): 1–10.

Preyer, Kathryn. "Jurisdiction to Punish: Federal Authority, Federalism and the Common Law of Crimes in the Early Republic." *Law and History Review* 4 (1986): 223–65.

Price, Jacob M. "One Family's Empire: The Russell-Lee-Clerk Connection in Maryland, Britain, and India, 1707–1857." *Maryland Historical Magazine* 72 (1977): 165–225.

Price, Polly J. "Natural Law and Birthright Citizenship in *Calvin's Case* (1608)." *Yale Journal of Law and the Humanities* 9 (1997): 73–145.

Rakove, Jack N. "Making a Hash of Sovereignty." *Green Bag* 2 (1998): 35–44; 3 (1999): 51–59.

Ramirez, Deborah A. "The Mixed Jury and the Ancient Custom of Trial by Jury *De Medietate Linguae*: A History and a Proposal for Change." *Boston University Law Review* 74 (1994): 777–818.

Reid, John P. "In Accordance with Usage: The Authority of Custom, the Stamp Act Debate, and the Coming of the American Revolution." *Fordham Law Review* 45 (1976): 335–68.

———. "Law and History." *Loyola of Los Angeles Law Review* 27 (1993): 193–223.

———. "The Ordeal by Law of Thomas Hutchinson." *New York University Law Review* 49 (1974): 593–613.

———. Review of *In English Ways*, by David G. Allen. *New York University Law Review* 56 (1981): 850–66.

———. "Some Lessons of Western History." *Western Law Review* 1 (1988): 2–21.

Rich, E. E. "The Population of Elizabethan England." *Economic History Review*, 2d ser., 2 (1949): 247–64.

Robbins, Caroline. " 'When It Is That Colonies May Turn Independent': An Analysis of the Environment and Politics of Francis Hutcheson (1694–1746)." *William and Mary Quarterly*, 3d ser., 11 (1954): 214–51.

Robbins, Keith. "Core and Periphery in Modern British History." *Proceedings of the British Academy* 70 (1984): 275–97.

Roche, John F. "The Uranian Society: Gentlemen and Scholars in Federal New York." *New York History* 52 (1971): 121–32.

Rose, Carol M. "The Ancient Constitution vs. the Federalist Empire: Antifederalism from the Attack on Monarchism to Modern Localism." *Northwestern Law Review* 84 (1988): 74–105.

Ross, Richard J. "The Commoning of the Common Law: The Renaissance Debate over the Meaning of Printing English Law, 1520–1640." *University of Pennsylvania Law Review* 146 (1998): 323–461.

———. "The Memorial Culture of Early Modern English Lawyers: Memory as Keyword, Shelter, and Identity, 1560–1640." *Yale Journal of Law and the Humanities* 10 (1998): 229–326.

Rubinstein, W. D. "The End of the 'Old Corruption' in Britain." *Past and Present*, no. 101 (1983): 55–86.

Ruger, Theodore W. " 'A Question Which Convulses a Nation': The Early Republic's Greatest Debate about the Judicial Review Power." *Harvard Law Review* 117 (2004): 826–97.

Russell, Conrad. "The British Problem and the English Civil War." *History* 72 (1987): 395–415.

Sacret, J. H. "The Restoration Government and Municipal Corporations." *English Historical Review* 45 (1930): 232–59.

Salisbury, Neal. "The Indians' Old World: Native Americans and the Coming of Europeans." *William and Mary Quarterly*, 3d ser., 53 (1996): 435–58.

Schechter, Frank I. "Popular Law and Common Law in Medieval England." *Columbia Law Review* 28 (1928): 269–99.

Seaberg, Robert B. "The Norman Conquest and the Common Law: The Levellers and the Argument from Continuity." *Historical Journal* 24 (1981): 791–806.

Seed, Patricia. "Taking Possession and Reading Texts: Establishing the Authority of Overseas Empires." *William and Mary Quarterly*, 3d ser., 49 (1992): 183–209.

Shammas, Carole. "Cadwallader Colden and the Role of the King's Prerogative." *New-York Historical Society Quarterly* 53 (1969): 103–26.

Sharpe, Jenny. "Is the United States Postcolonial? Transnationalism, Immigration, and Race." *Diaspora: A Journal of Transatlantic Studies* 4 (1995): 181–99.

Sherry, Suzanna. "The Founders' Unwritten Constitution." *University of Chicago Law Review* 54 (1987): 1127–77.

Siegel, Andrew M. " 'To Learn and Make Respectable Hereafter': The Litchfield Law School in Cultural Context." *New York University Law Review* 73 (1998): 1978–2028.

Skinner, Quentin. "The Limits of Historical Explanation." *Philosophy* 41 (1966): 199–215.

———. "Meaning and Understanding in the History of Ideas." *History and Theory* 8 (1969): 1–53.

Slemon, Stephen. "Unsettling the Empire: Resistance Theory for the Second World." *World Literature Written in English* 30 (1990): 30–41.

Smith, Joseph H. "Administrative Control of the Courts of the American Plantations." *Columbia Law Review* 60 (1960): 1210–53.

———. "An Independent Judiciary: The Colonial Background." *University of Pennsylvania Law Review* 124 (1976): 1104–56.

Steele, Ian K. "The Empire and Provincial Elites: An Interpretation of Some Recent Writings on the English Atlantic, 1675–1740." *Journal of Imperial and Commonwealth History* 8 (1980): 2–32.

Stein, Peter. "The Attraction of the Civil Law in Post-Revolutionary America." *Virginia Law Review* 52 (1966): 403–34.

Steppler, G. A. "British Military Law, Discipline, and the Conduct of Regimental Courts Martial in the Later Eighteenth Century." *English Historical Review* 102 (1987): 859–86.

Stokes, E. T. "Bureaucracy and Ideology: Britain and India in the Nineteenth Century." *Transactions of the Royal Historical Society*, 5th ser., 30 (1980): 131–56.

Stout, Neil R. "Captain Kennedy and the Stamp Act." *New York History* 45 (1964): 44–58.

Strauss, David A. "The Irrelevance of Constitutional Amendments." *Harvard Law Review* 114 (2001): 1457–1505.

Sutherland, Donald. "Conquest and Law." *Studia Gratiana* 15 (1972): 33–51.

Taylor, Alan. " 'A Kind of Warr': The Contest for Land on the Northeastern Frontier, 1750–1820." *William and Mary Quarterly*, 3d ser., 46 (1989): 3–26.

———. Review of *The Developer's Frontier*, by William Wycoff. *William and Mary Quarterly*, 3d ser., 46 (1989): 621–23.

Taylor, Miles. "The Radical Critique of Empire." *Journal of Imperial and Commonwealth History* 19 (1991): 1–23.

Thompson, Martyn P. "The History of Fundamental Law in Political Thought from the French Wars of Religion to the American Revolution." *American Historical Review* 91 (1986): 1103–28.

Thorne, Samuel E. "Dr. Bonham's Case." *Law Quarterly Review* 54 (1938): 543–52.

Tiedemann, Joseph S. "Patriots by Default: Queens County, New York, and the British Army, 1776–1783." *William and Mary Quarterly*, 3d ser., 43 (1986): 35–63.

Treanor, William M. "The Original Understanding of the Takings Clause and the Political Process." *Columbia Law Review* 95 (1995): 782–887.

Ullmann, Walter. "The Mediaeval Theory of Legal and Illegal Organizations." *Law Quarterly Review* 60 (1944): 285–91.

———. " 'This Realm of England Is an Empire.' " *Journal of Ecclesiastical History* 30 (1979): 175–203.

Varga, Nicholas. "Election Procedures in Colonial New York." *New York History* 41 (1960): 249–77.

———. "The New York Restraining Act: Its Passage and Some Effects." *New York History* 37 (1956): 233–58.

Voorhees, David W. "The 'Fervent Zeale' of Jacob Leisler." *William and Mary Quarterly*, 3d ser., 51 (1994): 447–72.

Warren, Charles. "New Light on the Federal Judiciary Act of 1789." *Harvard Law Review* 37 (1923): 49–132.

Webb, Stephen S. " 'Brave Men and Servants to His Royal Highness': The Household of James Stuart in the Evolution of English Imperialism." *Perspectives in American History* 8 (1974): 55–80.

———. "The Data and Theory of Restoration Empire." *William and Mary Quarterly*, 3d ser., 43 (1986): 431–59.

Webking, Robert H. "Melancton Smith and the *Letters from the Federal Farmer*." *William and Mary Quarterly*, 3d ser., 44 (1987): 510–28.

Wessel, Thomas R. "Agriculture and Iroquois Hegemony in New York, 1610–1779." *Maryland Historian* 1 (1970): 93–104.

Wheeler, Harvey. "Calvin's Case (1608) and the McIlwain-Schuyler Debate." *American Historical Review* 61 (1956): 587–97.

White, G. Edward. "The Constitutional Journey of *Marbury v. Madison*." *Virginia Law Review* 89 (2003): 1463–1573.

Wiecek, William M. "The Statutory Law of Slavery and Race in the Thirteen Mainland Colonies of British America." *William and Mary Quarterly*, 3d ser., 34 (1977): 258–80.

Wilf, Steven. "The First Republican Revival: Virtue, Judging, and Rhetoric in the Early Republic." *Connecticut Law Review* 32 (2000): 1675–98.

Wilkenfeld, Bruce. "The New York City Common Council, 1689–1800." *New York History* 52 (1971): 249–73.

Williams, Robert, Jr. "Jefferson, the Norman Yoke, and American Indian Lands." *Arizona Law Review* 29 (1987): 165–94.

Williston, Samuel. "History of the Law of Business Corporations before 1800." *Harvard Law Review* 2 (1888): 105–24, 149–66.

Wilson, Judith A. "My Country Is My Colony: A Study in Anglo-American Patriotism, 1739–1760." *Historian* 30 (1968): 333–49.

Wolfram, Charles W. "The Constitutional History of the Seventh Amendment." *Minnesota Law Review* 57 (1973): 639–747.

Wood, Gordon S. "The Origins of Judicial Review Revisited, or How the Marshall Court Made More out of Less." *Washington and Lee Law Review* 56 (1999): 787–809.

———. "The Origins of Vested Rights in the Early Republic." *Virginia Law Review* 85 (1999): 1421–45.

Wright, Benjamin. "The Origins of the Separation of Powers in America." *Economica* 13 (1933): 169–85.

Wright, Langdon. "Local Government and Central Authority in New Netherland." *New-York Historical Society Quarterly* 57 (1973): 7–29.

Zagorin, Perez. "The Court and the Country: A Note on Political Terminology in the Earlier Seventeenth Century." *English Historical Review* 77 (1962): 306–11.

Zeichner, Oscar, ed. "William Smith's 'Observations on America.' " *New York History* 23 (1942): 328–40.

Ashton, Rick J. "The Loyalist Experience, New York, 1763–1789." Ph.D. diss., Northwestern University, 1973.

Bailyn, Bernard. "The Idea of Atlantic History." Working paper 96–01, International Seminar on the History of the Atlantic World, Harvard University, 1996.

Christenson, Jack H. "The Administration of Land Policy in Colonial New York." Ph.D. diss., State University of New York, Albany, 1976.

Coit, Kent A. "The Diffusion of Democracy: Politics and Constitutionalism in the States, 1790–1840." Ph.D. diss., Harvard University, 1981.

Colvin, David L. "The Bicameral Principle in New York Legislature." Ph.D. diss., Columbia University, 1913.

Fingerhut, Eugene R. "Assimilation of Immigrants on the Frontier of New York, 1764–1776." Ph.D. diss., Columbia University, 1962.

Fisher, William W., III. "The Law of the Land: An Intellectual History of the American Property Doctrine, 1776–1880." Ph.D. diss., Harvard University, 1991.

Fitch, Keith. "American Nationalism and the Revolution, 1765–1776: A Case Study of the Movement in the Colony of New York." Ph.D. diss., Purdue University, 1972.

Games, Alison. "Sir Thomas Roe and the Integration of the First British Empire." Paper, Columbia University Seminar on Early American History and Culture, February 1999.

Guzzardo, John C. "Sir William Johnson's Official Family: Patron and Client in an Anglo-American Empire, 1742–1777." Ph.D. diss., Syracuse University, 1975.

Haley, Jacquetta M. "Voluntary Organizations in Pre-revolutionary New York City, 1750–1776." Ph.D. diss., State University of New York, Binghamton, 1976.

Hurley, J. D. "Children or Brethren: Aboriginal Rights in Colonial Iroquoia." Ph.D. diss., University of Cambridge, 1985.

Jopp, Jennifer Lee. " 'Kingly Government': English Law in Seventeenth-Century New York." Ph.D. diss., State University of New York, Binghamton, 1992.

McAnear, Beverly. "Politics in Provincial New York, 1689–1761." Ph.D. diss., Stanford University, 1935.

Milford, Timothy A. "Advantage: The Gardiners in Anglo-America, 1750–1820." Ph.D. diss., Harvard University, 1999.

Moglen, Eben. "American Federalisms: The Structure of 18th Century North American Law." Paper, American Society for Legal History Conference, Atlanta, February 1990.

———. "Settling the Law: Legal Development in Provincial New York." Forthcoming.

Moss, Laura-Eve. "Democracy, Citizenship and Constitution-Making in New York, 1777–1894." Ph.D. diss., University of Connecticut, 1999.

Murrin, John M. "Anglicizing an American Colony: The Transformation of Massachusetts." Ph.D. diss., Yale University, 1966.

Palumbo, Rina. "Imperial Fantasies: The Stuart Conquest of British North America." Working paper no. 97–03, International Seminar on the History of the Atlantic World, Harvard University, 1997.

Pole, J. R. "English Law and the Republican Concept of the State." Paper, Legal History Workshop, Harvard Law School, February 1998.

Russo, Raymond Joseph. "The Political Process in New York State, 1816–1824: A Study in Political Morality and Changing Attitudes toward the Party System." Ph.D. diss., Fordham University, 1973.

Shannon, Timothy J. "The Crossroads of Empire: The Albany Congress of 1754 and the British Atlantic Community." Ph.D. diss., Northwestern University, 1993.

Smith, David L. "The Idea of the Rule of Law in England and France in the Seventeenth Century." Paper, British History Workshop, Harvard University, February 1997.

Steacy, Stephen C. "Cadwallader Colden: Statesman and Savant of Colonial New York." Ph.D. diss., University of Kansas, 1987.

Sugarman, David. "The English Constitution." Paper, Harvard Law School Seminar in Legal History, April 1996.

Taylor, Clifton J. "John Watts in Colonial and Revolutionary New York." Ph.D. diss., University of Tennessee, 1981.

Terry, Wyllys C. "Buying the Frontier: The Experience of Colonial New York." Paper, Conference on New York State History, Brockport, New York, June 1995.

Tripp, Wendell E. "Robert Troup." Ph.D. diss., Columbia University, 1973.

Varga, Nicholas. "New York Government and Politics during the Mid-Eighteenth Century." Ph.D. diss., Fordham University, 1960.

Wright, Langdon G. "Local Government in Colonial New York, 1640–1710." Ph.D. diss., Cornell University, 1974.

ACKNOWLEDGMENTS

It is a joy to thank those who have helped me with this book, though it's also saddening to realize not just how long this project has taken but also how many favors I've received and how few I have returned. Deep thanks are due to anyone who was willing to talk about this project. It is common to refer to historiography as an ongoing dialogue; what I recall looking back on the past decade are the actual conversations. I know they will continue. I am grateful to have found an area of study, and a place to pursue it, where everyone seems bursting with dialogue.

With Eben Moglen of the Columbia Law School I began an early conversation about whether the joint degree I had planned before I entered law school was still a good idea after completing one year of it. From him I learned much about studying history and even more about how to approach the law. The debt is the kind authors acknowledge as unpayable. I hope that someday I can give someone what Eben gave me: help to locate areas of interest and to develop skills to explore them.

It is astonishing how many unselfish people inhabit the academy. Historians perhaps more than anyone know the value of time. Yet they give so much of it away. At Harvard, Morton Horwitz and Donald Fleming gave me countless hours as I wrote seminar papers, studied for generals, looked for a dissertation topic, processed research, and developed arguments. They taught me to distinguish the compelling from the ordinary and reminded me that people read books not just to learn something new but also to find new ways to organize what they think they already know. This project began in Bernard Bailyn's graduate seminar on colonial history, and he always made time to read proposals, drafts, and articles. I would not have undertaken a study of the eighteenth century without witnessing the enthusiasm that he brought to the classroom and to his research, moving swiftly through the Widener stacks, following one lead to another, for years.

The Samuel I. Golieb Fellowship at New York University School of Law provided a year of support and unparalleled intellectual community. Under the direction of William Nelson and John Reid, the members of the Legal History Colloquium read several chapters closely, and four years later they read the entire manuscript. Helpful comments from Louis Anthes, John Baker, Felice Batlan, Richard B. Bernstein, Peter Hoffer, William LaPiana,

Assaf Likhovski, Greg Mark, Nathan Newman, Andrew Siegel, Dahlia Tsuk, and other members of the colloquium have made this a better book.

Over the years in graduate school and at conferences, many people read parts of this book. For especially helpful comments on one or more chapters, deep thanks are due to Barbara Black, Alfred Brophy, George Eliades, Martin Flaherty, Richard Johnson, Stanley Kratz, David Konig, Tim Milford, Kent Newmyer, Julie Peters, and Chris Tomlins.

At Saint Louis University School of Law I found a welcoming community and the support of Dean Jeffrey Lewis and Associate Dean for Faculty Joel Goldstein. Conversations over five years with Eric Claeys, Tim Greaney, Camille Nelson, David Sloss, Dennis Tuchler, and Doug Williams helped sharpen my arguments.

The Studies in Legal History Series at the University of North Carolina Press was a perfect home for the manuscript. Hendrik Hartog believed in the project from the first time he heard twenty minutes of it, and Thomas Green encouraged me to make all readers believe in it too. The reader reports of John Murrin and Larry Kramer were models of the genre. One forced me to wrestle with the sources I had known for so long; the other compelled me to grapple with issues beyond my original reach. They were the ideal readers for which every author hopes. I am also grateful to Charles Grench and Ron Maner at UNC Press for guiding the manuscript through the publication process and to Grace Carino for excellent copyediting.

Finally, I am grateful for my family's support. My sister Betsy, without whose generosity and good humor I would not have been able to write this book, deserves special thanks.

Fortescue, John, 33

Founders and framers: American conception of law and, 9; concept of empire for, 207–8; context for, 4; ideologies of, 208. *See also names of specific individuals*

France: in American Revolution, 158

Franchise: power of, 28, 200

Franklin, Benjamin, 79, 350 (n. 33)

Freedom of press, 59

Freedom of religion: in N.Y. constitution (1777), 182–87

Freeman: Antifederalists' use of term, 222

French cession, 116, 134–35

French settlers: in Quebec Act, 135

"Friendly Club," 285

Frontier settlers: authority among, 97–98; common law used by, 101–4, 143–44; land development by, 98–101; law enforcement and, 101–3, 105; legal arguments of, 103–4; as measure of Federalist success, 293, 294–95; perspective on N.Y. constitution, 76, 96–104; property rights of, struggle for, 107–14; in ratification debate, 219–20; violence among, 101–3, 112–13

Fundamental law: in American constitutionalism, 237–38; common law distinguished from, 212, 237, 247; constitutional law equated with, 237, 247; constitutions as source of, 237; definition of, 34; English common law as, 28–32, 34, 146; vs. English constitutionalism, 6; English use of term, 34; publication of, 35–36; royal power subject to, 33

Gage, Thomas, 81; on frontier settlers, 105, 112, 348–49 (n. 12); on legal profession, 123; on military jurisdiction in French cession, 116

Garrisons: in New York City, 161

Geography: and Jay on divine destiny, 224; and land development, 99–100

Geopolitics: of land development, 96–101

George III (king), 132, 138

Georgia: imperial agents in, 3; restoration of civil government in, 159; sovereign immunity for officials in, 254–55

Germain, George, 147–48, 163

German Empire, Hamilton on, 227–28

Gerry, Elbridge, 245

Glorious Revolution (1688–89), 36, 37, 40, 53

Goebel, Julius, Jr., 254, 256, 327 (n. 58), 375 (n. 126)

Gorham, Nathaniel, 245

Gould, Charles, 157–58

Governors, colonial: and appeals of jury verdicts, 118; Board of Trade questions to, 71–73; complaints about N.Y. assembly, 71–72; dependence on N.Y. assembly, 72, 77; duties of, 56; imperial agents as check on, 79; James's selection of, 46; land grants by, 110–11; law licenses granted by, 127, 129; limitations on, 56; power of, 56; salary of, 72, 333 (n. 4). *See also names of specific individuals*

Governors, state: appointment power of, 179–80, 262, 265–68; election of, 175; in N.Y. constitution (1777), 175–76, 179–80; summary of powers, 175–76; veto power of, 176, 269. *See also names of specific individuals*

Grammatical Institute of the English Language, A (Webster), 274

Great Britain: as core of British Empire, 18; establishment of, 225–26; in ratification debate, 225–26, 228. *See also* British Empire

Human body: constitution of, 33
Humble Petition and Advice (1657), 35, 319 (n. 105)
Hume, David, 38–39, 226, 227
Humphreys, David, 274
Hunter, Robert, 56, 61, 78, 79
Hutchinson, Thomas, 160

Identity: of Creole New Yorkers, 84–85; cultural, of N.Y., 84; English, nation vs. crown in, 37; U.S., role of law in, 204–5
Ideology: of British Empire, 19–20; of framers, 208
Immigrants: influence on ratification debate, 217–18; Irish, 296; need for, in land development, 99. *See also* Aliens
Imperial agents: balance with provincial elite, 3; Board of Trade in appointment of, 137; as check on governors, 79; common-law reform attempted by, 105–33, 142; correspondence of, 83, 131–33, 337 (n. 44); educational institutions for, 133; failure of, 305; Federalist strategies compared to, 210; on jury trials, 105, 114–22; on legal profession, 105, 122–33; loyalty of, 78, 80, 156; perspective on N.Y. constitution, 76–83; profiles of prominent, 78–81; on property law, 105–14; salaries of, 77, 131; transcolonial perspective of, 82
Imperialization, 9
Imperium in imperio, 88, 96
Improvement: 18th-century spirit of, 85; incorporation and, 88; provincial constitution of, 84–87; and sailors, 97
Incorporation. *See* Corporations
In Defence of the Constitution (Seabury), 89
Independence, American: British recognition of, 167

Independence, Declaration of (1776): confusion in government after, 145; N.Y.'s refusal to sign, 172
Independence movements: outside U.S., 204, 375–76 (n. 6)
Independent Reflector (periodical), 85, 89, 99
India, colonial, 136, 168
Indian affairs: Johnson as superintendent of, 79–80, 82. *See also* Native Americans
Individual rights: in N.Y. constitution (1777), 187, 189
Inherited lands, vs. conquered lands, 25–27, 313 (n. 30)
Inns of Court, 128, 133
Institutes of Roman Law (Justinian), 281–82
Institutes of the Laws of England (Coke), 24–25, 28, 31
Institutionalists: goals of, 280
Instructions: relationship between commission and, 110–11
Instrument of Government (1654), 35, 319 (n. 105)
International law: American law distinguished from, 280
Intolerable acts, 93–94
Iredell, James, 254, 391 (n. 197)
Ireland: in British Empire, 18; English jurisdiction in, 313 (n. 26); Parliament of, 295, 314 (n. 47); taxation in, 91–92; United Irish movement in, 295–97
Irish immigrants, 296
Iroquois: Colden's history of, 79, 80; concept of property among, 111–12; influence of, 117; Johnson's relationship with, 80, 109, 112, 117, 335 (n. 20); land of, 2, 100, 108; N.Y. assembly relations with, 72; population size of, 345 (n. 126); in ratification debate, 217; in Stanwix Treaty, 113. *See also* Six Nations

Local autonomy: common law supporting, 43; English liberties and, 43, 90–94

Local government: institutions of, in colonial N.Y., 45–56; power returned to, 260, 271

Localism: of Antifederalists, 220–21, 224; in state constitutionalism, 260

Long Island, 46–47

Low, Isaac, 149, 150

Loyalists: as aliens, 194; as Federalists, 218; Hamilton's defense of, 192–94, 373 (n. 96); property of, British confiscation of, 161–64; property of, N.Y. state laws on, 192–94; Provincial Congress prosecution of, 154–55; on restoration of civil government, 158, 159, 160–61; in south, 159

Loyalty: in Continental army, 151, 155; of imperial agents, 78, 80, 156; motivations for, 156–57; of provincial elite, 90, 95–96, 156

Ludlow, George Duncan, 158, 163

Lydius, John Henry, 109

Macaulay, Catherine, 95

MacDougall, Alexander, 125–26, 149, 154

Machiavelli, Niccolo, 19

Madison, James: American empire envisioned by, 215; on bill of rights, 253; on common law, 247, 390 (n. 174); *Federalist Papers* by, 209, 227; on federal judiciary, 246; goal of writings of, 209; Hamilton's coordination with, 209, 377 (n. 11); on legislative review, 239; on Native Americans, 188; New York's influence on, 209; at Philadelphia Convention, 209; on representative government, 234; republicanism of, 226–27; on size of Union, 226–27; on slavery, 227, 380 (n. 44), 384

(n. 95); on state politics, 155, 194; on states as corporations, 223

Magna Carta: Article 39 of, 49; and jury trials, 114; and N.Y. constitution (1777), 187

Maier, Pauline, 371 (n. 62)

Maine, Henry, 15, 29

Maitland, Frederic W., 28, 87, 344 (n. 115)

Manifest destiny, 10

Manors: land users competing with, 98; in provincial government, 47–48, 327 (n. 59)

Mansfield, William Murray, Lord: Colden's correspondence with, 140; on conquered land, legal system of, 135; on constitutional law, 320 (n. 120); in legal unification efforts, 289–90; on parliamentary authority, 138; on settlement doctrine, 57; on slavery, 188

Marchland, origin of term, 333–34 (n. 2)

"Marcus," 234–35

Marshall, John, 258, 260

Marshall, Peter, 352 (n. 47)

Martial law: Adye's treatise on, 164–65, 366 (n. 88); in England, 21, 313 (n. 20); in New York, 145, 157–69; trials in, 165–66; in Virginia, 21, 313 (n. 20)

Martin, Luther, 389 (n. 161)

Mary II (queen), 37, 53

Mason, George: on equal footing for states, 220, 381 (n. 59); on federal judiciary, 245; on judicial review, 239

Massachusetts: liberties claimed in, 3; N.Y. land claimed by, 100; port closed in, 148

Matthews, David, 163

Mayor's Court: in *Rutgers* case, 195–201

McCulloch v. Maryland, 258

Mercantilism, 78

Merchants: economic classification of, 232

Migration, 10–11; and common law, as causes of Revolution, 143–44; constitution in context of, 97; ratification debate affected by, 219–20; reasons for, 97–98; after Revolution, 219–20; right of, Vermont on, 114

Military. *See* British military; Continental military

Military jurisdiction: provincial courts in conflict with, 64–68, 116; during Revolution, 157–58

Miller, Perry, 286

Mitchell, Samuel Latham, 285

Mobility, 10–11, 143–44. *See also* Migration

Moglen, Eben, 50, 357 (n. 96)

Mohawk Indians: Johnson's relationship with, 112, 117; land of, 107, 109–10, 112, 350 (n. 26)

Mohawk River, 99

Mohawk Valley: Johnson's control of, 123; land development in, 100; Madison in, 209

Molasses, duties on, 92, 342 (n. 91)

Molasses Act (1733), 342 (n. 91)

Monckton, Robert, 92, 118, 139, 147

Monopolies, in English law, 30

Monroe, James, 209

Montesquieu, Charles Louis de Secondat, baron de, 33, 221, 394 (n. 5)

Montgomerie, Robert, 61, 66

Moore, Harry, 140

Moore, Henry, 115

Moot, the (society), 129

Morris, Gouverneur: on bill of rights, 173; on constitutions, 207; on Council of Appointment, 179; in drafting of N.Y. constitution (1777), 171, 173, 174, 179, 182; on elections for legislature, 174; on equality for states, 381 (n. 59); and *Federalist Papers*, 377 (n. 9); on formation of government, 142–43; in Provin-

cial Congress, 171; on religious toleration, 182; on slavery, 188

Morris, Lewis: on Colden, 79; Colden on, 124; removal from supreme court, 59, 62–63

Morris, Lewis, Jr., 354 (n. 69)

Morris, Richard, 354 (n. 69)

Morris, Robert, 218

Morris, Roger, 164

Morris, Sarah Gouverneur, 164

Municipal law, vs. constitutional jurisprudence, 281

Murray, Joseph, 63–64, 67–68

Murrin, John M., 324 (n. 39)

Mutiny Act for North America (1765), 116, 157

Nation: U.S. as, 225

Nationalism, American: language and, 275

Nations, law of: crimes against, in ratification debate, 246; in Kent's *Commentaries*, 282–83, 286; vs. state laws, 194–201

Native Americans: Colden's history of, 79, 80, 82; concept of property among, 111–12; jury trials for, 115–17; justice for, vs. integrity of common law, 111; land of, 100, 106–13, 187–88, 217; in N.Y. constitution (1777), 187–88; peace with, 112–13; in ratification debate, 217; in Revolution, 156; violence with settlers, 112–13. *See also* Iroquois; Mohawk Indians; Six Nations

Naturalization: in N.Y. constitution (1777), 186–87

Natural law: in Kent's *Commentaries*, 286

Natural rights: in ratification debate, 251–52

Navigation Acts: First (1651), 36; jurisdiction over violations of, 121–22; rise of parliamentary power and, 53; theory of empire in, 78

Status law, 282

Statute law: common law distinguished from, 212, 237; in hierarchy of American law, 212, 279

Stokes, Anthony, 42, 70, 133

Story, Joseph, 210, 289, 291–92, 401 (n. 118)

Stuart, John, 82

Subinfeudation, 47

Subjectship, mutual: in Scotland and England, 20–22

Substantive law: common law as, 29; development of, 29

Suffrage: for African Americans, 263–65; in N.Y. constitution (1777), 174–75, 183, 369 (n. 19); in N.Y. constitutional convention (1821), 262–65; political parties and, 262; property qualifications for, 49, 175, 263–65, 324 (n. 34); in state elections, 219

Summary procedure, 114–15

Supermajority requirements: in N.Y. constitution (1821), 271

Supremacy Clause: judicial review and, 239

Supreme court, colonial (New York), 50, 59–62; and appeal of jury verdicts, 118, 119; assembly's creation of, 50; jurisdiction over violations of Navigation Acts, 121–22; during Revolution, 160, 162

Supreme court, state (New York): dismissal of justices, by N.Y. constitutional convention (1821), 270–71; first meeting of, 180–81; jurisdiction of, 181

Supreme Court, U.S.: Hamilton on, 248; judicial review by, 248, 258; ratification literature influencing, 210, 256; role in making constitutional law, 254–56; on state sovereignty, 254–56; treaty interpretations by, 241; for uniform interpretation of national law, 241

Taxation: by Confederation vs. states, 189–91; in English Civil War, 91; Hamilton on, 189–91; local, power of, 92; N.Y. Assembly on parliamentary regulation of, 91–92; N.Y. Assembly's role in, 50, 51; in N.Y. constitution (1777), 177; parliamentary right of, 91–92, 138; petitions against, 92–94; provincial resistance to, 90–94, 139–40; in ratification debate, 222, 223, 381–82 (nn. 66, 72); in Stamp Act, 139–40; vs. trade regulation, 91–92

Tea Act (1773), 121

Tenant farming: and land development, 98–99; and law enforcement, 102

Tenure, good behavior: judicial review and, 200; in N.Y. constitution (1777), 180; in provincial courts, 123–24, 127, 358 (n. 107); in ratification debate, 250

Thomson, James, 87

Tocqueville, Alexis Charles Henri Clerel de, 300–302, 305, 401 (n. 118)

Tompkins, Daniel, 269

Tort law, 289

Townsend, Freelove, 160

Trade, Board of: creation of, 57, 136; under Halifax, 137; Johnson's recommendations to, 106–7; legal precedents established through, 131–32; and legal profession, 124; membership in, 137; on Native Americans, trials for, 116–17; N.Y. assembly criticized by, 72; N.Y. assembly laws reviewed by, 53–54, 55; parliamentary alliance with, 137; power of, 137; problems with, 136–37; questions submitted to governors by, 71–73, 83; on quitrents, 61–62; recommendations of, 72, 333 (n. 4)

Trade regulation: in rebellious colonies, 157; vs. taxation, 91–92; violations of, jury trials on, 120–22

216, 275; *A Grammatical Institute,*
274; Hamilton and, 397 (n. 47);
Kent influenced by, 285; life of, 394
(n. 1); U.S. Constitution supported
by, 275–76
Wedderburn, Alexander, 135
Wentworth, Benning, 103
West Indies, 2, 18, 79, 82, 85, 96, 113,
166, 217
Wheaton, Henry, 298
Whig politics, constitutionalism in,
36–39
White, G. Edward, 399 (n. 79)
William III of Orange (king), 37, 43,
53–54, 137
Williams, Elisha, 259
Williams, Micah, 164
Williams, Nathan, 268
Wilson, James: in *Chisholm* case, 255,
392 (n. 197); electoral college pro-
posed by, 235–36; on judicial
review, 248; on law of nations, 282;
on legislative review, 239; life of,
218; on state vs. popular sov-
ereignty, 255

Wood, Gordon S., 6, 257
Woolsey, William, 285
Wraxall, Peter, 335 (n. 20)
Writing and publication: of assembly
laws, 55, 328 (n. 63); of constitutions, vs. unwritten constitutions, 8;
in English constitutionalism, 35–
36. *See also* Legal literature; Ratification literature; *titles of specific
works*

Yates, Abraham, 102, 190, 218
Yates, Robert: on common law in N.Y.
constitution, 181; on corporate
autonomy, 222; on federal judiciary,
242–43, 250–51; on judicial review,
250–51; life of, 218; on size of
Union, 221–22; writing as "Brutus," 209, 242–43, 250–51, 387
(n. 120)
York, Duke of, 191
Young, Samuel, 264, 265, 393 (n. 21)
Young, Thomas, 108, 109

Zenger, John Peter, 59, 61, 62, 126